DRUG DISCOVERY AND DEVELOPMENT IN MEDICINAL CHEMISTRY

Dr. KRATIKA DANIEL
Associate Professor
Deptt. of Pharmaceutical Chemistry
Mandsaur Institute of Pharmacy
Mandsaur

Dr. SWAPNIL GOYAL
Associate Professor
Deptt. of Pharmacology
Mandsaur Institute of Pharmacy
Mandsaur

Dr. NAVEEN CHOUDHARY
Associate Professor
Deptt. of Pharmacognosy
Mandsaur Institute of Pharmacy
Mandsaur

Dr. VIVEK DANIEL
Associate Professor
Deptt. of Pharmaceutical Chemistry
Mandsaur Institute of Pharmacy
Mandsaur

Price ₹ 290.00

NIRALI PRAKASHAN

DRUG DISCOVERY & DEVELOPMENT IN MEDICINAL CHEMISTRY   ISBN 978-93-83971-39-8

Second Edition : June 2015

© : **Authors**

The text of this publication, or any part thereof, should not be reproduced or transmitted in any form or stored in any computer storage system or device for distribution including photocopy, recording, taping or information retrieval system or reproduced on any disc, tape, perforated media or other information storage device etc., without the written permission of Authors with whom the rights are reserved. Breach of this condition is liable for legal action.

Every effort has been made to avoid errors or omissions in this publication. In spite of this, errors may have crept in. Any mistake, error or discrepancy so noted and shall be brought to our notice shall be taken care of in the next edition. It is notified that neither the publisher nor the authors or seller shall be responsible for any damage or loss of action to any one, of any kind, in any manner, therefrom.

Published By :
NIRALI PRAKASHAN
Abhyudaya Pragati, 1312, Shivaji Nagar,
Off J.M. Road, PUNE – 411005
Tel - (020) 25512336/37/39, Fax - (020) 25511379
Email : niralipune@pragationline.com

Printed By :
REPRO INDIA LTD.
50/2 T.T.C. MIDC,
Industrial Area, Mahape, Navi Mumbai
Tel - (022) 2778 2011

DISTRIBUTION CENTRES
PUNE

Nirali Prakashan
119, Budhwar Peth, Jogeshwari Mandir Lane
Pune 411002, Maharashtra
Tel : (020) 2445 2044, 66022708, Fax : (020) 2445 1538
Email : bookorder@pragationline.com

Nirali Prakashan
S. No. 28/27, Dhyari,
Near Pari Company, Pune 411041
Tel : (020) 24690204 Fax : (020) 24690316
Email : dhyari@pragationline.com
bookorder@pragationline.com

MUMBAI
Nirali Prakashan
385, S.V.P. Road, Rasdhara Co-op. Hsg. Society Ltd.,
Girgaum, Mumbai 400004, Maharashtra
Tel : (022) 2385 6339 / 2386 9976, Fax : (022) 2386 9976
Email : niralimumbai@pragationline.com

DISTRIBUTION BRANCHES

NAGPUR
Pratibha Book Distributors
Above Maratha Mandir, Shop No. 3, First Floor,
Rani Jhanshi Square, Sitabuldi, Nagpur 440012,
Maharashtra, Tel : (0712) 254 7129

BENGALURU
Pragati Book House
House No. 1, Sanjeevappa Lane, Avenue Road Cross,
Opp. Rice Church, Bengaluru – 560002.
Tel : (080) 64513344, 64513355,
Mob : 9880582331, 9845021552
Email:bharatsavla@yahoo.com

JALGAON
Nirali Prakashan
34, V. V. Golani Market, Navi Peth, Jalgaon 425001,
Maharashtra, Tel : (0257) 222 0395
Mob : 94234 91860

KOLHAPUR
Nirali Prakashan
New Mahadvar Road,
Kedar Plaza, 1st Floor Opp. IDBI Bank
Kolhapur 416 012, Maharashtra. Mob : 9850046155

CHENNAI
Pragati Books
9/1, Montieth Road, Behind Taas Mahal, Egmore,
Chennai 600008 Tamil Nadu, Tel : (044) 6518 3535,
Mob : 94440 01782 / 98450 21552 / 98805 82331, Email : bharatsavla@yahoo.com

RETAIL OUTLETS
PUNE

Pragati Book Centre
157, Budhwar Peth, Opp. Ratan Talkies,
Pune 411002, Maharashtra
Tel : (020) 2445 8887 / 6602 2707, Fax : (020) 2445 8887

Pragati Book Centre
Amber Chamber, 28/A, Budhwar Peth,
Appa Balwant Chowk, Pune : 411002, Maharashtra,
Tel : (020) 20240335 / 66281669
Email : pbcpune@pragationline.com

Pragati Book Centre
676/B, Budhwar Peth, Opp. Jogeshwari Mandir,
Pune 411002, Maharashtra
Tel : (020) 6601 7784 / 6602 0855

PBC Book Sellers & Stationers
152, Budhwar Peth, Pune 411002, Maharashtra
Tel : (020) 2445 2254 / 6609 2463

MUMBAI
Pragati Book Corner
Indira Niwas, 111 - A, Bhavani Shankar Road, Dadar (W), Mumbai 400028, Maharashtra
Tel : (022) 2422 3526 / 6662 5254, Email : pbcmumbai@pragationline.com

www.pragationline.com   info@pragationline.com

PREFACE

It gives us immense pleasure to present the Textbook on **'Drug Discovery and Development in Medicinal Chemistry'**. This book is written with the aim of providing a basic knowledge of pharmacy and pharmaceutical methods pertaining to Medicinal Chemistry to undergraduates and postgraduate students who are pursuing a career in the pharmaceutical industry. The book attempts to cover topics that overlap the disciplines of Pharmaceutical Chemistry, Pharmacognosy and Pharmacology.

The chapters on Drug Discovery, Development Process and Pharmacological Screening Methods, in-vivo and in-vitro models included in this book describe the general strategies employed in developing an effective drug and also the difficulties faced by the medicinal chemist and pharmacologist in achieving this task.

Understanding the various metabolic pathways is extremely important in the study of Pharmacognosy, Medicinal Chemistry and Pharmacology. We have therefore taken all efforts to illustrate and explain these pathways in a very simple and lucid manner to enable the reader to thoroughly understand them.

The modern extraction techniques and quantitative and qualitative estimation of herbals with the sophisticated analytical techniques and modern facilities that are explained in the book will be extremely beneficial to researchers who deal with different aspects of plant derived products.

We hope this book will also be useful for graduates and postgraduates for their research in various aspects of drug discovery for herbal and synthetic drugs.

Any suggestions and constructive criticism from the readers that could lead to further improvement of the book will be highly appreciated.

We would like to thank Dr S. B. Gokhale (Former, Head of Pharmacy, Govt. Polytechnic, Jalgaon) and our publishers Shri Dineshbhai Furia and Shri Jignesh Furia, Nirali Prakashan, Pune for providing us the opportunity to pen down this book.

Authors

CONTENTS

1. Drug Discovery, Development Process and Optimisation of Lead Molecules — 1.1 – 1.42

2. Various Metabolic Pathways with Special Reference to Production of Secondary Metabolites — 2.1 – 2.10

3. Modern Extraction Technology — 3.1 – 3.18

4. Quantitative and Qualitative Estimation of Herbals — 4.1 – 4.46

5. Antibiotics Derived from Microorganisms — 5.1 – 5.40

6. Biosynthesis and Isolation of some Phytochemicals — 6.1 – 6.92

7. Principles and Applications of Radiotracer Techniques and Autoradiography — 7.1 – 7.18

8. Constitution and Application of Various Hormones — 8.1 – 8.74

9. Pharmacological Screening Methods-In-vivo and in-vitro Models — 9.1 – 9.22

Glossary — G.1 – G.14

Index — I.1 – I.6

Chapter ... 1

DRUG DISCOVERY, DEVELOPMENT PROCESS AND OPTIMISATION OF LEAD MOLECULES

The primary objective of medicinal chemistry is the design and discovery of new compounds that are suitable for use as drugs. This process involves a team of workers from a wide range of disciplines such as chemistry, biology, biochemistry, pharmacology, mathematics, medicine and computing, amongst others.

The discovery or design of a new drug not only requires a discovery or design process but also the synthesis of the drug, a method of administration, the development of tests and procedures to establish how it operates in the body and last but not the least safety assessment. Drug discovery may also require fundamental research into the biological and chemical nature of the diseased state. These and other aspects of drug design and discovery require inputs from specialists of many fields and so medicinal chemists need to have outline knowledge of the relevant aspects of these fields.

Before the twentieth century, medicines consisted mainly of herbs and potions. It was not until the mid-nineteenth century that the first serious efforts were made to isolate and purify the active principles of these remedies (i.e. the pure chemicals responsible for the medicinal properties). The success of these efforts led to the birth of many of the pharmaceutical companies we know today. Since then, many naturally occurring drugs have been obtained and their structures determined (e.g. morphine from *Opium*, cocaine from coca leaves, and quinine from the bark of the *Cinchona* tree).

These natural products sparked off a major synthetic effort where chemists made literally thousands of analogues in an attempt to improve on what nature had provided. Much of this work was carried out on a trial and error basis, but the results obtained revealed several general principles behind drug design.

An overall pattern for drug discovery and drug development also evolved, but there was still a high element of trial and error involved in the process. The mechanism by which a drug worked at the molecular level was rarely understood and drug research was focused on what is known as the lead compound – an active principle isolated from a natural source or a synthetic compound prepared in the laboratory.

In recent years, medicinal chemistry has undergone revolutionary changes as rapid advances in biological sciences have resulted in a much better understanding of how the body functions at the cellular and molecular level. As a result, most research projects in the pharmaceutical industry or in universities now begin by identifying a suitable target in the body and designing a drug to interact with that target. An understanding of the structure and function of the target, as well as the mechanism by which it interacts with potential drugs is crucial to this approach. Generally, we can identify the following stages in drug discovery, design and development

- **Drug discovery involves the following steps**
  - Choose a disease.
  - Choose a drug target.
  - Identify a bioassay.
  - Find a lead compound.
  - Isolate and purify the lead compound if necessary.
  - Determine the structure of the lead compound if necessary.

- **Drug design**
  - Identify structure-activity relationships (SARs).
  - Identify the pharmacophore.
  - Improve target interactions (pharmacodynamics).
  - Improve pharmacokinetic properties.

- **Drug development**
  - Patent the drug.
  - Carry out preclinical trials (drug metabolism, toxicology, formulation and stability test, pharmacology studies, etc).
  - Design a manufacturing process (chemical and process development).
  - Carry out clinical trials.
  - Register and market the drug.
  - Make money.

Many of these stages run concurrently and are dependent on each other. For example, preclinical trials are usually carried out in parallel with the development of a manufacturing process. Even so, the discovery, design and development of a new drug can take 15 years or more, involve the synthesis of over 10,000 compounds and cost in the region of $800 million or £450 million.

DRUG DISCOVERY AND DESIGN: A HISTORICAL OUTLINE

Since ancient times, people have had a wide range of natural products that they use for medicinal purposes. These products, obtained from animal, vegetable and mineral sources, were sometimes very effective. However, many of the products were very toxic and it is interesting to note that the Greeks used the same word *pharmakon* for both poisons and medicinal products. Information about these ancient remedies was not readily available to users until the invention of the printing press in the fifteenth century. This led to the widespread publication and circulation of Herbals and Pharmacopoeias, which resulted in a rapid increase in the use, and misuse, of herbal and other remedies. Misuse of tartar emetic (antimony potassium tartrate) was the reason for its use being banned by the Paris parliament in 1566, probably the first recorded ban of its type. The usage of such remedies reached its height in the seventeenth century. However, improved communication between practitioners in the eighteenth and nineteenth centuries resulted in the progressive removal of preparations that were either ineffective or too toxic. It also led to a more rational development of new drugs.

The early nineteenth century saw the extraction of pure substances from plant material. These substances were of consistent quality but only a few of the compounds isolated proved to be satisfactory as therapeutic agents. The majority were found to be too toxic although many, such as morphine and cocaine for example, were extensively prescribed by physicians. The search to find less toxic medicines than those based on natural sources resulted in the introduction of synthetic substances as drugs in the late nineteenth century and their widespread use in the twentieth century. This development was based on the structures of known pharmacologically active compounds, now referred to as leads. The approach adopted by most nineteenth century workers was to synthesise structures related to that of the lead and test these compounds for the required activity. These lead-related compounds are now referred to as analogues.

The first rational development of synthetic drugs was carried out by **Paul Ehrlich** and **Sacachiro Hata** who produced arsphenamine in 1910 by combining synthesis with reliable biological screening and evaluation procedures. Ehrlich, at the beginning of the nineteenth century, had recognised that both the beneficial and toxic properties of a drug were important to its evaluation. He realised that the more effective drugs showed a greater selectivity for the target microorganism than its host. Consequently, to compare the effectiveness of different compounds, he expressed a drug's selectivity and hence its effectiveness in terms of its chemotherapeutic index, which he defined as

$$\text{Chemotherapeutic index} = \frac{\text{Minimum curative dose}}{\text{Maximum tolerated dose}}$$

At the start of the nineteenth century Ehrlich was looking for a safer antiprotozoal agent to treat syphilis than the then used atoxyl. He and Hata tested and catalogued in terms of his therapeutic index over 600 structurally related arsenic compounds. This led to their discovery in 1909 that arsphenamine (Salvarsan) could cure mice infected with syphilis. This drug was found to be effective in humans but had to be used with extreme care as it was very toxic. However, it was used up to the mid- 1940s when it was replaced by penicillin.

Ehrlich's method of approach is still one of the basic techniques used to design and evaluate new drugs in medicinal chemistry. However, his chemotherapeutic index has been updated to take into account the variability of individuals and is now defined as its reciprocal, the therapeutic index or ratio

$$\text{Therapeutic index} = \frac{LD_{50}}{ED_{50}}$$

where LD50 is the lethal dose required to kill 50 per cent of the test animals and ED50 is the dose producing an effective therapeutic response in 50 per cent of the test animals. In theory, the larger a drug's therapeutic index, the greater is its margin of safety. However, because of the nature of the data used in their derivation, therapeutic index values can only be used as a limited guide to the relative usefulness of different compounds.

The term **structure–activity relationship (SAR)** is now used to describe Ehrlich's approach to drug discovery, which consisted of synthesising and testing a series of structurally related compounds. Although attempts to quantitatively relate chemical structure to biological action were first initiated in the nineteenth century, it was not until the 1960s that **Hansch** and **Fujita** devised a method that successfully incorporated quantitative measurements into structure–activity relationship determinations. The technique is referred to as **QSAR (quantitative structure–activity relationship)**.

QSAR methods have subsequently been expanded by a number of other workers. One of the most successful uses of QSAR has been in the development in the 1970s of the antiulcer agents cimetidine and ranitidine. Both SAR and QSAR are important parts of the foundations of medicinal chemistry.

At the time when Ehrlich was investigating the use of arsenical drugs to treat syphilis, John Langley formulated his theory of receptive substances. In 1905, Langley proposed that the so-called receptive substances in the body could accept either a stimulating compound, which would cause a biological response, or a non-stimulating compound, which would prevent a biological response. These ideas have been developed by subsequent workers and the theory of receptors has become one of the fundamental concepts of medicinal chemistry. Receptor sites usually take the form of pockets, grooves or other cavities in the surface of certain proteins and glycoproteins in the living organism. They should not be confused with active sites which are the regions of enzymes where metabolic chemical reactions occur. It is now accepted that the binding of a chemical agent, referred to as a ligand, to a receptor, sets in motion, a series of biochemical events that result in a biological or physiological effect. Further more, a drug is most effective when its structure or a significant part of its structure, both as regards molecular shape and electron distribution (stereo electronic structure), is complementary with the stereo electronic structure of the receptor responsible for the desired biological action. Since most drugs are able to assume a number of different conformations, the conformation adopted when the drug binds to the receptor is known as its active conformation.

The section of the structure of a ligand that binds to a receptor is known as it pharmacophore. The sections of the structure of a ligand that comprise a pharmacophore may or may not be some distance apart in that structure. They do not have to be adjacent to one another. For example, the quaternary nitrogens that are believed to form the pharmacophore of the neuromuscular blocking agent tubocrarine are separated in the molecule by a distance of 115.3 nm.

Tubocrarine

The concept of receptors also gives a reason for side effects and a rational approach to ways of eliminating their worst effects. It is now believed that side effects can arise when the drug binds to either the receptor responsible for the desired biological response or to different receptors.

The mid- to late twentieth century has seen an explosion of our understanding of the chemistry of disease states, biological structures and processes. This increase in knowledge has given medicinal chemists a clearer picture of how drugs are distributed through the body, transported across membranes, their mode of operation and metabolism. This knowledge has enabled medicinal chemists to place groups that influence its absorption, stability in a bio-system, distribution, metabolism and excretion into the molecular structure of a drug. For example, the *in situ* stability of a drug and hence its potency could be increased by rationally modifying the molecular structure of the drug. Esters and N-substituted amides, for example, have structures with similar shapes and electron distributions (**Fig. 1.1 (a)**) but N-substituted amides hydrolyse more slowly than esters.

Consequently, the replacement of an ester group by an N-substituted amide group may increase the stability of the drug without changing the nature of its activity. This could possibly lead to an increase in either the potency or time of duration of activity of a drug by improving its chances of reaching its site of action. However, changing a group or introducing a group may change the nature of the activity of the compound.

For example, the change of the ester group in procaine to an amide (procainamide) changes the activity from a local anaesthetic to an antiarrhythmic **(Fig. 1.1 (b))**.

Ester group   Amide group

(a)

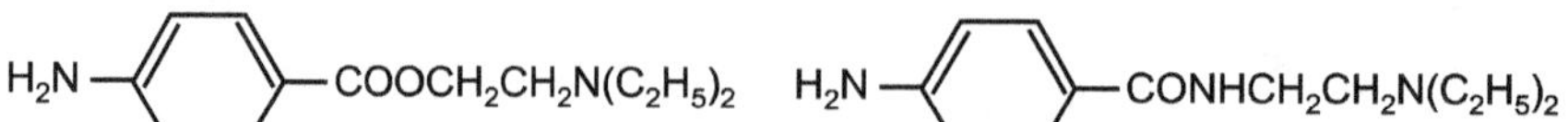

Procaine   Procainamide

(b)

Fig. 1.1 : (a) The similar shapes and outline electronic structures (stereoelectronic structures) of amide and ester groups (b) Procaine and procainamide

Drugs normally have to cross non-polar lipid membrane barriers in order to reach their site of action. As the polar nature of the drug increases, it usually becomes more difficult for the compound to cross these barriers. In many cases, drugs whose structures contain charged groups will not readily pass through membranes. Consequently, charged structures can be used to restrict the distribution of a drug. For example, quaternary ammonium salts, which are permanently charged, can be used as an alternative to an amine in a structure in order to restrict the passage of a drug across a membrane. The structure of the anticholinesterase neostigmine, developed from physostigmine, contains a quaternary ammonium group that gives the molecule a permanent charge. This stops the molecule from crossing the blood–brain barrier, which prevents unwanted CNS activity. However, its analogue miotine can form the free base. As a result, it is able to cross lipid membranes and causes unwanted CNS side effects.

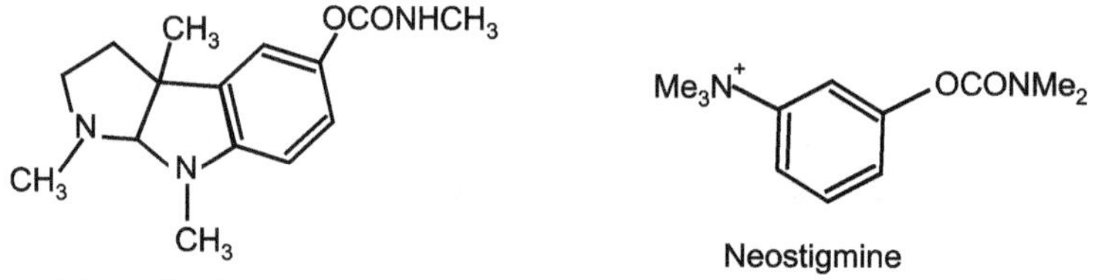

Physostigmine   Neostigmine

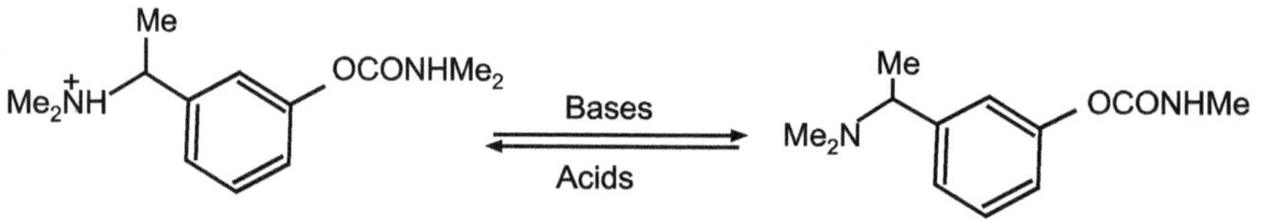

Miotine

Serendipity has always played a large part in the discovery of drugs. For example, the development of penicillin by Florey and Chain was only possible because Alexander Fleming noted the inhibition of *Staphylococcus* by *Penicillium notatum*. In spite of our increased knowledge, it is still necessary to pick the correct starting point for an investigation if a successful outcome is to be achieved and luck still plays a part in selecting that point. This state of affairs will not change and undoubtedly luck will also lead to new discoveries in the future. However, modern techniques such as computerised molecular modelling and combinatorial chemistry introduced in the 1970s and 1990s, respectively, are likely to reduce the number of intuitive discoveries. Two of the factors necessary for drug action are that the drug fits and binds to the target. Molecular modelling allows the researcher to predict the three-dimensional shapes of molecules and target. It enables workers to check whether the shape of a potential lead is complementary to the shape of its target. It also allows one to calculate the binding energy liberated when a molecule binds to its target. Molecular modelling has reduced the need to synthesise every analogue of a lead compound. It is also often used retrospectively to confirm the information derived from other sources. Combinatorial chemistry originated in the field of peptide chemistry has now been expanded to cover other areas. It is a group of related techniques for the simultaneous production of large numbers of compounds, known as libraries, for biological testing. Consequently, it is used for structure–activity studies and to discover new lead compounds. The procedures may be automated.

The general steps in the discovery of a new drug for a specific disease state.

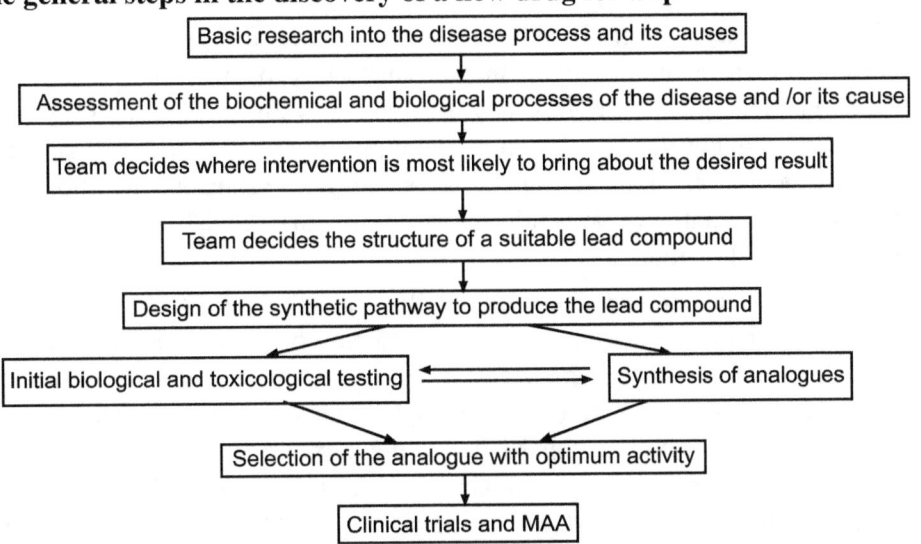

VARIOUS TECHNIQUES INVOLVED IN DISCOVERY OF MOLECULES

The starting point for the discovery of a new drug may be reached in several ways. The genesis of a research programme in pharmaceutical establishments, from where most of the drugs came today, is mainly by the following five procedures:

(i) **Random screening:** In this procedure, new chemical entities are subjected to a battery of screening tests designed to determine different types of biological activities. Such tests include studies on animal behaviour, isolated tissues, intact animals, and sometimes even animal models of disease. It is a sort of "blind hitting to hit a nail head". Such studies are time consuming, expensive and have low yield. It has been estimated that only one in every 4000 to 5000 new chemical entities screened is marketed. It is possible that the new drug thus found may ultimately turn out to be similar in its action to already existing drugs, with no added advantage. Such "me too drugs" add to the existing drug explosion.

(ii) **Molecular manipulation:** In this procedure, chemical analogues of existing drugs are synthesised and tested for their biological activity. This is a more logical approach, and may yield new compounds with certain advantages like better absorption, greater potency, more selective action, and fewer side effects e.g., hydrogenation of the parent thiazide diuretic, chlorothiazide has increased the sodium losing, and decreased the potassium losing potential of the resultant compounds, thereby raising their potency and lessening side effects. The thiazides and the oral hypoglycemic sulphonylureas represent slight modifications of the old antibacterial drug, sulphanilamide. Many synthetic penicillins and cephalosporins have been developed in this manner.

(iii) **Molecular designing:** This is the most rational form of drug research and development. It aims at designing of substances to fulfill a specific biological task. In its simplest form, this may involve the synthesis of a naturally occurring substance, a hormone, a vitamin, or a precursor of a neurotransmitter, e.g., dopamine for cardiogenic shock; levodopa for Parkinsonism; allopurinol, an analogue of xanthine, preventing synthesis of uric acid by inhibiting xanthine oxidase, used in gout.

(iv) **Metabolites of drugs:** Sometimes active metabolites of drugs are found to possess therapeutic advantages over the parent compound, e.g., paracetamol is a metabolite of phenacetin and is effective as an analgesic, but does not cause renal damage; chlordiazepoxide is metabolised to other active benzodiazepines which have a shorter action, and this has led to the introduction of drugs like oxazepam; the active metabolite of procainamide, N-acetyl-procainamide, is an effective antiarrhythmic drug, but does not cause a lupus-like syndrome that can occur with procainamide; suiphasalazine is metabolised to 5-aminosalicylic acid and sulphapyridine, the former has therapeutic activity and the latter (sulphapyridine) causes adverse effects; thus 5-aminosalicylic acid is now being used to treat ulcerative colitis.

(v) **Serendipity:** It means "happy observation by chance" and has led to the introduction of many useful remedies in the past, e.g., use of organo mercurials for cardiac oedema; penicillin as an antibacterial agent; lignocaine and phenytoin as antiarrhythmics, amphetamine to control hyperkinetic behaviour in children;

methotrexate for severe psoriasis; cyclophosphamide and azathiopurine to prevent tissue rejection in kidney transplants, and to treat autoimmune diseases. Thus, new uses are found for old drugs and the side effects find therapeutic applications. (**Table 1.1**)

Table 1.1 : Therapeutic applications of some drugs

Drug	Original proposed use	Side effect	Derived use
Merbaphen	Antitreponemal	Diuresis	Mercurial diuretics
Sulphanilamide	Antibacterial	Hypoglycaemia	Sulphonylureas
		Diuresis	Carbonic anhydrase inhibitors, Thiazides
		Thyroid inhibition	Thiouracils
Amphetamine	CNS stimulant	Appetite loss	Anorexiants
Iproniazid	Antituberculosis	Euphoria	Antidepressants (MAOIs)
Chlorpromazine	Antihistamine	Sedation	Phenothiazine antipsychotics
Reserpine	Antihypertensive	Sedation	Antipsychotic
Nalorphine	Narcotic antagonist	Analgesia	Agonist-antagonist analgesics
Diazoxide	Antihypertensive	Hyperglycaemia	Hyperglycaemia agent

The following steps are involved in the discovery of a new drug

1. Preliminary synthesis and physicochemical analysis.
2. Preliminary biological evaluation.
3. Secondary and specific biological evaluation.
4. Range-finding toxicological studies.
5. Target organ toxicological studies.
6. Acute and subacute toxicological studies.
7. Metabolic studies.
8. Synthesis and quality control of bulk material.

Note: These steps are shown in **Fig. 1.2**

9. Phase I clinical evaluation (human toxicity and metabolic studies).
10. Final (formulation, and final physicochemical analysis).
11. Phase II clinical evaluation (dose titration and limited efficacy studies).
12. Phase III clinical evaluation (broad efficacy and tolerance studies in a large population of patients; chronic, toxicological studies).
13. Phase IV clinical evaluation (surveillance during general clinical use).

Note: These steps are shown in **Fig. 1.3** and **Fig. 1.4**.

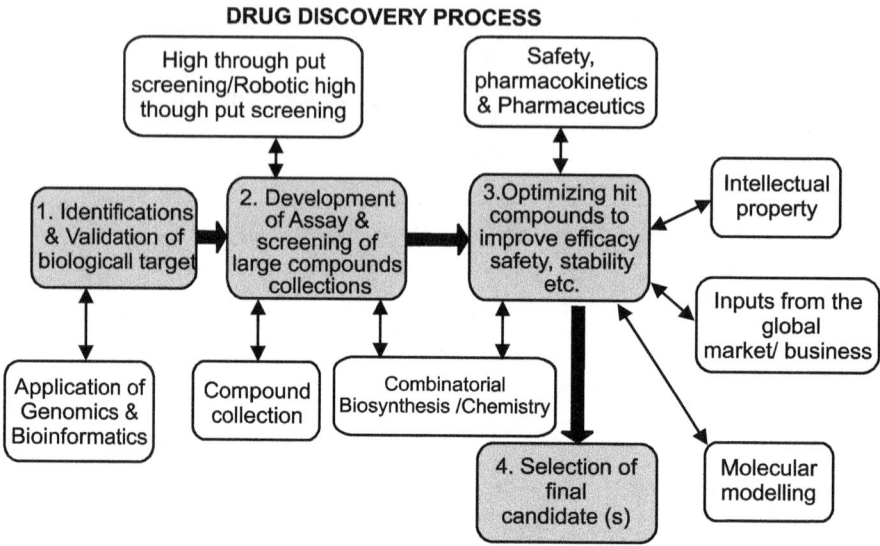

Current Methods Used in Drug Discovery Process Include :

1. Identification of novel pathways that is associated with disease, selection of targets in the pathway and development of screens.

2. Screening large compounds and natural compounds (from plants, animal products or microorganisms) for desired activity.

3. Molecular modeling using powerful software graphics and simulation program to generate 3D structures of target molecules and model the affinity of different molecules at these targets.

4. Targeted Synthesis i.e., the creation of original molecules with biological activities that target particular stages of a disease process. researchers design and synthesize molecules that bind to a particular locus on a target.

5. Combination chemistry, consist of systematically modifying an existing compound chemically to act on selected target. Screening of multiple compounds sometimes produce hint about how structural modifications alter the action of a compound.

Subsequent chemical modification of a load compound can result in a compound with enhanced properties, such as improved absorption enhanced safety, longer duration of action or increased efficiency. Hence, once a lead compound is developed, chemist will look up optimize the desirable characteristics of the compound.

Fig. 1.2 : Drug Discovery Process

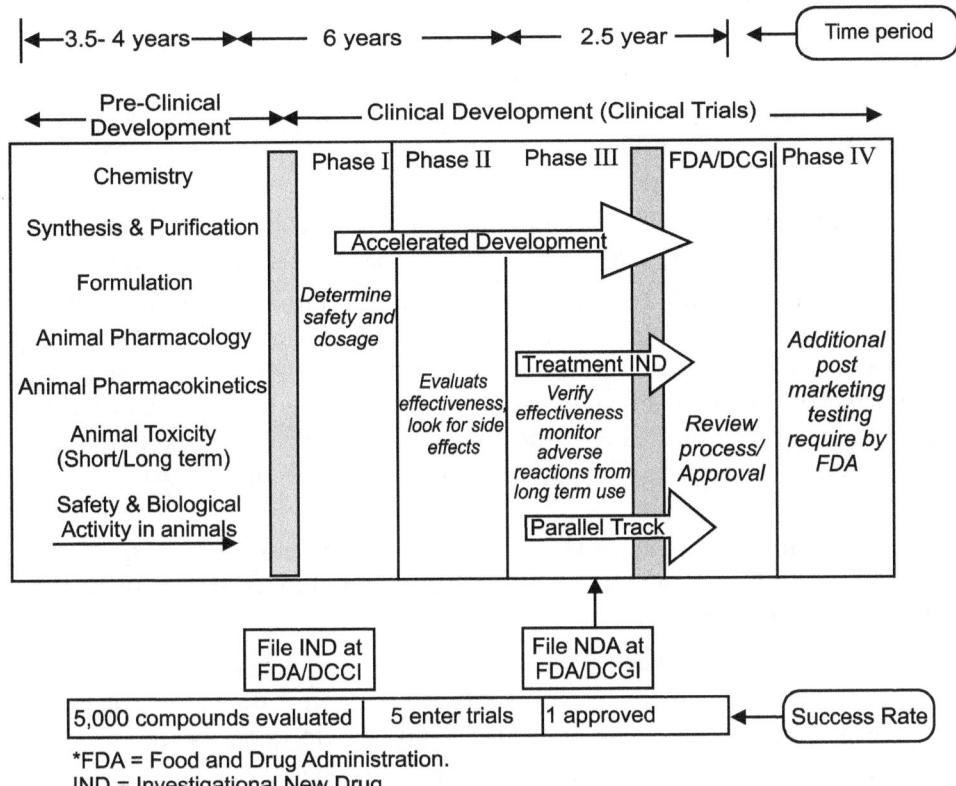

Fig 1.3 : New drug development process

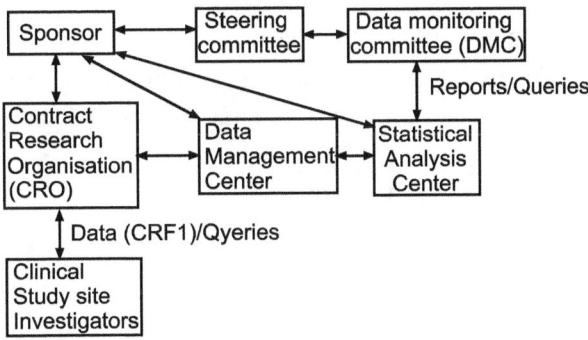

Fig. 1.4 : Trial organisation

PHYSICOCHEMICAL PROPERTIES OF DRUG

The biological response of a drug molecule is elicited when it interacts with bodies such as receptors, enzymes, membrane or certain small molecules in biological system.

The physicochemical properties and stereo chemical features of the drug greatly affects such interaction by influencing the process of drug transport from the site of administration to the site of action.

The main physicochemical properties affecting action are solubility, partition co-efficient, acid-base properties, chemical bonding, chelation and surface activity.

Solubility: On oral administration, a drug must go into solution before it can pass through the G.I.T. The dissolution of drug is dependent on several factors such as chemical structure, particle size, surface and crystal form. When given as a tablet, type of coating and tablet matrix govern the ability of the drug to dissolve. Since reaction is based on molecules dissolved in an aqueous phase, solubility is a significant property. Only a solution can interact with cellular and sub molecular structures that carry receptors.

The polar non-ionic compounds form hydrogen bond with water through –OH, –NH, –SH, and C=O groups or with non-bonding electron pairs of oxygen, nitrogen atom. The molecule is thus hydrated resulting in dissolution.

Non-polar compounds interact with lipids through hydrophobic bonds and get dispersed. The solubility of a drug can be changed by simple derivatisation. e.g. methyl prednisolone acetate is water insoluble but methyl prednisolone sodium succinate is water soluble and used orally and parentally. Solubility depends on rate of dissolution:

$$\frac{dc}{dt} = \text{rate of dissolution}$$

$$\frac{dc}{dt} \propto A \text{ (surface area of GIT)}$$

Partition co-efficient: In general, the higher the partition co-efficient, the greater is the rate of diffusion of drug into the membrane.

The partition co-efficient of the drug as the equilibrium constant is defined as P, which is the ratio of drug concentration in lipid phase and water phase.

$$p = \frac{[\text{drug}] \text{ Lipid}}{[\text{drug}] \text{ Water}}$$

$$\frac{dc}{dt} \propto K \text{ (partition coefficients)}$$

$$\frac{dc}{dt} \propto \frac{1}{h} \text{ (h = thickness)}$$

so, $$\frac{dc}{dt} \propto \frac{A.K (C_s - C_b)}{h}$$

Where, Cs = concentration of adjacent layer, Cb = concentration of bulk GIT fluid.

so,
$$\frac{dc}{dt} = D \frac{A.K(Cs - Cb)}{h}$$

Where D = diffusion coefficient

Acid-base properties: Mostly drugs are either acids or bases and so to a great extent acid-base properties of drugs affect their distribution and partition in a biological system.

For acids:
$$HA + H_2O \rightleftharpoons H_3O^+ + A^-$$
Acid　　　　　　　Conjugate base

$$B + H_2O \rightleftharpoons BH^+ + OH^-$$
Base　　　　　　　Conjugate acid

The physico-chemical parameters pKa are the measurements which determine in which direction acid-base reaction lies.

$$HA + H_2O \rightleftharpoons H_3O^+ + A^-$$
Acid　　　　　　　Conjugate base

$$K_{eq} = \frac{[H_3O^+][A^-]}{[HA][H_2O]}$$

Since water is in excess, it's the molar concentration can be treated as a constant and equation can be simplified as:

$$K_a = \frac{[H_3O^+][A^-]}{[HA]} \text{ Or } \frac{[\text{Conjugate Acid}][\text{Conjugate Base}]}{\text{Acid}}$$

$$pK_a = -\log K_a$$

Above equation can be written in log form as

$$pH = pK_a + \log \frac{[A^-]}{[HA]} \text{ Henderson Hassel batch equation}$$

Or
$$pH = pK_a + \log \frac{[\text{Conjugate Base}]}{[\text{Acid}]}$$

The above equation is known as **Henderson Hassel batch equation** and used for calculating the pH of weak acids and weak bases.

For weak bases

$$B + H_2O \rightleftharpoons BH^+ + OH^-$$
Base　　　　　　　Conjugate acid

To express the basicity of a drug in terms of pK_a using the following relationship

$$pK_a = pK_b - 14$$

The % ionisation of acid drug can be calculated as

$$\% \text{ ionisation} = \frac{100}{1 + 10^{(pK_a - pH)}}$$

Drug transport and distribution are also influenced by pK_a value.

Chemical Bonding: Most common drug action is initiation by interaction of the small molecules of drug with macromolecular system of the receptor. This interaction is promoted by various chemical bonds which are as follows

- van der waal Forces (London Dispersion Forces)
- Hydrophobic interaction
- Hydrogen bonding
- Charge transfer
- Dipole moment interaction
- Ion- dipole interaction
- Ionic-bond(electrovalent bond)
- Covalent bond

Chelation: Metal ion complexes are formed from electrons donating molecules or ions (ligands) and metal ions with incomplete valency shell. Amine, sulphide are neutral molecules which act as electron donors. Electron donating atoms in ligand`s molecule are N, O, S.

Depending upon the number of electron donating groups, a complexing agent can be di, tri or polydentate ligands .E.g. Ethyl diamine tetra acetic acid (EDTA)

When such an agent forms a complex with metal ion, a ring structure is formed which is called chelate and the process is called as chelation. Water soluble chelating agents which are soluble in water is called sequestering agent. The phenomena is known as sequestration.

The phenomena of chelation is significantly involved in the biological system and to some extent in explaining the drug action. Numerous enzyme systems contain metal ions chelated to them -haemoglobin and cyanocobalamin are naturally occurring chelates.

Surface activity: Many of the compounds such as detergents, transport agents for ions, several disinfects and antibiotics act through surface phenomena. In a living system, bio membrane form the largest functioning part of the cells.

STEREOCHEMICAL FEATURES

The significance of stereochemistry on drug disposition, receptor affinity and overall activity is being increasingly realised. Stereo chemical specificity in drug action, transport, biotransformation and elimination have been well established for a number of therapeutic agents. The therapeutic activity may reside in only one of the stereo isomers. Stereoisomer may show essentially similar qualitative and quantitative activity. The isomer may exhibit qualitatively similar but quantitatively different activities. The isomer may show quite distinct pharmacological activity. The three-dimensional details of a drug molecule may provide information about the nature of drug receptor interaction and receptor characteristics

Eg. (+)-lactic acid and (−) glyceric acid are corresponding enantiomorphs.

Optical Isomers: Optical isomerism is the most common isomerism encountered in medicinal agents. Optical isomerism is the result of molecular dissymmetry. There are several examples where difference in biological activities for 2-isomers (enantiomer) is observed in a drug molecule with one chiral centre. Stereo specificity of optical isomer in biological action is due to one isomer being able to achieve a 3-point attachment with its receptor molecule.

Eg. (a) Adrenaline (−) isomer is more active (because it contact with 3-site of receptor) than (+) adrenaline isomer.

(b) Warafarin is an anticoagulant drug which is administered as a racemate but the antihypoprothrombic effect of (−) warafarin is more than (+) warafarin.

Geometric isomerism: It is represented by cis/trans isomerism resulting from rotation due to carbon- carbon double bond or in a rigid ring system. Isomers have significantly different physical and chemical properties. Therefore, distribution patterns of these isomers is also different in biological systems. The receptor binding of these isomers is structurally in a specific manner.

E.g. The trans isomers called E- isomer of stilbestrol and cis or Z – isomer of oestrogenic is more active.

Conformational characteristics

Different arrangement of atoms that can be converted into another by rotation about single bonds is called conformation.

E. g. Acetylcholine produced muscarinic action if it is in staggered form.

BIOISOSTERISM

(Isosteric modification in drug design)

The term isosterism was introduced by *I. Langmuir* in 1919.

Isosteric compounds are defined as *"Compounds or groups of atoms having same number and arrangement of electrons"*.

It can also be defined as, those entities which have the same total charge as well as same number of electrons. E.g. Molecules of nitrogen (N_2) and carbon mono oxide (CO) show similarity in physical properties because both possess 14 electron and both are unchanged.

This term explains similarities in physical properties for non-isomeric molecules. Since, the biological properties of classically related isosteric compounds have to be more similar than their physical and chemical properties, the term bioisosteres was coined.

According to Burger – *"Bioisosterism is defined as compounds or groups that possess near equal molecular shape and volume, approximately the same distribution of electrons, and which exhibit similar physical properties".*

They are of two types

1. Classical bioisoester.
2. Non-classical bioisoester.

(1) Classical bioisoester : They are similar in shape and electronic configuration of atom, group and molecule which they replace.

Replacement of univalent atoms or groups- The analogous groups are –F, Cl, –OH, NH_2 and CH_3.

E.g. - Modification of oral hypoglycemics have involved successive replacement of amino (–NH_2) group or chlorine (Cl_2) to give tolbutamide and chlorpropamide, which possess extended biological half-lives and reduced toxicity.

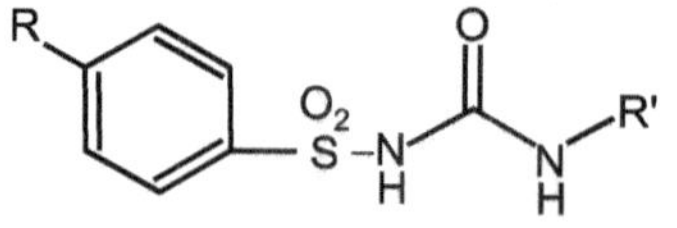

Drugs	R	R'	Half – lives (hrs)
Tolbutamide	–CH_3	–nC_4H_9	5.7
Chlorpropamide	–Cl	–nC_3H_7	33

Interchange of divalent atom or groups- Bioisosterism occurs more frequently between divalent atoms and groups. Steric similarities here are contributed by similarities in bond angles, so that the attached groups are oriented in a particular manner. This is due to isomeric relationship of ester and amides.

In ester rotation of C-O-C, bond is restricted by resonance and aliphatic ester exist in cis-configuration rather than trans.

Groups	O (ether)	S (thioether)	NH	CH₂
Bond angle	108 ± 3	112 ± 2	111 ± 3	111.5 ± 3

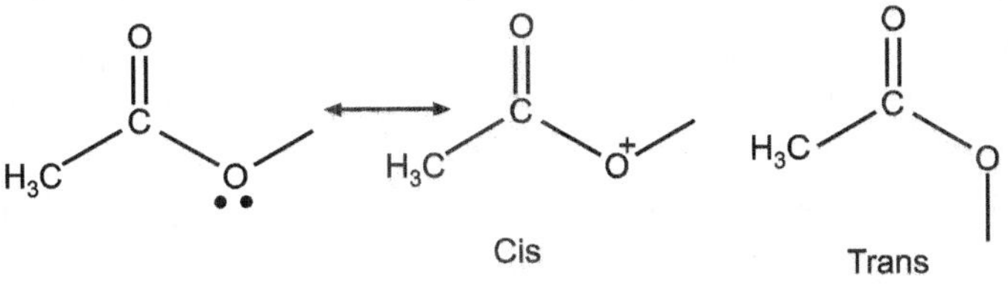

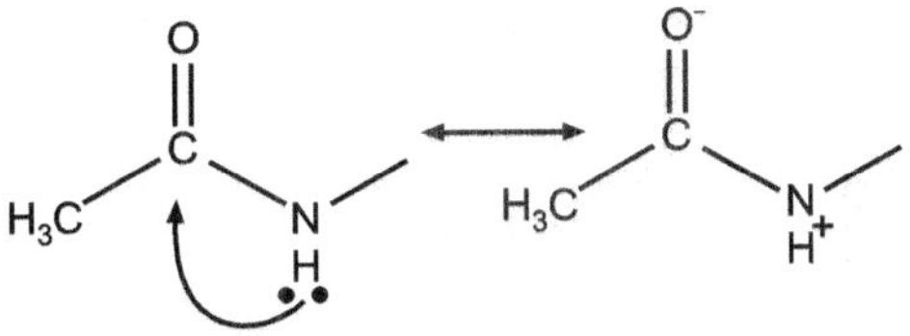

Local anesthetic activity of procaine is greater than procainamide because the dipolar character of carbonyl group is required for activity.

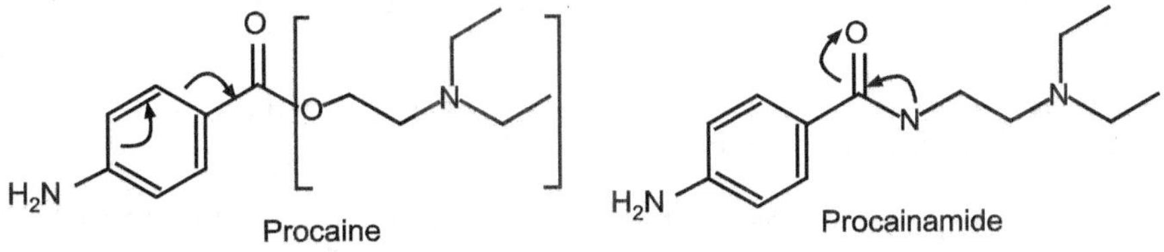

In procainamide, the amine group resonance (+M) is offset by amide resonance so that magnitude of C=O dipole is decreased.

Procaine activity is due to an optimum confirmation, and its lipid solubility enables its transport across the membrane.

Interchange of trivalent atom or ring equivalent : The substitution of –CH = by –N = in aromatic ring of antihistamine, mepyramine has evolved from replacement of phenyl group antigran by pyridyl.

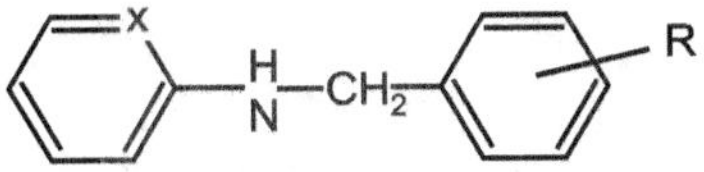

Drugs	X	R
Antegran	CH	H
Mepyramine	N	OCH₃ (p)
Chlorpheniramine	N	Cl (p)

The π electron deficiency of pyridine nucleus enables the nitrogen electron pair to hydrogen bond with water molecules, effecting an increase in hydrophilicity which is significant in determining the high level of biological activity. Substitution of pyridinyl amino –N = by –CH = in mepyramine produces chlorpheniramine that has a short powerful action and reduces sedation which is significant side effect of mepyramine.

The electron withdrawing effect of pyridyl and para chloro, phenyl substitution on –CH = group promotes formation of electron deficient centre, which may determine mechanism by which bioisoester- receptor interactions occur.

Tetrasubstitution atoms : In this type of interchange, quaternary charged atoms are changed with tertiary carbon atom.

E.g. Replacement of quaternary ammonium group with phosphonium in cholinergic agonist and arsonium analogues have greater toxicity than nitrogen analogue.

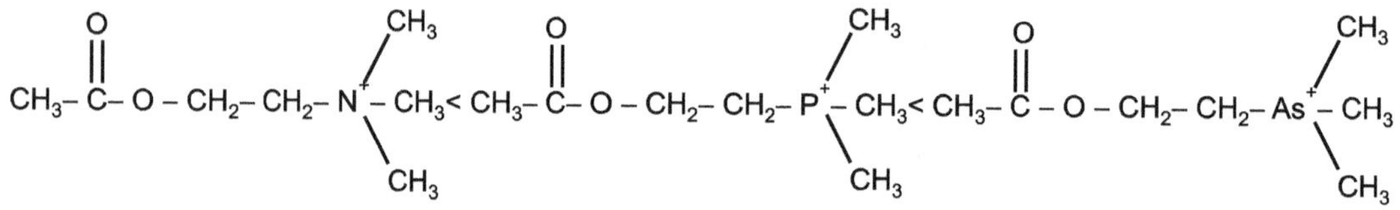

$$CH_3-\overset{O}{\underset{\|}{C}}-O-CH_2-CH_2-\overset{CH_3}{\underset{CH_3}{N^+}}-CH_3 < CH_3-\overset{O}{\underset{\|}{C}}-O-CH_2-CH_2-\overset{CH_3}{\underset{CH_3}{P^+}}-CH_3 < CH_3-\overset{O}{\underset{\|}{C}}-O-CH_2-CH_2-\overset{CH_3}{\underset{CH_3}{As^+}}-CH_3$$

(2) Non – classical isosteres : They do not obey the steric and electronic definition of classical isosteres.

They do not have same number of carbon atoms as replacement.

E. g. –CO– ; COOH– ; –SO$_2$NH$_2$; H; –CH.

The above groups when substituted in a certain molecules, give rise to a compound where steric arrangement and electronic configuration are similar to those of the parent compound, e.g. pair of these isosteres are H and F, CO and SO$_2$, etc.

(a) Reversal of group: Trimaperidine is the propanoate ester of piperidyl alcohol, while pethidine (mepridine) is an ethyl ester of piperidyl carboxylic acid. First compound is related to second by reversal of an ester group.

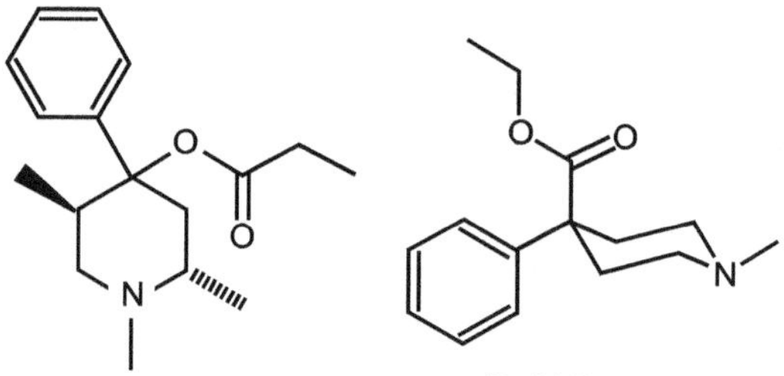

Trimeperidine   Pethidine

(b) Ring opening and closure: Cyclic v/s non – cyclic bioisosteric replacement: Sulfathiazole derivative lowers the blood sugar to fatal levels. Modification involving opening of thiazole ring give a thiourea unit in which = S was replaced by –O– yielding carbutamide which has less toxicity than tolbutamide.

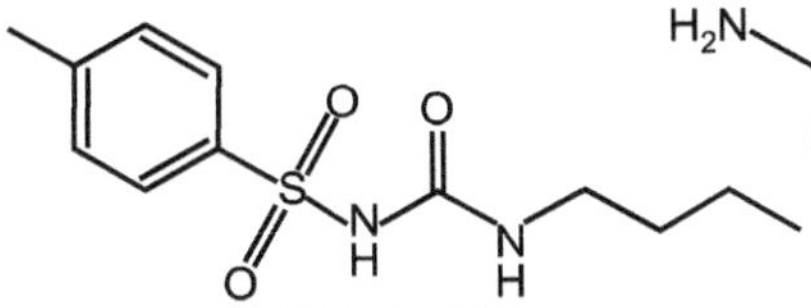

[Structures: Tolbutamide and Carbutamide]

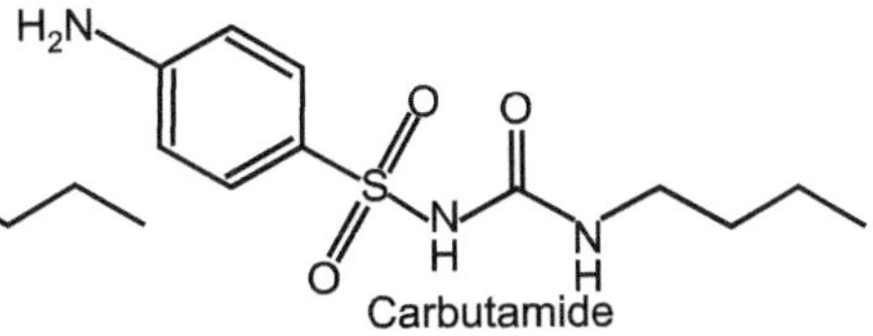

(c) Groups with similar polar effects: Correlation of metabolite – antimetabolite relationship in antagonism of PABA, by sulphonamide has focussed attention on groups with similar polar effects. e.g. –COOH and SO_2NHR which give antagonistic or analogous biological effects. E.g. Antagonism of nikethamide by pyridine –3– sulfonic acid and stimulation of respiratory stimulant effect by nitrophenyl analogue.

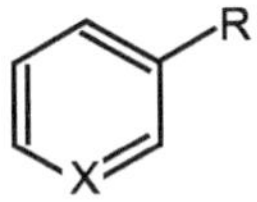

[Structure: Nikelhamide R]

Nikethamide R = $CONC_2H_5$, X = N

Pyridine - 3 - sulfonic acid R = SO_3H, X = N

Nitro Phenyl analogue R = $CONC_2H_5$, X = C – NO_2

(d) Amide group bioisosteres: (Amide bond is important for peptide). It is possible to convert amide bond into chemically stable and orally available molecules.

E.g. Amide (NH–CO), reversed amide (–CO–NH–), thioamide (–NH–CS), Urea (–NHCONH–).

Amide bond is required as hydrogen donor and acceptor functionalities for maintaining biological activity.

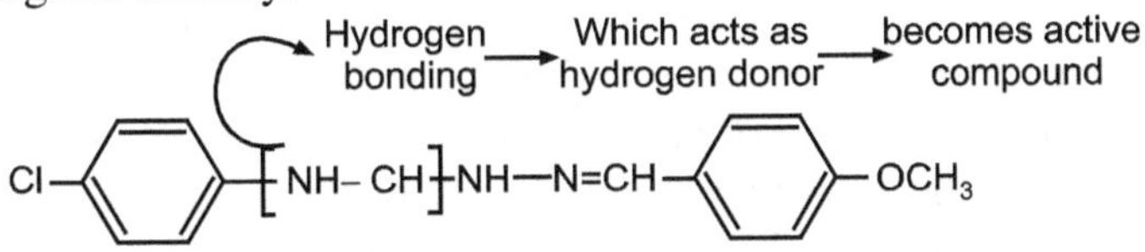

[Structure: Active anticonvulsant agent — Cl–C6H4–[NH–CH]–NH—N=CH–C6H4–OCH3, with Hydrogen bonding → Which acts as hydrogen donor → becomes active compound]

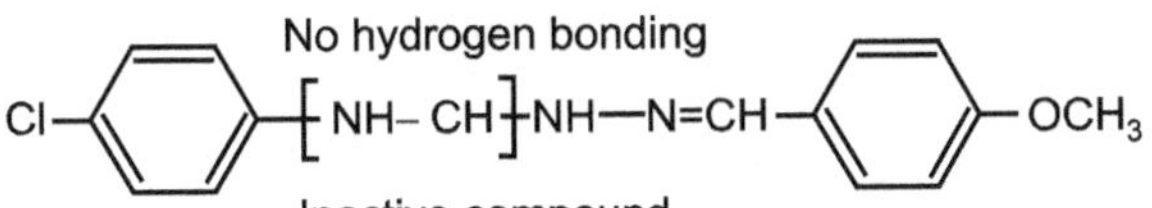

[Structure: Inactive compound — Cl–C6H4–[NH–CH]–NH—N=CH–C6H4–OCH3, No hydrogen bonding]

(e) Thiourea bioisosteres: Employed as H_2 receptor antagonist (for treatment of peptide ulcer). Isosteric modification of imidazole nucleus in cimetidine gives ranitidine without the side effects associated with cimetidine.

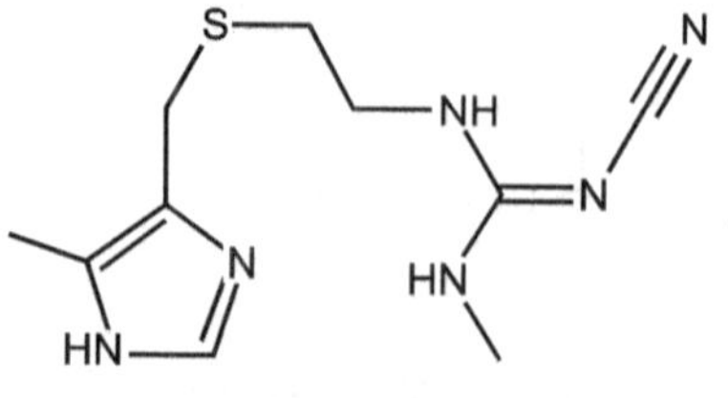

(f) Halogen bioisosteres: Halogens have been replaced by electron - withdrawing groups such as cyano or trifluoro methyl group. In a series of 5- benzyl uracil developed as uridine phosphorylase inhibitors, the activity is decreased by strong electron with drawing group like CF_3.

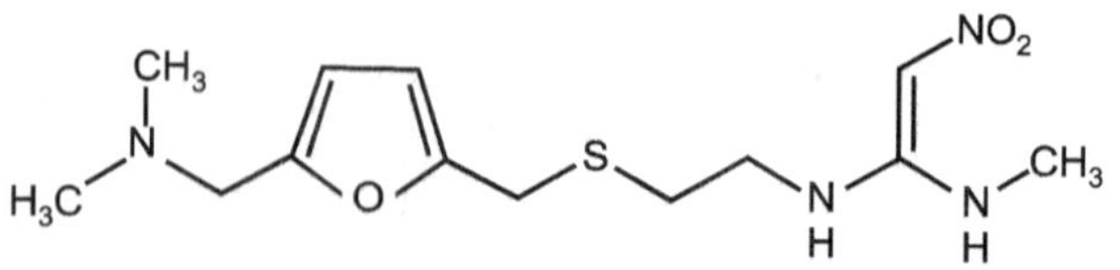

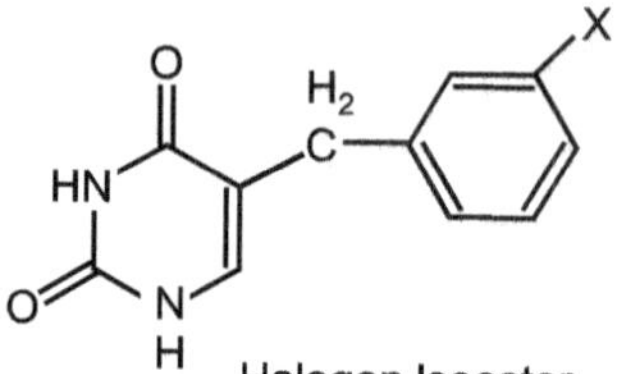

Halogen Isoester

X = Cl, IC_{50} (mm) = 2.5
X = CN, IC_{50} (mm) = 13.2

IMPORTANCE OF STRUCTURAL ACTIVITY RELATIONSHIP (SAR) IN DEVELOPMENT OF MOLECULES

Once the structure of a lead compound is known, the medicinal chemist moves on to study its structure activity relationships (SAR). The aim here is to ascertain which parts of the molecule are important to biological activity and which are not. If it is possible to crystallise the target with the drug bound to the binding site, the crystal structure of the complex could be solved by X-ray crystallography and then studied with molecular modelling software to identify important binding interactions. However, this may not be possible, either because the target structure cannot be crystallised or because the target structure has not been identified. If that is the case, it will be necessary to revert to the traditional method of synthesising a selected number of compounds that vary slightly from the original structure, then studying what effect it has on the biological activity.

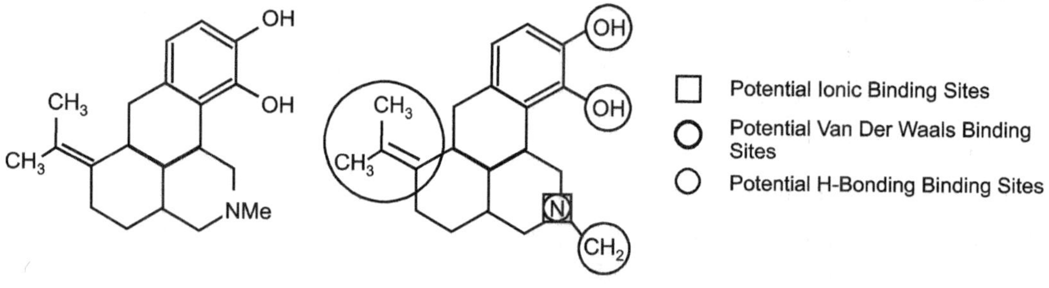

□ Potential Ionic Binding Sites
◯ Potential Van Der Waals Binding Sites
◯ Potential H-Bonding Binding Sites

(a) Glipine

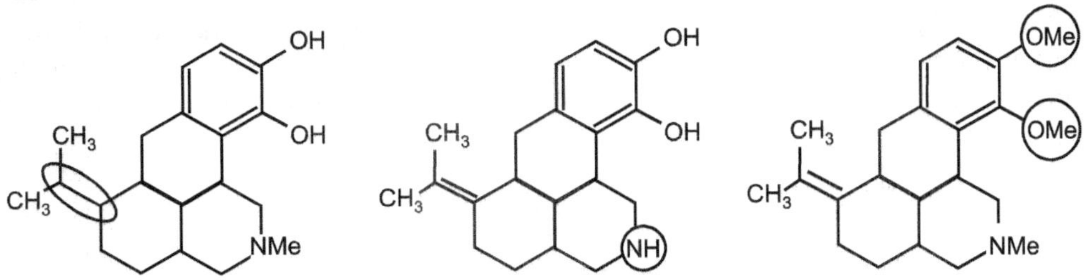

(b) Modifications of glipine

Fig. 1.5

Let us imagine that we have isolated a natural product with the structure shown in **Fig. 1.5 (a)**. We shall name it glipine. There are a variety of groups present in the structure and the diagram shows the potential bonding interactions which are possible with a receptor. It is unlikely that all of these interactions take place, so we have to identify those which do. By synthesising compounds (such as the examples shown in **Fig. 1.5 (b)** where one particular group of the molecule is removed or altered, it is possible to find out which groups are essential and which are not.

The ease with which this task can be carried out depends on how easily we can carry out the necessary chemical transformations to remove or alter the relevant group. For example, the importance or otherwise of an amine group is relatively easy to establish, whereas the importance of an aromatic ring might be more difficult. Hydroxyl groups, amino groups, and aromatic rings are particularly common binding groups in medicinal chemistry, so let us consider what analogues could be synthesised to establish whether they are involved or not.

1. The binding role of hydroxyl groups

Hydroxyl groups are commonly involved in hydrogen bonding. Converting such a group to a methyl ether or an ester is straightforward **(Fig. 1.6)** and will usually destroy or weaken such a bond.

$$R\text{-}OH \xrightarrow{CH_3I} R\text{-}OMe$$

$$R\text{-}OH \xrightarrow{CH_3COCl} R\text{-}O\text{-}\overset{\overset{O}{\|}}{C}\text{-}CH_3$$

$$R\text{-}OH \xrightarrow{CH_3SO_2Cl} R\text{-}O\text{-}\overset{\overset{O}{\|}}{\underset{\underset{O}{\|}}{S}}\text{-}CH_3 \xrightarrow{LiAlH_4} R\text{-}H$$

Fig 1.6 : Conversions of hydroxyl groups

Alcohols and phenols are functional groups which are common in many drugs and are often involved in hydrogen bonding. The oxygen can act as a hydrogen bond acceptor, and the hydrogen can act as a hydrogen bond donor **(Fig. 1.7)**. The directional preference for hydrogen bonding is indicated by the arrows in the figure, but it is important to realise that slight deviations are possible. One or all of these interactions may be important in binding the drug to the binding site. Synthesising a methyl ether or an ester analogue would be relevant in testing this, as it is highly likely that the bonding would be disrupted in either analogue.

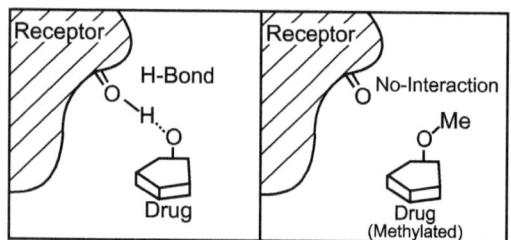

Fig. 1.7 : Possible hydrogen bonding interactions for an alcohol or phenol

Let us consider the methyl ether first.

There are two reasons why the ether might hinder or prevent the hydrogen bonding of the original alcohol or phenol. The obvious explanation is that the proton of the original hydroxyl group is involved as a hydrogen bond donor and if it is removed, the hydrogen bond is lost (Frames 1 and 2 in **Fig. 1.8**). However, suppose the oxygen atom is acting as a hydrogen bond acceptor (Frame 3 in **Fig. 1.8**), the oxygen is still present in the ether analogue and takes part in hydrogen bonding. The extra bulk of the methyl group should hinder the close approach that was previously attainable and should disrupt hydrogen bonding (Frame 4 in **Fig. 1.8**). The hydrogen bonding may not be completely destroyed, but we could reasonably expect it to be weakened.

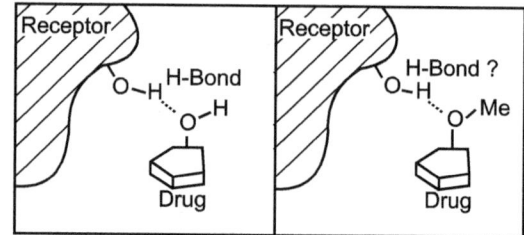

Fig. 1.8 : Possible hydrogen bond interactions

The oxygen is still present in the ether or the ester analogue, but we could still expect the hydrogen bonding to be effected on. The hydrogen bonding may not be completely destroyed, but we could reasonably expect it to be weakened, especially in the case of an ester. The reason is straight forward. When we consider the electronic properties of an ester compared to an alcohol, then we observe an important difference. The carboxyl group can 'pull' electrons from the neighbouring oxygen to give the resonance structure shown in **Fig. 1.9**. Since the lone pair is involved in such an interaction, it cannot take part so effectively in a hydrogen bond. Steric factors also count against the hydrogen bond.

The extra bulk of the acyl group will hinder the close approach which was previously attainable.

This steric hindrance also explains how a methyl ether could disrupt hydrogen bonding. If there is still some doubt over whether a hydroxyl group is involved in hydrogen bonding or not, it could be replaced with an isosteric group such as methyl. This would be more conclusive, but synthesis is more difficult.

Another possibility is to react the hydroxyl group with methane sulfonyl chloride followed by lithium aluminum hydride. This would replace the hydroxyl with a proton, but any group which is prone to reduction would have to be protected first.

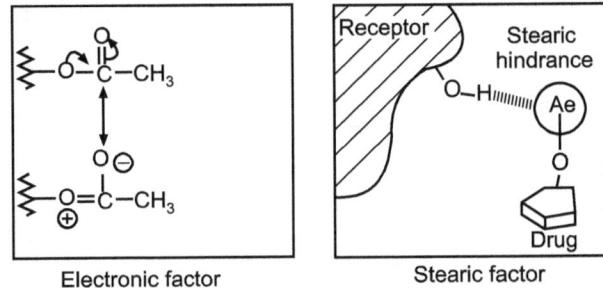

Fig. 1.9 : Factors by which an ester group can disrupt hydrogen bonding of the original hydroxyl group

2. The binding role of aromatic rings

Aromatic rings are commonly involved in van der Waals interactions with flat hydrophobic regions of the binding site. If the ring is hydrogenated to a cyclohexane ring, the structure is no longer flat and interacts far less efficiently with the binding site (**Fig. 1.10**).

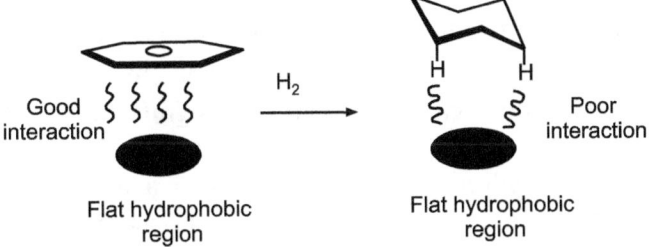

Fig. 1.10 : Reduction in the binding efficiency of aromatic rings by hydrogenation

However, carrying out the reduction may well cause problems elsewhere in the structure, since aromatic rings are difficult to reduce and need forcing conditions. Replacing the ring altogether with a bulky alkyl group could reduce van der Waals bonding for the same reason given above, but obtaining such compounds could involve a major synthetic effort.

3. The Binding Role of Double Bonds :

Unlike aromatic rings, double bonds are easy to reduce and this has a significant effect on the shape of that part of the molecule. The planar double bond is converted into a bulky alkyl group. If the original alkene was involved in vander Waals bonding with a flat surface on the receptor, reduction should weaken that interaction, since the bulkier product is less able to approach the receptor surface **Fig 1.11 (a) and (b)**.

(a) The binding role of double bonds

(b) Binding comparison of an alkene with an alkane

Fig. 1.11

4. Binding role of ketones and aldehydes

A ketone group is common in many of the structures studied in medicinal chemistry. It is a planar group that can interact with a binding site through hydrogen bonding where the carbonyl oxygen acts as a hydrogen bond acceptor (**Fig1.12**). Two such interactions are possible, as two lone pairs of electrons are available on the carbonyl oxygen. The lone pairs are in sp^2 hybridised orbitals, which are in the same plane as the functional group. The carbonyl group also has a significant dipole moment and so a dipole--dipole interaction with the binding site is also possible.

Fig 1.12 : Binding interactions that are possible for 3 carbonyl group

It is relatively easy to reduce a ketone to an alcohol and it may be possible to carry out this reaction directly on the lead compound. This significantly changes the geometry of the functional group, from planar to tetrahedral. Such an alteration in geometry may well weaken any existing hydrogen bonding interactions and will certainly weaken any dipole-dipole interactions, as both the magnitude and orientation of the dipole moment will be altered (**Fig. 1.13**). If it was suspected that the oxygen present in the alcohol analogue might still be acting as a hydrogen bond acceptor then the ether or ester analogues could be studied as described above. Reactions are available that can reduce a ketone completely to an alkane and remove the oxygen, but they are likely to be impractical for many of the lead compounds studied in medicinal chemistry.

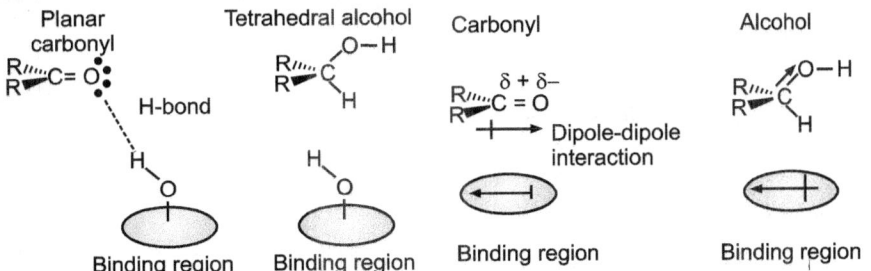

Fig. 1.13 : Effect on binding interaction following the reduction of a ketone or aldehyde

Aldehydes are less common in drugs since they are more reactive and are susceptible to oxidation to carboxylic acids. However, they could interact in the same way as ketones, and similar analogues could be studied.

5. Binding role of amines

Amines are extremely important functional groups in medicinal chemistry and are present in many drugs. They may be involved in hydrogen bonding either as a hydrogen bond acceptor or a hydrogen bond donor (**Fig. 1.14**). The nitrogen atom has one lone pair of electrons and can act as a hydrogen bond acceptor for one hydrogen bond. Primary and secondary amines have N-H groups and can act as hydrogen bond donors. Aromatic and hetero aromatic amines act only as hydrogen bond donor, because the lone pair interacts with the aromatic or hetero aromatic ring.

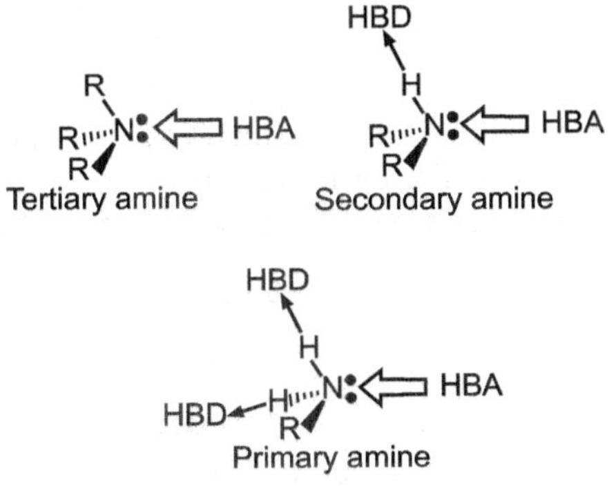

Fig. 1.14 : Possible binding interactions for amines

In many cases, the amine may be protonated when it interacts with its target binding site, which means that it is ionised and cannot act as a hydrogen bond acceptor. However, it can still act as a hydrogen bond donor and will form a stronger hydrogen bond than if it was not ionised (**Fig. 1.15**). Alternatively, a strong ionic interaction may take place with a carboxylate ion in the binding site (**Fig. 1.16**).

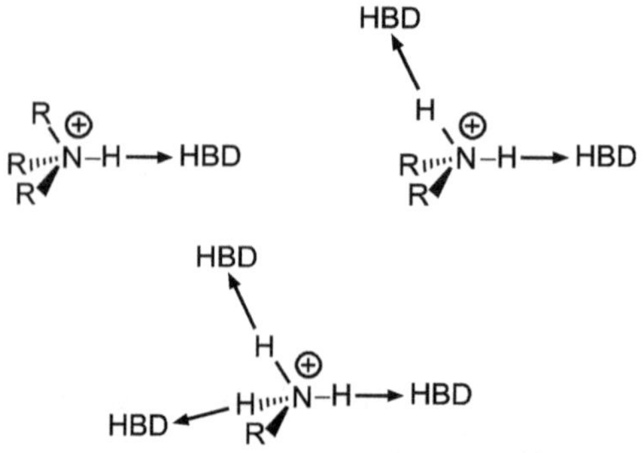

Fig 1.15 : Possible hydrogen bonding interactions for ionised amines

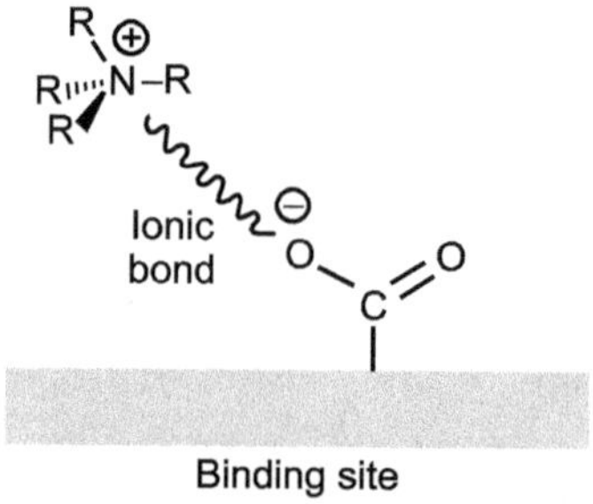

Fig 1.16 : Ionic interaction between an ionised amine and a carboxylate ion

To test whether ionic or hydrogen bonding interactions are taking place, an amide analogue could be studied. This will prevent the nitrogen acting as a hydrogen bond acceptor, as the nitrogen's lone pair will interact with the neighbouring carbonyl group instead (**Fig.1.17**). This interaction also prevents protonation of the nitrogen and rules out the possibility of ionic interactions. The right-hand structure in **Fig. 1.17** has a positive charge on the nitrogen and could still take part in an ionic interaction. However, this structure is not present as a distinct entity and the figure is only used to represent the fact that the lone pair can interact with the carbonyl group to produce double-bond character in the amide group. Any positive charge is extremely weak in comparison to that present in an ionised amine.

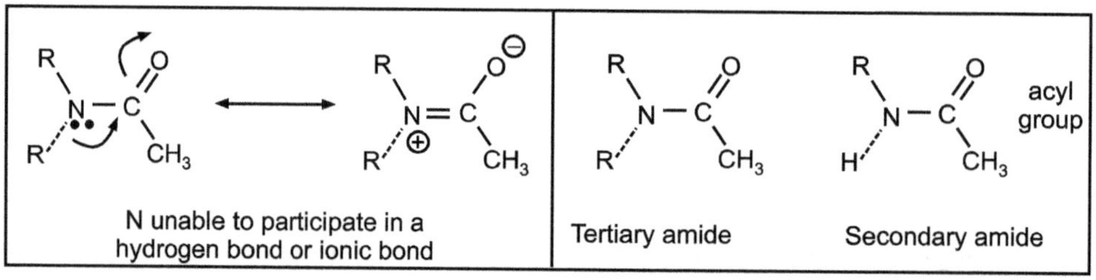

Fig 1.17 : Interaction of the nitrogen lone pair with the neighbouring carbonyl group in amides

It is relatively easy to form secondary and tertiary amides from primary and secondary amines respectively and it may be possible to carry out this reaction directly on the lead compound. A tertiary amide lacks the N-H group of the original secondary amine and would test whether this is involved as a hydrogen bond donor. The secondary amide formed from a primary amine still has an N-H group present, but the steric bulk of the acyl group should hinder it acting as a hydrogen bond donor.

Tertiary amines cannot be converted directly to amides, but if one of the alkyl groups is a methyl group, it is often possible to remove it with vinyloxycarbonyl chloride (VOC-Cl) to form a secondary amine which could then be converted to the amide (**Fig. 1.18**). The demethylation reaction is extremely useful and has been used to good effect in the synthesis of morphine analogues.

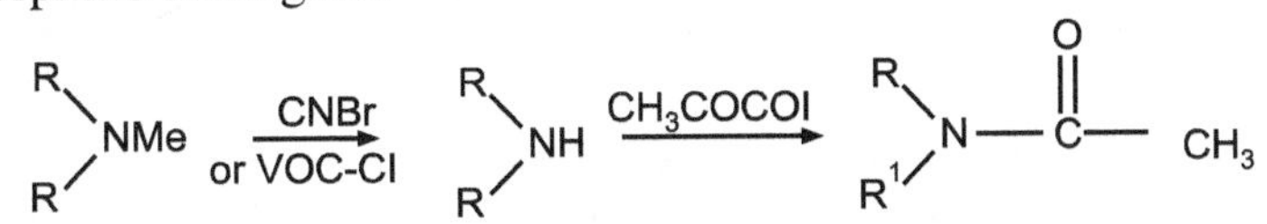

Fig. 1.18 : Dealkylation of a tertiary amine and formation of a secondary amide

6. Binding Role of Amides

Many of the lead compounds currently studied in medicinal chemistry are peptides or polypeptides, consisting of amino acids linked together by peptide or amide bonds. Amides are likely to interact with binding sites through hydrogen bonding (**Fig. 1.19**). The carbonyl oxygen atom can act as a hydrogen bond acceptor and has the potential to form two hydrogen bonds. Both the lone pairs involved are in sp^2 hybridised orbitals which are located in the same plane as the amide group. The nitrogen cannot act as a hydrogen bond acceptor because the lone pair interacts with the neighbouring carbonyl group. Primary and secondary amides have an N-H group, which allows the possibility of this group acting as a hydrogen bond donor.

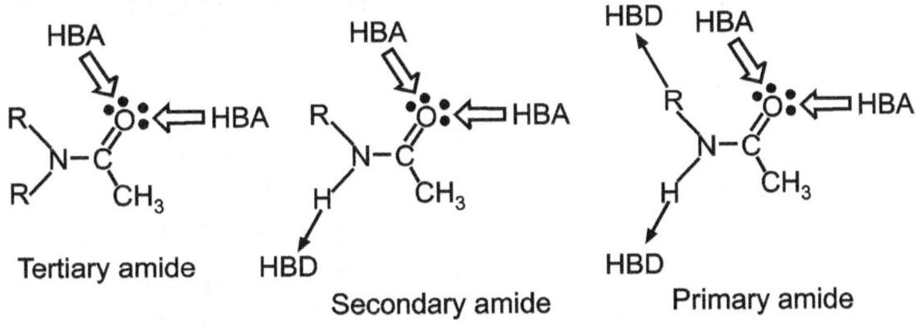

Fig 1.19 : Possible hydrogen bonding interaction for amides

The most common type of amide in peptide lead compounds is the secondary amide. Suitable analogues that could be prepared to test out possible binding interactions are shown in **Fig. 1.20**. All the analogues apart from the primary and secondary amines could be used to check whether the amide is acting as a hydrogen bond donor, and the alkenes and amines could be tested to see whether the amide is acting as a hydrogen bond acceptor. However, there are traps for the unwary. The amide group is planar and does not rotate, because of its partial double bond character. The ketone, the secondary amine, and the tertiary amine shown have a single bond at the equivalent position, which can rotate. This would alter the relative positions of any binding groups on either side of the amide group and lead to a loss of binding even if the amide itself was not involved in binding. Therefore, a loss of activity would not necessarily mean that the amide is important as a binding group. With these groups, it would only be safe to say that the amide group is not essential if activity is retained. Similarly, the primary amine and carboxylic acid may be found to have no activity, but this might be due to the loss of important binding groups in one half of the molecule. These particular analogues would only be worth considering if the amide group is peripheral to the molecule (e.g. R-NHCOMe or R-CONHMe) and not part of the main skeleton.

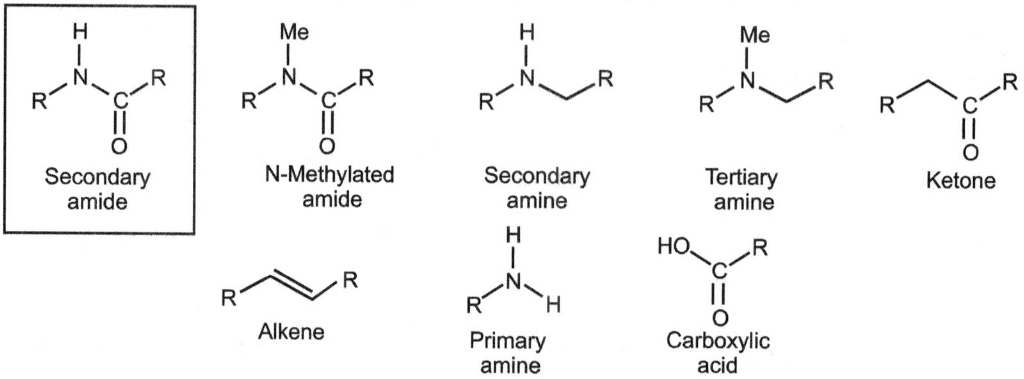

Fig 1.20 : Possible analogues to test the binding interactions of a secondary amide

The alkenes would be a particularly useful analogue to test, since it is planar, cannot rotate, and cannot act as a hydrogen bond donor or hydrogen bond acceptor. However, the synthesis of this analogue may not be simple. In fact, it is likely that all the analogues described would have to be prepared using a full synthesis. Amides are relatively stable functional groups and although several of the analogues described might be attainable from the lead compound directly, it is more likely that the lead compound would not survive the forcing conditions required.

Amides which are within a ring system are called **lactams.** They too can form intermolecular hydrogen bonds. However, if the ring is small and suffers ring strain, the lactam can undergo a chemical reaction with the target leading to the formation of a covalent bond. The best examples of this are the penicillins, which contain a four membered β – lactam ring. This acts as an acylating agent and irreversibly inhibits a bacterial enzyme by acylating a serine residue in the active site (**Fig. 1.21**).

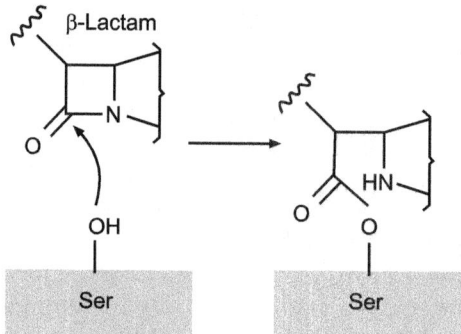

Fig. 1.21 : β - lactam ring acting as an acylating agent

7. Binding role of quaternary ammonium salts

Quaternary ammonium salts are ionised and can interact with carboxylate groups by ionic interactions. (**Fig. 1.22**) Another possibility is an induced dipole interaction between the quaternary ammonium ion and any aromatic ring in the binding site. The positively charged nitrogen can distort the π electrons of the aromatic ring such that a dipole is induced, whereby the face of the ring is slightly negative and the edges are slightly positive. This allows an interaction between the slightly negative faces of the aromatic rings and the positive charge of the quaternary ammonium ion.

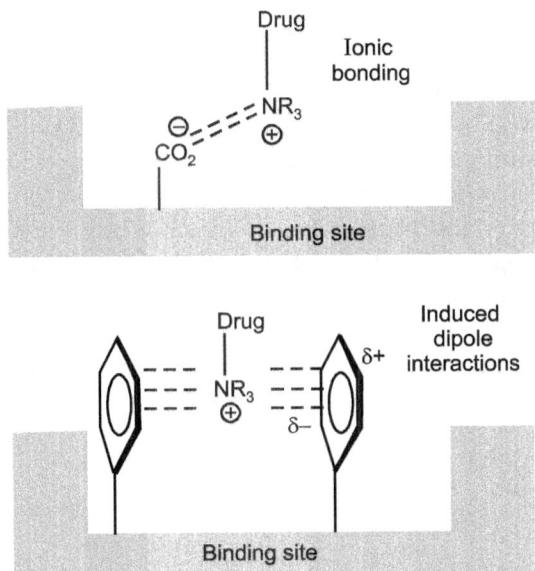

Fig. 1.22 : Possible binding interactions of a Quaternary ammonium ion

The importance of these interactions could be tested by synthesising an analogue that has a tertiary amine group rather than the quaternary ammonium group. Of course, it is possible that such a group could become ionised by being protonated, and interact in the same way. Converting the amine to an amide would prevent this possibility. The neurotransmitter acetylcholine has a quaternary ammonium group which is thought to bind to the binding site of its target receptor by ionic bonding and/or induced-dipole interactions

8. Binding Role of Carboxylic Acids

The carboxylic acid group is reasonably common in drugs. It can act as a hydrogen bond acceptor in various ways, or as a hydrogen bond donor (**Fig.1. 23**). Alternatively, it may exist as the carboxylate ion. This allows the possibility of an ionic interaction or a strong hydrogen bond where the carboxylate ion acts as the hydrogen bond acceptor. The carboxylate ion has also been found to be a good ligand for zinc ions, which are present as cofactors in enzymes known as *zinc metalloproteinases*.

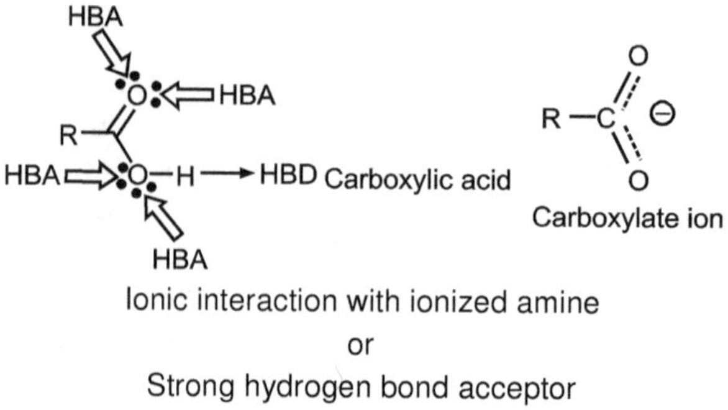

Fig. 1.23 : Possible binding interactions for a carboxylic acid and carboxylate ion

In order to test the possibility of such interactions, analogues such as esters, primary alcohols, and ketone could be synthesised and tested (**Fig. 1.24**). None of these functional groups can ionise, so a loss of activity could imply that an ionic bond is important. The primary alcohol could shed light on whether the carbonyl oxygen is involved in hydrogen bonding, whereas the ester and ketone could indicate whether the hydroxyl group of the carboxylic acid is involved in hydrogen bonding. It may be possible to synthesise the ester analogue directly from the lead compound, but the reduction of a carboxylic acid to a primary alcohol requires harsher conditions and this sort of analogue would normally be prepared by a full synthesis. The ketone would also have to be prepared by a full synthesis.

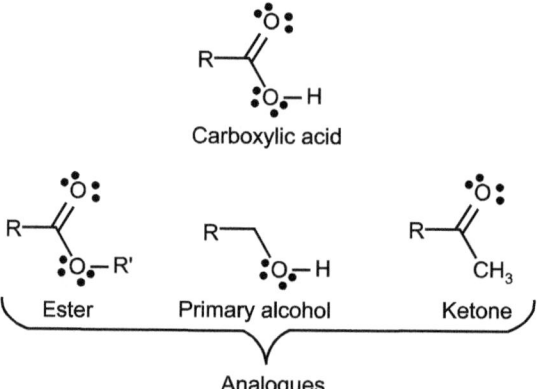

Fig. 1.24 : Analogues for carboxylic acid

9. Binding role of esters

An ester functional group has the potential to interact with a binding site as a hydrogen bond acceptor only (**Fig.1.25**). The carbonyl oxygen is more likely to act as the hydrogen bond acceptor than the alkoxy oxygen, as it is sterically less hindered and has a greater electron density. The importance or otherwise of the carbonyl group could be judged by testing an equivalent ether, which would require a full synthesis.

Esters are susceptible to hydrolysis *in vivo* by metabolic enzymes called esterases. This may pose a problem if the lead compound contains an ester that is important to binding, as it means the drug might have a short lifetime *in vivo*. There are several drugs that do contain esters and are relatively stable to metabolism, due to either electronic factors that stabilise the ester or steric factors that protect it.

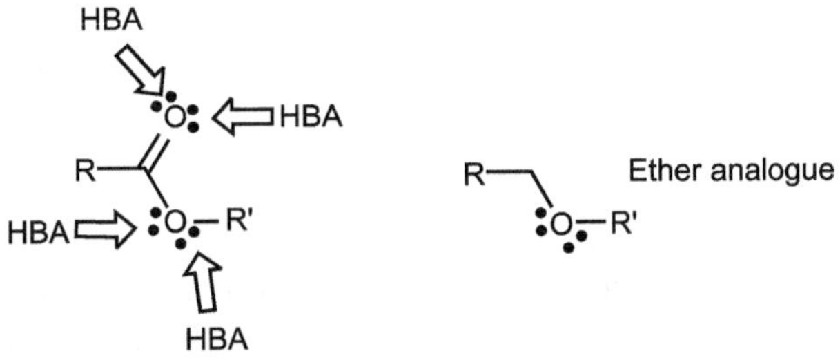

Fig. 1.25 : Possible binding interactions for an ester

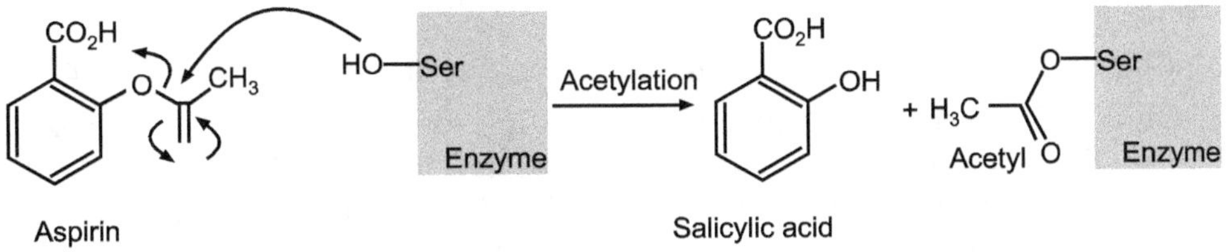

Fig. 1.26 : Aspirin acting as an acylating agent

10. Binding Role of Alkyl and Aryl Halides

Alkyl halides involving chlorine, bromine, or iodine tend to be chemically reactive, since the halide ion is a good leaving group. As a result, a drug containing an alkyl halide is likely to react with any nucleophilic group that it encounters and become permanently linked to that group by a covalent bond - an alkylation reaction (**Fig. 1.27**). This poses a problem, as the drug is likely to alkylate a large variety of macromolecules which have nucleophilic groups, especially proteins and nucleic acids. It is possible to moderate the reactivity to some extent, but selectivity is still a problem and leads to severe side effects. These drugs are therefore reserved for life threatening diseases such cancer.

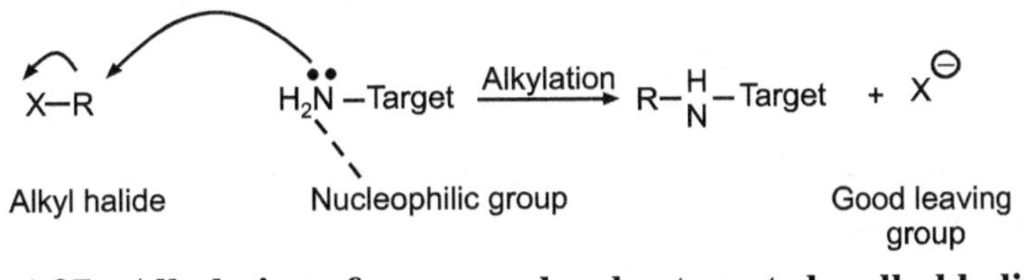

Fig. 1.27 : Alkylation of macromolecular targets by alkyl halides

Alkyl fluorides, on the other hand, are not alkylating agents, because the C-F bond is a strong one and is not easily broken. Fluorine is commonly used to replace a proton as it is approximately the same size, but has different electronic properties. It may also protect the molecule from metabolism.

Aliphatic and aromatic analogues lacking the halogen substituent could be prepared by a full synthesis to test whether the halogen has any importance in the activity of the lead compound.

11. Binding Role of Thiols

The thiol group (S-H) is known to be a good ligand for a zinc ion and has been incorporated into several drugs designed to inhibit enzymes containing a zinc cofactor. Such enzymes are known as zinc metalloproteinases. If the lead compound has a thiol group, the corresponding alcohol could be tested. This would have a far weaker interaction with a transition metal such as zinc.

12. Binding Role of Other Functional Groups

A wide variety of other functional groups may be present in lead compounds that have no direct binding role, but could be important in other respects. Some may influence the electronic properties of the molecule (e.g. nitro groups or nitriles). Others may restrict the shape or conformation of a molecule (e.g. alkynes). Functional groups may also act as metabolic blockers (e.g. alkynes, aryl halides).

13. Binding Role of Alkyl Groups and Carbon Skeleton

The alkyl substituents and carbon skeleton of a lead compound are hydrophobic and may bind with hydrophobic regions of the binding site through van der Waals and hydrophobic interactions. The relevance of an alkyl substituent to binding can be determined by synthesising an analogue which lacks the substituent. Such analogues generally have to be synthesised using a full synthesis if they are attached to the carbon skeleton of the molecule. However, if the alkyl group is attached to nitrogen or oxygen, it may be possible to remove the group from the lead compound as shown in **Fig 1.28**. The analogues obtained may then be expected to have less activity, if the alkyl group was involved in important hydrophobic interactions.

$$R_2N-Me \xrightarrow{VOC-Cl} R_2N-H$$

$$RO-Me \xrightarrow{HBr} RO-H$$

$$R-\underset{\underset{OMe}{|}}{\overset{O}{\|}}C \xrightarrow{NaOH} R-\underset{\underset{OH}{|}}{\overset{O}{\|}}C$$

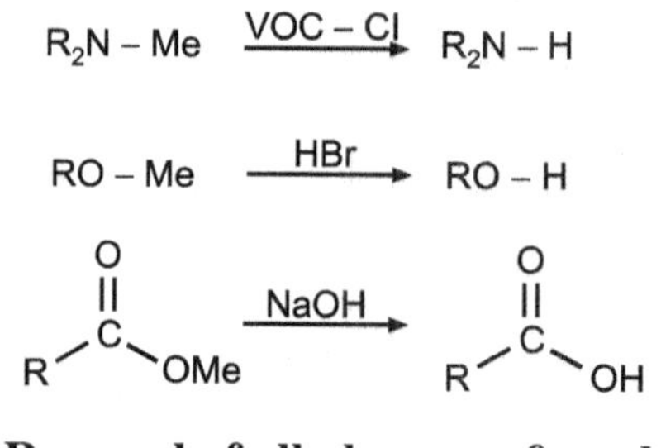

Fig. 1.28 : Removal of alkyl groups from heteroatom

14. Binding role of heterocycles

There is a large diversity of heterocycles to be found in lead compounds. Heterocycles are cyclic structures that contain one or more heteroatoms such as oxygen, nitrogen, or sulfur. Nitrogen-containing heterocycles are particularly prevalent. The heterocycles can be aliphatic or aromatic in character, and have the potential to interact with binding sites through a variety of bonding forces. For example, the overall heterocycles can interact through van der Waals and hydrophobic interactions, while the individual heteroatoms present in the structure could interact by hydrogen bonding or ionic bonding.

As far as hydrogen bonding is concerned, there is an important directional aspect. The position of the heteroatom in the ring and the orientation of the ring in the binding site can be crucial in determining whether or not a good interaction takes place. For example, a purine ring can take part in six hydrogen bonding interactions, three as a hydrogen bond donor and three as a hydrogen bond acceptor. The ideal directions for these interactions are shown in (**Fig.1.29**). van der Waals interactions are also possible, to regions of the binding site above and below the plane of the ring system.

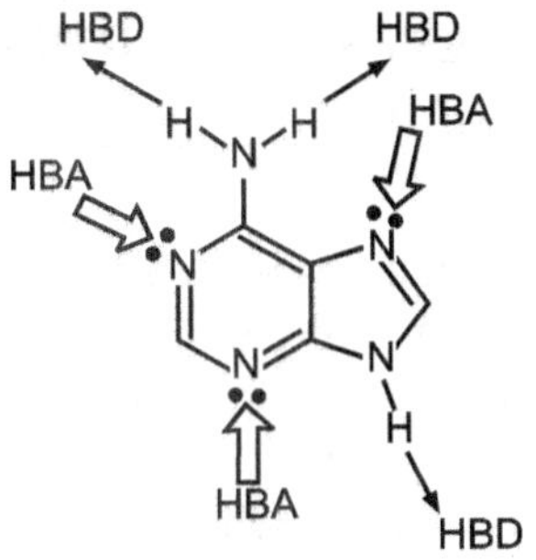

Fig. 1.29 : Possible hydrogen bonding interactions for adenine

Heterocycles can be involved in quite complicated, hydrogen bonding networks within a binding site. For example, the anticancer drug methotrexate contains a pteridine ring system that interacts with its binding site as shown in (**Fig. 1.30**).

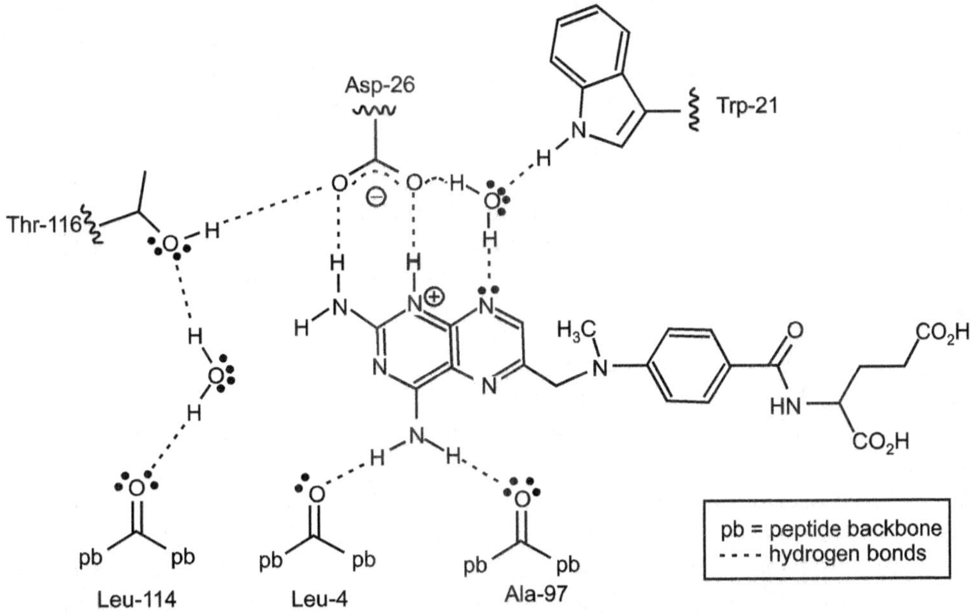

Fig.1.30. Binding interactions for the purine ring of methotrexate in its binding site

15. Isosteres

Isosteres are compounds or groups of atoms having same number and arrangement of electrons. These entities which have same total charge as well as same number of electrons (isoelectric) would possess similar physical properties e.g. Molecules of nitrogen (N_2) and carbon - monooxide (CO) show similar physical properties as both possess a total of 14 electrons and both are uncharged.

IMPORTANCE OF TOXICITY STUDIES IN DRUG DISCOVERY AND VARIOUS METHODS FOR DETERMINATION OF ACUTE AND CHRONIC TOXICITY AND LD 50 DETERMINATION

Introduction

Toxicology can be defined as that *"branch of science that deals with the study of poisons."* A poison can be defined as any substance that causes a harmful effect when administered, either by accident or design, to a living organism. Broader definitions of toxicology include the study of the detection, occurrence, properties, effects, and regulation of toxic substances. Toxicity itself cannot be defined as a single molecular event but is, a cascade of events starting with exposure, proceeding through distribution and metabolism, and ending with interaction with cellular macromolecules (usually DNA or protein) and the expression of a toxic end point. The study of toxicology is useful and necessary not only to protect humans and the environment from the deleterious effects of toxicants but also to facilitate the development of more selective toxicants such as anticancer and other clinical drugs and pesticides. The measurement of toxicity is also complex. Toxicity may be acute or chronic, and may vary from one organ to another. Toxicity also varies with age, genetics, gender, diet, physiological condition, or the health status of the organism. As opposed to experimental animals, which are highly inbred, genetic variation is the most important factor in human toxicity since the human population is highly out bred and shows extensive genetic variation. Even the simplest measure of toxicity, the LD50 (the dose required to kill 50% of a population under stated conditions) is highly dependent on the extent to which the above variables are controlled. LD50 values, therefore, vary greatly from one laboratory to another.

Brief History of Toxicology

Early references to toxicology in ancient manuscripts is to do primarily with medicine. Some, however, deal more specifically with toxic action or with the use of poisons for judicial execution, suicide or political assassination. Given the need for people to avoid toxic animals and plants, toxicology must rank as one of the oldest practical sciences. The Egyptian papyrus, *Ebers*, dating about 1500 BC, is the earliest surviving pharmacopeia, and the surviving medical works of Hippocrates, Aristotle, and Theophrastus published during the period 400 to 250 BC all include some mention of poisons. The early Greek poet Nicander mentions, in two poetic works, animal toxins (*Therica*) and antidotes to plant and animal toxins (*Alexipharmica*). The earliest surviving attempt to classify plants according to their toxic and therapeutic effects is that of Dioscorides, a Greek employed by the Roman emperor Nero in about AD 50. There appear to have been few advances in either medicine or toxicology between the time of Galen (AD 131–200) and Paracelsus (1493–1541). It was the latter who laid the groundwork for the development of modern toxicology by recognising the importance of the dose response relationship. His famous statement—"All substances are poisons; there is none that is not a poison. The right dose differentiates a poison and a remedy" summarises that concept. His belief in the value of experimentation was also a break with earlier tradition. There were some important developments during the eighteenth century. The publication of Ramazini's *Diseases of Workers* in 1700, led to his recognition as the father of occupational medicine. The correlation between the occupation of chimney sweeps and scrotal cancer by Percival Pott in 1775 is almost as well known, although it was foreshadowed by Hill's correlation of nasal cancer and snuff use in 1761.

Orfila, a Spaniard working at the University of Paris in the early nineteenth century, is generally regarded as the father of modern toxicology. He clearly identified toxicology as a separate science and, in 1815, published the first book devoted exclusively to toxicology. An English translation in 1817, was entitled *A General System of Toxicology or, A Treatise on Poisons, Found in the Mineral, Vegetable and Animal Kingdoms, Considered in Their Relations with Physiology, Pathology and Medical Jurisprudence.* Workers of the late nineteenth century who produced treatises on toxicology include Christian, Kobert, and Lewin. With the recognition of the site of action of curare by Claude Bernard (1813–1878), began the modern study of the mechanisms of toxic action. Since then, advances in the field of toxicology have been numerous. They have increased our knowledge of the chemistry of poisons, the treatment of poisoning, the analysis of toxicants and toxicity, modes of toxic action and detoxication processes, as well as specific molecular events in the poisoning process.

With the publication of her controversial book, *The Silent Spring*, in 1962, Rachel Carson became an important influence in initiating the modern era of environmental toxicology. Her book emphasised stopping the widespread, indiscriminate use of pesticides and other chemicals and advocated use patterns based on sound ecology. Although sometimes inaccurate and with arguments often based on anecdotal evidence, her book is often credited as the catalyst leading to the establishment of the US Environmental Protection Agency and she is regarded, by many, as the mother of the environmental movement. Since the 1960s, toxicology has entered a phase of rapid development and has changed from a science that was largely descriptive to one in which the importance of mechanisms of toxic action is generally recognised. Since the 1970s, with increased emphasis on the use of the techniques of molecular biology, the pace of change has increased even further, and significant advances have been made in many areas, including chemical carcinogenesis and xenobiotic metabolism, among many others.

DOSE-RESPONSE RELATIONSHIPS

Toxicity is a relative event that depends not only on the toxic properties of the chemical and the dose administered but also on individual and interspecific variation in the metabolic processing of the chemical. The first recognition of the relationship between the dose of a compound and the response elicited has been attributed to Paracelsus. His statement includes that not only that all substances can be toxic at some dose but that "the right dose differentiates a poison from a remedy," a concept that is the basis for pharmaceutical therapy. For many chemicals and effects there will be a dose below which no effect or response is observed. This is known as the *threshold dose*. This concept is of significance because it implies that a *no observed effect level* (NOEL) can be determined and that this value can be used to determine the safe intake for food additives and contaminants such as pesticides. Although this is generally accepted for most types of chemicals and toxic effects, for chemical carcinogens acting by a genotoxic mechanism, the shape of the curve is controversial and for regulatory purposes their effect is assumed to be a no-threshold phenomenon.

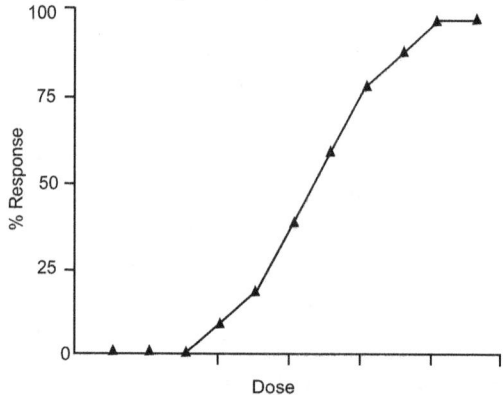

Fig. 1.31 : A Typical dose –response curve

The mammalian body has several inherent defense mechanisms and membrane barriers that tend to prevent the entry or absorption and distribution of these toxicants once an exposure event has occurred. However, if the toxicant is readily absorbed into the body, there are still other anatomical and physiological barriers that may prevent distribution to the target tissue to elicit a toxic response. As the toxicological response is often related to the exposed dose, interactions between the toxicant and the body's barriers and defense mechanisms will have an effect on toxicant`s movement in the body, and ultimately modulate the rate and extent of toxicant absorption and distribution to the target tissue. The skin represents the largest organ in the human body, and one of its primary functions is to act as a physical barrier to absorption of toxicants. The other major routes of toxicant entry into the body are through the respiratory and gastrointestinal tract, which offer less resistance to toxicant absorption than the skin. In general, the respiratory tract offers the most rapid route of entry, and the dermal the least rapid. One reason for this major difference is primarily because membrane thickness, which is really the physical distance between the external environment (skin surface, air in the lung, or lumen of the gut) and the blood capillaries, varies across these portals of entry. The overall entry depends on both the amount present and the saturability of the transport processes involved. Liver metabolism will have the most significant effect on toxicant bioavailability following gastrointestinal absorption, but microbial activity and various enzymes in the gastrointestinal tract and the skin can play a significant role in oral and dermal absorption, respectively. Physicochemical characteristics of the toxicant such as the chemical form is a useful indicator of whether the toxicant will be absorbed and distributed in the body. In this regard, toxicant molecular weight, ionisation (pKa), and octanol/water partition coefficient (log P) are useful indexes of predicting chemical transport from an environmental media across biological membranes to the blood stream. For those toxicants that are readily ionised, the pH gradient across membranes can determine the extent of toxicant transport and accumulation in tissues.

The two most important pharmacokinetic parameters that describe the disposition of a chemical are volume of distribution and systemic (body) clearance. *Pharmaco- and toxicodynamics* is the study of the biochemical and physiological effects of drugs and toxicants and determines their mechanism of action. Physiologically based pharmaco- or toxicokinetic models are used to integrate this information and to predict disposition of toxicants for a given exposure scenario.

CELL MEMBRANES

During absorption, distribution, and elimination processes, the toxicant will encounter various cell membranes before interacting with the target tissue. Each step of these processes involves translocation of the chemical across the various membrane barriers starting from the skin or mucosa through the cellular and organelle membranes. These membrane barriers could be the relatively thick areas of the skin to the relatively thin lung membranes. However, the membranes of tissue, cell, and cell organelle are all relatively similar. Proteins, which have many physiological roles in normal cell function, are closely associated with lipids and may be located throughout lipid bilayers. These proteins may be located on either the surface or traverse the entire membrane. Hydrophobic forces are responsible for maintaining the structural integrity of proteins and lipids within membranes, but movement within the membranes may occur. External and internal membrane proteins can function as receptors. Many proteins that traverse the membrane are transport proteins, and are involved in translocation of ligands; that is, they are involved in active and facilitated transport.

Mechanisms of Transport

In general, there are four main ways by which small molecules cross biological lipid membranes

1. **Passive diffusion :** Diffusion occurs through the lipid membrane.
2. **Filtration :** Diffusion occurs through aqueous pores.
3. **Special transport :** Transport is aided by a carrier molecule.
4. **Endocytosis :** Transport takes the form of pinocytosis for liquids and phagocytosis for solids.

The first and third routes are important in relation to pharmacokinetic mechanisms. The aqueous pores are too small in diameter for diffusion of most drugs and toxicants, although important for movement of water and small polar molecules (e.g., urea). Pinocytosis is important for some macromolecules (e.g., insulin crossing the bloodbrain barrier).

Passive Diffusion

Most drugs and toxicant pass through membranes by *simple diffusion* down a concentration gradient the driving force being the concentration gradient across the membrane. This diffusion process can continue until equilibrium, although in reality there is always movement but the net flux is zero. Eventually, the concentration of unionised or unbound (free) toxicant is the same on either side of the membrane. In other words, there is no competition of molecules and there is generally a lack of saturation. We can now quantitate the *rate* at which a toxicant can be transported by passive diffusion, and this can be described by Fick's law of diffusion given below.

$$\text{Rate of diffusion} = D \times Sa \times Pc \, d \, (CH - CL),$$

where D is the diffusion coefficient, Sa is the surface area of the membrane, Pc is the partition coefficient, d is the membrane thickness, and CH and CL are the concentrations at both sides of the membrane (high and low, respectively). The first part of this equation (DPc/d) represents the permeability coefficient of the drug. The permeability expresses the ease of penetration of a chemical and has units of velocity, distance/time (cm/h).

Carrier-Mediated Membrane Transport

This mechanism is important for compounds that lack sufficient lipid solubility to move rapidly across the membrane by simple diffusion. A membrane-associated protein is usually involved; *Michaelis-Menten enzyme kinetic models* best describe specificity, competitive inhibition, the saturation phenomenon and their kinetics. Membrane penetration by this mechanism is more rapid than simple diffusion and, in the case of active transport, may proceed beyond the point where concentrations are equal on both generally; there are two types of specialised carrier-mediated transport processes

Passive facilitated diffusion involves movement down a concentration gradient without an input of energy. This mechanism, which may be highly selective for specific conformational structures, is necessary for transport of endogenous compounds whose rate of transport by simple diffusion would otherwise be too slow. The classical example of facilitated diffusion is transport of glucose into red blood cells.

Active transport requires energy, and transport is against a concentration. Maintenance against this gradient requires energy. It is often coupled to energy-producing enzymes (e.g., ATPase) or to the transport of other molecules (e.g., Na+, Cl–, H+) that generate energy as they cross the membranes. Carrier-mediated drug transport can occur only in a few sites in the body such as

BBB, neuronal membranes, choroid plexus, renal tubular cells, hepatocytes, and the biliary tract.

VARIOUS TOXICITY STUDIES

Mainly toxicokinetic studies (generation of pharmacokinetic data either as an integral component of non-clinical toxicity studies or in specially designated studies) should be conducted to assess the systemic exposure achieved in animals and its relationship to dose levels and duration of treatment. A drug effect seen both in rat and in dog probably involve a common physiologic mechanism that is likely to be present in the human. For instance, a toxic effect observed only in rats or dog would indicate its probability of occurring in about 25% in case of human; while an effect observed in both rat and dog would indicate a probability of 80% in case of man. These studies are conducted with the assumption that man will behave in the same manner as animals. Toxicity studies are of the following types.

1. Acute Toxicity Studies
2. Sub-acute Toxicity Studies
3. Chronic Toxicity Studies

1. Acute Toxicity Studies (Single dose study)

Acute toxicity is defined as toxicity elicited as a result of short-term exposure to a toxicant. This study is conducted to determine the median lethal dose (LD 50) or LD 90, the dose required to kill 50% or 90% population of laboratory animals. Such studies may also indicate the probable target organ of the toxicant and its specific toxic effects. These toxicity studies form a complete programme of toxicity testing that provides the basis on which further testing programmes can be designed. LD 50 value is determined in a 24-hour test using two species; one is rodent (mice or rat) and one non-rodent (rabbit), and two routes of administration. Basically following signs are recorded during acute toxicity studies.

- Clonic convulsion
- Spasmicity
- Loss of righting reflex
- Lacrimation
- Diarrhoea
- Sedation
- Muscle relaxation
- Ataxia
- Tremors
- Muscle spasm
- Anaesthesia
- Respiration
- Skin colour
- Hypnosis

Experimental Design for acute toxicity design : The main aim of the study is to establish therapeutic index (LD50/ED50), i.e. the ratio between the pharmacologically effective dose and the lethal dose on the same strain and species. The greater the index safer the compounds and lower the index more toxic the compounds.

(a) Selection of species : Study is carried out in at least two rodents (rats or mice). These animals are preferred because they are easily available, easy to handle and economical. These animals are used only under conditions in which the process of biotransformation is same as human. In case, if it isn't so then non-rodent (rabbit) is desirable. Animals of both sexes and young animals are used because of their difference in susceptibility. Mainly, these studies are carried out by using 6-9 animals in a group.

(b) Dose : The study is performed in each species and at same dose levels for the treatment. Three other doses are also to be used for administration: the dose that can kill half of the animals (LD_{50}), another dose that can kill more than half (LD_{90}) and third dose that will kill less than half of the animals (more than 10%).

(c) Routes of administration and duration of study : The routes of administration depends upon the nature of the drug, but usually the oral route is preferred and it is most common. Parenteral route is also preferred in case of acute toxicity study of parenteral drug. If routes of administration in human is only IV, then another routes is also used to ensure the systemic absorption of drug. The duration of acute toxicity studies are only 24 hrs but in some cases it is also performed for 48 hrs.

(d) Evaluation : The number and time of death should be examined in order to estimate LD 50. The observation period is 7-14 days and during this period signs of toxicity should also be recorded.

There are some other methods which are used for the determination of acute toxicity studies, and are described as under.

Graphical Method of Miller and Tainter (1944) : This method is simple, accurate enough in most cases and should always be performed first. In this method, the observed percentage of mortality is converted into probit value by referring to the appropriate values thus these values are plotted against log dose. The LD_{50} value and its standard error may be determined from graph if the line is straight.

Estimation of dose range 4% of mortality : LD_{50} can be determined by stair case method. In this method, there is use of minimum number of animals and increasing the doses of drug. Five doses can be chosen for determination of LD_{50} starting from no death to 100% mortality. Animals were observed for first 2 hrs. and then at 6th and 24th hrs. for any toxic symptoms. After 24 hrs. the no. of diseased animals were counted in each group and percentage mortality were calculated. The percentage of animals that had died at each dose level is than transformed to probit.

Arithmetical method : This Karber's method is the modified form of arithmetical method for the determination of LD50. It does not involve any plotting of dose-response curve. This method is specially resorted to when a small number of animals are used. The mean interval of the number of dead in each group of animals is used as well as the difference between doses for the same interval. Results from doses larger than the least dose lethal to all in a group and doses from smaller than maximal tolerated doses are excluded. The sum of the product is divided by the number of animals in a group and resulting quotient is subtracted from the least lethal dose in order to obtain the LD50 value.

2. Sub-acute Toxicity Studies (daily dose study)

These studies are conducted to determine the organs affected by different dose levels. In this study, the nature of toxic affects is assessed under more realistic situations than the acute toxicity studies. The main purpose of this study is to determine maximum tolerated dose so that chronic studies can be designed to evaluate fully the toxic potential of the compounds. The animals are dosed daily and the dosage is increased stepwise every two to three days until toxic signs are observed and maintained at the maximum tolerated dose for a period of two to three weeks to allow the development of any pathological changes. Hematological and biochemical monitoring is carried out and blood levels of the compound are checked to ensure its absorption.

Experimental Design for Sub-acute Toxicity Design

(a) **Selection of animal species:** This study is carried out in at least two phylogenetically different mice, of which one should be non-rodent and the other a rodent species. The animals selected for the study should be identical in biotransformation to humans.

(b) **Dose:** The compounds should be given in three dose levels. A dose that is enough to elicit definite signs of toxicity but not high enough that can kill many animals, a low dose that is expected to induce no toxic effects, and an intermediate dose.

(c) **Routes of administration:** Routes of administration are same as that in human.

(d) **Duration of study:** Generally these studies are performed for 90 days. In dog it may be extended to 6 months or even 1 year.

(e) **Evaluation:** This study provides information about the effects on organ, dose-effect and dose-response relationship. Gross histopathological study provides useful information about toxicity of chemicals.

Parameters to be studied during acute, sub acute and chronic study

S. No.	Haematological parameters	Urine analysis parameters	Blood biochemical parameters	Gross and microscopic pathology
1.	Haemoglobin	Colour	Glucose	Brain
2.	Total RBC count	Appearance	Cholesterol	Parathyroid
3.	Haematocrits	Specific gravity	HDL	Adrenal
4.	Reticulocytes	Reaction	LDL	Trachea
5.	Total WBC count	Albumin	SGOT	Lungs
6.	Platelets count	Acetone	SGPT	Pancreas
7.	ESR	Bile pigments	Creatinine	Kidney
8.	Coagulation parameters	Urobilinogen	Total proteins	Uterus

3. Chronic Toxicity Studies (daily dose study)

In these studies, the animals are exposed over a long period of time to the toxic effects of the drug in order to mimic a more realistic situation. The main aim of these studies is to determine the organs affected and determine whether the drug is potentially carcinogenic or not. The duration of long term studies in rat is generally 1-2 years and it can extend for 7 years in case of dogs. Mainly one rodent and one non-rodent is dosed daily for six months. Three dose levels are chosen so that the high dose will produce significant retardation of growth or some pathological changes, the low dose is about twice the expected maximum clinical dose while the third dose is fixed midway between high and low dose. During the course of the study, body weight, food intake, water intake, hepatic function, hematology, pulse rate, B.P. and blood levels of tested compounds are measured at regular interval (at least every 14 days).

Chapter ... 2

VARIOUS METABOLIC PATHWAYS WITH SPECIAL REFERENCE TO PRODUCTION OF SECONDARY METABOLITES

All living organisms transform one organic molecule to another in order to live, grow and reproduce. All these interconversions require/ produce energy in the form of ATP. An integrative network of energy and enzyme mediated chemical reactions are called intermediate metabolic reactions and the pathways are called metabolic pathways.

Living plants are biosynthetic laboratories which manufacture glucose and large amount of energy using air, water, minerals and sunlight by a process termed as photosynthesis. The glucose produced during photosynthesis is the basic metabolite useful in biosynthesis of various primary and secondary metabolites through different metabolic pathways.

Plants and their products form the basis of medicines and several compounds which are pharmaceutically and medicinally important. However, the medicinal value of a plant depends on the nature of plant constituents present in it, which is known as active principal or active constituent.

Active constituents are those chemical substances, which are solely responsible for the therapeutic activity of the plant. Many theories have been proposed as to why these compounds are formed in plants, it is likely that many of them are produced as part of chemical defense system to protect the producing organism. The chemical constituents present in plants that do not possess any definite therapeutic value are known as inactive constituents. As the formation of different active and inactive constituents of plants involves various metabolic pathways, the inactive plant constituents are termed as primary plant metabolites whereas active plant constituents are termed as secondary plant metabolites.

Primary plant metabolites are simple molecules or polymers of simple molecules synthesised by plants, which generally do not possess therapeutic properties as such but are essential for the life of plants and contain high-energy bonds. These are used up for the biosynthesis of secondary metabolites. e.g. carbohydrates, proteins, lipids and nucleic acids. Secondary metabolites are complex organic molecules biosynthesised from primary plant metabolites in plant cells (Fig.2.1).They are unique to plants or group of plants, and they generally do not possesses activity essential for plant life nor contain high energy bonds. These are usually stored in vacuoles. Secondary metabolites are classified as alkaloids, glycosides, tannins, phenolic compounds, volatile oils, terpenoids, saponins, steroids, resins and bitter principles. These are used as medicine, food, flavours, colours, dyes, poisons, perfumes, etc.

KEGG PATHWAY

Each step of biosynthesis of plant secondary metabolites is shown in Kegg's pathway **(Fig. 2.2) Refer to the end of book**. It starts from glycolysis whose precursor is glucose/ carbohydrate which is derived in plant from photosynthesis and end product is pyruvic acid. Further, this pyruvic acid is the starting material for Citric Acid Cycle, which is essential for alkaloid biosynthesis and also for Acetate Mevalonate pathway which yield steroids, terpenoids as secondary metabolites.

Glucose/ Carbohydrate is also a precursor of Pentose Phosphate Pathway which yields erythrose 4-phosphate. Erythrose 4-phosphate is the starting material for shikimic acid pathway, which is an essential link for alkaloids, volatile oil biosynthesis.

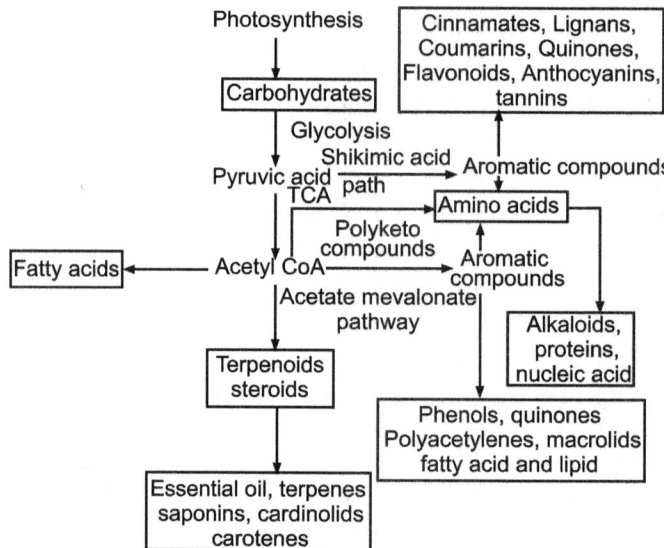

Fig 2.1 : Production of Primary and Secondary Metabolites

GLYCOLYSIS

Glycolysis is the metabolic pathway that converts glucose into pyruvate or phosphorylated derivatives of glucose before being processed any further. The free energy released in this process is used to form the high energy compounds such as ATP and NADH. It takes place both in aerobic and anaerobic organisms. The overall reaction occurs in the cytoplasm and is represented as

$C_6H_{12}O_6 + 2\ NAD^+ + 2\ ADP + 2\ P \longrightarrow 2$ pyruvic acid $+ 2\ ATP + 2\ NADH + 2\ H^+$

Pyruvate generated in the end of the glycolysis is fed into the citric acid cycle. The pathway for glycolysis is shown in **Fig. 2.3**.

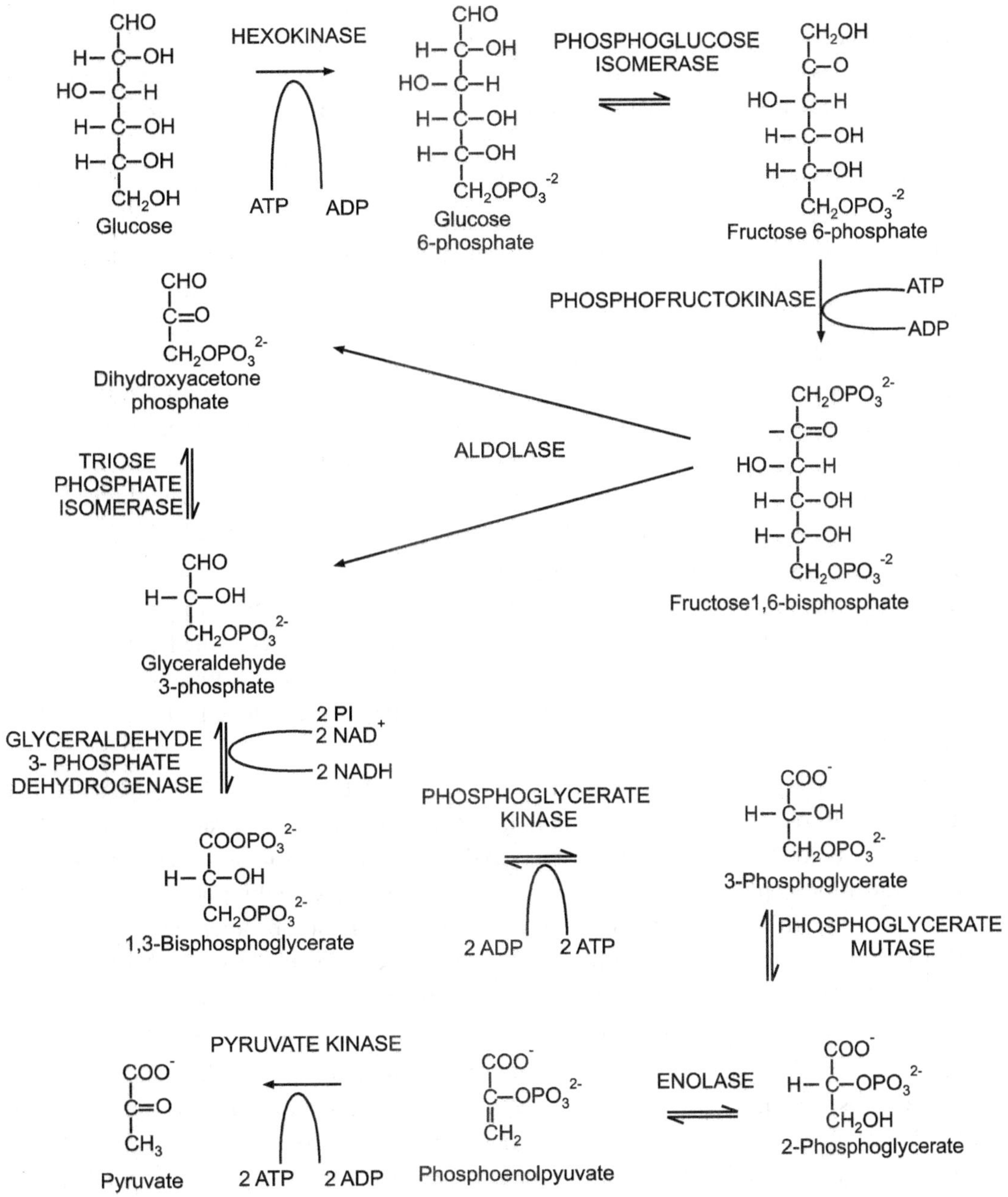

Fig. 2.3 : Glycolysis

CITRIC ACID CYCLE

Citric acid cycle or Kreb Cycle or Tricarboxylic acid Cycle (TCA Cycle) is the common pathway for generating energy through the oxidation of acetate derived from carbohydrates, fats and proteins into carbon dioxide and chemical energy in the form of adenosine triphosphate (ATP) occuring in eukaryotes and prokaryotes. The reaction of glycolysis is localised in cytosol whereas TCA cycle reactions takes place in mitochondria where oxygen is utilised to generate energy.

The pyruvic acid generated in cytosol during glycolysis from carbohydrate, protein and fats is converted into acetyl Co-A by release of one CO_2 molecule and formation of one molecule of NADH. The enzyme is pyruvate dehydrogenase. Acetyl Co-A enters into mitochondria for the first reaction of Krebs' cycle. An important stage in catabolism is the citric acid cycle (sometimes called the Krebs cycle or tricarboxylic acid cycle), which is the series of nine enzyme-catalysed reactions illustrated here. In the first step of the cycle, acetyl-CoA (formed from glucose in the body) reacts with oxaloacetic acid to form citric acid. Citric acid then undergoes a series of eight reactions in a cycle that reforms oxaloacetic acid and produces two molecules of CO_2. In the process, 11 molecules of ADP are converted into ATP. The cycle continues by reaction of oxaloacetic acid with another molecule of acetyl-CoA. The citric acid cycle is shown in **Fig. 2.4**.

In step 1 of the Krebs cycle, the two-carbon compound, acetyl-S-CoA, participates in a condensation reaction with the four-carbon compound, oxaloacetate, to produce citrate. Then isomerisation of citrate molecule occurs which involves moving the hydroxyl group in the citrate molecule by a sequential dehydration and hydration reaction, to form the D-isocitrate isomer with cis-aconitate as the intermediate. A single enzyme, *Aconitase,* performs this two-step process.

The next step involves the first oxidative decarboxylation step of Krebs' Cycle. The reaction is catalysed by the enzyme *isocitrate dehydrogenase.* Isocitrate is converted to α-ketoglutaric acid. The reaction involves dehydrogenation to oxalosuccinate, an unstable intermediate which spontaneously decarboxylates to give α-ketoglutarate. In addition to decarboxylation, this step produces a reduced nicotinamide adenine dinucleotide (NADH) cofactor. Furthur, α-ketoglutarate is converted into succinyl Co-A by a multi-enzyme complex, known as the *α-ketoglutarate dehydrogenation complex.*

Succinyl-CoA is a high potential energy molecule. The energy stored in this molecule is used to form a high energy phosphate bond in a guanine nucleotide diphosphate (GDP) molecule. Most of the GTP formed is used in the formation of ATP, by the action of *nucleoside diphosphokinase*. In plants and bacteria, ATP is formed in the *succinyl-CoA synthase* catalysed reaction by direct phosphorylation of ADP. In animals, GDP is the substrate in the reaction with formation of GTP (which is then used to form ATP by *nucleoside diphosphokinase*).

The succinate produced by *succinyl CoA-synthetase* in the prior reaction needs to be converted to oxaloacetate to complete the Krebs cycle. Both succinate and oxaloacetate are 4-carbon compounds. The first step in the conversion is the dehydrogenation of succinate to yield fumarate. Fumarate undergoes a stereo-specific hydration of the C=C double bond, catalysed by *fumarate hydratase* (also known as *Fumarase*), to produce L-malate. *fumarase* is the enzyme. It hydrates Fumarate. L-Malate (Malate) is dehydrogenated to produce oxaloacetate by the enzyme *malate dehydrogenase*. This is a highly endergonic reaction, and so, the equilibrium strongly favours the reactants over the products.

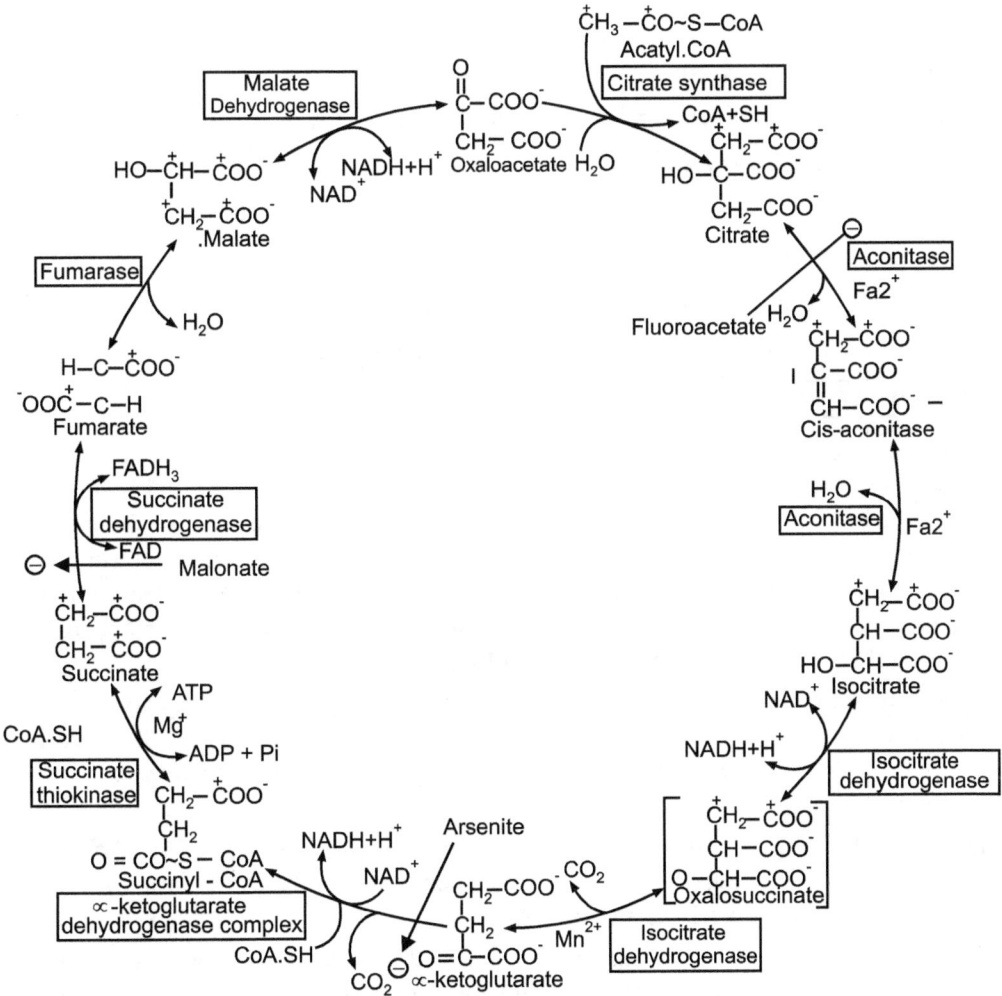

Fig. 2.4 : Citric acid cycle

In terms of energy, one Krebs cycle generates 4 NADH, 1 FADH$_2$ and 1 ATP. One NADH in terms of ATP is equal to 3, whereas one FADH$_2$ is equal to 2 molecules of ATP. So overall, 15 ATP molecules are generated during one Krebs cycle. Acetyl Co-A which is the starting material of Kreb's Cycle has three carbons as it is formed from the 3-C pyruvate in cytosol. Pyruvate is produced from 6 –C glucose during Glycolysis. It means that 2 pyruvates are generated during glycolysis. Overall acetyl Co-A generated from 2 pyruvates enter into Krebs Cycle. So, one glucose molecule gives 30 ATP in Krebs cycle.

Total NADH in one Krebs' cycle = 4 molecules

From one glucose molecule = 8 NADH molecules.

8 NADH molecules would yield $8 \times 3 = 24$ ATP

Total FADH$_2$ in one Krebs' cycle = 1 molecule

From one glucose molecule = 2 FADH2 molecules.

2 FADH$_2$ molecules would yield $2 \times 2 = 4$ ATP

Total ATP in one Krebs' cycle = 1×2

From one glucose molecule = 2 ATP

Total ATP generation from one glucose molecule in Krebs' cycle source = 30 ATP

The Krebs cycle provides precursor for biosynthesis of certain amino acids.

SHIKIMIC ACID PATHWAY

The shikimic acid pathway converts simple carbohydrate precursors derived from glycolysis and the pentose phosphate pathway to the aromatic amino acids. One of the pathway intermediates is shikimic acid, which has given its name to this whole sequence of reactions. The shikimic acid pathway is present in plants, fungi, and bacteria but is not found in animals. Animals have no way to synthesise the three aromatic amino acids— phenylalanine, tyrosine, and tryptophan- which are therefore essential nutrients in animal diets. The shikimic acid pathway is shown in **Fig. 2.5**.

Synthesis starts from erythrose – 4 –phosphate and phosphoenolpyruvic acid. The first step in the pathway is an aldol condensation that results in synthesis of a 7 carbon 3-deoxy- arabino-heptulosonic acid-7-phosphate (DAHP). *DAHP synthases* catalyses the aldol condensation.

DAHP in the presence of enzyme *dehydroquinate synthases* (*DHQ Synthases*) forms a cyclic intermediate, 3-dehydroquinic acid. The enzyme catalyses oxidation followed by a reduction that requires NAD as a cofactor.

3-dehydroquinic acid is the substrate for *dehydroquinase* that catalyses removal of water molecule and introduces double bond in a ring forming 3-dehydroshikimic acid. Enzyme *Shikimate dehydrogenase* further catalyses reduction of ketone to alcohol forming the first unique intermediate as **shikimic acid.**

Shikimic acid is further metabolised to chorismic acid through phosphorylation of one of the Meta hydroxyls catalysed by *shikimate kinase* to produce shik-mic acid-3-phosphate. This intermediate is further condensed with another molecule of phosphoenol pyruvate to give 5-enol-pyruvyl shikimate 3- phosphate (EPSP). EPSP is the substrate for *EPSP synthase* that removes phosphate from C-3 and introduces double bond into ring. This results in formation of chorismic acid.

The chorismic acid is the precursor for the biosynthesis of salicylic acid, prephenic acid, P-aminobenzoic acid, anthralinic acid and L-tryptophan.

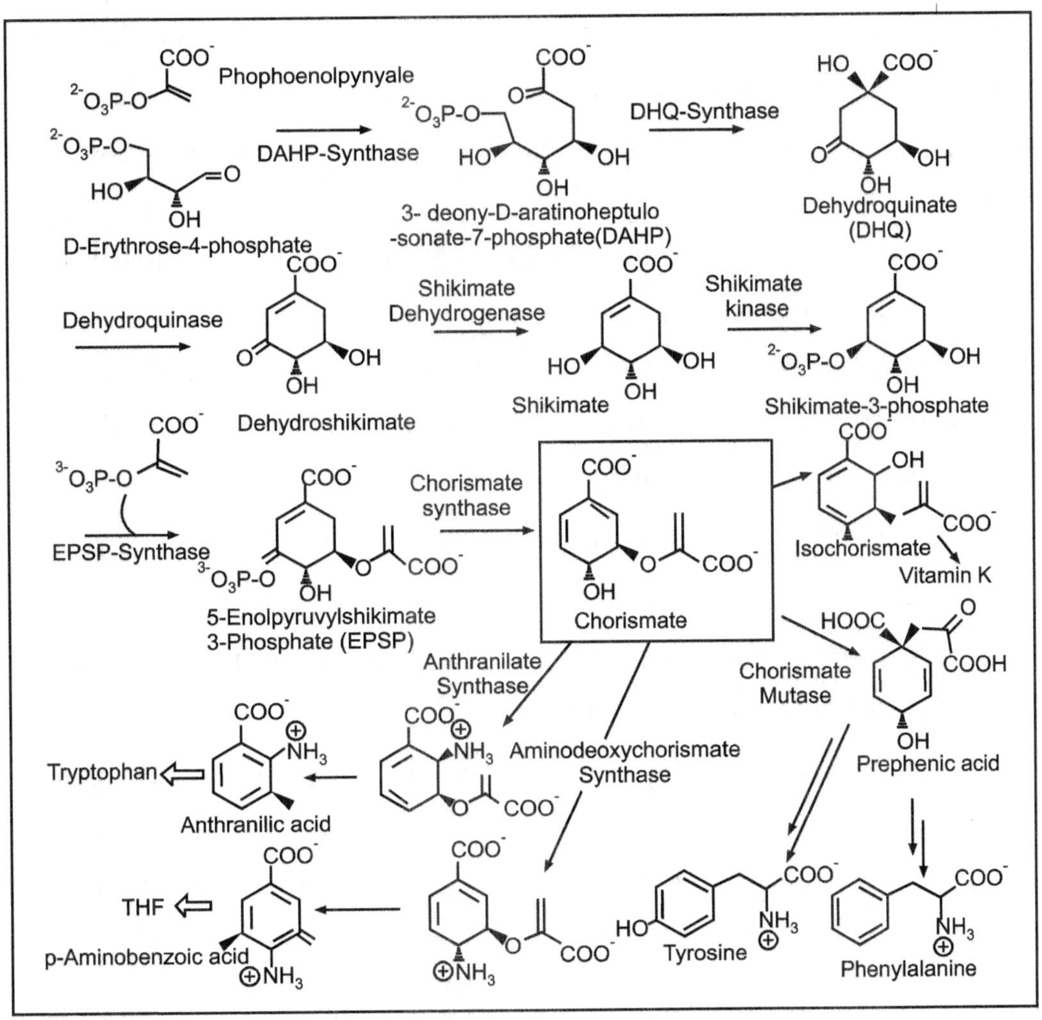

Fig. 2.5 : Shikmic acid Pathway

ACETATE MEVALONATE/ ISOPRENOID PATHWAY

The pathway begins with the acetyl CoA, produced from the pyruvic acid, the end product of glycolysis. The two molecule of acetyl CoA condense to form acetoacetyl CoA, catalysed by *acetyl-CoA transferase*. Further, one more molecule of acetyl CoA condenses with acetoacetyl CoA in presence of HMG-CoA synthase to form β-hydroxy β-methyl glutaryl CoA (HMG CoA).

In the next step of the pathway, HMG CoA is reduced in two consecutive steps to form mevalonate/ mevalonic acid. The reduction is catalysed by *HMG CoA reductase*, each step requires NADPH. Mevalonic acid is the main precursor for biosynthesis of terpenoids.

Mevalonic acid is finally converted to isopentyl pyrophosphate (IPP) mediated through two step phosphorylation. In the first step, mevalonic acid is converted into 5-phosphomevalonate; this step is ATP mediated. Similarly, one more phosphate condenses to 5-phosphomevalonate resulting into 5-pyrophosphomevalonate, which on decarboxylation produces Isopentyl pyrophosphate.

Isopentyl pyrophosphate has five carbons and it is the first isoprene unit.

IPP by an isomerase enzyme is converted into a second isoprene unit known as dimethyl allyl pyrophosphate (DMAPP), which further yields carbonium ion, a reactive alkylating group which easily reacts with IPP.

Electrophillic addition of IPP with carbonium ion of DMAPP yields 10 carbon geranyl diphosphate (GPP) precursor of monoterpenes. Furthermore, combination of another IPP unit with GPP yields farnesyl pyrophosphate (15 carbons). It is the precursor of sesquiterpene synthesis (30 Carbons) such as cholestrol, pregnenolone, diosgenin, digitoxin, etc. These steps are shown in **Fig. 2.6** and **Fig. 2.7**.

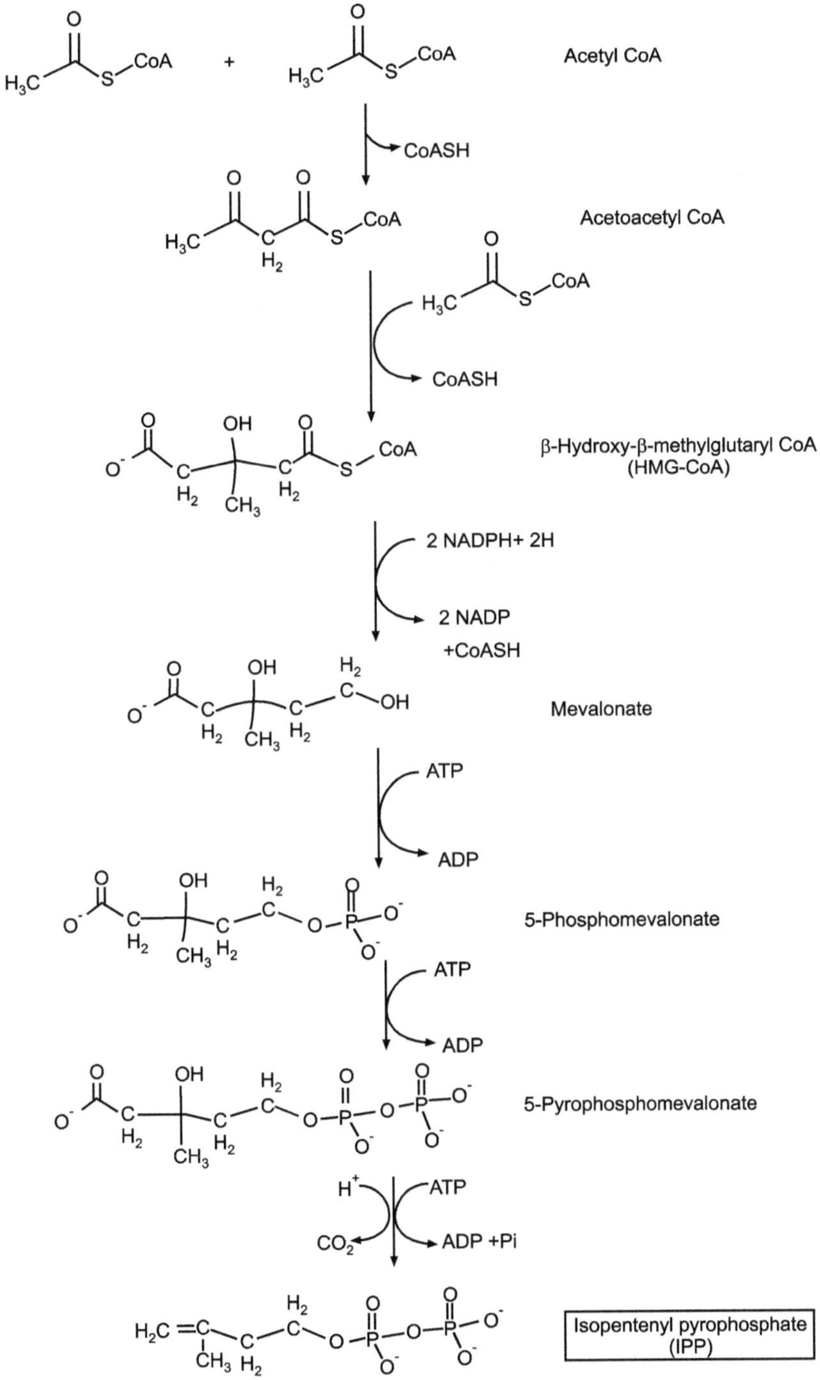

Fig. 2.6 : Isopentyl pyrophosphate Synthesis from Acetyl CoA (Acetate Mevalonate pathway)

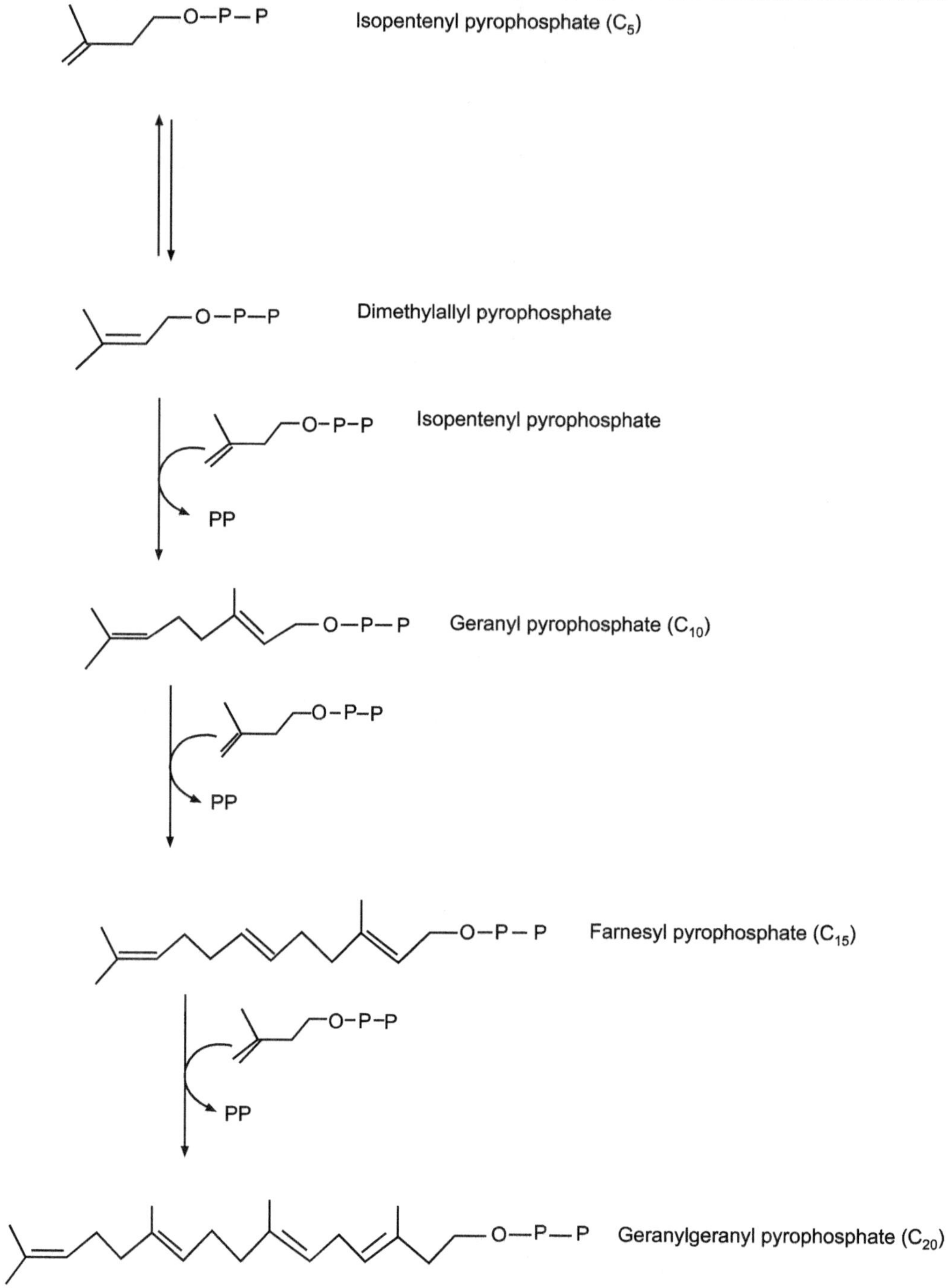
O–P–P
Isopentenyl pyrophosphate (C_5)
O–P–P
Dimethylallyl pyrophosphate
O–P–P
Isopentenyl pyrophosphate
PP
O–P–P
Geranyl pyrophosphate (C_{10})
O–P–P
PP
O–P–P
Farnesyl pyrophosphate (C_{15})
O–P–P
PP
O–P–P
Geranylgeranyl pyrophosphate (C_{20})

Fig. 2.7 : Acetate Mevalonate Biosynthesis Pathway

Chapter ... 3

MODERN EXTRACTION TECHNOLOGY

Recent years have shown a growing popularity and faith in the use of herbal medicine worldwide. This may be because of the realisation that modern synthetic drugs have failed to provide a "cure all" guarantee to most of the human diseases with often producing undesirable side- effects, which at the end turnout to be more problematic than the actual disease itself. Herbal medicine provides a ray of hope through its cocktail of phyto-compounds, which are believed to act in a synergistic manner, providing excellent healing touch with practically no undesirable side effect provided its quality is assured of.

Extraction is an important step in studies involving the discovery and isolation of active compounds of plant materials. It serves not only to remove and separate compounds of interest from the insoluble, high – molecular weight parts of the plants but also from other extractives, which could interfere with later steps. Extraction, as the term is used pharmaceutically, involves the separation of medicinally active portions of plant or animal tissues from the inactive or inert components by using selective solvents in standard extraction procedures. The products so obtained from plants are relatively impure liquids, semisolids, or powders intended only for oral or external use. These include classes of preparations known as decoctions, infusions, fluid extracts, tinctures, pilular (semisolid) extracts and powered extracts.

The various conventional extraction processes including maceration, digestion, percolation, and soxhelation are available for the extraction of the phyto-constituents from plants. Conventional extraction techniques for the solvent extraction of nutraceuticals from plant matrices are based on the choice of solvent coupled with the use of heat and/or agitation. Soxhlet, which has been used for a long time, is a standard technique and the main reference for evaluating the performance of other solid-liquid extraction methods. The lengthy time requirement makes it more labour-intensive and requires an additional recovery step and limits the number of samples that can be processed which may not be entertained from commercial aspects. Use of large amounts of organic solvents requires an additional recovery step and subsequent evaporation to concentrate the extract, resulting in a more cumbersome process.

In the last decade, alternative extraction techniques (non-conventional extraction methods) that introduce some form of additional energy to the extraction process in order to facilitate the transfer of analysts from sample to solvent have been considered. These methods include ultrasound assisted extraction, pressurised liquid extraction, microwave extraction and supercritical fluid extraction. The main advantage of these non-conventional methods compared to conventional methods is the increased extraction efficiency, which leads to increased yield and/or shorter extraction time.

MICROWAVE EXTRACTION TECHNOLOGY

Commercially, microwave devices have been available in late seventies. Randall and Booth designed magnetron, a device for generating fixed microwaves. Further investigation showed that microwave could cook food much quicker. This work led to introduction of first commercial microwave oven for domestic use. As this system heats rapidly, the experimental microwave extractions were performed. The results showed that microwaves have special properties such as quicker process, higher yield, less expensive etc. In 1980's the companies began to manufacture industrial microwaves specially designed for the use in laboratory.

Microwave energy consists of non-ionising electromagnetic waves that causes molecular motion by migration of ions and rotation of dipoles. The frequency range is between 300 MHz to 300 GHz. (Singh 2001). Commercially, for extraction, frequency of 2450 MHz is commonly used, which corresponds to an energy output of 600-700 Watts.

Electromagnetic field is an oscillating electric and magnetic disturbance that spreads as a harmonic wave through space. The electromagnetic field plays an important role to describe physical reality. Electromagnetic fields interact with matter resulting in energy transfer that are quantized which leads to heating. The two basic phenomena: ionic conduction and dipole rotation governed the heating. Ionic conduction refers to electrophoretic migration of ions under the influence of changing electric field. The resistance offered by solution to the migration of ions generates friction, which eventually heats up the solution. Dipole rotation means realignment of the dipoles of the molecule with the rapidly changing electric field. The electric component of the waves changes 4.9×10^4 times per second. With changing electric field, the alignment of solvent molecules gets disturbed and every time the solvent molecule tries to align itself with the electric field to keep itself in the same phase. This generates heat through frictional force.

The optimum frequency to produce the maximum heat is 2450 MHz. If the frequency is greater than 2450 MHz, the electrical component changes at a much higher speed as a result of which the molecule doesn't get sufficient time to even start to align itself with the external field. Therefore there is no friction and no heat is generated.

If the frequency is lesser than 2450 MHz, the electrical component changes at a much lower speed as a result the molecules get sufficient time to even start to align itself with the external field as a result of which there is no friction and no heat is generated. The above mechanism clearly indicates that only dielectric material / solvents with permanent dipoles get heated up under microwave.

Two parameters define the dielectric properties of materials. The first one is dielectric constant (ε') which describes the polarisability (ability to absorb microwave energy) of the molecule in an electric field. Second one is the dielectric loss factor (ε'') which measures the efficiency with which the absorbed microwave can be converted into heat. The ratio of the two is termed as dissipation factor (δ).

i.e. $\delta = \varepsilon''/\varepsilon'$

Three parameters must be considered for microwave extraction i.e.
1. Solubility
2. Dielectric constant
3. Dissipation factor

One must choose a solvent in which the target analyte is soluble and have high extracting power, depending on the interactions between the analyte and solvent. Usually, higher the dielectric constant, higher is the microwave absorption. Water has the highest dielectric constant but significantly lower dissipation factor which leads to superheating effect. In superheating, the rate at which water absorbs microwave energy is higher than the rate at which the system can dissipate heat. Localised superheating can have positive or negative effects, depending on the solvent. In some cases it can increase the diffusivity of analyte in a solvent. In other cases, intense heating can cause degradation of the analyte. So, one must choose the solvent that has a high dielectric constant as well as high dissipation factor. **Table 3.1** represents the dielectric constant and dissipation factor of some commonly used solvents. The table shows that ethanol and methanol have lower dielectric constant than water but higher dissipation factor, which ultimately produces higher heat.

Table 3.1: The dielectric constant and dissipation factor of some commonly used solvents

Solvent	Dielectric constant (ε')	Dissipation factor ($\varepsilon'' \times 10^4$)
Water	80	1500
Ethanol	7	2286
Acetone	20.7	5555
Methanol	23.9	6400
Hexane	1.88	0.10
Ethyl acetate	6.02	5316

Extraction Principle

Usually, dried plant material is used for extraction, but here the plant material with little moisture is useful for maximum yield due to microwave heating. The moisture present inside the plant cell evaporates and generates tremendous pressure on cell wall due to microwave heating. The pressure results in rupturing the cell wall, which facilitates the leaching out of active constituents from the cell into the surrounding medium. The yield of phytoconstituent increases even more if the solvent has higher dissipation factor. Higher temperature attainted by the microwave radiation can hydrolyse ether linkage of cellulose easily and reduces mechanical strength of cell wall which in turn helps the solvent to access the phytoconstituents inside the cell.

Instrumentation

There are two types of commercially available microwave extractors: a closed-system and an open-vessel system. The parameters which must be considered while developing a protocol for the closed system are: solvent, temperature, pressure, power applied and the length of the extraction time. Although, open systems are simple and usually safe, the optimisation parameters are limited to solvent, power applied and time. Both types of systems depend on power applied and time.

Both types of icrowave systems comprise of 4 major devices.

1. **Microwave generator:** Which generates microwave energy
2. **Wave guide:** Used to propagate the microwave from the source to the microwave cavity
3. **The applicator:** Where the sample is placed
4. **Circulator:** This allows the microwave to move only in the forward direction.

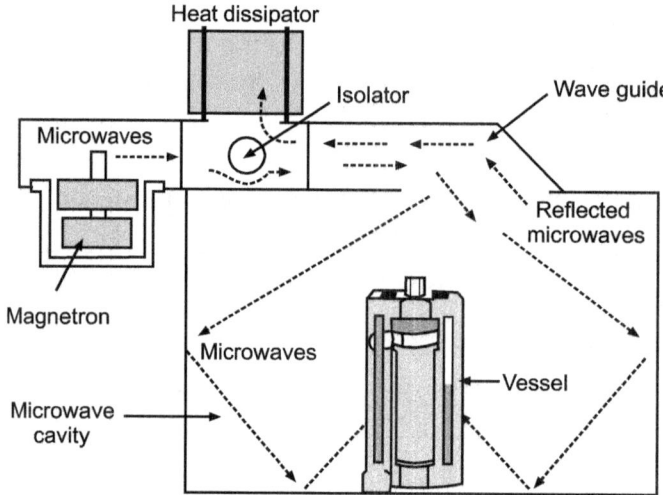

Fig. 3.1 : Schematic ray diagram of Microwave guide, Magnetron, vessel, wave guide and radiation pathway of reflected waves

The closed vessel system and open vessel system both are available as multimode and single- mode systems. A multimode system allows random dispersion of microwave radiation within the microwave cavity, so every zone in the cavity and sample it contains is evenly irradiated. Single mode or focused systems allow focused microwave radiation on a restricted zone where the sample is subjected to a much stronger electric field than in the multimode.

The closed-vessel system operates under controlled pressure and temperature. The closed system allows the temperature of the solvent to be raised above its boiling point. The maximum allowable temperature is 200°C and the maximum pressure is 120 psi. The technique exploits the Arrhenius relationships of temperature to rate of desorption; increased mass transfer as a result of higher temperatures.

The advantages of the closed type system are as follows
1. In a closed system, higher temperature can be reached in lesser time than in open system.
2. Less solvent is required as compared to open system as no evaporation occurs.
3. The risk of contamination is minimal.
4. As it is closed, loss due to evaporation of volatile substances during irradiation is completely avoided.
5. During acid extraction, the possibility of exposure to hazardous fumes is negligible.
6. Most closed vessel systems have high extraction efficiency i.e. 12 to 24 samples at a time.

Disadvantages of closed type system are as follows
1. The probability/ risk of explosion is maximum.
2. Closed-system outputs the same amount of energy as the focused system but this energy is split between the 12-24 extraction vessels, which can reduce the heating rate of the solvent. Therefore, it is generally accepted that the sample size should be limited to 0.5- 1.0 gram.
3. It takes a lot of time for the samples to cool and depressurise.

Extractions using the open-system are performed at atmospheric pressures so the temperature inside the extraction vessel is normally within +/- 5°C of the solvent boiling point. The heating process is more efficient because all of the energy is focused on one sample instead of being split among several samples. When the temperature of the solvent approaches the boiling point, the solvent vaporizes, rises to a reflux condenser where it is condensed and returned to the extraction vessel.

The advantages of the open type system are as follows
1. Easy to add reagent at any time during the operation.
2. Much safer than closed vessel system.
3. No time required for the samples to cool and depressurise.
4. The sample capacity for most open commercial microwave systems can be as large as 10 grams.
5. The low cost of the equipment required.
6. As in open system, energy is focused on limited sample, so it will have a higher heating rate.
7. Analysis is generally twice as fast because of the more efficient heating and the shorter cooling time of the vessel.

Disadvantages of open type system are as follows
1. Loss due to evaporation is higher as compared to closed vessel system.
2. The ensuing methods are usually less precise than those developed using closed-vessel systems.

Practical Approach of Microwave Assisted Extraction

Duvernay et al. (2005) described the microwave assisted extraction technology and analysed the effect of extraction temperature and extraction time on rice bran oil and vitamin E from rice bran. Results showed that extraction time has minimal effect on yield whereas more Vitamin E was extracted at 140°C.

Kormin et al. described microwave assisted extraction simple as an inexpensive and valuable tool in applied chemistry due to lesser amount of solvent needed, simplified manipulation and higher purity of final product with lower cost. They extracted bioactive component from two traditionally used ferns *Dicranopteris linearis* (Burm.) and *Stenochleana palustris* (Bedd.). They concluded that water can penetrate easily into the cells of the plant matrix and facilitate better heating of the plant matrix and increases the mass transfer of the active constituents into the extracting solvent. The optimum time for extraction is 5 min. Short extraction time was more significant than long extraction time.

Oufnac et al. (2007) studied total phenolic, tocopherol contents and free radical scavenging capability of wheat bran extracted using conventional and microwave assisted in three different solvents methanol, hexane and acetone. Conclusion was made that methanol was the most effective solvent, producing higher extraction yield (4.86 %). Microwave-assisted solvent extraction using methanol significantly increased the total phenolic compound content to 467.5 and 489.5 µg of catechin equivalent; total tocopherol content to 18.7 and 19.5 µg; and free radical scavenging capability to 0.064 and 0.072 µmol of trolox equivalent/g of wheat bran at extraction temperatures of 100 and 120°C, respectively. However, extraction yields of conventional methanol solvent and microwave-assisted methanol extractions at different temperatures were not significantly different.

Raman and Gaikar (2002) optimised the parameters such as nature of the solvent, microwave energy input, and solid loading for the microwave-assisted extraction of piperine from coarsely powdered black pepper (*Piper nigrum*). They described the mechanism of the enhancement of extraction rates. Studies have revealed that dielectric heating of the polar cellular matrix resulted in remarkable swelling and coalescence of the oil cells and other constituents. The resulting pressure, built-up within the cell, breaks open the cell, releasing the constituents and providing easy access for solvent penetration and subsequent solubilisation of piperine and other substances. Because the cell wall is mainly composed of slightly ionic cellulose, there is a marked increase in the dielectric heating rates. Rapid degradation of the cellulosic cell wall occurs, thereby further increasing the permeability of the wall toward solvent penetration. Selective extraction of piperine in nonpolar solvents to the extent of 94% with a purity of 85% has been achieved. The MAE procedure is simple, rapid, and reliable.

Wang et al. (2010) optimised microwave-assisted extraction (MAE) technique protocol for the extraction of flavonoids from *Radix puerariae*. Several influential parameters of the MAE procedure (ethanol concentration, solvent volume, microwave power and extraction time) were studied through single factor experiments and orthogonal experiments for the optimisation of the extraction protocol. The optimal conditions of MAE were: ethanol concentration 70%, solvent volume 35 ml, microwave power 255W and extraction time 6.5 min, while extraction yield of *Radix puerariae* was 8.37 mg/g. The developed MAE method provided a good alternative for the extraction of flavonoids from *R. puerariae*.

Some more interesting results on microwave assisted extraction have recently been published. For example, the extraction of vanillin from *Vanilla planifolia* pods using Microwave assisted extraction and ultrasound-assisted extraction has been described. Using absolute ethanol as the solvent at room temperature, the yield of vanillin was 1.25 wt% at each of the three conventional extractions performed over 24 h. Using ultrasound-assisted extraction, the yield was 0.99 wt%, while it was 1.86 wt% using MAE. These investigations clearly showed that vanillin extraction by Microwave assisted extraction is superior to other techniques in terms of yield, purity of vanillin, and the time taken to extract the same percentage of the vanillin from the pods.

SUPER CRITICAL FLUID EXTRACTION

In recent years, the supercritical fluids are increasingly replacing the organic solvents that are used in extraction and recrystallisation operations because of regulatory and environmental pressures on hydrocarbon and ozone-depleting emissions. Super critical fluid processes have helped to eliminate the use of hexane and methylene chloride as solvents. This technique has some advantages over more conventional separation techniques, largely due to the unique physical properties of supercritical fluids. Supercritical fluids exhibit a liquid-like density, while their viscosity and diffusivity remain between gas-like and liquid-like values. Also, the recovery of a supercritical solvent after extraction can be carried out relatively simply by reducing the pressure and evaporating the solvent, because a supercritical solvent is usually a gas at normal temperature and pressure.

Supercritical Fluids

A supercritical fluid is made up of liquid and gas and not of solid. When a liquid/ gas is compressed under high pressure and heated above the corresponding critical values it enters the phase called supercritical phase and the fluid is called as supercritical fluid. Above the critical temperature, there is no phase transition in that the fluid cannot undergo a transition to a liquid phase, regardless of the applied pressure.

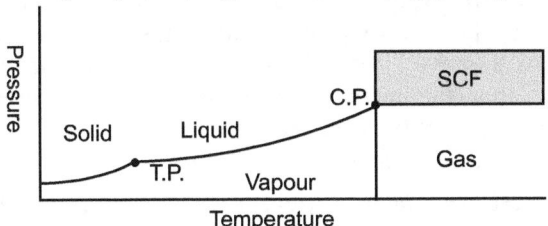

Fig. 3.2 : Relationship between pressure and temperature for supercritical fluids

A supercritical fluid (SCF) is characterised by physical and thermal properties that are between those of the pure liquid and gas. The fluid density is a strong function of the temperature and pressure. The diffusivity of SF is much higher than for a liquid and SCF readily penetrates porous and fibrous solids. Consequently, SCF can offer good catalytic activity.

Critical Temperature (Tc): The highest temperature at which a gas can be converted to a liquid by an increase in pressure.

Critical Pressure (Pc): The highest pressure at which a liquid can be converted to a traditional gas by an increase in liquid temperature.

Triple Point (Tp): The point at which the gas, liquid and solid phases all exists in equilibrium.

The compressibility of a supercritical fluid just above the critical temperature is large compared to the compressibility of ordinary liquids. A small change in the pressure or temperature of a supercritical fluid generally causes a large change in its density. A commonly accepted opinion is that the solvent power of a supercritical fluid is mainly related to its density in the critical point region. A high density generally implies a strong solvating capacity. The unique property of a supercritical fluid is that its solvating power can be tuned by changing either its temperature or pressure.

A significant cost factor for many conventional liquid-liquid extraction processes is the recovery of the spent extraction solvent. The separation of the solvent from the solute is usually done by distillation, which can sometimes be very energy-consuming. If a supercritical solvent is applied, the solute can be separated from the mixture by e.g. lowering the pressure of the mixture. One should remember that to recycle the supercritical solvent, it must be compressed again. This can be a significant cost factor, if the difference between the pressure in the extraction vessel and the pressure in the separator is relatively large.

Even though the density of a supercritical fluid increases with pressure and becomes liquid-like, the viscosity and diffusivity remain between liquid-like and gas-like values. Additionally, supercritical fluids exhibit almost zero surface tension, which allows facile penetration into micro porous materials. As a result of the advantageous combination of physicochemical properties, the extraction process can often be carried out more efficiently with a supercritical solvent than it can with an organic liquid one.

The critical temperature (Tc) of the compound depends on the polarity of the compound. The critical temperatures of non-polar gases, such as carbon dioxide or ethane, are below 50°C, whereas for polar compounds, such as methanol or water, the critical temperature is well above 200°C. In practice, especially in food-related industries, it is usually desirable that the critical temperature of the solvent is below 100°C. Therefore, the solvents commonly used for supercritical operations are low molecular weight gases, such as carbon dioxide, ethane and propane.

Carbon Dioxide as a Best Solvent in Supercritical Fluid Extraction

Carbon dioxide is the most commonly used solvent in industrial practice for several reasons. Carbon dioxide has a technically convenient critical pressure and temperature of 73.8 bar and 31.1°C, respectively. It is non-toxic, nonflammable, non-reactive, non-corrosive, and abundant. Furthermore, it is the second least expensive solvent after water and it does not leave any solvent residue after extraction. Also, unlike solvents, the carbon dioxide is readily recycled by pressure and temperature adjustment, which is very mild and does not harm the product.

Botanicals can be fractionated to produce a natural colour fraction, an aroma fraction, an anti-oxidant fraction and/or a flavour fraction. This is important in producing nutraceuticals because unwanted strong flavours in certain botanicals such as garlic and rosemary can be separated from the nutraceutical components.

Supercritical carbon dioxide is finding broad acceptance in the nutraceutical industry because it does not harm products and produces higher concentration (quality) extracts.

Principle and Process

Supercritical Fluid Extraction (SFE) is based on the principle that, near the critical point of the solvent, its properties change rapidly with only slight variations of pressure.

The fluid is stored in the work tank, as a liquid at high pressure from where it is sub-cooled before being fed to the pump. The pump increases the pressure of the fluid which is then heated to the desired temperature. The operating conditions vary between processes, so the standard pumping loop has a maximum pressure of 500 bar and a maximum temperature of 200°C. The fluid then enters the application dependant part of the process, extractor, reactor or washing chamber, to extract an oil or convert reactants to products.

The fluid then passes through a pressure control valve, which reduces the pressure of the product mixture to subcritical conditions.

The product mixture enters the separators where heat can be added, to assist in the separation of the product and gaseous fluid. The liquid product will stay in the separator vessel and is periodically drained away to an atmospheric product storage vessel. The gas phase from the separator enters the condenser where the fluid is condensed and returned to the work tank.

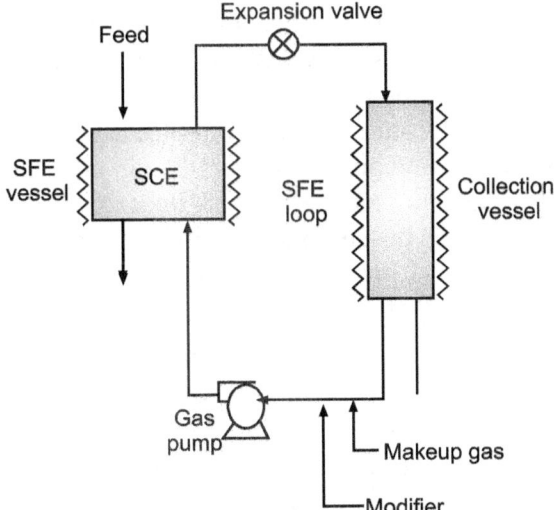

Fig. 3.3 : Basic Ray Diagram of Supercritical Fluid Extraction

Advantages of SFE

1. SCFs have solvating powers similar to liquid organic solvents, but with higher diffusivities, lower viscosity, and lower surface tension.
2. Since the solvating power can be adjusted by changing the pressure or temperature, separation of analytes from solvent is fast and easy.
3. By adding modifiers to a SCF (like methanol to CO_2) its polarity can be changed for having more selective separation power.
4. In industrial processes involving food or pharmaceuticals, one does not have to worry about solvent residuals.
5. SCFs are generally cheap, simple and safe. Disposal costs are much less and in industrial processes, the fluids can be simple to recycle.
6. SCF technology requires sensitive process control. In addition, the phase transition of the mixture of solutes and solvents has to be measured or predicted accurately.

Practical approach of Supercritical Extraction

Gainar et al. concluded that peppermint oil extracted by supercritical fluid extraction optimum conditions (p = 90 bar, T = 40 C) had a better aroma than hydrodistillation. Chemical analysis revealed that oils extracted under different supercritical fluid extraction conditions possessed a widely different percentage composition. Although, practically the same compounds were present in the hydrodistilled oil, its composition was similar to supercritical fluid extraction oil extracted under non-optimised conditions.

Hadolin et al. (2001) studied the extraction of vitamin E-rich oil from a plant (*Silybum marianum*) that naturally grows in Mediterranean area. It was pointed out that extractions at 60°C and 200 bar produced the most concentrated extracts in terms of α-tocopherol (0.08 %), while the extraction yield was relatively high (19 %).

Tsuda et al. (1995) studied the antioxidant activity of extracts obtained from tamarind (*Tamarindus indica* L.) seed coat using SFE (with CO_2) at different conditions. Results showed that the antioxidant activity of the extracts increased when the extraction pressure and temperature were raised. Besides, the addition of a co-solvent suitable for the food industry (ethanol) on the extraction process was studied in order to show the influence of polar compounds on the final antioxidant activity of the extracts. In any case, the addition of 10% modifier (V/V) increased the antioxidant activity of the extracts.

Yépez et al. (2002) demonstrated the possibility to obtain odourless and flavourless extracts from coriander (*Coriander sativum*), with high antioxidant activity, using supercritical fluid extraction with CO_2. Extraction at moderate conditions (45°C and 177 bar), that means CO_2 densities close to 0.74 g/ml, provides extracts with high antioxidant activity and high yields.

Zancan et al. (2002) carried out a study to prove the effect of temperature and pressure as well as the addition of a co-solvent on the kinetics of ginger (*Zingiber officinale*) extraction and on the extract`s antioxidant activity. By means of a factorial design it was possible to conclude that the addition of a co-solvent was not necessary to increase the mass transfer rate or the extraction yield. The factors selected to carry out the factorial design were: extraction temperature (25 to 35 ºC), extraction pressure (200 to 250 bar) and solvent (i.e. CO_2, CO_2 + ethanol, CO_2 + isopropyl alcohol). The best results in terms of antioxidant activity were obtained when the extraction was carried out with a modifier at low temperatures and pressures and relatively long extraction times, apparently, due to the extraction of gingerols at these conditions.

ULTRASONIC EXTRACTION

Ultrasound is an efficient non-thermal alternative method of extraction. Ultrasonic wave is referred to the acoustic wave with the frequency between 20 kHz and 10 MHz, but to achieve maximum extraction efficiency frequencies between 20 to 40 kHz are generally used.

The power supply transforms line voltage to high frequency 20 kHz electrical energy. This electrical energy is transmitted to the probe or water bath where it is converted to mechanical energy. The vibrations from the probe are coupled to and intensified by the titanium tip. The probe vibrates in a longitudinal direction and transmits this motion to the titanium tip immersed in the solution. The high intensity of ultrasound travels across a medium where it can generate the growth and collapse of bubbles inside liquids and the phenomenon is known as cavitation. The asymmetric implosions of the cavitation bubbles close to a solid surface generate microjets in the direction of the surface that can affect mass transfer and will produce great force (shear forces) to penetrate into the cells and improve material transfer. Some other effects of ultrasound are the heating of the medium, the microstirring at interfaces and several structural effects such as the ''sponge effect'' or the generation of micro channels.

Several concomitant physical effects, such as the mechanics, thermotics and cavatition effect, present themselves during the propagation of ultrasonic wave in various media, and these effects have been recognised to be beneficial to many physical and chemical processes.

Importance of Cavitation

Cavitation is usually considered playing the most important role in ultrasonic enhancement of membrane process for liquid–liquid and liquid–solid system. The collapse of the micro bubbles bring significant mechanical and thermal effects, generating temperature and pressure that is above 5000 K and 500 atm (50 MPa) in the bubbles and associated with which powerful shock wave and microstreaming with the speed of about 110 m/s are created. The implosions occur within very short lifetime, less than 0.1 µs. These effects are considered beneficial to the mass transfer of membrane process. The macroflow of liquid resulted from the mechanical effect can promote turbulence, reduce the boundary layer, and intensify eddy diffusion. Secondly, microstreaming, shock wave and acoustic streaming can continuously stimulate the interfaces between liquid–liquid and liquid–solid, therefore refresh the interfaces. Finally, microstreaming and shock wave also lead to the disturbance of fluid in microporous medium and accelerate the fluid diffusion through the pores.

Cavitation increases with the increase of surface tension, viscosity of liquid or the hydrostatic pressure, and with the decrease of temperature. An increase in ultrasonic intensity leads to an increase in cavitation. Ultrasonic frequency is another important factor, under the same ultrasonic intensity, an increase of ultrasonic frequency reduces the production and intensity of cavitation in liquid.

Procedure

This method is divided into two procedures, based on the expected concentration of organic compounds. The low concentration procedure is for individual organic components expected at less than or equal to 20 mg/kg and uses the larger sample size and three serial extractions and the medium/high concentration procedure is for individual organic components expected at greater than 20 mg/kg and uses the smaller sample and a single extraction.

Low concentration procedure : The sample is mixed with anhydrous sodium sulfate to form a free-flowing powder. The mixture is extracted with solvent three times, using ultrasonic extraction. The extract is separated from the sample by vacuum filtration or centrifugation. The extract is ready for final concentration, cleanup, and/or analysis.

Medium/high concentration procedure : The sample is mixed with anhydrous sodium sulfate to form a free-flowing powder. This is extracted with solvent once, using ultrasonic extraction. A portion of the extract is collected for cleanup and/or analysis.

Benefits of Ultrasonic

Ultrasonic cavitation creates shear forces that break cell walls mechanically and improve material transfer. This effect is being used in the extraction of liquid compounds from solid cells (solid-liquid extraction). In this case, the compound to be dissolved into a solvent is enclosed in an insoluble structure. In order to extract it, the cell membrane must be ruptured. For this, ultrasound is faster and more complete than maceration or stirring. The particle size reduction by the ultrasonic cavitation increases the surface area in contact between the solid and the liquid phase significantly. The mechanical activity of the ultrasound enhances the diffusion of the solvent into the tissue. As ultrasound breaks the cell wall mechanically by the cavitation shear forces, it facilitates the transfer from the cell into the solvent.

Practical Approach of Ultrasound Assisted Extraction

More recently, ultrasound-assisted extraction has been applied to the separation of inorganic compounds and metal ions from the matrix, to facilitate their analytical determination. Other application areas of ultrasound-assisted extraction include the selective extraction of different physicochemical forms of elements for speciation. In this case, advantage is taken of the nondestructive character of ultrasound treatments which, under suitable conditions, maintain the integrity of the extracted species. But, ultrasonic extraction is not appropriate for applications where high extraction efficiencies of analyte at very low concentrations is necessary. Following are examples where ultrasound is employed in extraction of active constituent from herbals.

Herrera et.al (2005) reported the use of ultrasound-assisted extraction for the determination of phenolic compounds present in strawberries. The optimisation study of the extraction was carried out using spiked samples (100 mg/kg). The sample immersed in an aqueous solution containing hydrochloric acid (0.4 M) was sonicated for 2 min Subsequent separation was carried out by liquid chromatography (LC) with photodiode array UV detection. Calibration curves using the standard addition in green strawberries typically gave linear dynamic ranges of 2–300 mg/l for all analytes. The method was applied to two types of strawberries to demonstrate the applicability of the proposed method, which is much faster and produces less analyte degradation than methods as solid–liquid, subcritical water and microwave-assisted extraction.

Kadkhodaee and Kakhki (2009) extracted the active compounds of saffron using high power ultrasound at a constant frequency of 30 kHz and at 20°C. The efficiency of the process was compared with that of cold water extraction method. The results showed that ultrasound largely improved the extraction rate and incredibly reduced the process time. The extraction yield increased with the increase of time and amplitude of sonication. It was also found that the use of pulsed ultrasound with short pulse intervals was more efficient than continuous sonication.

Shukor et. al (2008) reported the effect of ultrasonic waves and type of solvent on extraction process, ultrasonic assisted extraction and soxlet extraction was performed using ethanol, hexane and acetone as a solvent of dried Patchouli (*Pogostemon cablin*) leaves and their qualitative and quantitative analysis has been done. Qualitative analysis involved the chromatogram analysis from GCMS while quantitative analysis is based on the percent yield. From qualitative analysis, ethanol gives the highest peak area (27.92%) than hexane (20.01%) and acetone (20.42%). In addition, average peak area for ultrasonic method (50.18%) is better than soxlet (42.40%). Meanwhile, for qualitative analysis, ethanol can extract highest yield (2.87%) compared to hexane (2.53%) and acetone (2.00%). By using ultrasonic waves, it gives higher average yield (2.27%) than soxlet (1.67%). Therefore, from these analyses, the best solvent used for solvent extraction is ethanol because it produced highest quality yield of patchouli oil. This experiment also has the better result when it involves the ultrasonication method.

In this research, fish oil was extracted from eel (*Monopterus albus*) by using ultrasonic extraction method. Effects of different ultrasonic power, solvent to solid ratio and sonication time on extraction yields were investigated. Then, the extracted fish oil was analysed using 785 DMP Titrino and Gas Chromatography Mass Spectrometer. The ultrasonic power was used at 100, 200, 300 and 450W. The solvents used were 50, 100, 200 and 500ml of ethanol. In terms of sonication time it was set at 20, 30, 50, and 60 minutes. Results obtained show that the ultrasonic power of 200 W, solvent amount of 500 ml and 60 minutes of sonication time produced higher yields of extracted fish oil at 7.20 %. The Free Fatty Acid and acid value content of the extracted fish oil was higher at 100 W of ultrasonic power with content of 0.53 g/100 g and 0.30 Mg KOH/1 g.

The application of ultrasound during extraction and trans-esterification of oil from rapeseed was evaluated. Two methods of extraction were used, batch wise extraction and soxhlet extraction. In batch wise extraction procedure, ground rapeseeds were added to solvent and subjected to ultra sonication. Conventional soxhlet extraction assisted in the soxhlet chamber by ultrasound has been developed. Ultrasonic technique reduced time required to extract oil. Using batch wise extraction procedure, percent recovery of oil increased to almost 17.83% by using cleaning bath rather than control after 2 hrs, while in using soxhlet extraction percent recovery reached 85% after 1.5 hr in case of ultrasonic and after 4 hrs without using ultrasonic. Physical and chemical properties of rapeseed oil were tested. Then the alkaline trans-esterification of rapeseed oil with methanol and potassium hydroxide for production of biodiesel was studied, using ultra-sonication and magnetic stirring. In trans-esterification the use of ultra-sonication and magnetic stirring led to similar high yields of 90% of methyl esters after approximately 10 min. of reaction time. Comparison between biodiesel obtained and standard biodiesel and diesel fuel was done.

SOLID PHASE MICRO-EXTRACTION

Solid phase micro-extraction (SPME) was developed in the 1990s by Professor J. Pawliszyn to provide a quick and solvent less technique for the isolation of analytes from a sample matrix. The traditional methods by which the analytes of interest were isolated are typically time and labor intensive and involve multistep procedures, which could reduce sensitivity. Also, the use of solvents can be hazardous to the operators' health and can damage the environment. SPME was developed from the technique of solid phase extraction, but the sorbing material is permanently attached to the fiber, allowing reuse of the extracting phase. SPME uses a small volume of sorbent, typically dispersed on the surface of small fibers, to isolate and concentrate analytes from the sample matrix. After contact with the sample, analytes are absorbed or adsorbed by the fiber phase (depending on the nature of the coating). After the extraction step, the fibers are transferred, with a syringe like handling device, to the analytical instrument, for separation and quantify cation of the analytes. This technique integrates sampling, extraction and sample introduction, and is a simple way of performing on-site monitoring. Applications of this technique include environmental monitoring, fragrance drug analysis, and in-laboratory and on-site analyses.

The configuration of SPME is a small, fused silica fiber, usually coated with a polymeric phase. The fiber is mounted for protection in syringe like device. The analytes are absorbed or adsorbed by the fiber phase until equilibrium is reached in the system. The amount of an analyte extracted by the coating at equilibrium is determined by the magnitude of the partition coefficient of the analyte between the sample matrix and the coating material.

SPME Device

The commercial SPME device manufactured by Supelco (Bellefonte, USA) is presented in **Fig. 3.4**. The fiber glued into a piece of stainless steel tubing is mounted on a special holder. The holder is equipped with an adjustable depth gauge, which makes it possible to control repeatedly, how far the needle of the device penetrates the sample container or the injector. This is important, as the fiber can break if it hits an obstacle. The movement of the plunger is limited by a small screw that moves in the z-shaped slot of the device. For protection during storage or septum piercing, the fiber is withdrawn into the needle of the device, with the screw in the uppermost position. During extraction or desorption, the fiber is exposed by depressing the plunger. The plunger is moved to its lowermost position only for replacement of the fiber assembly. Each type of fiber has a hub of a different colour.

If the sample is in a vial, the septum of the vial is first pierced with the needle (with the fiber in the retracted position), and the plunger is lowered, which exposes the fiber to sample. The analytes are allowed to partition into the coating for a pre-determined time, and the fiber is then retracted back to the needle. The device is then transferred to the SPME instrument. When gas chromatography is used for analyte separation and quantification, the fiber is inserted into a hot injector, where thermal desorption of the trapped analyte takes place.

For spot sampling, the fiber is exposed to a sample matrix until partitioning equilibrium is reached between sample matrix and the coating material. In the time average approach, on the other hand, the fiber remains in the needle during exposure of the SPME device to the sample. The coating works as a trap for the analytes that diffuse into the needle, resulting in integral concentration over time measurements.

SPME sampling can be performed in three basic modes: direct extraction, headspace trapping, and extraction with membrane protection.

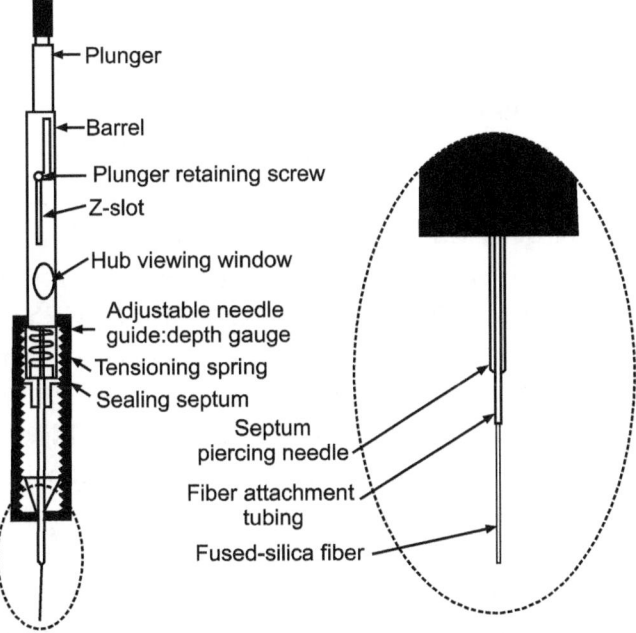

Fig. 3.4 : Commercial SPME device manufactured by Supelco (Bellefonte, USA)

Advantages

The primary advantages of SPME are its ability to decouple sampling from matrix effects that would distort the apparent sample composition or disturb the chromatographic separation; its simplicity and ease of use; and its reduced or non-existent solvent consumption. These characteristics combine to make SPME an attractive alternative to classic headspace or thermal-desorption sampling, solid-phase extraction and classic liquid–liquid extraction.

As with several related sample preparation and injection techniques such as headspace GC and thermal desorption, SPME lends itself well to handling difficult sample matrices and has the added benefits of low cost and simplicity. SPME doesn't require elaborate and expensive instrument accessories for occasional use, and yet it seems to be capable of delivering very good manual results when in the hands of skilled users, which cannot necessarily be said of manual headspace or thermal-desorption sampling. Auto samplers are also available to perform repetitive unattended SPME sampling.

SPME requires careful optimisation and consistent operating conditions for success, but this statement is true of the related techniques as well. Any poorly characterised sampling technique has no valid use in analytical laboratories, and the burden of developing an SPME method is no greater than for developing a method for any of the other techniques. SPME has a significant place in analysts' arrays of sample preparation techniques.

Practical Approach of Solid Phase Micro Extraction

Zhannan Yang et al. (2009) compared the sampling techniques headspace solid-phase microextraction (HS-SPME), petroleum ether extraction (PEE) and steam distillation extraction (SDE) for the GC-MS of volatile constituents present in ginger (*Zingiber officinale*). The effects of different parameters, such as extraction fibers, extraction time, extraction temperature and particle size ranges, on the HS-SPME of rhizome of ginger were investigated. Zingiberene (53.12%) was the predominant component of ginger samples obtained by HS-SPME whereas those levels were 39.01% in the same samples by PEE and 35.05% in those by SDE, respectively as shown in **Fig. 3.5**. HS SPME with polydimethylsiloxane (PDMS) fiber was more selective and particularly efficient for the isolation of volatile phytochemical composition and afforded a higher yield of total compounds than PEE and SDE. The specific compound isolated by SPME, which due to effective fiber, was much larger than that isolated by PEE or SDE. HS-SPME is a powerful tool for determining the volatile constitutes present in the traditional Chinese medicines.

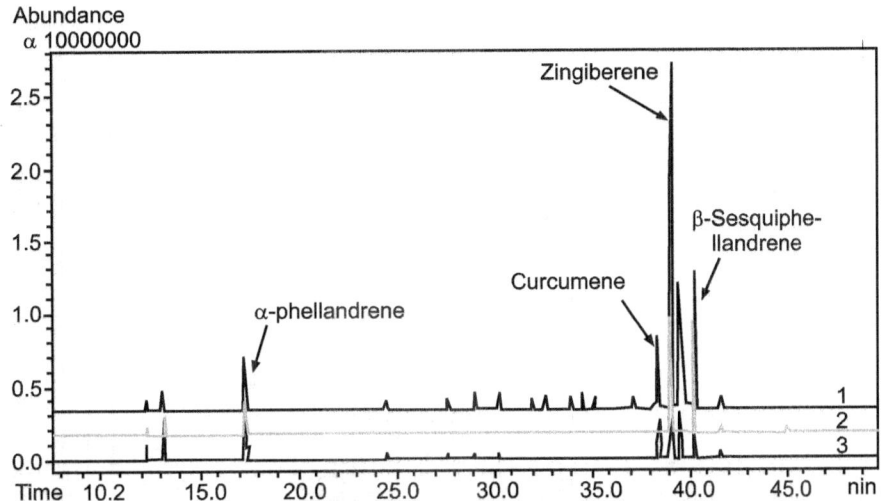

Fig. 3.5 : Comparison of HS.SPME PEE and SDE for GC.MS of volatile constituents present in ginger

Solid Phase Microextraction (SPME) as a modern sample preparation method was discussed by Magdalena Ligor et al (2004). Based on theoretical and practical aspects of the SPME method, a comparison of extraction efficiency of aromatic hydrocarbons (benzene, toluene, ethylbenzene, m,p-xylene (BTEX)) as testing substances was performed. The various SPME coated fibers: commercial (polydimethylsiloxane – PDMS, polyacrylate – PA) and home-made (etoxy polydimethylsiloxane – PDES, polyurethaneacrylate, fused silica, and fused silica after etching of hydrogen fluoride acid) were compared in these experiments. The extraction efficiency was displayed as the extracted mass for BTEX after extracting of standard solution with various SPME fibers. Various extraction times of BTEX isolation were taken into consideration, but 20 min was a sufficient time for reproducible results obtained for the extracted mass of BTEX.

The most efficient extraction (adsorption on the fiber surface) is for the ethoxypolydimethyl siloxane - coated fibers after drying at 200°C than for other tested fibers as shown in the figure given below. On the other hand, the adsorption of BTEX on fused silica fiber etched with hydrofluoric acid HF (0.5%) is much better compared to untreated fused silica fiber. An interesting problem is that for the studied volatile organic compounds with larger molecular weight (more CH_3 – groups in the molecule) a higher sorption level was observed. A comparison of new modified fibers with commercial fiber PDMS (7 μm coating thickness) shows a higher recovery of extraction (ca. 20%) for PDES (ca. 10 μm coating thickness). This data also confirms that the thickness of the fiber coating and chemical properties of coatings exert an influence on extraction recoveries. Many advantages, as well as disadvantages of the SPME method are described in details.

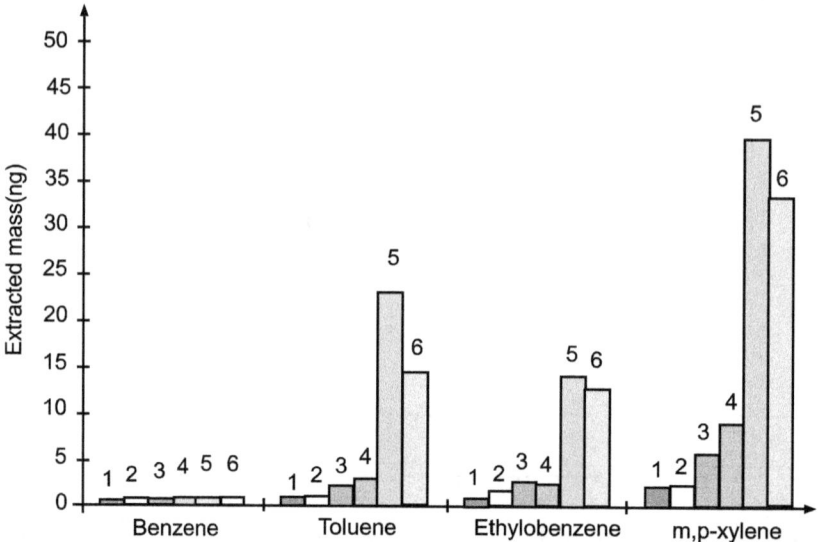

Fig. 3.6 : Comparison of extraction efficiency for BTEX for five different coated fibers (1) fused silica, (2) fused silica after etching by HF, (3) polyuethaneacrylate, (4) ethoxy polydimethylsiloxane (PDES) after drying at 450° C, (5) ethoxy-polydimethylsiloxane (PDES) after drying at 200° C, (6) polydimethylsiloxane (PDMS).

Mari R. Tellez et al. (2004) reported a new method involving concurrent solid-phase microextraction combined with continuous hydrodistillation of essential oil. This new methodology allowed for the detection by GC–MS of very small amounts of a diagnostic peak for the authentication of *Ephedra sinica*, in a short period of time and using only small sample sizes. This diagnostic peak was identified as 4-vinylanisole, and elucidated from the chromatographic profile allowed for the identification of a sample as *E. sinica* among other species investigated in this study. A total of 46 collections representing 21 species of *Ephedra* were studied. As per the results, SD–SPME is an excellent technique that compliments existing methodology in the investigation of volatile components in *E. sinica*, and for any plant sample in general. The method should also be ideal for the analysis of trace amounts of volatile components from large volumes of aqueous matrices, with 1mg of 4-vinyl-anisole in 3: 1 ratio with water (333 µg/ml) easily detected by GC–MS. We also found the SD–SPME set-up to be superior to currently available automated SPME protocols. Several experiments with an automated SPME autosampler at temperatures ranging from 65 to 200°C with varying amounts of water (2 to 10 ml) led to an optimised protocol that used 2ml of water and 140°C. However, even after optimising, this method afforded signals for 4-vinyl-anisole that were about an order of magnitude smaller than using SD–SPME. SD–SPME suffers from the fact that there are currently no available systems that allow for automated sampling.

Chapter ... 4

QUANTITATIVE AND QUALITATIVE ESTIMATION OF HERBALS

The use of herbs as medicine is the oldest form of healthcare known to humanity and has been used in all cultures throughout history. Many countries, including Japan, Korea, America, Britain, China countries in Africa etc. have benefited from traditional herbal medicine for thousands of years. Early humans recognised their dependence on nature for a healthy life and since that time humanity has depended on the diversity of plant resources for food, clothing, shelter, and medicine to cure myriads of ailments. Led by instinct, taste, and experience, primitive men and women treated illness by using plants, animal parts, and minerals that were not part of their usual diet. Primitive people learned by trial and error to distinguish useful plants with beneficial effects from those that were toxic or inactive, and also which combinations or processing methods had to be used to gain consistent and optimal results. Even in ancient cultures, tribal people methodically collected information on herbs and developed well-defined herbal pharmacopeia.

Indeed, well into the twentieth century, much of the pharmacopeia of scientific medicine was derived from the herbal lore of native people. The knowledge of plant-based drugs developed gradually and was passed on, thus, laying the foundation for many systems of traditional medicine all over the world. In some communities herbal medicine is still a central part of their medical system.

Medicinal plants are widely distributed throughout the world but most abundantly in tropical countries. It is estimated that about 25% of all modern medicines are directly or indirectly derived from higher plants (WHO, 2005). Thus, herbal medicine has led to the discovery of a number of new drugs, and non-drug substances.

A herb is a plant or part of a plant valued for its medicinal, aromatic, or savoury qualities. Herbs can be viewed as biosynthetic chemical laboratories, producing a number of chemical compounds. Herbal remedies or medicines consist of portions of plants or unpurified plant extracts containing several constituents, which often work together synergistically. Herbal medicine or herbalism is the use of herbs or herbal products for their therapeutic or medicinal value. They may come from any part of the plant but are most commonly made from leaves, roots, bark seeds, and flowers. They are eaten, swallowed, drunk, inhaled, or applied topically to the skin. Herbal products often contain a variety of naturally-occurring biochemicals from plants, many of which contribute to the plant's medicinal benefits. Chemicals known to have medicinal benefits are referred to as "active ingredients" or "active principles" and their presence depends on a number of factors including the plant species, the time and season of harvest, the type of soil, the way the herb is prepared, etc.

During the past decade, in the developed countries, people are attracted to herbal therapies for many reasons, the most important reason being that, like our ancestors, it is believed they will help us live healthier lives. Herbal medicines are often viewed as a balanced and moderate approach to healing. Individuals who use them as home remedies and over-the-counter drugs spend billions of dollars on herbal products. As such, they represent a substantial proportion of the global drug market.

To achieve the desired benefit from herbal preparations, an individual must take the required dose over a certain length of time. Although it is generally believed that most herbal preparations are safe for consumption, some herbs like most biologically active substances could be toxic with undesirable side effects.

Herbal drugs possess great advantage in curing and preventing diseases as compared to man-made synthetic drugs. Herbal medicines contain many components which are pharmacologically active. However, herbal medicines also have their shortcomings since the concentration of their active components may vary from batch to batch thus affecting their efficiency in treating diseases. The variability of the constituents in herbs or herbal preparations due to genetic, cultural and environmental factors has made the use of herbal medicines more challenging than it would necessarily have been. For instance, the availability and quality of the raw materials are frequently problematic, the active principles are diverse and may be unknown, and quality of different batches of preparation may be difficult to control and ascertain. In most countries, herbal products are launched into the market without proper scientific evaluation, and without any mandatory safety and toxicological studies. There is no effective machinery to regulate manufacturing practices and quality standards. Consumers can buy herbal products without a prescription and might not recognise the potential hazards in an inferior product. A well-defined and constant composition of the drug is therefore, one of the most important prerequisites for the production of a quality drug. Given the nature of products of plant origin, which are not usually constant and are dependent on and influenced by many factors, ensuring consistent quality of products is vital for the survival and success of the industry.

QUALITY CONTROL AND STANDARDISATION OF HERBAL MEDICINES

Generally, all medicines, whether they are synthetic or of plant origin, should fulfill the basic requirements of being safe and effective. The term "herbal drugs" denotes plants or plant parts that have been converted into phytopharmaceuticals by means of simple processes involving harvesting, drying, and storage. Hence they are capable of variation. This variability is also caused by differences in growth, geographical location, and time of harvesting.

The quality control involves three steps:
1. False and true identification.
2. Distinguish originating regions of herbs.
3. Quality evaluation.

The false and true identification aims to distinguish the species by means of many qualitative analytical methods. The qualities of herbs are closely related to their producing areas; for this reason the determination of producing regions is critical. The quality of herbs depends on the growing environments, methods of harvesting, drying, storage, transportation, and processing (for example, mode of extraction and polarity of the extracting solvent, instability of constituents, etc.) as well, since the growth of herbs is easily affected by geographical and climate conditions.

Standardisation of herbal medicines is the process of prescribing a set of standards or inherent characteristics, constant parameters, definitive qualitative and quantitative values that carry an assurance of quality, efficacy, safety and reproducibility. It is the process of developing and agreeing upon technical standards. Specific standards are worked out by experimentation and observations, which would lead to the process of prescribing a set of characteristics exhibited by the particular herbal medicine. Hence standardisation is a tool in the quality control process.

Several problems often influence the quality of herbal drugs. For instance:
1. Herbal drugs are usually mixtures of many constituents.
2. The active principle(s) is (are), in most cases unknown.
3. Selective analytical methods or reference compounds may not be available commercially.
4. Plant materials are chemically and naturally variable.
5. Chemo-varieties and chemo-cultivars exist.
6. The source and quality of the raw material are variable.

At present no official standards are available for herbal preparations. Those manufacturers, who are currently doing some testing for their formulations, have their own parameters, many of which are very preliminary in nature.

The quality control methods underwent many developments since ancient times, from the botany shapes, microscopy structure identification to the physical and chemical properties based on the major component identification to almost all components identification depending on fingerprint spectra.

Presently it is very difficult to identify the presences of all the ingredients as claimed in a formulation. Hence the first important task is to evolve such parameter by which the presence of the entire ingredient can be identified, various chromatographic and spectrophotometric methods such as HPLC, HPTLC, Mass Chromatography GC etc. and evaluation of physicochemical properties can be tried to evolve pattern for identifying the presence of different ingredient. Wherever possible, these methods can be applied for quantitative estimation of bioactive group of compounds like alkaloids, flavonoids, polyphenolic components or estimation of a particular compound.

The Need for Standardisation

In the global perspective, there is a shift towards the use of medicines of herbal origin, as the dangers and the shortcoming of modern medicine are getting more apparent. It is the cardinal responsibility of the regulatory authorities to ensure that consumers get the medication, which guarantees purity, safety, potency and efficacy. The regulatory authorities rigidly follow various standards of quality prescribed for raw materials and finished products in pharmacopoeias, formularies and manufacturing operations through statutory imposed good manufacturing practices (GMP). These procedures logically would apply to all types of medication whether included in modern system of medicine or one of the traditional systems.

Though herbal products have become increasingly popular throughout the world, one of the impediments in its acceptance is the lack of standard quality control profile. The quality of herbal medicine that is, the profile of the constituents in the final product has implications in efficacy and safety. However, due to the complex nature and inherent variability of the constituents of plant-based drugs, it is difficult to establish quality control parameters, though modern analytical technique are expected to help in circumventing this problem. Furthermore, the constituents responsible for the claimed therapeutic effects are frequently unknown or only partly explained. This is further complicated by the use of combination of herbal ingredients as being used in traditional practice. It is common to have as many as five different herbal ingredients in one product. Thus batch to batch variation starts from the collection of raw material itself in the absence of any reference standard for identification. These variations multiply during storage and further processing. Hence for herbal drugs and products, standardisation should encompass the entire field of study from cultivation of medicinal plant to its clinical application.

HPLC (HIGH PERFORMANCE LIQUID CHROMATOGRAPHY)

Liquid chromatography though more troublesome than gas chromatography, has the main advantage of operating at low temperatures and can be used with advantage for separation of substances as proteins, nucleosides which are thermolabile.

In conventional liquid chromatography, a dilute solution of sample is passed through a column packed with solid particles. Thus, liquid is passed through vertical columns under gravitational flow. This is passed with slow speed and especially if the packing granules were small enough to give efficient separation, then the delivery under gravity decreases even upto a few drops per minute.

The way to increase the flow rate and get efficient separation is to force the liquid by a positive displacement pump or by gas pressure. This versatility can be achieved by making certain modifications in columns and by using smaller diameter and smaller surface area of column particles and by using other suitable packing structure. This is HPLC i.e. **High Pressure/Performance Liquid Chromatography.**

Thus, HPLC is a high resolution and high speed liquid chromatography. It has several times more resolving power than open column liquid chromatography. Hence it is used for speedy resolution of complex mixtures.

Theory

The particle size of the stationary phase material plays a very vital and crucial role in HPLC. In fact, high-efficiency-stationary-phase materials have been researched and developed exclusively for HPLC having progressively smaller particle size termed as microparticulate column packings. These silica particles are mostly uniform, porous, with spherical or irregular shape, and having diameter ranging from 3.5 to 10 μm.

Bonded-Phase Supports: The bonded-phase supports usually overcome plethora of the nagging problems which is mostly encountered with adsorbed-liquid phases. Here the molecules, comprising the stationary phase, *i.e.*, the surfaces of the silica particles, are covalently bonded to a silica-based support particle.

However, the most popular bonded-phase, **siloxanes**, is formed by heating the silica particles in dilute acid for a day or two so as to generate the reactive silonal group

$$\begin{array}{ccc} OH & OH & OH \\ | & | & | \\ -Si-O-Si-O-Si- \\ | & | & | \end{array}$$

which is subsequently treated with an organochlorosilane

$$-Si-OH + Cl-\underset{\underset{CH_3}{|}}{\overset{\overset{CH_3}{|}}{Si}}-R \longrightarrow -Si-O-\underset{\underset{CH_3}{|}}{\overset{\overset{CH_3}{|}}{Si}}-R + HCl$$

These bonded phases are found to be fairly stable between the pH range 2 to 9 and upto temperatures of about 80°C. The nature of the R group of the silane solely determines the surface polarity of the bonded phase.

A fairly common bonded phase is made with a linear C18 hydrocarbon, also known as ODS (octadecyl silane) bonded phases, wherein the groups appear to be protruding out from the silica particle surface just as the bristles on a toothbrush. It takes care of almost 75% of the samples in HPLC.

Note : The exact mechanism by which the respective bonded phases actually alter the nature of the sorption mechanism is still not yet clear.

When such microparticulate-bonded-phases are packed compactly into a column by means of a suitable device, the small size of these particles offers a significant resistance to solvent flow; therefore, the mobile phase has to be pumped through the column under a high positive pressure. For an analytical HPLC, the mobile-phase is pumped through the column at a flow rate of 1-5 cm^3. min^{-1}.

At this juncture usually two varying situations arise. These are- isocratic elution - *i.e.*, when the composition of the mobile-phase is constant, and gradient elution *i.e.*, when the composition of the mobile phase can be made to change in a predetermined fashion during the course of separation.

Instrumentation

A schematic diagram of a **High-Performance Liquid Chromatography** is shown in **Fig. 4.1.** It consists of five major components :

- Solvent delivery system.
- Sample injection valve.
- Column.
- Detection and recording system.
- Microcomputer with control and data-processing software.

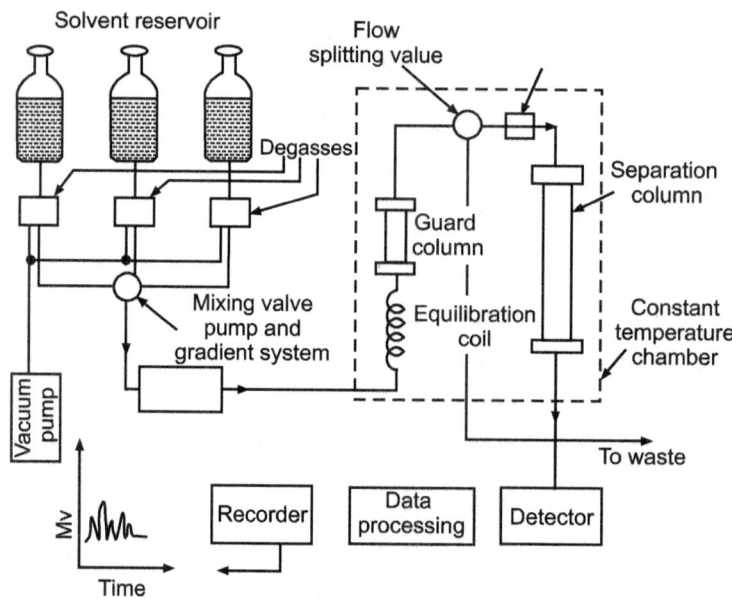

Fig. 4.1 : Schematic Diagram of a High-Performance Liquid Chromatography

In order to attain reasonably high flow rates and yet keep particle size of packing very low (3-10 μm), pumping pressures of several hundred atmospheres (2000 - 8000 psi) are required. Thus, the equipment for HPLC is quite elaborate though simple.

Application of HPLC

Unlike the single chemical entity that forms the basis of modern pharmacology and drug development, the paradigm of traditional herbal medicine views the multi-compound, multi-ingredient preparations typical of herbal medicine as representing the activity of the herbal drug. Selection of individual analytical compounds for determining either efficacy or quality is contrary to traditional medicine principles.

The common clinical use of herbal medicine requires the combination of two or more herbals based on recipes and formulae derived from historical references and empirical evidence of traditional medicine practitioners. Herbal drugs, singularly and in combinations, contain a myriad of compounds in complex matrices in which no single active constituent is responsible for the overall efficacy. This creates a challenge in establishing quality control standards for raw materials and the standardisation of finished herbal drugs.

This problem is compounded when one substance that contains a specific class of compounds is combined with others containing the same or different classes of compounds. Thus, it is necessary to develop a type of quality assessment system that adequately meets the complex characteristics of traditional herbal medicine. Chromatographic fingerprint analysis by which multiple compounds in single herbal drug and finished traditional herbal medicine can be identified represents a rational approach for the quality assessment of traditional herbal medicine. It utilises chromatographic techniques such as Gas Chromatography, HPLC, HPTLC, etc.

Chromatographic fingerprint analysis of herbal drugs represents a comprehensive qualitative approach for the purpose of species authentication, evaluation of quality, and ensuring the consistency and stability of herbal drugs and their related products.

Some of examples of Chromatography fingerprint analysis are-

Hydrastis canadensis L., is one of the oldest herbal medicinal plants and is of current interest as a natural medicine. It has been used as an anti-inflammatory and antibiotic. It has also been used to treat nasal congestion, cold, flu, and a variety of intestinal disorders. There are two alkaloids present in the plant that are the expected active components, berberine and hydrastine. Canadine, hydrastinine, berberastine, and canadaline are minor alkaoloids.

For HPLC, 0.5gm of root powder was extracted in a sonicator with 100 ml of acetonitrile: water: H_3PO_4 (70:30:0.1) for 5 minutes and then shake it for 10 min and centrifuge for 5 min. The filtrate thus obtained were analysed in HPLC.

The HPLC analysis of the plant extract was required to identify the quality and quantity of alkaloids present in the plant. The specification required for the HPLC are mentioned below in **Fig. 4.2**.

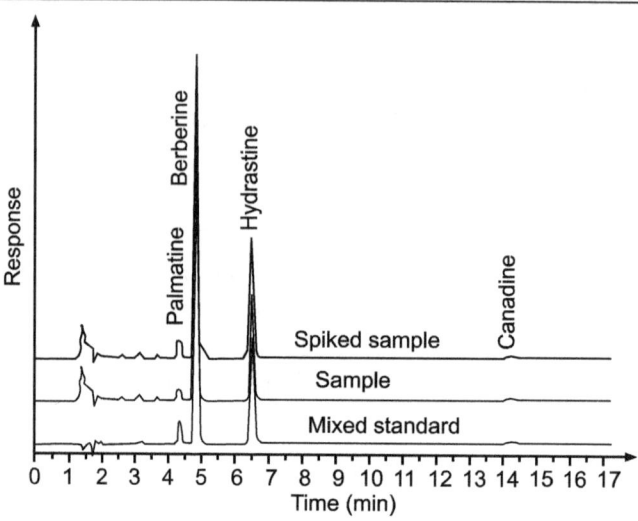

Fig. 4.2 : HPLC Separation of *Hydrastis canadensis* L.

The immature fruits of *Terminalia chebula* were collected and ground to a coarse powder (50 mg) and extracted with 50 ml acetone, filtered, the filtrate evaporated to dryness, the residue dissolved in 10ml of water and refrigerated at 5°C for 1 h. It is then filtered, and the filtrate used as the sample solution. Similarly, the sample was prepared for the marketed formulation of fruits of *Terminalia chebula* (5 mg).

HPLC Specification

Column: Lichrospher 100 RP-18, 4mm×125 mm, 5μm (Merck);

Column temperature: 20°C;

Mobile phase: (A) 0.05 mol/L phosphoric acid aqueous solution and 0.05 mol/L KH_2PO_4 aqueous solution; (B) methanol; (C) ethyl acetate

Flow rate (ml/min): 1.0; injection volume: 5μL;

Detection wavelength: 280 nm;

Run time: 35 min;

Relative retention time of reference substances: gallic acid 1.0 min; chebulagic acid 6.3 min; chebulinic acid 7.2 min.

Observation and comparison of the chromatograms of the sample and standard solutions reflects some changes in the extract fingerprint in comparison to that of standard. In sample as shown in **Fig. 4.3 (a)**, the total fingerprint was divided into three sections; section I contains peaks 1–5, peak 3 corresponds to gallic acid (retention time region from 2 to 10.6 min); section II contains peak 6–11 (retention time region from 11 to 22.5 min); section III contains peak 12–15, peak 13 corresponds to chebulagic acid and peak 15 to chebulinic acid (retention time region from 23 to 40 min). In standard as shown in **Fig 4.3 (b)**, the intensity of peak 3 (gallic acid) in section I is dramatically increased, while the intensity of peak 13 (chebulagic acid) and peak 15 (chebulinic acid) in section III is proportionately decreased.

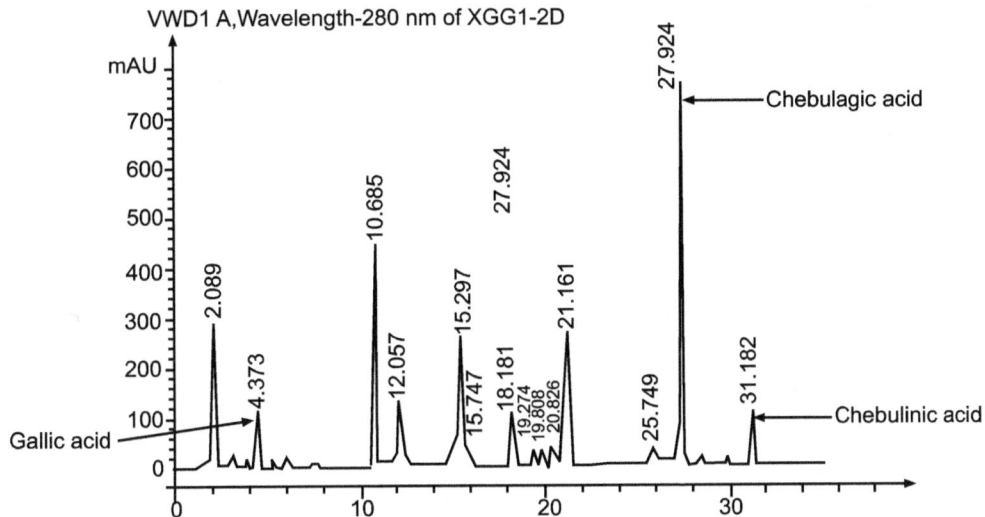

(a) HPLC Separation of *Terminalia chebula* sample

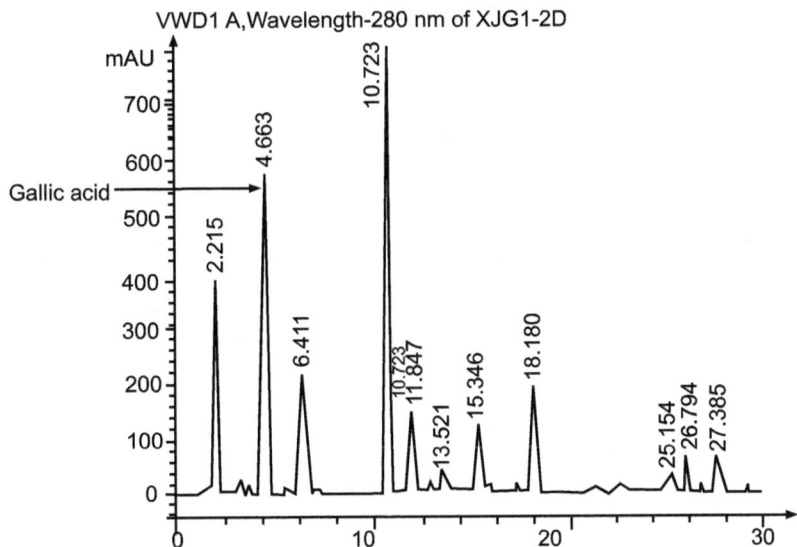

(b) HPLC Separation of *Terminalia chebula* standard
Fig. 4.3

The leaves of *Ginkgo biloba* was collected from 19 different places, their extract prepared and their HPLC pattern compared with the standard reference preparation of flavonoids.

Ginkgo biloba leaves were dried and extracted, 80 mg of extract dissolved in 5 ml of methanol, filtered and the filtrate is used as the sample solution. Similarly, 0.2 mg of rutin, heteroside A and heteroside B are dissolved individually in 1 ml of methanol to be used as a reference standards for *Ginkgo biloba* analysis. HPLC Specifications are as described-

Column: Spherisorb ODS2 C-18, 4 mm × 250 mm, 5μm (Waters);

Column temperature: 25°C;

Mobile phase: (A) water–acetonitrile–isopropanol–citric acid (1000:200:30:4.92 g); (B) water–acetonitrile–isopropanol–citric acid (1000:470:50:6.08 g)

Gradient: 0 min: 100% A; 25 min 100% B

Flow rate (mL/min): 1.0; injection volume: 5μL; detection wavelength: 250 nm, 360 nm

Run time: 25 min.

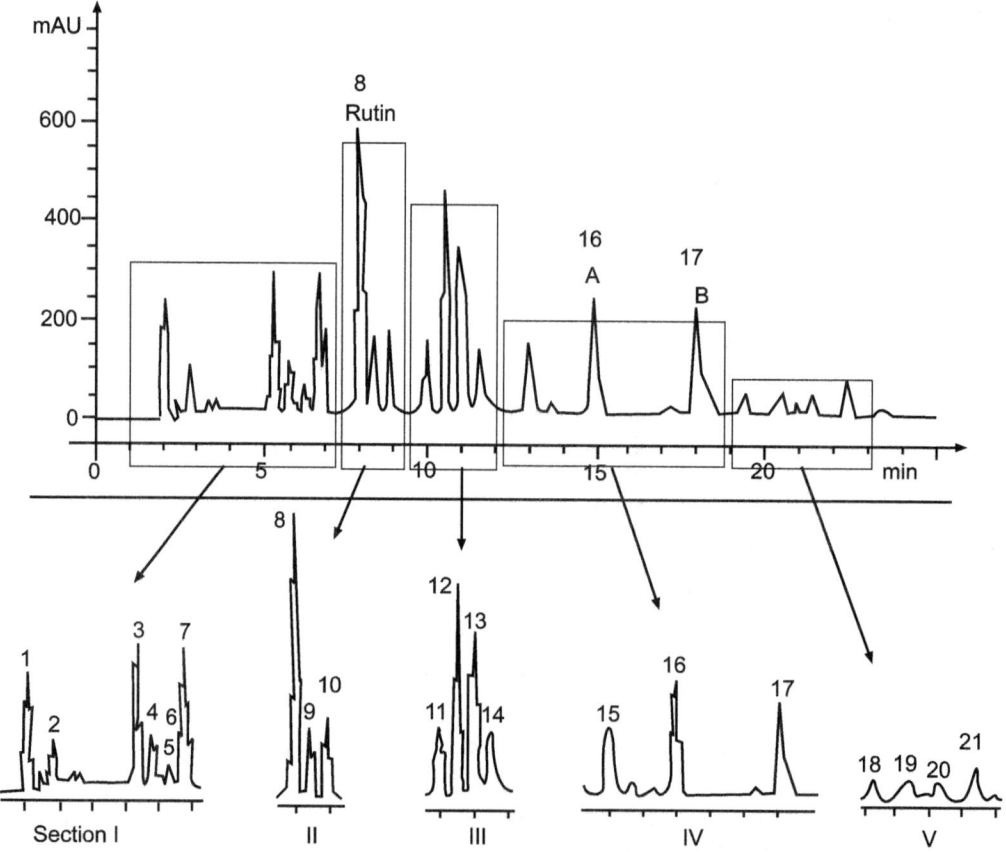

Fig. 4.4 : HPLC fingerprint of standard reference of *Gingko biloba*

The chromatogram was divided into five sections and characterised as follows: seven peaks in section I (*t*R region from 2 to 7 min), three peaks in section II (*t*R region from 7.5 to 9 min), four peaks in section III (*t*R region from 9 to 12 min), three peaks in section IV (*t*R region from 12 to 18.5 min), and several minor peaks in section V (*t*R region from 19 to 23 min). These minor peaks are of less significance to the overall characteristics of the pattern. A simple review of the chromatogram allows the analyst to quickly and reliably identify a characteristic pattern, including peak height and peak-to-peak ratios before reading peak area values. In the chromatogram presented (**Fig. 4.4**), the highest peak (8) in the fingerprint is attributed to rutin (quercetin-3-rutinoside); peak 16 to heteroside A (quercetin cinnamoyl-glycoside), and peak 17 to heteroside B (kaempferol cinnamoyl glycoside); the approximate peak to peak ratios of peaks 3, 16, and 17 are approximately 1:0.5:0.45.

Using the HPLC fingerprint (**Fig. 4.4**) as the standard pattern against which to compare other preparations, 19 samples of leaves of *Gingko biloba* from different sources were comparatively analysed. Calculating the raw signal points set for all samples by using the computer-aided similarity-evaluation (CASE) software, the results showed a high degree of similarity for the samples collected to the standard represented by a correlation coefficient of more than 0.94; five batches showed a lower degree of similarity represented by a correlation coefficient of less than 0.87 (Fig. 4.5). This indicates that the proportion and distribution of the total flavonoids in most extracts of *Ginkgo biloba* leaves possess a high level of consistency. Additionally, the fingerprint analysis shows that three of the products (sample numbers 1, 2, and 4) were adulterated, likely with the inexpensive flavonoid rutin, which can be used to artificially increase the total flavonoid content. In this fingerprint chromatogram, peak no. 8 was uncharacteristically predominating (Fig. 4.6).

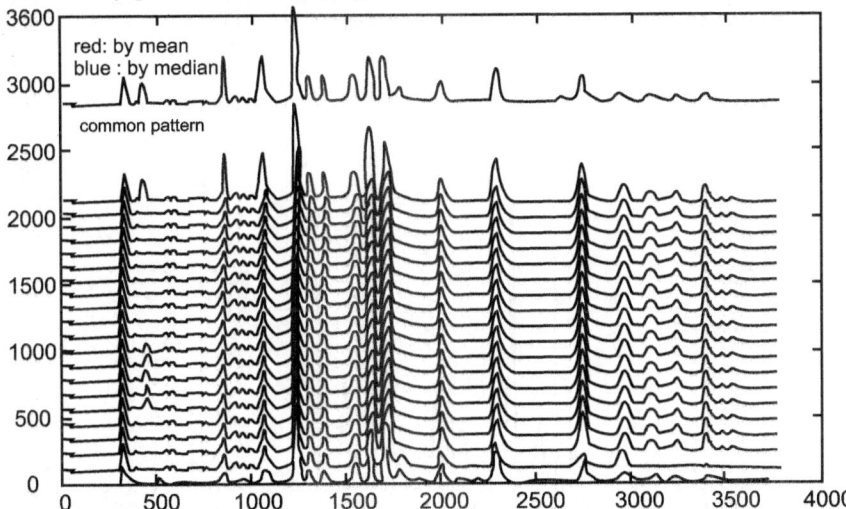

Fig. 4.5 : The similarity of HPLC fingerprints of 19 commercial samples of *Ginkgo biloba* extracts from different sources derived from computer-aided similarity-evaluation (CASE) software

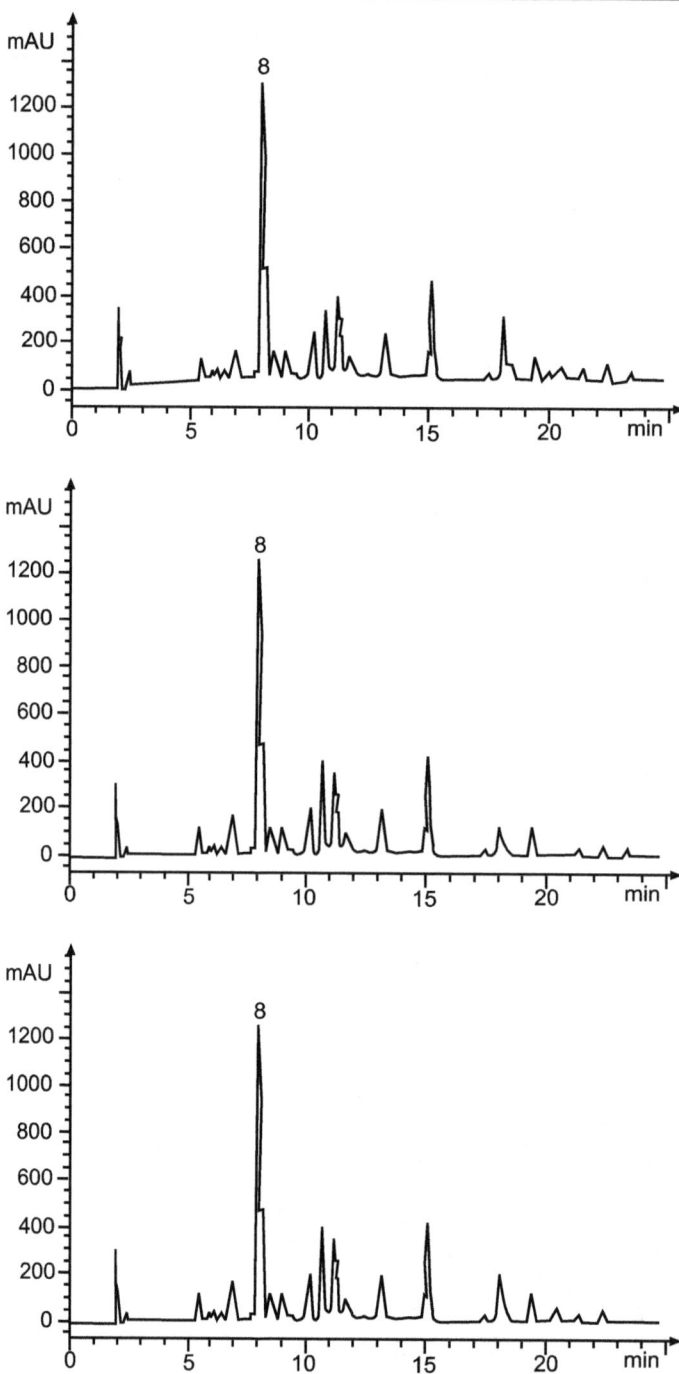

Fig. 4.6 : The HPLC fingerprint of *Gingko biloba* samples nos. 1, 2, and 4 showing adulteration with the flavonoid rutin; note abnormally increased peak dominating the fingerprint in comparison with the fingerprint of standard reference

Rhizoma chuanxiong were dried first at 30°C and then extracted using a stirrer at 11000 rpm with 30 ml of methanol for 2 min. After centrifugation for about 20 min, the solution was filtered through a glass filter covered with a filter paper. Next, the solution was evaporated under reduced pressure to about 1 ml and then diluted with methanol to 5 ml in a volumetric flask and then the sample was standardised using HPLC. The chromatographic fingerprints from *Rhizoma chuanxiong* are shown in Fig. 4.7.

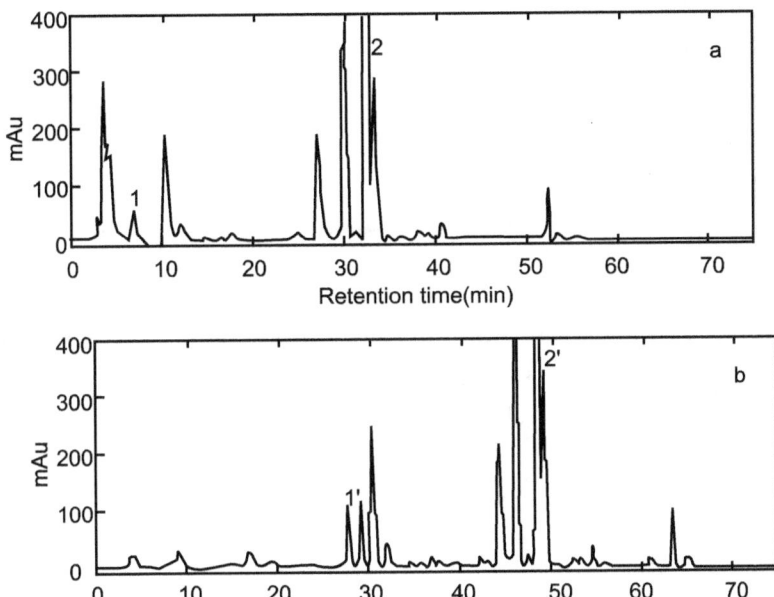

Fig. 4.7 : Chromatographic fingerprints from *Rhizoma chuanxiong*

Here we use reverse phase high performance liquid chromatography for quantitative analysis of piperine from ayurvedic polyherbal formulations such as Arkavati vati, Kravyada rasa and Marichyadi taila using standard piperine solution as all the three formulations have black piper. The main constituent of black piper is piperine. 0.5 gm powder of Arkavati and Kravyada Rasa were extracted using soxhlet apparatus in HPLC grade methanol (150ml) at 70°C for 6hrs. The extract was filtered through Whatman filter paper no. 1, filtrate collected and the final volume was made to 150 ml with the help of HPLC grade methanol. Extraction of Marichyadi taila was done by adding 1ml of taila to 9 ml of methanol. The mixture was vortexed for 30 sec and kept overnight. Next day, the upper methanolic layer was separated and used for further analysis using HPLC.

Column: C_{18} column (150 mm × 4.6 mm, 5 μm particle)

Column temperature: 25°C;

Mobile phase: Methanol: water 70:30 (v\v)

Flow rate (mL/min): 1.0; injection volume: 5 μL; detection wavelength: 342 nm

Run time: 25 min.

The peak of standard piperine was appeared at retention time of 6.10 min as shown in **Fig. 4.8**. The samples of piperine such as Arkavati vati, Kravyada rasa and Marichyadi taila also shows peak at 6.0 min approximately which shows that all the formulations has black piper or piperine (**Fig. 4.9 - 4.11**).

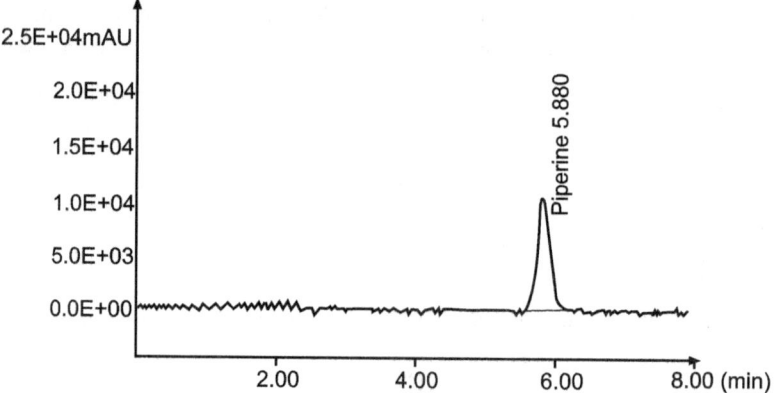

Fig. 4.8 : HPLC chromatogram of Piperine standard (1000 ng/ml)

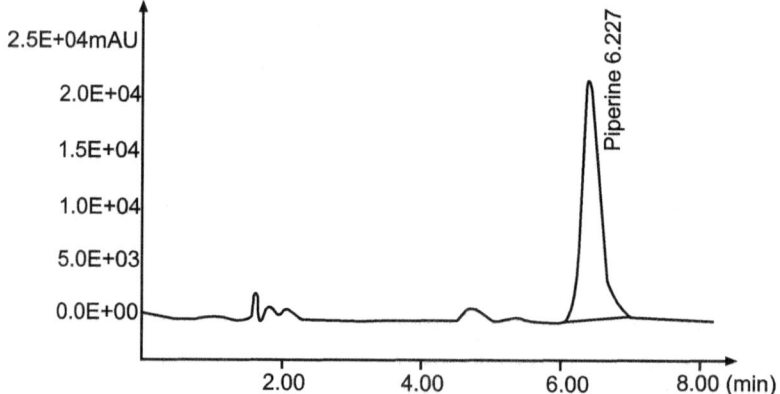

Fig. 4.9 : HPLC chromatogram of Arkavati

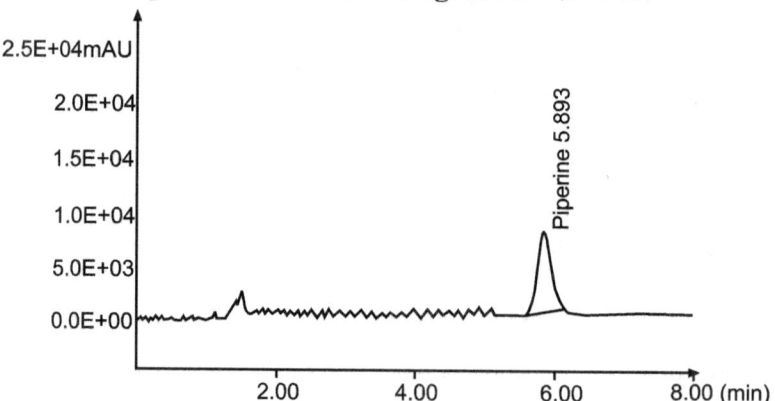

Fig. 4.10 : HPLC chromatogram of Kravyada rasa

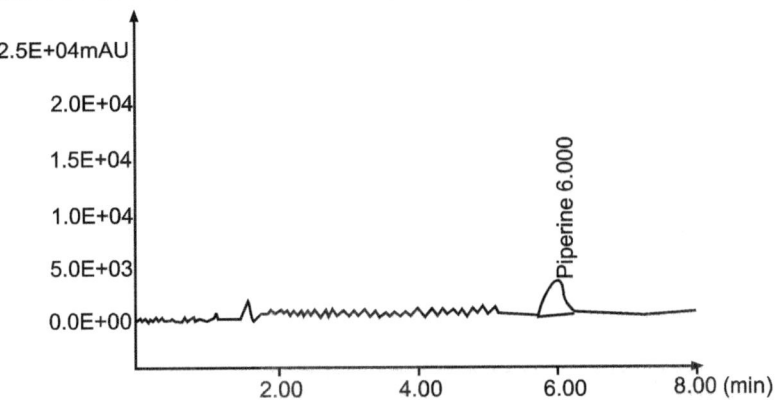

Fig. 4.11 : HPLC chromatogram of Marichyadi taila

Eclipta alba (L.) Hassk. (Asteraceae), a small, branched annual herb with white flower heads, is native to the tropical and subtropical regions of the world. It is used as a tonic and diuretic in hepatic and spleen enlargement. It is also used in catarrhal jaundice and for skin diseases. Decoction of the plant is used to invigorate the liver, to prevent premature greying of the hair and to stop bleeding, especially from the uterus. The plant contains specified compounds like ecliptin and wedelolactone. To identify the major and minor constituent in *Eclipta alba* the HPLC was used.

Sample preparation: 50 g of dried powdered samples were soaked in 125 ml of HPLC grade methanol for 16 hours in a rotatory shaker. Whatman No.1 filter paper was used to separate the extract of both plants. The filtrates were used for further HPLC analysis.

Column: C_{18} column (150 mm × 4.6 mm, 5 μm particle), Water's (USA), Tiger- LC System

Column temperature: 25°C;

Mobile phase: 0.5% Formic acid : Acetonitrile (70 : 30)

Flow rate (mL/min): 1.0; injection volume: 5 μL; detection wavelength: 270 nm

Run time: 25 min.

The HPLC chromatogram of *Eclipta alba* methanolic extract is shown in **Fig. 4.12**. The HPLC results revealed the presence of a good percentage of flavanoid content. The flavanoid content of *Eclipta alba* was 0.280%.

Emilia sonchifolia (Asteraceae), is a herbaceous plant found in India and in other Asian countries. The plant is used in treatment of tumour, inflammation, cough, rheumatism, cuts and wounds. In China, the plant is used for fever and dysentery. The plant exhibits different properties like antimicrobial, antifungal etc. The samoolam or whole plant is taken fresh and crushed well, juice is extracted and given in the dose of 5 – 10 ml daily for three days to cure intestinal worms. The karkam or the paste of samoolam of the plant is given in the dose of 2 – 5 grams preferably with butter milk for bleeding piles. The decoction of the whole plant is effective for fever. To identify the major and minor constituent in *Emilia sonchifolia* the HPLC was used.

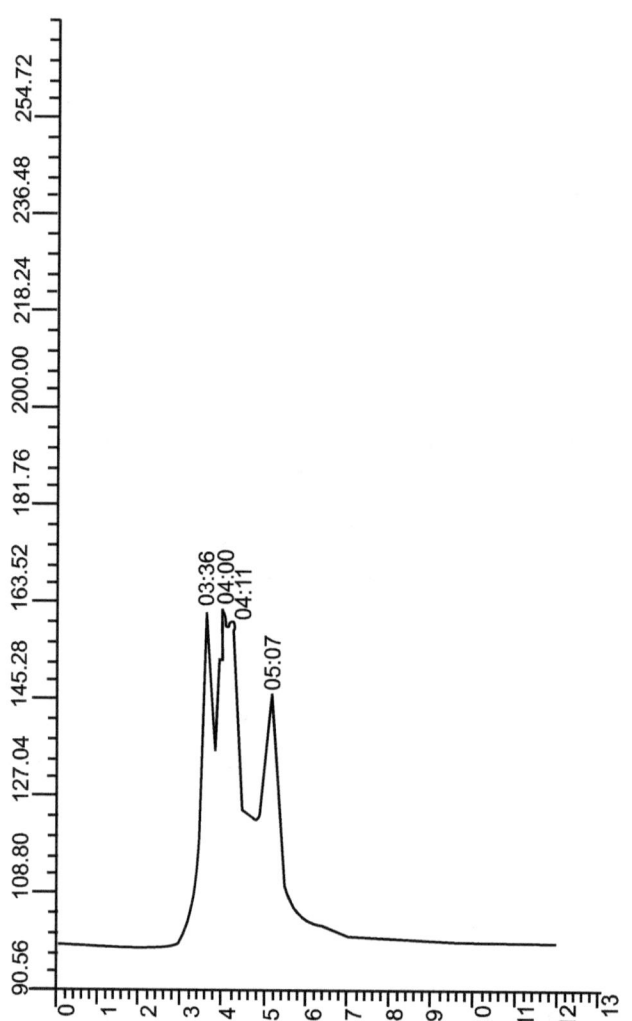

Fig. 4.12 : HPLC chromatogram of *Eclipta alba* methanolic extract

Sample preparation: 50 g of dried powdered samples were soaked in 125 ml of HPLC grade methanol for 16 hours in a rotatory shaker. Whatman No.1 filter paper was used to separate the extract of both plants. The filtrates were used for further HPLC analysis.

Column: C_{18} column (150 mm × 4.6 mm, 5 μm particle), Water's (USA), Tiger- LC System

Column temperature: 25°C;

Mobile phase: 0.5% Formic acid : Acetonitrile (70 : 30)

Flow rate (mL/min): 1.0; injection volume: 5 μL; detection wavelength: 270 nm

Run time: 25 min.

The HPLC chromatogram of *Emilia sonchifolia* methanolic extract is shown in **Fig. 4.13**. The HPLC results revealed the presence of a good percentage of flavanoid content. The flavanoid content of *Emilia sonchifolia* was 0.147%.

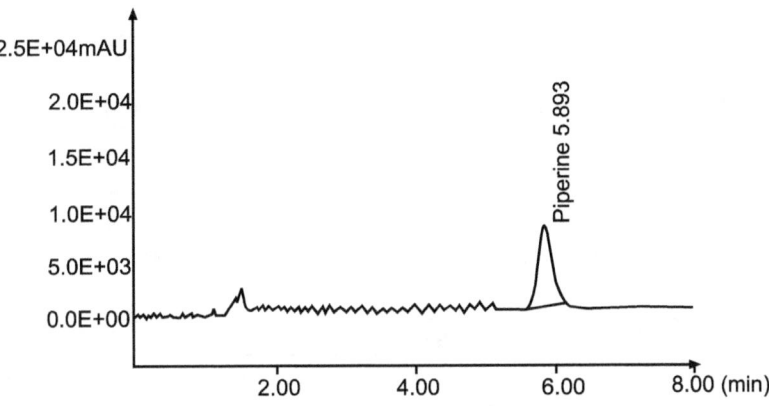

Fig. 4.13 : HPLC chromatogram of *Emilia sonchifolia* methanolic extract

HIGH PERFORMANCE THIN LAYER CHROMATOGRAPHY (HPTLC)

Among the modern analytical tools HPTLC is a powerful analytical method equally suitable for qualitative and quantitative analytical tasks. HPTLC is playing an important role in today's analytical world, not in competition to HPLC but as a complementary method. One of the most obvious orthogonal features of the two techniques is the primary use of reversed phases in HPLC versus unmodified silica gel in HPTLC, resulting in partition chromatography and adsorption chromatography respectively. Unlike other methods, HPTLC produces visible chromatograms so that complex information about the entire sample is available at a glance. Multiple samples are seen simultaneously so that reference and test samples can be compared for identification.

Principle

HPTLC takes place in high speed capillary flow range of the mobile phase. There are three main steps HPTLC procedure.

1. Sample to be analysed is loaded onto the chromatogram and volume precision and exact position are achieved by use of suitable instrument.

2. Solvent (mobile phase) migrates the planned distance in the layer (stationary phase) by capillary action. In this process, sample separated into it's components.

3. Separation tracks are scanned in densitometer with light beams in visible or UV region.

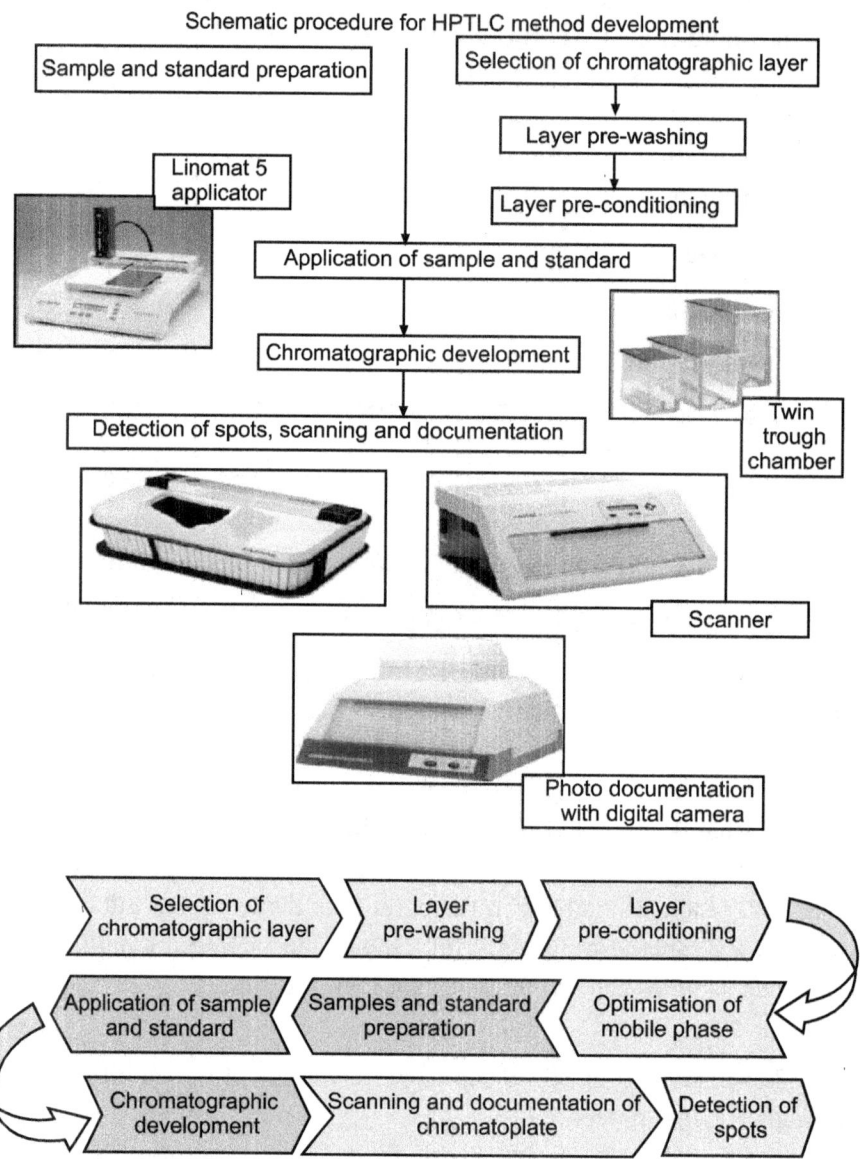

Fig. 4.14 : Steps involved in HPTLC

HPTLC Applications

Most of the modern medicines have originated from plant metabolites. There is a growing focus on the importance of medicinal plants in the traditional health care system (viz. Ayurveda, Unani, Homoeopathy, Yoga) in solving health care problems. Because of this awareness, plant materials and herbal remedies derived from them represent substantial portion of the global market. Most of the developing countries have reviewed the traditional medical practices as an integral part of their culture so much so a large number of herbal remedies are becoming popular to treat many deadly ailments. But we are still facing problems for the standardisation of herbal products and there are no specific prescribed provisions for herbal drugs in current Drug Legislation enforced in our country. But in view of the growing interest in herbal medicines and photochemicals, scientists are trying to develop methods for standardisation of herbal drugs used in different formulations.

Analysis of herbal drugs are carried out in all stages of extraction and isolation processes. These analytical techniques provide more accurate and precise data, not only supporting drug discovery and development but also postmarket surveillance. Analytical methods used in drug analysis are diversified and are still being improved to find better solutions to satisfy manufacturers and institutions that test drug quality. Official documents dealing with the problem of QC of pharmaceutical products recommend diversified analytical techniques, with chromatographic methods playing a significant role in pharmaceutical analysis.

Thin layer chromatography studies are among the key identity tests in most pharmacopeial monographs. An extension of TLC is the high performance thin layer chromatography (HPTLC). It is robust, simplest, rapid and efficient tool in quantitative analysis of compounds. HPTLC is an analytical technique based on TLC, but with enhancements intended to increase the resolution of the compounds to be separated and to allow quantitative analysis of the compounds.

HPTLC in Natural Products

HPTLC not only confirms but also establishes the identity of the compound present in the sample. The technique is rapid, comparatively simple, robust and extremely versatile. It is also an ideal screening tool for adulterations and is highly suitable for evaluation and monitoring of cultivation, harvesting, extraction processes and test of stability.

Syzygium jambolanum is commonly known as *Syzygium cuminii* (Linn) Skeel and belongs to the family of Myrtaceae. It is also known as Black plum (*Eugenia jambolana*). It contains glycoside Jamboline, tannin, ellagic acid and gallic acid. As it has immediate effect on increasing the blood sugar, glycosuria results. It is chiefly used in homoeopathy as remedy for diabetes mellitus. **Khandagale *et al.*** made an in-house standard mother tincture and compared it with different marketed samples using HPTLC fingerprint characteristics. Camag HPTLC system comprising of Linomat 5 as sample applicator and TLC Scanner 3 controlled by win CATS software version 1.3.4 was used for quantitative evaluation. Stationary phase used for quantitative evaluation was Merck's percolated TLC aluminum foil Silica Gel 60F254 and the mobile phase used was Toluene: Ethyl Acetate: 100 % Formic Acid (100:60:50) v/v. Samples and standard were applied at

8 mm bands with 6 mm distance between the tracks. Tank saturation was carried out with filter paper for 15 min. Ascending development for a distance of 80 mm in a twin trough chamber was completed in *ca.* 15 min. Volume of standard mother tincture was first optimised at 5 μL for fingerprinting. The λmax of *ellagic acid* was found to be 279 nm after taking the spectra of the standard of *ellagic acid*. Quantitative measurement in the absorbance mode was at 225 nm using a slit dimension of 5.00 × 0.45 mm. The results obtained were that many fractions of standard mother tincture were matched with the help of its characteristic spectra with that of other marketed samples. Individual λ_{max} of each fraction was also found with the help of spectral scanning and then the plate was scanned with this selected wavelength in MWL mode. The pattern of the peaks was compared for the standard mother tincture and marketed samples (**Table 4.1**).

Table 4.1 : HPTLC pattern of peaks for standard and marketed mother tinture

Peak	A			A1			A2			A3			A4		
	R_f	Max. Ht.	Area %	R_f	Max. Ht.	Area %	R_f	Max. Ht.	Area %	R_f	Max. Ht.	Area %	R_f	Max. Ht.	Area %
1	0.09	162.5	34.07	0.07	374.7	57.98	0.10	340.9	95.25	0.08	319.2	53.23	0.07	186.6	61.95
2	0.20	24.8	5.15	0.21	225.8	32.81	0.22	16.0	3.40	0.21	57.5	10.07	0.20	58.6	22.17
3	0.33	41.0	13.29	0.36	34.4	3.95	0.27	14.7	1.36	0.38	29.7	4.66	0.39	30.2	11.02
4	0.48	15.0	2.25	0.46	19.4	1.21	-	-	-	0.70	125.9	30.58	0.77	18.8	4.87
5	0.72	141.0	45.24	0.54	38.1	3.35	-	-	-	-	-	-	-	-	-

Chothani et al. performed the identification, isolation and quantification of marker in various extracts and fractions of *Ruellia Tuberose* using HPTLC finger printing analysis. TLC plate consists of 20 × 10 cm, precoated with silica gel 60 F254 TLC plates (E. Merck) (0.2mm thickness) with aluminum sheet support. The spotting device was a CAMAG Linomat V Automatic Sample Spotter (Camag Muttenz, Switzerland); the syringe, 100 μL (from Hamilton); the developing chamber was a CAMAG glass twin trough chamber (20 × 10 cm); the densitometer consisted of a CAMAG TLC scanner 3 linked to WINCATS software. Mobile phase was chloroform: toluene: ethyl acetate (6: 3: 1, v/v). Saturation time for mobile phase was 2 hours. Various extracts of roots, leaf, and stem of *R. tuberosa* were applied on TLC plate and the plate was developed in chloroform: toluene: ethyl acetate (6 : 3 : 1, v/v) solvent system to a distance of 8 cm. The plates were dried at room temperature in air. The plate was scanned at 254 nm and 366 nm before spraying and at 600nm (**Fig. 4.15**) after spraying with detection reagent (Anisaldehyde sulfuric acid reagent) and plate was heated at 110°C for 5 minutes. The HPTLC finger print showed R_f value at 0.56 and purple colour of the resolved bands of leaf, root, and stem of *R. tuberosa*.

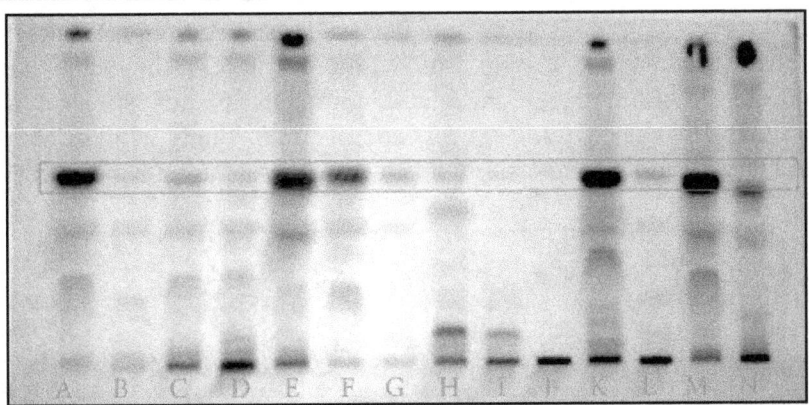

**Fig. 4.15 : HPTLC fingerprint of various extracts of *R. tuberosa* at 600 nm. (A) Petroleum Ether extract (R). (B) Toluene extract (R). (C) Chloroform extract (R). (D) Ethanol extract (R). (E) Petroleum Ether Fraction (R). (F) Hexane Fraction (R). (G) Toluene Fract (R). (H) Chloroform Fract (R). (I) Ethanol Fract (R). (J) Methanol Fract (R). (K) Ethanol extract (R). (L) Methanol extract (R). (M) Petroleum Ether extract (S). (N) Petroleum ether (L). R: Root; Fract: Hydroalcoholic fraction;
L: Leaf; S: Stem.**

Rumex vesicarius L. (Polygonaceae) is a edible green used as a sorrel eaten fresh or cooked, commonly called as "Bladder dock". It is a common vegetable green used in daily diet, it is known for its important medicinal uses, used in treatment of tumours, hepatic diseases, bad digestion, constipation, calcules, heart troubles, and pains.

The shade dried powdered sample was sonicated with respective solvents of 25 ml for thirty minutes. The extracts obtained were evaporated to dryness in China dish on water bath to get the residue. Each extract residue was re-dissolved in 1 ml of chromatographic grade solution, which was used for sample application on pre-coated silica gel 60 GF 254 aluminium sheets. Application of bands of each extract was carried out (14 mm in length and 1 µl in concentration) using spray technique. Samples were applied in duplicate on pre-coated silica gel 60GF254 aluminium sheets [(3x10) cm] with the help of Linomat 5 applicator attached to CAMAG HPTLC system, which was programmed through WIN CATS software. After the application of spots, the chromatogram was developed in twin trough glass chamber [(20 × 10) cm saturated with solvent Toluene and ethyl acetate in the ratio 7:3 for 15 min. The air-dried plates were viewed in ultra violet radiation to midday light. The chromatograms were scanned by densitometer at 405 nm after spraying with anisaldehyde sulphuric acid. Photo documentation of different extract solvents was observed at 366 and 254 nm respectively. The R_f values at fingerprint data were recorded by WINCATS software.

The HPTLC fingerprinting of *Rumex vesicarius* L. extracts revealed several peaks. The chloroform and ethanol extracts showed 9 spots of 5 µl concentration and 10 spots of 10 µl concentrations. n-Hexane extract showed 8 spots in 5 µl concentration and 7 spots in 10 µl concentrations. While ethyl acetate showed 7 spots in 5 µl concentration and

10 spots in 10 μl concentrations. The aqueous extract showed only 2 spots in both 5 μl and 10 μl concentration of the sample. **Fig. 4.16** and **Fig. 4.17** shows the chromatogram photo documentation of the plant extracts at 254 nm and 366 nm. The peak formation of the extracts and the Rf values of the extracts are given separately with the spots formed at Rf values and purity of the sample was confirmed by comparing the absorption spectra at start, middle and end position of the band.

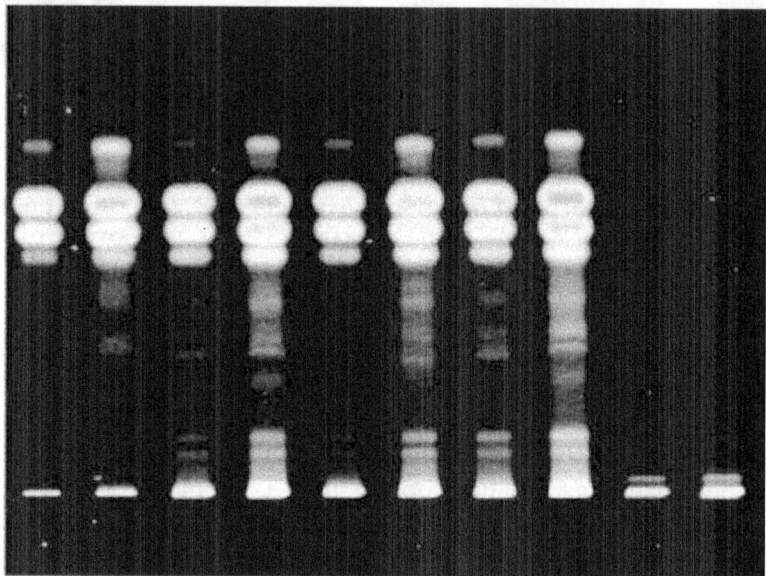

Fig. 4.16 : Photo documentation of different solvent extracts of *R. vesicarius* L. at 366 nm

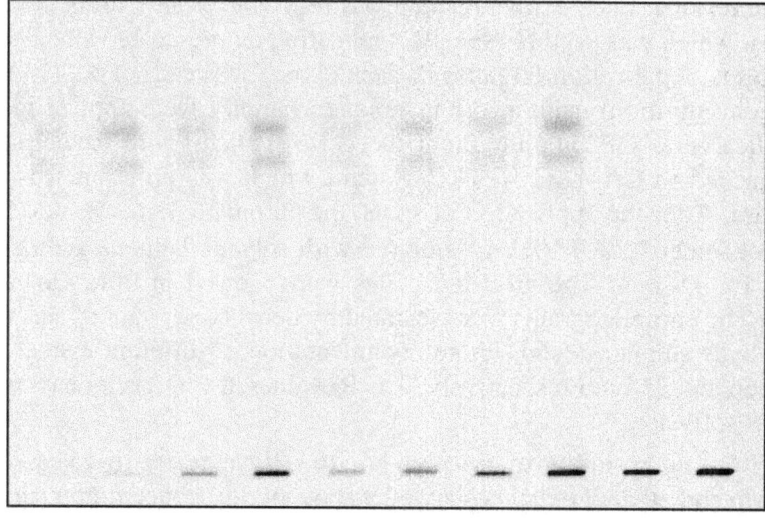

Fig. 4.17 : Photo documentation of different solvent extracts of *R. vesicarius* L. at 254 nm

Acacia catechu Willd. (Mimosaceae), also known as Khair, is a medium sized deciduous tree with crooked and forked trunk. It is found growing in both natural and plantation forms in most of the parts of India. *Acacia catechu* is used in traditional medicinal system for its wider range of therapeutic properties. Various parts of the tree such as leaf, bark, heartwood possess medicinal value. Main chemical constituents of *Acacia catechu Willd* are catechin, (−) epicatechin, epigallocatechin, epicatechin gallate, epigallocatechin, phloroglucin, protocatechuic acid, quercetin, poriferasterol glucosides, poriferasterol acyglucosides, lupenone, kaempferol, dihydrokaempferol, taxifolin, (+)-afzelchin gum and minerals. Both rutin and quercetin possess antioxidant activity and reduce low density lipoproteins (LDL) oxidation. Rutin and quercetin have shown regulatory activity of hormones like affect the transport, metabolism and action of thyroid hormones. High Performance Thin Layer Chromatography (HPTLC) method is the suitable method for estimation of chemical constituents present in plant materials.

200 mg of *Acacia catechu* leaf extract was accurately weighed into a 10 mL volumetric flask, was extracted by heating 40°C for 10 minutes, dissolved in methanol and then solution was filtered through Whatman filter paper and the filtrate was made up to the mark with methanol and proceed for spotting. The samples were spotted in the form of bands with hamilton syringe on a precoated silica gel plates 60F 254 [10 cm × 10 cm with 0.2 mm thickness, E.Merck] using Camag linomat IV applicator. Automatic sample spotter of band width 7 mm was used. Mobile phase was ethyl acetate: glacial acetic acid: formic acid:water [10:10:80: 5v/v]. The plates were developed in a solvent system in CAMAG glass twin through chamber previously saturated with the solvent for 30 min, the distance travelled was 8 cm. Subsequent to scanning, TLC plates were air dried and scanning was performed on a Camag TLC Scanner 3 in absorbance at 366 nm and operated by LC Solutions Version 1.21 SP1 software on a Pentium computer (Hewlett Packard). The HPTLC graph was shown in **Fig. 4.18**.

Standard: Rutin 1mg/ml [5 μL],

Standard: Quercetin 1 mg/ml [5 μL],

Sample : Herbal extract 10 mg/ml [10 μL],

Migration distance : 60 mm,

Detection wavelength: 366 nm,

Mode of scanning: Absorption

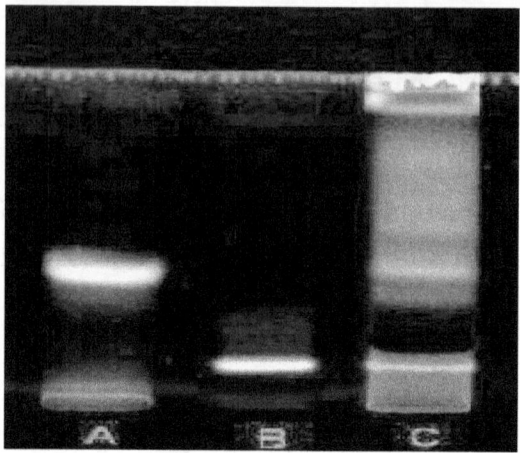

Fig. 4.18 : HPTLC chromatogram of A – Quercetin/Std/99.0%, B – Rutin/Std/98.0% and C – *Acacia catechu* **ethanolic leaf extract**

The chromatogram obtained with the reference solutions shows in the middle part, a light greenish blue fluorescent zone (quercetin) and in the lower part, a bluish fluorescent zone (Rutin). The chromatogram obtained with the test solution shows a light greenish blue fluorescent zone corresponding in position to the zone due to quercetin in the chromatogram obtained with the reference solution and it shows a bluish fluorescent zone corresponding to the zone due to Rutin in the chromatogram obtained with the reference solution.

Bauhinia variegata linn. (Mandharai) is a medium sized, deciduous tree, found throughout India, ascending to an altitude of 1,300 m in the Himalayas. *B.variegata* mainly consist of lupeol, β-sitosterol, tannins, kaempferol-3-glucoside[17], amides, carbohydrates, reducing sugars, crude protein, vitamin C, fibers[18], calcium, phosphorus[19], rutin, quercetin, quercitrin, apigenin, apigenin -7-O-glucoside. The chromatographic finger print profile of *Bauhinia variegata* leaves by HPTLC finger printing method.

A Camag HPTLC system (Muttenz,Switzerland) equipped with a sample applicator LinomatV, twin trough plate development chamber, TLC Scanner 3, winCATS software and Hamilton (Reno, Nevada, USA) were used for the finger printing analysis.

The leaves were washed with water and then shade dried. Crude extract was obtained after maceration with 95% ethanol at room temperature for 72 hrs, and repeated till exhaustion of the material. Thereafter, the ethanol crude extract was distilled, evaporated and dried under reduced pressure to yield ethanol extract of *B.variegata* leaves, EBV(yield 8%). A stock solution was prepared for analysis.

Chromatograph was performed on 10 × 10 cm aluminum packed TLC plate coated with 0.2 mm layer of silica gel 60F254 ((E. Merck Ltd, Darmstadt, Germany) stored in a dessicator. Application was done by Hamilton microsyringe (Switzerland), mounted on a Linomat V applicator. Spotting was done on the TLC plate, ascending development of the plate was for a migration distance of 80 mm (distance to the lower edge was 10 mm) was performed at 25+/-20°C with n-Hexane:ethyl acetate: formic acid: acetic acid

(70:30:1.0:1.0 v/v)as a mobile phase in a camag chamber previously saturated for 30 min. Various concentrations of the sample (2.5 µl, 5 µl and 10µl) were applied in four tracks as 8 mm bands at a spraying rate of 15s µL^{-1}. After development the plate was dried at 60°C in an oven for 5 minutes. Densitometric scanning was then performed with a Camag TLC Scanner 3 equipped with win CATS Software Version 1.3.0 at λ_{max} = 254 nm and 366nm using Deuterium light source, the slit dimensions were 6.00 X 0.45 mm and at λ_{max} = 620 nm using tungsten light source. The chromatograms were recorded.

The chromatograms shown in **Fig. 4.19** indicate that all sample constituents were clearly separated without any tailing and diffuseness. It is evident from **Table 4.2** that in 2.5 µl of ethanol extract of *Bauhinia variegata* leaves, there are 11 spots at the following R_f 0.24, 0.36, 0.55, 0.6, 0.63, 0.69, 0.75, 0.79, 0.89, 0.96, 0.99 as shown in **Fig. 4.20**, indicating the occurrence of atleast 11 different components in 2.5 µl of ethanol extract. Out of 11 components, the component with R_f values 0.51, 0.67, 0.73, 0.76 and 0.83 were found to be more predominant as the percentage area was more with 23.04%, 13.91%, 10.15%, 13.84% and 27.65% respectively. The remaining components were found to be very less in quantity as the percent area for all the spots were less than 4.0%.

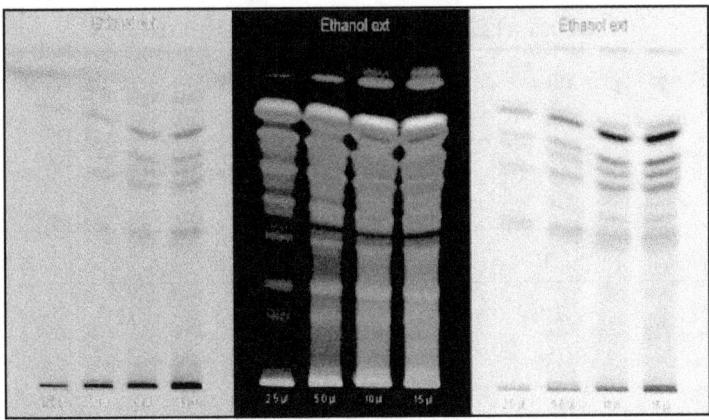

Fig 4.19 : HPTLC chromatogram of ethanol extract of *B.variegata*

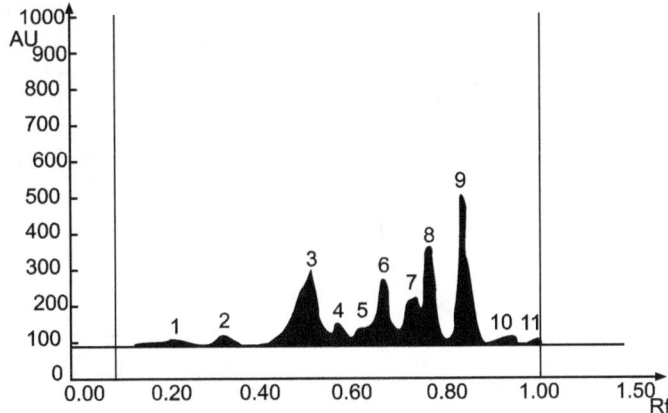

Fig. 4.20 : Fingerprint of *B.variegata* of 2.5 µl of ethanol extract leaves ↓case

As shown in **Table 4.2**, 5 µl of ethanol extract of *Bauhinia variegata* leaves there are 13 spots as shown in **Fig. 4.21** indicating the presence of at least 13 different components in ethanol extract. Out of 13 components, the component with Rf values 0.49, 0.64, 0.7, 0.73 and 0.8 were found to be more predominant as the percentage area was more with 21.21%, 15.03%, 10.86%, 14.85% and 27.3% respectively. The remaining components were found to be very less in quantity as the percent area for all the spots were less than 5.5%. 10 µl of ethanol extract of *Bauhinia variegata* leaves there are 13 spots as shown in **Fig. 4.22** indicating the presence of at least 13 different components in ethanol extract. Out of 13 components, the component with Rf values 0.46, 0.6, 0.65, 0.68 and 0.76 were found to be more predominant as the percentage area was more with 19.99%, 14.24%, 10.03%, 14.87% and 27.41% respectively. The remaining components were found to be very less in quantity as the percent area for all the spots were less than 6.1%.

Table 4.2: Peak list and Rf value of the chromatogram of 2.5, 5 and 10µl of Ethanol Extract of *Bauhinia variegata* Linn. leaves

Peak	Chromatogram of 2.5µl of Ethanol Extract			Chromatogram of 5µl of Ethanol Extract			Chromatogram of 10 µl of Ethanol Extract		
	Max Rf	Max Height	Area %	Max Rf	Max Height	Area %	Max Rf	Max Height	Area %
1	0.22	16.2	0.96	0.15	11.8	0.29	0.17	29.3	0.95
2	0.32	29.6	2.19	0.21	27.2	1.08	0.21	49.9	1.41
3	0.51	191.3	23.04	0.26	6.9	0.21	0.25	20.7	0.48
4	0.57	56.6	3.9	0.31	49.2	2.55	0.3	76.7	3.03
5	0.62	46.1	2.46	0.49	275.4	21.21	0.46	357.6	19.99
6	0.67	172.5	13.91	0.55	114.3	5.21	0.52	201.8	6.09
7	0.73	128.9	10.15	0.64	284.8	15.03	0.6	397.2	14.24
8	0.76	252.6	13.84	0.7	232.8	10.86	0.65	386.7	10.03
9	0.83	407.7	27.65	0.73	357	14.85	0.68	466.5	14.87
10	0.93	19.1	1.58	0.8	519.3	27.3	0.76	595.6	27.41
11	0.99	13	0.33	0.9	12.9	0.34	0.88	23.7	0.53
12	-	-	-	0.93	20.1	0.76	0.92	28.8	0.72
13	-	-	-	0.99	16.2	0.29	0.98	23.3	0.26

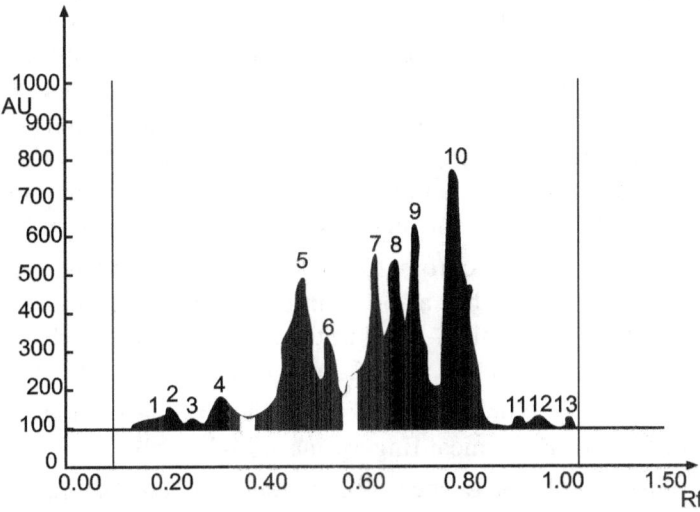

Fig. 4.21 : Fingerprint of *B.variegata* of 5 µl of ethanol extract of leaves

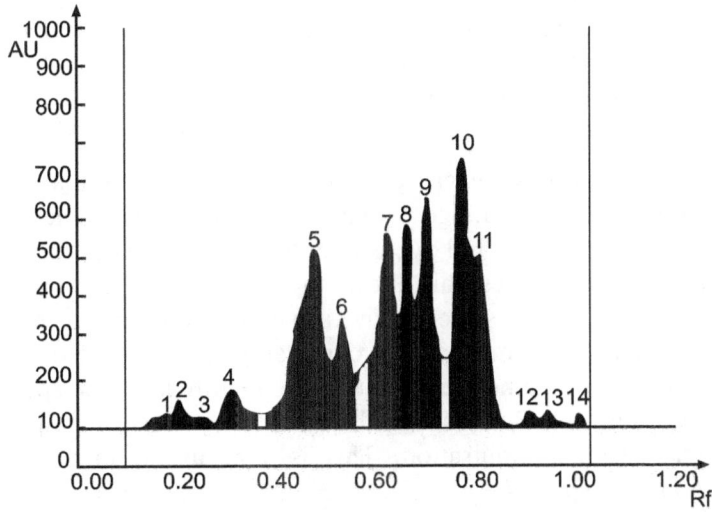

Fig. 4.22 : Fingerprint of *B.variegata* of 10 µl of ethanol extract of leaves

COMBINED SPECTROSCOPY

I. GC- MS

Mass spectrometry is the most sensitive and selective method for molecular analysis and can yield information on the molecular weight as well as the structure of the molecule. Combining chromatography with mass spectrometry provides the advantage of both chromatography as a separation method and mass spectrometry as an identification method. In mass spectrometry, there is a range of methods to ionise compounds and then separate the ions. Common methods of ionisation used in conjunction with gas chromatography are electron impact (EI) and electron capture ionisation (ECI). EI is primarily configured to select positive ions, whereas ECI is usually configured for negative ions (ECNI). EI is particularly useful for routine analysis and provides reproducible mass spectra with structural information which allows library searching. GC–MS was the first successful online combination of chromatography with mass spectrometry, and is widely used in the analysis of essential oil in herbal medicines.

With the GC–MS, not only a chromatographic fingerprint of the essential oil of the herbal medicine can be obtained but also the information related to its most qualitative and relative quantitative composition. Used in the analysis of the herbal medicines, there are at least two significant advantages for GC–MS, that is

(1) With the capillary column, GC–MS has in general very good separation ability, which can produce a chemical fingerprint of high quality

(2) When coupled with mass spectroscopy and the corresponding mass spectral database, the qualitative and relatively quantitative composition information of the herb investigated could be provided by GC–MS, which will be extremely useful for the further research for elucidating the relationship between chemical constituents in herbal medicine and its pharmacology in further research. Thus, GC–MS should be the most preferable tool for the analysis of volatile chemical compounds in herbal medicines.

Principle

The separation of mixtures by gas chromatography requires that they are volatile within the operating temperature range of the instrument. Since stable stationary phases are available for use up to 400°C and ovens may be temperature- programmed to operate from ambient to high temperatures, this allows the separation of many samples, provided they do not decompose in the system. The separated components may be classified according to their retention times or by chromatographing spiked samples, but for unambiguous identification, other techniques are required. Mass spectrometry is an important identification tool. Solutes may be ionised by electron impact, or by softer techniques such as chemical ionisation. This is very useful in the identification of biological and less stable species.

Instrumentation

The effluent gases from the gas chromatograph enclose both the carrier gas and the separated components at a pressure close to atmospheric. Detection by a flame ionisation detector (FID) or one of the other GC detectors is possible, and affected by splitting the effluent stream at the column exit, allowing most of the sample to enter the mass spectrometer. It is then necessary to reduce the pressure to the operating pressure of the mass spectrometer, which is around $10-8$ $Nm-2$. With a capillary GC column, the flow of carrier gas is small, and the effluent can be fed through a fine capillary directly into the mass spectrometer. For a packed GC column, an interface between the GC and the MS is required. This may either be a porous tube separator, or a jet separator. In both of these, the low-mass carrier gas, usually helium, diffuses away and is removed by pumps, while the larger sample molecules continue through into the MS. A complete GC-MS system is shown in the **Fig. 4.23**. The interface should be maintained at the temperature of the GC outlet, usually by enclosing it in the GC oven. Most types of mass spectrometer are suitable for GC-MS work, although those with a quadrupole analyzer are very often used because of their ability to scan rapidly. The chromatogram will be recorded by the GC detector and data system, but can also be derived by continuously measuring the total ion current (TIC) for the ions generated as a function of the elapsed time. This total ion current chromatogram matches that from the GC detector, and may also detect other solutes. By selecting a particular mass/charge (m/z) ratio, selected ion monitoring (SIM) may be used to detect a particular ion; for example, m/z 320, 322 and 324 may be studied in analysing mixed dioxins, since these ions are characteristic of a particular tetrachlorodibenzo-p-dioxin. Detection down to 10–15 g of a solute is possible.

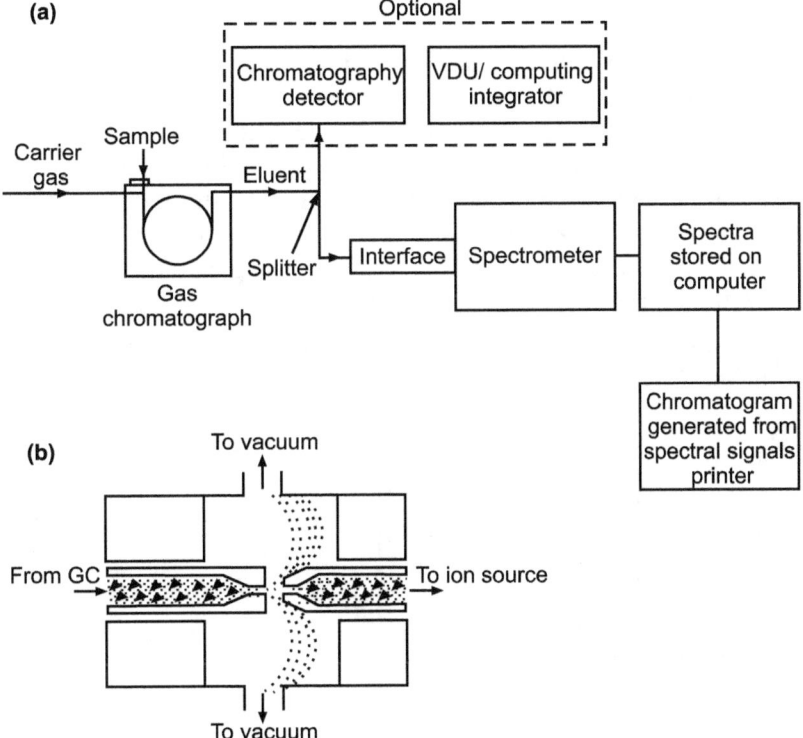

Fig 4.23 : (a) Schematic of a GC-MS system; (b) Jet separator

Application of GC-MS

Pesticide contamination of foodstuffs has become a matter of major concern worldwide, prompting various levels of regulation and monitoring. Pesticides are quantified with gas chromatography (GC) combined with selective detectors (ECD, FID, etc.). Selective GC detectors are favoured tools to quantify one or two pesticide classes at a time. However, screening for a number of different pesticides requires multiple runs utilising various GC configurations. Gas chromatography/mass spectrometry (GC/MS) various pesticides in a single analytical run; its superior selectivity allows interference-free quantification even with peak coelution. As a result, GC/MS has become a preferred technique for pesticide analysis because of its single-run capability.

The PerkinElmer 600 GC/MS with programmable split/splitless injector was used for this experiment. Sample volumes of 1.0 μL were injected into the programmable split/splitless injector, incorporating a 2-mm deactivated fused-silica liner. The injection-port temperature was set at 275°C (isothermal). The capillary column used incorporated a proprietary phase specifically suited for pesticides (Elite-CLPesticides) with the dimensions of 30 m × 0.25 mm × 0.25 μm df. The helium carrier gas was programmed with a constant velocity of 30 cm/sec. The oven-temperature programme was initially set at 80°C with no hold and ramped to 290°C at 20°C/min with a hold of 4.5 minutes. The total oven programme is 15 minutes, with an injection-to-injection time of less than 20 minutes.

The standards analysed here contain over 50 pesticides, of which 25 are pictured in **Fig. 4.24**. The chromatogram shown in **Fig. 4.24** is a composite of extracted ions from the full-scan acquisition of a 100-ppm standard. The spectral data provided by the mass spectrometer allows for the use of chromatographic conditions that resolve only peaks with similar spectra, allowing for faster oven programs and short analysis times. **Fig. 4.25** and **Fig. 4.26** show the background-subtracted spectra of Fenarimol and Fluridone respectively. The spectra of Fenarimol are quite complex and fragment into many different ions, while Fluridone is quite simple with only three major ions.

(**Source:** The application of GC/MS to the Analysis of Pesticides in food stuffs - By William Goodman, Perkin Elmer, Inc. U.S.A.)

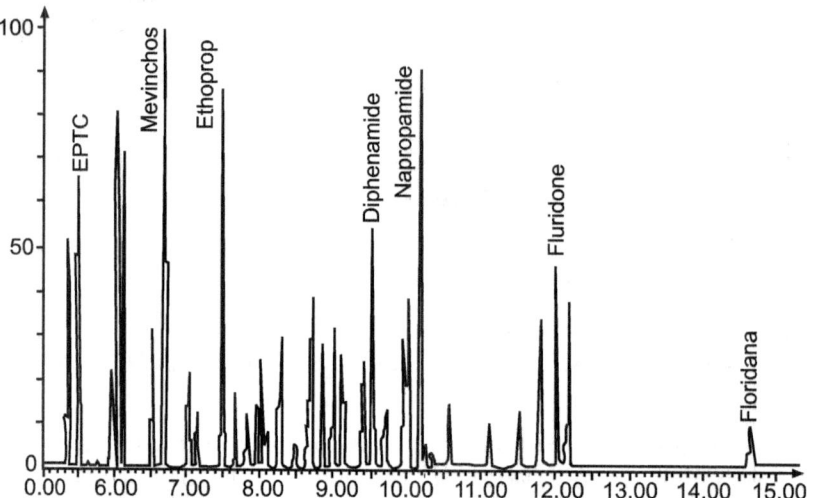

Fig. 4.24 : Extracted ion chromatogram of 100-ppm pesticide standard

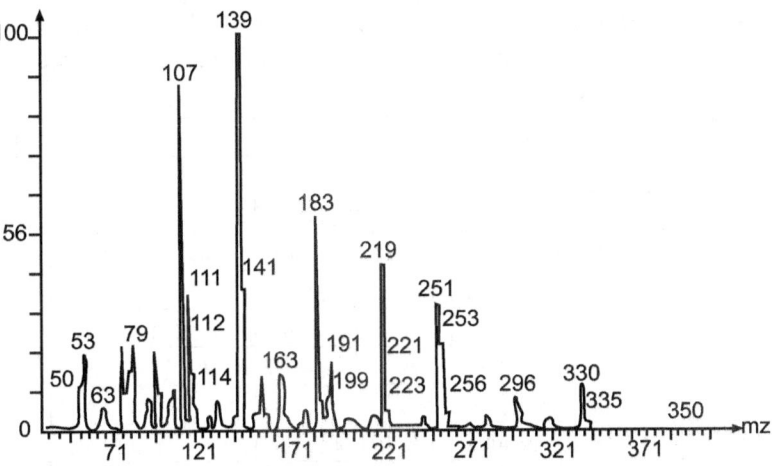

Fig. 4.25 : Background subtracted spectra of Fenarimol

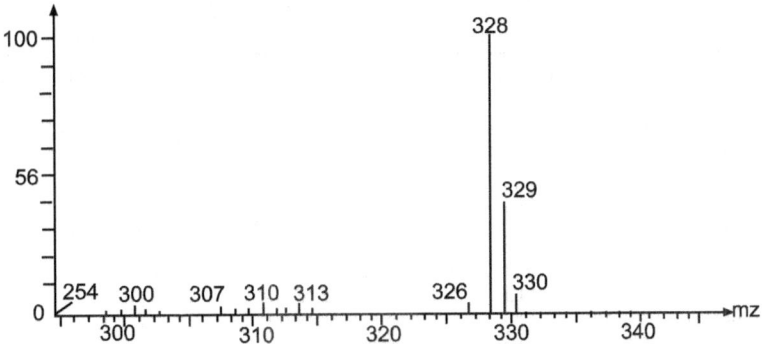

Fig. 4.26 : Background subtracted spectra of Fluridone

To establish a representative chromatographic fingerprint for fresh *Houttuynia cordata*, 10 authentic batches of fresh *H. cordata* acquired from Emei (major production area in Sichun Province, P. R. China) (EM-1 to EM-10) were analysed using the established GC-MS method. By similarity match, using the mass spectrometric libraries (NIST147, NIST27), a majority of the chemical components were identified. Individual results indicated that their chromatographic patterns were generally consistent to one another, although there existed some variations in peak abundance. The correlation coefficient of each chromatogram to their simulative mean chromatogram was found to be 0.962_0.034 (mean S.D., n=10). Among the 10 acquired chromatograms, peaks having matched RRT with a reasonable abundance of RPA were chosen and assigned as common peaks for representing the characteristics pattern of fresh *H. cordata*. Altogether, 16 common peaks were located in the chromatograms (**Table 4.3**). Peak 13 (2-undecanone) was assigned as the reference peak because of its highest content and definite pharmacological actions. Relative retention time (RRT) and relative peak area (RPA) were used as the parameters for the analysis between each characteristic peak and the reference peak.

Table 4.3 : The Relative Retention Time (RRT) and Relative Peak Area (RPA) of sixteen identified peaks of samples from various sources

Peak	Chemical Compound	YA (n = 8)		GD (n = 2)		HK (n = 2)		EM (n = 10)	
		RRT	RPA	RRT	RPA	RRT	RPA	RRT	RPA
1.	α-phellandrene (1)	0.16	0.03 ± 0.008	0.16	0.01 ± 0.001	-	-	0.16	0.01 ± 0.004
2.	α-Pinene (2)	0.17	0.30 ± 0.062	0.17	0.18 ± 0.009	0.17	0.24 ± 0.012	0.17	0.11 ± 0.014
3.	Camphone (3)	0.18	0.04 ± 0.005	0.18	0.02 ± 0.001	0.18	0.05 ± 0.002	0.18	0.02 ± 0.005
4.	3-Carene (4)	0.22	1.04 ± 0.366	0.21	0.14 ± 0.006	0.21	0.01 ± 0.001	0.21	0.27 ± 0.043
5.	β-Pinene (5)	0.22	0.40 ± 0.064	0.22	0.37 ± 0.018	0.22	0.39 ± 0.016	0.22	0.14 ± 0.020
6.	β-Mycrene (6)	0.25	1.27 ± 0.354	0.24	1.06 ± 0.056	0.24	1.79 ± 0.467	0.24	0.30 ± 0.044
7.	Terpinolene (7)	0.28	0.14 ± 0.090	0.28	0.02 ± 0.001	0.28	0.01 ± 0.001	0.28	0.07 ± 0.012
8.	Limonene (8)	0.31	0.10 ± 0.008	0.30	0.04 ± 0.001	0.30	0.14 ± 0.004	0.30	0.03 ± 0.008
9.	β-Ocimene (9)	0.32	0.45 ± 0.144	0.32	0.02 ± 0.004	0.32	0.68 ± 0.011	0.32	0.40 ± 0.118
10.	γ-Terpinene (10)	0.35	0.32 ± 0.070	0.35	0.03 ± 0.001	0.34	0.03 ± 0.001	0.35	0.10 ± 0.015
11.	Terpinen-4-ol (11)	0.59	0.68 ± 0.160	0.58	0.06 ± 0.001	0.58	0.01 ± 0.001	0.59	0.22 ± 0.028
12.	Bornyl acetate (12)	0.94	0.05 ± 0.016	0.93	0.07 ± 0.001	0.94	0.16 ± 0.001	0.94	0.08 ± 0.018
13.	2-Undecanone (13)	1	1	1	1	1	1	1	1
14.	Geraniol acetate (14)	1.35	0.04 ± 0.016	1.35	0.02 ± 0.001	1.35	0.14 ± 0.013	1.35	0.20 ± 0.035
15.	Isopentyl decanoate (15)	2.32	0.02 ± 0.008	2.31	0.03 ± 0.002	2.31	0.02 ± 0.001	2.32	0.07 ± 0.022
16.	n-Hexadecanoic acid (16)	2.49	0.12 ± 0.102	2.47	0.01 ± 0.003	2.47	0.01 ± 0.001	2.48	0.06 ± 0.035

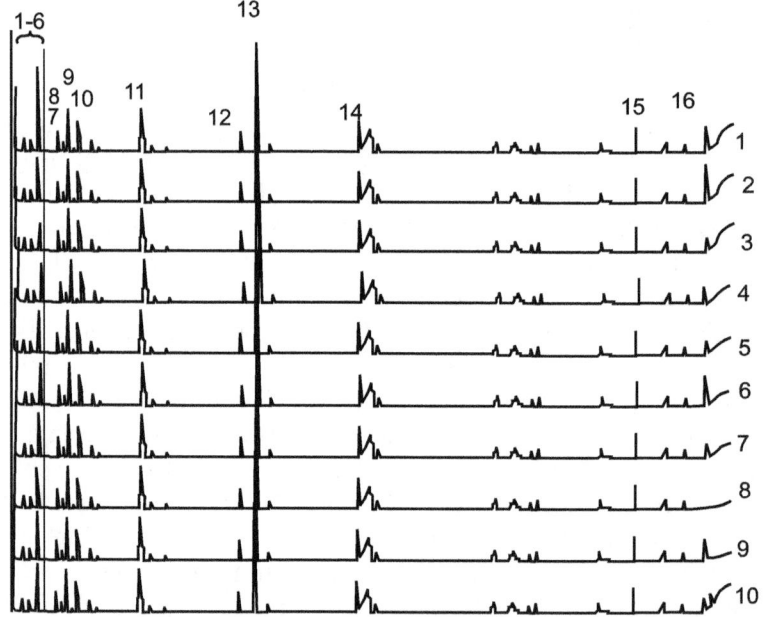

Fig. 4.27 : GC-MS Fingerprint of 10 batches of fresh *H. cordata*

To evaluate the extraction efficiency of the solid phase micro extraction method from peppermint leaves using the GC-MS were used by Ligor et al. The results of quantitative analysis of menthol and menthone from peppermint candies confirmed the concentration of menthol to be 0.023% w/w and the concentration of menthone 0.019% w/w. For peppermint candy preparation, peppermint oil (customarily obtained by steam distillation), is widely used. The presence of menthol, menthone and other terpenes in peppermint leaves is confirmed by SPME-GC/MS analysis. The GC/MS chromatogram obtained from *Mentha piperita* extract is presented in **Fig. 4.28**.

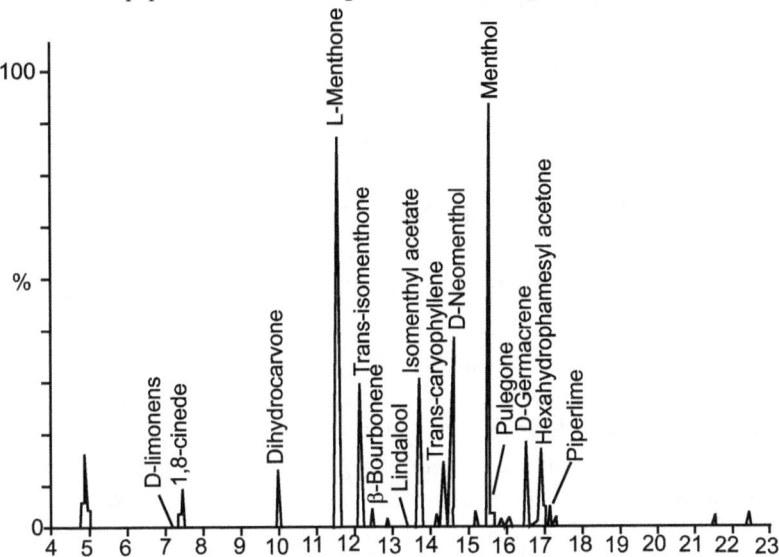

Fig. 4.28: GC/MS chromatogram of volatile organic compounds obtained from *Mentha piperita* extract

II. LC-MS

Liquid chromatography-mass spectrometry (LC-MS) is an analytical chemistry technique that combines the physical separation capabilities of liquid chromatography with the mass analysis capabilities of mass spectrometry. LC-MS is a powerful technique used for many applications which has very high sensitivity and selectivity. Generally, its application is oriented towards the specific detection and potential identification of chemicals in a complex mixture. There are two common atmospheric pressure ionisation (API) LC/MS process: Electrospray Ionization (ESI) & Atmospheric Pressure Chemical Ionization (APCI). Both are soft ionisation technique. Both of these processes are compatible with most chromatographic separations.

Principle

The wide variety of modes of liquid chromatography available and since these employ liquid mobile phases, sometimes containing inorganic salts, the most difficult problem is the transfer of the separated component of the analyte to the mass spectrometer without interference from the solvent.

Materials of high relative molecular mass are readily separated by liquid chromatography and, consequently, ionisation methods that produce less fragmentation in the mass spectrometer may have to be employed.

Instrumentation

The interface between the liquid chromatograph and the mass spectrometer is the most vital part of the combined instrument. Early systems using a moving belt interface have been superseded by spray devices and interfaces, which operate near atmospheric pressure. In atmospheric pressure chemical ionisation (APCI) interfaces, nitrogen is introduced to nebulise the mobile phase producing an aerosol of nitrogen and solvent droplets, which are passed into a heated region. Desolvation occurs, and ionisation is achieved by gas-phase ion-molecule reactions at atmospheric pressure, electrons and the primary ions being produced by a corona discharge.

Since the pressure is close to atmospheric, the collision frequency is high and pseudomolecular ions, $(M + H)+$ and $(M - H)+$, are formed with high efficiency by chemical ionization. The analyte ions are accelerated into the mass spectrometer and the uncharged solvent molecules are removed by vacuum pumps.

In the electrospray (ES) interface, also operating at atmospheric pressure, the liquid mobile phase is ejected from a metal capillary tube into an electric field obtained by applying a potential difference of 3–6 kV between the tube and a counter electrode. The drops accumulate charge on their surface, and as they shrink by evaporation they break into ever smaller charged droplets. The uncharged solvent molecules are pumped away and the charged ions pass into the mass spectrometer. These interfaces can deal with a wide range of solvent polarities, although for ionic mobile phases the electrospray is preferable.

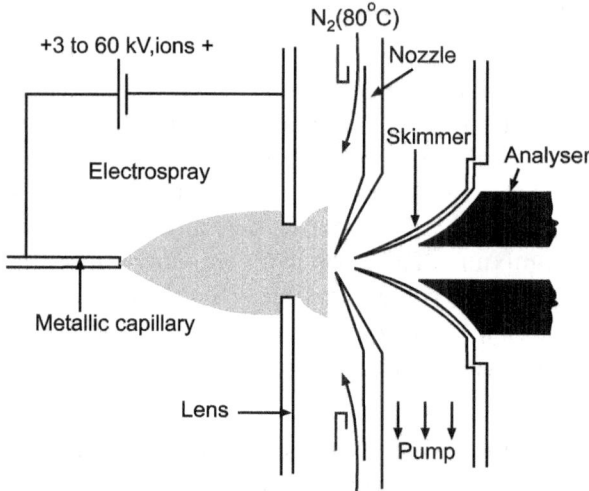

Fig. 4.29 : Electrospray (ES) interface

LC-MS Applications

LC/MS has been playing a more and more significant role in herbal medicine research because the technique is capable of characterising active components ranging from small polar molecules to macromolecules such as peptides/protein, carbohydrates and nucleic acids. Recent scientific results and publications show that the application of LC/MS has been expanding rapidly into the area of structural elucidation and characterisation of active components, in addition to valuable quantitative analysis. Several papers discussing LC/MS analysis of ginseng extracts and ginsenosides were published recently.

Lin *et al.* applied LC/ESIMS to analyse chemical constituents of *Danggui* (rhizome of *Angelica sinensis*). DiPaola *et al.* used LC/MS analysis to support the study of clinical and biological activity of an estrogenic herbal combination for the treatment of prostate cancer. Xue and co-workers studied the precipitate produced in the preparation of a complex prescription of Chinese herbal medicines *Xiexin* (*Shanhuangxiexin Tang*) decoction by LC/MS/MS. The authors demonstrated that their LC/MS method was reliable for determining active components and their metabolites in support of pre-clinical and clinical studies. Kasimu *et al.* conducted a comparative study on the compositions and inhibitory activities of seven *Salvia* plants (*Danshen*) by examining their water and methanol extracts using LC/MS. Liu *et al.* analysed cholic, deoxycholic and chenodeoxycholic acids in the traditional Chinese medicine by LC/MS/MS. After the identification of these acids, a quantitative method to determine cholic acid in the medicine was developed. LC/MS, combined with other analytical tools, was used by Hamasaki *et al.* to study highly selective antibacterial activity of novel quinolone alkaloids from a Chinese herbal medicine named *Wu-Chu-Yu*. Similarly, Gu *et al.* isolated and identified triptolide and tripdiolide and found that they were responsible for the anti-rheumatic properties of crude aqueous extracts of *Tripterygium wilfordii* which represented a novel class of immunosuppressive drugs with potential clinical utility.

Olive leaf is the leaf of *Olea europaea* and since olive oil is well known for its flavour and health benefits the leaf has been used medicinally. Olive leaf, olive oil and olive leaf extracts (OLE) are now marketed as anti-aging, immunostimulator, and antibiotic agents. The olive leaf contains many active principles, but the major active constituent is a seco-iridoid called oleuropein. To identify the compound and for its quantitation, Liquid chromatography- Mass spectroscopy (LCMS) is a preferred tool.

LC-MS can be applied for both compound identification and quantitation. It involves two steps :

- Marker compound selection
- Confirmation of specificity

For marker compound selection, the extract of olive leaf was utilised and **Fig. 4.30** shows the HPLC and mass spectrum of extract. The extract shows m/z value of 558 at retention time of 9.5 min of oleuropein.

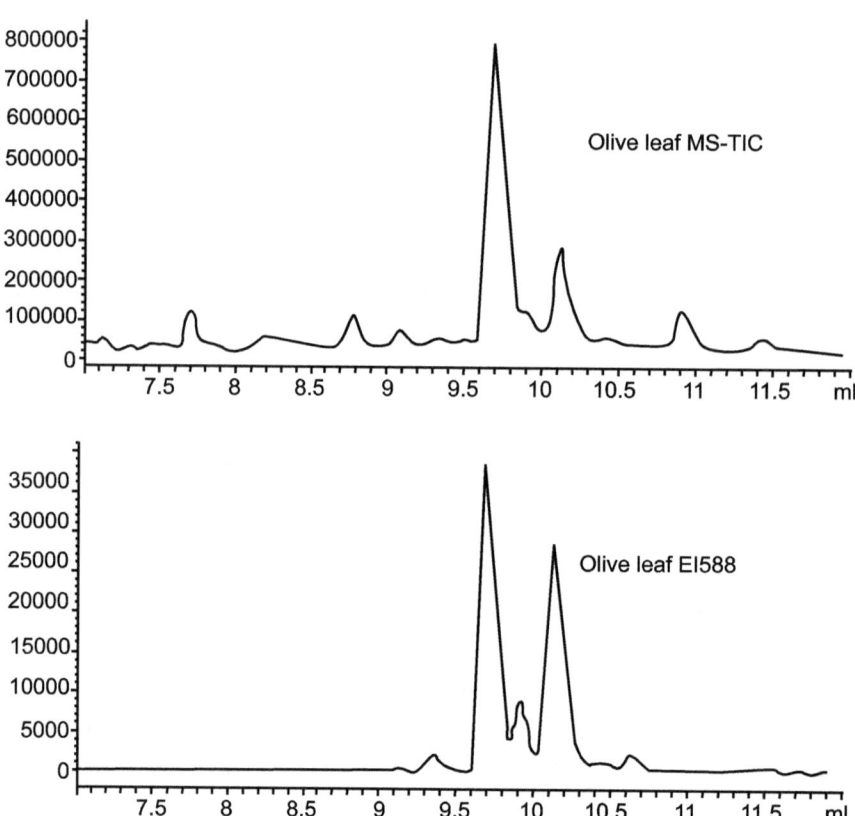

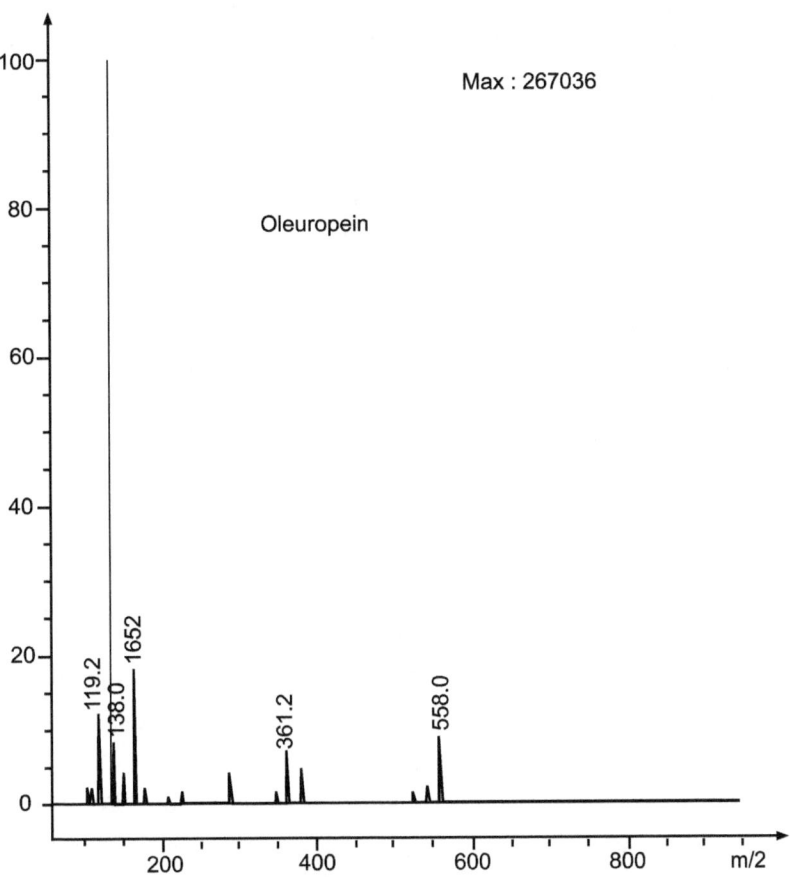

Fig. 4.30 : HPLC and Mass spectrum of extract of olive leaf

For confirmation of specificity of olive leaf marker i.e. oleuropein, the mass spectra was performed for olive leaf extract which also shows m/z at 588, 447 and 465 as represented in **Fig. 4.30**.

Ginseng refers to plants of the genus *Panax*, which include *Panax ginseng*, *Panax quinquefolius* L. (American ginseng) and *Radix notoginseng* (*Sanqi*). *Panax ginseng* is one of the most popular natural tonics and is widely used in many Chinese medicinal prescriptions. Chemical and pharmacological studies on ginseng have demonstrated numerous constituents and actions. Active components in ginseng include *O*-glycosides of the triterpene dammarane structure, known as ginsenosides (ginseng saponins).

LC/MS with electro spray ionization (ESI) and collision induced dissociation (CID) MS/MS has been used increasingly for the structure characterization of ginsenosides.

Both positive and negative ionisation of ginsenosides have been studied. Some alkali and transition metal cations form strongly bonded attachment ions with the ginsenosides. As a result, their CID spectra of the metal attachment ions show a variety of structurally characteristic fragmentation patterns. Ackloo et al. conducted CID experiments on metal-attachment ions for the characterization of ginseng saponins. Positive ion ESI-MS experiments with alkali metal cations such as Li^+ and Na^+ and transition metal cations such as Co^{2+}, Ni^{2+} and Zn^{2+} were found to be useful in determining the molecular masses of ginsenosides, and their CID mass spectra show a variety of structure related fragmentation patterns. The results can be used to determine the identity of the triterpene core, the type and attachment positions of sugars to the core and the nature of the O-glycosidic linkages in the appended disaccharides.

III. Gel Electrophoresis

Capillary electrophoresis was introduced in early 1980s as a powerful analytical and separation technique and has since been developed almost explosively. It allows an efficient way to document the purity/complexity of a sample and can handle virtually every kind of charged sample components ranging from simple inorganic ions to DNA. Thus, there was an obvious increase of electrophoretic methods, especially capillary electrophoresis, used in the analysis of herbal medicines in last decades. The more or less explosive development of capillary electrophoresis since its introduction has to a great extent paralleled that of liquid chromatography. Most of the used techniques are capillary zone electrophoresis (CZE), capillary gel electrophoresis (CGE) and capillary isoelectric focusing (CIEF). CE is promising for the separation and analysis of active ingredients in herbal medicines, since it needs only small amounts of standards and can analyse samples rapidly with very good separation ability.

Electrophoresis is a technique for the separation of components of mixtures by differential migration through a buffered medium across which an electric field is applied. In the slab gel method, the supporting gel is pre-formed into thin rectangular slabs on which a number of samples and standards can be separated simultaneously. Alternatively, it can be polymerised in a set of short tubes. The whole assembly is enclosed in a protective perspex chamber for safety reasons because of the high voltages employed (500 V–2 kV DC, or up to 50 V cm-1). A separation may take from about 30 minutes to several hours, after which the gels are treated with a suitable visualising agent to reveal the separated solutes (vide infra). Slab gels dissipate Joule heat more efficiently than column gels and have a superior resolving power.

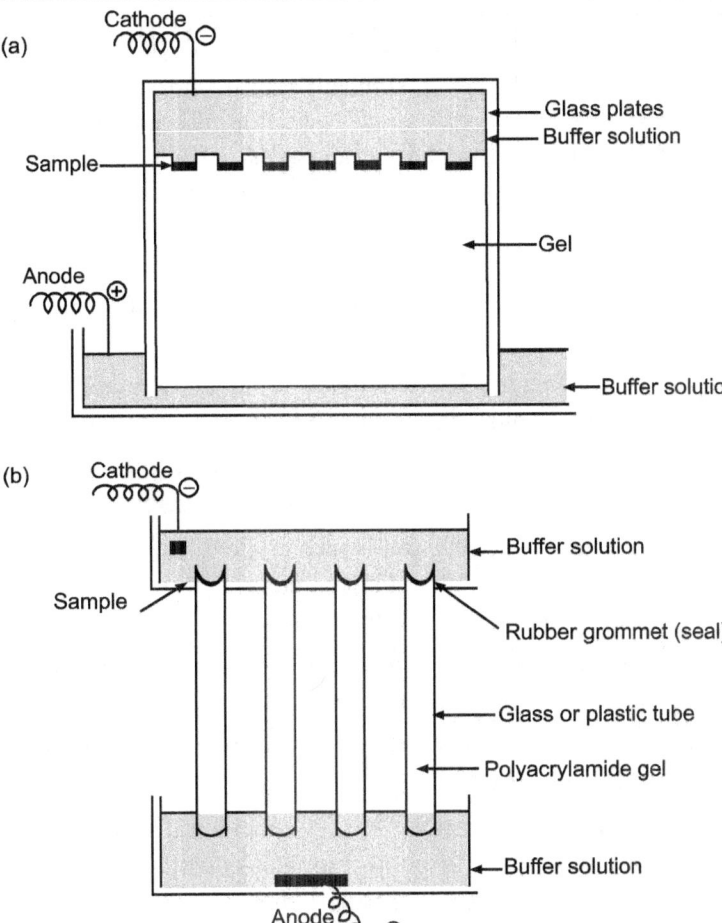

Fig. 4.31 : Gel electrophoresis (a) Slab gel (b) Tube gel

It is a good tool for generating the chemical fingerprints of herbal medicines, since it has similar technical characteristics of liquid chromatography. Recently, several studies dealing with herbal medicines have been reported and two kinds of medicinal compounds, i.e. alkaloids and flavonoids, have been studied extensively. In general, CE is a versatile and powerful separation tool with high separation efficiency and selectivity when analysing mixtures of low-molecular-mass components However, the rapid development in capillary electrophoresis causes improvement of resolution and throughput rather than reproducibility and absolute precision. One successful approach to improve the reproducibility of both mobility and integral data has been based on internal standards. But many papers were published unfortunately revealed limited image on the real possibilities of CE in the field of fingerprinting herbal medicines. CE and capillary electrochromatography approaches, contribute to be a better understanding of the solution behaviour of herbal medicines, especially when additionally combined with the powerful spectrometric detectors.

WHO GUIDELINES FOR HERBAL DRUGS STANDARDISATION

According to WHO (1996a and b, 1992), standardisation and quality control of herbals is the process involved in the physicochemical evaluation of crude drug covering aspects, such as selection and handling of crude material, safety, efficacy and stability assessment of finished product, documentation of safety and risk based on experience, provision of product information to consumer and product promotion. Attention is normally paid to such quality indices such as-

1. **Macro and microscopic examination:** For identification of right variety and search of adulterants.

2. **Foreign organic matter:** This involves removal of matter other than source plant to get the drug in pure form.

3. **Ash values:** These are criteria to judge the identity and purity of crude drug – total ash, sulphated ash, water soluble ash and acid insoluble ash etc.

4. **Moisture content:** Checking moisture content helps reduce errors in the estimation of the actual weight of drug material. Low moisture suggests better stability against degradation of product.

5. **Extractive values:** These are indicative weights of the extractable chemical constituents of crude drug under different solvents environment.

6. **Crude fibre:** This helps to determine the woody material component, and it is a criterion for judging purity.

7. **Qualitative chemical evaluation:** This covers identification and characterisation of crude drug with respect to phytochemical constituents. It employs different analytical techniques to detect and isolate the active constituents. Phytochemical screening techniques involve botanical identification, extraction with suitable solvents, purification, and characterisation of the active constituents of pharmaceutical importance.

8. **Chromatographic examination:** Include identification of crude drug based on the use of major chemical constituents as markers.

9. **Quantitative chemical evaluation:** To estimate the amount of the major classes of constituents.

10. **Toxicological studies:** This helps to determine the pesticide residues, potentially toxic elements, safety studies in animals like LD50 and microbial assay to establish the absence or presence of potentially harmful microorganisms.

The processes mentioned above involves a wide array of scientific investigations, which include physical, chemical and biological evaluation employing various analytical methods and tools. The specific aims of such investigation in assuring herbal quality are as varied as the processes employed.

Physical Evaluation

Each monograph contains detailed botanical, macroscopic and microscopic descriptions of the physical characteristics of each plant that can be used to ensure both identity and purity. Each description is accompanied by detailed illustrations and photographic images which provide visual documentation of accurately identified material.

Microscopic evaluation

Full and accurate characterisation of plant material requires a thorough physical examination. Microscopic analyses of plants are invaluable for assuring the identity of the material and as an initial screening test for impurities.

Chemical evaluation

This covers screening, isolation, identification and purification of the chemical components. Chemical analysis of the drug is done to assess the potency of vegetable material in terms of its active principles. The chemical screening or tests may include colour reaction test, which help to determine the identity of the drug substance and possible adulteration.

Biological evaluation

Pharmacological activity of certain drugs has been applied to evaluate and standardise them. The assays on living animal and on their intact or isolated organs can indicate the strength of the drug or their preparations. These assays are known as biological assays or bioassay.

Purity determination

Each monograph includes standards for purity and other qualitative indices already mentioned above.

Analytical methods

Critical to compliance with any monograph standard is the need for appropriate analytical methods for determining identity, quality, and relative potency. There are a plethora of analytical methods available. However, it is often difficult to know which is the most appropriate to use, but critical among know analytical tools in monograph standardisation is chromatography.

Chromatography

Chromatography is the science which studies the separation of molecules based on differences in their structure and/or composition. In general, chromatography involves moving a preparation of the materials to be separated, "the "test preparation", over a stationary support. The molecules in the test preparation will have different interactions with the stationary support leading to separation of similar molecules. Test molecules which display tighter interactions with the support will tend to move more slowly through the support than those molecules with weaker interactions. In this way, different types of molecules can be separated from each other as they move over the support material. Chromatographic separations can be carried out using a variety of supports, including immobilised silica on glass plates (thin layer chromatography), very sensitive High Performance Thin Layer Chromatography (HPTLC), volatile gases (gas chromatography), paper (paper chromatography), and liquids which may incorporate hydrophilic, insoluble molecules (liquid chromatography). High performance thin layer chromatography (HPTLC) is a valuable quality assessment tool for the evaluation of botanical materials. It allows for the analysis of a broad number of compounds both efficiently and cost effectively. Additionally, numerous samples can be run in a single analysis thereby dramatically reducing analytical time. With HPTLC, the same analysis can be viewed collectively in different wavelengths of light thereby providing a more complete profile of the plant than is typically observed with more specific type of analysis.

Authentication and reproducibility of herbal ingredients

The problems associated with unregulated herbal products highlight the major public health issues that can arise when their herbal ingredients have not been authenticated correctly. Herbal ingredients must be accurately identified by macroscopic and microscopic comparison with authentic material or accurate descriptions of authentic herbs (Houghton, 1998). It is essential that herbal ingredients are referred to by their binomial Latin names of genus and species; only permitted synonyms should be used. Even when correctly authenticated, it is important to realise that different batches of the same herbal ingredient may differ in quality due to a number of factors such as

1. **Inter- or intra-species variation:** The variation in constituents is mostly genetically controlled and may be related to the country of origin.
2. **Environmental factors:** The quality of a herbal ingredient can be affected by environmental factor like climate, altitude and other conditions under which it was cultivated.
3. **Time of harvesting:** For some herbs, the optimum time of harvesting should be specified as it is known that the concentrations of constituents in a plant can vary during the growing cycle or even during the course of a day.
4. **Plant part used:** Active constituents usually vary between plant parts and it is not uncommon for a herbal ingredient to be adulterated with parts of the plant not normally utilised. In addition, plant material that has been previously subjected to extraction and is therefore 'exhausted' is sometimes used as adulterants to increase the weight of a batch of herbal ingredient.
5. **Post-harvesting factors:** Storage conditions and processing treatments can greatly affect the quality of a herbal ingredient. Inappropriate storage after harvesting can result in microbial contamination, and processes such as drying may result in a loss of thermo-labile active constituents.

Adulteration/substitution

There are instances when herbal remedies have been adulterated with other plant material and conventional medicines. Reports of herbal products devoid of known active constituents have reinforced the need for adequate quality control of herbal remedies.

Identity and Purity

In order to try to ensure the quality of licensed herbal medicines, it is essential not only to establish the botanical identity of a herbal ingredient but also to ensure batch-to-batch reproducibility. Thus, in addition to macroscopic and microscopic evaluation, identity tests are necessary. Such tests include simple chemical tests, e.g. colour or precipitation and chromatographic tests. Thin-layer chromatography is commonly used for identification purposes but for herbal ingredients containing volatile oils, a gas–liquid chromatographic test may be used. Although the aim of such tests may be to confirm the presence of active principles, it is frequently the case that the nature of the active principle has not been established. In such instances chemical and chromatographic tests help to provide batch-to-batch comparability and the chromatogram may be used as a 'fingerprint' for the herbal ingredient by demonstrating the profile of some common plant constituents such as flavonoids, alkaloids and terpenes. Identity and purity ask the most important question "is the herb the one it should be?" In answering this, a lot of quality determinants are critically examined. Such determinants as purity and chemical constituents are very important. To prove identity and purity, criteria such as type of preparation, sensory properties, physical constants, adulteration, contaminants, moisture, ash content and solvent residues have to be checked. Identity can be achieved by macro- and microscopical examinations. Voucher specimens are reliable reference sources. Outbreaks of diseases among plants may result in changes to the physical appearance of the plant and lead to incorrect identification. At times an incorrect botanical quality with respect to the labelling can be a problem. For example, in the 1990's, a South American product labelled as "Paraguay Tea" was associated with an outbreak of anticholinergic poisoning in New York. Subsequent chemical analysis revealed the presence of a class of constituents that was different from the metabolites normally found in the plant from which Paraguay tea is made.

Assaying for those herbal ingredients with known active principles is another method of ensuring product's identity and purity. An assay should be established in order to set the criterion for the minimum accepted percentage of active substances. Such assays should, wherever possible, be specific for individual chemical substances, and high-pressure liquid chromatography and gas–liquid chromatography are the methods of choice. Where such assays have not been established, then non-specific classical methods such as titration or colorimetric assays may be used to determine the total content of a group of closely related compounds.

Purity is closely linked with the safe use of drugs and deals with factors such as values, contaminants (e.g. foreign matter in the form of other herbs), and heavy metals. However, due to the application of improved analytical methods, modern purity evaluation also includes microbial contamination, aflatoxins, radioactivity, and pesticide residues. Analytical methods such as photometric analysis, thin layer chromatography (TLC), high performance liquid chromatography (HPLC), and gas chromatography (GC) can be employed in order to establish the constant composition of herbal preparations. Depending on whether the active principles of the preparation are known or unknown, different concepts such as "normalisation versus standardisation" have to be applied in order to establish relevant criteria for uniformity.

Content assay is the most difficult area to perform in quality control since in most herbal drugs the active constituents are not known. Sometimes markers can be used. In all other cases, where no active constituent or marker can be defined for the herbal drug, the percentage extractable matter with a solvent may be used as a form of assay, an approach often seen in pharmacopeias. The choice of the extracting solvent depends on the nature of the compounds involved, and might be deduced from the traditional uses. For example, when an herbal drug is used to make a tea, the hot water extractable matter, expressed as milligrams per gram of air-dried material, may serve this purpose (WHO, 1998b,1996b). A special form of assay is the determination of essential oils by steam distillation. When the active constituents (for example, sennosides in Senna) or markers (for example, alky amides in Echinacea) are known, a vast array of modern chemical analytical methods such as ultraviolet/visible spectroscopy (UV/VIS), TLC, HPLC, GC, mass spectrometry (MS), or a combination of GC and MS (GCMS), can be employed.

GOOD AGRICULTURAL/MANUFACTURING PRACTICES

Quality control and the standardisation of herbal medicines also involve several other steps like source and quality of raw materials, good agricultural practices and good manufacturing practices. These practices play a pivotal role in guaranteeing the quality and stability of herbal preparations (WHO, 2004, 2003, 2000). The quality of a plant product is determined by the prevailing conditions during growth, and accepted Good Agricultural Practices (GAP) can control this. These include seed selection, growth conditions, fertilisers application, harvesting, drying and storage. In fact, GAP procedures are integral part of quality control. Factors such as the use of fresh plants, age and part of plant collected, period, time and method of collection, temperature of processing, exposure to light, availability of water, nutrients, drying, packing, transportation of raw material and storage, can greatly affect the quality, and hence the therapeutic value of herbal medicines. Apart from these criteria, factors such as the method of extraction, contamination with microorganisms, heavy metals, and pesticides can alter the quality, safety, and efficacy of herbal drugs. Using cultivated plants under controlled conditions instead of those collected from the wild can minimise most of these factors. Sometimes, the active principles are destroyed by enzymatic processes that continue for long periods from collection to marketing, resulting in a variation of composition. Thus, proper standardisation and quality control of both the raw material and the herbal preparations should be conducted.

Contaminants of herbal ingredients

Herbal ingredients of high quality should be free from insects, animal matter and excreta. It is usually not possible to remove completely all contaminants, hence specifications should be set in order to limit them

1. **Ash values:** Incineration of a herbal ingredient produces ash which constitutes inorganic matter. Treatment of the ash with hydrochloric acid results in acid-insoluble ash which consists mainly of silica and may be used to act as a measure of soil present. Limits may be set for ash and acid-insoluble ash of herbal ingredients.

2. **Foreign organic matter:** It is not possible to collect a herbal ingredient without small amounts of related parts of plant or other plants. Standards should be set in order to limit the percentage of such unwanted plant contaminants.

3. **Microbial contamination:** Aerobic bacteria and fungi are normally present in plant material and may increase due to faulty growing, harvesting, storage or processing. Herbal ingredients, particularly those with high starch content, may be prone to increased microbial growth. Pathogenic organisms including *Enterobacter, Enterococcus, Clostridium, Pseudomonas, Shigella* and *Streptococcus* have been shown to contaminate herbal ingredients. It is essential that limits be set for microbial contamination and the European Pharmacopoeia now gives non-mandatory guidance on acceptable limits.

4. **Pesticides:** Herbal ingredients, particularly those grown as cultivated crops, may be contaminated by DDT (dichlorodiphenyltrichloroethane) or other chlorinated hydrocarbons, organophosphates, carbamates or polychlorinated biphenyls. Limit tests are necessary for acceptable levels of pesticide contamination of herbal ingredients. The European Pharmacopoeia includes details of test methods together with mandatory limits for 34 potential pesticide residues.

5. **Fumigants:** Ethylene oxide, methyl bromide and phosphine have been used to control pests which contaminate herbal ingredients. The use of ethylene oxide as a fumigant with herbal drugs is no longer permitted in Europe.

6. **Toxic metals:** Lead, cadmium, mercury, thallium and arsenic have been shown to be contaminants of some herbal ingredients. Limit tests for such toxic metals are essential for herbal ingredients.

7. **Radioactive contamination:** There are many sources of ionisation radiation, including radionuclides, occurring in the environment. Hence, a certain degree of exposure is inevitable. (WHO, 2000).

8. **Other contaminants:** As standards increase for the quality of herbal ingredients it is possible that tests to limit other contaminants such as endotoxins and mycotoxins will be utilised to ensure high quality for medicinal purposes.

Standardisation of herbal medicines

This involves adjusting the herbal drug preparation to a defined content of a constituent or a group of substances with known therapeutic activity by adding excipients or by mixing herbal drugs or herbal drug preparations. Botanical extracts made directly from crude plant material show substantial variation in composition, quality, and therapeutic effects. Standardised extracts are high-quality extracts containing consistent levels of specified compounds, and they are subjected to rigorous quality controls during all phases of the growing, harvesting, and manufacturing processes. No regulatory definition exists for standardisation of dietary supplements. As a result, the term "standardisation" may mean many different things. Some manufacturers use the term standardisation incorrectly to refer to uniform manufacturing practices, but following a recipe is not sufficient for a product to be called standardised. Therefore, the presence of the word "standardised" on a supplement label does not necessarily indicate product quality. When the active principles are unknown, marker substances should be established for analytical purposes and standardisation. Marker substances are chemically defined constituents of a herbal drug that are important for the quality of the finished product. Ideally, the chemical markers chosen would also be the compounds that are responsible for the pharmacological effects in the body. There are two types of standardisation. In the first category, "true" standardisation, a definite phytochemical or group of constituents is known to have activity. Ginkgo with its 26% ginkgo flavones and 6% terpenes is a classic example. These products are highly concentrated and no longer represent the whole herb, and are now considered as phytopharmaceuticals. In many cases they are vastly more effective than the whole herb. However the process may result in the loss of efficacy and the potential for adverse effects and herb–drug interactions may increase. The other type of standardisation is based on the guarantee of the manufacturers for the presence of a certain percentage of marker compounds which are not indicators of therapeutic activity or quality of the herb.

In the case of herbal drug preparations, the production and primary processing of the medicinal plant or herbal drug has a direct influence on the quality of the active pharmaceutical ingredients (APIs). Due to the inherent complexity of naturally growing medicinal plants and the limited availability of simple analytical techniques to identify and characterize the active constituents solely by chemical or biological means, there is a need for an adequate quality assurance system. This assurance is also required during cultivation, harvesting, primary processing, handling, storage, packaging, and distribution. Deterioration and contamination through adulteration, especially microbial contamination, can occur at any one of these stages. It is extremely important to establish good agricultural, harvesting, and manufacturing practices for herbal starting materials in order to minimise these undesirable factors. In this regard producers, processors, and traders of medicinal plants or herbal drugs have an obligation and a role to play. The manufacturers and suppliers of herbal products should adhere to quality control standards and good manufacturing practices. Currently, only a few manufacturers adhere to complete quality control and good manufacturing procedures including microscopic, physical, chemical, and biological analysis. Organisations, such as, National Agency for Food and Drugs Administration and Control (NAFDAC) help safeguard Nigerians' health, and Health Canada help safeguard Canadians' health by carrying out premarket reviews of all drugs before they are authorised for sale. The products available in the market are analysed regularly to ensure that they are free of unsafe ingredients and that the products actually contain the ingredients indicated on the labels.

The potency and quality of an individual herbal product may be unclear because of lack of regulation. It is obvious that for a given plant product, its quality will also be determined by the prevailing conditions during the growth cycle of the plant. Therefore, for cultivated plants, the good agricultural practice (GAP) system has been introduced, under which each step, including seed selection, growing conditions, use of fertilisers, and optimisation of harvest time, harvesting, and drying, has to adhere to a set of criteria. It is likely that GAP procedures will become an integral part of quality control in the near future.

Chapter ... 5

ANTIBIOTICS DERIVED FROM MICRO-ORGANISMS

Chemotherapy is the term originally used to describe the use of drugs that are 'selectively toxic' to invading micro-organisms while having minimal effects on the host. The term also embraces the use of drugs that target tumors and in fact has now come to be associated specifically with that branch of pharmacology.

The term *chemotherapy* was coined by Ehrlich himself at the beginning of the 20th century to describe the use of synthetic chemicals to destroy infective agents. In recent years, the definition of the term has been broadened to include antibiotic-substances produced by some micro-organisms (or by pharmaceutical chemists) that kill or inhibit the growth of other micro-organisms. Chemotherapeutic agents then, are chemicals that are intended to be toxic for the pathogenic organism (or cancer cells) but innocuous to the host. Before discussing the molecular basis of such selective toxicity, we need to define what we mean by infectious organism. The word 'microbe' is generally used to describe bacteria, viruses and fungi, and the word 'parasite' to describe protozoa and helminths. However, we are concerned only with those organisms that cause disease, and the immune response of the human host makes no distinction between the above categories, which are of purely semantic convenience.

The term "*Antibiotic*' was coined by Vuillemin in 1889, to name the active participant in the process of "*antibiosis*" or the opposition of one living micro-organism by another or in simple words "*an antibiotic is a chemical that is produced by a micro-organism and that., in a relatively high dilution, inhibits the growth or reproduction of some other microorganism*".

Living organisms are classified as either prokaryotes (cells without nuclei such as bacteria), or eukaryotes, (cells with nuclei e.g. protozoa, fungi, helminths). In a separate category are the viruses, which are not really cells at all because they do not have their own biochemical machinery for generating energy or for any sort of synthesis. Viruses need to utilise the metabolic machinery of the host cell, and they thus present a particular kind of problem for chemotherapeutic attack.

The function of the cell wall is to support the underlying plasma membrane, which is subject to an internal osmotic pressure of about 5 atmospheres in Gram-negative organisms, and about 20 atmospheres in Gram-positive organisms. The plasma membrane and cell wall together comprise the bacterial envelope.

Within the plasma membrane is the cytoplasm, which this contains soluble enzymes and other proteins, the ribosomes involved in protein synthesis, and the small-molecule intermediates involved in metabolism, as well as inorganic ions. However, unlike the eukaryotic cell, the bacterial cell has no nucleus; instead, the genetic material, in the form of a single chromosome containing all the genetic information, lies in the cytoplasm with no surrounding nuclear membrane. In further contrast to eukaryotic cells, there are no mitochondria therefore cellular energy is generated by enzyme systems located in the plasma membrane.

The Molecular Basis of Chemotherapy

Chemotherapeutic drugs should be toxic to invading organisms and innocuous to the host. Such selective toxicity depends on the discovery of biochemical differences between the pathogen and the host that can be appropriately exploited.

Three general classes of biochemical reactions are potential targets for chemotherapy of bacteria.

- **Class I:** reactions that utilise glucose and other carbon sources are used to produce ATP and simple carbon compounds.
- **Class II:** pathways utilising energy and class I compounds to make small molecules (e.g. amino acids and nucleotides).
- **Class III:** pathways that convert small molecules into macromolecules such as proteins, nucleic acids and peptidoglycan.

Table 5.1 : Antibiotics derived from microorganisms

Sr. No.	Fungi	Bacteria	Actinomycetes
1.	Penicillin	Polymyxin-B	Aminoglycoside
2.	Cephalosporin	Colistin	Tetracycline
3.	Griseofulvin	Bacitracin	Macrolide
4.		Aztreonam	Polyenes
5.		Tyrothricin	Chloramphenicol

ANTIBIOTICS DERIVED FROM FUNGI

[I] Penicillin

The penicillins are classified as β-lactam drugs because of their unique four-membered lactam ring. All penicillins have the basic structure. A thiazolidine ring is attached to a β- lactam ring that carries a secondary amino group (RNH–). If the β-lactam ring is enzymatically cleaved by bacterial β-lactamases, the resulting product, penicilloic acid, lacks antibacterial activity.

In 1928, **Alexander Fleming**, working at St Mary's Hospital in London, observed that a culture plate on which *Staphylococci* were being grown had become contaminated with a mould of the genus *Penicillium*, and that bacterial growth in the vicinity of the mould had been inhibited. He isolated the mould in pure culture and demonstrated that it produced an antibacterial substance, which he called **penicillin**. This substance was subsequently extracted and its antibacterial effects analysed by **Florey, Chain** and their colleagues at Oxford in 1940. They showed that it had powerful chemotherapeutic properties in infected mice, and that it was non-toxic.

Penicillin is a generic term which refers to a class of compounds of the molecular formula $C_9H_{11}N_2O_4SR$, produced by various strains of *Penicillium notatum*, *Penicillium chrysogenum*, and various other moulds (fermentation).

Production

Various culture methods have been developed for the production of penicillin on a commercial scale. The strains of *Penicillium* species are allowed to grow on a nutrient medium containing carbohydrates *(e.g.* glucose sucrose. lactose. maltose, starch) and protein. Commercially, penicillin may be produced by three methods, *viz.,* surface culture, bran and submerged culture method.

(i) **Surface culture method:** It was the first method used for the production of penicillin on commercial scale, now-a-days this method is applied only for laboratory studies. In this method, an aqueous solution of molasses adjusted to pH 7-8 is used as a medium for the growth of micro-organisms as the molasses under this condition contain sucrose, mineral salts and nitrogenous material almost ideally suited for mould growth. In a few days, the growth of micro-organisms begin and after 6 or 7 days, the concentration of penicillin reaches up to 0.3-0.4 mg. per c.c. Although, this process is simple, its high cost of labour restricted its use for the commercial production of penicillin.

(ii) **Bran method :** The use of bran is an alternative to liquid surface production. Moist bran is a good substrate for mould growth and the resultant penicillin can be extracted as in liquid production, or the, penicillin containing bran can be used directly. Since bran is a bad conductor of heat, it is difficult to sterilise it owing to the length of time taken for the interior to reach the desired temperature. Moreover, the developing mould produces heat which is difficult to dissipate and thus partly destroys the penicillin.

(iii) **Submerged culture method :** Submerged culture methods are the exclusive methods for the commercial production of penicillin. In this process, the inoculum is introduced into large tanks and the medium usually contains lactose as sugar source and corn-steep liquor as an adjuvant. The medium is agitated by a stream of sterile air, and the temperature is maintained at about 24°C. Under these conditions of agitation and aeration, the mould grows throughout the bulk of the liquid as globular pellicles consisting mainly of mycelium.

Isolation

The next stage in the process is the extraction of the penicillin from the dilute solution of the broth which posed many problems. Close control of conditions is needed because the product is readily decomposed by too acidic or too alkaline solution, by the presence of heavy metals, by bacterial contamination of the culture filtrate or by an elevated temperature. The sensitivity to high temperature means that evaporation at a high temperature could not be used to obtain the final solid; and freeze drying methods were developed instead. The effect of bacterial contamination of the culture filtrate on the yield of penicillin is because of the fact that some bacteria, notably strains of *Escherichia coli*, secrete an enzyme, "penicillinase", which inactivates penicillin by breaking up the basic structure. Since such a bacterial contamination results in the complete loss of all the penicillin in a large batch; maintaining complete aseptic conditions during penicillin production is very important.

In practice, for the isolation of penicillin, the metabolic solution is rapidly cooled and adjusted to a low pH and the solvent is then extracted. If amyl alcohol is used, the pH is reduced to 2-3, while if butyl alcohol is used, it is adjusted to 6.4 after adding ammonium sulphate. Petroleum ether is now added to the cold solvent extract and this is shaken with dilute sodium bicarbonate solution. The solution is adjusted to pH 6-7 and then rapidly freeze-evaporated to give the sodium salt. Since the final product should be absolutely dry as well as pure, the sodium salt of penicillin is dried in a high vacuum. During all these operations, the penicillin solution must be maintained at a temperature just above its freezing point to avoid inactivation. Lastly, since most of the penicillin is administered by injection, the final sample must be non-toxic, sterilised and free from pyrogens for which the concentrated and purified solution of penicillin is passed through asbestos pads which absorb micro-organisms and pyrogens.

Although commercial penicillin consists of a mixture of benzyl, pentenyl, and heptyl penicillins; by making use of certain chemical compounds in the culture medium, it is possible to increase the yield of the desired penicillin. For example, by the use of phenylacetamide. $C_6H_5CH_2CONH_2$, as precursor, it is possible to cause a strain usually producing pentenyl-penicillin to produce benzyl penicillin and by adding 2-phenylethylamine the yield of benzyl penicillin is increased. Similarly, by adding suitable precursors, new types of penicillins have been produced.

Thus, by selecting or inducing mutants of the mould or by adding precursors, it is possible to produce almost any desired penicillin.

Properties

Inspite of being highly unstable, sustained effort by research workers has elucidated the structure of all the penicillins.

The general molecular formula for the penicillins is $\mathbf{C_9H_{11}N_2O_4SR}$.

They form mono salts indicating the presence of a carboxyl group.

Penicillins are not found to possess a free amino or thiol group.

1. On hydrolysis with hot dilute inorganic acids, all the penicillins are degraded to the equimolecular amount of an amine, *penicillamine*. and an *aldehyde, penilloaldehyde*, along with the elimination of one carbon atom as carbon dioxide.

$$C_9H_{11}N_2O_4SR + 2H_2O \xrightarrow{HCl} C_5H_{11}NO_2S + C_3H_4NO_2R + CO_2$$

Penicillins　　　　　　　　　Penicillamine　Penilloaldehyde

Now since the fragment R comes in the aldehyde portion, all penicillins give the same amine, but different aldehydes.

Penicillin on treatment with diazomethane is converted into its methyl ester which on treatment with an aqueous solution of mercuryl chloride gives the methyl ester of penicillamine. This set of reactions clearly indicates that the carboxyl group of penicillamine is the carboxyl group of penicillin itself.

Penicillin is a monocarboxylic acid and the carboxyl group is present in the penicillamine molecule which is from the thiazolidine nucleus, the second carboxyl group of penicilloic acid may be present either as oxazolone or as, β-lactam and thus penicillin might be I or II.

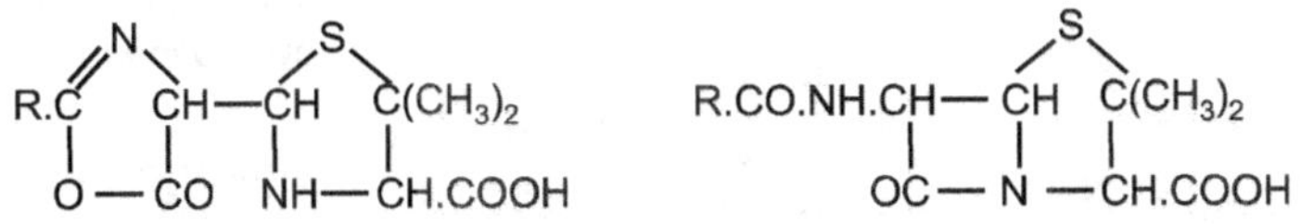

Oxazolone structure　　　　　　　β-Lactam structure

Biosynthesis of Peniciilin

Penicillin is a modified tripeptide made from aminoadipic acid, cysteine and valine. The principle enzyme involved in penicillin biosynthesis is ACV-synthetase, which forms the tripeptide ACV (δ-(L-α-aminoadipyl)-L-cysteinyl-D-valine) from the three constituent amino acids. The second step in penicillin biosynthesis is the formation of the β-lactam ring (as penicillin-N) from ACV by the enzyme isopenicillin-N synthetase; oxygen is involved in the ring closure process but is not incorporated into the molecule. Finally, side chains are added or exchanged by acetyl-CoA : isopenicillin-N acyltransferase. **Fig. 5.1 (a)**.

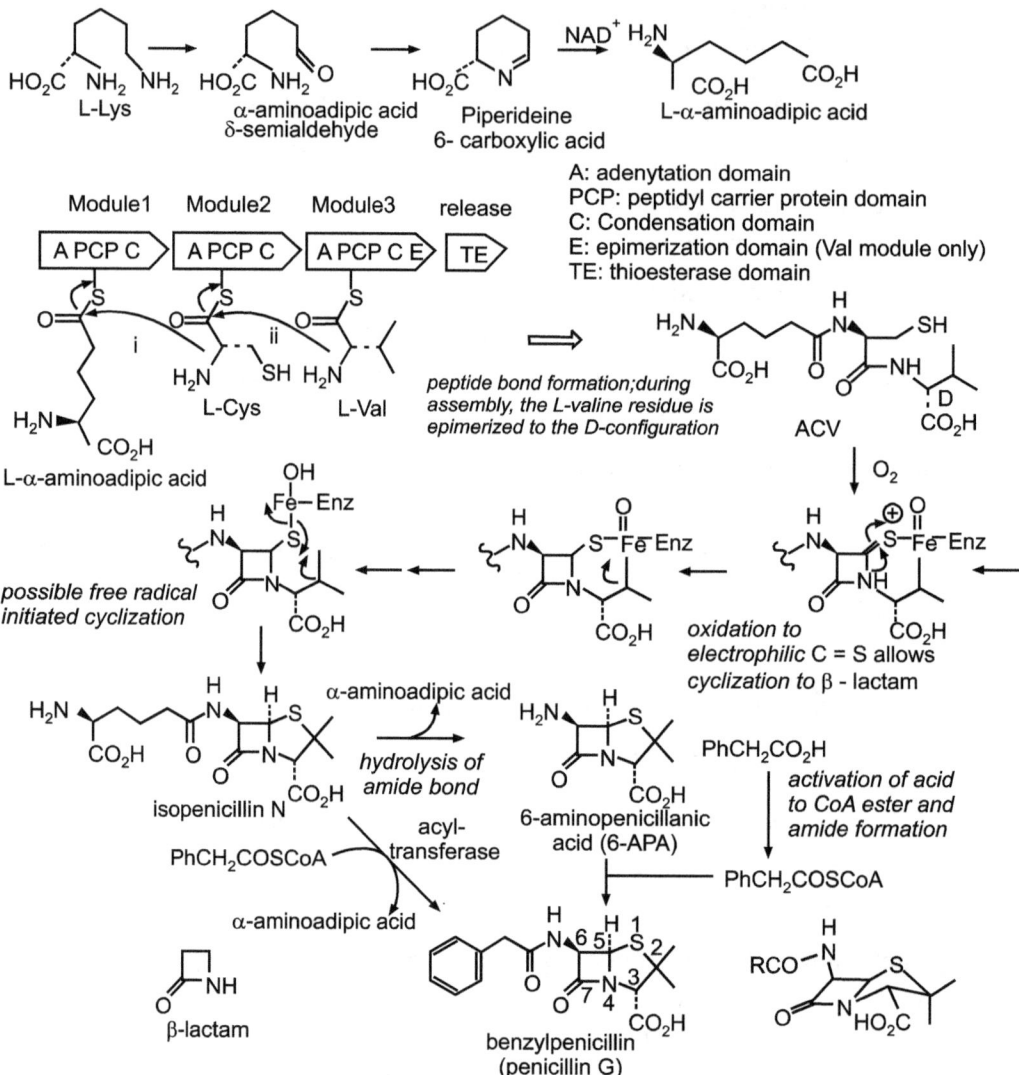

Fig. 5.1(a) : Biosynthesis of Penicillin

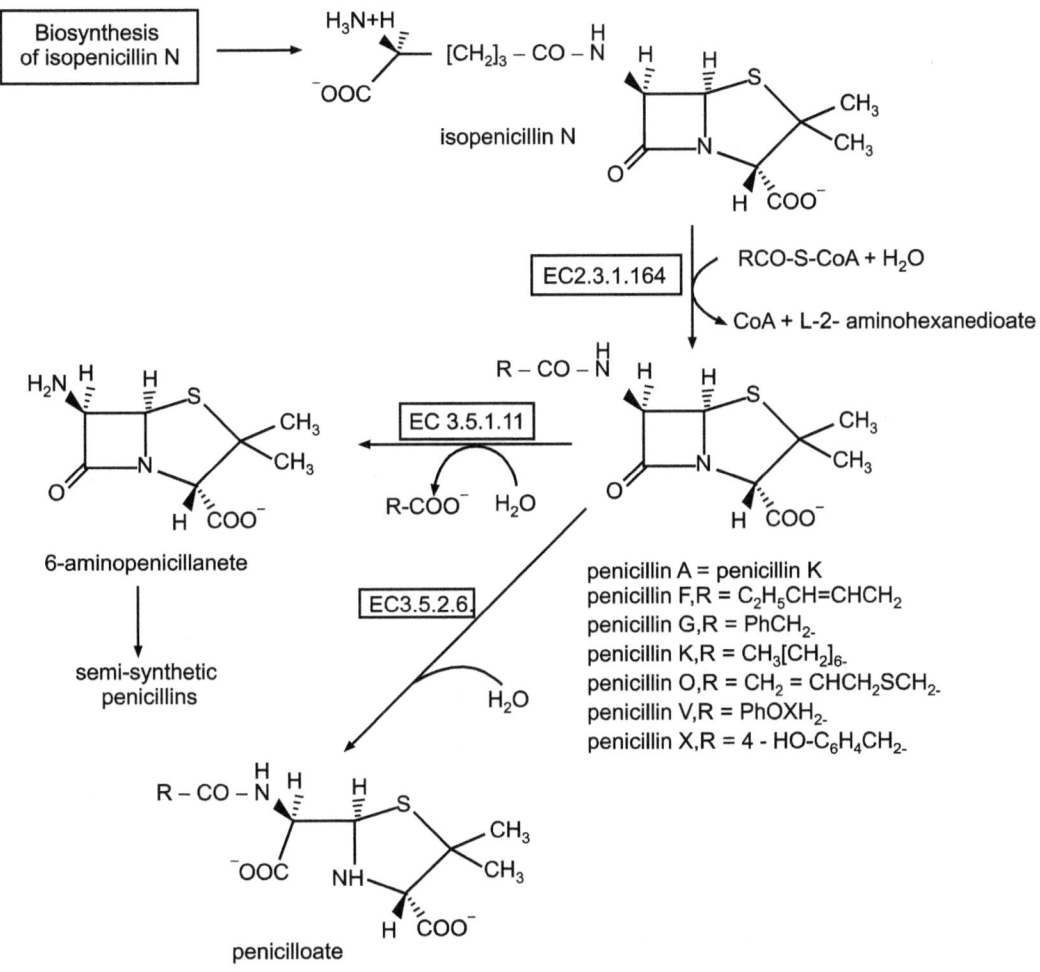

5.1 (b) : Metabolism of Penicillin

Chemistry

All penicillins have the basic structure as shown in **Fig. 5.2.** A thiazolidine ring (A) is attached to a β-lactam ring (B) that carries a secondary amino group (RNH-).

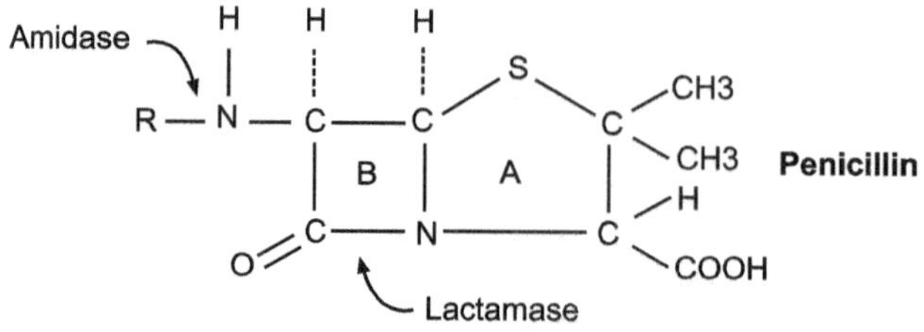

Penicillin — Substituted 6-aminopenicillanic acid

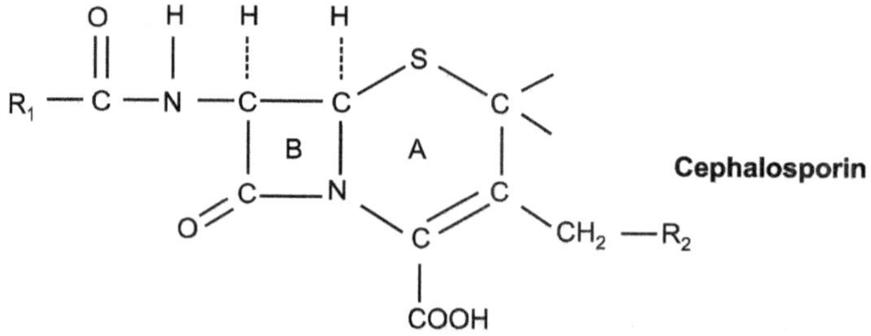

Cephalosporin — Substituted 7-aminocephalosporanic acid

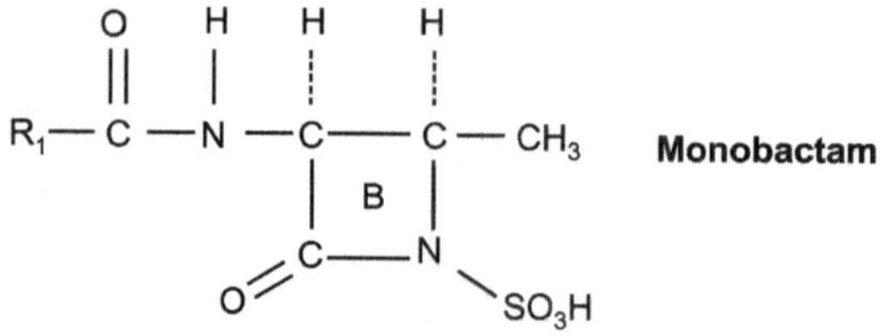

Monobactam — Substituted 3-amino-4-methylmonobactamic acid (azreonam)

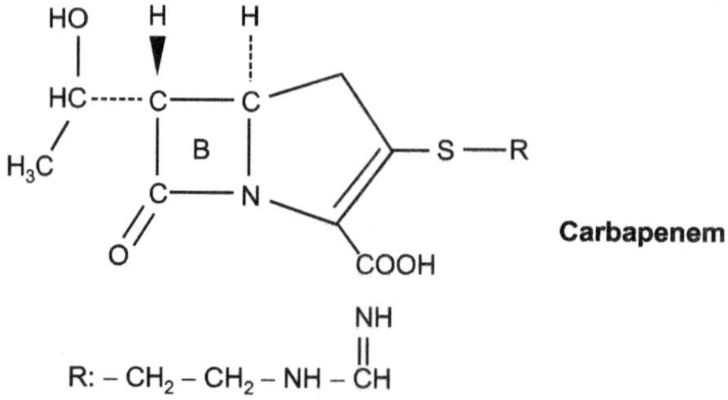

Carbapenem — Substituted 3-hydroxyethylcarbapenemic acid (imipenem)

R: – CH_2 – CH_2 – NH – CH=NH

Fig. 5.2 : Core structures of four β-Lactam antibiotic families. The ring marked B in each structure is the β lactam ring. The penicillins are susceptible to bacterial metabolism and inactivation by amidases and lactamases at the points shown. Note that the carbapenems have a different stereochemical configuration in the lactam ring that apparently imparts resistance to β-lactamases

Substituents (R; examples shown in **Fig. 5.3**) can be attached to the amino group. Structural integrity of the 6-aminopenicillanic acid nucleus is essential for the biologic activity of these compounds. Hydrolysis of the β-lactam ring by bacterial β-lactamases yields penicilloic acid, which lacks antibacterial activity.

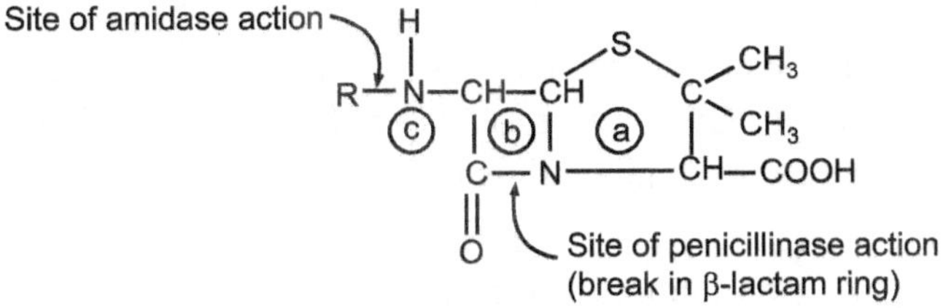

6-Aminopenicillanic acid

The following structures can each be substituted at the R to produce a new penicillin

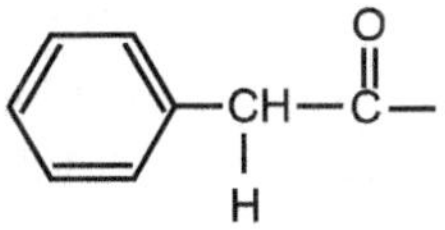

Penicillin G (benzylpenicillin)
High activity against gram-positive bacteria. Acid-labile. Destroyed by β-lactamase 60% protein-bound

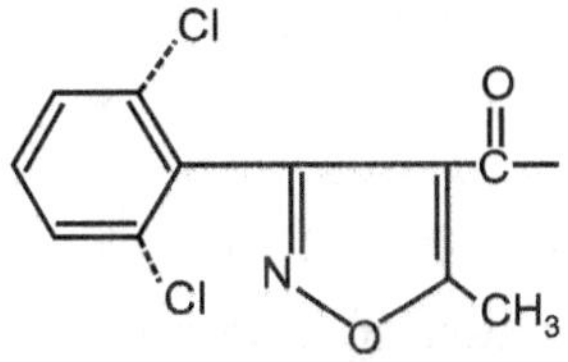

Oxacillin (no Cl atoms); cloxacillin (one Cl in structure); diclexacillin (2 Cls in structure); fluclaxacillin (one Cl and one F in structure) (isoxazolyl penicillins):
Similar to methicillin in β-lactamase resistance, but acid-stable can be taken orally. Highly protein-bound (95–98%).

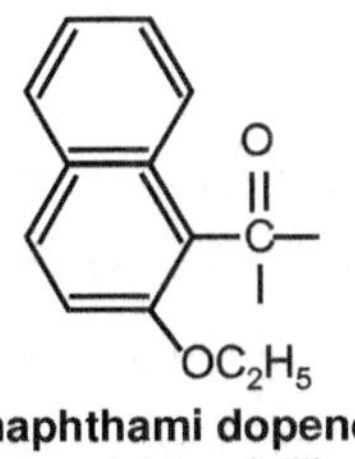

Nafcillin (ethoxynaphthami dopencilin):
Similar to osoxazolyl penicillins. Less strongly protein-bound (90%). Resistant to staphylococcal β-lactamase.

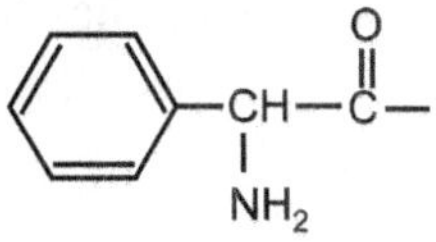

Ampicillin (alpha-aminobenzylpenicillin):
Similar to Penicillin G (destroyed by β-lactamase) but acid-stable and more active against gram-negative because. Carbenicillin has –COONa instead of NH_2 group.

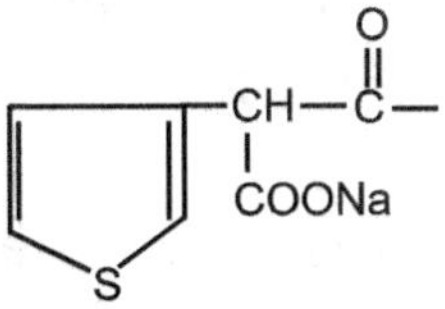

Ticarcillin:
Similar to carbenicilin but gives higher blood levels. Piperacillin, azlocillin, and mezlocillin resemble ticarcillin in action against gram-negative aerobes.

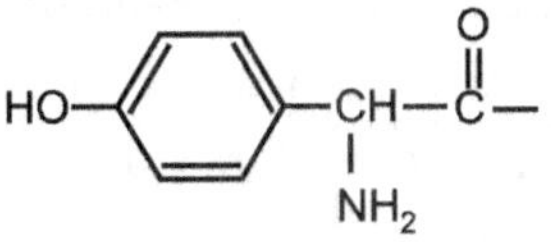

Amoxicillin:
Similar to ampicillin but better absorbed, gives higher blood levels.

Fig. 5.3 : Side chains of some Penicillins

Structure Activity Relationship

1. 6-Acyl side chain : Benzyl penicillin has serious limitations i.e., narrow spectrum of activity, with acids and alkali degradation occurs, and susceptible to all known β-lactamases.

Introduction of α-aryloxyalkyl penicillins in the side chain gives increased acid stability and oral absorption. Other substituents on the α-carbon of the side chain such as amino (ampicillin), chloro, and guanidine display good resistance to inactivation by acids.

Substitution of α-carbon atom of the side chain with bulky groups confers β-lactamase resistance, for example, methicillin, naficillin, oxacillin etc. In all these penicillins, an aromatic ring is attached directly to the side chain carbonyl, and there is substitution at both positions ortho to the point of attachment. The size of the ring system plays an important role in determining the ability of the ortho substituent to confer penicillinase resistance. By steric hinderance, this group interferes with the β-lactamase attachment to the penicillins and cause a conformational change and loss of activity.

Introduction of an ionised or polar group into the α-position of the side chain benzyl carbon atom of peniciilin G confers activity against gram-negative bacilli. Amino, hydroxyl, carboxyl and sulfonyl increase gram-negative activity, i.e., ampicillin and carbeniciilin.

The D-isomer is 2-8 times more active than L-isomer in ampicillin.

The acyl side chain has recently been replaced with hydroxymethyl groups with increased gram-negative activity.

(a) N-acylated ampicillin have increased activity against *Pseudomonas*.

2. Many esters of carboxyl group attached to C-3 have been prepared as prodrugs to increase lipophillicity and acid stability. Acetoxy methyl ester and the $HOCH_2OCOOCH_3$, $HOCHO(CH_3)COCH_3$, [lactone structure] are used for preparing prodrugs.

3. Introduction of C-6 α-methoxy group confers greater stability against β-lactamase without significant loss of potency. Another group NHCHO at C-6 α postion as in fomadicillin also confers stability to chemical hydrolysis.

4. The sulphur of the thiazolidine ring can be replaced with O, CH_2, CH-β-CH_3 and S_+(O) CH_2 with increased broad spectrum antibacterial activity.

5. The C-2 methyl groups have been recently replaced. The 2-exomethylene penicillin V is active. One of the methyl groups has been replaced with 3,4-diacetoxy benzoic acid to yield better activity against *Pseudomonas*.

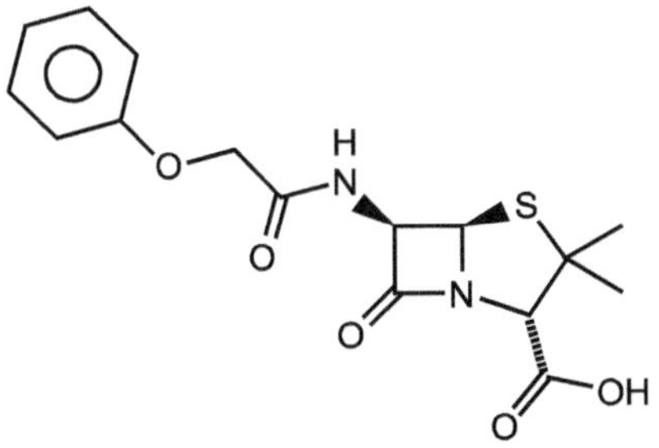

6. Novel 2-carboxypenam analogs (1) and (2) in which both the (C2) and (C3) substituents have been changed, displayed potent antibacterial activity against gram-negative organism including *P. aeruginosa*, with stability to β-lactamase generally greater than for natural penicillin.

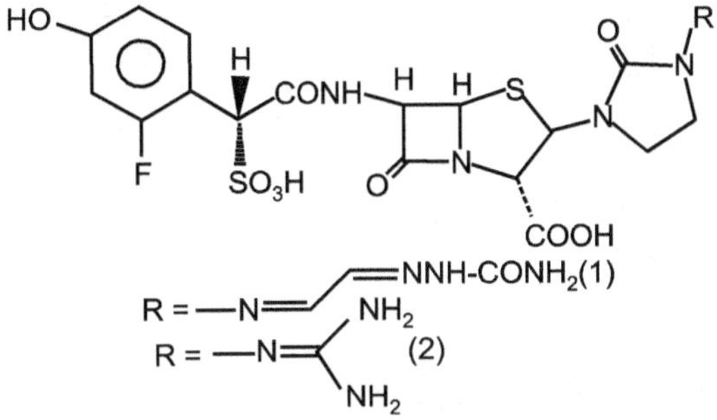

Mechanism of Action

Penicillins, like all β-lactam antibiotics, inhibit bacterial growth by interfering with a specific step in bacterial cell wall synthesis. The cell wall is a rigid outer layer that is not found in animal cells. It completely surrounds the cytoplasmic membrane maintaining the shape of the cell and preventing cell lysis from high osmotic pressure. The cell wall is composed of a complex cross linked polymer, peptidoglycan (murein, mucopeptide), consisting of polysaccharides and polypeptides. The polysaccharide contains alternating amino sugars, *N*-acetylglucosamine and *N*-acetylmuramic acid. A five-amino-acid peptide is linked to the *N*-acetylmuramic acid sugar. This peptide terminates in D-alanyl-D-alanine. Penicillin-binding proteins (PBPs) catalyse the transpeptidase reaction that removes the terminal alanine to form a crosslink with a nearby peptide, which gives cell wall its structural rigidity. β-Lactam antibiotics are structural analogs of the natural D-

Ala-D-Ala substrate and they are covalently bound by PBPs at the active site. After a β-lactam antibiotic has attached to the PBP, the transpeptidation reaction is inhibited peptidoglycan synthesis is blocked, and the cell dies.

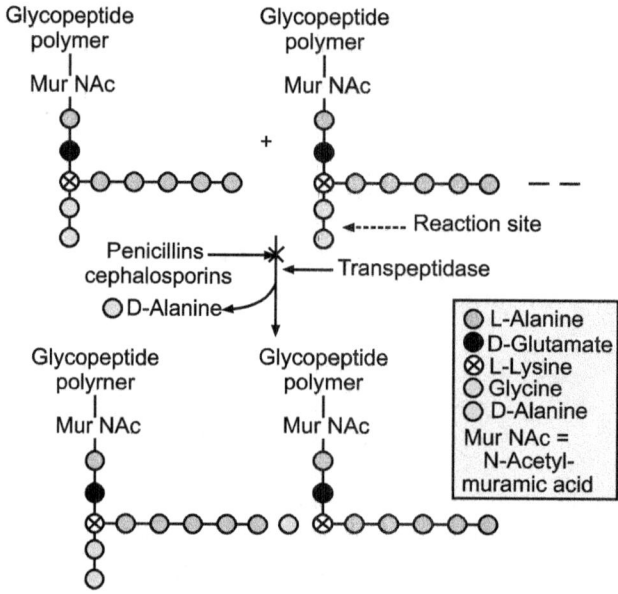

Fig. 5.4 : Action of β-lactam antibiotics in *Staphylococcus aureus*

The bacterial cell wall consists of glycopeptide polymers linked via bridges between amino acid side chains. In *S. aureus*, the bridge is (Gly)5-D-Ala between lysines. The cross-linking is catalysed by a transpeptidase, the enzyme that penicillins and cephalosporins inhibit.

CEPHALOSPORINS

Cephalosporin is an antibiotic produced by a species of *Cephalosporium*. It was found to be a penicillin in which the value of R is $-CH_2CH_2CH_2CH(NH)_2COOH$ (Abraham et al, 1954). **Abraham et al (1956)** isolated another antibiotic from crude cephalosporin N and called it cephalosporin C. Cephalosporin C was shown

(i) to have antibacterial activity (ii) to be much more stable to acid than cephalosporin N. (iii) to be resistant to the action of enzyme penicillinase.

Production

Cephalosporin C (**Fig. 5.5 (a)**) is produced commercially by fermentation using cultures of a high-yielding strain of *Acremonium chrysogenum* (formerly *Cephalosporium acremonium*).Initial studies of the antibiotic compounds synthesised by *C. acremonium* identified penicillin N (originally called cephalosporin N) as the major component, with small amounts of cephalosporin C. In contrast to the penicillins, cephalosporin C was stable under acidic conditions and also was not attacked by penicillinase (β-lactamase). Antibacterial activity was rather low, however, and the antibiotic was poorly absorbed after oral administration. However, the structure offered considerable scope for side-chain modifications, more so than with the penicillins since it has two side-chains, and this has led to a wide variety of cephalosporin drugs, many of which are currently in clinical use. As with the penicillins, removal of the amide side-chain by the hydrolysis of cephalosporin C to 7-aminocephalosporanic acid (7-ACA) (**Fig. 5.5 (b)**) was the key to semi-synthetic modifications, and this may be achieved chemically by the procedure used for penicillins. Removal of this side-chain by suitable microorganisms or enzymes has proved elusive. The ester side-chain at C-3 maybe hydrolysed enzymatically by fermentation with a yeast, or, alternatively, the acetoxy group is easily displaced by nucleophilic reagents. It is also possible to convert readily available benzylpenicillin into the deacetoxy derivative of 7-ACA through a chemical ring expansion process and enzymatic removal of the side-chain

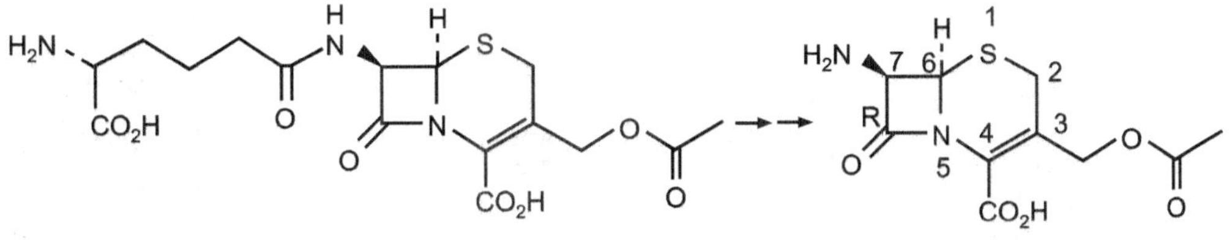

(a) Cephalosporin C

(b) 7-aminocephalosporanic acid (7-ACA)

Fig. 5.5 : Hydrolysis of Cephalosporin

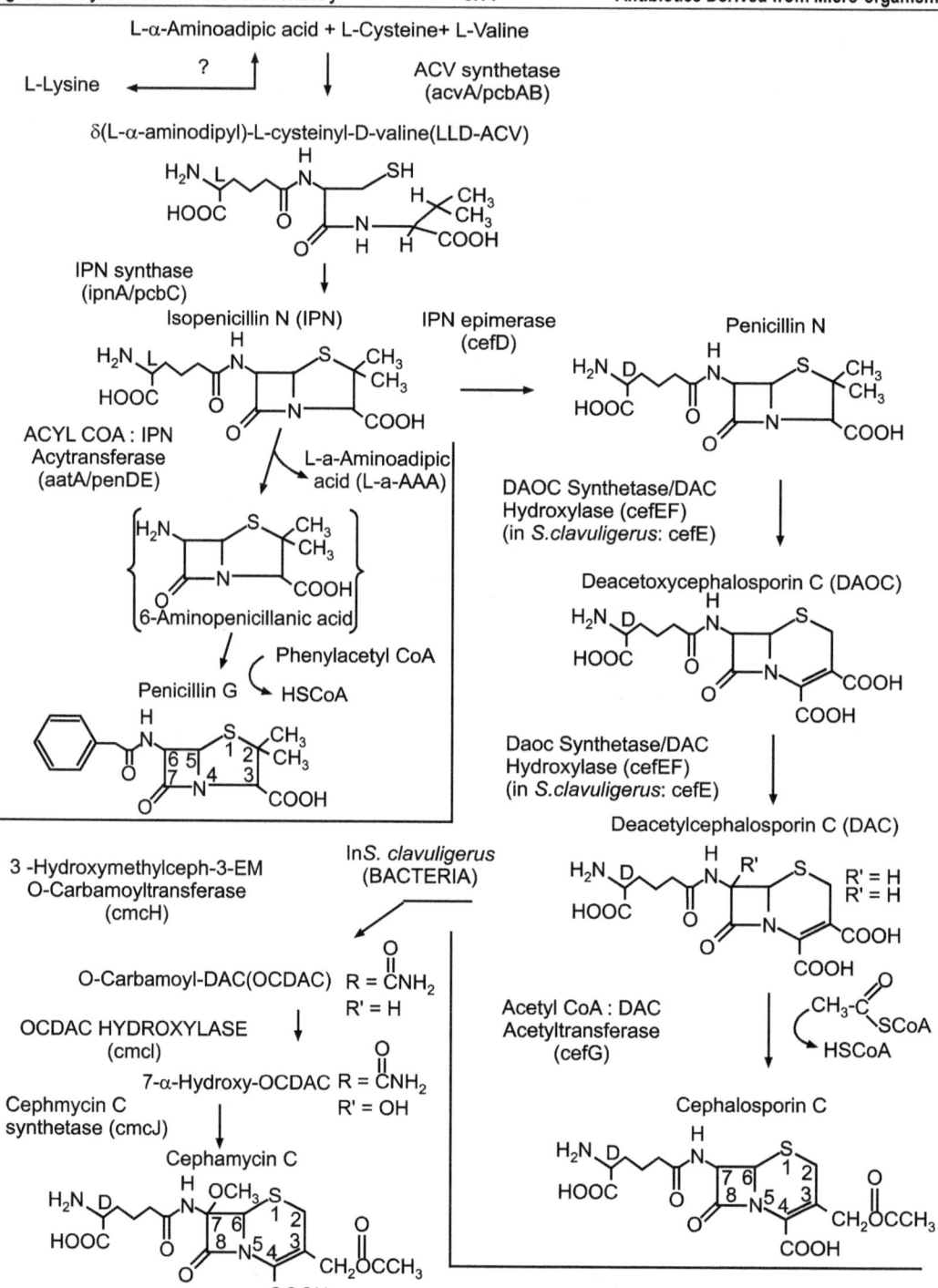

Fig. 5.6 : Biosynthesis of cephalosporin

Structure of cephalosporin C was established **by Abraham** *et al (1961)*.

1. Its molecular formula was found to be $C_{16}H_{21}N_3O_8S$.

2. It gave a positive ninhydrin reaction, indicating the presence of an α-amino acid.

3. On the basis of titration experiments, cephalosporin C was found to have an aminodicarboxylic acid; further the three ionisable groups were found with *pKa* values of < 2.6, 3.1 and 9.8 respectively.

4. The IR spectrum showed a band at 1783 cm^{-1} which was believed to be due to the carbonyl group in the β-lactam ring (recall that a similar band is also observed at 1770 cm^{-1} in penicillins). However, unlike penicillins, cephalosporin C did not give penicillamine on hydrolysis showing thereby that the structures of the fragment attached to the β-lactam ring in cephalosporin C and penicillins are different.

5. Hydrolysis of cephalosporin C with acid gave one molecule of D-α-arninoadipic aeid (I), one rnolecule of CO_2 and two molecules of ammonia.

Chemistry

The nucleus of the cephalosporins, 7-aminocephalosporanic acid bears a close resemblance to 6-aminopenicillanic acid. The intrinsic antimicrobial activity of natural cephalosporins is low, but the attachment of various R_1 and R_2 groups has yielded hundreds of potent compounds of low toxicity. Cephalosporins can be classified into four major groups or generations, depending mainly on the spectrum of antimicrobial activity. The cephalosporins have molecular weights of 400–450. They are soluble in water and relatively stable to pH and temperature changes.

Cephalosporins can be classified into four major groups or generations, depending mainly on the spectrum of antimicrobial activity. As a general rule, first-generation compounds have better activity against gram-positive organisms and the later compounds exhibit improved activity against gram-negative aerobic organisms

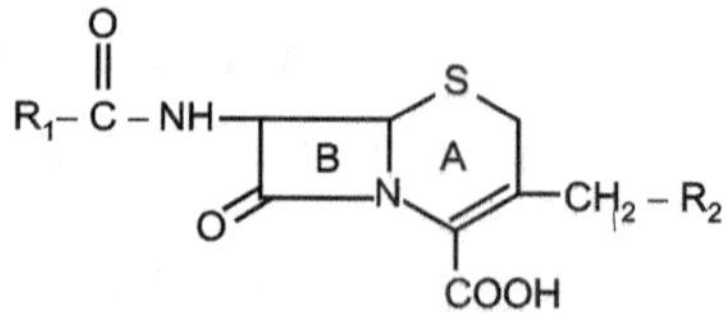

7-Aminocephalosporanic acid nucleus. The following structures can each be substituted at R_1 and R_2 to produce the named derivatives

"First generation"

R_1	Name	R_2
2-thienyl-CH_2-	Cephalothin	$-O-CO-CH_3$
phenyl-$CH(NH_2)-$	Cephalexin	$-H$
tetrazolyl-CH_2-	Cefazolin	$-S-$(5-methyl-1,3,4-thiadiazol-2-yl)
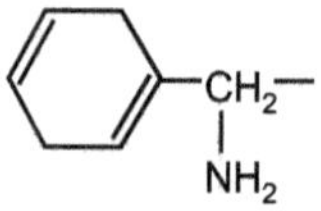 1,4-cyclohexadienyl-$CH(NH_2)-$	Cephradine CH_3	$-H$
(pyridin-4-yl)-$S-CH_2-$	Cephapirin	$-O-CO-CH_3$
phenyl-$CH(OH)-$	Cefamandole	$-S-$(1-methyl-1,3,4-thiadiazol-2-yl)

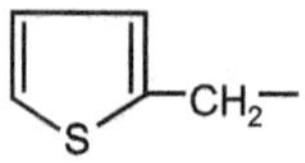

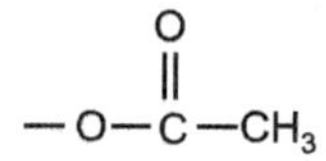

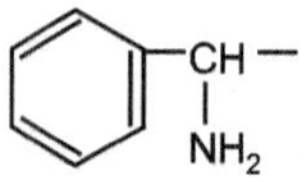

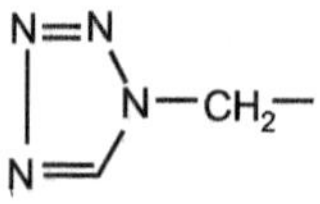

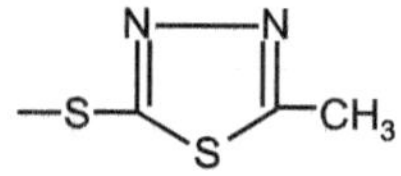

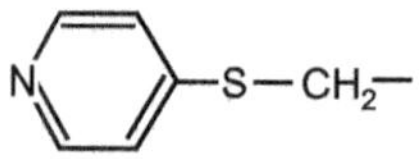

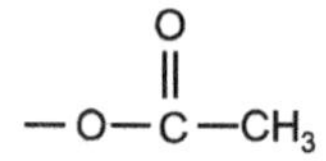

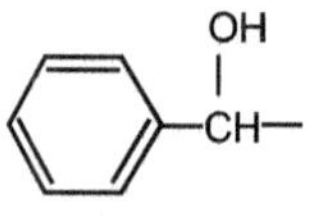

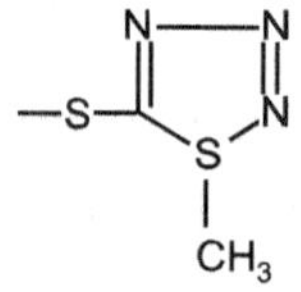

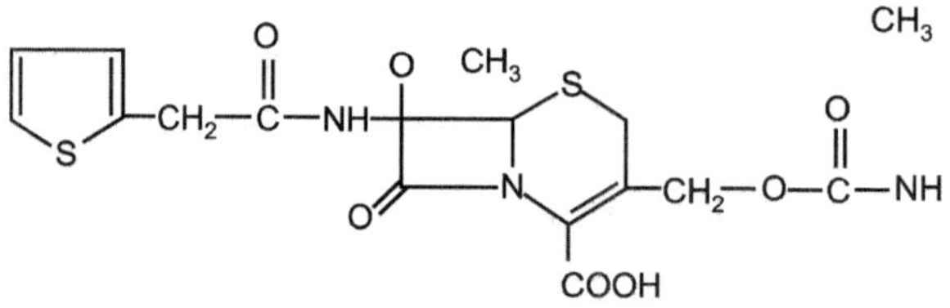

Cefoxitin (a cephamycin)

"Third generation"

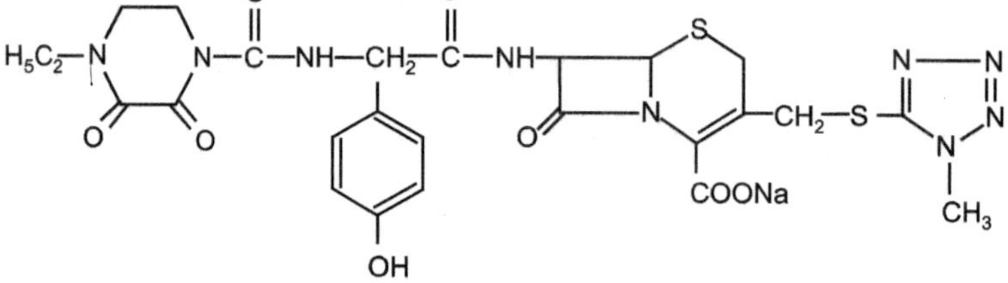

Cefoperazone

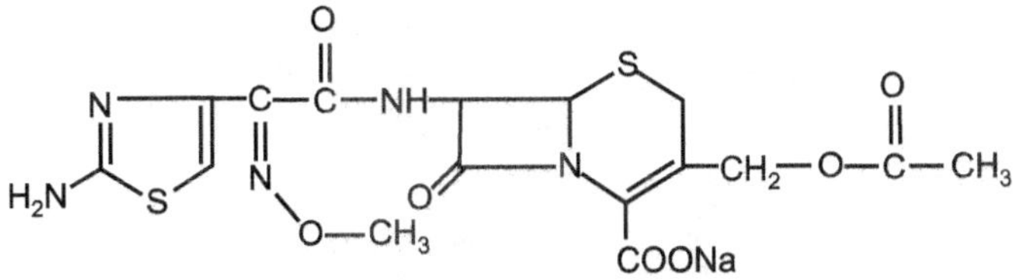

Fig. 5.7 Structures of some cephalosporins R₁ and R₂ structures are substituents on the 7-aminocephalosporanic acid nucleus pictured at the top. Other structures (cefoxitin and below) are complete in themselves

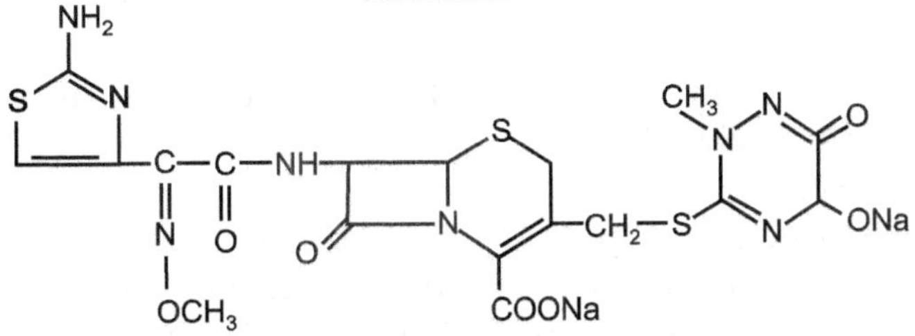

Structure Activity Relationship

The low potency of cephalosporin C soon made it clear that natural product itself was unsuitable as a clinical antibiotic. The structure would have to be modified in the laboratory to give more potent semi-synthetic analog. The semisynthetic cephalosporins are obtained by attaching a side chain to 7-aminocephalosporanic acid just as penicillin.

The basic skeletons involved in cephalosporin chemistry are

1. Cephalosporins X = H
2. Cephamycins X = OCH_3

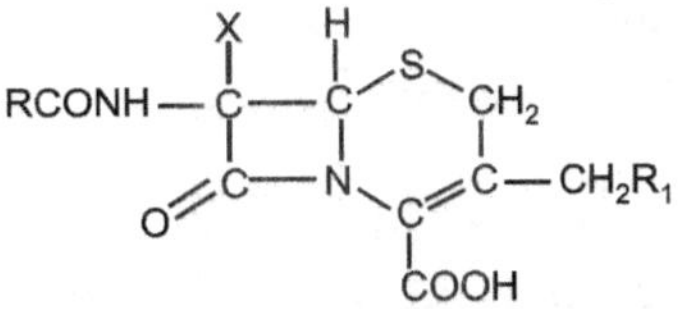

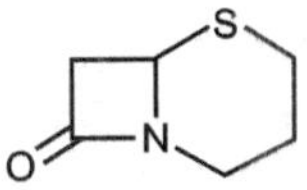

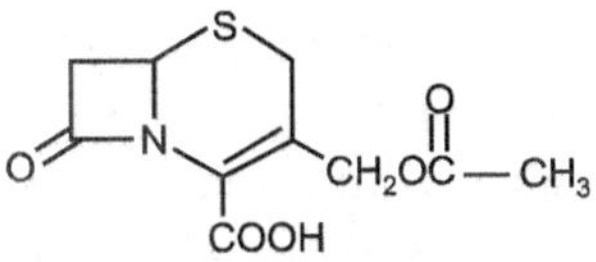

Cepham   Cephalosporanic acid

1. The cephalosporins are considered as broad spectrum antibiotics with patterns of antibacterial effectiveness similar to ampicillins.

2. Cephalosporins are significantly less sensitive than β - lactamase resistant penicillin to hydrolysis by the enzymes from *Staphylococcus aureus* and *Bacillus subtilis*. This may be due to the bicyclic cephem ring system rather than the acyl group.

3. Drug design in cephalosporin series followed the prominent footprints marked in penicillin evolution. Cefadroxyl is an example. The design of this drug seems to have derived from the success of amoxycillin.

Cefadroxyl

4. Similar to penicillin series, phenylglycine moiety if attached to 7 - amino cephalosporanic acid, affords a compound with increased oral activity: example is cephaloglycin.
5. The allylic acetoxy group at C - 3 is apparently not necessary for antibiotic activity e.g. cephalexin. Cephradine does not contain this group.
6. Analogous to azlocillin - mezloclllin, acylation of the amino group of 2-phenylglycine containing cephalosporins (e.g. cephaloglycin) is consistent with anti-pseudomonal activity e.g. cefoperazone.
7. A sulphonic acid moiety if present in acyl side-chain, confers antipseudomonal activity to certain penicillins. The analogy works with cephalosporins as well, resulting into cefsulodin.
8. While screening for β-lactam antibiotics, stable to β- lactamases, a strain of *Streptomyces lactamdurans* was found to release certain agents containing 6 - α - methoxy group whose electronic and steric properties protect the antibiotic from enzymatic attack. This generates a new series of compounds. known as cephamycins. Cefoxitin is one of the clinically useful agent from this class.
9. Several cephalosporins penetrate into CSF in sufficient concentration to be useful for the treatment of meningitis. For example, cefuroxime, cefotaxime and moxalactam.
10. Cephalosporins are still useful as alternatives to penicillins for a variety of infections in patients who cannot tolerate penicillins. These include streptococcal and staphylococcal infections.

Mechanism of Action

Like penicillin, the beta-lactam ring is also responsible for the antibacterial spectrum of cephalosporin (**Fig. 5.3**). Many organisms produce beta lactamase enzyme that causes destruction of this beta lactam ring and causes decrease in antibacterial activity. They also cause inhibition of bacterial cell wall synthesis by inhibiting transpeptidase enzyme and causes inhibition of cross linkage so that rigidity is not restored in cell wall and the cell dies. Like penicillin, cephalosporin binds to CBS (cephalosporin binding protein) and causes inhibition of cell wall synthesis.

Griseofulvin

Griseofulvin is fungistatic in vitro for various species of the dermatophytes.

Griseofulvin is an antifungal agent produced by cultures of *Penicillium griseofulvum* and a number of other *Penicillium* species, including *P. janczewski, P. nigrum,* and *P.*

patulum. Griseofulvin is the drug of choice for widespread or intractable dermatophyte infections, but is ineffective when applied topically. However, it is well absorbed from the gut and selectively concentrated into keratin, so may be used orally to control dermatophytes such as *Epidermophyton, Microsporium, and Trichophyton.* Treatment for some conditions, e.g. infections in finger nails, may have to be continued for several months, but the drug is generally free of side-effects. The antifungal action appears to be through disruption of the mitotic spindle, thus inhibiting fungal mitosis.

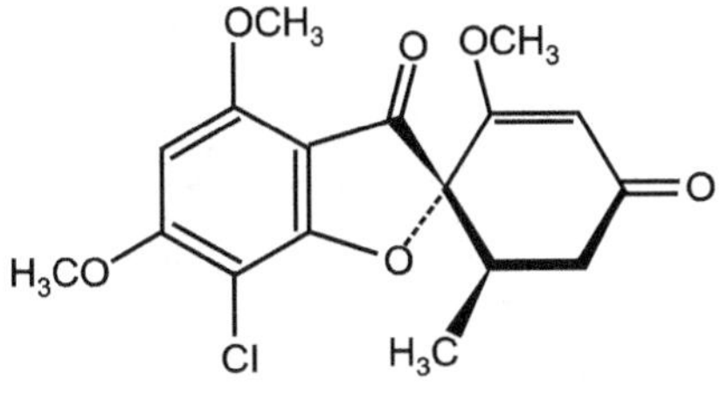

Griseofulvin

Structural Features

Of the four possible stereoisomers only the natural product is active. Synthesis of some derivatives revealed the following points

1. None of these shows activity superior to that of griseofulvin.
2. Few analogs anyhow manage to retain the activity e.g. 7 - fluoro analog.
3. Most of the modifications lead to decrease in activity.
4. It is remarkably non - toxic though less often gastric upset, diarrhoea, headache, transient leukopenia and allergic reactions are observed.

Biosynthesis (Acetate Pathway)

Phenolic oxidative coupling is widely encountered in natural product biosynthesis, and many other examples are described in subsequent sections. A further acetate-derived metabolite formed as a result of oxidative coupling is the antifungal agent ***griseofulvin***

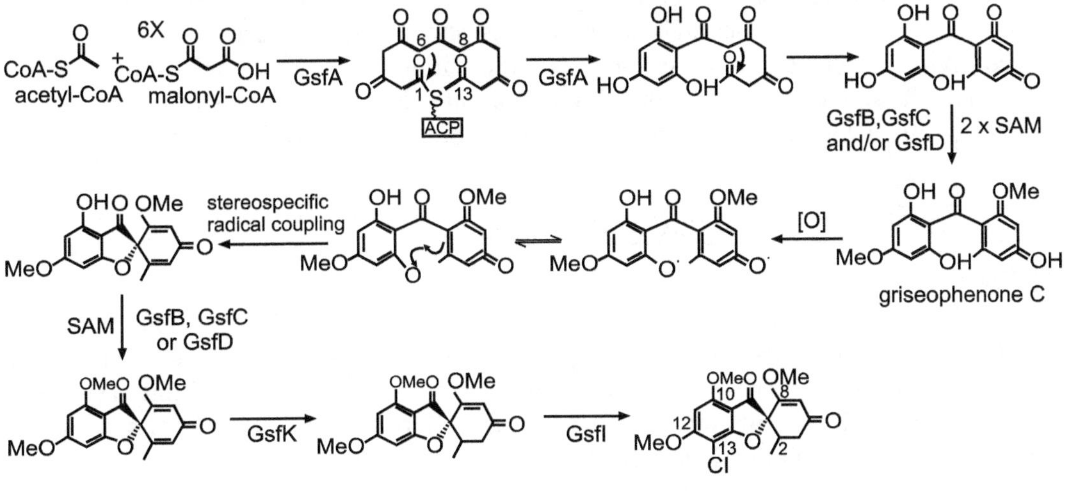

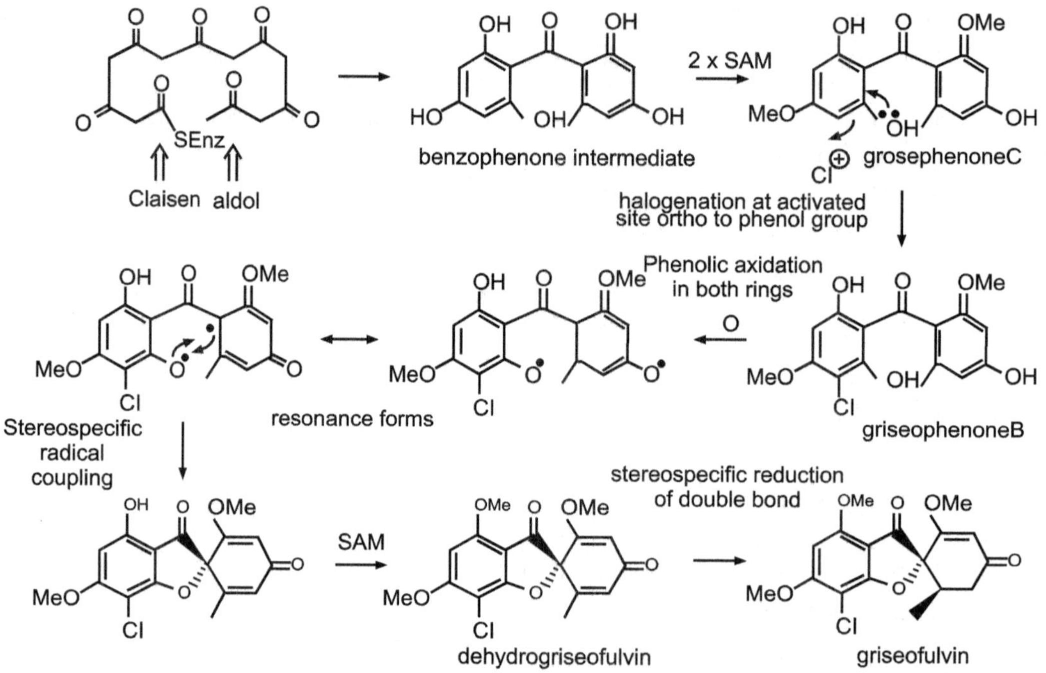

Fig. 5.8 : Biosynthesis of Griseofulvin

Mechanism of Action

Griseofulvin inhibits fungal mitosis, presumably disrupting the mitotic spindle by interacting with polymerised microtubules. Griseofulvin also may bind to a microtubule-associated protein.

Griseofulvin is deposited in keratin precursor cells and persists in keratin to provide prolonged resistance to fungi. The new growth of hair or nails is the first to become free of disease. As the fungus-containing keratin is shed, it is replaced by normal tissue. Griseofulvin is detectable in the stratum corneum within 4–8 hours of oral administration. Sweat and transepidermal fluid loss play important roles in drug transfer to the stratum corneum. Only a very small fraction of the drug is present in body fluids and tissues.

ANTIBIOTICS DERIVED FROM BACTERIA

[I] Bacitracin

Bacitracin is a cyclic peptide mixture first obtained from the Tracy strain of *Bacillus subtilis* in 1943. It is active against gram-positive microorganisms. Bacitracin inhibits cell wall formation by interfering with dephosphorylation in cycling of the lipid carrier that transfers peptidoglycan subunits to the growing cell wall. There is no cross-resistance between bacitracin and other antimicrobial drugs.

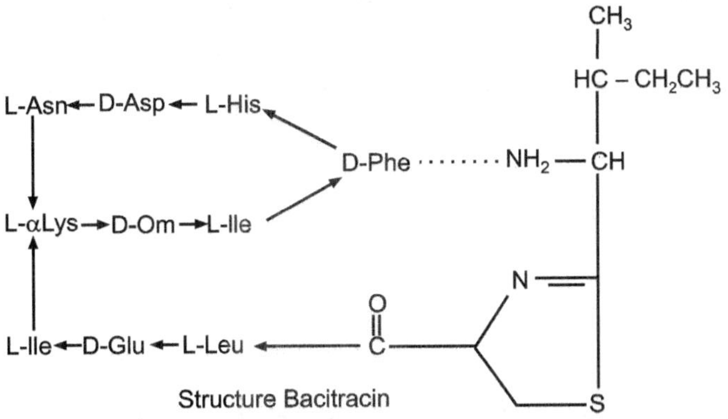

```
L-Asn ← D-Asp ← L-His
  ↓                    ↘
L-αLys → D-Orn → L-Ile    D-Phe ······ NH₂ — CH — CH(CH₃) — CH₂CH₃
  ↑                    ↗                      |
L-Ile ← D-Glu ← L-Leu ← C(=O) — [thiazoline ring with N, S]
           Structure Bacitracin
```

Fig. 5.9: Structure of Bacitracin

The structure contains a cyclic peptide portion, involving the carboxyl terminus and the ε-amino of lysine, and at the N-terminus an unusual thiazoline carboxylic acid, which is a condensation product from isoleucine and cysteine residues.

Bacitracin is active against a wide range of Gram-positive bacteria, and appears to affect biosynthesis of the bacterial cell wall by binding to and sequestering a polyprenyl diphosphate carrier of intermediates; this binding also requires a divalent metal ion, with zinc being especially active. It is rarely used systemically because some bacitracin components are nephrotoxic, but as zinc bacitracin, it is a component of ointment formulations for topical application. The vast majority of bacitracin manufactured is used at subtherapeutic doses as an animal feed additive, to increase feed efficiency, and at therapeutic dosage to control a variety of disorders in poultry and poultry

Bacitracin is markedly nephrotoxic if administered systemically, causing proteinuria, hematuria, and nitrogen retention. Hypersensitivity reactions (e. g, skin rashes) are rare. Because of its marked toxicity when used systemically, it is limited to topical use. Bacitracin is poorly absorbed. Topical application results in local antibacterial activity without significant systemic toxicity. The small amounts of bacitracin that are absorbed are excreted by glomerular filtration.

[II] Aztreonam

Aztreonam is a monocyclic β-lactam. Aztreonam is resistant to the β-lactamases that are elaborated by most gram-negative bacteria. The antimicrobial activity of aztreonam differs from those of other β-lactam antibiotics and resembles that of an aminoglycoside. Aztreonam has activity only against gram-negative bacteria; it has no activity against gram-positive bacteria and anaerobic organisms. Activity against Enterobacteriaceae is excellent, as is that against *P. aeruginosa*. It is also highly active against *H. influenzae* and gonococci.

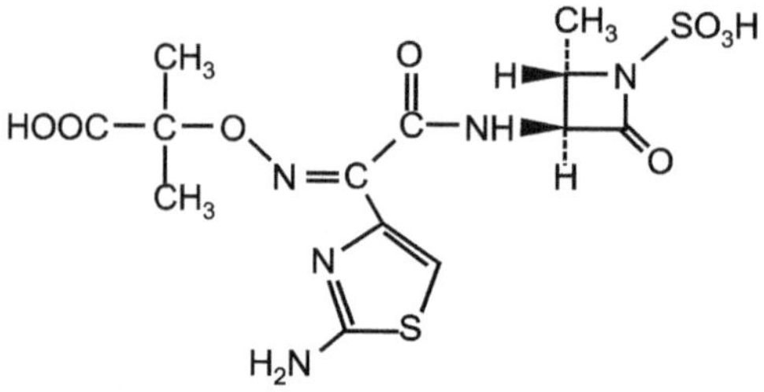

Aztreonam

[III] Polymyxin

The polymyxins are a group of closely related antibiotics elaborated by various strains of *Bacillus polymyxa*. Colistin is produced by *Bacillus colistinus*. These drugs, which are cationic detergents, are basic peptides of ~1000 Da.

The polymyxins are a group of cyclic polypeptide antibiotics produced by species of *Bacillus*. Polymyxins A–E were isolated from *Bacillus polymyxa*, though polymyxin B and polymyxin E were both subsequently shown to be mixtures of two components. A polypeptide mixture called colistin isolated from *Bacillus colistinus* was then found to be identical to polymyxin E. Polymyxin B and colistin (polymyxin E) are both used clinically. These antibiotic mixtures respectively contain mainly polymyxin B1 with small amounts of polymyxin B2, or predominantly polymyxin E1 (≡ colistin A) with small amounts of polymyxin E2 (≡colistin B). These molecules contain ten amino acids, six of which are L-α, γ-diaminobutyric acid (L-Dab), with a fatty acid (6-methyloctanoic acid or 6-methylheptanoicacid) bonded to the N-terminus, and a cyclic peptide portion constructed via an amide bond between the carboxyl terminus and the γ -amino of one of the Dab residues. The γ-aminogroups of the remaining Dab residues confer a strongly basic character to the antibiotics. This results in detergent-like properties and allows them to bind to and damage bacterial membranes. These peptides have been used for the treatment of infections with Gram-negative bacteria such as *Pseudomonas aeruginosa*, but are seldom used now because of neurotoxic and nephrotoxic effects. However, they are included in some topical preparation such as ointments, eye drops, and ear drops, frequently in combination with other antibiotics

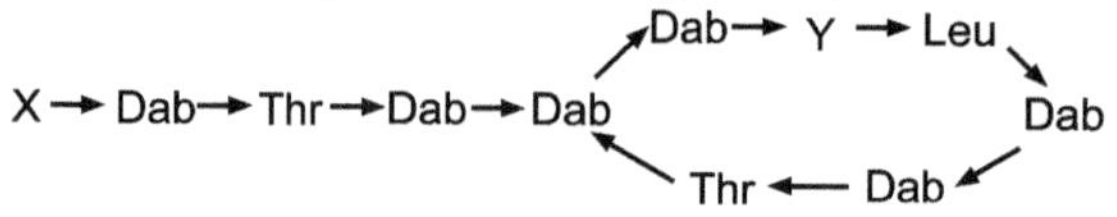

X → Dab → Thr → Dab → Dab → Dab → Y → Leu → Dab → Thr ← Dab

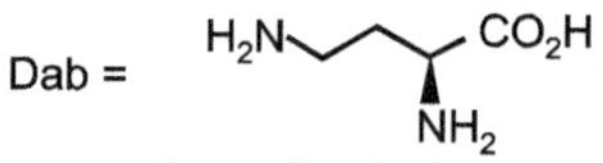

Dab = L-α,γ-diaminobutyric acid

	X	Y
polymyxin B₁	6-methyloctanoic acid	D-Phe
polymyxin B₂	6-methylheptanoic acid	D-Phe
polymyxin E₁ (colistin A)	6-methyloctanoic acid	D-Leu
polymyxin E₂ (colistin B)	6-methylheptanoic acid	D-Leu

Mechanism of Action : Polymyxins are amphipathic agents that interact with phospholipids and disrupt the structure of cell membranes to increase permeability. Polymyxin B sensitivity apparently is related to the phospholipid content of the cell wall–membrane complex, which may prevent access of the drug to the cell membrane.

These drugs are not absorbed when given orally and poorly absorbed from mucous membranes and burnt surfaces. They are cleared renally, and dose modification is required with impaired renal function. Polymyxin B sulphate is available for ophthalmic, otic, and topical use in combination with a variety of other compounds. Colistin is available as otic drops. Parenteral preparations are rarely used, but colistin may be useful as a salvage regimen for infections caused by multiple-drug-resistant organisms. Because of their extreme nephrotoxicity, these drugs are rarely if ever used, except topically.

Polymyxin B applied to intact or denuded skin or mucous membranes produces no systemic reactions because of its almost complete lack of absorption.

ANTIBIOTICS DERIVED FROM ACTINOMYCETES

[I] Chloramphenicol

Chloramphenicol (chloromycetin) was initially isolated from cultures of *Streptomyces venezuelae*, but is now obtained for drug use by chemical synthesis.

Crystalline chloramphenicol is a neutral, stable compound with the following structure

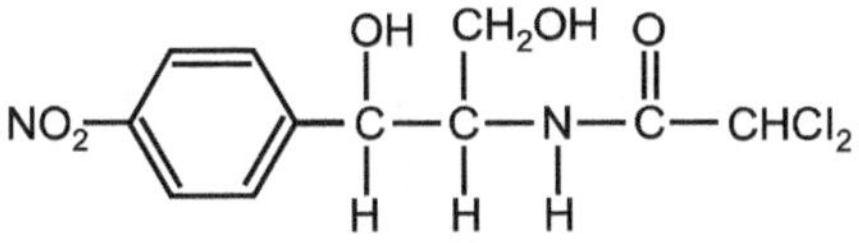

$$NO_2-C_6H_4-\underset{\underset{H}{|}}{\overset{\overset{OH}{|}}{C}}-\underset{\underset{H}{|}}{\overset{\overset{CH_2OH}{|}}{C}}-\underset{\underset{H}{|}}{N}-\overset{\overset{O}{\|}}{C}-CHCl_2$$

Chloramphenicol

It is soluble in alcohol but poorly soluble in water. Chloramphenicol succinate, which is used for parenteral administration, is highly water-soluble. It is hydrolysed in vivo with liberation of free chloramphenicol.

Production of Chloramphenicol

In the biological process, the master cultures of *Streptomyces venezuelae* strains are preserved with soil, and slope cultures are prepared from time to time. From these, suspensions in a soapy solution are made and are kept in refrigerator until required. As usual, inocula are made in a stepwise fashion manner. First a 50 gallon tank is inoculated and growth is allowed to go on for 24 hours, the contents of this pre-seed tank are transferred aseptically by air pressure to the seed tank of 500 gallons capacity, where growth goes on further for 2 hours; and finally the 5,000 gallon fermenter is seeded by transferring the contents of the seed tank and fermentation goes on for about 72 hours.

In the culture solution, protein source is wheat gluten, the main carbon source is glycerol; sodium carbonate and sodium chloride are used for adjusting the pH: and anti-foaming agents are also required. Growth conditions are aerobic and the temperature is maintained carefully at 27.8°C.

Isolation of Chloramphenicol

Unlike penicillin, the isolation of chloramphenicol is rendered easier partly because of its stability and because of the fact that little pH adjustment is needed. It is extracted on the counter-current principle by amyl acetate, the amyl acetate solution is concentrated, washed with sulphuric acid, alkali and finally with water, and then evaporated. The crude crystals are recrystallised from water containing charcoal. Chloramphenicol is sufficiently stable in hot water to be used at about 93°C. Chloramphenicol is a stable, neutral compound, bitter in taste with a sharp melting point of 150.1°C. It is soluble in many organic solvents but sparingly soluble in water. It is optically active.

Constitution

The chemical structure of chloramphenicol was elucidated by analysis and confirmed by synthesis (**Controulis *et al*. 1949; Long & Troutman, 1949**).

1. Its molecular composition is $C_{11}H_{12}N_2O_5Cl_2$.
2. Chloramphenicol on reduction with tin and hydrochloric acid followed by diazotization and coupling with β-naphthol gives an orange red precipitate indicating the presence of an aromatic nitro group.
3. Its ultraviolet spectrum is found to be similar to that of nitrobenzene.
4. On catalytic reduction over palladium as a catalyst, chloramphenicol gives a product which shows an absorption spectrum similar to that of p-toluidene, and the solution contains ionic chlorine. The observation indicates that chloramphenicol is a p-nitrobenzene substituted compound and its chlorine atom is present in the side chain.
5. It contains neither free amino group nor carbonyl group.
6. On acetylation by means of acetic anhydride in pyridine, it gives diacetyl derivative indicating presence of two hydroxyl groups.
7. On hydrolysis with either acids or alkalis, it gives dichloroacetic acid and an optically active base.

    $C_{11}H_{12}N_2O_5Cl_2$ + H_2O $\longrightarrow$ $C_9H_{12}N_2O_4$ + $CHCl_2.COOH$
    Chloromycetin   Base   Dichloroacetic acid

8. **Structure of base,** $C_9H_{12}N_2O_4$
    (i) It is found to have one primary amino group,
    (ii) The base on acetylation with acetic anhydride in pyridine yields triacetyl derivative confirming the presence of two hydroxyl groups of the drug and amino group derived by hydrolysis.
    (iii) The base on treatment with methyl dichloroacetate gives a dichloracetamide identical with chloramphenicol.

(iv) On oxidation with periodic acid, it utilises two equivalents of periodic acid to form p-nitro benzaldehyde, formaldehyde and ammonia. This suggests that in the base, a propyl group is present *para* to the nitro group with an amino group on the second carbon atom, i.e., the base is 2-amino-1-1-*p*-nitrophenylpropane -1, 3-diol.

$$C_{11}H_{12}N_2O_5Cl_2 \text{ (Chloromycetin)} \xrightleftharpoons[Cl_2CHCOOCH_3]{H^+ \text{ or } OH^-} \text{Base}$$

Base → (Ac$_2$O) → Acetylated derivative

Base + 2HIO$_4$ → O$_2$N-C$_6$H$_4$-CHO + NH$_3$ + CH$_2$O

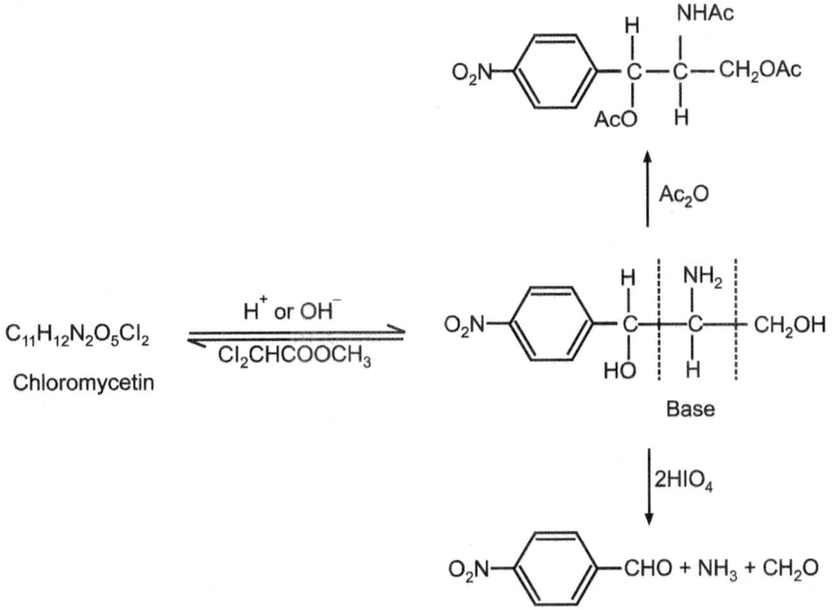

Biosynthesis

It was one of the first broad spectrum antibiotics to be developed, and exerts its antibacterial action by inhibiting protein biosynthesis. It binds reversibly to the 50S subunit of the bacterial ribosome, and in so doing disrupts peptidyl transferase, the enzyme that catalyses peptide bond formation. This reversible binding means that bacterial cells not destroyed may resume protein biosynthesis when no longer exposed to the antibiotic. Some microorganisms have developed resistance to chloramphenicol by an inactivation process involving enzymic acetylation of the primary alcohol group in the antibiotic. The acetate binds only very weakly to the ribosomes, so has little antibiotic activity. The value of chloramphenicol as an antibacterial agent has been severely limited by some serious side-effects. It can cause blood disorders including irreversible aplastic anaemia in certain individuals, and these can lead to leukaemia and perhaps prove fatal. Nevertheless, it is still the drug of choice for some life-threatening infections such as typhoid fever and bacterial meningitis. The blood constitution must be monitored regularly during treatment to detect any abnormalities or adverse changes. The drug is orally active, but may also be injected. Eye-drops are useful for the treatment of bacterial conjunctivitis.

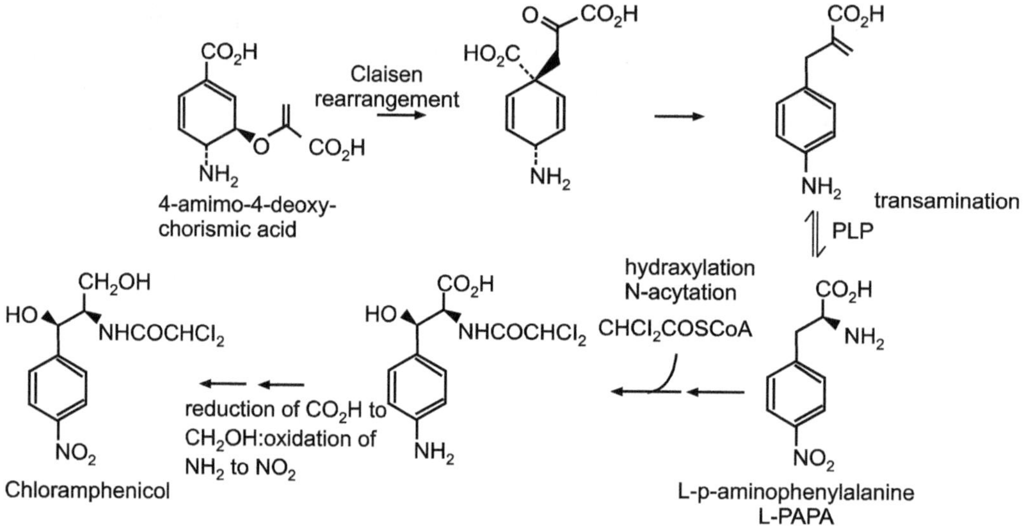

Biosynthesis of Chloramphenicol

[Scheme: 4-amino-4-deoxychorismic acid → (Claisen rearrangement) → intermediate → transamination (PLP) → L-p-aminophenylalanine (L-PAPA) → hydroxylation, N-acylation with $CHCl_2COSCoA$ → intermediate → (reduction of CO_2H to CH_2OH; oxidation of NH_2 to NO_2) → Chloramphenicol]

Structure Activity Relationship

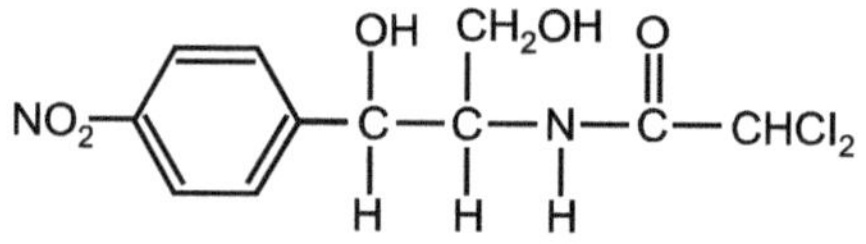

[Structure of Chloramphenicol: NO_2-C$_6$H$_4$-CH(OH)-CH(CH$_2$OH)-NH-CO-CHCl$_2$]

Chloramphenicol

SAR of cloraphenicol can be studied under the following headings

1. SAR of p-nitrophenyl Group

Substitution of the nitro group by other substituents leads to reduction in activity.

(a) Shifting of the nitro group from *para* position reduces antibacterial activity.

(b) Replacement of phenyl group by the alicyclic moieties results in less potent compounds.

(c) The p-nitrophenyl group may be replaced by other aryl structures without significant loss of activity.

2. SAR of Dichloroacetamido Group

Other dihaloderivatives of side-chain are less potent though major activities are retained.

While in case of trihaloderivatives, Hansch et. al in the light of QSAR calculation claimed that $NHCOCF_3$ derivative would be about 1.7 times as active as the chloramphenicol.

3. SAR of 1, 3-propanediol

The primary alcoholic group on C-1 atom if modified, results in a decrease in activity hence the alcoholic group seems to be essential for activity.

Of the four stereoisomers of chloramphenicol, the antibacterial activity resides in only d-threo compound. Other isomers are inactive.

```
       CH₂OH                    CH₂OH
        |                        |
   H—C—NHCOCHCl₂            H—C—NHCOCHCl₂
        |                        |
   HO—C—H                   H—C—OH
        |                        |
      (phenyl)                 (phenyl)
        |                        |
       NO₂                      NO₂
 threo-Chloramphenicol    erythro-Chloramphenicol
```

Mechanism of Action

Chloramphenicol is a potent inhibitor of microbial protein synthesis. It binds reversibly to the 50S subunit of the bacterial ribosome. It inhibits the peptidyl transferase step of protein synthesis. Chloramphenicol is a bacteriostatic broad-spectrum antibiotic that is active against both aerobic and anaerobic gram-positive and gram-negative organisms. It is active also against rickettsiae but not chlamydiae. Most gram-positive bacteria are inhibited at concentrations of 1–10 g/mL, and many gram-negative bacteria are inhibited by concentrations of 0.2–5 g/mL.

Haemophilus influenzae, Neisseria meningitidis, and some strains of bacteroides are highly susceptible, and for them chloramphenicol may be bactericidal.

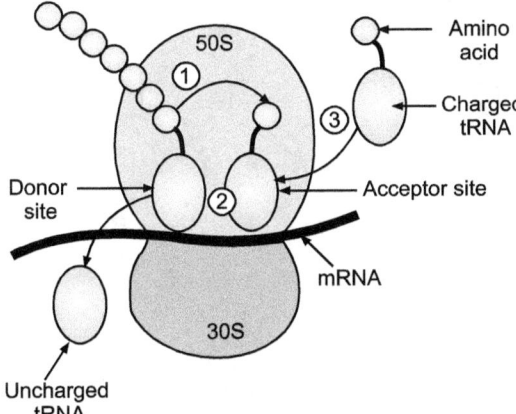

Fig. 5.10 : Steps in bacterial protein synthesis and targets of chloramphenicol (1), macrolide (2), tetracycline (3)

The 70S ribosomal mRNA complex is shown with its 50S and 30S subunits. The peptidyl tRNA at the donor site donates the growing peptide chain to the aminoacyl tRNA at the acceptor site in a reaction catalyzed by peptidyl transferase. The tRNA, discharged of its peptide, is released from the donor site to make way for translocation of the newly formed peptidyl tRNA. occupied by the next "charged" aminoacyl tRNA.

[II] Tetracyclines

The tetracycline antibiotics contain the hydro naphthacene skeleton as a characteristic structural unit. These are yellow amphoteric substances, forming salts with acids or bases, or complexes with such metals as aluminium, magnesium, calcium, or iron. The three most important members of the group **are tetracycline. chlortetracycline (aureomycin) and oxytetracycline (terramycin),** all of which are produced by actinomycetes.

Production

Chlortetracycline is produced by a strain of *Streptomyces aureofaciens.* Its isolation is said to follow the following stages

(a) adsorption on activated charcoal or magnesium silicate;

(b) washing the chromatogram with an acidified organic solvent such as methanol or acetone;

(c) selection of the fraction which appears to be yellow under U.V. light;

(d) finally, recovery of the antibiotic by extraction with butanol, precipitation with dry ether, re-solution in dilute hydrochloric acid and freezing to remove water.

Tetracycline is also produced by *Streptomyces aureofaciens* as well as other *Streptomyces* organisms; while oxytetracycline (terramycin) is produced by *Streptomyces rimosus.*

All of the tetracyclines have the basic structure shown below

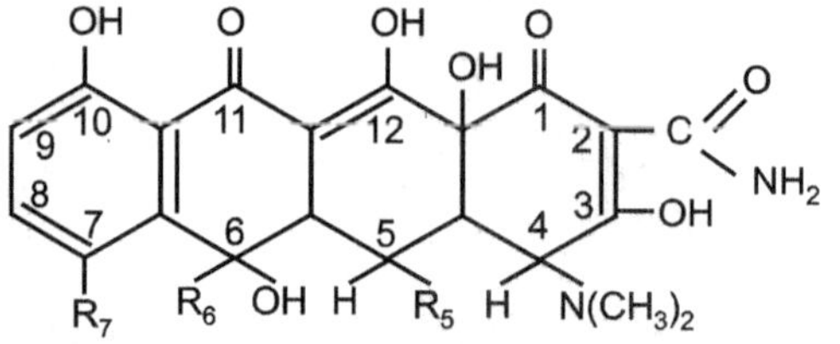

	R_7	R_6	R_5	Renal Clearance (mL/min)
Chlortetracycline	–Cl	–CH$_3$	–H	35
Oxytetracycline	–H	–CH$_3$	–OH	90
Tetracycline	–H	–CH$_3$	–H	65
Demeclocycline	–Cl	–H	–H	35
Methacycline	–H	=CH$_2$*	–OH	31
Doxycycline	–H	–CH$_3$*	–OH	16
Minocycline	–N(CH$_3$)$_2$	–H	–H	10

There is no –OH at position 6 on methacycline and doxycycline.

Free tetracyclines are crystalline amphoteric substances of low solubility. They are available as hydrochlorides, which are more soluble. Such solutions are acidic and, with the exception of chlortetracycline, fairly stable. Tetracyclines chelate divalent metal ions, which can interfere with their absorption and activity.

Structure Activity Relationship

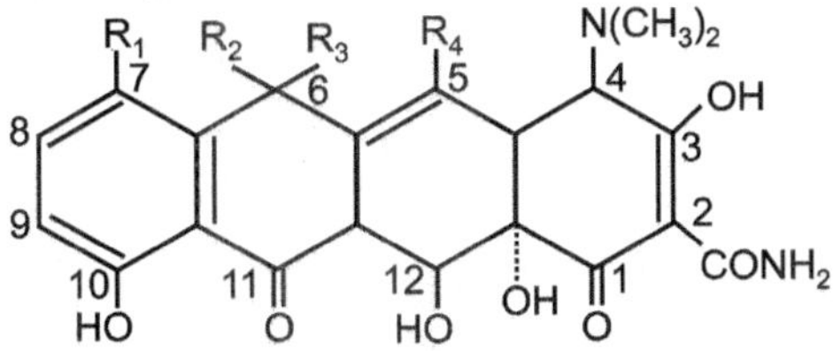

1. The tetracyclines are truly broad spectrum antibiotics with the broadest spectrum than any of the presently available antibiotics. The basic nucleus common to all tetracyclines is a polycyclic napthacene carboxamide which is comprised of four fused, six, membered rings A. B. C and D. The group name tetracycline thus describes the pattern of backbone skeleton. A tetracyclic backbone skeleton is essential for activity.
2. The enolized system present at carbons 1 to 3 must be intact for good activity.
3. The amide function at C - 2 is essential for activity.
4. Epitetracyclines are very much less active than neutral isomers.
5. Substitution at C - 6 decreases chemical stability e.g. oxytetracycline is chemically less stable than doxycycline.
6. In general, C - 6 methylated analogs achieve higher blood levels.
7. C - 7 substitution results in increased potency and the drug may sometimes be active against resistant microbial strains.
8. Strong acid dehydrates tetracyclines utilising a 6 - hydroxyl group and the 5 α-hydrogen. This route led to development of 6 -deoxytetracycline.
9. A cis type fusion between A/B with an α-hydroxyl group at 1, 2 position is necessary for retention of activity.
10. Electron withdrawing groups and electron donating groups both are equally effective at C - 7. e.g. chlortetracycline contains an electron withdrawing group at C - 7 and minocycline possesses an electron releasing (dimethyl amino) group at C - 7.
11. The SAR of 8 - substituted analogs is not yet documented.

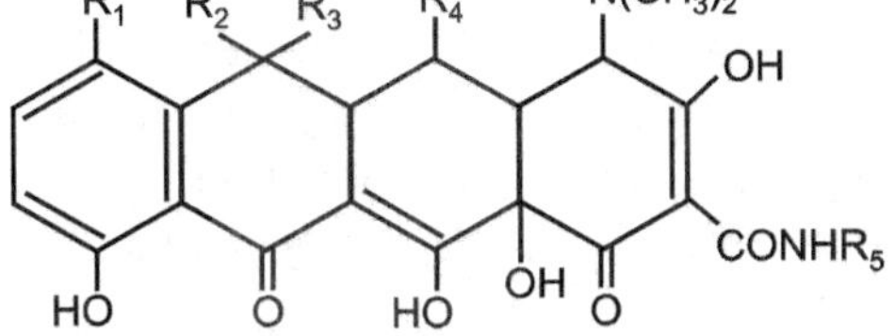

Table 5.2 : Tetracyclines, their substituents and source

Name	R_1	R_2	R_3	R_4	R_5	Source
7-chlorotetracycline	Cl	CH_3	OH	H	H	*S.aureofaciens*
Oxytetracycline	H	CH_3	OH	OH	H	*S.rimosus*
Tetracycline	H	CH_3	OH	H	H	Semi-synthetically from chlortetracycline
Demeclocycline	Cl	H	OH	H	H	Mutant strain of *S.aureofaciens*
Methacycline	H		$-CH_2$	OH	H	Semi-sythetically from oxytetracycline
Doxycycline	H	CH_3	H	OH	H	Semi-synthetically from oxytetracycline
Minocycline	$N(CH_3)_2$	H	H	H	H	Semi-synthetically from oxytetracycline
Rolitetracycline	H	CH_3	OH	H	X	Semi-synthetically from tetracycline
Lymecycline	H	CH_3	OH	H	Y	Mannich base of tetracycline
Sancycline	H	H	H	H	H	
Clomocycline	Cl	CH_3	OH	H	CH_2OH	Semi-synthetically from chlortetracycline

In rolitetracycline X = $-CH_2N\langle$ ⬠

In lymecycline Y = $-CH_2NH-CH-(CH_2)_4-NH_2$
                                  |
                                 COOH

12. The SAR of positions 5, 6, 7 and 9 can be modified by various substituents resulting into retention and in some cases, improvement of antibiotic activity.
13. 6-thiatetracyclines in a preliminary report are showing excellent superior pattern of activity. They contain a sulphur atom at C-6. A recent derivative thiacycline is found to be more active than minocycline against tetracycline-resistant bacteria.
14. Tetracyclines have low solubility in water which may be overcome by aminoalkylation at carboxamido group using Mannich reaction. The clinically effective mannich bases are rolitetracycline (pyrrolidinomethyltetracycline), lymecycline (Tetracycline-L-methylenelysine) and domocycline (N-methylol-7-chlortetracycline).

15. Semisynthetic analogs have also been obtained in an attempt to achieve advances in chemotherapy. Methacycline, doxycycline and minocycline are some results of such efforts. For example, chlortetracycline through a catalytic dehalogenatlon can be converted to tetracycline. Methacycline is obtained from oxytetracycline while hydrogenation of methacycline offers doxycycline.

Mechanism of Action

Tetracyclines enter microorganisms in part by passive diffusion and in part by an energy-dependent process of active transport. Susceptible cells concentrate the drug intracellularly. Once inside the cell, tetracyclines bind reversibly to the 30S subunit of the bacterial ribosome, blocking the binding of aminoacyl-tRNA to the acceptor site on the mRNA-ribosome complex. This prevents addition of amino acids to the growing peptide.

[III] Macrolides

The macrolides are a group of closely related compounds characterised by a macrocyclic lactone ring (usually containing 14 or 16 atoms) to which deoxy sugars are attached. The prototype drug, erythromycin, which consists of two sugar moieties attached to a 14-atom lactone ring, was obtained in 1952 from *Streptomyces erythreus*.

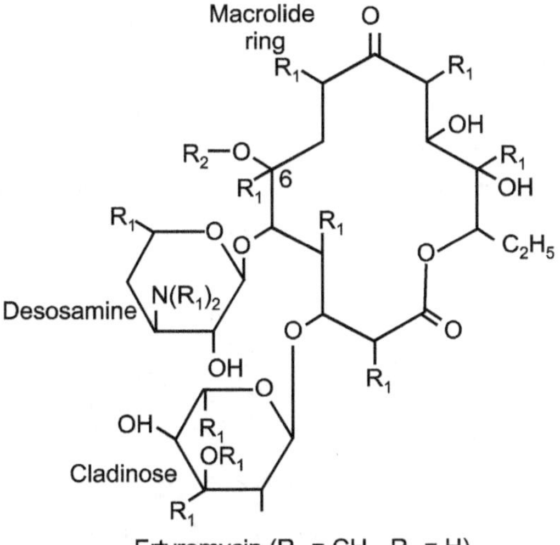

Ertyromycin (R_1 = CH_3, R_2 = H)
Clarithromycin (R_1, R_2 = CH_3)

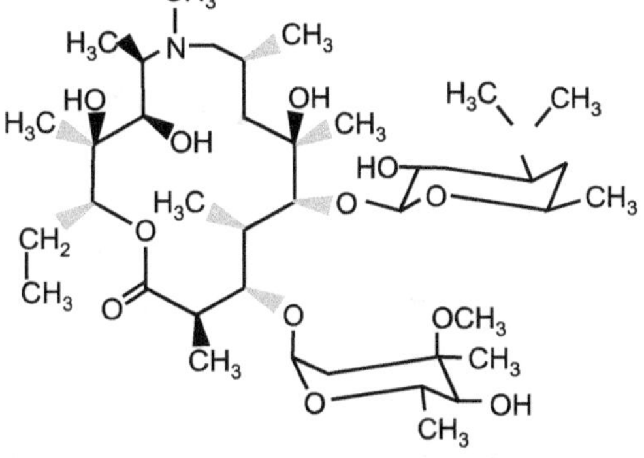

Azithromycin

Chemistry

Clarithromycin and azithromycin are semisynthetic derivatives of erythromycin. The general structure of erythromycin is shown above with the macrolide ring and the sugars desosamine and cladinose. It is poorly soluble in water (0.1%) but dissolves readily in organic solvents. Solutions are fairly stable at 4 °C but lose activity rapidly at 20 °C and at acid pH.

The macrolide antibiotics have three common chemical characteristics
1. A large lactone ring.
2. A ketone group.
3. A glycosidically linked amino group.

Usually, the lactone ring has 12, 14 or 16 atoms in it and is often partially unsaturated, with an oliefinic group conjugated with a ketone function. They may have, in addition to the amino sugar, a neutral sugar that is glycosidically linked in lactone ring.

Biosynthesis

Erythromycin A from *Saccharopolyspora erythraea* is a valuable antibacterial drug and contains a 14-membered macrocycle composed entirely of propionate units, both as starter and extension units, the latter *via* methyl malonyl-CoA (acetate pathway). In common with many anti-bacterial macrolides, sugar units, including aminosugars, are attached through glycoside linkages. These unusual 6-deoxy sugars are frequently restricted to this group of natural products. In erythromycin A, the sugars are L-cladinose and D-desosamine. Chain extension and appropriate reduction processes lead to an enzyme-bound polyketide in which one carbonyl group has suffered total reduction, four have been reduced to alcohols, whilst one carbonyl is not reduced, and remains throughout the sequence. These processes ultimately lead to release of the modified polyketide as the macrolide ester deoxyerythronolide ,a demonstrated intermediate in the pathway to erythromycins.The stereochemistry in the chain is controlled by the condensation and reduction steps during chain extension, but a reassuring feature is that there appears to be a considerable degree of stereochemical uniformity throughout the known macrolide antibiotics. In the later stages of the biosynthesis of erythromycin, hydroxylations at carbons 6 and 12, and addition of sugar units, are achieved.

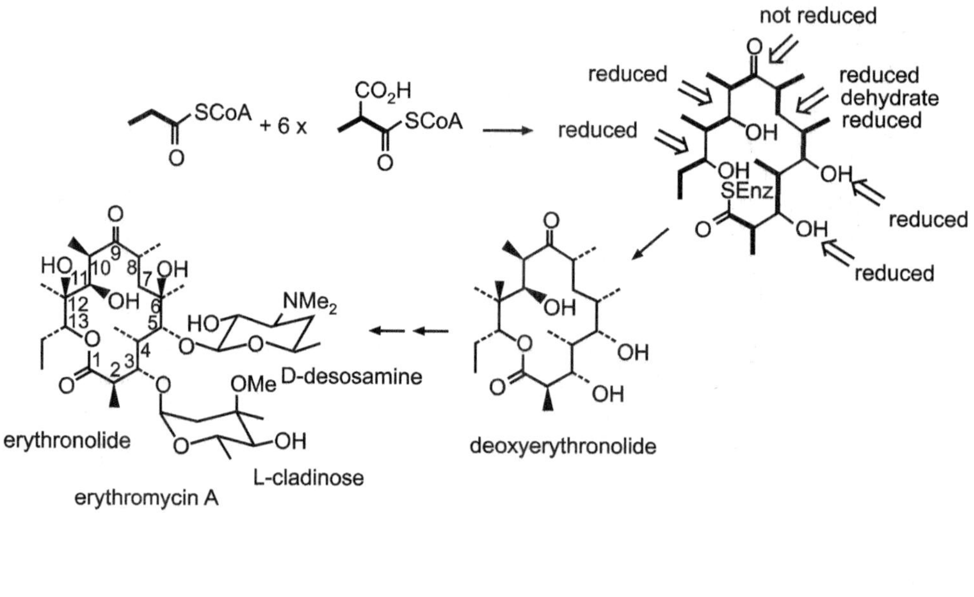

Structure Activity Relationship

1. A number of strategies have been utilised to improve the acid stability of erythromycin.

    The first approach involved the addition of hydroxylamine to ketone to form ozime e.g. roxithromycin.

    The second approach involves an alteration of C-6 hydroxyl group, which is of nucleophilic functionality that initiates erythromycin degradation. Modification that removes the nucleophilic nature of this hydroxyl group that retain antibacterial properties if the size of the group is kept small so as not to affect the ribosomal binding e.g., clarithromycin.

2. Tha azithromycin are semisynthetic 15-membered congoners in which a nitrogen atom has been introduced to expand a 14-membered precursor, and this leads to an extended spectrum of action.

Mechanism of Action : The antibacterial action of erythromycin may be inhibitory or bactericidal, particularly at higher concentrations, for susceptible organisms. Activity is enhanced at alkaline pH. Inhibition of protein synthesis occurs via binding to the 50S ribosomal RNA. Protein synthesis is inhibited because amino acyl translocation reactions and the formation of initiation complexes are blocked.

[IV] Clindamycin

Clindamycin is a chlorine-substituted derivative of lincomycin, an antibiotic that is elaborated by *Streptomyces lincolnensis.*

Lincomycin, although structurally distinct, resembles erythromycin in activity, but it is toxic and no longer used.

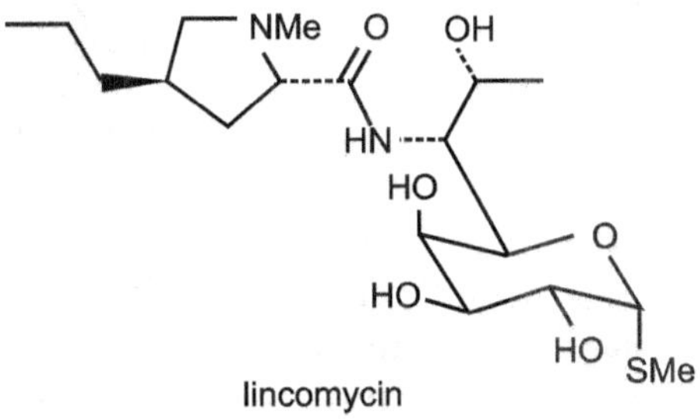

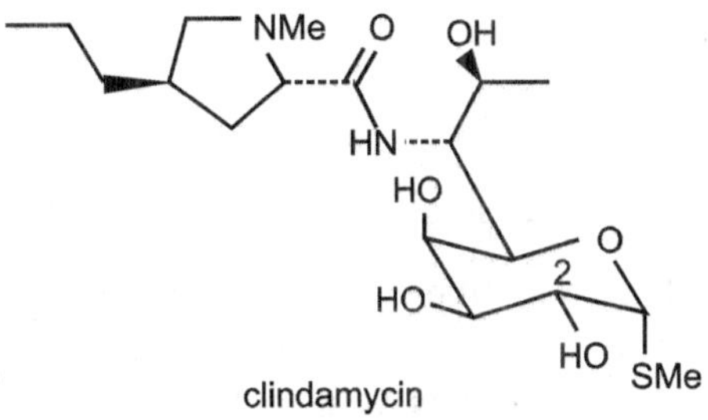

The semi-synthetic derivative clindamycin obtained by chlorination of the lincomycin with resultant inversion of stereochemistry is more active and better absorbed from the gut, and has largely replaced lincomycin. Both antibiotics are active against most Gram-positive bacteria, including penicillin-resistant staphylococci. Their use is restricted by side-effects. These include diarrhoea and occasionally serious pseudomembraneous colitis, caused by over growth of resistant strains of *Clostridium difficile*, which can cause fatalities in elderly patients. However, this may be controlled by the additional administration of vancomycin. Clindamycin finds particular application in the treatment of staphylococcal joint and bone infections such as osteomyelitis since it readily penetrates into bone. Clindamycin 2-phosphate is also of value, especially in the topical treatment of acne vulgaris and vaginal infections. Lincomycin and clindamycin inhibit protein biosynthesis by blocking the peptidyltransferase site on the 50S subunit of the bacterial ribosome. Microbial resistance may develop slowly, and in some cases has been traced to adenylylation of the antibiotic.

It bears a superficial similarity to the aminoglycosides, but has a rather more complex origin. The sugar fragment termed methyl α-thiolincosaminide, contains a thio-methyl group, and is known to be derived from two molecules of glucose, one of which provides a five-carbon unit, the other a three-carbon unit. The 4-propyl- N -methyl proline fragment does not originate from proline, but is actually a metabolite from the aromatic amino acid L-DOPA. Oxidative cleavage of the aromatic ring provides all the carbons for the pyrrolidine ring, the carboxyl, and two carbons of the propyl side-chain. The terminal carbon of the propyl is supplied by L-methionine, as are the N -methyl, and the S -methyl in the sugar fragment. Two carbons from DOPA are lost during the biosynthesis.

Mechanism of Action

Clindamycin, like erythromycin, inhibits protein synthesis by interfering with the formation of initiation complexes and with aminoacyl translocation reactions. The binding site for clindamycin on the 50S subunit of the bacterial ribosome is identical with that for erythromycin.

Resistance to clindamycin, which generally confers cross-resistance to other macrolides, is due to mutation of the ribosomal receptor site or modification of the receptor by a constitutively expressed methylase and enzymatic inactivation of clindamycin. Gram-negative aerobic species are intrinsically resistant because of poor permeability of the outer membrane.

[V] Aminoglycosides

The aminoglycosides consist of two or more amino sugars joined in glycosidic linkage to a hexose nucleus. Different aminoglycosides are distinguished by the amino sugars attached to the aminocyclitol. Streptomycin differs from the other aminoglycoside antibiotics in that it contains streptidine rather than 2-deoxystreptamine, and the aminocyclitol is not in a central position. Aminoglycosides are a group of bactericidal antibiotics originally obtained from various *Streptomyces* species and sharing chemical, antimicrobial, pharmacologic, and toxic characteristics.

The group includes streptomycin, neomycin, kanamycin, amikacin, gentamicin, tobramycin, sisomicin, netilmicin, and others. Aminoglycosides are used most widely against gram-negative enteric bacteria, especially in bacteremia and sepsis, in combination with vancomycin or a penicillin for endocarditis, and for treatment of tuberculosis. Streptomycin is the oldest and best-studied of the aminoglycosides. Aminoglycosides have a hexose ring, either streptidine (in streptomycin) or 2-deoxystreptamin (other aminoglycosides), to which various amino sugars are attached by glycosidic linkages. They are water-soluble, stable in solution, and more active at alkaline than at acid pH. Aminoglycosides frequently exhibit synergism with β-lactams or vancomycin in vitro.

In combination, they eradicate organisms more rapidly than would be predicted from the activity of either single agent.

In 1940, Waksman commenced an examination of various strains of *Actinomyces* and in short time (in 1944) isolated from A. *griseus* (commonly known as S*treptomyces griseus)* a compound to which he called streptomycin. In 1952, Waksman received a Noble prize for his work on streptomycin.

Production of Streptomycin

Like penicillin, streptomycin was first produced by surface cultures cultures but after a short time they were replaced by submerged cultures. Again, as in penicillin, the culture medium must contain protein materials such as soyabean meal and cottonseed meal, in addition to other constituents. The culture solution is kept in large vats, growth of the micro-organism begins at 24 -28°C and the maximum yield is achieved after three to five days.

Isolation of Streptomycin

The mycelium and waste materials are separated, and the antibiotic from the filtrate, either by adsorption on charocoal or on base exchange resins. It is eluted from the adsorbent by means of dilute aqueous or alcoholic mineral acids and the acidic eluate is purified by passing it through an ion exchange resin. The pure streptomycin is isolated either as sulphate or as the crystalline trihydrochloride with calcium chloride. Aseptic handling must be done during the production and isolation of the drug.

For obtaining completely sterile drug, the crystalline compounds (obtained above) are redissolved to give 25% solution which is cleared from solvent (if present), heavy metals, colour, and other impurities by passing through a seitz filter, and freeze-dried. The freeze-dried powder is transferred aseptically to small vials as in case of penicillin.

Streptomycin is a colourless, water soluble, laevorotatory base and has not yet been obtained in a crystalline compound. Its aqueoos solutions are stable in the pH range 1-10 and streptomycin in fact is more stable than penicillin.

Biosynthesis

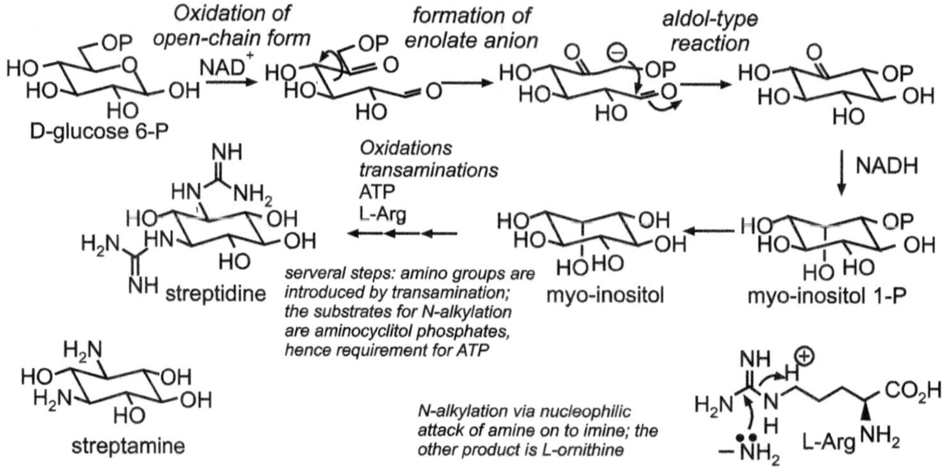

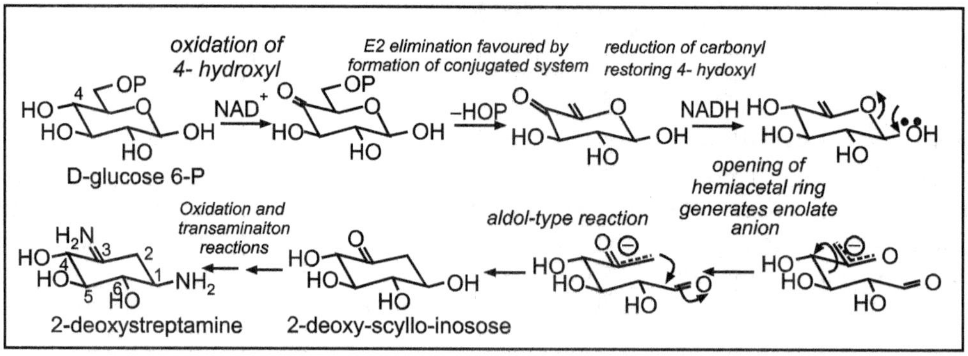

Constitution

1. The base streptomycin itself has an empirical formula $C_{21}H_{39}N_7O_{12}$.
2. Since the molecule forms a trihydrochloride, its three nitrogen atoms must be basic.

   $C_{21}H_{39}N_7O_{12}$ + 3HCl $\longrightarrow$ $C_{21}H_{39}N_7O_{12}.3HCl$
   Streptomycin   Streptomycin trihydrochloride
                                             (crystalline)

3. Mild acidic hydrolysis cleaves streptomycin into two products, namely streptidine. $C_8H_{18}N_6O_4$ and streptobiosamine, $C_{13}H_{23}NO_9$

   $C_{21}H_{39}N_7O_{12}$ + H_2O $\longrightarrow$ $C_8H_{18}N_6O_4$ + $C_{13}H_{23}NO_9$
   Streptomycin   Streptidine   Streptobiosamine

Structure Activity Relationship

The aminoglycoside consists of two or more amino sugars joined in glycoside linkage to a highly substituted 1,3-diaminocyclohexane (aminocyclitol) centrally placed ring. This ring is 2-deoxystreptamine in all aminoglycosides except streptomycin and dihydrostreptomycin where it is streptidine.

Thus, In kanamycin and gentamicin families, two amino sugars are attached to 2-deoxy-streptamine.

In stretomycin, two amino ugars are attached streptidine.

In neomycin family, there are three amino sugars attached to 2-deoxy streptamine.

So, in summary, the aminoglycoside antibiotics contain two important structural features.

1. Amino sugar portion and,
2. Centrally placed hexose ring either 2-deoxystreptamine or streptidin.

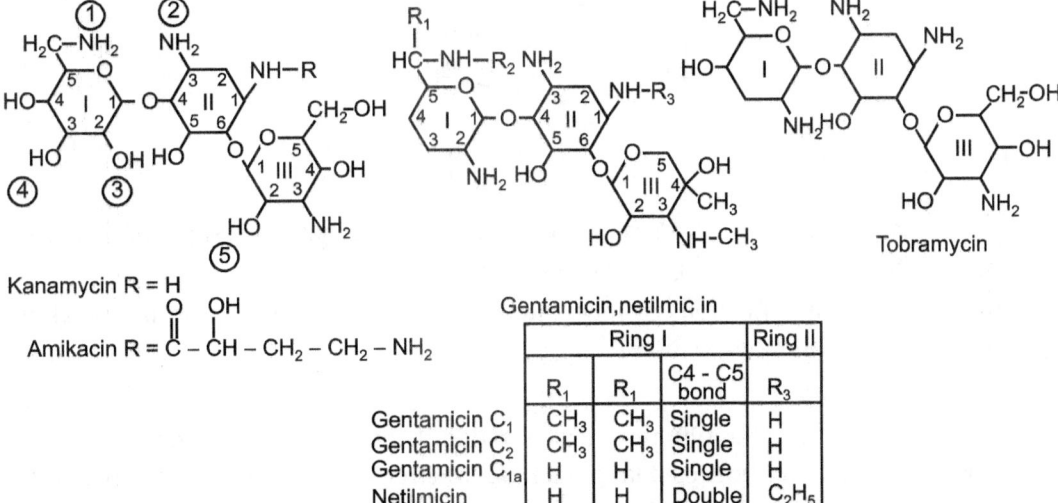

Fig. 5.11 : Structures of several important aminoglycoside antibiotics

Ring II is 2-deoxystreptamine. The resemblance between kanamycin and amikacin and between gentamicin, netilmicin, and tobramycin can be seen. The circled numerals on the kanamycin molecule indicate points of attack of plasmid-mediated bacterial transferase enzymes that can inactivate this drug. 1, 2 and 3 acetyltransferase; 4 phosphotransferase; 5 adenylyltransferase. Amikacin is resistant to modification at 2, 3, 4, and 5.

(I) SAR of aminosugar portion

The amino function at C - 6 and C - 2 serve as major target sites for bacterial inactivating enzymes.

Methylation at C - 6 position does not decrease the activity; instead increases enzyme resistance.

Cleavage of 3 - hydroxyl or the 4 - hydroxyl or both groups does not affect the activity.

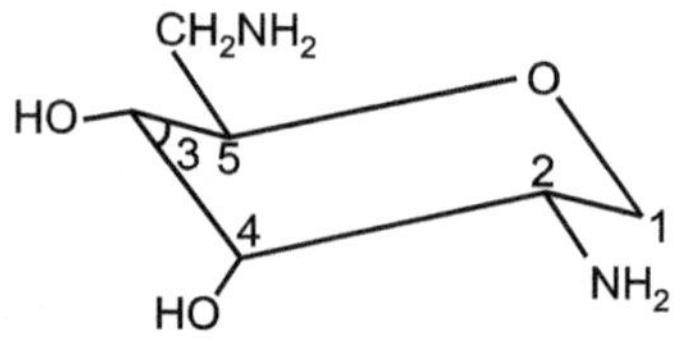

(II) SAR of centrally placed hexose ring (aminocyclitol ring)

Various modifications at C - 1 amino group have been tested. The acylation (e.g., amikacin) and ethylation (e.g. 1 - N - ethylsisomicin) though do not increase the activity, help to retain antibacterial potency.

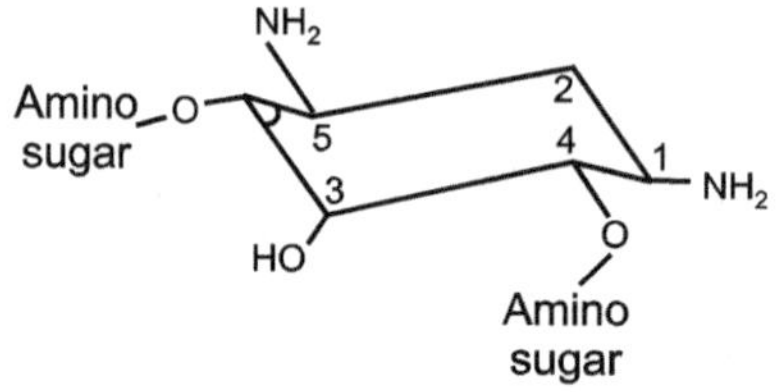

In sisomicin series, 2 - hydroxylation and 5-deoxygenation results in increased inhibition of bacterial inactivating enzyme systems.

Thus, very few modifications of the central ring are possible which do not break the activity spectrum of aminoglycosides.

Mechanism of Action

The aminoglycoside antibiotics are rapidly bactericidal. Bacterial killing is concentration-dependent, but residual bactericidal activity persists even after the serum concentration has fallen below the minimum inhibitory concentration. These properties account for the efficacy of once-daily dosing regimens.

Driven by the membrane electrical potential (interior negative), aminoglycosides diffuse through aqueous channels formed by porin proteins in the outer membrane of gram-negative bacteria and enter the periplasmic space. This rate-limiting process (and thus the antimicrobial efficacy of aminoglycosides) can be blocked or inhibited by a reduction in pH or anaerobic conditions, as in an abscess. Once inside the cell, aminoglycosides bind to polysomes and interfere with protein synthesis by causing misreading and premature termination of mRNA translation.

The resulting unusual proteins may be inserted into the cell membrane, altering permeability and further stimulating aminoglycoside transport.

The primary site of action of the aminoglycosides is the 30S ribosomal subunit; some aminoglycosides also bind to several sites on the 50S ribosomal subunit. Aminoglycosides disrupt the normal cycle of ribosomal function by interfering with the initiation of protein synthesis, leading to the accumulation of abnormal initiation complexes. Aminoglycosides also cause misreading of the mRNA template and incorporation of incorrect amino acids into the growing polypeptide chains. Aminoglycosides vary in their capacity to cause misreading, presumably owing to differences in their affinities for specific ribosomal proteins; bactericidal activity and the ability to induce misreading are strongly correlated. (**Fig. 5.12**)

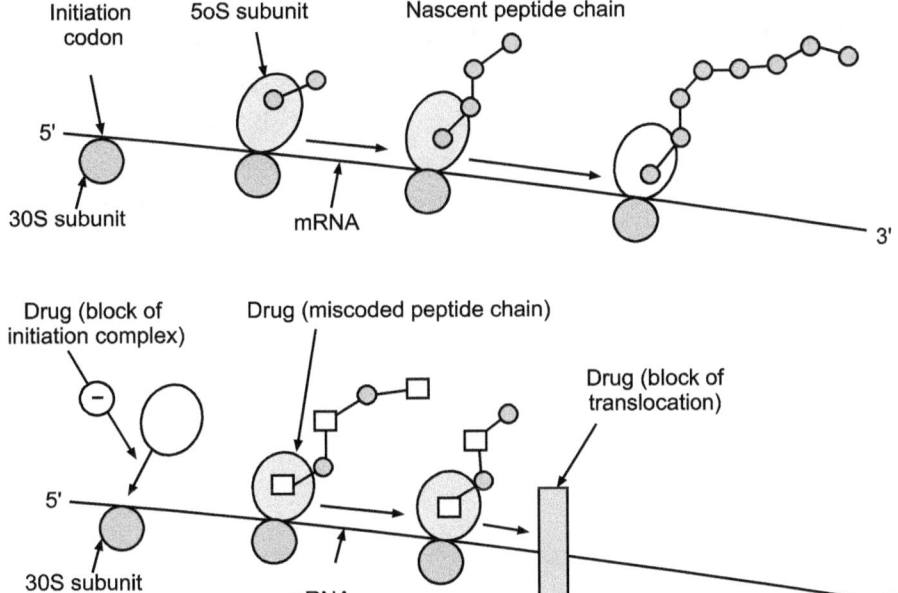

Fig. 5.12 : Inhibition of protein synthesis

Putative mechanisms of action of the aminoglycosides. Normal protein synthesis is shown in the top panel. At least three aminoglycoside effects have been described, as shown in the bottom panel: block of formation of the initiation complex; miscoding of amino acids in the emerging peptide chain due to misreading of the mRNA; and block of translocation on mRNA. Block of movement of the ribosome may occur after the formation of a single initiation complex, resulting in an mRNA chain with only a single ribosome on it, a so-called monosome.

Linezolid

It is a member of the oxazolidinones, a new class of synthetic antimicrobials. It is active against gram-positive organisms including staphylococci, streptococci, enterococci, gram-positive anaerobic cocci, and gram-positive rods such as corynebacteria and *Listeria monocytogenes*. It is primarily a bacteriostatic agent except for streptococci for which it is bactericidal. There is modest in vitro activity against *Mycobacterium tuberculosis*.

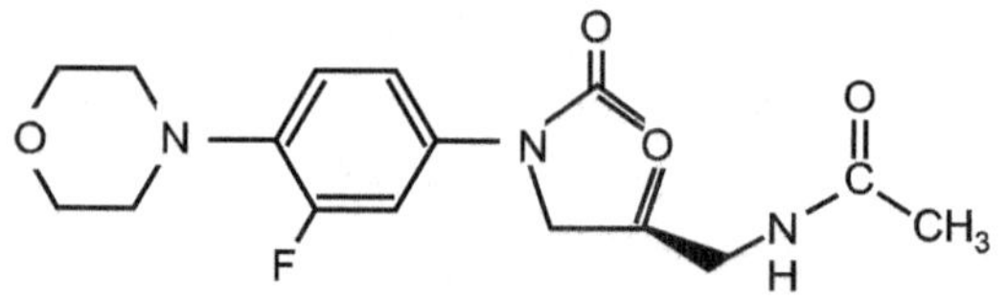

Linezolid

Linezolid inhibits protein synthesis by preventing formation of the ribosome complex that initiates protein synthesis. It acts in the early translation stage, preventing the formation of a functional initiation complex. Its unique binding site, located on 23S ribosomal RNA of the 50S subunit, results in no cross-resistance with other drug classes. Resistance is caused by mutation of the linezolid binding site on 23S ribosomal RNA.

Chapter ... 6

BIOSYNTHESIS AND ISOLATION OF SOME PHYTOCHEMICALS

Chemotherapy is the term originally used to describe the use of drugs that are 'selectively toxic' to invading micro-organisms while having minimal effects on the host. The term also embraces the use of drugs that target tumors and in fact has now come to be associated specifically with that branch of pharmacology.

Biosynthesis (*also called biogenesis or anabolism*) is an enzyme-catalysed process in cells of living organisms by which substrates are converted to more complex products. The biosynthesis process often consists of several enzymatic steps in which the product of one step is used as substrate in the following step. Examples for such multi-step biosynthetic pathways are those for the production of amino acids, fatty acids, and natural products. Biosynthesis plays a major role in all cells, and many dedicated metabolic routes combined, constitute general metabolism.

The prerequisites for biosynthesis are precursor compounds, chemical energy (such as in the form ATP), and catalytic enzymes, which may require reduction equivalents (e.g., in the form of NADH, NADPH).

ALKALOIDS

Alkaloid Chemistry: **Sertuerner** in 1806 laid the foundation of alkaloid chemistry. It is the branch of pharma phytochemistry, which deals with the study of alkaloids. He reported isolation of morphine from opium.

Alkaloid means alkali likes. The pharmacist **W. Meissner** proposed the term alkaloids in 1819. According to him **"alkaloids (alkali = base, oid = like)** are basic nitrogenous compounds of plant origin which have complex molecular structure and many pharmacological activity."

According to **Landenberg** "*Alkaloids are defined as natural plant compounds that have a basic character and contain at least one nitrogen atom in a heterocyclic ring and having biological activities.*"

There are some exception to this definition, for example –

Colchicine: Colchicine is regarded as an alkaloid although it is not heterocyclic and is scarcely basic.

Thiamine: It is heterocyclic nitrogenous base but not as a alkaloid because it is universally distributed in living matter.

Nitrogen as side chain: Some compound is grouped under alkaloids but they do not contain nitrogen in the heterocyclic ring, but contain nitrogen inside the chain e.g. ephedrine, hordenine, betanine, choline, muscarine, strychnine and tryptamine etc.

Naturally occurring open chain basic compound: These compounds have physiological activity but do not fall under alkaloids e.g. cholines, amino acid, phenylethylamines etc.

Piperine: It is neither basic in character nor does it possess any physiological activity but is included under alkaloids.

Those compounds, which fully satisfy the definitions, like physiological activity, heterocyclic basic nitrogenous ring but they do not fall under alkaloids e.g. Thiamine, caffeine, purine, theobromine, and xanthenes.

According to **Pelletier** (1983) *"an alkaloid is cyclic compound containing nitrogen in negative of oxidation state which is of limited distribution in living organisms"*.

From the above discussion, a conclusion can be drawn that it is still difficult to define an alkaloid.

Occurrence of Alkaloids

Alkaloids are chemically, nitrogenous heterocyclic basic compounds that occur in nature. They are present in about 15% of vascular plants and widely distributed in higher plants e.g. Apocynaceae, papaveraceae, papillionaceae, ranunculaceae, solanaceae.

They are present in the form of salts of organic acids, like acetic acid, oxalic acid, malic, lactic, tartaric, tannic, aconitic acid, a few are associated with sugar e.g. Solanum and veratrum groups. According to parts of plants.

Leaves: Nicotine (Nicotine and derivatives are among the earliest known and most potent insecticides)

Bark: Cinchonine, Quinine.

Seeds: Strychnine, Nibidine.

Roots: Rawelfinine, Glycyrrhizin, Punarnavine I and II.

Alkaloids are distributed in different parts of plants like in seeds (nux-vomica, colchicum); fruits (black pepper, opium); leaves (*Datura, belladonna, Hyoscyamus, Vinca,* tobacco); barks (*Cinchona,* cinnamon, kurchi); roots and rhizomes (*Rauwolfia,* ipecac, aconite) and also in whole plant (*Ephedra, Lobelia*).

Some *animals* also contain alkaloids like butterflies contain pyrrolizidine alkaloids because they feed upon the plants containing these alkaloids. Salamanders, amphibians and arthropods also contains small amount of alkaloids. Insects, marine organisms and lower plants have also been reported to contain small amount of alkaloids like ergot alkaloids from fungus.

Nomenclature

There was no systematic nomenclature. But there are some methods for nomenclature are mention below.

1. **According to their source:** These are named according to the family in which they are found. e.g. papavarine, punarnavin, ephedrin.
2. **According to their physiological response:** These are named according to their physiological response.
   e.g.. Morphine means God of dreams, Emetine means to vomit.
3. **According to their discoverers:** These are named according to their discoverer.
   e.g.. pelletierine group has been named after its discoverer, P.J. Pelletier.
4. **Prefixes:** These are named by some prefixes. e.g. epi, iso, neo, pseudo, nor- CH_3 (group not attached to nitrogen).

Physical Properties

- They are colourless, crystalline solids. Exceptions are - berberin (yellow), nicotine, coniine (liquid).
- They are insoluble in water (exceptions are the liquid alkaloids which are soluble in water) and soluble in organic solvent ($CHCl_3$, Ethyl alcohol ether)
- Taste: They are bitter in taste.
- Optically active, most are levoratatory but a few are dextrorotatory e.g. Coniine, some inactive e.g. papaverine
- Alkaloids are available in the form of salt, less toxic and don't show addiction property like morphine. Free bases of alkaloids are insoluble in water and soluble in organic solvents like chloroform, ether etc. (caffeine and colchicine are soluble in water), whereas alkaloidal salts and quaternary alkaloids are highly soluble in water but insoluble in organic solvents (lobelline HCl is soluble in $CHCl_3$, quinine sulphate is sparingly soluble in water). Alkaloids, taken in their broadest sense, may have nitrogen atom which is primary e.g. mescaline, secondary e.g. ephedrine, tertiary e.g. atropine and quaternary e.g. tubocurarine.
- Most alkaloid skeletons are derived from amino acids whereas some are derived from other groups of molecules also, such as the steroidal alkaloids with the nitrogen from glutamine or another N donor being added in later biosynthetic steps.

Classification of alkaloids on the basis of origin

(a) **True Alkaloids:** These are basic in nature, derivatives of amino acids having nitrogen in heterocyclic ring, occurs in plants as salts of organic acids. e.g. Quinine, morphine, atropine.

(b) **Proto/amino-alkaloids:** These are simple biological amines, basic in nature, derivatives of amino acids, don't have heterocyclic nitrogen atom in ring system (but in side chain). e.g. ephedrine, colchicine and mescaline.

(c) **Pseudo alkaloids:** These weakly basic nitrogenous compounds, are not derived from amino acids but have heterocyclic nitrogen atom. e.g. purine bases like caffeine and steroidal alkaloids like solasodine.

1. True and proto alkaloids (amino acid derived alkaloids)
   (a) Ornithine and lysine derived alkaloids
      (i) Pyrolidine alkaloids e.g. Nicotine
      (ii) Tropane alkaloids e.g. Atropine, Hyoscine
      (iii) Pyrrolizidine alkaloids e.g. Alkaloids of Borage and Symphytum
      (iv) Quinolizidine alkaloids e.g. Lupanine and sparteine
      (v) Indolizidine alkaloids e.g. Castanospermine (Anti-HIV)
      (vi) Piperidine alkaloids e.g. Lobeline, piperine, pelleterine and coniine
   (b) Phenylalanine and tyrosine derived alkaloids
      (i) Phenyl ethyl amine alkaloids e.g. Ephedrine
      (ii) Isoquinoline alkaloids e.g. Papaverine
      (iii) Aporphine alkaloids e.g. Apomorphine
      (iv) Morphinans e.g. Morphine, codine, thebaine
   (c) Tryptophan derived alkaloids
      (i) Tryptamine and carbolines e.g. Muscarine, serotonine, harmine and harmaline
      (ii) Indolines e.g. Neostigmine and physiostigmine
      (iii) Ergolines e.g. Lysergic acid derivative ergot alkaloids
      (iv) Monoterpenoid indole e.g. *Vinca, Cinchona, Nux-vomica, Rauwolfia* and *Camptotheca* alkaloids.
   (d) Histidine derived alkaloids e.g. Pilocarpine
2. Pseudo alkaloids (non amino acid derived alkaloids)
   (a) Alkaloids derived from terpene metabolism
      (i) Mono and sesquiterpene alkaloids e.g. alkaloids of *Nymphea* sp.
      (ii) Diterpene alkaloids e.g. alkaloids of *Aconitum* sp.
      (iii) Steroidal alkaloids e.g. alkaloids of *Solanum* and *Veratrum* sp. and kurchi alkaloids.
   (b) Purine bases e.g. caffeine and theine.
   (c) Miscellaneous alkaloids like peptide alkaloids of *Ziziphus* sp. and maytansinoids.

Chemical classification of alkaloids on the basis of heterocyclic ring

Alkaloids are mainly divided into two categories on the basis of their chemical structure i.e. heterocyclic rings (Table 6.1).

1. **Atypical alkaloids:** These are also known as non-heterocyclic alkaloids and contain nitrogen in aliphatic chain.
2. **Typical alkaloids:** These are also known as heterocyclic alkaloids and contain nitrogen in heterocyclic ring system.

Table 6.1: Classification of Alkaloids

Groups	Example	Source	Chemical structure	Uses
1. Non-Heterocyclic Alkaloids				
Phenyl ethyl amine alkaloid	Ephedrine, Mescaline, Hordenine	*Ephedra sp.* *Lophophora wiliamsii*	(phenyl-CH₂-CH₂-NH₂)	Asthama
Tropolone alkaloids	Colchicine	*Colchicum sp.*	(tropone)	Gout
Modified diterpene	Taxol	*Taxus sp.*	—	Anti cancer
2. Heterocyclic Alkaloids				
(a) Mono-nuclear Heterocyclic Alkaloids				
Pyridine	Lobeline	*Lobelia sp.*	(pyridine ring)	Asthama
Piperidine	Piperine	*Piper sp.*	(piperidine ring)	Gonorrhea, Anti oxidant
Pyrrole	Hygrine	*Coca sp.*	(pyrrole ring)	CNS-Stimulant
Pyrrolidine	Nicotine	*Tobacco sp.*	(pyrrolidine ring)	CNS Stimulant
Indiazole	Pilocarpine	*Pilocarpus sp.*	(imidazole ring)	Contraction of pupil
(b) Poly-nuclear Hetero-cyclic alkaloids				
Isoquinoline	Morphine, papervine	*Opium*	(isoquinoline ring)	Narcotic analgesic
Quinoline	Quinidine, quinidine	*Cinchona*	(quinoline ring)	Anti-malarial
Indole	Ergotamine, reserpine, vincrystrine strychinine	*Ergot, Rauwolfia, Vinca, Nux-vomica*	(indole ring)	Oxytoxic, Anti HT, Anti-cancer, CNS-stimulant

Quinazoline	Vasicine	*Vasaka*		Anti-tussive
Tropane	Atropine, hyoscine	*Datura belladonna*		Parasym-patholytic
Purine	Caffeine Theine	*Coffee, tea*		CNS stimulant
Steroid	Solasodine	*Solanum sp.*		Steroidal precursor
Terpenoid	Aconitine	*Aconite sp.*	–	CNS

Extraction and isolation of alkaloids: Alkaloids can be extracted by the following two methods
1. Direct extraction using non polar organic solvent
2. Extraction using polar solvent

1. **Direct extraction using non polar organic solvent**
   (a) The powdered material is moistened with limewater, which combines with acids, tannins and other phenolic substances and the alkaloids are extracted (exists in the plant as salts).
   (b) The extraction is then carried out with organic solvents such as ether or chloroform, filtered and the filtrate is concentrated.
   (c) The concentrated organic extract is then mixed with aqueous acid solution to form alkaloidal salts, which are soluble in aqueous acidic layer. The impurities present in the extract remain in the organic liquid.
   (d) The aqueous acidic phase is separated and alkaloidal salts present are precipitated using strong ammonia solution (make alkaline).
   (e) Precipitated alkaoidal bases are back extracted with chloroform or ether and evaporated to dryness.
   (f) The dried residue is weighed, which gives total alkaloidal content of drug.

2. **Extraction using polar solvent**
   (a) Powered drug is extracted with aqueous or alcoholic dilute acid solution, filtered and concentrated on water bath till complete evaporation of alcohol.
   (b) The concentrated extract is mixed well with organic solvent like chloroform or ether to remove pigments and other unwanted materials.
   (c) Excess of ammonia solution is then added to concentrated extract containing alkaloidal salts to precipitate alkaloidal bases.
   (d) Alkaline extract is extracted with chloroform or ether and evaporated to dryness.
   (e) The dried residue is weighed, which gives total alkaloidal content of drug.

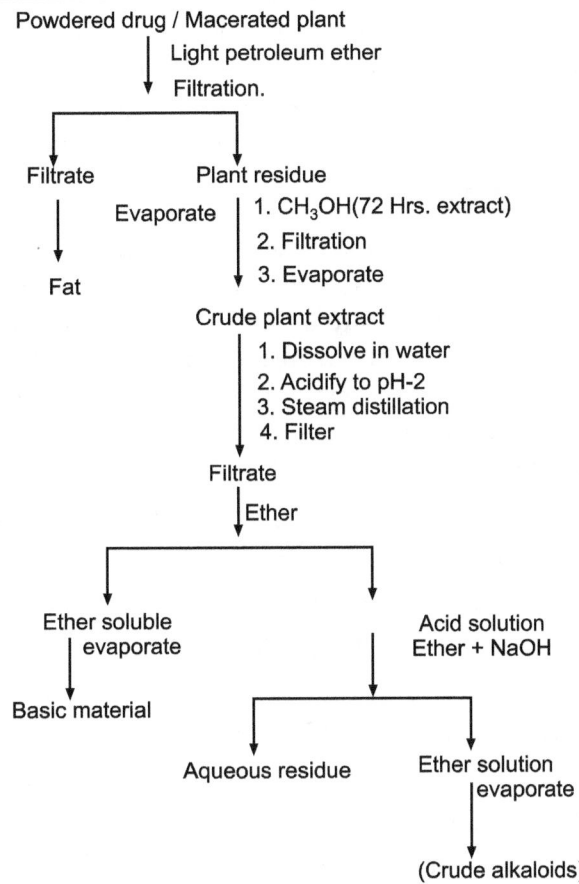

3. Separation of Alkaloids: After detection, the next step is separation of a relatively small percentage of alkaloids from a large amount of crude drugs. E.g.- Opium contains 10% morphine, Cinchona contains 5-8 % quinine, belladona- 0.2% of hyoscyamine. The required alkaloid is separated from the mixture from fractional crystallisation, chromatography and ion exchange method.

CHEMICAL TESTS FOR ALKALOIDS

Chemical tests are performed using a neutral or slightly acidic solution of a drug. The following chemical reaction given by alkaloids are-

1. **Dragendorff's Test:** Drug solution + Dragendroff's reagent (potassium bismuth iodide). Presence of alkaloids is confirmed by the formation of orangish red colour.
2. **Mayer's Test:** Drug solution + few drops of Mayer's reagent (K_2HgI_4). Formation of creamy-white precipitant confirms the presence of alkaloids.
3. **Hager's Test:** Drug solution + few drops of Hagers reagent (saturated aq. solution of picric acid), formation of crystalline yellow precipitate indicates the presence of alkaloids.

4. **Wagner's Test:** Drug solution + few drops of Wagner's reagent (dilute Iodine solution) results in the formation of reddish-brown precipitate.

5. **Tannic Acid Test:** Drug solution + few drops of tannic acid solution. Formation of buff coloured precipitate indicates the presence of alkaloids.

BIOSYNTHESIS OF ALKALOIDS

As more and more structures of alkaloids were elucidated, it becomes increasingly probable that the precursor in the biosynthesis of many alkaloids were amino acids and amino-aldehyde or amines derived from them. **Woodward** in 1948, proposed a biosynthesis of strychnine. Because of the great diversity of structure of alkaloids, it not possible to develop only one hypothesis of biosynthesis of alkaloids. Thus many pathways have been proposed, each one accounting for the biosynthesis of a number of alkaloids of related structure.

The most common amino acids that act as precursor in biosynthesis of alkaloids are

(i) Ornithine **$H_2N(CH_2)CHNH_2COOH$**

(ii) Lysine **$H_2N(CH_2)_3 CHNH_2COOH$**

(iii) Phenylalanine (R=H) **$RC_6H_5CH_2CH(NH_2)COOH$**

(iv) Tyrosine (R=OH)

(v) Methionine **$MeSCH_2CH_2CH(NH_2)COOH$**

(vi) Tryptophan

Some common reactions are

Decarboxylation : Formation of amine

$$RCH(NH_2)COOH \longrightarrow RCH_2NH_2 + CO_2$$

Oxidation : Formation of aldehyde

$$RCH(NH_2)COOH \longrightarrow RCOCOOH \longrightarrow RCHO$$

Shiff base formation

$$R_1CHO + R_2NH_2 \longrightarrow R_1CH = NR_2$$

Physical Method

These following physical methods are applied to elucidate the structure of alkaloids

- U.V. Spectroscopy
- IR Spectroscopy
- Nuclear Magnetic Resonance Spectroscopy
- Mass Spectroscopy
- Optical Rotatory Dispersion and Circular Dichroism.
- Conformational Analysis

- X-Ray Diffraction
    o Alkaloids in most cases are formed from L-amino acids.
    o Tryptophan, tyrosine, phenylalanine, lysine and arginine are common precursors.
    o Produced alone from the above precursors or in combination with other chemicals such as terpenoid moieties.
    o One or two transformations can covert the above amino acid precursors to very specific secondary metabolites.

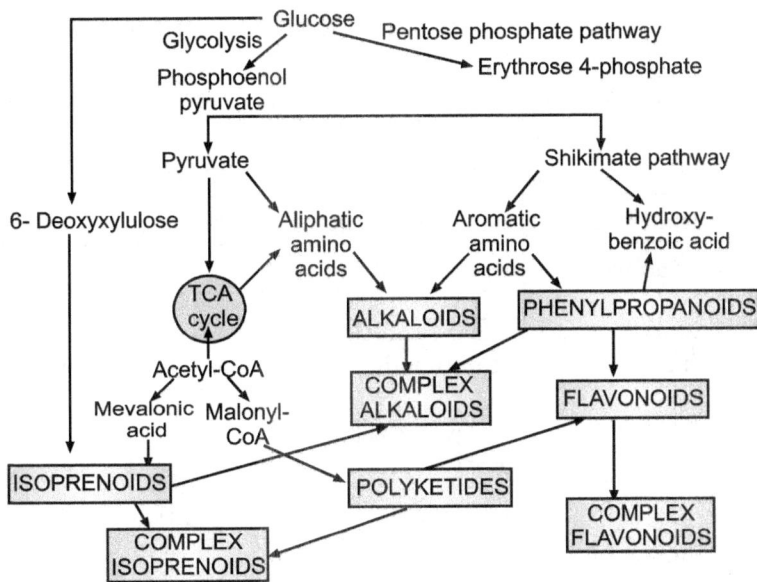

Fig. 6.1 : Production of secondary metabolites

TROPANE ALKALOIDS

Tropane alkaloids from solanaceae family arise from the esterification of acids, such as acetic acid, propanoic acid, isobutyric acid, isovaleric acid, 2-methylbutyric acid, tiglic acid, α-hydroxy-β-phenylpropionic acid, tropic acid, and atropic acid with various hydroxytropanes (α-tropanol, ∝-tropane-diol or α-tropane-triol) whereas tropane alkaloids from *Erythroxylaceae* family produces esters of benzoic acid, cinnamic acid; 3,4,5-trimethoxybenzoic and 3,4,5-trimethoxycinnamic acid residues with 2-carbomethoxytropane-3α-ol; 6,7- dihydroxytropane-3α-ol; or 6-hydroxytropane-3α-ol.

Tropane is a bicyclic amine, characterised by fusion of pyrolidine and piperidine ring sharing a single nitrogen and two carbon atoms. IUPAC name is 8-methyl, 8-aza-bicyclooctane (**Fig. 6.2**).

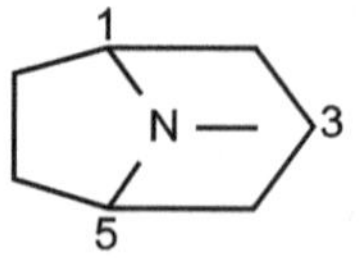

Fig 6.2: Tropane alkaloids

The tropane alkaloids are mostly found in plants of families-solanaceae, erythroxylaceae and convolvulaceae. Sometimes, they are also found in Brassicaceae (Cruciferae), Euphorbiaceae, Oleaceae, Proteaceae, and Rhizophoraceae families. The family *Solanaceae* comprises of about 100 genera and 3000 species and the most commonly found genera are *Datura, Brugmansia, Hyoscyamus, Atropa, Scopolia, Anisodus, Przewalskia, Atropanthe, Physochlaina, Mandragora, Anthotroche, Cyphanthera,* and *Duboisia*.

The most important natural tropane alkaloids are hyoscyamine, scopolamine, and cocaine.

Table 6.2: Important tropane alkaloids

Sr. No.	Alkaloid Name	Hydroxy Tropane	Acid
1.	Hyoscyamine	tropane-3α-ol	Tropic acid
2.	Scopolamine	6,7-epoxytropane-3α-ol	Tropic acid
3.	Cocaine	2-carbomethoxytropane-3α-ol	Tropic acid

L-Hyoscyamine

L-Scopolamine

L-Cocaine

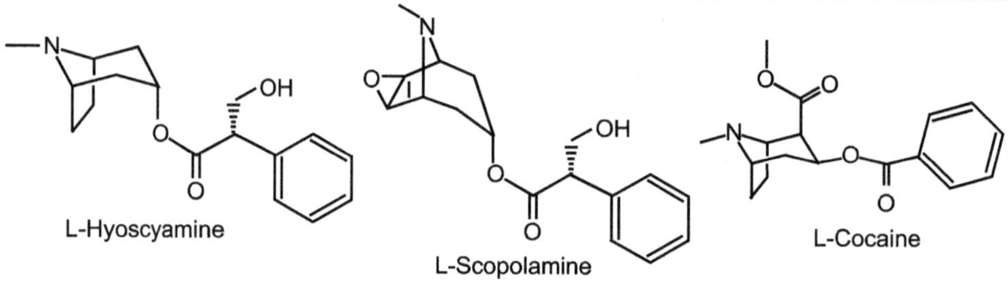

Chemistry and Properties
Structure

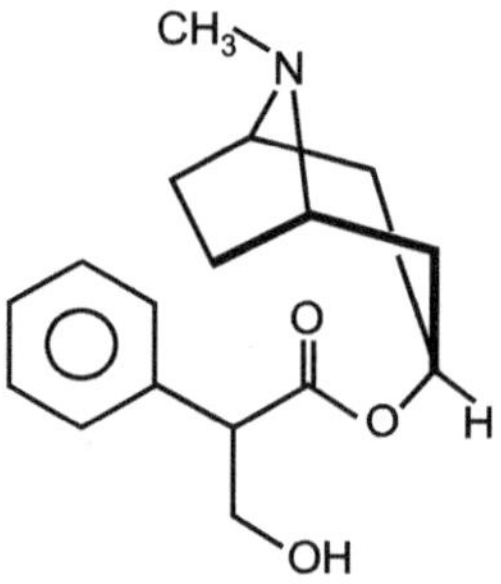

- Melting point −116°C to 118°C.
- Molecular formula −$C_{17}H_{23}NO_3$

- On hydrolysis it gives alcohol, tropine, and tropic acid which indicates that atropine is an ester.

  $C_{17}H_{23}NO_3 + H_2O \longrightarrow C_8H_9NO + C_{19}H_{10}O_3$
  atropine   tropine   tropic acid

- It is optically inactive (±) atropine is racemate form of hyoscyamine.
- **Solubility:** Insoluble in ether. Easily soluble in chloroform and alcohol. Sparingly soluble in water.
- **UV (Ethanol):** λ_{max} at 246, 251.6, 257, 263.5, 271 nm
- **IR (KBr):** V_{max} 3070 (OH⁻ Hydrogen bonding), 2930 (C–H stretching for aliphatic), 2810 (N–CH$_3$ stretch for amine), 1725 (O–C = O stretching for ester), 1595, 1580 (C = C stretching for Aromatic), 1155, 1030 (C–C–O stretching for ether), 770, 725 and 690 (mono substituted for aromatic) cm^{-1}.
- **^{1}H NMR (CDCl$_3$):** δ 7.23 (5H, s, Ar-H), 4.96 (1H, t, H-3), 3.9 (1H, m, H 10), 2.93 (2H, s, H-5), 1.66 (8H, m, H-2,4,6,7). [s = singlet, t = triplet, m = multiplet, Ar = Aromatic, H = hydrogen (proton)]

Identification Test
1. **Vitali –Morin reaction :** Add 2 to 3 drops of sulphuric acid on atropine or alkaloids (1μg) than evaporate this to dryness, and add 0.3 mL of 3% solution of potassium hydroxide in methanol, which produces purple colour which indicates the presence of atropine
2. Addition of AgNO$_3$ solution to solution of hyoscine hydrobromide gives yellowish white precipitate which is soluble in dilute ammonia and insoluble in nitric acid.

Thin Layer Chromatography
- 1% solution of atropine dissolved in 2N acetic acid is spotted over silica gel G plate and eluted in the solvent system of strong NH$_3$ solution – methanol (1 : 5 : 100).
- TLC plate is spread with an acidified iodoplatinate solution.
- Rf – 0.18.
- Solvent system – Acetone : 0.5% sodium chloride solution (1 : 5).
- Spraying reagents – Dragendroff's reagent.

Biosynthesis

The biosynthesis of tropane alkaloids commences from L-ornithine which is a part of the citric acid cycle / Krebs cycle and mainly formed from glutamic acid. L-ornithine is converted into putrescine by decarboxylation, which further on N-methylation, is converted into N-methyl putrescine; the enzyme responsible is putrescine N-methyl transferase. N-methyl putrescine is further converted into N-methyl-Δ^1-pyrolinium cation through the action of N-methyl putrescine oxidase and there is formation of Schiff base. The attack of acetyl Co-A moieties on cation forms an intermediate. This intermediate acts as a chief precursor for the biosynthesis of different tropane alkaloids as represented for biosynthesis of three types of tropane alkaloids. Hydrolysis and decarboxylation generates tropinone which on reduction yields tropine (a hydroxy tropane). The reaction between tropine and tropic acid obtained from phenylalanine gives L-hyoscyamine and L-scopolamine.

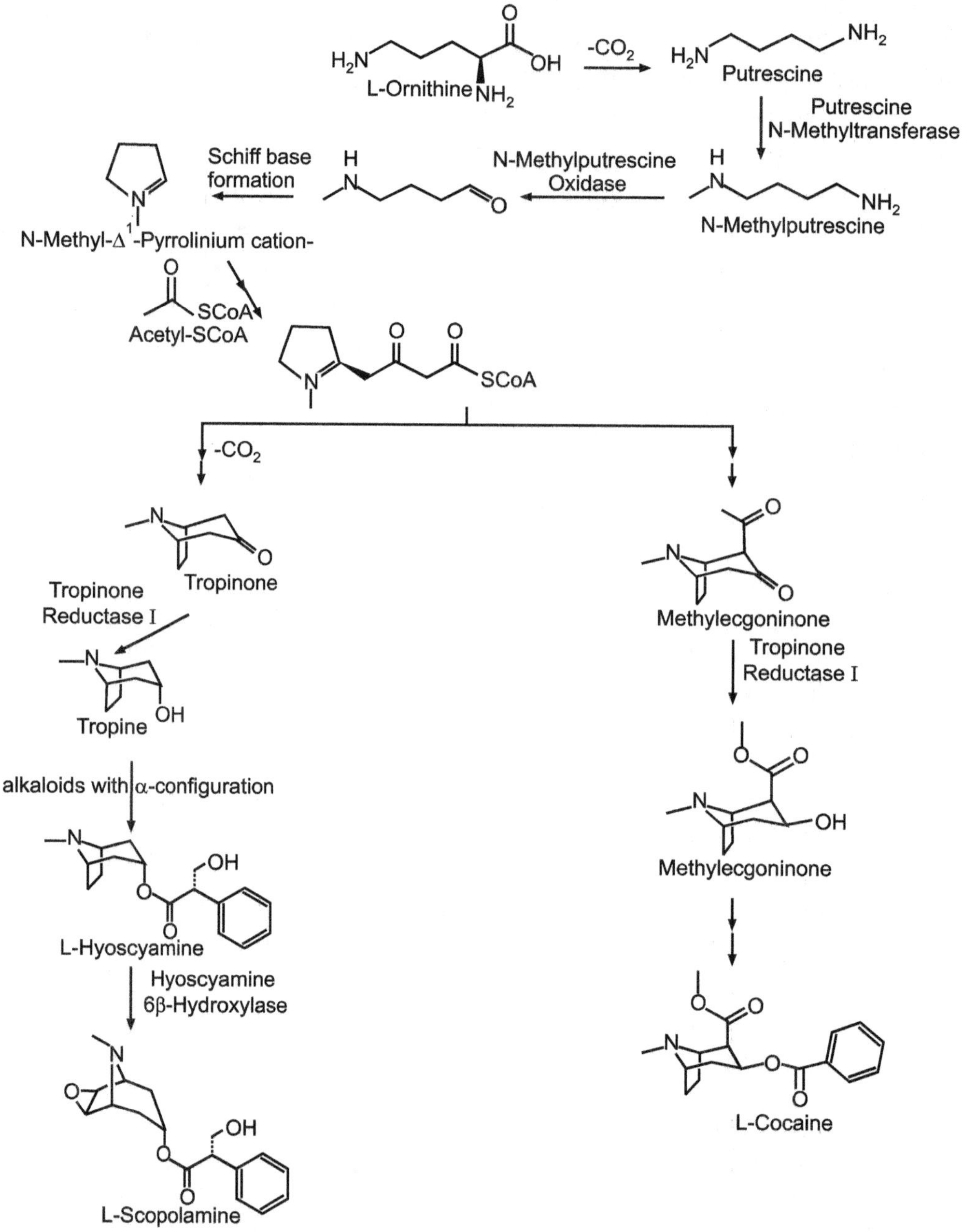

Fig. 6.3: Biosynthesis of tropane alkaloid

Extraction of Tropane Alkaloids

Tropane alkaloids like other alkaloids are usually found in the seeds, root, leaves, or bark of the plant. A common method of isolation of these alkaloids is as follows. The plant is dried, then finely powdered and extracted with boiling methanol. The solvent is distilled off, and the residue is treated with inorganic acids, whereupon the bases are extracted as their soluble salts. The free bases are liberated by the addition of sodium carbonate and extracted with various solvents, e.g., ether, chloroform, etc. The mixtures of bases thus obtained are separated by various methods into individual compounds. Most recent methods of separation involve the use of chromatography. Now-a-days most tropane analogs are synthesised but alkaloids like atropine, hyoscyamine and scopolamine are still obtained from natural sources.

Isolation

Powdered drug/juice + moisten drug with aqueous solution of K_2CO_3
↓
Extract with $CHCl_3$
↓
Evaporate solvent
↓
Extract with dil. H_2SO_4
↓
Acidic extract made alkaline by K_2CO_3
↓
Atropine precipitates out
↓
Crystallise by use of alcohol

Structure Activity Relationship

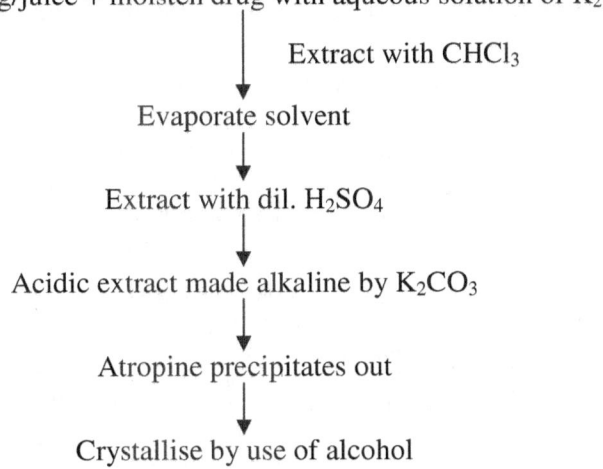

1. The primary part of attachment to cholinergic sites is through the positively charged nitrogen (cationic head). In tertiary amines, they are quaternised by protonation at physiological pH which causes lack of CNS activity.
2. For hydrophobic bond formation and vander waal interaction an aryl group (phenyl thienyl) and cycloaliphatic (cyclohexyl) group is necessary.
3. The presence of free hydroxyl or carbamide is also important for hydrogen bonding with receptor.
4. L – hyoscyamine is more active than d-isomer.
5. Difference between hydroxyl group and quaternary nitrogen is between $2°$ to $3°$.

6. It is similar in structure to acetylcholine but contains an additional substituent which enhances binding to receptor.
7. It has acetic acid ester of amino alcohol which is therapeutically useful. Minimal structure necessary for pure antagonistic activity is due to following structure

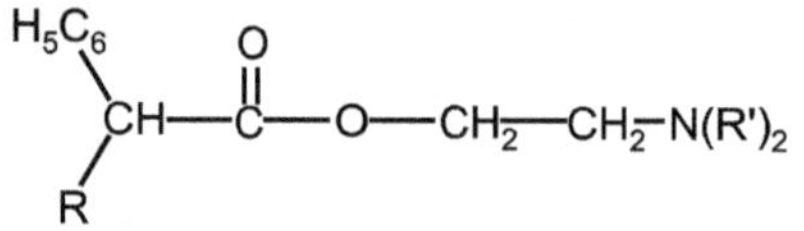

H_5C_6―CH(R)―C(=O)―O―CH_2―CH_2―N(R')$_2$ R = hydroxyl alkyl, alkyl, cycloalkyl, or heterocyclic
R' = alkyl.

8. In the above general structure, the antagonist may contain larger groups than methyl on the nitrogen atom. In general, these groups should not be larger than butyl, if the compound is to be an effective antagonist.
9. The nitrogen atom in an antagonist need not always be quaternised Since pH of the receptor is acidic, this amino group gets protonated and carries a positive charge that interacts with the anioinic site of the receptor.
10. The acyl group in an antagonist, is always larger than the acyl group in acetylcholine. The larger acyl group ensures that the compound is not a partial agonist.
11. Hydrophobhic substituents increases the affinity of the antagonist by binding to receptor area. However receptor area is not uniform in its hydrophobic nature. The fact that esters of triphenyl acetic acid have low potency can be justified only if the hydrophobic area does not accomodate binding by a third phenyl ring.
12. The high potency of ester and amides of tropic acid result from their ability to H – bond with suitable group to the receptor, surrounded by hydrophobic area.

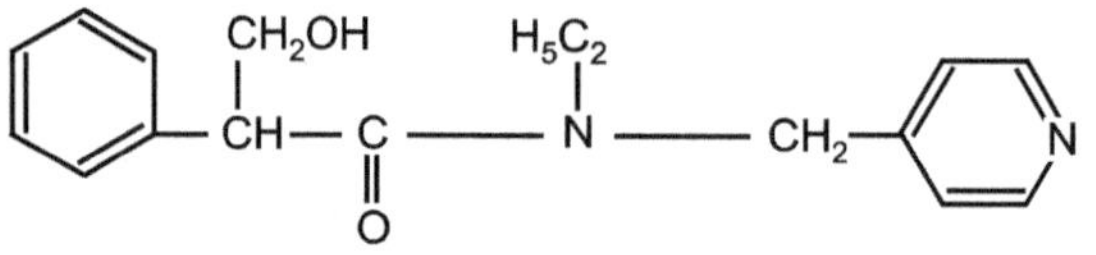

[Structure: Phenyl―CH(CH$_2$OH)―C(=O)―N(C$_2$H$_5$)―CH$_2$―pyridyl]

Tropicamide
It is used to produce mydriasis and cycloplegia.

Mechanism of Action of Tropane

Atropine and other muscarinic antagonists competitively bind to receptors with acetylcholine or other agonists. Muscarinic receptors are GPCRs (G-protein coupled receptors). They have 7-helicalamino acid structure, the aspartate present on the –NH$_2$ end of the receptor. If concentration of acetylcholine is increased, antagonistic activity occurs.

Tropane alkaloids are commonly described as anti-cholinergic compounds, due to their ability to bind to muscarinic acetylcholine receptors and hence acting as competitive antagonists at these receptors. According to the organ distribution, different subtypes of muscarinic receptors have been described, denoted M_1 to M_5, all belonging to the class of G-protein coupled receptors. M_1 represents a population of receptors localised in the central nervous systems, as well as in gastric and salivary glands. M_2 receptors occur in the atria of the heart, at smooth muscles of the gastrointestinal tract as well as in the central nervous system. M_3 receptors dominate at exocrine glands including the salivary glands, occur in the gastro-intestinal tract as well as in the eye, and on the endothelium of blood vessels. M_4 receptors are predominantly found in the central nervous system and M_5 receptors are found especially in the substantia nigra of the central nervous system, in the salivary glands and in the ciliary muscle of the iris of the eye. Atropine is a non-selective antagonist of all classes of muscarinic receptors, but known to have a stimulating effect on the central nervous system, whereas scopolamine is a depressant of the central nervous system.

Intoxications with tropane alkaloids are characterised by dryness of the mucosa in the upper digestive and respiratory tract, constipation, pupil dilation (mydriasis) and disturbance of vision, photophobia and changes in heart rate, dose-dependent hypertension or hypotension, bradycardia or tachycardia as well as arrhythmias, nervousness, restlessness, irritability, disorientation, ataxia, seizures and respiratory depression. As anticholinergic compounds disturb the balance between cholinergic and adrenergic regulation of organ functions, secondary effects may occur. A prominent example is the effect of atropine on the heart rate, which commences as bradycardia at low (therapeutic) doses, progressing into tachycardia and arrhythmia at higher (toxic) doses.

Pharmacological Properties: The Prototypical Alkaloids Atropine and Scopolamine

Atropine and scopolamine differ quantitatively in antimuscarinic actions, particularly in their ability to affect the CNS. Atropine has almost no detectable effect on the CNS at doses that are used clinically. In contrast, scopolamine has prominent central effects at low therapeutic doses. The basis for this difference is probably the greater permeation of scopolamine across the blood–brain barrier. Because atropine has limited CNS effects, it is preferred to scopolamine for most purposes.

Table 6.3: Effects of Atropine in Relation to Dose

Dose	Effects
0.5 mg	Slightly cardiac slowing; some dryness of mouth; inhibition of sweating.
1 mg	Definite dryness of mouth; thirst; acceleration of heart, sometimes preceded by slowing; mild dilation of pupils.
2 mg	Rapid heart rate; palpitation; marked dryness of mouth; dilated pupils; some blurring of near vision.
5 mg	All the above symptoms marked; difficulty in speaking and swallowing; restlessness and fatigue; headache; dry, hot skin; difficulty in micturition; reduced intestinal peristalsis.
10 mg and more	Above symptoms more marked; pulse rapid and weak; iris practically obliterated; vision very blurred; skin flushed, hot, dry and scarlet, ataxia, restlessness, and excitement; hallucinations and delirium, coma.

Central Nervous System Atropine in therapeutic doses (0.5–1 mg) causes only mild vagal excitation as a result of stimulation of the medulla and higher cerebral centers. With toxic doses of atropine, central excitation becomes more prominent, leading to restlessness, irritability, disorientation, hallucinations, or delirium (see discussion of atropine poisoning, below). With still larger doses, stimulation is followed by depression, leading to circulatory collapse and respiratory failure after a period of paralysis and coma.

Scopolamine in therapeutic doses normally causes CNS depression manifested as drowsiness, amnesia, fatigue, and dreamless sleep, with a reduction in rapid eye movement (REM) sleep. Scopolamine also causes euphoria and is therefore subject to some abuse. Scopolamine is effective in preventing motion sickness.

The belladonna alkaloids and related muscarinic receptor antagonists have long been used in parkinsonism. These agents can be effective adjuncts to treatment with levodopa. Muscarinic receptor antagonists also are used to treat the extrapyramidal symptoms that commonly occur as side effects of conventional antipsychotic drug therapy. Certain antipsychotic drugs are relatively potent muscarinic receptor antagonists, and these cause fewer extrapyramidal side effects.

Eye

Muscarinic receptor antagonists block the cholinergic responses of the pupillary sphincter muscle of the iris and the ciliary muscle controlling lens curvature. Thus, they dilate the pupil (mydriasis) and paralyse accommodation (cycloplegia). Locally applied atropine and scopolamine produce ocular effects of considerable duration; accommodation and pupillary reflexes may not fully recover for 7–12 days; thus, other muscarinic antagonists with shorter durations of action are preferred as mydriatics. Muscarinic receptor antagonists administered systemically have little effect on intraocular pressure except in patients predisposed to narrow-angle glaucoma, in whom the pressure may occasionally rise dangerously.

Cardiovascular System

Heart

Although the dominant response to atropine is tachycardia, the heart rate often decreases slightly (4–8 beats/min) transiently with average clinical doses (0.4–0.6 mg). The slowing is usually absent after rapid intravenous injection. Larger doses of atropine cause regressively increasing tachycardia by blocking vagal effects on M2 receptors on the SA node. Resting heart rate increased by 35–40 beats/min in young men given 2 mg of atropine intramuscularly. The maximal heart rate (e.g., in response to exercise) is not altered by atropine. The influence of atropine is most noticeable in healthy young adults, in whom vagal tone is considerable. In infancy and old age, even large doses of atropine may fail to accelerate the heart. Atropine often produces cardiac arrhythmias, but without significant cardiovascular symptoms. With low doses of scopolamine (0.1–0.2 mg), the cardiac slowing is greater than with atropine. With higher doses, a transient cardioacceleration may be observed. Adequate doses of atropine can abolish many types of reflex vagal cardiac slowing or a systole

For example, from inhalation of irritant vapors, stimulation of the carotid sinus, pressure on the eyeballs, peritoneal stimulation, or injection of contrast dye during cardiac catheterisation. Atropine also prevents or abruptly abolishes bradycardia or a systole caused by choline esters, acetylcholinesterase inhibitors, or other parasympathomimetic drugs, as well as cardiac arrest from electrical stimulation of the vagus. The removal of vagal influence on the heart by atropine also may facilitate AV conduction.

Circulation

Atropine, alone, has little effect on blood pressure, an expected result since most vessels lack cholinergic innervation. However, in clinical doses, atropine completely counteracts the peripheral vasodilation and sharp fall in blood pressure caused by choline esters. Atropine in toxic, and occasionally therapeutic doses can dilate cutaneous blood vessels, especially those in the blush area (atropine flush).

Respiratory Tract

Belladonna alkaloids inhibit secretions of the nose, mouth, pharynx, and bronchi, and thus dry the mucous membranes of the respiratory tract. Reduction of mucous secretion and mucociliary clearance resulting in mucus plugs are undesirable side effects of atropine in patients with airway disease. Inhibition by atropine of bronchoconstriction caused by histamine, bradykinin, and the eicosanoids presumably reflects the participation of parasympathetic efferents in the bronchial reflexes elicited by these agents. The ability to block the indirect bronchoconstrictive effects of these mediators that are released during attacks of asthma forms the basis for the use of anticholinergic agents, along with β-adrenergic receptor agonists, in the treatment of asthma.

Gastrointestinal Tract

Atropine can completely abolish the effects of Acetylcholine (and other parasympathomimetic drugs) on the motility and secretions of the Gastrointestinal tract, but can only incompletely inhibit the effects of vagal impulses. This difference is particularly striking in the effects of atropine on gut motility. Preganglionic vagal fibers that innervate the Gastrointestinal tract synapse not only with postganglionic cholinergic fibers, but also with a network of noncholinergic intramural neurons. These neurons of the enteric plexus release numerous neurotransmitters and neuromodulators (e.g., 5-Hydroxytryptamine, Dopamine and myriad peptides) whose actions atropine does not block and which can effect changes in motility. Similarly, while vagal activity modulates gastrin-elicited histamine release and gastric acid secretion, the actions of gastrin can occur independently of vagal tone. Histamine H_2 receptor antagonists and proton pump inhibitors have replaced nonselective muscarinic antagonists as inhibitors of acid secretion.

Secretions

Salivary secretion, mediated through M3 receptors, is particularly sensitive to inhibition by muscarinic receptor antagonists, which can completely abolish the copious, watery, parasympathetically induced secretion. The mouth becomes dry, and swallowing and talking may become difficult. Gastric secretions during the cephalic and fasting phases are reduced markedly by muscarinic antagonists; the intestinal phase of gastric secretion is only partially inhibited. Atropine also reduces the cytoprotective secretions (HCO_3-, mucus) of the superficial epithelial cells

Motility

The parasympathetic nerves enhance both tone and motility and relax sphincters, thereby favouring intestinal transit. Muscarinic antagonists produce prolonged inhibitory effects on the motor activity of the Gastrointestinal tract; relatively large doses are needed to produce such inhibition. The complex myenteric nervous system can regulate motility independently of parasympathetic control,

Other Smooth Muscles

1. **Urinary Tract:** Muscarinic antagonists decrease the normal tone and amplitude of contractions of the ureter and bladder, and often eliminate drug-induced enhancement of ureteral tone, but at doses of atropine that inhibit salivation and lacrimation and cause blurring of vision. Control of bladder contraction is complex, involving mainly M_2 receptors at multiple sites and also M_3 receptors that can mediate detrusor muscle contraction.

2. **Biliary Tract:** Atropine exerts a mild antispasmodic action on the gallbladder and bile ducts, an effect that usually is insufficient to overcome or prevent the marked spasm and increase in biliary duct pressure induced by opioids, for which nitrites are more effective.

Sweat Glands and Temperature

Small doses of atropine or scopolamine inhibit the activity of sweat glands innervated by sympathetic cholinergic fibers, making the skin hot and dry. After large doses or at high environmental temperatures, sweating may be sufficiently depressed to raise the body temperature.

CINCHONA ALKALOIDS

Quinoline alkaloids is a heterocyclic aromatic organic compound include two fold carbon rings comprising one nitrogen. The chemical formula is C_9H_7N.

These are biosynthetically derived from tryptophan amino acid. e.g. Cinchona alkaloids. Cinchona is the dried stem and root barks of *Cinchona succirubra* (known as Red Cinchona), *C. Ledgeriana.*, *C. calisaya* (known as yellow cinchona), and *C. officinalis* (known as pale cinchona) Family Rubiaceae.

Quinoline is a basic structure of quinine, the malarial remedy found in cinchona tree (*Cinchona calisaya, Cinchona ledgeriana, Cincohna succiruba* and *Cinchona officinalis*) bark. The alkaloid quinine is poisonous to *Plasmodium vivax* and three supplementary classes, that cause malaria, although many synthetic anti-malarial drugs such as chloroquine and primaquine have been developed currently.

In general, the alkaloids containing essentially the **'quinoline'** nucleus include a series of alkaloids obtained exclusively from the **cinchona bark**, the major members of this particular group are, namely: **quinine, quinidine, cinchonine** and **cinchonidine.** Interestingly, more than twenty five alkaloids have been isolated and characterised either from the Yellow *Cinchona i.e., Cinchona calisaya* Wedd and *Cinchona ledgeriana* Moens e.g. Trimen, or from the Red *Cinchona i.e., Cinchona succirubra* Pavon e.g. Klotzsch (Family: *Rubiaceae*). The aforesaid alkaloids are also found in their hybrids as well as in the *Cuprea* Bark obtained from *Remijia pedunculata* and *Remijia purdieana* belonging to the natural order *Rubiaceae*.

However, it has been revealed that an average commercial yield of the **cinchona alkaloids** in the dry bark materials from the said plant materials are as follows: **quinine** (5.7%); **quinidine** (0.1-0.3%); **cinchonine** and **cinchonidine** (0.20.4%). Nevertheless, the other closely related minor alkaloids are present in relatively smaller quantities.

Chemistry

Basic Structures of Cinchona Alkaloids: The various quinoline alkaloids, which possess potent medicinal activities are **quinine, quinidine, cinchonine,** and **cinchonidine.** It is interesting to observe that these alkaloids not only have a closely related structure but also similar medicinal characteristics. These alkaloids possess the *basic skeleton* of 9'-rubanol that is derived from the parent compound known as ruban. Thus, ruban is obtained from the combination of *two* distinct heterocyclic nuclii, namely: (*a*) 4-methyl quinoline nucleus, and (*b*) quinuclidine nucleus. However, this particular nomenclature was suggested by **Rabe** so as to simplify the naming of such compounds and also to signify its origin from the natural order *Rubiaceae*.

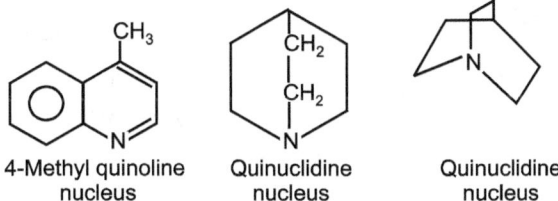

Fig. 6.4: Structure of 4-methyl quinoline nucleus, and (*b*) quinuclidine nucleus

The basic skeleton of *Cinchona* alkaloids is Ruban-9-Ol.

- Ruban nucleus is a combined skeleton formed from a quinoline ring attached through a methylene group to a quinuclidine ring (a bicyclic ring contain N).

- In Rubanol, the methylene group is oxidised to a secondary alcoholic group and the carbon atom becomes asymmetric.
- *Cinchona* alkaloids are di-acidic bases (due to presence of 2N atoms).

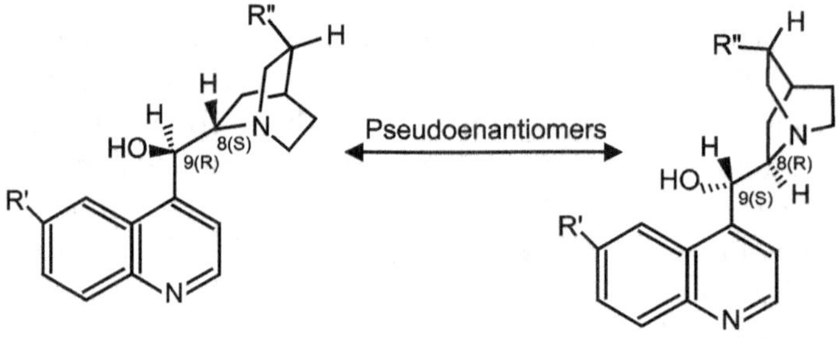

Cinchona alkaloids contains two groups of diastereo-isomers [Quinine (levo) and Quinidine (dextro)] and [Cinchonine (dextro) and Cinchonidine (levo)].

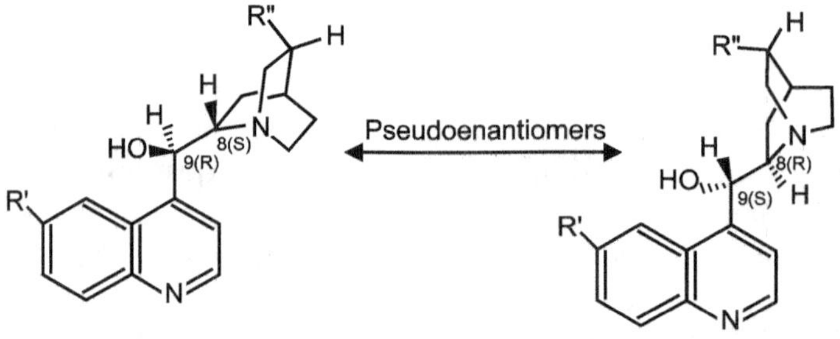

R' = OMe		R' = OMe	
Quinine	R" = vinyl	Quinine	R" = vinyl
Dihydroquinine	R" = Et	Dihydroquinine	R" = Et

R' = H		R' = H	
Cinchonidine	R" = vinyl	Cinchonine	R" = vinyl
Dihydrocinchondine	R" = Et	Dihydrocinchonine	R" = Et

Isolation

The isolation of all the four important quinoline alkaloids, such as: **quinine, cinchonine; cinchonidine** and **quinidine** may be accomplished by adopting the following steps carefully and sequentially.

Step 1: The *Cinchona* bark is dried, powdered, sieved and treated with calcium oxide (slaked lime), NaOH solution (10% w/v) and water and kept as such for 6-8 hours.

Step II: The resulting mixture is treated with benzene in sufficient quantity and refluxed for 12-16 hours. The mixture is then filtered while it is hot.

Step III: The hot filtrate is extracted successively with 6N. sulphuric acid. The mixture of alkaloidal bisulphate is heated upto 90°C and maintained at this temperature upto 20-30 minutes.

Step IV: The resulting solution is cooled to room temperature and made alkaline by the addition of solid pure sodium carbonate till a pH of 6.5 is attained.

Step V: The alkaloidal sulphate solution thus obtained is treated with sufficient quantity of activated charcoal powder (1g per 1L), boiled, mixed vigorously and filtered.

Step VI: Cool the hot filtrate slowly in a refrigerator (2-10°C) overnight and again filter. Collect the residue and the filtrate separately.

Step VII: The residue (or precipitate) of quinine sulphate is boiled with water and made alkaline by adding cautiously solid sodium carbonate. The resulting precipitate is that of **quinine.**

Step VIII: The filtrate obtained from step-VI comprises of **cinchonine, cinchonidine** and **quinidine;** which is treated with NaOH solution (10% w/v) very carefully to render it just alkaline. It is successively extracted with adequate quantity of ether. The lower (aqueous layer) and the upper (ethereal layer) are collected separately.

Step IX: The aqueous layer contains **cinchonine.** It is evaporated to dryness in a rotary film evaporator, extracted with absolute ethanol, decolourised with activated charcoal powder and allowed to crystallise slowly in a refrigerator (2-10°C) overnight. The crystals of **cinchonine** are obtained.

Step X: The ethereal layer obtained in step-VIII contains **quinidine** and **cinchonidine.** It is extracted with dilute HCl (2N) several times till a drop of the extract on evaporation does not give a positive test for alkaloids. The combined acidic extract is neutralised by adding solid sodium potassium tartrate carefully. The resulting mixture is filtered and the precipitate and the filtrate collected separately.

Step XI: The precipitate of **cinchonidine tartrate** is treated with dilute HCl carefully. The resulting solution of alkaloid hydrochloride is made alkaline by the addition of dilute ammonium hydroxide when **cinchonidine** is obtained as a precipitate.

Step XII: The filtrate obtained from Step-X contains quinidine tartrate which is treated with solid potassium iodide powder carefully till the whole of quinidine gets precipitated as quinidine hydroiodide salt. It is filtered and the solid residue is finally treated with dilute NH_4OH to obtain the precipitate of **quinidine.**

Schematic Method of Isolation of *Cinchona* Alkaloids

```
Powdered crude drug + NaOH + CaO + Water
          (Reflux with Benzene)
                │ Filter while hot
                ▼
           Hot filtrate
   [Extract with dilute sulphuric acid(2N)]
                │
                ▼
        Alkaloids bisulphate
              Δ │ 90°C
                ▼
  Alkalify to pH 6.5 with pure sodium carbonate
                │
                ▼
  Alkaloids sulphate, boil with activated charcoal powder
                │ Filter
                ▼
        Chill the clear filtrate
         ┌──────────┴──────────┐
         ▼                     ▼
      Filtrate          Precipitate of quinine sulphate
[Quinidine, Cinchonine, Cinchonidine]
         │                     │ Add boiling water
   Add NaOH and Extract        │ + Sodium Carbonate
   with Ether (4/5-Times)      ▼
   ┌─────┴─────┐            Quinine
   ▼           ▼
Aqueous layar  Ethereal layar
(Cinchonine)   (Quinidine + Cinchoridine)
   │                 │ Extract with
   │                 │ dilute HCl
   │                 ▼
   │         Neutralise acid solution
   │         with Sod.Pot. Tartarate
   │                 │
Evaporate to dryness,│
extract with ethanol,│
decolourise with charcoal,
and allow it to      │
crystallise gradually│
   ▼          ┌──────┴──────┐
Cinchonine   ▼             ▼
         Precipitate      Filtrate
     (Cinchonidine Tartrate)  (Quinidine Tartrate)
            │ Add HCl        │ Add KI
            ▼                ▼
      Cinchonidine HCl   Precipitate of quinidine HI
            │ +NH₄OH         │ +NH₄OH
            ▼                ▼
       Cinchonidine       Quinidine
```

Biosynthesis

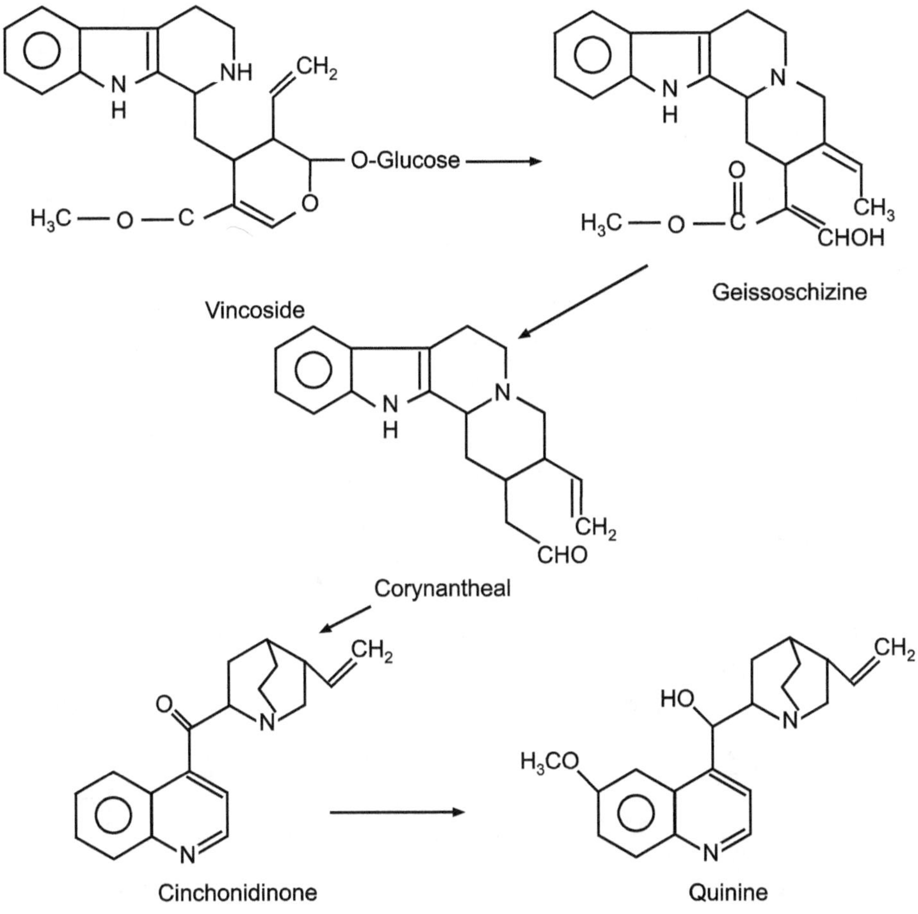

Fig 6.5 : Biosynthesis of Quinine

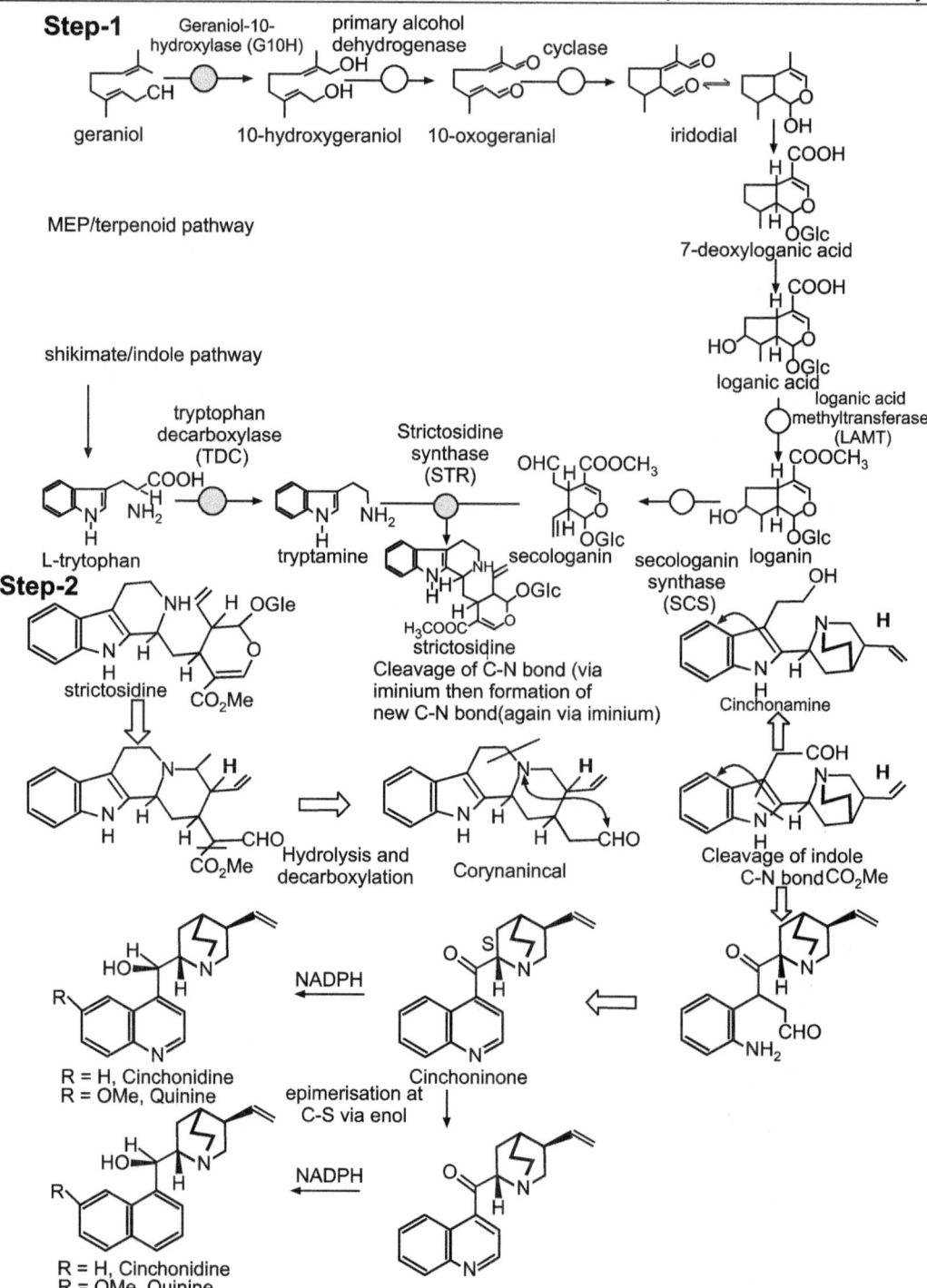

Fig. 6.6 : Biosynthesis of cinchonine and quinidine

Properties
1. Bisulphates of *Cinchona* as alkaloids [B.H$_2$SO$_4$] are readily soluble in water.
2. **Quinine sulphate** [Br.H$_2$SO$_4$] is sparingly soluble in water [1:720].
3. **Cinchonine** is practically insoluble in ether.
4. Tartrates of **Quinine** and **Cinchonidine** are insoluble, whereas the tartrates of **Cinchonine** and **Quinidine** are soluble in water.

Characteristic Features
1. The orthorhombic needles obtained from absolute ethanol are triboluminescent and having melting point of 177°C (with some decomposition).
2. It sublimes in high vacuum at 170-180°C.
3. Its specific rotation is $[\alpha]_D^{15}$ −169° (C = 2 in 97% ethanol); $[\alpha]_D^{17}$ −117° (C = 1.5 in chloroform); and $[\alpha]_D^{15}$ −285° (C = 0.4 M in 0.1 N H$_2$SO$_4$).
4. Its dissociation constant pK$_1$ (18°) is 5.07 and pK$_2$ 9.7.
5. **Neutral Salt of Quinine [(B)$_2$.H$_2$SO$_4$.8H$_2$O]:** It is formed by neutralisation from boiling water, which is sparingly soluble in water (1 in 720 at 25°C). The octahydrate neutral salts of quinine undergoes efflorescence on being exposed to air and gets converted to the corresponding dihydrate salt which is more stable.
6. **Acid Sulphate of Quinine [(B).H$_2$SO$_4$.7H$_2$O]:** The quinine bisulphate is soluble in water (1 in 8.5 at 25°C) and in ethanol (1 in 18). The aqueous solution is acidic to litmus.
7. **Tetrasulphate Salt of Quinine [(B)$_2$.2H$_2$SO$_4$.7H$_2$O]:** The tetrasulphate salt of quinine is very soluble in water.

Cinchonine Characteristic
1. Its prisms, needles are obtained from ether and ethanol having mp 265°C.
2. It begins to sublime at 220°C.
3. Its specific rotation is $[\alpha]_D$ +229° (in ethanol).
4. One gram of it dissolves in 60 ml ethanol, 25 ml boiling ethanol, 110 ml chloroform and 500 ml ether. It is practically insoluble in water.

Identification Tests
1. Fluorescence Test: Quinine gives a distinct and strong blue fluorescence when treated with an oxygenated acid, such as: acetic acid, sulphuric acid. This test is very marked and pronounced even to a few mg concentration of quinine.

Note: The hydrochloride and hydroiodide salts of quinine do not respond to this fluorescence test.

2. Thalleioquin Test: Add to 2-3 ml of a weakly acidic solution of a quinine salt, a few drops of bromine-water followed by 0.5 ml of strong ammonia solution, a distinct and characteristic emerald green colour is produced. The coloured product is termed as **thalleioquin**, the chemical composition of which is yet to be established. This test is so sensitive that quinine may be detected to a concentration as low as 0.005%.

Notes: Quinidine and cupreine (a Remijia alkaloid) give also a positive response to this test; but cinchoninine and cinchonidine give a negative test.

3. Erythroquinine Test (or Rosequin Test): Add to a solution of quinine in dilute acetic acid, 1-2 drops of bromine water, a drop of a solution of potassium ferrocyanide [$K_4(FeCN)_6$] (10% w/v), and to it add a drop of strong ammonia solution, the solution turns red instantly. In case, it is shaken immediately with 1 ml of chloroform, the red colour is taken up by the chloroform layer.

4. Herpathite Test: To a boiling mixture containing 0.25 g of quinine in 7.5 ml glacial acetic acid add 3 ml ethanol (90% v/v), 5 drops of conc. sulphuric acid and 3.5 ml of 1% iodine solution in ethanol. The appearance of crystals of **iodosulphate of quinine** (*i.e.*, **sulphate of iodo-quinine**) is known as **Herpathite** after the name of its discoverer. It has the chemical composition [$(B_4).3H_2SO_4.2HI.I_4.3H_2O$] which separates out as crystals (on cooling), having a metallic lustre that appears dark green in reflected light and olive green in transmitted light.

Structure Activity Relationship

Amino alcohol is a basic nucleus.

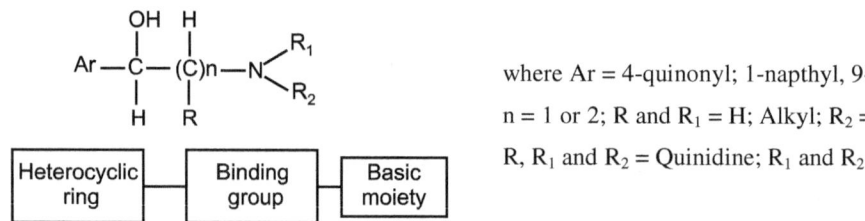

where Ar = 4-quinonyl; 1-napthyl; 9-phenanthryl;

n = 1 or 2; R and R_1 = H; Alkyl; R_2 = Alkyl;

R, R_1 and R_2 = Quinidine; R_1 and R_2 = piperidyl

Quinine derivative: Erythrocytic schizontocidal activity.

General structure

Sr. No.	Compound	R
1.	Quinine	OCH_3
2.	Quinidine	OCH_3
3.	Cinchonine	H
4.	Cinchonidine	H

1. Asymmetry at position 3 and 4 is not essential for anti malarial activity.
2. The configuration at position 8 and 9 affect the juxtaposition of hydroxy group and non - aromatic nitrogen atom, a relationship i.e., associated with antimalarial activity.

   The distance between the oxygen and non - aromatic nitrogen should be $3°A$.

   In all active amino alcohols, the orientation of hydroxy hydrogen and amine nitrogen should be such that hydrogen bonding is possible.
3. The presence of methoxy group in quinine is not essential. Replacement of methoxy group by a halogen, especially chlorine enhances activity.

   A further increase in activity resulted from introduction of phenyl group at position 2. In general, blocking of position 2 of quinloine ring with a phenyl group, but not with aliphatic hydrocarbon, lead to highly active compound.
4. 2 hydroxy quinine is less active than quinine due to biological oxidation in second position.
5. All high active 2-phenyl -4-quinolinyl amino alcohol were highly phototoxic.
6. Blocking second position with trifluoromethyl group, lead to development of mefloquine.
7. Activity is usually enhanced by introduction of a halogen at position 8.
8. Modification of secondary alcohol at C-9, through oxidation, esterification diminishes the activity.
9. The quinuclidine portion is not necessary for activity.
10. An alkyl tertiary amine linked to C-9 is necessary for activity.
11. Quinine is dextrorotatory and has antimalarial activity while quinidine is antiarrhythmic drug.
12. Structurally, quinidine is composed of a quinoline ring and the bicyclic quinuclidine ring system with a hydroxymethylene bridge connecting these two components. Examination of quinidine reveals two basic nitrogens, with the quinuclidine nitrogen being the stronger of the two. Because of the basic character of quinidine, it is always used as water soluble salt forms.

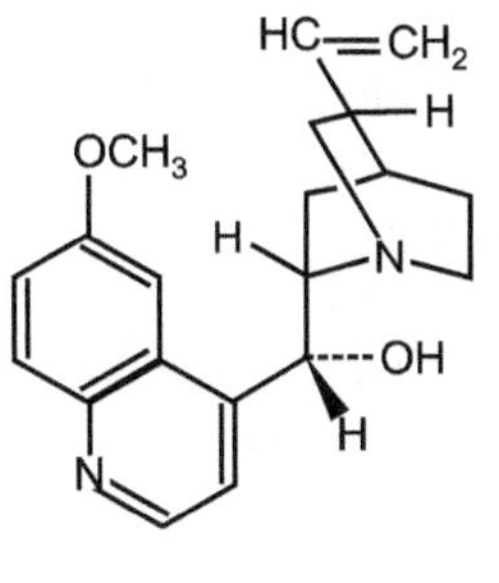

Mechanism of Action of *Cinchona* Alkaloids

The precise modes of action of the **quinoline** antimalarials are still not completely understood, although various mechanisms have been proposed for the action of cinchona and related compounds. Some of the proposed mechanisms would require higher drug concentrations than those that can be achieved in vivo and, therefore, are not considered as convincing as other arguments. Such mechanisms include the inhibition of protein synthesis, the inhibition of food vacuole phospholipases, the inhibition of aspartic proteinases and the effects on DNA and RNA synthesis. *Cinchona* is active against the erythrocytic stages of malaria parasites but not against pre-erythrocytic or hypnozoite-stage parasites in the liver or mature gametocytes. Since cinchona acts exclusively against those stages of the intra-erythrocytic cycle during which the parasite is actively degrading haemoglobin, it was assumed that cinchona somehow interferes with the parasite-feeding process.

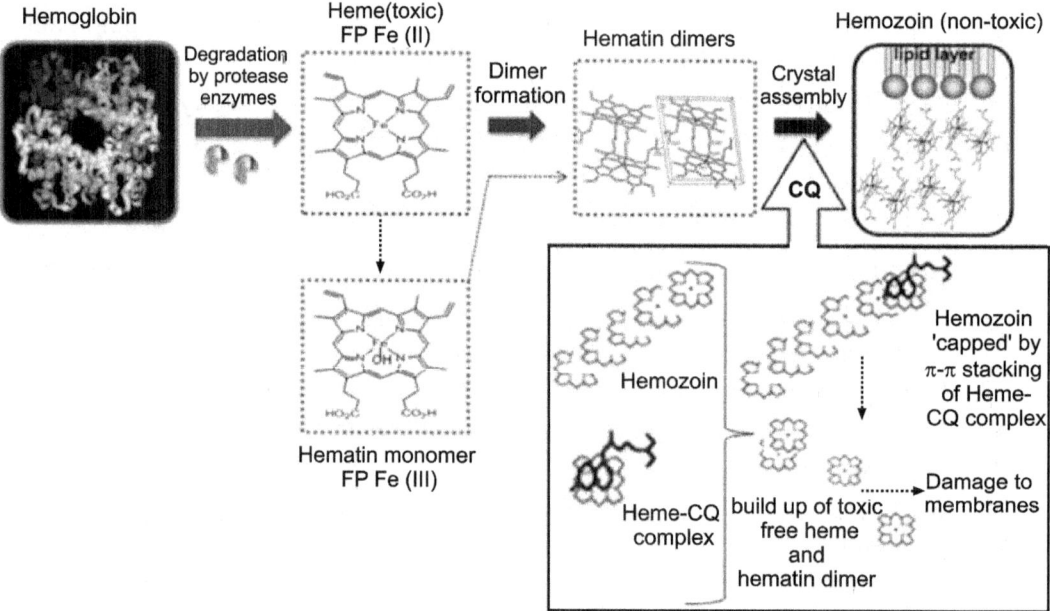

Fig. 6.7: Degradation of haemoglobin and detoxification mechanisms of the parasite and proposed target of *Cinchona*

Mechanism of Action of Quinidine

Quinidine is a very important alkaloid fron *Cinchona* bark. Bark contains two active principles namely quinine and quinidine. Quinine is a potent antimalarial agent while quinidine is a potent anti-arrhythmic agent. It is a Class I category drug which is sodium channel blocker. Subclasses of this action reflect effects on the action potential duration (APD) and the kinetics of sodium channel blockade. Drugs with class 1A action prolong the APD and dissociate from the channel with intermediate kinetics. Quinidine slows the upstroke of the action potential and conduction, and prolongs the QRS duration of the

ECG, by blockage of activated sodium channels. Recovery from block occurs with intermediate kinetics and is slowed further in partially depolarised cells. Sodium channel-blocking concentrations of quinidine also prolong the action potential duration as a result of potassium channel blockage. This action is relatively nonspecific as most types of potassium channels are blocked by therapeutic concentrations of quinidine although the resting potential is not altered. The action potential prolonging action is greatest at slow rates. Its major cardiac effects are excessive QT interval prolongation and induction of torsade de pointes arrhythmia, and syncope. Toxic concentrations of quinidine also produces excessive sodium channel blockage with slowed conduction throughout the heart, increased PR interval, and further QRS duration prolongation.

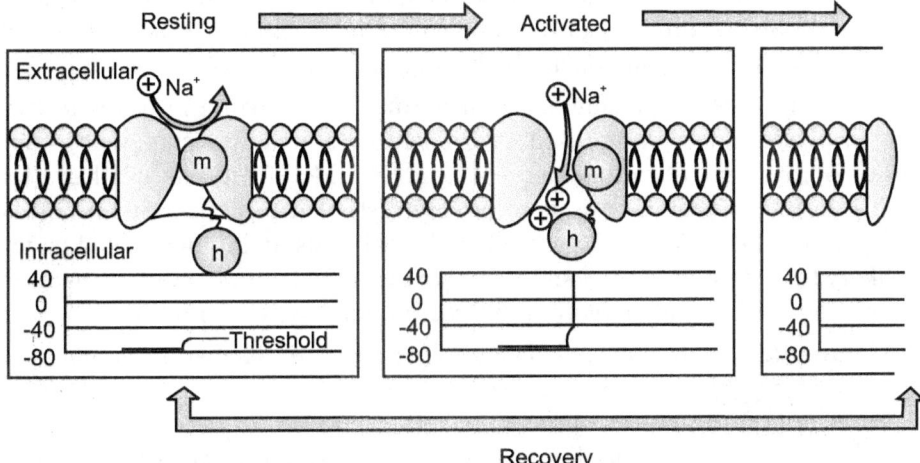

Fig. 6.8: Quinidine blocks this activation of sodium channel and also prevents entry of sodium ions inside the membrane

Phamacological Action

Antimalarial action: Quinine acts primarily against asexual erythrocytic forms and has little effect on hepatic forms of malarial parasites. The alkaloid also is gametocidal for *P. vivax* and *P. malariae* but not for *P. falciparum*. Quinine is more toxic and less effective than chloroquine against malarial parasites susceptible to both drugs. However, quinine, along with its stereoisomer quinidine, is especially valuable for the parenteral treatment of severe illness owing to drug-resistant strains of *P. falciparum*, even though these strains have become more resistant to both agents in certain parts of Southeast Asia and South America. Because of its toxicity and short $t_{1/2}$, quinine generally is not used for prophylaxis. Quinine resistance in *P. falciparum* more closely resembles resistance to mefloquine and halofantrine than to chloroquine. A number of different transporter genes may confer resistance to quinine.

Action on Skeletal Muscle: Quinine increases the tension response to a single maximal stimulus delivered to muscle, but it also increases the refractory period of muscle so that the response to tetanic stimulation is diminished. The excitability of the motor end-plate region decreases so that responses to repetitive stimulation and to acetylcholine are reduced. Thus, quinine can antagonise the actions of physostigmine on skeletal muscle. Quinine also may produce respiratory distress and dysphagia in patients with myasthenia gravis.

CVS: Quinidine is used to maintain sinus rhythm in patients with atrial flutter or atrial fibrillation and to prevent recurrence of ventricular tachycardia or ventricular fibrillation.

Extracardiac Effects

Gastrointestinal side effects of diarrhea, nausea, and vomiting are observed in one third to half of patients. A syndrome of headache, dizziness, and tinnitus (cinchonism) is observed at toxic drug concentrations. Idiosyncratic reactions including thrombocytopenia, hepatitis, angioneurotic edema, and fever are observed rarely.

Quinidine is used for the maintenance of normal sinus rhythm in patients with atrial flutter or fibrillation. It is also used occasionally to treat patients with ventricular tachycardia. Because of its cardiac and extracardiac side effects, its use has decreased considerably in recent years and is now largely restricted to patients with normal (but arrhythmic) hearts. In randomised, controlled clinical trials, quinidine-treated patients are twice as likely to remain in normal sinus rhythm compared with controls. However, drug treatment was associated with a twofold to threefold increase in mortality.

Anti-rheumatic: Cinchonine and cinchonidine are used as anti-rheumatic.

OPIUM ALKALOIDS

Morphine was the first alkaloid to be isolated from serturner plant (1806). Morphine named for Morpheus, the god of dreams in the Greek mythology

In opium, it is present in a quantity of 10-23 percent along with other substances like fats, resins, proteins, carbohydrates, mineral salts, meconic acid and about 20 or more alkaloids.

Morphine, the prototypical opioid agonist, has long been known to relieve severe pain with remarkable efficacy. The opium poppy is the source of crude opium from which Serturner in 1803 isolated the pure alkaloid morphine—named after Morpheus, the Greek god of dreams. Incision of the poppy seed pod reveals a white substance that turns into a brown gum that is crude opium. Opium contains many alkaloids, the principle one being morphine which is present in a concentration of about 10%. Codeine is synthesised commercially from morphine. Opioid alkaloids (eg, morphine) produce analgesia through actions at regions in the brain that contain peptides which have opioid-like pharmacologic properties. The general term currently used for these endogenous substances is endogenous opioid peptides, which replaces the previous term endorphin.

Codeine and thebaine are the other closely related alkaloids to morphine. These three are commonly known as *morphine alkaloids* and from a sub-group of the *opium alkaloids*. In all morphine alkaloids, phenanthrene nucleus is present. Due to this, these are also known as phenanthrene alkaloids.

The morphine alkaloids have been studied comparatively more due to the following reasons:

(i) These are widely used as analgesic agents, and

(ii) These undergo a wide variety of molecular rearrangements.

Opium is the air-dried milky exudate, or latex, obtained by incising the unripe capsules of the poppy plant *Papaver somniferum (Papaveraceae).*

For opium production, the ripening capsules, which are just changing colour from blue-green to yellow, are carefully incised with a knife to open the latex tubes

Opium alkaloids usually occur naturally combined with a specific acid (meconic acid).

Meconic acid is present only in *Papaver* species and is considered as a chemotaxonomic marker of plants of this genus.

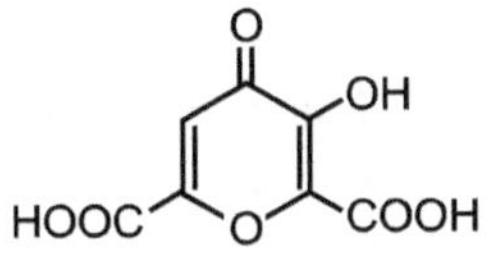

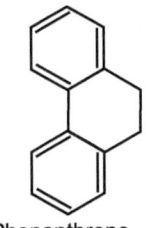

Meconic acid gives a deep purplish red-coloured complex with $FeCl_3$

Classification of Opium Alkaloids

(1) Benzylisoquinoline Alkaloids

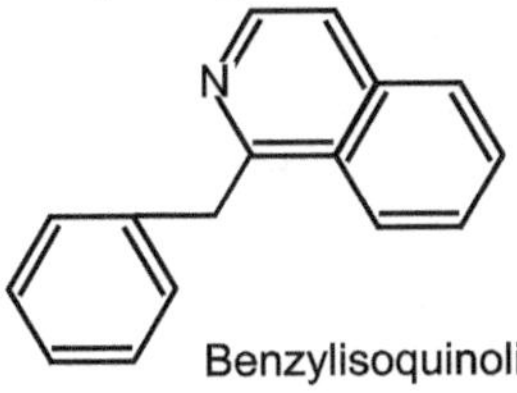

Benzylisoquinoline

e.g. Papaverine
Noscapine

(2) Phenylethylamine Alkaloids

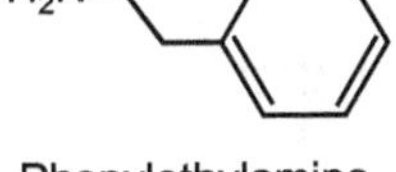

Phenylethylamine

e.g. Narceine

(3) Phenanthrene Alkaloids

Phenanthrene

e.g. Morphine
Codeine
Thebaine

1. Benzylisoquinoline Group

(a) **Papaverine:** Papaverine is a benzylisoquinoline alkaloid, and is structurally very different from the morphine, codeine, thebaine group of alkaloids (morphinans)

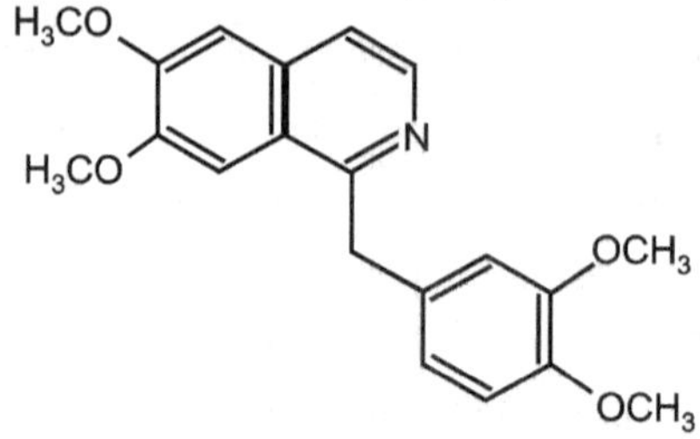

- It has little or no analgesic or hypnotic properties but possesses spasmolytic and vasodilator activity.
- It is sometimes used as an effective treatment for male impotence, being administered by direct injection to achieve erection of the penis.

Chemical Test For Papaverine

(i) **Warren's test:** Add some crystal of $KMnO_4$ on a sample of papaverine and add Marqui's reagent ($HCHO/H_2SO_4$) which gives green colour and finally turns to blue colour which indicates the prsence of papaverine.

(ii) Add concentrated sulphuric acid to papaverine which gives violet colour on heating

(b) **Noscapine (Narcotine)**

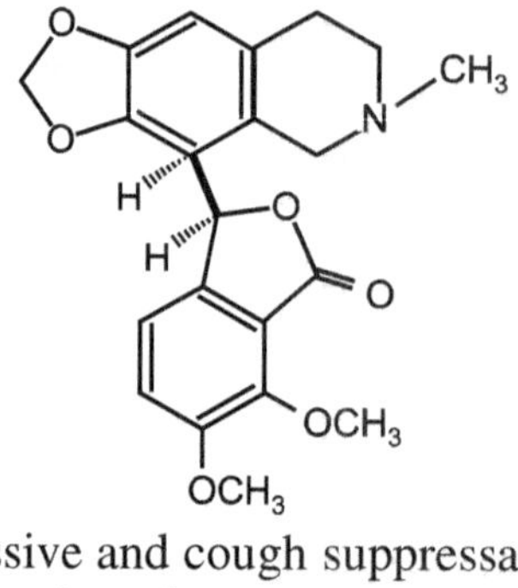

Noscapine has good anti-tussive and cough suppressant activity comparable to that of codeine, but no analgesic or narcotic action.

- Its original name 'narcotine' was changed to reflect this lack of narcotic action.

Chemical Test For Narcotine

Add concentrated sulphuric acid to narcotine which give violet colour on heating. This test is negative with morphine.

2. Ethylamine Group

Narceine

- It is a weakly basic alkaloid.
- It is an example of amphoteric alkaloid.
- It is not used medicinally.

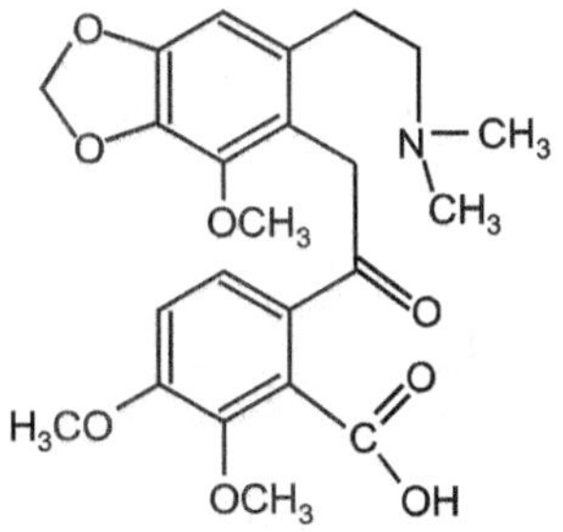

3. Phenanthrene Group (Morphinans)

Thebaine is tetrahydro-phenanthrene type differs structurally from morphine/codeine mainly by its possession of a conjugated diene ring system.
- Morphine and codeine are hexahydro-phenanthrene type.
- Morphine is the major alkaloid of opium (about 10%).

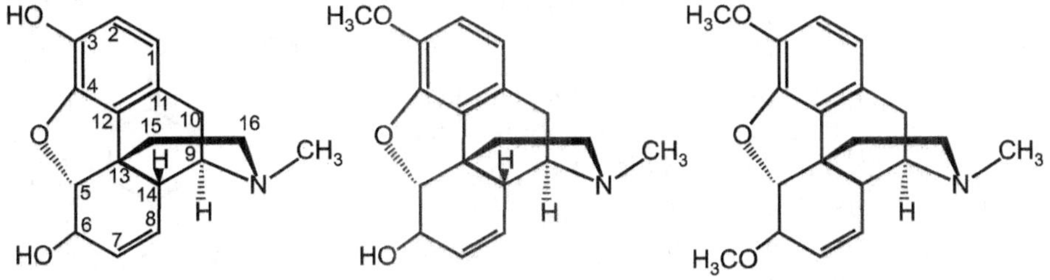

Morphine   Codeine   Thebaine

Table 6.4: Properties of Opium Alkaloids

Morphine	Codeine	Thebaine
Insoluble in H_2O, ether, benzene, ethanol and $CHCl_3$	Soluble in H_2O, ether, benzene, ethanol and $CHCl_3$	Insoluble in H_2O, but soluble in ether, benzene, and $CHCl_3$
It contains two OH groups, one is phenolic at C-3 and the other is alcoholic at C-6	It contains one alcoholic OH group at C-6	No phenolic or alcoholic OH groups
It can be precipitated from its acid solutions by addition of NH_4Cl, or NH_4OH	It dissolves in NH_4OH due to formation of codeline NH_4OH complex	
Has basic $N-CH_3$ group and a phenolic OH group (has acidic character)	Has basic $N-CH_3$ group	
Dissolve is in both acids and bases (Amphoteric)		
Methylation of the phenolic OH group → Codeline	It is prepared from morphine by methylation of the phenolic OH group	

Heroin (Diacetylmorphine)

It is a semi-synthetic alkaloid. Its action is more pronounced than morphine and there is also increased risk of addiction.

It is not used therapeutically.

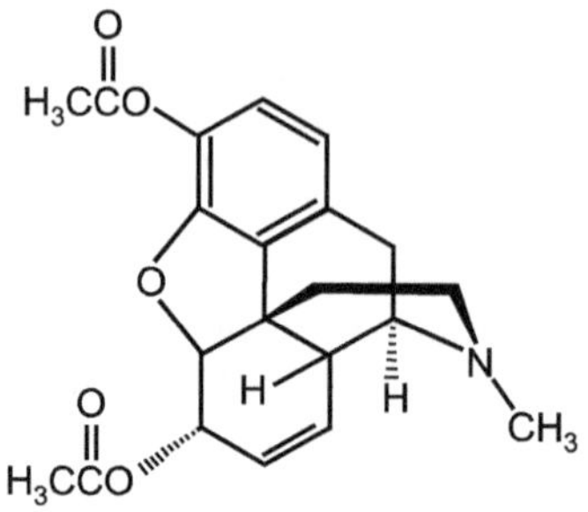

Apomorphine

Heating of morphine with concentrated hydrochloric acid results in dehydration and rearrangement of the morphinan skeleton to produce a compound known as apomorphine.

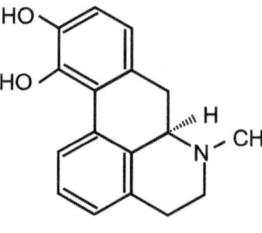

Apomorphine

Apomorphine does not possess the central depressant effect of morphine.

It has an emetic action(*s.c.* or *i.v.* injection) and antiparkinsonism effect.

Chemical Test

1. **Morphine**
   (a) **Test due to phenolic properties**
      (i) To morphine sample, add $FeCl_3$ which gives blue colour.
      (ii) **Nitrous acid test:** to morphine sample solution add hydrochloric acid, sodium nitrite and sodium hydroxide which gives red colour.
   (b) **Tests due to reducing properties**
      (i) **Iodic acid test:** to morphine sample solution add H_2SO_4 which reduces iodic acid or KIO_3 (K-iodate) to iodine, which on shaking with chloroform gives violet colour in the chloroform layer.
      (ii) Morphine solution gives purple red colour with sucrose and conc. H_2SO_4

2. **Codiene**

   To Codeine solution, add concentrated H_2SO_4 and $FeCl_3$, which on heating on water bath gives blue colour and then on adding HNO_3 gives red color.

Spectral Peaks

UV (Ethanol): λ_{max} 286, 250 and 298 nm (log c 3.256, 3.275, 3.360 respectively).

IR (KBr): V_{max} 3480, 3350 (OH), 3210 (OH bonded), 2940, 2920 (CH stretch), 2840 (N–CH_3 stretch), 1640 (C=C alkene), 1605 (C=C, Ar), 1250, 1090 (X–O stretch), 760 (monosubs. Ar) cm^{-1}.

^{1}**H NMR (HCl):** δ 6.76 (d, H-1), 6.68 (d, H-2), 5.75 (d, H-7), 5.40 (d, H-8), 5.06 (d, H$_{-5}$, J5, 6 = 2Hz), 4.37 (m, H$_{-9}$), 4.20 (d, H$_{-14}$), 3.0 (s,N-Me), 2.16 (d, H$_{-10}$)

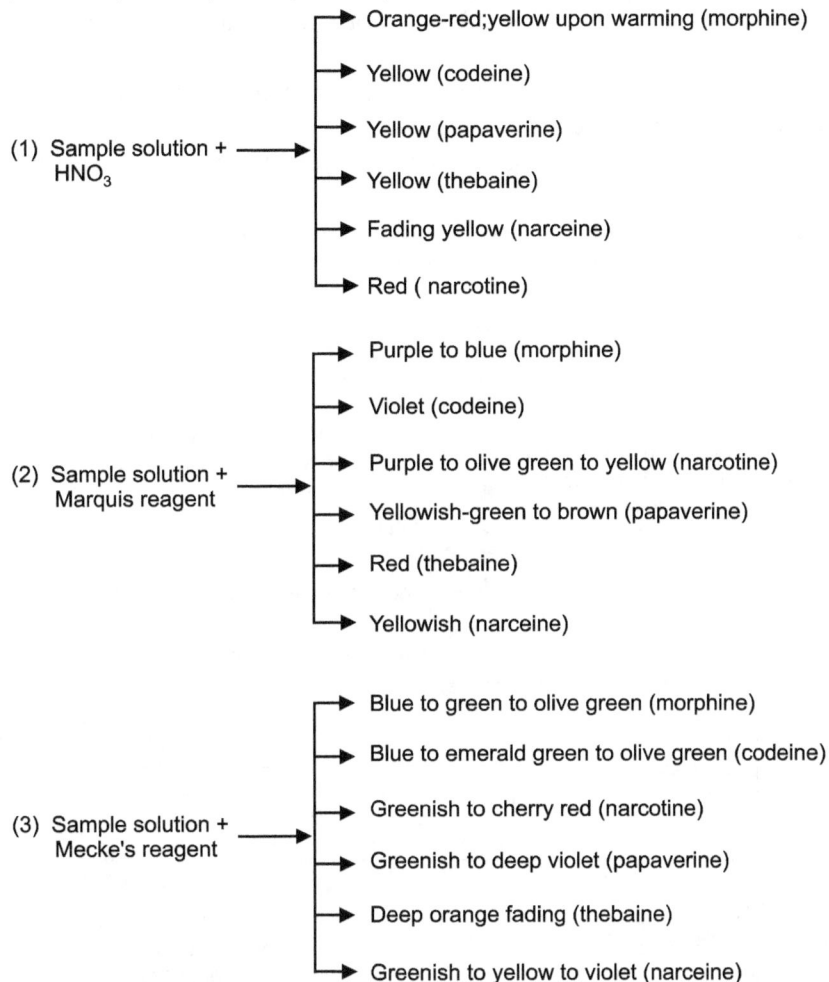

Isolation of Opium Alkaloids

The latex obtained by incision on the unripe capsule of opium poppy is first collected in clean, plastic containers, and the process of incision is repeated at least four times on the same capsule after an interval of two days. Care must be taken to make the incisions on the superficial surface only so as to collect exclusively the external exudation of latex. Subsequently, the latex is dried carefully either by exposing to air on metallic shallow plates or by passing a stream of hot air.

Thus the '*opium*' or the dried latex is stored for the isolation of **morphine.** It is found to contain usually 9.5% **morphine** when calculated as anhydrous morphine.

The morphine may be isolated form **'powdered opium'** by adopting the following steps sequentially

Step-1: The powdered opium is shaken with calcium chloride solution and filtered.

Step-2: The resulting filtrate is concentrated and to it is added 10% w/v sodium hydroxide solution carefully *i.e.*, to solubilise morphine, codeine and narceine. It is now filtered.

Step-3: The filtrate containing morphine, codeine and narceine is extracted with chloroform. The resulting mixture is separated.

Step-4: The lower chloroform layer contains codeine, whereas the upper aqueous layer comprises of **morphine** and **narceine.**

Step-5: The aqueous layer is first acidified and subsequently made alkaline with ammonia, whereby morphine gets precipitated and collected as a while solid residue (Yield = 9.5%).

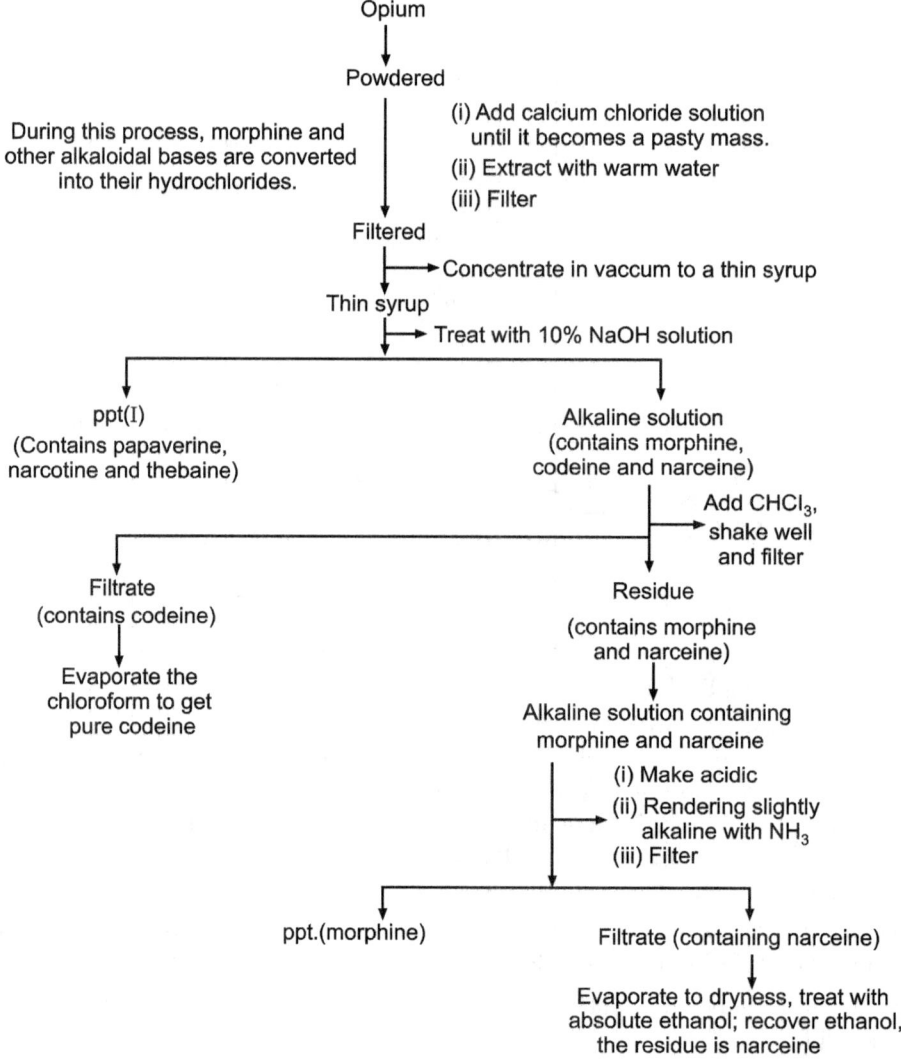

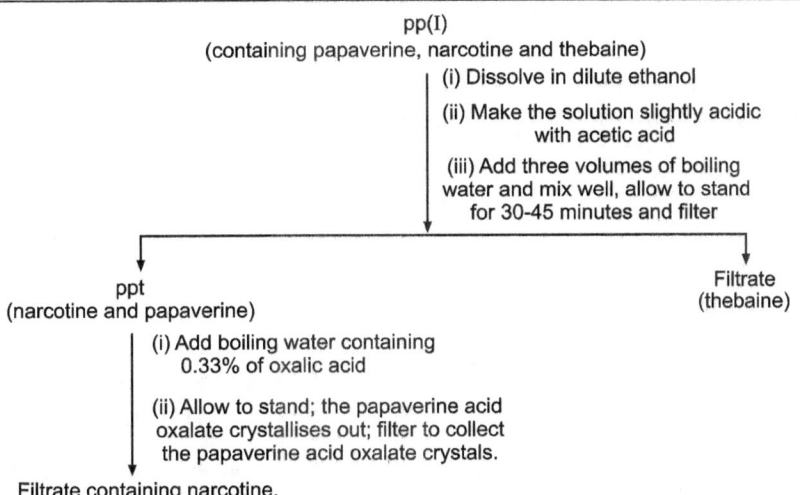

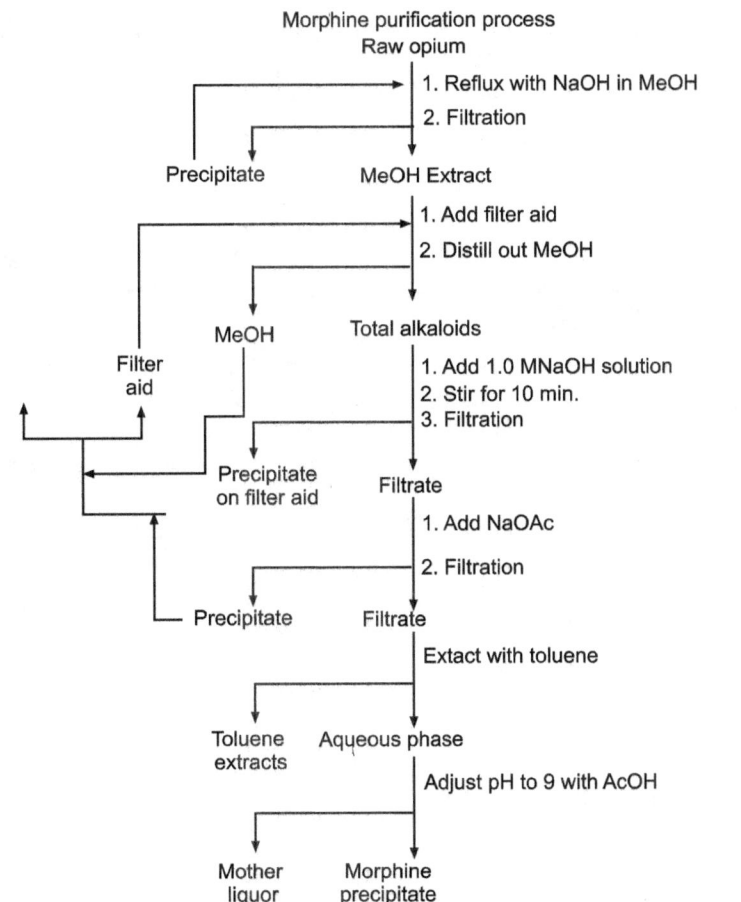

Biosynthesis of Opium Alkaloids (Morphine and Codiene)

Structure Relationship Activity

Modifications in morphine structure are as follows
1. The peripheral groups and simple skeletal modifications on *alicyclic ring*.
2. The peripheral groups and simple skeletal modifications on *aromatic ring*.
3. The tertiary nitrogen.

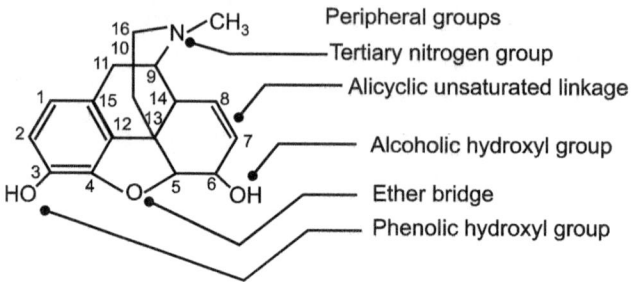

Modifications in morphine structure

Peripheral Groups of Morphine	Modification (On Morphine Unless Otherwise Indicated)
Phenolic hydroxyl	–OH → –OCH$_3$ (codeine)
	–OH → –OC$_2$H$_5$ (ethylmorphine)
	–OH → –OCH$_2$CH$_2$–N⌒O (pholcodine)
Alcoholic hydroxyl	–OH → –OCH$_3$ (heterocodeine)
	–OH → –OC$_2$H$_5$
	–OH → –OCOCH$_3$
	–OH → =O (morphone)
	–OH → =O (dihydromorphine to dihydromorphinonne
	–OH → =O (dihydrocodeine to dihydrocodeinone)
	–OH → –H (dihydromorphine to dihydrodesoxymorphine-D)
Ether bridge	=C–O–CH– → =C–OH HCH– (dihydrodesoxymorphine-D to tetrahydrodesoxymorphine)
Alicyclic unsaturated linkage	–CH=CH– → –CH$_2$CH$_2$– (dihydromorphine)
	–CH=CH– → –CH$_2$CH$_2$– (codeine to dihydrocodeine)
Tertiary nitrogen	⟩N–CH$_3$ → ⟩N–H (normorphine)
	⟩N–CH$_3$ → ⟩N–CH$_2$CH$_2$–C$_6$H$_5$
	⟩N–CH$_3$ → ⟩N–R
	⟩N–CH$_3$ → ⟩N(CH$_3$)(CH$_3$) Cl–
	Opening of nitrogen ring (morphimethine)

Nuclear substitution	Substitution of
	– NH$_2$ (most likely at position 2)
	– Cl or – Br (at position 1)
	– OH (at position 14 in dihydromorphinone)
	– OH (at position 14 in dihydrocodeinone)
	– CH (at position 6)
	– CH$_3$ (at position 6 in dihydromorphine)
	– CH$_3$ (at position 6 in dihydrodesoxymorphine-D)
	= CH$_2$ (at position 6 in dihydrodesoxymorphine-D)

1. **Modification on Alicyclic Ring**
   (a) The **C-6** α hydroxyl group is methylated, esterified, oxidised, removed or replaced by halogen in order to get more potent analgesics. e.g. codeine, heroin, chloromorphide. but there is also parallel increase in toxicity.
   (b) **The C-8 presents the next site for modification:** It has an hydrogen atom and a double bond. The outcome of catalytic hydrogenation is the compounds dihyrocodeine and dihydromorphine which are the precursors of more potent ketones, dihydrocodeinone and dihydromorphinone. Similarly, C-8 β-halo derivatives are found to be more potent analgesics than morphine.
   (c) **C-14:** Introduction of 14-OH group in dihydro forms yielded the still more potent and 14-hydroxydihydromophinone. Bridging of C_6 and C_{14} through ethylene limkage is also tried e.g., etorphine. It is about 200 times more potent than morphine.
   (d) Introduction of any new substituents at 5th position does not enhance the activity, except 5 – methyl dihydro morphine and azidomorphines.

Modifications on aromatic ring system
   (a) An aromatic phenyl ring is essential for activity.
   (b) Modifications of C-3 phenolic hydroxyl group decreases analgesic activity.
   (c) Making the phenolic – OH group by etherification to methyl ether (codeine) and ethyl ether (ethyl morphine) results in about one tenth of analgesic activity of morphine, because phenolics – OH group binds with opiate receptor by hydrogen bonding easily. But ethers are not easily subject to hydrolysis.
   (d) Esterification of 3–OH group gives compounds more active than morphine. Substances other than 3-position in the aromatic ring results in a reduction of opiod actions.
   (e) But 1-fluoro codeine possess the same analgesic activity as that of codeine.

Modifications of Nitrogens

(a) Replacement of N-CH$_3$ by N-C$_2$H$_5$ results slight fall in analgesic response. More hydrophobic groups such as propyl, pentyl, hexyl and phenylethyl gave an increase in activity.

(b) N-allyl and N-cycloalkyl methyl functions give the narcotic antagonistic properties.

(c) N-phenyl ethyl group enhances the analgesic activity in desmorphine, codeine and heterocodeine.

Modifications of ether bridge

Breaking of ether bridge and opening of piperidine ring decreases the activity.

Mechanism of Action

Opioid agonists produce analgesia by binding to specific G protein-coupled receptors, located primarily in brain and spinal cord regions involved in the transmission and modulation of pain. At the molecular level, opioid receptors form a family of proteins that physically couple to G proteins and through this interaction affect ion channel gating, modulate intracellular Ca^{2+} disposition, and alter protein phosphorylation. The opioids have two well-established direct actions on neurons: (1) they close voltage-gated Ca^{2+} channels on presynaptic nerve terminals and thereby reduce transmitter release and (2) they hyperpolarize and thus inhibit postsynaptic neurons by opening K$^+$ channels. The presynaptic action is depressed, transmitter release has been demonstrated for release of a large number of neurotransmitters including glutamate, the principle excitatory amino acid released from nociceptive nerve terminals, as well as acetylcholine, norepinephrine, serotonin, and substance.

Pharmacological Action

Central Nervous System Effects

The principal effects of opioid analgesics with affinity for receptors are on the CNS; the more important ones include analgesia, euphoria, sedation, and respiratory depression. With repeated use, a high degree of tolerance occurs to all of these effects.

Analgesia

Pain consists of both sensory and affective (emotional) components. Opioid analgesics are unique in that they can reduce both aspects of the pain experience, especially the affective aspect.

Euphoria

Typically, patients or intravenous drug users who receive intravenous morphine experience a pleasant floating sensation with lessened anxiety and distress. However, dysphoria, an unpleasant state characterised by restlessness and malaise, may sometimes occur.

Sedation

Drowsiness and clouding of mentation are frequent concomitants of opioid action. There is little or no amnesia. Sleep is induced by opiates more frequently in the elderly than in young, healthy individuals. Ordinarily, the patient can be easily aroused from this sleep. However, the combination of morphine with other central depressant drugs such as the sedative-hypnotics may result in very deep sleep.

Respiratory Depression

All of the opioid analgesics can produce significant respiratory depression by inhibiting brainstem respiratory mechanisms. Alveolar PCO_2 may increase, but the most reliable indicator of this depression is a depressed response to a carbon dioxide challenge. The respiratory depression is dose-related and is influenced significantly by the degree of sensory input occurring at the time.

Cough Suppression

Suppression of the cough reflex is a well-recognised action of opioids. Codeine, in particular, has been used to advantage in persons suffering from pathologic cough and in patients in whom it is necessary to maintain ventilation via an endotracheal tube. However, cough suppression by opioids may allow accumulation of secretions and thus lead to airway obstruction and atelectasis.

Miosis

Constriction of the pupils is seen with virtually all opioid agonists. Miosis is a pharmacologic action to which little or no tolerance develops thus, it is valuable in the diagnosis of opioid overdose.

Nausea and Vomiting

The opioid analgesics can activate the brainstem chemoreceptor trigger zone to produce nausea and vomiting. There may also be a vestibular component in this effect because ambulation seems to increase the incidence of nausea and vomiting.

Cardiovascular System

Most opioids have no significant direct effects on the heart and no major effects on cardiac rhythm (except bradycardia). Meperidine is an exception to this generalisation because its antimuscarinic action may result in tachycardia. Blood pressure is usually well maintained in subjects receiving opioids unless the cardiovascular system is stressed, in which case hypotension may occur.

Gastrointestinal Tract

In the stomach, motility (rhythmic contraction and relaxation) may decrease but tone (persistent contraction) may increase—particularly in the central portion; gastric secretion of hydrochloric acid is decreased. Small intestine resting tone is increased, with periodic spasms, but the amplitude of nonpropulsive contractions is markedly decreased. In the large intestine, propulsive peristaltic waves are diminished and tone is increased; this delays passage of the fecal mass and allows increased absorption of water, which leads to constipation.

Biliary Tract

The opioids constrict biliary smooth muscle, which may result in biliary colic. The sphincter of Oddi may constrict, resulting in reflux of biliary and pancreatic secretions and elevated plasma amylase and lipase levels.

Renal

Renal function is depressed by opioids. It is believed that in humans this is chiefly due to decreased renal plasma flow. Opioids can decrease systemic blood pressure and glomerular filtration rate. In addition, opioids have been found to have an antidiuretic effect in humans. Mechanisms may involve both the CNS and peripheral sites.

Neuroendocrine

Opioid analgesics stimulate the release of ADH, prolactin, and somatotropin but inhibit the release of luteinising hormone. These effects suggest that endogenous opioid peptides, through effects in the hypothalamus, play regulatory roles in these systems.

Miscellaneous

The opioids may modulate the actions of the immune system by effects on lymphocyte proliferation, antibody production, and chemotaxis. Natural killer cell cytolytic activity and lymphocyte proliferative responses to mitogens are usually inhibited by opioids. Although the mechanisms involved are complex, activation of central opioid receptors could mediate a significant component of the changes observed in peripheral immune function.

ERGOT ALKALOIDS

Ergot is the dried sclerotium of a fungus, *Claviceps purpurea* (Fam. Hypocreacea) that arise on the ovaries of the rye plant (*Secale cereale,* Family Gramineae.)

Consumption of flour contaminated with ergot led to many serious intoxications known as (Ergotism- Ignis sacer) in Europe.

Ergot alkaloids are amides of the terpenoid indole derivate D-lysergic acid, and are produced by a wide range of fungi, predominantly the *Clavicipitaceae*, but are also present in members of the plant family *Convolvulaceae*, e.g. *Ipomoea violacea* and *Turbina corymbosa*.

Classification of Ergot Alkaloids

(a) **Clavine Type Alkaloids:** Simple water soluble bases with little medicinal value. All end with "clavine: e.g. Agroclavine.

(b) **Lysergic acid Amides:** They are all derivatives of (l)-Lysergic acid and subclassified into

1. **Simple lysergic acid amides:** Composed of Lysergic acid and simple amines.
2. **Polypeptide Alkaloids:** Composed of Lysergic acid and at least 3 amino acids.

Ergot alkaloids are N-monosubstituted amide derivatives of both lysergic acid and its isomer isolysergic acid that differ only in configuration at C-8.

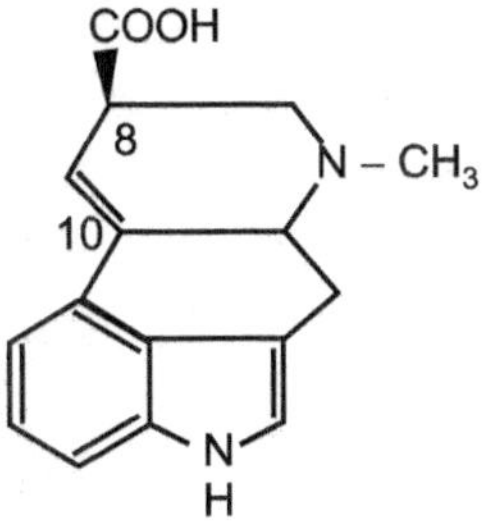

Lysergic acid

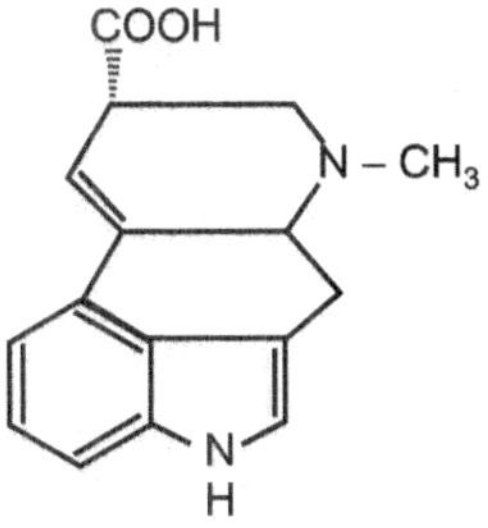

Isolysergic acid

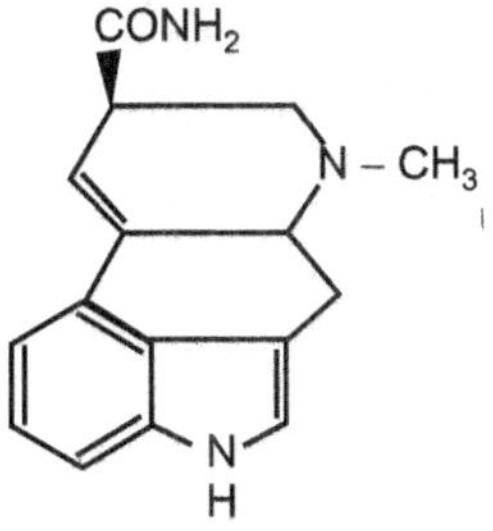

Ergine

On treatment with ammonia, lysergic and isolysergic acids give the corresponding amides ergine and isoergine respectively.

Members related to lysergic acid (e.g. ergotamine and ergometrine) are levorotatory, more active and designated by suffix "ine".

Members related to isolysergic acid (e.g. ergotaminine and ergometrinine), are dextrorotatory, less active and designated by suffix "inine".

1. Simple Lysergic acid amides

- Composed of lysergic acid and simple amines.
- Low molecular weight.
- Water Soluble.

Ergonovine (Ergometrine) Composed of (*l*)-lysergic acid and 2-aminopropanol. Its (*d*) isomer is called Ergometrinine. It causes vigorous contraction of the uterus. It is mainly used as an oxytocic in order to aid delivery or to prevent postpartum hemorrhage.

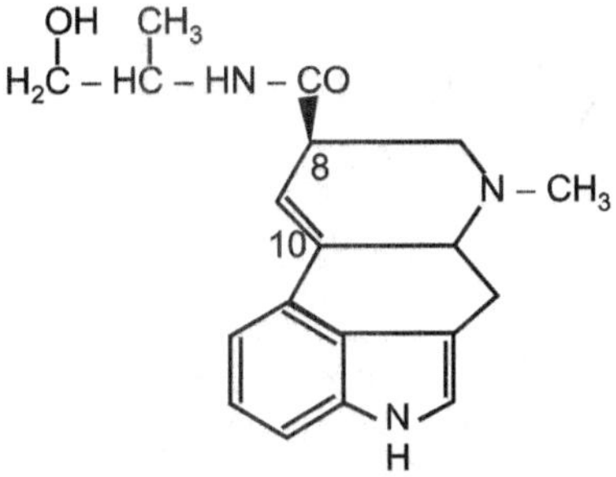

Ergonovine (*l*) (Ergometrine)
Ergonovine (*d*) (Ergometrinine)

Lysergic acid diethylamide (LSD)

- It is a semisynthetic product.
- LSD has potent CNS stimulant effect.
- LSD is one of the abused drugs.

2. Polypeptide Alkaloids

- They are derivatives of lysergic acid with a complex polypeptides of at least 3 amino acids.
- They have high molecular weight.
- They are insoluble in water.
- This class includes medicinally important members.

Ergotamine

- Its (*d*) isomer is called Ergotaminine.
- The peptide moiety is composed of three amino acids: α-hydroxylamine, proline, phenylalanine
- It is used in treatment of migraine as it constricts the peripheral blood vessels.
- It has some oxytocic activity.

Stablity

The active (*l*) form converts to the (*d*) isomer by the effect of alkalis or prolonged storage in alcohol.

(*l*) form   (*d*) form

Addition of water to the 9-10 double bond takes place in aqueous acidic solutions, upon exposure to day or UV light. The resulted Lumi alkaloids are inactive.

The particular alkaloids of ergot, and the corresponding amino acid obtained after hydrolysis, are as follows

Upon acid hydrolysis

Ergocornine	⟶	L-valine
Ergocristine	⟶	L-phenylalanine
Ergocryptine	⟶	L-leucine
Ergosine	⟶	L-leucine
Ergotamine	⟶	L-phenylalanine

Identification Test

- **Van-Urk's Reagent** (p-dimethyl aminobenzaldehyde (**PDAB**) in **15% H_2SO_4**, containing traces of $FeCl_3$ + Alkaloid gives deep blue colour.
- **Erlich Reagent** {p-dimethyl aminobenzaldehyde (**PDAB**) in H_2SO_4} + Alkaloid, gives deep blue colour.
- **Keller's test:** Solution of the alkaloids in acetic acid with traces of $FeCl_3$ + concentrated H_2SO_4 on the wall of the test tube, results in blue layer being formed between the two phases.
- **Identification by paper chromatography:** The amino acids produced by the acid hydrolysis of water insoluble alkaloids can be used for the identification of the members of the respective alkaloid.

Isolation

The following method is used by the Barger and Carr, for the isolation of different alkaloids of ergot.

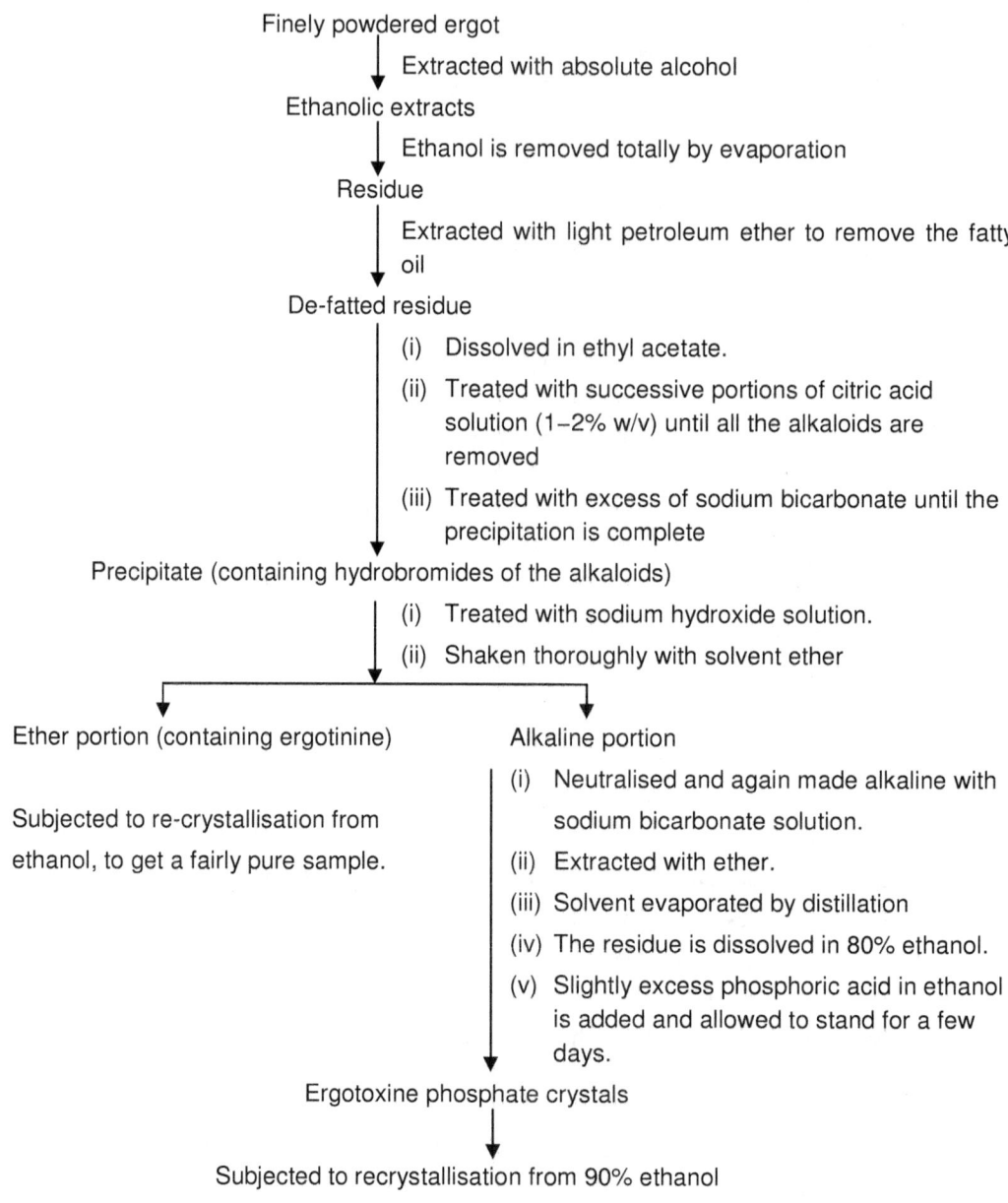

Isolation of Ergosine

De-fatted ergot powder
  | (i) Subjected to extraction with benzene.
  | (ii) The extract is allowed to cool.
  | (iii) Made alkaline with 1% NaOH, and again made acidic by the addition of dilute H_2SO_4 and filtered.
  ↓
Filtrate
  | (i) Made alkaline with $NaHCO_3$ until the precipitation is complete and filtered.
  | (ii) The precipitate is dried in a vacuum dessicator and later dissolved in methanol.
  | (iii) The crystalline precipitate containing crude ergosinine, is re-crystallised from hot aqueous acetone.
  ↓
Crystalline sample of ergosine

Isolation of Ergotomine

Coarse powder of ergot
  | (i) Mixed with aluminium sulphate and 300 ml of H_2O.
  | (ii) The total mixture is subjected to proper blending.
  | (iii) The above mixture is allowed to cool; finely divided powder sample is collected.
  | (iv) Subjected to continuous hot extraction with benzene.
  | (v) The solvent is diluted off.
  | (vi) The residue is stirred with sufficient quantity of benzene and made slightly alkaline with ammonia gas.
  | (vii) Subjected to shaking for several hours and filtered.
  | The residue is washed with benzene and the washings are added to the filtrate.
  ↓
Filtrate
  ↓
Concentrated to a small volume under reduced pressure, the ergotamine crystallises out. It is subjected to re-crystallisation from aqueous acetone.

Biosynthesis

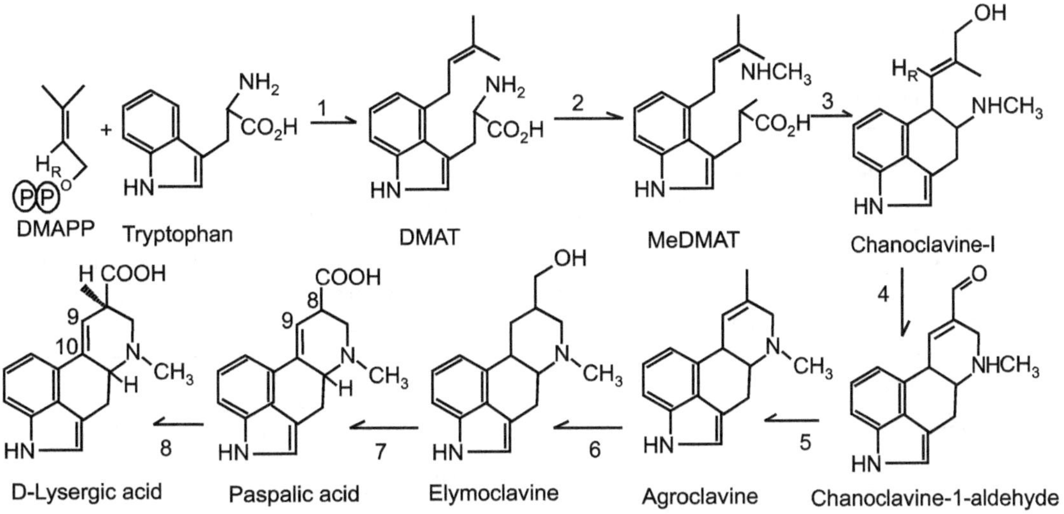

Pathway of ergoline ring synthesis up to the stage of D-lysergic acid.

Structure Activity Relationship

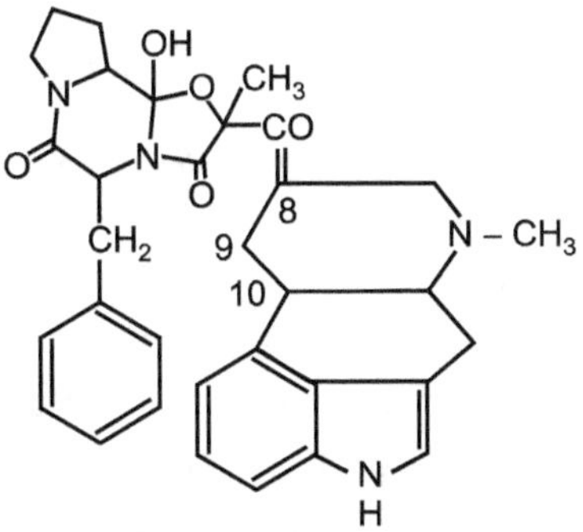

1. Lysergic acid must be in the (*l*) form. The (*d*) isomers are inactive.
2. Saturation of the 9-10 double bond of Ergotamine gives dihydroergotamine, a compound with antimigraine effect but no oxytocic effect.

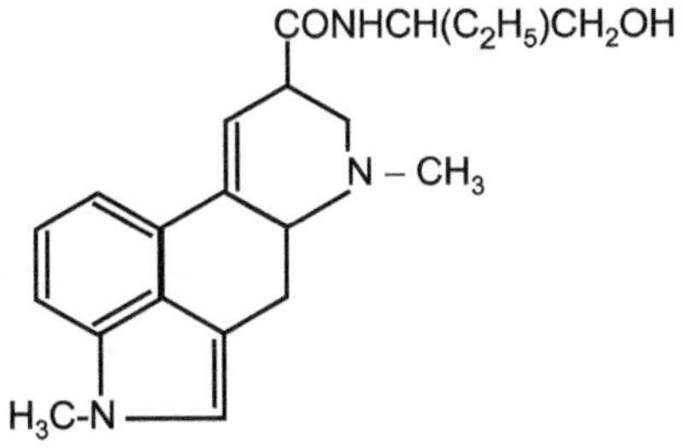

Methylsergide

Mechanism of Action

- **Targets:** Several receptor types
  - agonist effects
  - partial agonist effects
  - antagonist effects
  - Pre- and post-synaptic sites

Table 6.5: Targets of Ergot Alkaloids

Ergot Alkaloids	Alpha-adrenergic receptor	Dopamine receptor	Serotonin receptor (5 HT$_2$)	Uterine smooth muscle stimulation
Bromocryptine	-	+++	-	0
Ergonovine	+	+	- (partial agonist)	+++
Ergonovine	-- (partial agonist)	0	+ (partial agonist)	+++
LSD	0	+++	--	+
Methysergide	+/0	+/0	--- (partial agonist)	+/0

The ergot alkaloids act on several types of receptors. Their effects include agonist, partial agonist, and antagonist actions at adrenoceptors and serotonin receptors (especially 5-HT1A and 5-HT1D; less for 5-HT$_1$C, 5-HT$_2$, and 5-HT$_3$); and agonist or partial agonist actions at central nervous system dopamine receptors. Furthermore, some members of the ergot family have a high affinity for presynaptic receptors, while others are more selective for postjunctional receptors. There is a powerful stimulant effect on the uterus that seems to be most closely associated with agonist or partial agonist effects at 5-HT2 receptors. Structural variations increase the selectivity of certain members of the family for specific receptor types.

Pharmacological Action

Central Nervous System

As indicated by traditional descriptions of ergotism, certain of the naturally occurring alkaloids are powerful hallucinogens. Lysergic acid diethylamide (LSD; "acid") is a synthetic ergot compound that clearly demonstrates this action. The drug has been used in the laboratory as a potent peripheral 5-HT2 antagonist, but good evidence suggests that its behavioral effects are mediated by agonist effects at prejunctional or postjunctional 5-HT2 receptors in the central nervous system.

Vascular Smooth Muscle

The action of ergot alkaloids on vascular smooth muscle is drug-, species-, and vessel-dependent, so few generalisations are possible. Ergotamine and related compounds constrict most human blood vessels in a predictable, prolonged, and potent manner. This response is partially blocked by conventional-blocking agents. However, ergotamine's effect is also associated with "epinephrine reversal" and with blockage of response to other agonists.

Uterine Smooth Muscle

The stimulant action of ergot alkaloids on the uterus, as on vascular smooth muscle, appears to combine agonist, serotonin, and other effects. Furthermore, the sensitivity of the uterus to the stimulant effects of ergot changes dramatically during pregnancy, perhaps because of increasing dominance of α_1 receptors as pregnancy progresses. As a result, the uterus at term is more sensitive than earlier in pregnancy and far more sensitive than the nonpregnant organ.

Other Smooth Muscle Organs

In most patients, the ergot alkaloids have no significant effects on bronchiolar smooth muscle. The gastrointestinal tract, on the other hand, is quite sensitive in most patients. Nausea, vomiting, and diarrhea may be induced even by low doses in some patients. The effect is consistent with action on the central nervous system's emetic center and on gastrointestinal serotonin receptors.

Vinca (Catharanthus) Alkaloids

Catharanthus or *Vinca* is the dried whole plant of *Catharanthus roseus* G. Don (or *Vinca rosea* L), Fam. Apocynaceae.

It contains about 150 alkaloids, the most important ones are **vinblastine and vincristine**.

The French referred to it as "violet of the sorcerers"

Earlier used as a remedy for scurvy, toothaches, controlling hemorrhage, diabetes – investigated as a hypoglycemic agent by Eli Lily.

Anticancer activity first noted in 1957 in rats (bone marrow suppression and antileukemic effects).

Cytotoxicity activity occurs through the disruption of microtubules.

The aerial parts of the plant contain from 0.2 to 1% alkaloids.

About 150 alkaloids have been isolated from *Catharanthus roseus*

Of particular interest is a group of 20 dimeric alkaloids which contain thos ewith antineoplastic activity, including vincristine and vinblastine. These alkaloids are formed by the coupling of two moieties: an indole moiety and a dihydroindole moiety. Thus, this led to referring them as "dimer alkaloids" or "bisindolealkaloids.

Vinblastine is produced by coupling of two monomer alkaloids catharanthine (indole) and vindoline (dihydroindole), both of which occur free in the plant. Vincristine is structurally similar to vinblastine, but has a formyl group rather than a methyl on the indole nitrogen in the vindoline derived portion. Because these alkaloids are only minor constituents of the plant (vincristine is obtained in about 0.0002% yield from the crude drug), large quantities of raw materials are employed in the extraction procedures. Also there is a growing demand for vincristine rather than vinblastine, but the plant produces a much higher proportion of vinblastine. Fortunately, it is now possible to convert vinblastine into vincristine either chemically or via microbiological N-demethylation using *Streptomyces albogriseolus*.

Other binary alkaloids which are active are leurosidine (20'-epivinblastine), leurosine (15', 20'-epoxy vinblastine).

Some alkaloids, for example, ajmalicine, lochnerine, serpentine and tetrahydroalstonine, also occur in other genera of the family.

Classification

1. **Monomeric Alkaloids:** These are alkaloids that contain either indole or indoline:
   - Indole monomers e.g. Catharanthine
   - Indoline monomers e.g. Vindoline and Vincamine.
2. **Dimeric Alkaloids:**
   Homogenic dimmers: Composed of two indole or indoline monomers.
   Mixed dimmers: One indole and one indoline monomers e.g. Vincristine and Vinblastine.

   (1) **Monomeric Alkaloids**

Vincamine   Catharanthine   Vindoline

Vincamine: It enhances the cerebral blood flow, facilitate cerebral circulation metabolism and increase general activity. Vincamine is used in cerebral vascular deficiency and atherosclerosis in elderly patients.

(2) **Dimeric Alkaloids: Mixed dimers**

These are dimeric alkaloids having indole and indoline (dihydro-indole) nuclei e.g. Vinblastine and Vincristine

These alkaloids occur in very minute amounts in *Vinca* (0.003- 0.005); 500 Kg of the plant yields only 1 gm of vincristine.

These alkaloids are very important for cancer treatment.

Vincristine is more active but isolated in smaller amounts than vinblastine. Vinblastine (Vincaleukoblastine) is produced by coupling of catharanthine and vindoline.

- Vincristine (leurocristine) has CHO instead of CH_3 in the vindoline part of vinblastine.

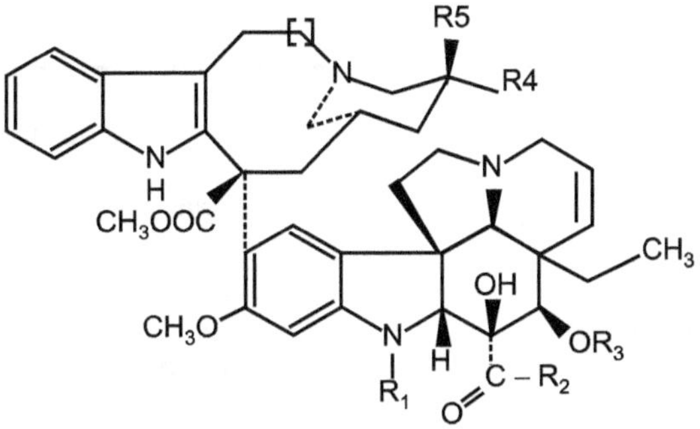

Table 6.5: *Vinca* Alkaloids and their Substitutions

	R1	R2	R3	R4	R5	[ ]
Vincristine	CHO	OCH_3	$OCOCH_3$	CH_2CH_3	OH	-
Vinblastine	CH_3	OCH_3	$OCOCH_3$	CH_2CH_3	OH	-
Vindesine	CH_3	NH_2	OH	CH_2CH_3	OH	-
Vinepidine	CHO	OCH_3	$OCOCH_3$	H	CH_2CH_3	-
Desformyl-vincrystine	H	OCH_3	$OCOCH_3$	CH_2CH_3	OH	-
Desacetyl-desformyl-vincristine	H	OCH_3	OH	CH_2CH_3	OH	-
Vinorelbine	CH_3	OCH_3	$OCOCH_3$	CH_2CH_3	H	remixed
Vinflunine	CH_3	OCH_3	$OCOCH_3$	CF_2CH_3	H	remixed

Identification Tests

- 1-Vanillin/HCl reagent gives pink color with vinblastine and orange-yellow colour with vincristine.
- 2-Van-Urk's reagent (Para-Dimethyl-amino-benzaldehyde reagent): on adding Van-Urk's reagent on sample of vinca alkaloids gives reddish-brown colour.

Extraction and Isolation of *Vinca* Alkaloids

Various extraction procedures employed are
- (a) Supercritical fluid extraction (SFE)
- (b) Soxhlet extraction
- (c) Solid-liquid extraction

(d) Hot water extraction

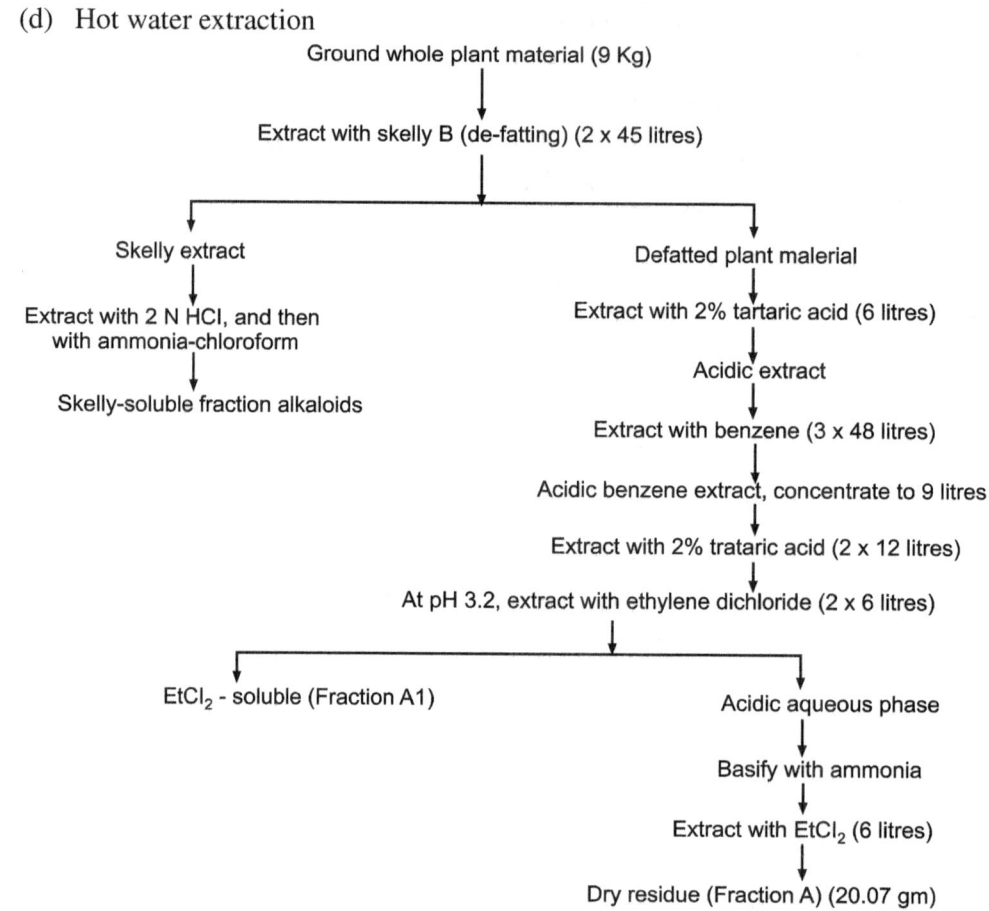

Biosynthesis

The various *Catharanthus* alkaloids belong to the class of terpenoid indole alkaloids, that is, they consist of two moieties derived from two separate metabolic pathways. The Mevalonate pathway which gives the non tryptophan moiety; and the tryptophan moiety is obtained from tryptophan. The complex structure of these alkaloids usually contains two nitrogen atoms; one is the indole nitrogen (in the tryptophan-derived moiety) and the second is generally two carbons removed from the Beta- position of the indole ring. The non- tryptophan moiety is derived from mevalonic acid and it is a C-10-geraniol (monoterpenoid) contribution in the case of these alkaloids. This portion with suitable rearrangements leads to formation of three types of alkaloids : (i) Corynanthe-type alkaloids (ii) Iboga-type alkaloids, (iii) Aspidosperma-type alkaloids. It is believed that the corynanthe- type monoterpenoid moiety is metabolically most primitive. The reactive form of terpene involves an aldehyde group. The loss of one carbon atom during biogenesis, to give C9 unit is largely common. Geraniol by a series of conversions forms loganin and then secologanin (a monoterpenoid glucoside). The molecular characterisation of CYP72A1 from *Catharanthus roseus* was described nearly a decade ago, but the enzyme's function remained unknown. However in a recent study conducted, it was shown that CYP72A1 converts loganin into secologanin. A key intermediate in the biogenesis of the monoterpene indole alkaloids is 3 alpha (S)-strictosidine, formed by the enzymatic condensation of tryptamine and secologanin. The enzyme responsible for this important reaction, strictosidine synthase, has been isolated and characterised from cell cultures of a number of species including *Catharanthus roseus*. Strictosidine then leads to formation of cathenamine (a coryanthe-type of alkaloid); enzyme involved is cathenamine synthase. Cathenamine further gives rise to ajmalicine (enzyme- ajmalicine synthase) and serpentine. Both ajmalicine and serpentine are also coryanthe- type alkaloids. Cathenamine through a series of reactions also leads to formation of catharanthine and vindoline. Catharanthine and vindoline are monomeric indolealkaloids and occur free in the plant. 3',4'-Anhydrovinblastine is a key intermediate from the coupling of catharanthine and vindoline and the enzymes involved are peroxidases. It is further converted to vinblastine.

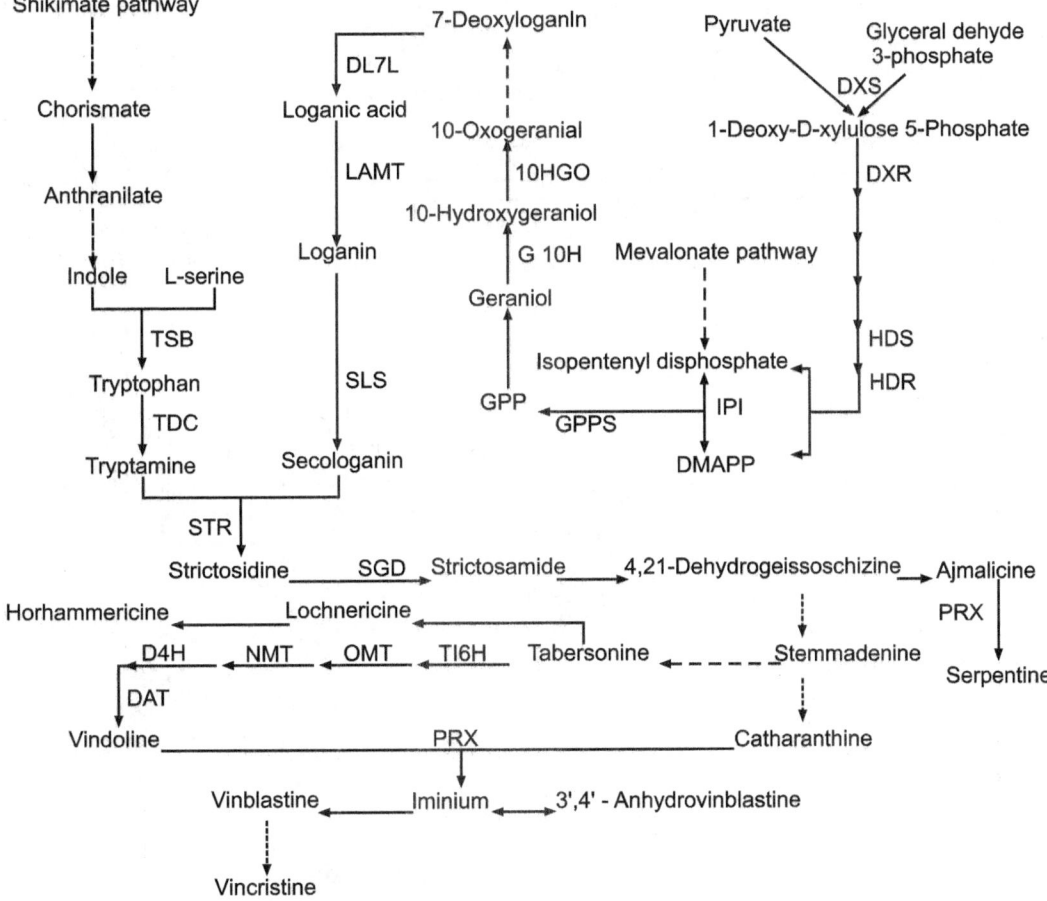

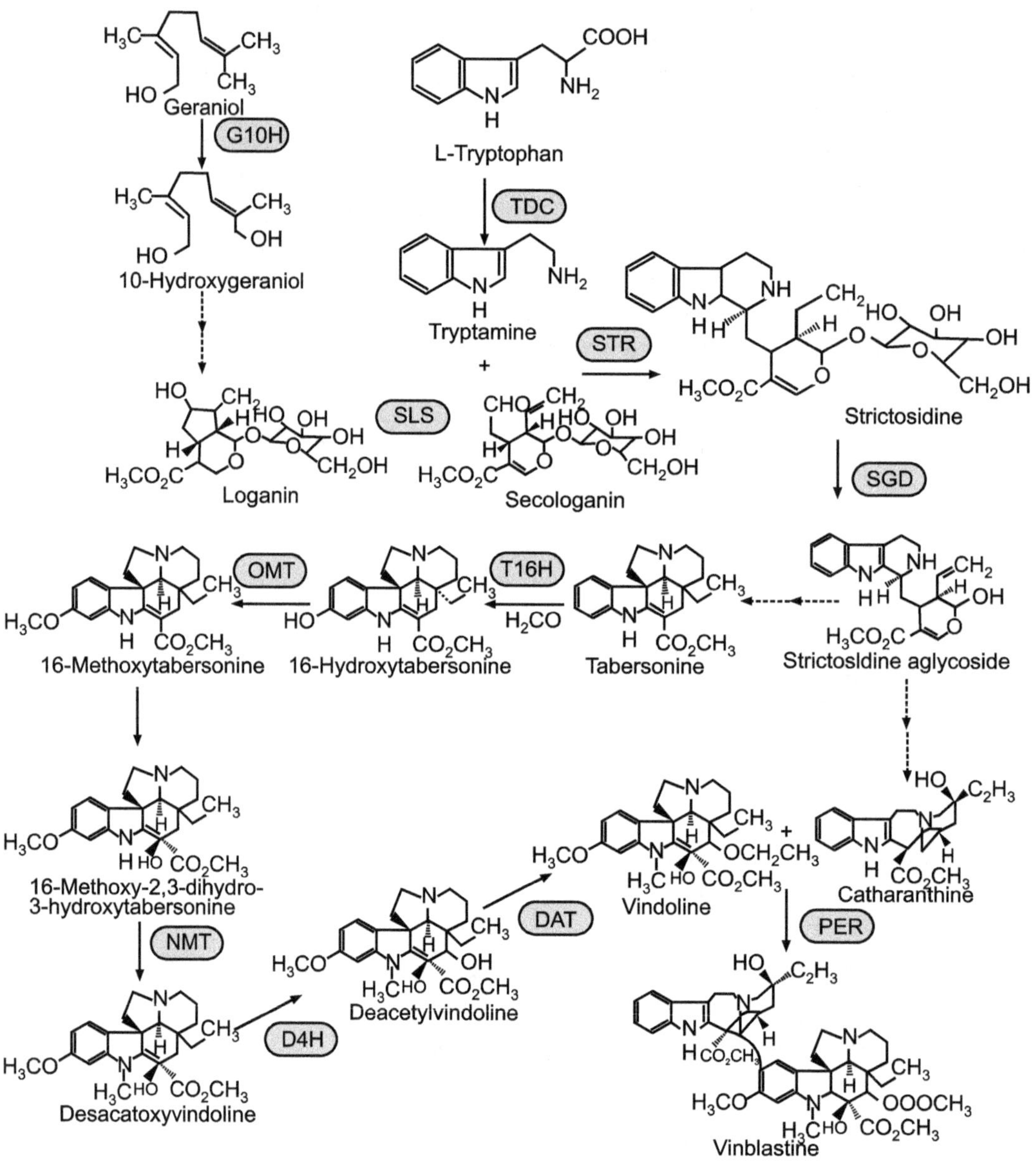

Fig. 6.30 : Biosynthesis of vinca alkaloids

Mechanism of Action

Vinblastine

Vinblastine is an alkaloid derived from *Vinca rosea,* the periwinkle plant. Its mechanism of action involves depolymerisation of microtubules, which are an important part of the cytoskeleton and the mitotic spindle. The drug binds specifically to the microtubule protein tubulin in dimeric form; the drug-tubulin complex adds to the forming end of the microtubules to terminate the assembly, and depolymerisation of the microtubules then occurs. This results in mitotic arrest at metaphase, dissolution of the mitotic spindle, and interference with chromosome segregation. Toxicity includes nausea and vomiting, bone marrow suppression, and alopecia. It has clinical activity in the treatment of Hodgkin's disease, non-Hodgkin's lymphomas, breast cancer, and germ cell cancer.

Vincristine

Vincristine is also an alkaloid derivative of *Vinca rosea* and is closely related in structure to vinblastine. Its mechanism of action is considered to be identical to that of vinblastine, in that it functions as a mitotic spindle poison leading to arrest of cells in the M phase of the cell cycle. Despite these similarities to vinblastine, vincristine has a strikingly different spectrum of clinical activity and qualitatively different toxicities.

Vincristine has been effectively combined with prednisone for remission induction in acute lymphoblastic leukemia in children. It is also active in various hematologic malignancies such as Hodgkin's and non-Hodgkin's lymphoma and multiple myeloma and in several pediatric tumors including rhabdomyosarcoma, neuroblastoma, Ewing's sarcoma, and Wilms' tumor. The main dose limiting toxicity is neurotoxicity, usually expressed as a peripheral sensory neuropathy, although autonomic nervous system dysfunction with orthostatic hypotension, sphincter problems, and paralytic ileus cranial nerve palsies, ataxia, seizures, and coma have been observed. While myelosuppression can occur, it is generally milder and much less significant than with vinblastine. The other potential side effect that can develop is the syndrome of inappropriate secretion of antidiuretic hormone (SIADH).

Vinorelbine

Vinorelbine is a semisynthetic vinca alkaloid whose mechanism of action is identical to that of vinblastine and vincristine, i.e., inhibition of mitosis of cells in the M phase through inhibition of tubulin polymerisation. Despite its similarities in mechanism of action, vinorelbine has activity in non-small cell lung cancer and in breast cancer. Myelosuppression with neutropenia is the dose limiting toxicity, but nausea and vomiting, transient elevations in liver function tests, neurotoxicity, and SIADH are also reported.

PYRROLIZIDINE ALKALOIDS

- The leading plant toxins
- Over 360 different structures, found in 3% of the world's flowering plants

Mostly derived from either the polyamines putrescine and spermidine

Pyrrolizidine alkaloids (PAs) are a group of naturally occurring alkaloids based on the structure of pyrrolizidine. Pyrrolizidine alkaloids are produced by plants as a defense mechanism against insect herbivores. More than 660 PAs and PA N-oxides have been identified in over 6,000 plants, and about half of them exhibit hepatotoxicity. They are found frequently in plants in the Boraginaceae, Asteraceae, Orchidaceae and Leguminosae families; less frequently in the Convolvulaceae and Poaceae, and in at least one species in the Lamiaceae. It has been estimated that 3% of the world's flowering plants contain pyrrolizidine alkaloids. Honey can contain pyrrolizidine alkaloids, as can grains, milk, offal and eggs. To date (2011), there is no international regulation of PAs in food, unlike those for herbs and medicines.

Unsaturated pyrrolizidine alkaloids are hepatotoxic, that is, damaging to the liver. PAs also cause hepatic veno-occlusive disease and liver cancer. PAs are tumorigenic. Disease associated with consumption of PAs is known as pyrrolizidine alkaloidosis.

Of concern is the health risk associated with the use of medicinal herbs that contain PAs, notably borage leaf, comfrey and coltsfoot in the West, and some Chinese medicinal herbs.

Pyrrolizidine alkaloid

Isolation

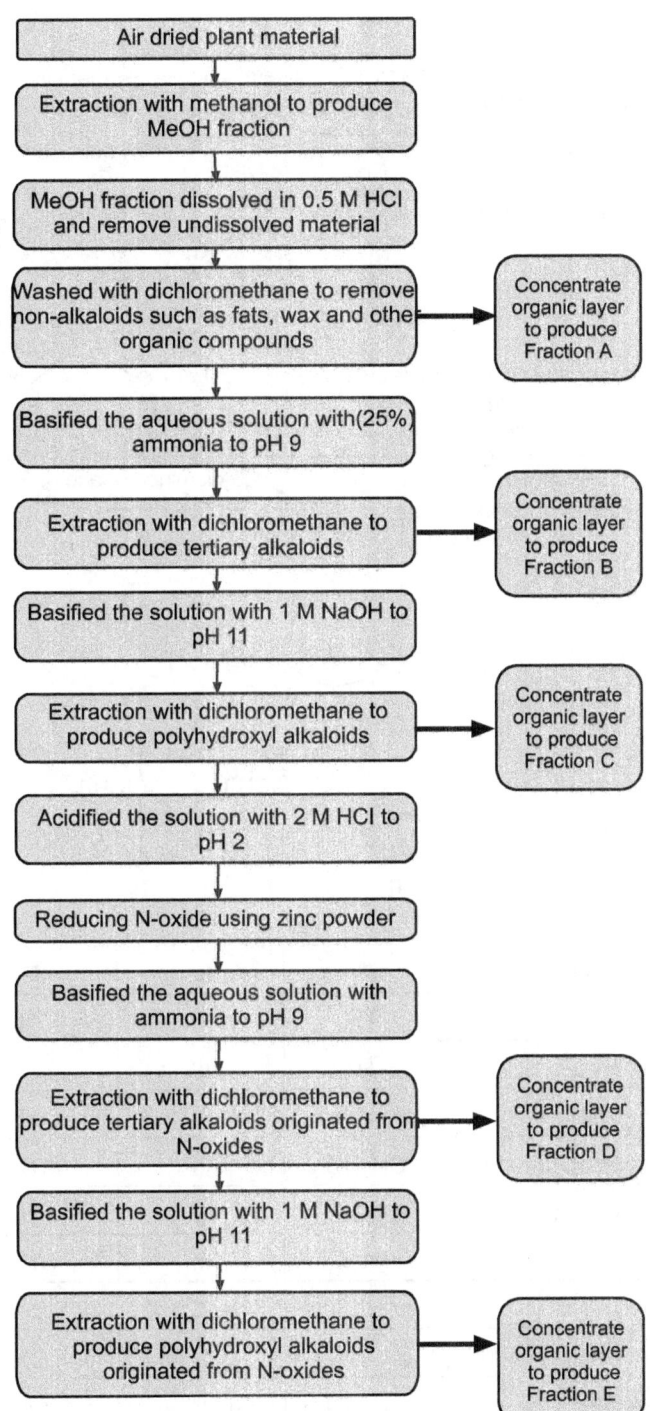

BIOSYNTHESIS

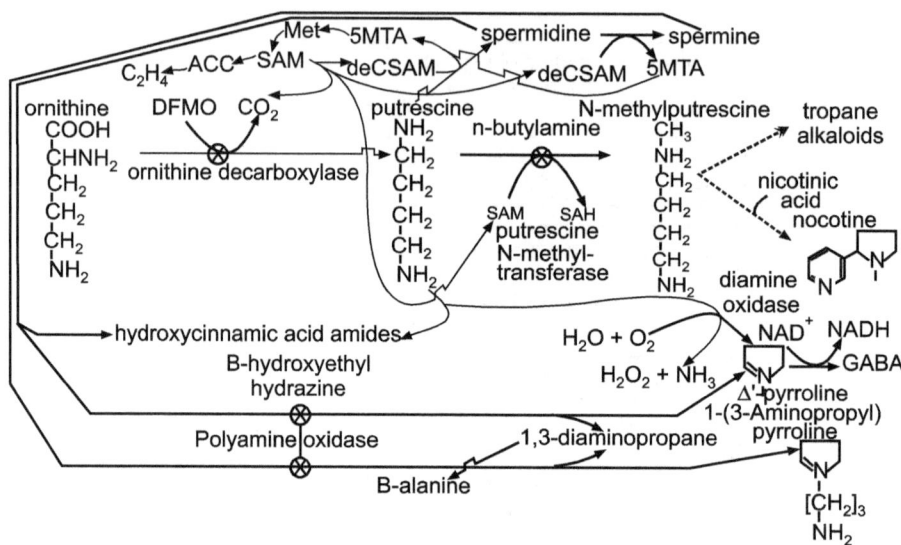

Name	R₁	R₂	R₃
retronecine	H	H	H
lycopsamine	H	III	H
intermedine	H	IV	H
7-acetyllycopsamine	CH₃CO	III	H
7-acetylintermedine	CH₃CO	IV	H
symphytine	I	III	H
symlandine	II	III	H
eschimidine	II	III or IV	OH
uplandicine	CH₃CO	III or IV	OH

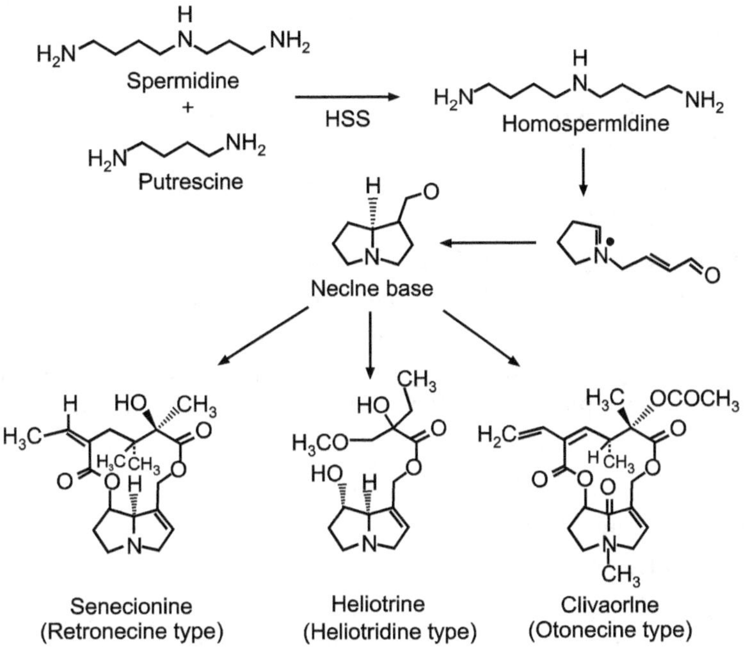

Biosynthesis & Isolation of Some Phyto.

Spermidine + Putrescine →(HSS)→ **Homospermidine** → [pyrrolidinium intermediate] → **Necine base**

Necine base gives rise to:
- **Senecionine** (Retronecine type)
- **Heliotrine** (Heliotridine type)
- **Clivaorine** (Otonecine type)

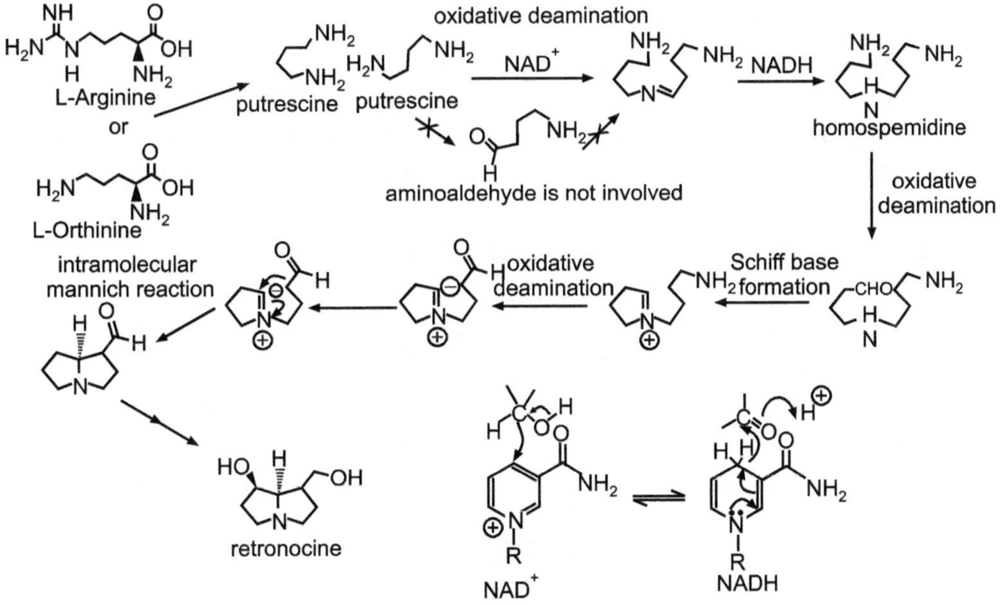

L-Arginine or **L-Ornithine** → putrescine + putrescine →(NAD$^+$, oxidative deamination)→ [iminium intermediate] →(NADH)→ **homospermidine**

aminoaldehyde is not involved

homospermidine →(oxidative deamination)→ [aldehyde-amine] →(Schiff base formation)→ [pyrrolinium-CHO] →(oxidative deamination)→ [pyrrolizinium dialdehyde] →(intramolecular mannich reaction)→ [pyrrolizidine aldehyde] → **retronecine**

NAD$^+$ ⇌ NADH

GLYCOSIDES

In nature, glycosides are formed by the interaction of nucleotide glycosides like uridine phosphate glucose with alcohol, phenol, steroid, triterpenoid and flavonoids etc. and joined by glycosidic linkage.

These are non-reducing (do not reduce Fehling solution) organic substances which on hydrolysis yield one or more sugar molecules along with non-sugar molecules. The sugar molecule is known as glycon and the non-sugar molecule termed as aglycon part. Sugars are hemiacetal and occur as oxide rings.

Glycosides are (usually) non-reducing compounds, which on hydrolysis by reagents or enzymes yield one or more reducing sugars among the products of hydrolysis

Glycosides can be defined as the condensation product of hydroxyl group of aglycon and hemiacetal hydroxyl group of sugar. The aglycon may be any compound containing at least one hydroxyl group to which glycosidal hydroxyl group of sugar joins.

$$\underset{\text{(genin)}}{\text{non-sugar}} \; \underset{\text{linkage}}{\text{glycoside}} \; \underset{\text{(glycone)}}{\text{sugar}}$$

Classification and Nomenclature

1. **On the basis of glycosidic linkage**

    (a) **O-glycosides:** Sugar molecule is combined with phenol or OH group of aglycon. e.g Amygdaline, indesine, arbutin, salicin, cardiac glycosides, anthraxquinone glycosides like sennosides etc.

    (b) **N-glycosides:** Sugar molecule is combined with N of the –NH (amino group) of aglycon. e.g. Nucleosides

    (c) **S-glycosides:** Sugar molecule is combined with the S or SH (thiol group) of aglycon. e.g. Sinigrine

    (d) **C-glycosides:** Sugar molecule is directly attached with C – atom of aglycon. e.g. Anthraquinone glycosides like aloin, barbaloin, cascaroside and flavan glycosides etc.

1. **Alcoholic or phenolic (aglycone): e.g., O-Glycoside**

$C_6H_{12}O_6$ + (phenol with CH$_2$OH and OH) $\xrightarrow{-H_2O}$ Salicin (with CH$_2$OH and O-$C_6H_{11}O_5$ — Glycosidic linkage)

Sugar

2. **Sulphur containing compounds: e.g., S-Glycoside**

$C_6H_{12}O_6$ + $CH_2 = CH - CH_2 - C \underset{N-OSO_3K}{\overset{SH}{\diagup}}$ ⟶ $CH_2 = CH - CH_2 - C \underset{N-OSO_3K}{\overset{S-C_6H_{11}O_5}{\diagup}}$ (Glycosidic linkage)

Sugar

Sinigrin

3. Nitrogen containing compounds: e.g., N-Glycoside

4. C-Glycoside

α and β Glycosides

- Sugars exist in isomeric α and β forms. Both α and β Glycosides are theoretically possible.
- All natural glycosides are of the β Type.
- Some α linkage exists in sucrose, glycogen and starch. Also the glycoside, K-strophanthoside (strophanthidin-link to strophanthotriose (Cymarose + β-glucose + α- glucose).

According to the nature of the simple sugar component of the glycoside
 (a) Glucosides (the glycone is glucose).
 (b) Galacosides (the glycone is galacose).
 (c) Mannosides (the glycone is mannose).
 (d) Arabinosides (the glycone is arabinose).

According to the number of the monosaccharides in the sugar moiety
 (a) Monoside (one monosaccharide) e.g., salicin.
 (b) Biosides (two monosaccharide) e.g., gentobioside.
 (c) Triosides (three monosaccharide) e.g., strophanthotriose.

According to the physiological or pharmacological activity they can be 'therapeutically classified as
 (a) Laxative glycosides.
 (b) Cardiotonic glycosides.

According to the correlation to the parent natural glycoside

    (a) Primary glycosides e.g., amygdalin, purpurea glycoside A,

    (b) Secondary glycosides e.g., prunasin, digitoxin.

According to the plant families.

According to the chemical nature of the aglycone

    (a) Alcoholic and phenolic glycosides -aglycones are alcohols or phenols

    (b) Aldehydic G - aglycones are aldehydes.

    (c) Cyanogenic G - aglycones are nitriles or derivatives of hydrocyanic acid.

    (d) Anthracene or anthraquinone G - aglycones are anthracene derivative.

    (e) Steroidal G-aglycones are steroidal in nature, derived from cyclopentanoperhydrophenanthrene.

    (f) Coumarin G-aglycones are derivative of benzo α-pyrone.

    (g) Chromone glycosides-aglycones are derivatives of benzo-δ-pyrone.

    (h) Flavonoidal G-aglycones are 2-phenyl chromone structure.

    (i) Sulphur containing or thioglycosides- aglycones are contain sulphur.

    (j) Alkaloidal glycosides-aglycone is alkaloidal in nature e.g., glucoalkaloids of solanum species.

Sugars in Glycosides

    (a) Monosaccharide (glucose in salicin, rhamnose in ouabain)

    (b) Disaccharides (gentiobiose in amygdalin).

    (c) Trisaccharides (strophanthotriose).

    (d) Tetrasaccharides (purpurea glycosides)

    (e) Rare sugars (deoxy sugars)

    (f) Sugar linked in one position to the aglycone rarely in 2 positions as sennosides.

(a) 6-deoxy sugars

    e.g.,   1- methylpentoses   2- α-L-rhamnose

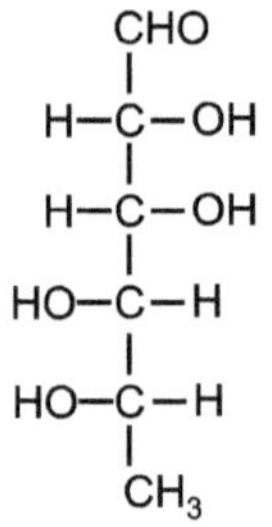

CHO
|
H—C—OH
|
H—C—OH
|
HO—C—H
|
HO—C—H
|
CH₃

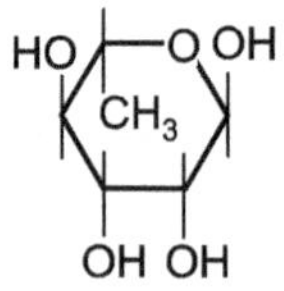

(b) 2, 6-deoxy sugars (called rare sugars)

e.g., 1- D.digitoxose 2-D.cymarose 3- diginose

```
CHO            CHO              CHO
|              |                |
CH₂            CH₂              CH₂
|              |                |
C—OH           C—OCH₃     H₃CO—C
|              |                |
C—OH           C—OH         HO—C
|              |                |
C—OH           C—OH        H—C—OH
|              |                |
CH₃            CH₃              CH₃
```

(c) 2-deoxy sugars   e.g. 2-deoxy-D-ribose

Physical and Chemical Properties

Diversity in structure makes it difficult to find general physical and chemical properties

1. (a) Most glycosides are water soluble and soluble in alcohols.
   (b) Either insoluble or less soluble in non polar organic solvents.
   (c) More sugar units in a glycoside lead to more solubility in polar solvents.
2. Glycosides do not reduce Fehling's solution, but when are susceptible to hydrolysis give reducing sugars (C-glycosides are exceptions).

Stability and Hydrolytic Cleavage

1. Acid Hydrolysis
(a) Acetal linkage between the aglycon and glycone is more unstable than that between two individual sugars within the molecule.

(b) All glycosides are hydrolysable by acids non specific (except C-glycosides).

(c) Glycosides containing 2-deoxy sugars are more unstable towards acid hydrolysis even at room temperature.

(d) C-glycosides are very stable (need oxidative hydrolysis).

2. Alkali Hydrolysis
(a) Mild alkali
(b) Strong alkali

3. **Enzyme Hydrolysis**
   (a) Enzymatic hydrolysis is specific for each glycoside as there is a specific enzyme that exerts a hydrolytic action on it.
   (b) The same enzyme is capable of hydrolysing different glycosides, but α and β sterio-isomers of the same glycoside are usually not hydrolysed by the same enzyme.
   (c) Emulsin is found to hydrolyse most β-glycoside linkages, those glycosides attacked by emulsin are regarded as β-glycosides.
   (d) Maltase and invertase are α-glycosidases, capable of hydrolysing α-glycosides only.

Extraction and Isolation of Glycosides

1. Water mixed with different proportions of methanol or ethanol (most suitable extracting solvent).
2. Non-polar organic solvents are generally used for de-fating process.
3. Glycosides are not precipitated from aqueous solutions by lead acetate.

General methods of isolation involve

1. Destruction of hydrolysing enzymes.
   (a) Drying for 15-30 min. at 100°C.
   (b) Place plant in boiling water or alcohol 10-20 min.
   (c) Boil with acetone.
   (d) Subject to cold acid pH treatment.
   (e) Extract at very low temperature.
2. De-fating or purification of the plant material (in case of seeds).
3. Extraction of the glycosidal constituents by alcohol, water or dilute alcohols.
4. Concentrate the alcoholic extract (to get rid of the organic solvent). Add water (or hot water) → filter any precipitate.
5. Purify aqueous extract
   (a) Extract non glycosidal impurities by organic solvent.
   (b) Water soluble impurities precipitate by lead acetate.
6. Precipitate excess lead salts.
7. Isolation of the glycosides from the purified aqueous solution, by crystallisation.

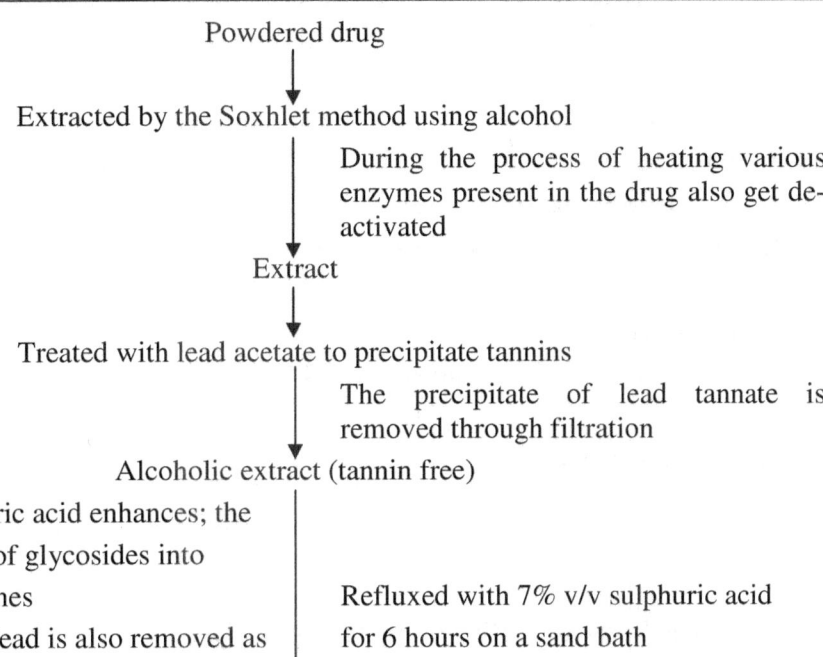

Chemical Tests of Glycosides: Glycosides are the compounds with organic molecules having attached glucose or any mono-oligosaccharide unit. Usually, these are crystalline or amorphous solids; optically active, soluble in water and alcohol but insoluble in organic solvents like ether, chloroform and benzene etc. Generally, aqueous or alcoholic extracts of crude drugs are tested with specific reagents for presence of various types of glycosides.

1. **Chemical tests for anthraquinone glycosides**
   - Borntrager's test
   - Modified Borntrager's test
2. **Chemical tests for saponin glycosides**
   - Heamolysis test
   - Foam test
3. **Chemical tests for steroid and triterpenoid glycosides**
   - Libermann Bruchard test
   - Salkowski test
   - Antimony trichloride test
   - Trichloroacetic acid test
   - Tetranitromethane test
   - Zimmermann test

4. Chemical tests for cardiac glycosides
- Keller Killiani test
- Legal test
- Baljet test
- 3, 5-dinitro benzoic acid test

5. Chemical tests for Coumarin glycosides
- $FeCl_3$ test
- Fluorescence test

6. Chemical tests for Cynophoric glycoside
- Sodium picrate test

7. Chemical tests for flavonoid glycosides
- Ammonia test
- Shinoda test
- Vanillin HCl test

(1) Chemical Tests for Anthraquinone Glycosides

(a) Borntrager's Test: To 1 gm of drug, is added 5-10 ml of dilute HCl, boiled on water bath for 10 minutes and filtered. Filtrate was extracted with CCl_4/benzene and equal amount of ammonia solution added to filtrate and shake. Formation of pink or red colour in ammonical layer due to presence of anthraquinone moiety is observed

(b) Modified Borntrager's Test: To 1 gm of drug, 5 ml dilute HCl is added, followed by 5 ml ferric chloride (5% w/v). The mixture is boil for 10 minutes on water bath, cooled and filtered, filtrate was extracted with carbon tetrachloride or benzene and equal volume of ammonia solution added. Formation of pink to red colour is due to presence of anthraquinone moiety. This test is used for C-type of anthraquinone glycosides.

(2) Chemical Tests for Saponin Glycosides

(a) Haemolysis test: A drop blood on slide was mixed with few drops of aq. saponin solution. RBCs rupture in presence of saponins.

(b) Foam test: To 1 gm of drug 10-20 ml of water is add and shaken for a few minutes. Formation of froth which persists for 60-120 seconds indicates the presence of saponins.

(3) Chemical Tests for Steroid and Triterpenoid Glycosides

(a) Libermann Bruchard test: Alcoholic extract of drug was evaporated to dryness and extracted with $CHCl_3$ A few drops of acetic anhydride was added, followed by conc. H_2SO_4 from side wall of test tube to the $CHCl_3$ extract. Formation of violet to blue coloured ring at the junction of two liquids, indicate the presence of steroid moiety.

(b) Salkowski test: Alcoholic extract of drug was evaporated to dryness and extracted with $CHCl_3$. conc. H_2SO_4 is added from the sidewall of the test tube to the $CHCl_3$ extract. Formation of yellow coloured ring at the junction of two liquids, which turns red after 2 minutes, indicates the presence of steroid moiety.

(c) Antimony trichloride test: Alcoholic extract of drug was evaporated to dryness and extracted with $CHCl_3$. Saturated solution of $SbCl_3$ in $CHCl_3$ containing 20% acetic anhydride is added. Formation of pink colour on heating indicates presence of steroids and triterpenoids. .

(d) Trichloro acetic acid test: Triterpenes on addition of saturated solution of trichloro acetic acid forms coloured precipitate.

(e) Tetranitro methane test: It forms yellow colour with unsaturated steroids and triterpenes.

(f) Zimmermann test: Meta dinitro benzene solution was added to the alcoholic solution of drug containing alkali, on heating, it forms violet colour in presence of keto-steroid.

(4) Chemical Tests for Cardiac Glycosides

(a) Keller Killiani test: To the alcoholic extract of drug, equal volume of water and 0.5 ml of strong lead acetate solution was added, shaked and filtered. Filtrate was extracted with equal volume of chloroform. Chloroform extract was evaporated to dryness and residue was dissolved in 3 ml of glacial acetic acid followed by addition of few drops of $FeCl_3$ solution. The resultant solution was transferred to a test tube containing 2 ml of conc. H_2SO_4. Reddish brown layer is formed, which turns bluish green after standing due to presence of digitoxose.

(b) Legal test: To the alcoholic extract of drug equal volume of water and 0.5 ml of strong lead acetate solution was added, shaked and filtered. Filtrate was extracted with equal volume of chloroform and the chloroform extract was evaporated to dryness. The residue was dissolved in 2 ml of pyridine and sodium nitropruside 2 ml was added followed by addition of NaOH solution to make alkaline. Formation of pink colour in presence of glycosides or aglycon moiety.

(c) Baljet test: Thick section of leaf of digitalis or the part of drug containing cardiac glycoside, when dipped in sodium picrate solution, it forms yellow to orange colour in presence of aglycones or glycosides.

(d) 3, 5-dinitro benzoic acid test: To the alcoholic solution of drug, a few drops of NaOH followed by 2% solution of 3, 5-dinitro benzoic acid was added. Formation of pink colour indicates the presence of cardiac glycosides.

(5) Chemical Tests for Coumarin Glycosides

(a) $FeCl_3$ test: To the concentrated alcoholic extract of drug few drops of alcoholic $FeCl_3$ solution was added. Formation of deep green colour, which turned yellow on addition of conc. HNO_3, indicates presence of coumarins.

(b) Fluorescence test: The alcoholic extract of drug was mixed with 1N NaOH solution (one ml each). Development of blue-green fluorescence indicates presence of coumarins.

(6) Chemical Tests for Cynophoric Glycoside

(a) Sodium picrate test: Powdered drug moistened with water in a conical flask and few drops of conc. sulphuric acid was added. Filter paper impregnated with sodium picrate solution followed by sodium carbonate solution was trapped on the neck of flask using cork. Formation of brick red colour due to volatile HCN is formed in presence of cynophoric glycosides.

(7) Chemical Tests for Flavonoid Glycosides

(a) Ammonia test: Filter paper dipped in alcoholic solution of drug was exposed to ammonia vapor. Formation of yellow spot on filter paper.

(b) Shinoda test:
   (i) To the alcoholic extract of drug, magnesium turnings and dil. HCl was added, formation of red colour indicates the presence of flavonoids.
   (ii) To the alcoholic extract of drug, zinc turnings and dil. HCl was added, formation of deep red to magenta colour indicates the presence of dihydro flavonoids.

(c) Vanillin HCl test: Vanillin HCl was added to the alcoholic solution of drug; there is formation of pink colour due to presence of flavonoids.

PHARMACEUTICAL APPLICATION OF GLYCOSIDES

Glycosides are widely used in pharmaceutical industries including production of steroidal hormones, vitamins, active pharmaceutical ingredients and also for therapeutic purposes. Some important applications are listed below:

1. **Digitalis:** Used in the treatment of conjustive heart failure.
2. **Strophanthus:** Used as a cardiotonic and diuretic.
3. **Squill:** Finds application as a rodenticide.
4. **Oleandrin and adynerin:** Used in the treatment of a cancer.
5. **Senna and rhubarb:** Used as a laxative and purgative.
6. **Aloe:** Used as a purgative.
7. **Diosgenin:** Used for production of steroidal hormones like estrogen and progesterone.
8. **Glycyrrhetinic acid:** Used as an anti inflammatory drug.
9. **Quillia:** Finds application as an emulsifier.
10. **Almond (Bitter):** Used as expectorant.
11. **Picrorrhiza and Kalmegh:** Bitter in tastes and used to treat liver disorders.
12. **Rutin:** Venoactive and as a source of Vit. P.

CARDIAC GLYCOSIDE

- The genins of all cardiac glycosides are steroidal in nature, that act as cardio tonic agents.
- They are characterised by their highly specific action on cardiac muscle, increasing tone, excitability and contractility of this muscle, thus allowing the weakened heart to function more efficiently.

Source and Chemical Constituents

It is obtained from *D. purpurea, D. lanata, D. lutea* and *D. thapsi*. Family – *Scrophularaceae*.

1. The glycoside K-strophanthoside (a trioside), K-strophanthin B (bioside) and cymarin (a monoside) were isolated from different *Strophanthus* species.
2. The primary glycoside K-strophanthoside gives, on hydrolysis, one molecule of glucose and the secondary glycoside K-strophanthoside B or K- strophanthin B.
3. It later, gives on hydrolysis, one molecule of glucose and the tertiary glycoside cymarin, which in turn hydrolyse into the genin K-strophanthidin and the deoxysugar cymarose.

Cardioactive agents includes the squill glycosides (the scillarins) and the toad poison (Bufotoxin).

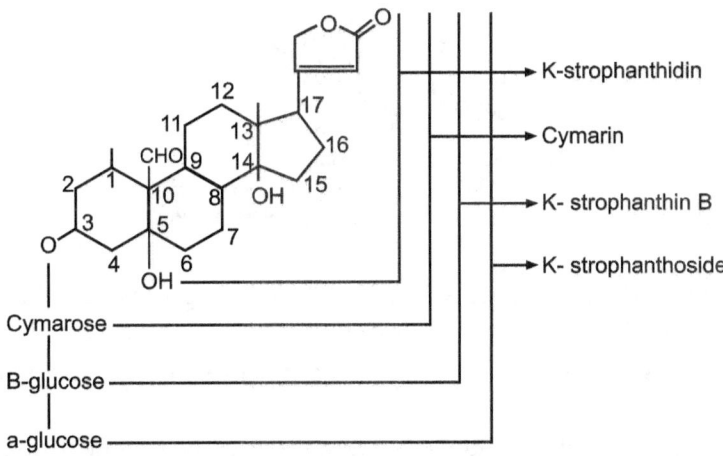

Fig. 6.36 : Structure of strophanthidin glycoside

The seeds of *Strophanthus gratus* contains another glycoside named Ouabain or (G-strophanthin), which on hydrolysis yields rhamnose and the aglycone ouabagenin.

Ouabagenin differs from K-strophanthidin in having 2 additional (OH) groups at C-1 and C-11 and having a primary alcoholic group at C-10 instead of the aldehydic group.

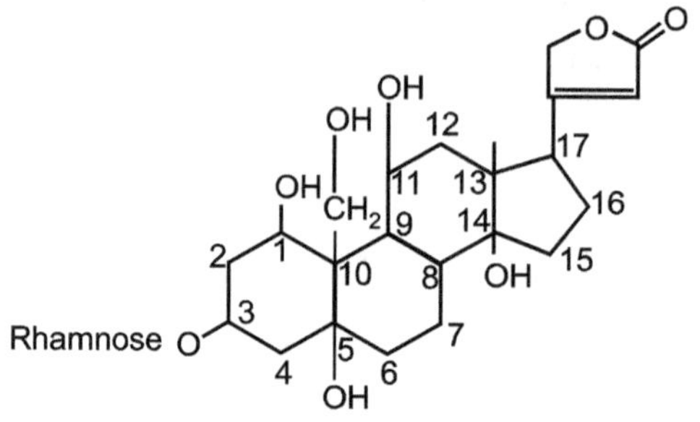

Fig. 6.37 : Ouabain (G-strophanthin)

The genins of squill glycosides differ from those of the cardenolides in two important aspects

1. They have six membered doubly unsaturated lactone ring in position C-17.
2. They have at least one double bond in the steroid nucleus.

Squill glycosides
Bufotoxin

Bufadienolides
R_1 = OH, R_2 = H
R_1 & R_2 = ester group

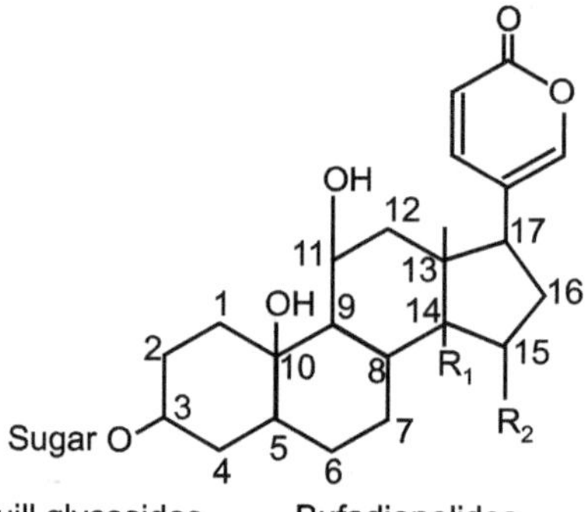

This group of cardioactive agents includes the squill glycosides (the scillarins) and the Toad poison (Bufotoxin).

The genins of squill glycosides differ from those of the cardenolides in two important aspects

1. They have six membered doubly unsaturated lactone ring in position C-17.
2. They have at least one double bond in the steroid nucleus.

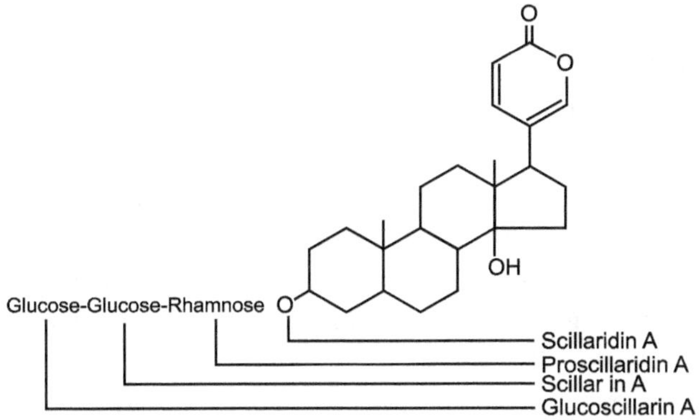

Table 6.6 : The Bufadienolides of *Squill*

Scillaridin A
Proscillaridin A
Scillar in A
Glucoscillarin A

Glucose-Glucose-Rhamnose

Name of glycosides	Structure
Glucoscillarin	Scillaridin A ---RH—G---G
Scillarin A	Scillaridin A ---RH—G
Proscillaridin A	Scillaridin A ---RH

All cardio active glycosides are characterised by the following structural features :

1. The presence of β-OH at position C-3, which is always involved in a glycosidic linkage to a mono, di, tri, or tetra saccharide.
2. The presence of another β-OH group at C-14.
3. The presence of unsaturated 5 or 6- membered lactone ring at position C-17, also in the β configuration.
4. The A/B ring junction is usually (cis), while the B/C ring junction is always (trans) and the C/D ring junction is in all cases (cis).
5. Additional OH groups may be present at C-5, C-11 and C-16.
6. Cardiac glycosides that α-β unsaturated 5-membered lactose ring in position C-17 are known as cardenolides. These are represented by the digitalis and straphanthus group.
7. Digitalis glycosides contain angular methyl group at C-10, while strophanthus glycoside are characterised by presence of either an aldehydic (CHO) or primary alcoholic (C`H$_2$OH) group at C-10.

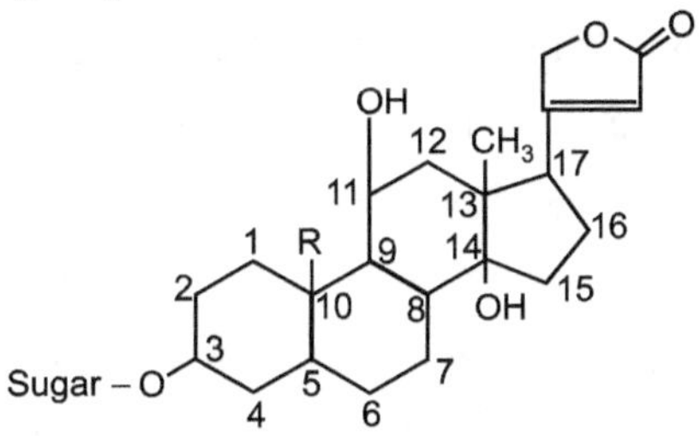

Cardenolides

Digitalis glycosides   R=CH$_3$
Strophanthus glycosides   R=CHO OR CH$_2$OH

8. Cardiac agents that have doubly unsaturated 6-membered lactone ring in position C-17 are referred to as Bufadienolides.
9. This group includes the squill glycosides and the toad venom, Bufotoxin.
10. The glycone portion at position C-3 of cardiac glycosides may contain four monosaccharide molecules linked in series. Thus, from a single genin one may have a monoside, a bioside, a trioside or a tetroside.
11. With the exception of D-glucose and L-rhamnose, all the other sugars that are found in cardiac glycosides are uncommon deoxy-sugars e.g., Digitoxose, cymarose, thevetose.

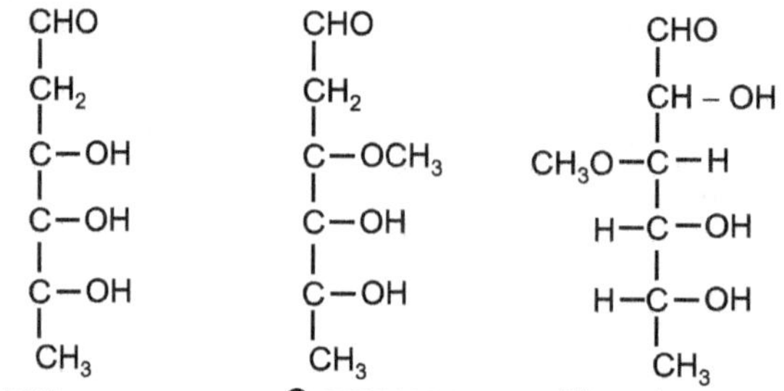

Dititoxose / Cyamarose / Thevetose

The structures of the common aglycones of the digitalis group are

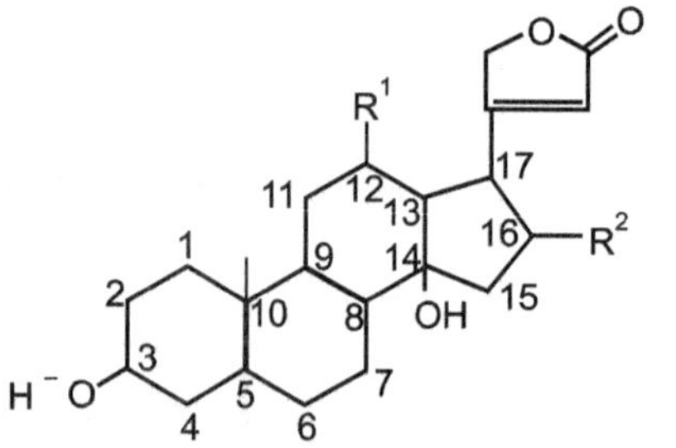

Compounds	R_1	R_2
Digitoxigenin	H	H
Gitoxigenin	H	OH
Digoxigenin	OH	H

DX = Digitoxose, DX (AC) = Acetyldigitoxose, G = Glucose.

1. **Glycosides derived from Digitoxigenin**
   (a) Lanatoside A = Digitoxigenin---DX---DX----DX(AC)---G.
   (b) Acetyl-digitoxin = Digitoxigenin---DX---DX----DX---(AC).
   (c) Digitoxin = Digitoxigenin------DX---DX----DX.
   (d) Purpurea gly A = Digitoxigenin---DX---DX----DX---G

2. **Glycosides derived from Gitoxigenin**
   (a) Lanatoside B = Gitoxigenin---DX---DX----DX(AC)---G.
   (b) Acetyl-gitoxin = Gitoxigenin---DX---DX----DX---(AC).
   (c) Gitoxin = Gitoxigenin------DX---DX----DX.
   (d) Purpurea gly B = Gitoxigenin---DX---DX----DX---G.

3. Glycosides derived from Digoxigenin

(a) Lanatoside C = Digoxigenin---DX---DX----DX(AC)---G.

(b) Acetyl-digoxin = Digoxigenin---DX---DX----DX---(AC).

(c) Digoxin = Digoxigenin------DX---DX----DX.

(d) Deslanoside = Digoxigenin---DX---DX----DX---G.

(i) The primary glycosides Lanatoside A, Lanatoside B, Lanatoside C are acted by specific enzyme which split the terminal glucose, give the secondary glycosides acetyldigitoxin, acetylgitoxin and acetyldigoxin respectively.

(ii) The deacetyl-lanatosides A, B and C can be obtained by the alkaline hydrolysis of the corresponding lanatosides.

(iii) Digitoxin, gitoxin and digoxin are obtained by the action of alkali on their acetyl-derivatives.

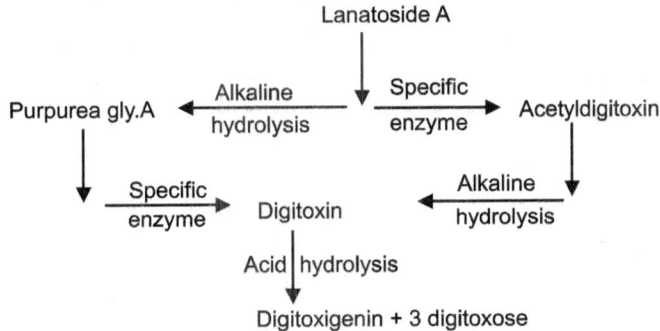

Properties

- It is recommended to heat stabilise these CG, by destroying the enzymes at higher temperatures. At higher temperature, the tertiary OH group at C-14 may split off as water, leading to formation of an inactive anhydro-form of CG.

- The gitoxin has in addition to tertiary OH at C-14, another secondary OH at C-16. Both OH groups split as water by the action of H_2SO_4 with the formation of two additional double bonds. These with the double bond of the lactone ring from a conjugated double bond system that makes the compound fluorescent in UV light.

- The detection of gitoxin in other digitalis G is based on the above mentioned reaction.
- **Molecular formula** – $C_{27}H_{44}O_5$
- **Melting point** – 230 – 265°C

Solubility
- The different cardiac glycosides show different solubilities in aqueous and organic solvents. They are usually soluble in water or aqueous alcohol and insoluble in the fat solvents with exception of chloroform and ethylacetate.
- Higher the number of sugar units in the molecule, greater is the solubility in water but lower is the solublility in chloroform.
- Alcohols are good solvents for both the glycosides and the aglycones.
- Petroleum ether and ether are used for defatting process of drug.

Stability
- Acid hydrolysis cleavage of the glycosides into aglycones and sugar residues.
- Specific enzyme usually coexist with CG in plants, which may split the primary G into G with less sugar units. Thus, CG deteriorate during drying and storage. These drugs should be stored in sealed containers over dehydrating agents.

Thin layer Chromatography: -

Solvent system: Ethyl acetate : chloroform : ethanol (9 : 5 : 0.5)

Cyclohexane : acetone : acetic acid (49 : 49 : 2)

Detecting reagent: - Antimony tri-chloride.

Chemical Test
1. **Raymond test:** A small quantity of glycoside is dissolved in 1ml of 50% ethanol followed by addition of 0.1 ml of 1% solution of dinitrobenzene in methanol. To this solution 2 – 3 drops of 20% sodium hydroxide solution is added. Appearance of violet colour changes to blue colour.
2. **Legal test:** Glycoside + few drops of pyridine and 1 drop of 2% sodium nitroprusside and a drop of 20% NaOH is added. Deep red colour appears.
3. **Tollens test:** A mixture of pyridine and ammonical silver nitrate gives silver mirror on wall of test tube.
4. **Keller Killani test:** Drug + 10ml of 70% alcohol for a few minutes and filtered. To 5 ml filtrate, 10ml of hydrogen peroxide and 0.5 ml of strong solution of lead acetate is added. To this mixture 1 or 2 drop of concentrated sulphuric acid is added. Appearance of blue colour confirms presence of deoxy sugar.
5. **Baljet test:** To transverse or longitudinal section of digitalis, add sodium picrate solution which gives yellow to orange color.

6. **Antimony trichloride test:** A solution of glycoside is heated with antimony trichloride and trichloroacetic acid to obtain blue or violet colour.
7. **Liebermann test:** A solution of glycoside in chloroform is added in acetic anhydride followed by conc. sulphuric acid gives violet to blue colour. This test is for confirmation of steroidal nucleus.
8. **Xanthohydral test:** Red colour is produced by deoxy sugar when they are heated with 0.125% solution of xanthohydral in glacial acetic acid.

Isolation

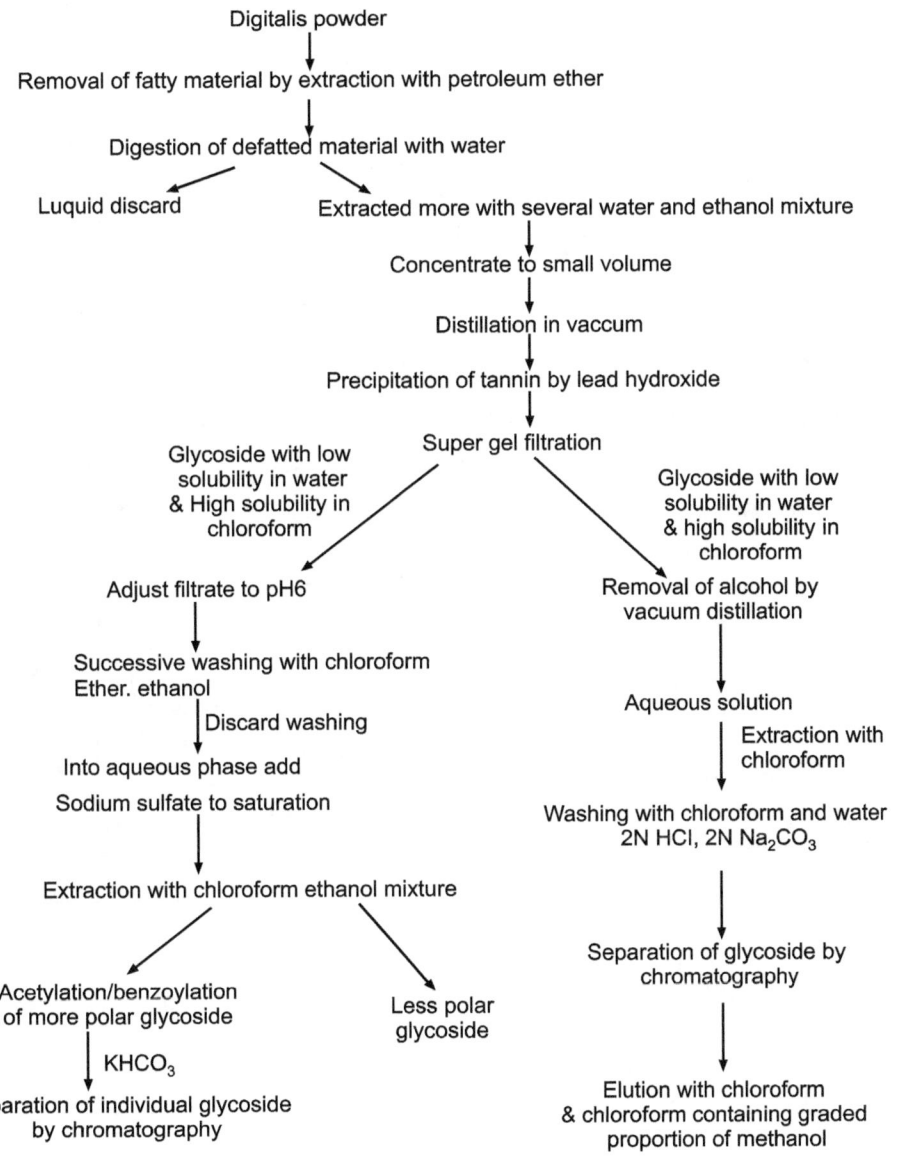

Biosynthesis

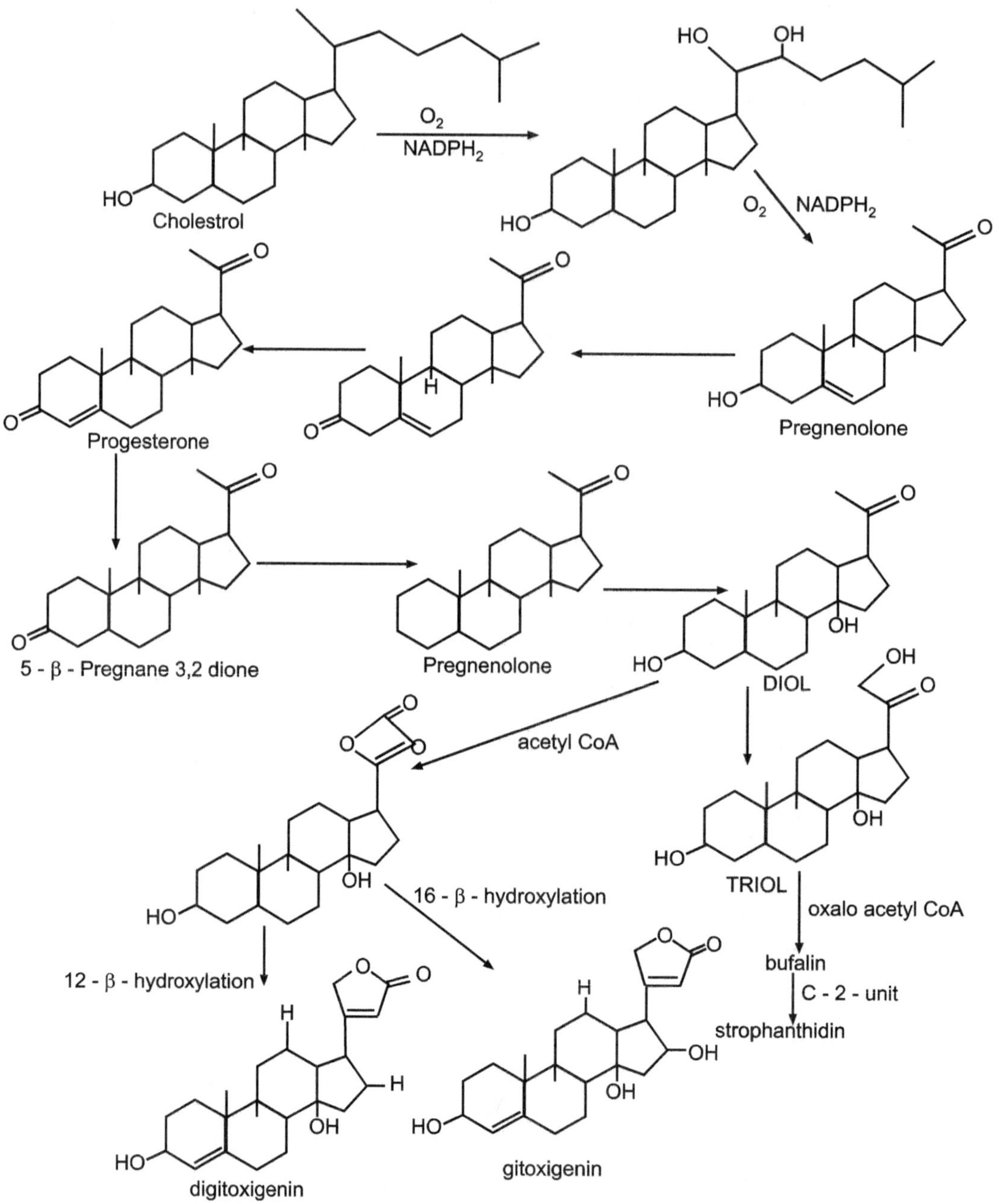

The biosynthetic pathway proceeds from Cholesterol through the following intermediates:

- **Cholesterol** → (O$_2$, NADPH$_2$) → 20,22-dihydroxycholesterol → (O$_2$, NADPH$_2$) → **Pregnenolone**
- Pregnenolone → (intermediate) → **Progesterone**
- Progesterone → **5-β-Pregnane 3,2 dione** → **Pregnenolone** → **DIOL**
- DIOL → **TRIOL** → (oxalo acetyl CoA) → **bufalin** → (C-2 unit) → **strophanthidin**
- DIOL → (acetyl CoA) → intermediate with malonyl group, 14-OH
  - → (12-β-hydroxylation) → **digitoxigenin**
  - → (16-β-hydroxylation) → **gitoxigenin**

Structure Activity Relationship

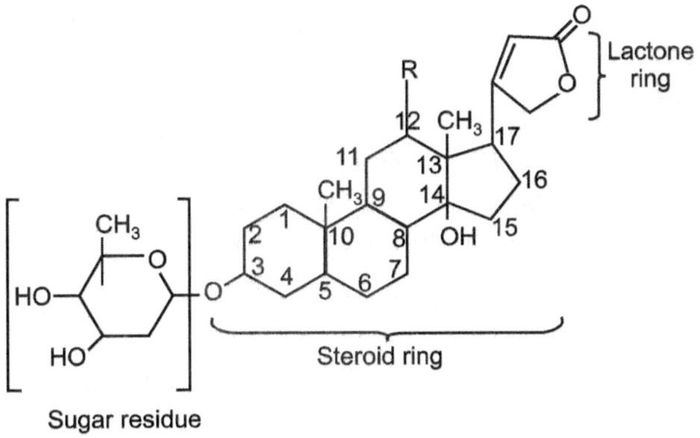

[Diagram of cardiac glycoside structure with sugar residue, steroid ring, and lactone ring labeled; carbons numbered 1–17; CH$_3$ groups at C-10 and C-13; OH at C-14; R at C-12]

Since cardiac glycoside comprise of:
(a) A genin or Aglycone portion or non-sugar portion.
(b) A sugar portion or glycon portion.

(I) A genin or Aglycone portion

(a) **C-17 side chain:** The substitution at C-17 of the genin portion of cardiac glycoside are generally of 2 types.

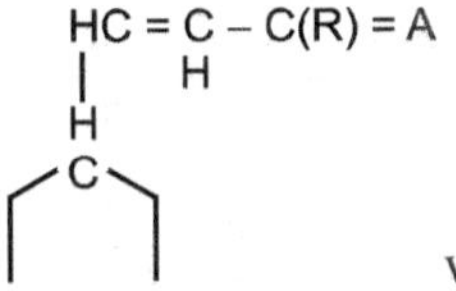

$$HC = C - C(R) = A$$

where A may be oxygen or nitrogen

A 5 or 6 membered lactone ring, in both types of C-17 substituents there is double bond conjugated with a carbonyl oxygen.

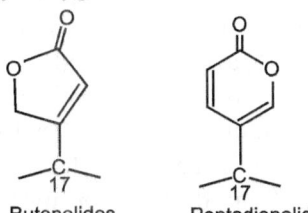

Butenolides   Pentadienolides

1. Reduction of C-17 side chain double bond results into decreased activity.
2. In the side chain –CH=CH–(R)=A where A may be heteroatom, activity falls, if 'R' is larger than -OCH$_3$. It is generally a hydrogen or small alkyl group.
3. The compound having –CH=CH–CH=NH, side chain (A=N) at C-17 exhibits higher activity.
4. If the conjugation system in C–17 side chain is extended (i.e., –CH=CH–CH=CH–CH=A) activity is abolished.
5. Since H bonding determines degree of Na$^+$, K$^+$, ATPase inhibition, the molecule dipole is an important parameter.

6. It is found that the distance between the position of particular carbonyl oxygen (or nitrile nitrogen) relative to digitoxigenin serves a nearly perfect index of its activity.

(b) Steroidal nucleus

1. Lactone ring at C-17 is essential for activity.
2. Since some compounds, not having C-17 hydroxyl group, exhibit more acivity than corresponding C-14 hydroxy derivatives, C-14 hydroxyl group does not seen to be essential for activity.

(II) Sugar Portion

Though the sugars are not directly involved in cardiotonic activity, their attachment to the steroid (at C-3) contributes greatly to both pharmacodynamic and pharmacokinetic parameters of cardiac glycosides.

Table 6.8 : Mechanism of Action

	Atrium	Purkinje Ventricle	AV Fibre	SA Node	Node
Contractility	↑	↑	–	–	–
Excitability	0	Variable	↑	–	–
Conductivity	↑	↑	↓	↓	–
Refractory period	↓	↓	↑	↑	–
Automaticity	–	–	↑	–	↓

Digitalis has multiple direct and indirect cardiovascular effects, with both therapeutic and toxic consequences. In addition, it has undesirable effects on the central nervous system and gut. At the molecular level, all therapeutically useful cardiac glycosides inhibit Na^+/K^+ ATPase, the membrane-bound transporter often called the sodium pump. The binding sites for Na^+, K^+, ATP, and digitalis all appear to reside on the subunit. Different isomers of the subunits have been identified, thus providing for different isomers of the complete enzyme with differing affinities for cardiac glycosides in various tissues. Very low concentrations of these drugs have occasionally been reported to stimulate the enzyme. In contrast, inhibition over most of the dose range has been extensively documented in all the tissues studied. It is probable that the inhibitory action is largely responsible for the therapeutic effect (positive inotropy) in the heart. Since the sodium pump is necessary for maintenance of normal resting potential in most excitable cells, it is likely that a major portion of the toxicity of digitalis is also caused by this enzyme inhibiting action.

Electrical Effects

The effects of digitalis on the electrical properties of the heart are a mixture of direct and autonomic actions. Direct actions on the membranes of cardiac cells follow a well-defined progression: an early, brief prolongation of the action potential, followed by a protracted period of shortening (especially the plateau phase).

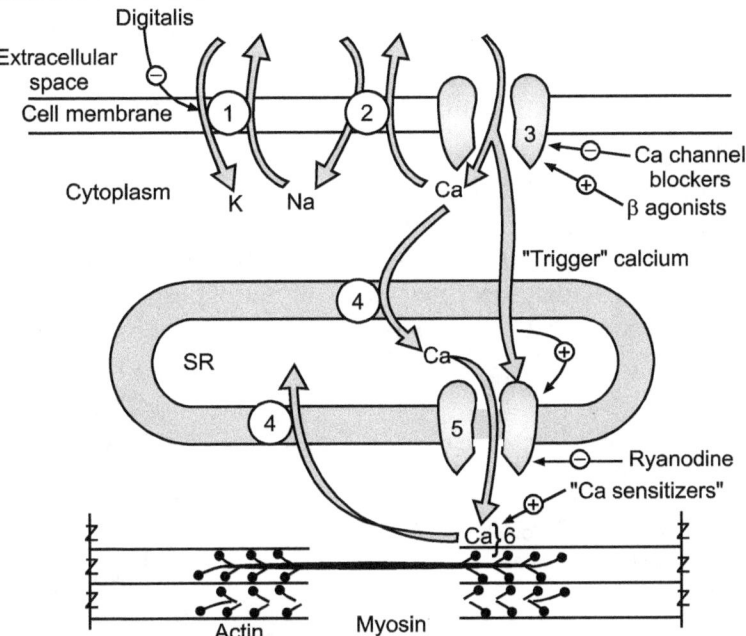

Figure: 6.8 : Schematic diagram of a cardiac muscle sarcomere, with sites of action of several drugs that alter contractility (numbered structures). Site 1 is Na^+/K^+ ATP_{ase}, the sodium pump. Site 2 is the sodium/calcium exchanger. Site 3 is the voltage-gated calcium channel. Site 4 is a calcium transporter that pumps calcium into the sarcoplasmic reticulum (SR). Site 5 is a calcium channel in the membrane of the SR that is triggered to release stored calcium by activator calcium. Site 6 is the actin-troponin-tropomyosin complex at which activator calcium brings about the contractile interaction of actin and myosin.

Main Action on Heart

The primary action may be divided into 3 parts

1. Positive inotropic effect on heart.
2. Partial blockade of A.V. conduction.
3. Reduction in heart rate.

- Direct stimulation of myocardium and increased contractility with a resultant increase in cardiac output, reduction in heart size, and improved cardiac efficiency.
- Depression of conduction, especially in A. V. node, which protects the ventricles from excessive bombardment by auricular impulses in auricular arrythmias. Due to this effect bradycardia occurs.
- Increased vagal activity, which decrease the auricular refractory period with conversion of flutter to fibrillation. The delay in A. V. conduction and bradycardia is also vagal origin.
- Increased cardiac excitability makes heart more vulnerable to arrythmias

- It has direct constrictor action on vascular smooth muscle. It may diminish clotting time.
- GIT – it causes emetic action due to stimulation of chemoreceptor trigger zone in medulla.

Biochemical Mechanism of Action

The mechanism whereby cardiac glycosides cause a positive inotropic effect and electrophysiologic changes is still not completely clear. Several mechanisms have been proposed, but the most widely accepted involves the ability of cardiac glycosides to inhibit the membrane bound Na^+-K^+-ATPase pump responsible for Na^+-K^+ exchange.

The process of muscle contraction can be pictured as shown below.

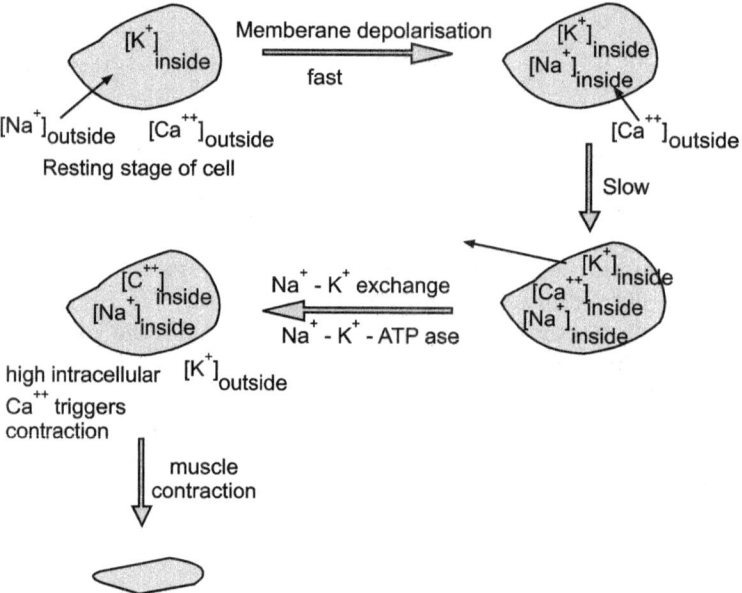

Fig 6.9 : Mechanism of muscle contraction

The process of membrane depolarisation / repolarisation is controlled by the movement of three cations, Na^+, Ca^{+2}, and K^+, in and out of the cell. At the resting stage, the concentration of Na^+ is high on the outside. On membrane depolarisation, sodium fluxes-in leading to an immediate elevation of the action potential. Elevated intracellular Na^+ triggers the influx of free of Ca^{++} that occurs more slowly. The higher intracellular $[Ca^{++}]$ results in the efflux of K^+. The reestablishment of the action potential occurs later by the reverse of the Na^+-K^+ exchange.

The Na^+ / K^+ exchange requires energy which is provided by an enzyme Na^+-K^+-ATPase. Cardiac glycosides are proposed to inhibit this enzyme with a net result of reduced sodium exchange with potassium that leaves increased intracellular Na^+. This results in increased intracellular $[Ca^{++}]$. Elevated intracellular calcium concentration triggers a series of intracellular biochemical events that ultimately result in an increase in the force of the myocardial contraction or a positive inotropic effect.

Pharmacological Action
Effects on Other Organs

Cardiac glycosides affect all excitable tissues, including smooth muscle and the central nervous system. Inhibition of Na^+/K^+ ATPase in these tissues depolarises and increases spontaneous activity both in neurons and in smooth muscle cells. The gastrointestinal tract is the most common site of digitalis toxicity outside the heart. The effects include anorexia, nausea, vomiting, and diarrhoea.

This toxicity may be partially caused by direct effects on the gastrointestinal tract but is also the result of central nervous system actions, including chemoreceptor trigger zone stimulation. Central nervous system effects commonly include vagal and chemoreceptor zone stimulation. Much less often, disorientation and hallucinations especially in the elderly and visual disturbances are noted. The latter effect may include aberrations of colour perception. Agitation and even convulsions are occasionally reported in patients taking digitalis.

Gynecomastia is a rare effect reported in men taking digitalis; it is not certain whether this effect represents a peripheral estrogenic action of these steroid drugs or a manifestation of hypothalamic stimulation.

Interactions with Potassium, Calcium, and Magnesium

Potassium and digitalis interact in two ways. First, they inhibit each other's binding to Na^+/K^+ ATPase; therefore, hyperkalemia reduces the enzyme-inhibiting actions of cardiac glycosides, whereas hypokalemia facilitates these actions. Second, abnormal cardiac automaticity is inhibited by hyperkalemia.

ANTHRAQUINONE GLYCOSIDES

They possess anthracene or it's derivatives as aglycone

Hydrolysis of these glycoside yields aglycone which are di, tri, or tetra hydroxy anthraquinone.

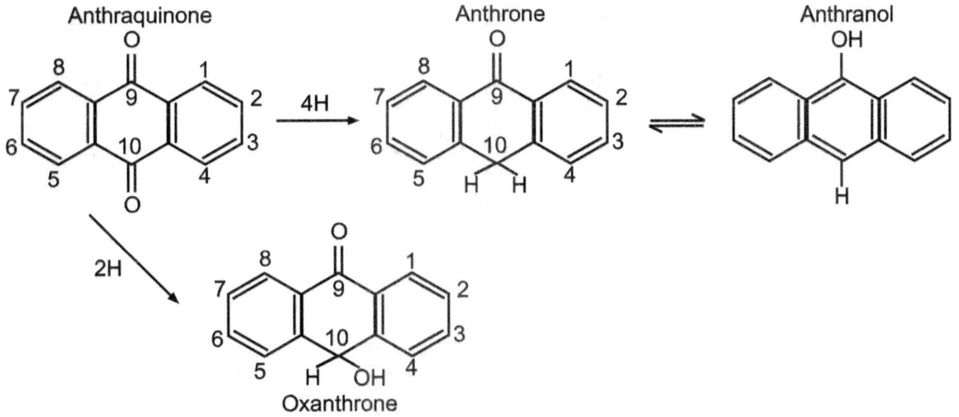

Types of Anthraquinone Glycoside

1. O-glycosides where the aglycone moiety is 1,8 dihydroxyanthraquinone derivatives, e.g.,

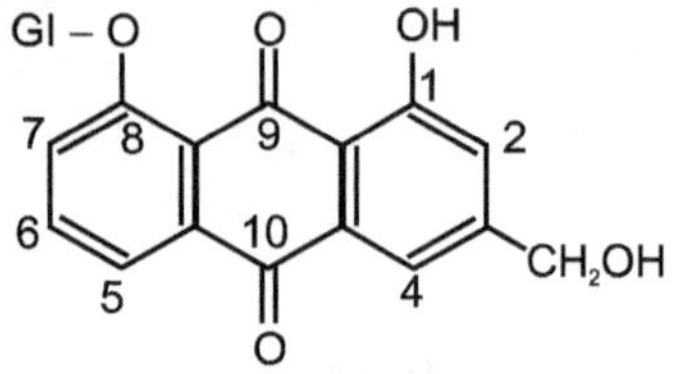

Aloe-emodin-8-glycoside 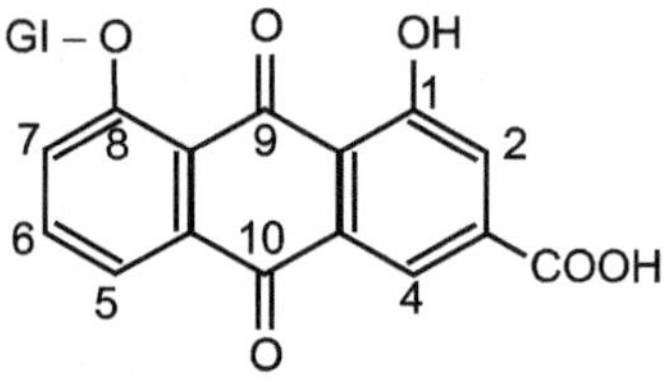   Rhein-8-glycoside 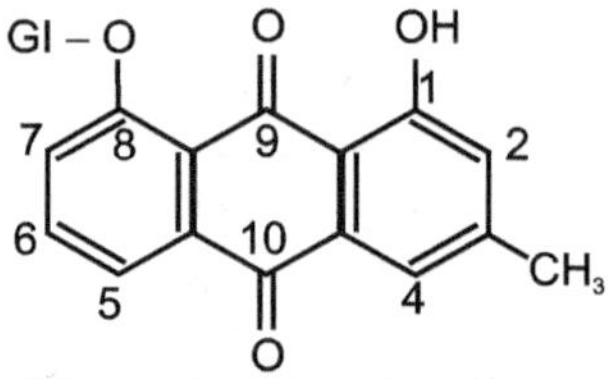   Chrysophanol-8-glycoside

2. O-glycoside where the aglycone moiety is partially reduced 1,8 dihydroxy anthraquinone, e.g., Oxanthrone type.

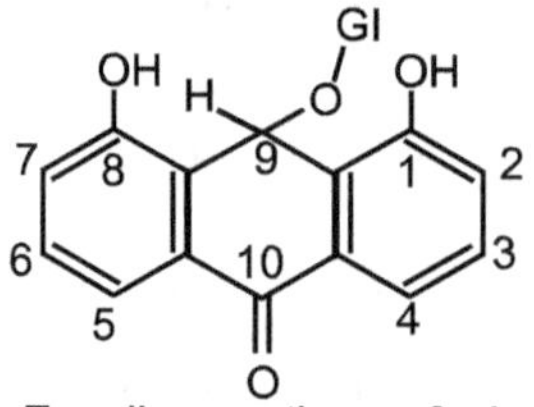

Emodin-oxanthrone-9-glucoside

3. C-glycoside where the aglycone structure is anthrone derivative. e.g. barbaloin

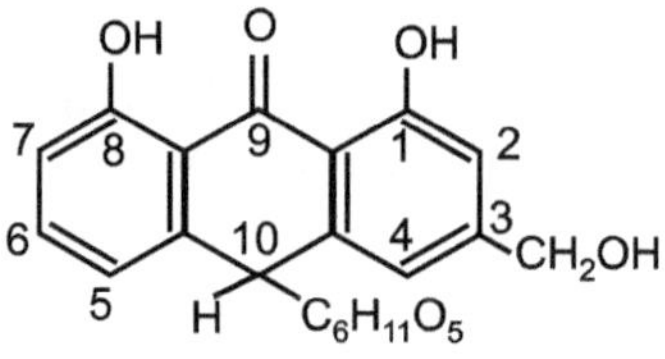

Barbaloin

4. O-glycosides where the aglycone moiety is di-anthrone derivative (i.e., **dimmer**) e.g., Sennosides where there is **C-C** bridge between the anthranol units. **Sennoside A and B**.

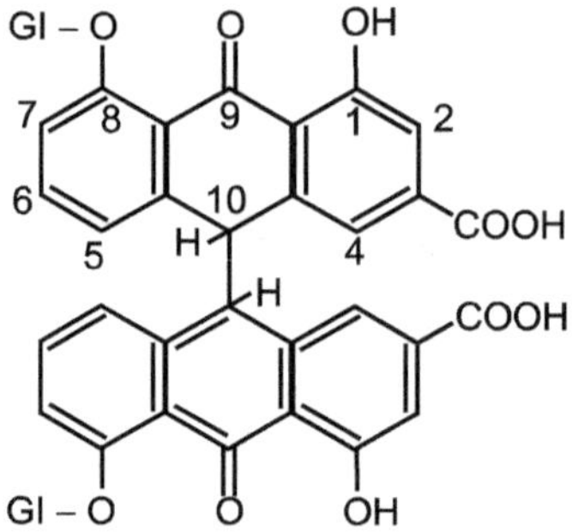

Source and Chemical Constituents

SENNA

The most widely used drugs that contain anthracene compounds are

Consists of the dried leaflet of Alexandrian or Khartoum senna, *Cassia senna* (*C. acutifolia*), *Tinnevelly senna* (*C. angustifolia*).

Constituents

Dimeric anthracene glycosides derived from two anthrones moieties which may be

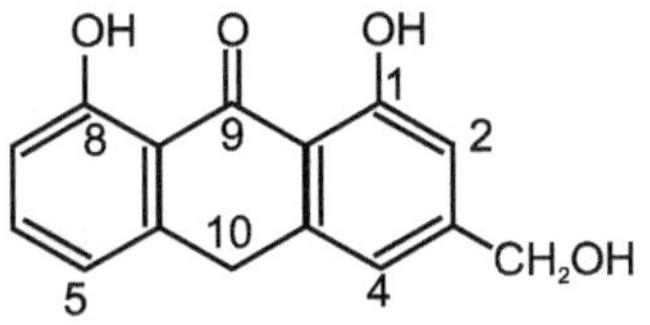

Aloe-emodin anthrone 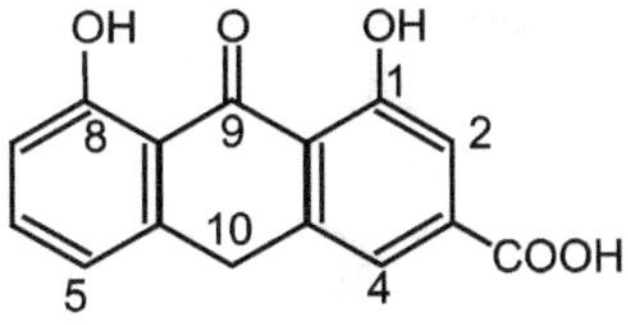   Rhein anthrone

1. Similar anthrone moiety (**Homo-dianthrones**) i.e., 2 rhein anthrone moieties condensate through two C-10 atomes. Thus, it can exist in two optical forms, Sennoside A (L- form) and Sennoside B (meso form).

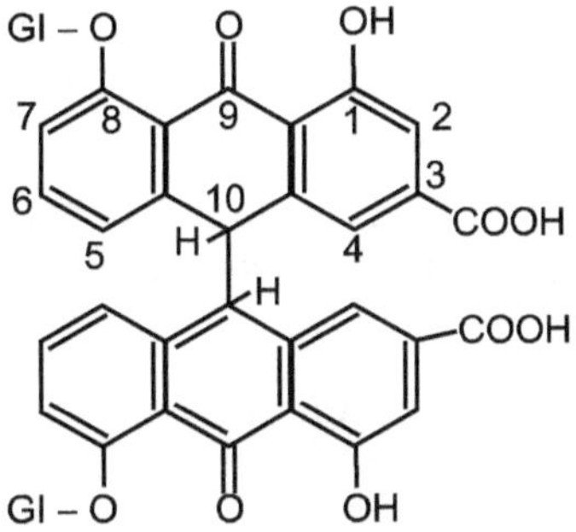

Sennoside A & B

2. Or different (**Hetero-dianthrones**) i.e., one rhein-anthrone and one emodin anthrone, Sennoside C (L-form) and Sennoside D (meso form).

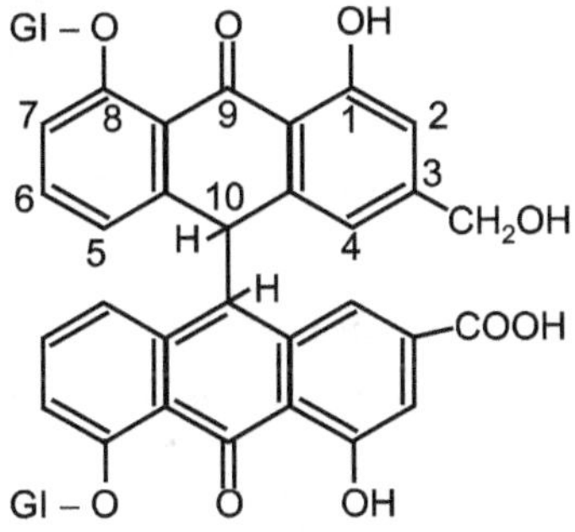

Sennoside C & D

CASCARA

The dried bark of *Rhamnus purshiana* Family **Rhamnaceae.** British Pharmacopoeia specified that the collection must be made at least one year before the bark is used (fresh bark contains an emetic principle).

Constituents

(a) Four primary glycosides

1. cascarosides A and B (glycosides of barbaloin)
2. cascarosides C and D (glycosides of chrysaloin)

[Structures: Barbaloin, Cascaroside A & B, Chrysaloin, Cascaroside C & D]

(b) Two aloins (secondary glycosides)

Barbaloin derived from (C-10-C-glycoside) of aloe-emodin anthrone and **chrysaloin** derived from (C-10-C-glycoside) of chrysophanol anthrone.

(c) A number of O-glycosides

e.g., derived from emodin, emodine oxanthrone, aloe emodin and chrysophanol.

[Structures: Aloe-emodin, Chrysophanol]

(d) Free anthraquinones

Aloe emodin, chysophanol and emodin.

FRANGULA BARK

1. Frangulin (frangula emodin rhamnoside).
2. Glucofrangulin (frangula emodin glucorhamnoside).

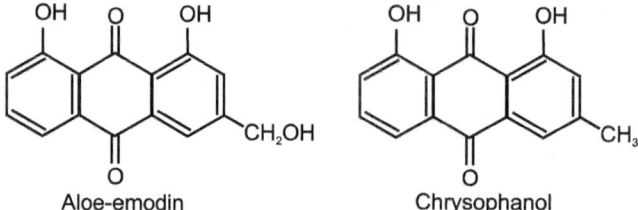

Frangulin   R = Rhamnose
Glucofrangulin R = Rhamnose-glucose

3. Hydrolysis of glucofrangulin yields frangulin and glucose.
4. Hydrolysis of frangulin gives frangula emodin and rhamnose.

RHUBARB

1. Consist of glycoside of rhein, rhein anthrone, chrysophanol and aloe emodin.
2. Dianthrones of heteroanthrone types are palmidin A, B, C, Rheidins, sennosides A and B and their oxalate esters (sennosides E and F).
3. The presence of tannins in rhubarb makes the drug constipating. So in small doses, rhubarb exerts no purgative action but acts only as intestinal astringent, but large doses cause purgation.

Properties of Anthraquinone Derivatives

The glycosides are extracted and hydrolysed by boiling the drug with acids.

The **aglycones** are extracted from the acidic solution with ether or benzene. Upon shaking the ether or benzene layer with aqueous alkali or ammonia solution, the aqueous layer assumes a deep red colour, because of the formation of anthraquinone salts.

Borntrager's reaction can distinguish anthraquinones from anthrones and anthranols which **do not** give the test unless they are converted to anthraquinone by oxidation with mild oxidants such as hydrogen peroxide or ferric chloride.

Sennoside occurs as a brownish powder.

Sennoside soluble in alcohol but sparingly soluble in acetone.

Purgative activity of senna is mainly due to sennoside A and B while C and D exerts a powerful synergistic effect upon purgative activity.

Stability is achieved as follows

1. In senna, there is dimeric glycoside in which a C-C bridge between two anthrone units is formed (the C-10 position of one anthrone is involved in a C-C-covalent bonding with C-10 of the other anthrone). Thus, the C-10 position can not be easily oxidised and the anthrone structure is stabilised.

2. In the aloe, the aloins (barbaloin and chrysaloin) contain C-C glycosidic linkage (anhydroglycosides) stabilise the anthrone structure.

3. In cascara, cascarosides have an additional O-glycosidic linkage (beside the C-10-C glycosidic linkage. The solubility of cascarosides is increased and thus, produce higher pharmacological activity.

Identification Test

(a) **Borntragor's Test:** To 1 gm of drug, 5-10 ml of dilute HCl is added and boiled on water bath for 10 minutes and filtered. Filtrate was extracted with CCl_4/benzene and equal amount of ammonia solution is added to filtrate and mixed well. Formation of pink or red colour in ammonical layer is due to presence of anthraquinone moiety.

(b) Modified Borntragor's Test: To 1 gm of drug 5 ml dilute HCl is added, followed by 5 ml ferric Chloride (5% w/v) and boiled for 10 minutes on water bath, cooled and filtered. Filtrate was extracted with carbon tetrachloride or benzene and equal volume of ammonia solution added. Formation of pink to red colour is due to presence of anthraquinone moiety. This is used for C-type of anthraquinone glycosides.

(c) Magnesium Acetate Solution Test: In methanolic extract magnesium acetate is added to give orange coloured solution.

Thin Layer Chromatography

Solvent system – dichloromethane: methanol: formamide (8:2:1) ethyl acetate: n–propanol: water (4:4:3)

Detecting reagent – ammonia vapours or spectrophotometry.

Isolation

I

Dry Senna powdered

↓ 90% methanol or 50% Acetone for 6 hrs.

Extraction with cold water for 4hrs

↓

17% of solid extract

Contains 60 - 65 % sennoside

II

Powdered Senna leaf

↓ Citric acid in methanol

Extraction with methanol - toluene Mixture & ammonia

↓

Extract treated with $CaCl_2$

↓

Calcium salt of sennoside A & B

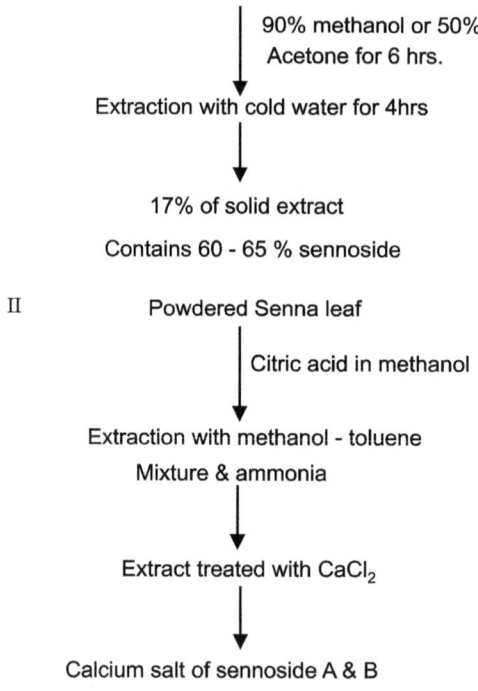

Biosynthesis

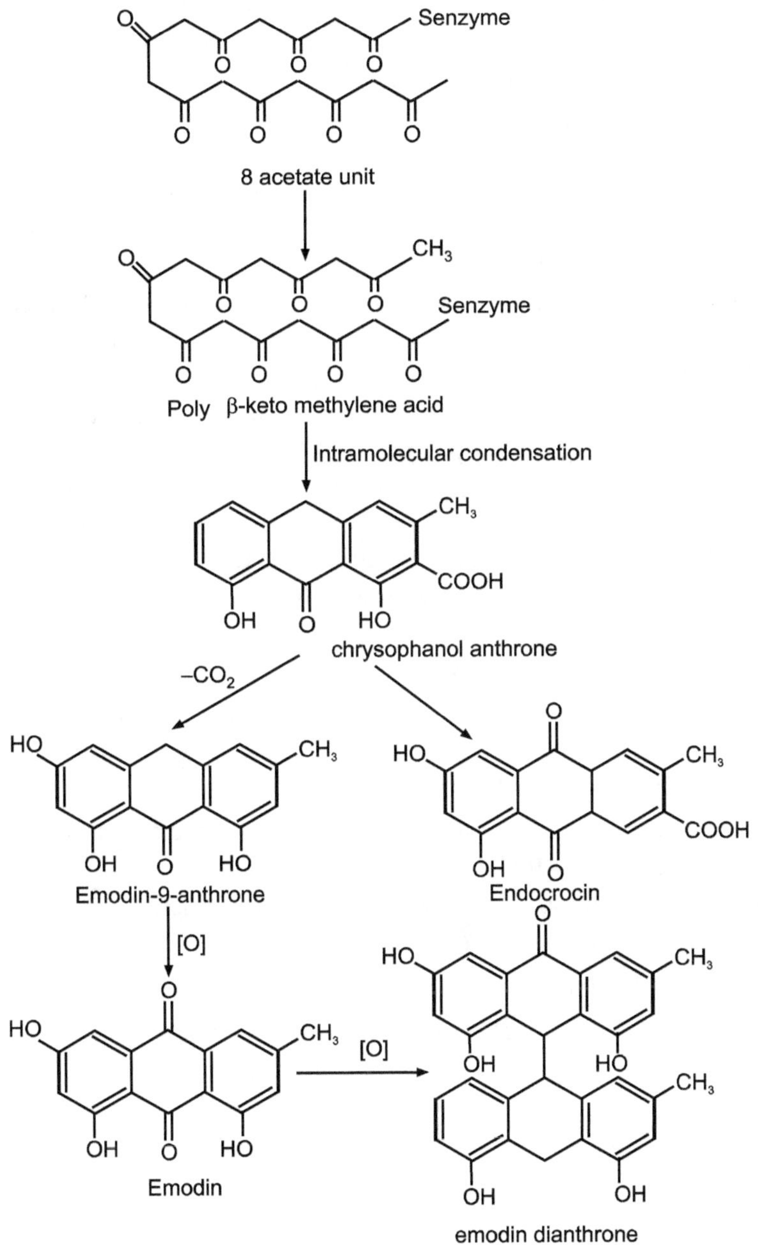
Senzyme
8 acetate unit
CH3
Senzyme
Poly β-keto methylene acid
Intramolecular condensation
CH3
COOH
OH
HO
chrysophanol anthrone
–CO2
HO
CH3
OH
HO
Emodin-9-anthrone
HO
CH3
COOH
OH
Endocrocin
[O]
HO
CH3
OH
HO
Emodin
[O]
HO
CH3
OH
HO
CH3
OH
OH
emodin dianthrone

Structure Activity Relationship

1. **Glycosylation:** The purgative action of anthracene containing drugs is due to their anthracene glycosidal content rather than their content of free anthracene aglycones (i.e., glycosylation is the main requirement for activity, as the sugar moiety serve to transport the aglycone to the site of action in the large intestine).

2. **Hydroxylation:** Hydroxylation of C-1, C-8 is essential for activity. Increased hydroxylation leads to increase in solubility.

3. **Oxidation level:** The degree of oxidation at positions C-9 and C-10 plays an important role in the pharmacological activity. Higher oxidation level at C-9 and C-10 causes lowering of activity. i.e., anthrones and anthranols are more potent than their corresponding oxanthrones, which in turn are more active than their corresponding anthraquinones. Complete reduction of C-10 and C-9 lead to complete loss of activity.

4. **The nature of substances at C-3:** Derivatives with CH_2OH (as in aloe emodin) are more active than those with CH_3 substitution. The latter is more active than derivative with COOH substitution at C-3.

Anthraquinone glycosides containing a dimer are more active than a monomer.

5. **Effect of storage on the active of anthracene glycosides:** Prolonged storage of anthracene bearing drugs may bring oxidation of anthranols and anthrones to give the less active anthraquinones. Thus, the activity of drugs decreases by time. However, anthraquinone glycosides do not cause any griping action (like anthranol and anthone), Senna preparations retain their activity for a long time

Action and Uses

1. Used as effective cathartic agents for long time.
2. Their action is due to their anthracene constituents acting on the large intestine. The sugar moiety helps to transport anthracene aglycon intact to large intestine, where aglycon is liberated by enzyme.
3. Anthracene derivative without sugar moiety are broken down and only small amount reaches to intestine to exert cathartic action.
4. It is also used as purgative, cathartic, laxative and in acute constipation.
5. Gripping action – occurs due to its resin or emodin.
6. Used in haemhoridial, after anorectal operation, anal fissure.
7. For evaluation of X – ray contrast media from intestine.

Chapter ... 7

PRINCIPLES AND APPLICATION OF RADIOTRACER TECHNIQUES AND AUTORADIOGRAPHY

Introduction

Living plants are considered as biosynthetic laboratories for primary as well as secondary metabolites

Different biosynthetic pathways found in plants are

- Shikimic acid pathway
- Mevalonic acid pathway
- Acetate pathway

Various intermediate steps are involved in biosynthetic pathways in plants and can be investigated by means of the following techniques

- Tracer techniques
- Use of isolated organs
- Grafting methods
- Use of mutant strains

TRACER TECHNIQUE

It can be defined as a technique which utilises a labelled compound to find out or to trace the different intermediates and the various steps in biosynthetic pathways in plants, at a particular rate and time.

OR

In this technique different isotopes, mainly the radioactive isotopes are incorporated into presumed precursors of plant metabolites and are used as markers in biogenic experiments.

Radioactive tracer, also called as a **radioactive label**, is a substance containing a radioisotope that is used to measure the speed of chemical processes and to track the movement of a substance through a natural system such as a cell or tissue.

- When the labelled compounds are administered into plant system they become part of the general metabolic pool and undergoes reaction characteristic to the metabolism of that particular plant system. The original compound remains unchanged or may get changed to become a part of new compound or intermediate in the series. This provides a convenient and suitable technique to trace and find out the biosynthetic pathway.
- The labelled compound can be prepared by the use of two types of isotopes.
  1. Radioactive isotopes.
  2. Stable isotopes.

Radioactive isotopes: Also called as radioisotopes, these are any of several species of the same chemical element with different masses whose nuclei are unstable and dissipate excess energy by spontaneously emitting radiation in the form of alpha, beta, and gamma rays. [e.g. ^1H, ^{14}C, ^{24}Na, ^{42}K, ^{35}S, ^{35}P, ^{131}I decay with emission of radiation]

- For biological investigation radioactive isotopes of carbon and hydrogen are widely used. ^3H compound is commercially available.
- For metabolic studies isotopes of sulphur, phosphorous, alkali and alkaline earth metals are used.
- For studies on protein, alkaloids, and amino acids labelled nitrogen atom gives more specific information.

Stable isotopes: [e.g. ^2H, ^{13}C, ^{15}N, ^{18}O]
- Used for labelling compounds as possible intermediates in biosynthetic pathways.
- Usual method of detection are
  - MASS spectroscopy [^{15}N, ^{18}O]
  - NMR spectroscopy [^2H, ^{13}C]

HISTORICAL PERSPECTIVE

At the beginning of 1910s, experiments conducted by F. Soddy gave the first demonstration that most of the elements in nature are composed of atoms identical from the chemical point of view but slightly different in weight. These characteristics were later explained by the fact that each element is identified by the number of protons but may have different number of neutrons, and the term "isotope" was introduced. Just after the discovery of deuterium, for which H. C. Urey was awarded the Nobel Prize in 1934, the idea of using stable isotopes in kinetic/dynamic investigations found useful applications in the early studies on fat metabolism in mice which was carried out with deuterium by R.Schoenheimer and D.Rittenberg. This was continued with studies in nutrition by using ^{15}N, ^{13}C and ^{18}O. During the successive three decades, with the advent of scintillation counting and the availability of radioactive isotopes, the use of stable isotopes was replaced by the radiotracer technique. The principle use of radiotracers was actually conceived by G.de Hevesy in the early 1910s, however their widespread use in clinical/biomedical applications really started after the development of the cyclotron as a source for massive production, and quickly expanded with the production of radionuclide in nuclear reactors.

The stable isotope approach remained confined to light elements as H, O, C and N (in particular for lack of suitable radioisotopes of N and O) in food science with some restricted applications towards other elements, such as the investigations by Lowman and Krivit in the '60s about plasma clearance of iron. In the mid '70s, stable isotopes regained some interest, due to a greater sensibility of the scientific community towards the use of radioactive substances in healthy volunteers as well as to the availability of new and improved analytical techniques such as ICPMS (Inductively Coupled Plasma Mass Spectrometry) and AMS (Accelerator Mass Spectrometry). Stable isotopes are now mainly used in the fields of nutrition and physiology for investigations on micronutrients and essential trace minerals, but applications to selected issues can be found. For example, the bio kinetics in human radionuclides is studied by combining the use of stable isotopes as tracers and complementary analytical techniques such as Charged Particle Activation Analysis (CPAA), Thermal Ionization Mass Spectrometry (TIMS) and ICPMS.

This note will exclusively deal with applications of isotopic tracers different than imaging purposes, and particularly with metabolic and molecular studies in the field of life science.

CRITERIA FOR TRACER TECHNIQUE

1. The starting concentration of tracer must be sufficient to withstand resistance with dilution in course of metabolism.
2. **Proper Labelling:** For proper labelling physical and chemical nature of the compound must be known.
3. Labelled compound should be involved in the synthesis reactions.
4. Labelling should not damage the system to which it is used.

Advantages

1. High sensitivity.
2. Applicable on all living organisms.
3. Wide ranges of isotopes are available.
4. More reliable, easily administration and isolation procedure.
5. Gives accurate result, if proper metabolic time and techniques are applied.

Limitations

1. **Kinetic effect:** Being chemically similar, the isotopes are expected to undergo the same reaction. This may be done at different rates. This effect is termed as kinetic isotope effect. These different rates are more or less proportional to the difference

in the mass between isotopes i.e. the effect is more on lighter element than on a heavier element.

2. **Chemical effect:** This effect may be caused by either extraneous element or the principle activity itself.

3. **Radiation effect:** These are important in some tracer experiments where total amount of radioactive material required is of such magnitude that radiation is harmful to the organism.

4. **Radiochemical purity:** It is effected by the presence of extraneous element, chemical state, colloidal state and production of radioactive nuclide.

5. High concentrations distort the result.

Requirements for Tracer Technique

- Preparation of labelled compound.
- Introduction of labelled compound into a biological system.
- Separation and determination of labelled compound in various biochemical fractions at later time.

(I) Preparation of Labelled Compound

- The labelled compound is produced by growing chlorella in an atmosphere of $^{14}CO_2$. As a result all carbon compounds are ^{14}C labelled.
- The ^3H (tritium) labelled compounds are commercially available. Tritium labelling is effected by catalytic exchange in aqueous media by hydrogenation of unsaturated compounds with tritium gas. Tritium is a pure β – emitter of low intensity and its radiation energy is lower than ^{14}C.
- By the use of organic synthesis

$$CH_3MgBr + {}^{14}CO_2 \longrightarrow CH_3{}^{14}COOHMgBr + H_2O$$
$$\downarrow$$
$$CH_3{}^{14}COOH + Mg(OH)Br$$

(II) Introduction of Labelled Compound

While introduction of a labelled compound the following precautions should be taken

1. The precursor should react at the required site of synthesis in plant.
2. Plant during the time of experiment should synthesise the compound under investigation
3. The dose given is for a short time period.

(a) Root feeding: This method is preferred in plants in which roots are the biosynthetic sites, as for biosynthesis of **tobacco** alkaloids. In this type of experiment, the plants are cultivated hydroponically to avoid microbial contamination from soil.

Disadvantage: Plant roots occasionally appear to be impermeable to some organic compounds such as mevalonate and acetate.

(b) Stem feeding: The substrate can be administered through cut ends of stems immersed in a solution.

Disadvantage: The presence of latex retards feeding through cut stem. Cutting of stem under water avoids blockage of transpiration by air. This technique is impractical for experiments extending over a period of weeks and can be used on if the duration of the experiment is for a short time period.

(c) Direct injection: It is applicable to plants with hollow stems and to capsules.

Disadvantage: With rigid tissue it is difficult to avoid loss of solution from the site of injection.

(d) Infiltration: It is desired to carry out feeding to plants rooted in soil or other support without disturbances to roots. Wick feeding is applicable.

(e) Floating method: This technique is used when small amounts of material is available, leaf discs or chopped leaves are floated on substrate solution. This technique is also used with vaccum filtration.

(f) Spray technique: This technique involves spraying of aqueous solution on leaves for its absorption.

(III) Separation and Detection of Compound

Following detector systems are used for determination of labelled compounds.

(a) Geiger – Muller counter.
(b) Liquid Scintillation counter.
(c) Gas ionisation chamber.
(d) Bernstein – Bellentine counter.
(e) Mass spectroscopy.
(f) NMR eletrodemeter.
(g) Autoradiography.
(h) Radio paper chromatography.

METHODS IN TRACER TECHNIQUE

- Precursor product sequence.
- Double and Multiple labelling.
- Competitive feeding.
- Isotope incorporation.
- Sequential analysis.

1. **Precursor Product Sequence:** It is the most widely used method in tracer technique. In this technique, the presumed precursor of the constituent under investigation in a labelled form is fed into the plant and after a suitable time the constituent is isolated, purified and radioactivity is determined.

Disadvantage: The radioactivity of isolated compound alone is not usually sufficient evidence that the particular compound fed is a direct precursor, because substance may enter the general metabolic pathway and from there may become randomly distributed through a whole range of products.

If this happens, degradation of the isolated constituent and determination of the activity of the fragment would probably show that the labelling was random throughout the molecule and not indicative of a specific incorporation of precursor.

Applications

- Stopping of hordenine production in barley seedling after 15 – 20 days of germination.
- Restricted synthesis of hyoscine, distinct from hyoscyamine in *Datura stramonium*.
- This method is applied to the biogenesis of morphine and ergot alkaloids.

2. **Double and Multiple Labelling:** This method gives proof about the nature of biochemical precursor which has double and triple labelling. In this method, specifically labelled precursors and their subsequent degradation of recovered product are more commonly employed.

Applications

- This method is extensively applied to study the biogenesis of plant secondary metabolites.
- Used for study of morphine alkaloid.

E.g. **Leete**, used doubly labeled lysine used to determine which hydrogen of lysine molecule was involved in formation of piperidine ring of anabasine in *Nicotina glauca*.

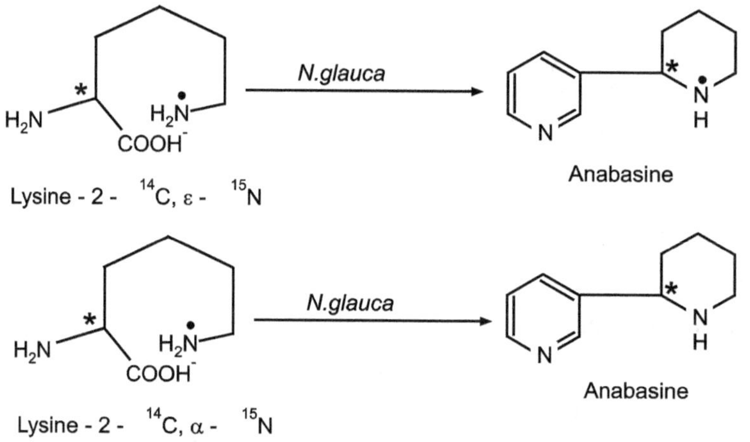

Lysine - 2 - ^{14}C, ε - ^{15}N → (N.glauca) → Anabasine

Lysine - 2 - ^{14}C, α - ^{15}N → (N.glauca) → Anabasine

Incorporation of doubly labeled lysine into anabasine

3. **Competitive Feeding:** If incorporation is obtained, it is necessary to consider whether this infact, is the normal route of synthesis in plant not the subsidiary pathway. Competitive feeding can distinguish whether B and B' is normal intermediate in the formation of C from A.

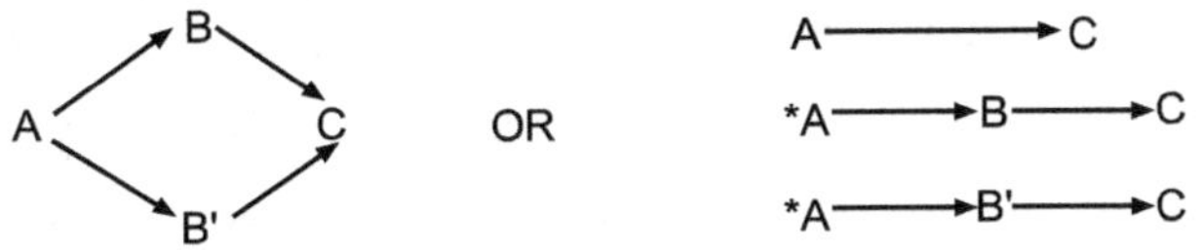

$$A \diagup^{B}\diagdown_{B'} C \quad OR \quad \begin{array}{l} A \longrightarrow C \\ *A \longrightarrow B \longrightarrow C \\ *A \longrightarrow B' \longrightarrow C \end{array}$$

Inactive B and B' are fed with labelled A, to a separate group of plants, and control is maintained by feeding labelled A only to another group. If the incorporation of activity into C is inhibited in the plant receiving B but is unaffected in the group receiving B', then it is concluded that the pathway from A to C is probably through B.

Applications

- This method is used for elucidation of biogenesis of propane alkaloids.
- Biosynthesis of hemlock alkaloids (conline, conhydrine etc) e.g. biosynthesis of alkaloids of *Conium maculactum* (hemlock) using ^{14}C labelled compounds.

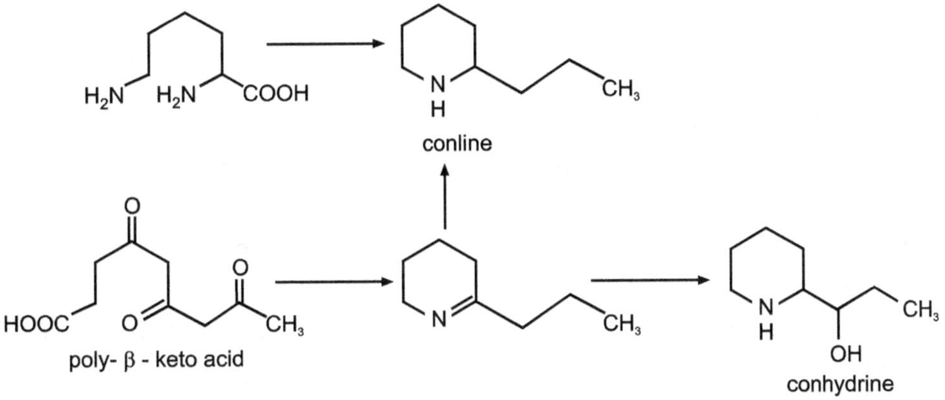

4. **Isotope Incorporation:** This method provides information about the position of bond cleavage and their formation during reaction.

   E.g. Glucose – 1- phosphatase cleavage is catalysed by alkaline phosphatase. This reaction occurs with cleavage of either C – O bond or P – O bond.

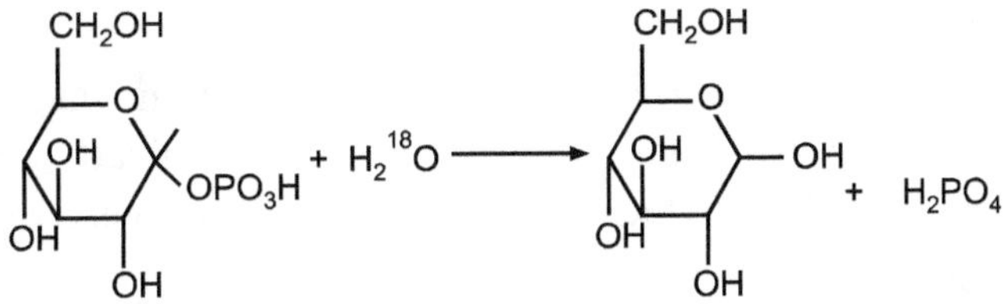

5. **Sequential Analysis:** The principle of this method of investigation is to grow the plant in atmosphere of $^{14}CO_2$ and then analyse the plant after a given time interval to obtain the sequence in which various correlated compounds become labelled.

Applications

- $^{14}CO_2$ and sequential analysis have been very successfully used in elucidation of carbon in photosynthesis.
- Determination of sequential formation of opium hemlock and tobacco alkaloids.
- Exposure as less as 5 min.to $^{14}CO_2$, is used in detecting biosynthetic sequence as

    Piperitone --------- (-) Menthone ---------- (-) Menthol in *Mentha piperita*.

Significance of Tracer Technique

1. Tracing of biosynthetic pathway: - e.g. By incorporation of radioactive isotope of ^{14}C into phenylalanine, the biosynthetic cyanogenetic glycoside, prunasin, can be detected.
2. Location and quantity of compounds containing tracer: - ^{14}C labelled glucose is used for determination of glucose in biological system
3. Different tracers for different studies: - For studies on nitrogen and amino acids, labelled nitrogen gives specific information than carbon.
4. Convenient and suitable technique.

Applications of Tracer Technique

1. Study of squalene cyclization by use of ^{14}C, ^3H labelled mevalonic acid.
2. Interrelationship among 4 – methyl sterols and 4, 4 dimethyl sterols, by use of ^{14}C acetate.
3. Terpenoid biosynthesis by chloroplast isolated in organic solvent, by use of 2- ^{14}C mevalonate.
4. Study of the pathway that leads to the formation of cinnamic acid from labelled coumarin.
5. Origin of carbon and nitrogen atoms of purine ring system by use of ^{14}C or ^{15}N labelled precursor.
6. Study of formation of scopoletin by use of labelled phenylalanine.
7. By use of ^{45}Ca as tracer, uptake of calcium by plants from the soil was studied. (CaO and $CaCO_2$).
8. By adding ammonium phosphate labelled with ^{32}P of known specific activity, the uptake of phosphorus is studied by measuring the radioactivity as label reaches the lower part of plant first, then the upper part i.e. branches, leaves etc.

Selected Applications

The two examples cited above give an idea of the different fields which can be investigated using tracer techniques and of the extent of the implications of the results obtained.

Molecular and Cellular Biology

Radioactive isotopes as ^{3}H, ^{14}C, ^{32}P, ^{35}S, ^{86}Rb, ^{125}I have played and still continue to play a key role in the understanding of the metabolic aspects in cells or bacteria, yeasts, plants and animals (including humans) and in the elucidation of the fundamental properties of genetic material. The radioisotopically labelled metabolites trace the corresponding stable molecules, and autoradiographic or counting measurements provide the information of interest. So, for example, ^{32}P-dATP is used in the phosphorylation of a protein in order to evaluate its kinetic activity. Similarly ^{35}S or ^{125}I labelled proteins are used in order to evaluate some specific expressions. ^{35}S-, ^{33}P- or ^{32}P-dideoxynucleotides are used for the synthesis of families of DNA labelled molecules (template DNA) in DNA sequence analysis, and as probes for the detection of specific genes (**Fig. 7.1**).

Recently, stable isotopes in combination with mass spectrometric techniques have been used for such labelling, especially when the molecules have to be injected into patients for in vivo studies.

The incorporation of ^{86}Rb into glial and neuronal cells is a method to trace the potassium entering the cell via the Na/K pump and therefore to monitor the Na$^+$/K$^+$ ATPase activity in these cells, which is an important information in the study of neurodegenerative diseases. The value of the uses of tracers in genetics will continue to improve, particularly considering that gene therapy is now beginning to find its way into ordinary clinical application.

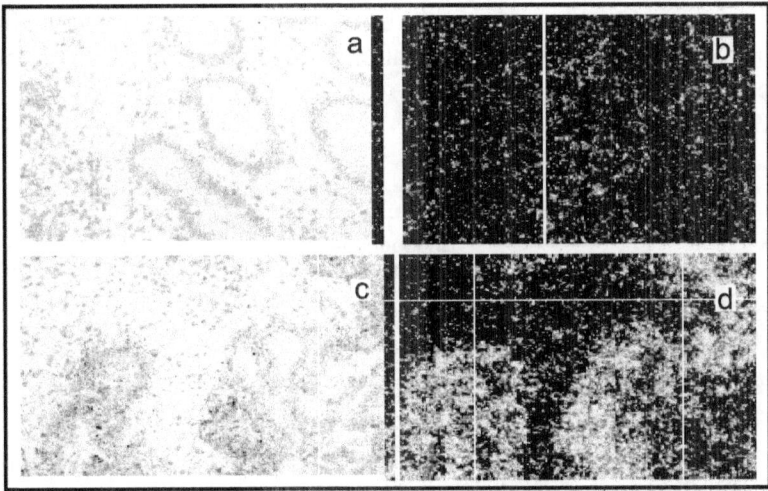

Fig. 7. 1 : Radioactive in situ hybridisation of normal and tumour colon tissue sections. RNA probes containing ^{35}S UTP were used to detect the presence of the transcript of a specific gene in the two samples. The incorporated radioactivity is detected by autoradiography using silver salt grains to impress a photo film. Panel a and c shows morphology of normal (a) and cancer (c) tissue viewed in bright field under the microscope. Switching to dark field (panels b and d), where luminescence of grains is the only source a, c d of light, the distribution of the specific RNA in the tissues can now be observed. In the case reported the gene is heavily expressed in the cancer cells, as showed by the intensity of the (white) signal.

Elemental Kinetics

The biokinetics of essential elements trace elements, micronutrients or any other elements of interest in nutrition, physiology, toxicology can be studied by tracer method. As already pointed out before, the use of stable tracers is the ethically justifiable choice when dealing with healthy volunteers, although this could mean less information and/or more cumbersome measurements than with radiotracers. Therefore a sound experimental design is required. The double (or multiple) tracer technique, for example, consists in the simultaneous administration of two (or more) tracers through different pathways (typically, one oral and one intravenous tracer), and thus permits to obtain dynamical pictures of relevant processes such as the intestinal absorption or the main excretion pathways (**Fig. 7.2**). Many analytical approaches are used for the determination of the stable tracers in biological samples, and many are the works which can be found in literature about the study of biokinetics of nutrient and non-nutrient elements. For some elements such as iron, molybdenum, ruthenium, zirconium, the combination of stable isotopes, charged particle activation analysis and thermal ionisation mass spectrometry has enabled to collect, for the first time ever, a detailed picture of the kinetics in blood plasma and of the renal elimination process. It has been therefore possible to revise the existing models, in order to provide a more realistic description of the biokinetics of ingested material. Radiation protection is, for example, a field which may greatly benefit from this improved realism, since the revised models may enable a more correct interpretation of control measurements in persons suspected of contamination and provide a sound support for the implementation of effective protective actions in case of radiological emergencies.

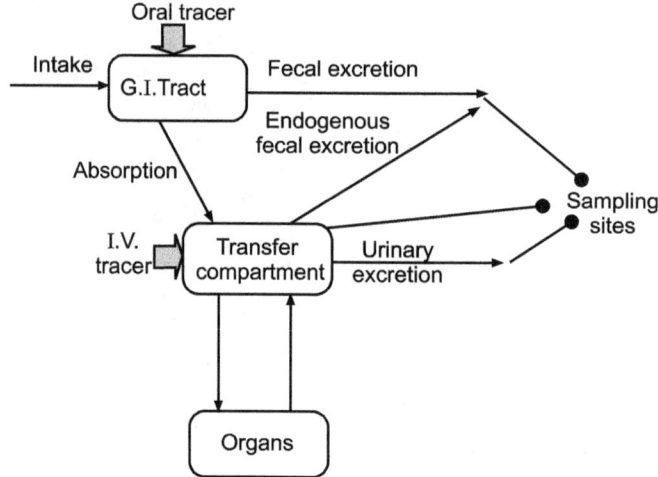

Fig. 7. 2 : Simplified scheme of the distribution of an element in the organism, as can be studied using the double stable tracer technique. One tracer is administered orally, the other tracer is injected intravenously. Blood, urine and faeces samples are then collected and analysed, in order to characterise the processes of interest

RADIOGRAPHY

Radiography is the visualization of the pattern of distribution of radiation. In general, the radiation consists of X-rays, gamma (γ) or beta (β) rays, and the recording medium is a photographic film. For classical X-rays, the specimen to be examined is placed between the source of radiation and the film, and the absorption and scattering of radiation by the specimen produces its image on the film.

In contrast, in **autoradiography,** the specimen itself is the source of the radiation, which originates from radioactive material incorporated into it. The recording medium which makes visible the resultant image is usually, though not always, photographic emulsion.

Radioisotopes

The mass of the atomic nuclei can vary slightly (=isotopes) for a particular element although the number of electrons remains constant and all the isotopes have the same chemical properties. The nuclei of radioactive isotopes are unstable and they disintegrate to produce new atoms and, at the same time, give off radiations such as electrons (β rays) or radiations (γ rays). Naturally occurring radioisotopes are rare because of their instability, but radioactive atoms can be produced in nuclear reactors by bombardment of stable atoms with high-energy particles. The disintegrations can be detected in three ways. *These detection methods are extremely sensitive and every radioactive atom that disintegrates can be detected.*

Detection

(i) Electrical: This depends on the production of ion pairs by the emitted radiation to give an electrical signal that can be amplified and registered: used in Geiger counter, ionisation counter and gas flow counter.

(ii) Scintillation: Some materials have the property of absorbing energy from the radiation and re-emitting this in the form of visible light. In a scintillation counter these small flashes of light are converted into electrical impulses. Both of these techniques count the pulses of the disintegrating atoms.

These are fast and quantitative.

(iii) Autoradiography differs from the pulse-counting techniques in several ways. Each crystal of silver halide in the photographic emulsion is an independent detector, insulated from the rest of the emulsion by a capsule of gelatin. Each crystal responds to the charged particle by the formation of a **latent** (hidden) image that is made permanent by the process of development. The record provided by the photographic emulsion is cumulative and spatially accurate. It provides information on the localization and distribution of radioactivity within a sample. Thus there is little point on doing autoradiography on a specimen that is homogeneously labeled. Although it can be quantitative, autoradiography is a much slower and more difficult approach.

Nuclear emulsions have a very high efficiency for β particles (electrons of nuclear origin), particularly those with low energies. Many of the isotopes of interest to biologists have suitable radioactive isotopes, e.g. tritium (= hydrogen-3), carbon-14, sulphur-35 and iodine-125. The effective volume of the detector emulsion in the immediate vicinity of the source may be as little as 100 cubic microns.

History

The first autoradiography was obtained accidently around 1867 by Victor de Niepce. He recorded that blackening was produced on emulsions of silver chloride and iodide by uranium salts. Such studies and the work of the Curies in 1898 demonstrated autoradiography before, and contributed directly to, the discovery of radioactivity. The development of autoradiography as a biological technique really started to happen after World War II with the development of photographic emulsions and then stripping film made of silver halide. Radioactivity is now no longer the property of a few rare elements of minor biological interest (such as radium, thorium or uranium) as now any biological compound can be labeled with radioactive isotopes, thus opening up many possibilities in the study of living systems.

Definition

"Autoradiography is a cytochemical method in which the location of a particular chemical constituent in a specimen is determined by observing the site at which radioactive material becomes positioned."

- This technique is based on the fact that photographic emulsion is darkened when exposed to ☐isualiz radiation.
- It is an important technique for tracing the route and conversion of a particular molecule in different biochemical reactions of the cell.
- It provides means to ☐isualize biochemical process by allowing an investigator to determine the location of radio labeled material within the cell.

Basic Principle

Based on PULSE and CHASE experiment **Fig. 7.3.**

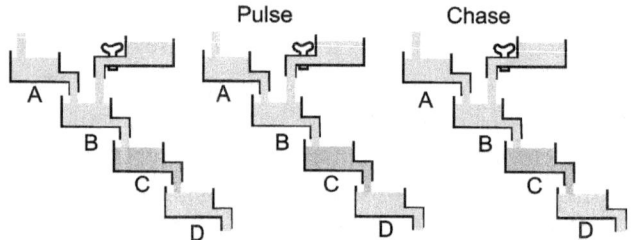

Fig. 7.3 : The logic of a typical pulse-chase experiment using radioisotopes

The chambers labelled A, B, C and D represent either different compartments in the cell (detected by autoradiography or by cell-fractionation experiments) or different chemical compounds (detected by chromatography or other chemical methods

PULSE – a brief incubation with radioactive material followed by – CHASE – exposure to unlabeled media, where normal reaction using incorporated radio labeled material occurs. (**Pulse chase** is used to sharpen the resolution of timing in many of these experiments.)

If the photographic emulsion is brought into close contact with a radioactive source, the particles emitted by the source leave tiny, black silver grains in the emulsion after photographic development.

AUTOGRAPHIC TECHNIQUES

Choice of technique depends on the type of study performed and information desired. There are three techniques as

1. Autoradiograph for macroscopic viewing.
2. Autoradiograph for light microscope.
3. Autoradiograph for electron microscope.

Autoradiograph for macroscopic viewing: It involves localisation of radioactivity rather than quantitative data. In this method, x-ray film is used for high sensivity, large grain size, reproducibility and simplicity of handling.

Autoradiograph for light microscope: In this technique, small grain sized nuclear emulsions are needed because of higher resolution and clear visibility. This technique includes two groups:

1. Grain Density Autoradiograph : In this method, radioactivity is detected by arrangement of silver grains produced in a relatively thin layer of emulsion.

2. Track Autoradiograph : In this method, passage of beta particles is recorded (as silver grain produced), when they pass through the specimen covered with a thin layer of photographic emulsion.

Autoradiograph for electron microscope : This will provide information about the distribution of radioactivity in structures which can only be viewed with an electron microscope. In this method, very fine grained crystal diameter (A^0) emulsion are used e.g. Eastman Kodak NTE and Gevaert NUC 307.It gives high resolution which depends on thickness of emulsion layer and specimen.

Method
- Living cells are briefly exposed to a 'pulse' of a specific radioactive compound.
- The tissue is left for different time intervals (3 minutes, 20 minutes and 120 minutes).
- Samples are taken, fixed, and processed for light or electron microscopy.
- Sections are cut and overlaid with a thin film of photographic emulsion.
- The thin film of photographic emulsion is left in the dark for days or weeks (while the radioisotope decays). This exposure time depends on the activity of the isotope, the temperature and the background radiation.

- The photographic emulsion is developed (as for conventional photography).
- Counterstaining e.g. with toluidine blue, shows the histological details of the tissue. The staining must be able to penetrate, but not have an adverse affect on the emulsion.
- Alternatively, pre-staining of the entire block of tissue can be done (e.g. with osmium) coated with stripping film [or dipping emulsion] as in papers by McGeachie and Grounds) before exposure to the photographic emulsion. This avoids the need for individually (post-) staining each slide.
- It is not necessary to coverslip these slides.
- The position of the silver grains in the sample is observed by light or electron microscopy Note: the grains are in a different plane of focus in the emulsion overlying the tissue section. Often oil with a 100 X objective is used for detailed observation with the light microscope.
- These autoradiographs provide a permanent record.
- Full details on the batch of emulsion used, dates, exposure time and conditions should be kept for each experiment.

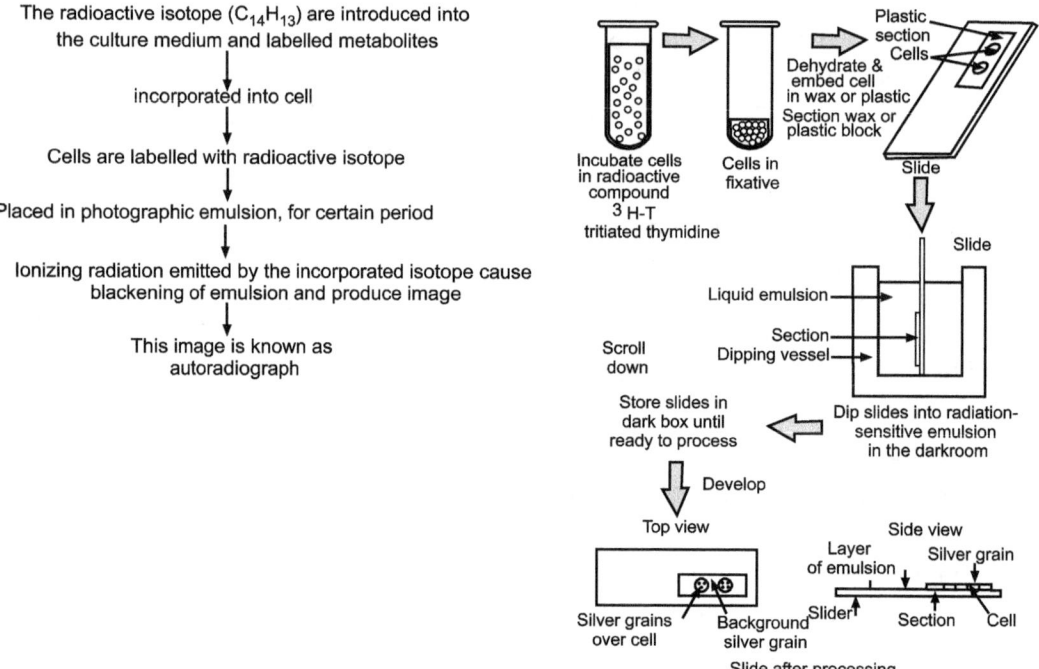

Fig. 7.4 : Autoradiography Method

Types of Photographic Detection Systems

Stripping film consists of an even layer of photographic emulsion on a supporting gelatin membrane (e.g. Kodak AR10). It is floated on water and then wrapped around the slide and forms a very close contact as it dries. This was once widely used but is now no longer made. It has the major advantage of uniform thickness but the disadvantage that the supporting membrane prevents counterstaining of the section and therefore the tissue block must be pre-stained before sections are coated.

Liquid photographic emulsion: This is the method routinely used today (see details below). It is simpler and much quicker to do, but the layer of liquid emulsion (e.g. Kodak NB2) can be **slightly uneven** in thickness as it flows down to the bottom of the slide as it is withdrawn: for most purposes this slight variation is not important, unless the number of grains are being strictly counted and compared across one slide.

Method for Coating and Developing Dipping Emulsion Coating the Slides

- Wear gloves and work in the darkroom (using only a red safety light).
- Allow Kodak-NB2 emulsion (which comes as a thick white gel and is stored in the dark at 4°C) to come to room temperature for 2 hours.
- Mix equal volumes of Kodak-NB2 and double distilled water together (say 5ml of each), place in water bath at 37°C and shake gently for about 15 mins.
- Dip slides vertically into a small amount of emulsion (about 2ml is all that is required) in a holder designed to take one slide at a time (economises on the amount of emulsion).
- Place horizontally for about 15 minutes to air dry. Then let it stand vertically for at least 2 hours to dry.
- Transfer to a black, light free box and store in the fridge (4°C) with dessicant.
- Allow exposure time as specified e.g. 2 weeks. Or remove test slides at various time intervals to determine optimal exposure time for your particular situation.

Developing the Film

- Use a dark room.
- Use Kodak D19 developer mixed 50:50 with water. Immerse slides for 4 mins.
- Wash in gently running tap water.
- Wash in double distilled water.
- Use Ilford Hypan Rapid Fixer (leaflet T1812). Mix 40ml + 160ml double distilled water +2ml Hypan hardener. Immerse slides for 5mins.
- Wash in gently running tap water.
- **Note:** Once it is fixed, the lights can be turned on and the workplace tidied up. But make sure all sensitive film is put away before it is done.

X-ray film

This is still widely used for macroscopic analysis of big specimens (not requiring a microscope). This film has much bigger crystal diameters and comes on hard sheets. It is traditionally used for analysing gels where the separated proteins or nucleic acids are labelled with radioisotopes.

Phosphoimager screen

This is a new variation on detection of bands in radioactively labelled gels This has (i) very high sensitivity, (ii) a shorter development time and (iii) a major advantage is that the amount of signal increases linearly over a wide range of labelling intensities making quantitation very easy. Radioactive signal activates fluorescence in the screen (nothing is visible = latent image). The screen is scanned on a special densitometer, hooked to a computer which produces a digital picture. The image can be enhanced and the intensity of the signal quantified. The screen can be easily cleared and re-used.

Latent Images

This image is the film caused by light or an electron passing through. This is due to silver halide crystals suspended in a gelatin layer. (The crystals are not perfect and contain defects called electron traps. This is an area which captures electrons and results in the form of metallic silver.) These changes are too small to be detected by electron microscopy so development of the latent image is required to give final image.

Resolution

It may be defined as the ability to distinguish two objects as seprate. Usually increase in resolution causes a decrease in sensitivity. Lower energy isotopes have better resolution than higher energy isotopes.

Factors affecting resolution are

1. Isotopic selection.
2. Distance of source from emulsion.
3. Emulsion thickness.
4. Exposure time.
5. Size of silver halide crystals.

Type of Emulsion Used in Autoradiography

Nuclear emulsion used for autoradiography differs from standard emulsion as it contains high ratio of silver halide and gelation.

Three types of emulsions are used

1. **Premounted:** It has a thick layer (25µ) of emulsion mounted on a glass microscopic slide.
2. **Liquid:** It is supplied as a gel. It hardens and forms a film whose thickness depends on the concentration of gelatin in liquid.
3. **Stripping:** It is supplied as a thin film (5µ). The slide is placed under a floating film and lifted up to film;a dry and thin emulsion adheres tightly.

Application of Autoradiography

1. To locate and determine the relative concentration of radio labeled compound of TLC.
2. To describe the distribution pattern of radio labeled drug in animals or organs.
3. This technique used to understand the mechanism of DNA replication i.e. transcription of RNA from DNA, protein synthesis and life cycle of cell.

4. By comparing autoradiograph with normal cell in tissue, the position of radioisotope can be localised in a radioactive material.
5. Radio labeled substances can be used in two different ways using autoradiographic technique as
   (a) Tracer to visualise the path.
   (b) Marker of biomolecules.

   (a) As tracers they can be used to study
   - Oxidative respiration.
   - Photosynthesis.
   - Time of events throughout the cell cycle.
   - Comparison of experimental treatments on the events.

   (b) As markers they can be used to locate biomolecules like
   - Enzyme inhibitors.
   - Antibodies.
   - Nucleic acid probes.

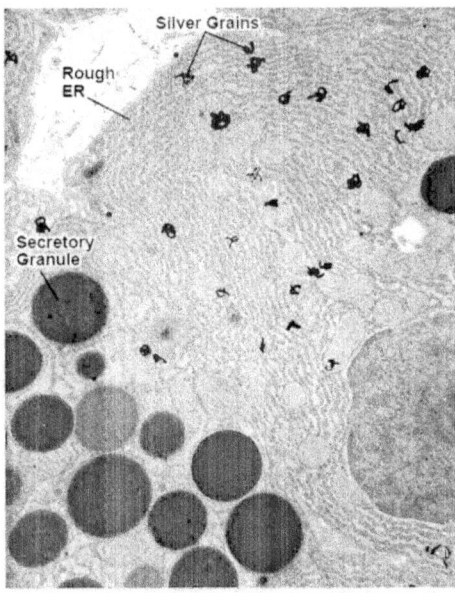

Fig. 7.5 : Autoradiography reveals the sites of synthesis and subsequent transport of secretory proteins
(COURTESY : JAMES D. JAMIESON AND GEORGE PALADE)

Fig. 7.5 (a) is an electron micrograph of a section of a pancreatic acinar cell that had been incubated for 3 minutes in radioactive amino acids and then immediately fixed and prepared for autoradiography.

The black silver grains that appear in the emulsion following development are localised over the endoplasmic reticulum. (**Fig. 7.5 (b), (c) and (d)**). Diagrams of a sequence of autoradiographs showing the movement of labelled secretory proteins (represented by the silver grains in red) through a pancreatic acinar cell.

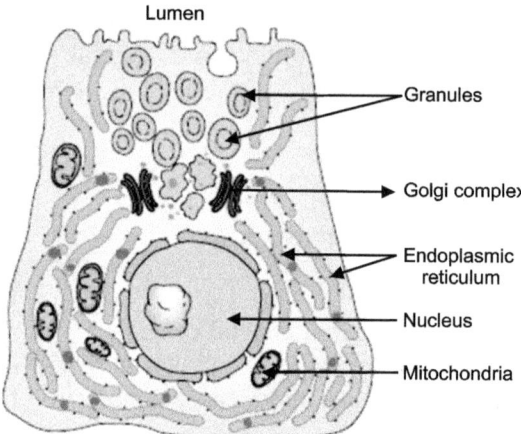

Fig. 7.5 (b) When the cell is pulse-labeled for 3 minutes and immediately fixed as shown in Figure a), radioactivity is localized in the endoplasmic reticulum

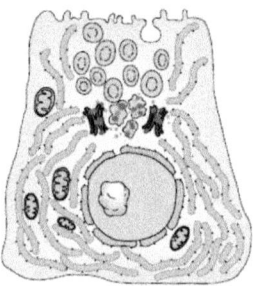

20 min

Fig. 7.5 (c) After a 3-minute pulse and 17 minute chase, radioactive label is concentrated in the Golgi complex and adjacent vesicles.

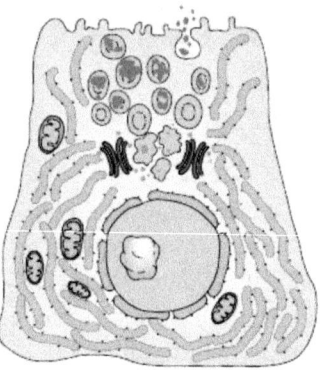

120 min

Fig. 7.5 (d) After a 3-minute pulse and 117-minute chase, radioactivity is concentrated in the secretory granules and is beginning to be released into the pancreatic ducts

Chapter ... 8

CONSTITUTION AND APPLICATIONS OF VARIOUS HORMONES

The endocrine system is involved in all of the integrative aspects of life, including growth, sex differentiation, metabolism, and adaptation to an ever-changing environment. This chapter focuses on general aspects of endocrine function, organisation of the endocrine system, hormone receptors and hormone actions, and regulation of hormone levels. The endocrine system uses chemical substances called *hormones* as a means of regulating and integrating body functions. The endocrine system participates in the regulation of digestion, use and storage of nutrients, growth and development, electrolyte and water metabolism, and reproductive functions. Although the endocrine system once was thought to consist solely of discrete endocrine glands, it is now known that a number of other tissues release chemical messengers that modulate body processes.

Hormones generally are thought of as chemical messengers that are transported in body fluids. They are highly specialised organic molecules produced by endocrine organs that exert their action on specific target cells. Hormones do not initiate reactions; they are modulators of systemic and cellular responses. A characteristic of hormones is that a single hormone can exert various effects in different tissues or, conversely, a single function can be regulated by several hormones. For example, estradiol, which is produced by the ovary, can act on the ovarian follicles to promote their maturation, on the uterus to stimulate its growth and maintain the cyclic changes in the uterine mucosa, on the mammary gland to stimulate ductal growth, on the hypothalamic-pituitary system to regulate the secretion of gonadotropins and prolactin, and on general metabolic processes to affect adipose tissue distribution.

Hormones are conventionally defined as organic substances, produced in small amounts by specific tissues (endocrine glands), secreted into the blood stream to control the metabolic and biological activities in the target cells. Hormones may be regarded as the chemical messengers involved in the transmission of information from one tissue to another and from cell to cell. The major endocrine organs in human body are depicted in **Fig. 8.1(a).**

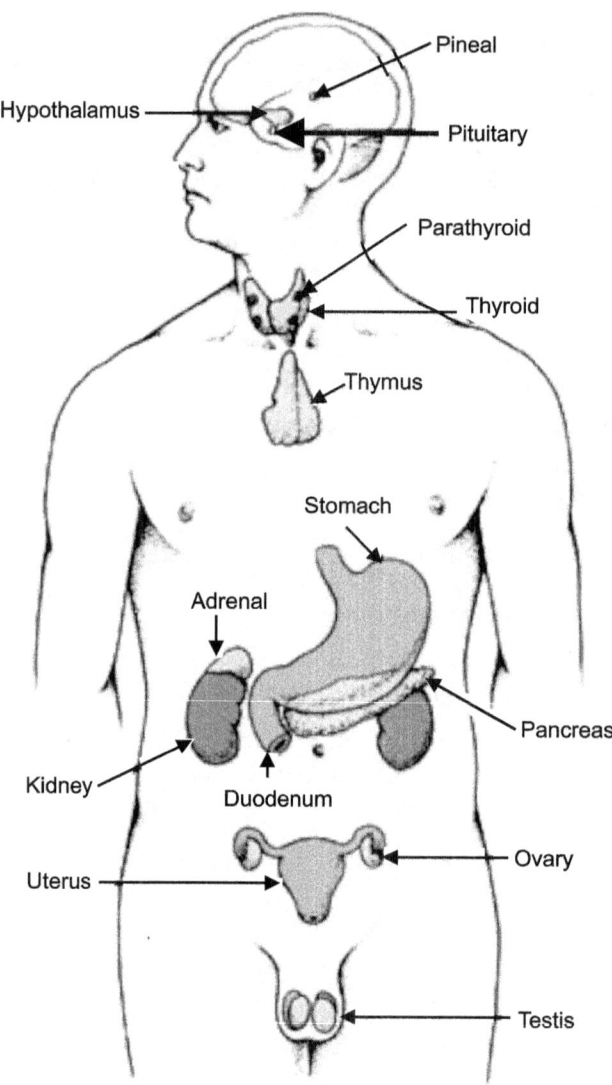

Fig. 8.1 (a) : The major endocrine organs of the human body

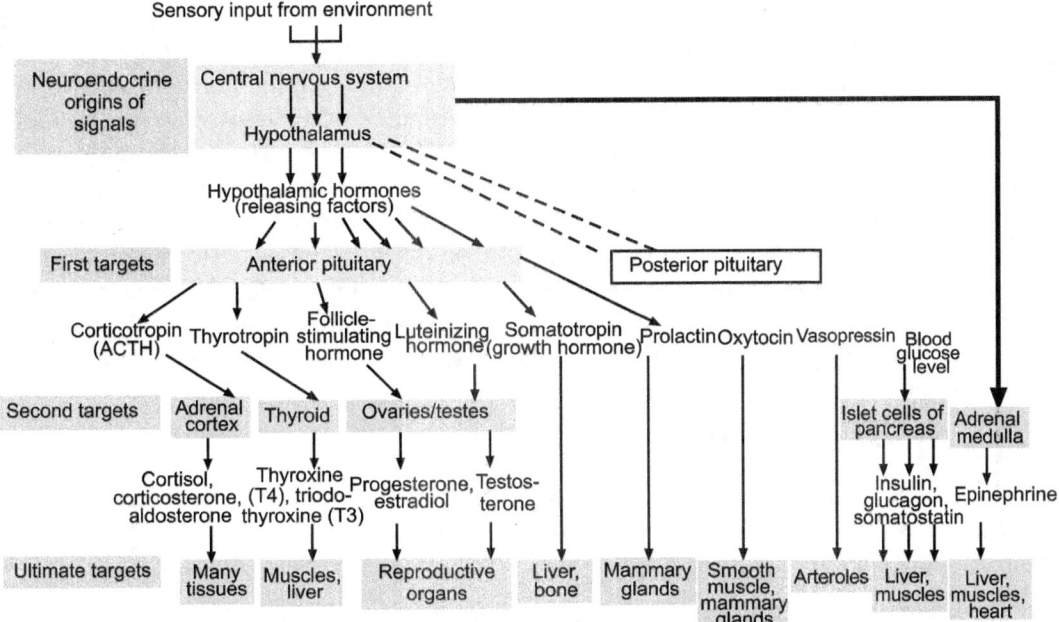

Fig. 8.1 (b) : The major endocrine systems and their target tissues. Signals originating in the central nervous system (top) are passed via series of relays to the ultimate target tissues (bottom). In addition to the systems shown, the thymus and pineal glands, as well as groups of cells in the gastrointestinal tract, also secrete hormones.

Paracrine and Autocrine Actions

In the past, hormones were described as chemical substances that were released into the bloodstream and transported to distant target sites, where they exerted their action. Some hormones and hormone-like substances never enter the bloodstream but instead act locally in the vicinity in which they are released. When they act locally on cells other than those that produced the hormone, the action is called *paracrine*. The action of sex steroids on the ovary is a paracrine action. Hormones also can exert an *autocrine* action on the cells from which they were produced. For example, the release of insulin from pancreatic beta cells can inhibit its release from the same cells.

Synthesis and Transport

The mechanisms for hormone synthesis vary with hormone structure. Protein and peptide hormones are synthesised and stored in granules or vesicles in the cytoplasm of the cell until secretion is required. The lipid-soluble steroid hormones are released as they are synthesised. Protein and peptide hormones are synthesised in the rough endoplasmic reticulum in a manner similar to the synthesis of other proteins. Appropriate amino acid sequence is dictated by messenger RNAs from the nucleus. Usually, synthesis involves the production of a precursor hormone, which is modified by the addition of peptides or sugar units. These precursor hormones often contain extra peptide units that ensure proper folding of the molecule and insertion of essential linkages. If extra amino acids are present, as in insulin, the precursor hormone is called a prohormone. After synthesis and sequestration in the endoplasmic reticulum, the protein and peptide hormones move into the Golgi complex, where they are packaged in granules or vesicles. It is in the Golgi complex that prohormones are converted into hormones. Steroid hormones are synthesised in the smooth endoplasmic reticulum, and steroid-secreting cells can be identified by the large amounts of smooth endoplasmic reticulum present in them. Certain steroids serve as precursors for the production of other hormones. Hormones that are released into the bloodstream circulate as either free, unbound molecules or as hormones attached to transport carriers. Peptide hormones and protein hormones usually circulate unbound in the blood. Steroid hormones and thyroid hormone are carried by specific carrier proteins synthesised in the liver.

CLASSIFICATION OF HORMONES

Hormones may be classified in many ways based on their characteristics and functions. Two types of classification are discussed here

(I) Based on the Chemical Nature

The hormones can be categorised into three groups considering their chemical nature.

1. *Protein or peptide hormones* e.g. Insulin, glucagon, anti-diuretic hormone, oxytocin.
2. *Steroid hormones* e.g. glucocorticoids, mineralocorticoids, sex hormones.
3. *Amino acid derivatives* e.g. epinephrine, norepinephrine, thyroxine (T_4), triiodothyronine (T_3)

(II) Based on the Mechanism of Action

Hormones are classified into two broad groups (I and II) based on the location of the receptors to which they bind and the signals used to mediate their action.

1. Group I hormones: These hormones bind to intracellular receptors to form receptor - hormone complex (the intracellular messenger) through which their biochemical functions are mediated. Group I hormones are lipophilic in nature and are mostly derivatives of cholesterol (exception T_3 and T_4).

e.g. estrogens, androgens, glucocorticoids, calcitriol.

2. Group II hormones: These hormones bind to cell surface (plasma membrane) receptors and stimulate the release of certain molecules namely the second messengers which in turn, perform the biochemical functions. Thus, hormones themselves are messengers.

Group II hormones are subdivided into three categories based on the chemical nature of the second messengers.

(a) The second messenger is cAMP e.g. ACTH, FSH, LH , PTH , glucagon and calcitonin.

(b) The second messenger is phosphotidylinositol/calcium e.g. TRH, GnRH, gastrin, CCK) The second messenger is unknown in case of growth hormone, insulin, oxytocin, and prolactin.

Table 8.1 : The principal human hormones, their classification based on the mechanism of action, and major functions

Hormone(s)	Origin	Major Function(s)
Group I: Hormones that Bind to Intracellular Receptors		
Estrogens	Ovaries and adrenal cortex	Female sexual characteristics, menstrual cycle
Progestins	Ovaries and placenta	Involved in menstrual cycle and maintenance of pregnancy
Androgenis	Testes and adrenal cortex	Male sexual characteristics, spermatogenesis.
Glucocorticoids	Adrenal cortex	Affect metabolisms, suppress immune system.
Mineralocorticoids	Adrenal cortex	Maintenance of salt and water balance.
Calcitriol (1.25-DHCC)	Kidney (final form)	Promotes absorption of Ca^{2+} from intestine, kidney
Thyroid hormones (T_3, T_4)	Thyroid	Promote general metabolic rate.
Group II: Hormones that Bind to Cell Surface Receptors		
(A) The second messenger is C Amp		
Adrenocorticotropic hormone (ACTH)	Anterior pituitary	Stimulates the release of adrenocorticosteroids.
Follicle stimulating hormone (FSH)	Anterior pituitary	In females, stimulates ovulation and estrogen? in males, promotes spermatogenesis.
Leuteinizing hormone (LH)	Anterior pituitary	Stimulates synthesis of estrogens and progesterone, causes ovulation. Promotes androgen synthesis.
Chorionic gonadotropin (HCG)	Anterior pituitary	Stimulates progesterone release from placenta.
Thyroid stimulating hormone (TSH)	Anterior pituitary	Promotes the release of thyroid hormones (T_3)
β-Endorphins and enkephalins	Anterior pituitary	Natural endogenous analgesics (pain relievers)
Antidiuretic hormone (ADH)	Posterior pituitary (stored)	Promotes water reabsorption by kidneys.
Glucagon	Pancreas	Increases blood glucose level, stimulates glycogenolysis and lipolysis.

Parathyroid hormone (PTH)	Parathyroid	Increases serum calcium, promotes Ca^{2+} release from bone
Calcitonin	Thyroid	Lowers serum calcium. Decreases Ca^{2+} uptake by bone and kidney
Epinephrine	Adrenal medulla	Increases heart rate and blood pressure. Promotes glycogenolysis in liver and muscle and lipolysis in adipose
Norepinephrine	Adrenal medulla	Stimulates lipolysis in adipose tissue
(B) The second messenger in phosphatidyl inositol/calcium		
Thyrotropin-releasing hormone (TRH)	Hypothalamus	Promotes TSH release.
Gonadotropin-releasing hormone (GnRH)	Hypothalamus	Stimulates release of FSH and LH.
Gastrin	Stomach	Stimulates gastric HCl and pepsinogen secretion
Cholecystokinin (CCK)	Intestine	Stimulates contraction of gall bladder and secretion enzymes.
(C) The second messenger is unknown/unsettled		
Growth hormone (GH)	Anterior pituitary	Promotes growth of the body (bones and organ)
Prolactin (PRL)	Anterior pituitary	Growth of mammary glands and lactation
Oxytocin	Posterior pituitary (stored)	Stimulates uterine contraction and milk ejection
Insulin	Pancreas	Lowers blood glucose (hypoglycemic effect) promotes protein synthesis and lipogenesis
Somatomedins (insulin-like growth factors, IGF-I, IGF-II)	Liver	Growth related functions of GH are mediated. Stimulates growth of cartilage.

Mechanisms of Action

Hormones produce their effects through interaction with high affinity receptors, which in turn are linked to one or more effector systems within the cell. These mechanisms involve many of the cell's metabolic activities, ranging from ion transport at the cell surface to stimulation of nuclear transcription of complex molecules. The rate at which hormones react depend on their mechanism of action. The neurotransmitters, which control the opening of ion channels, have a reaction time of milliseconds. Thyroid hormone, which functions in the control of cell metabolism and synthesis of intracellular signaling molecules, requires days for its action to take affect.

There are approximately 2000 to 100,000 hormone receptor molecules per cell. The number of hormone receptors on a cell may be altered for several reasons. Antibodies may destroy or block receptor proteins. Increased or decreased hormone levels often induce changes in the activity of the genes that regulator receptor synthesis. For example, decreased hormone levels often produce an increase in receptor numbers by means of a process called *up-regulation*; this increases the sensitivity of the body to existing hormone levels. Likewise, sustained levels of excess hormone often bring about a decrease in receptor numbers by *down-regulation*, producing a decrease in hormone sensitivity. The most widely distributed second messenger is cyclic adenosine monophosphate (cAMP). cAMP is formed from cellular adenosine triphosphate (ATP) by the enzyme adenylate cyclase, a membrane-bound enzyme that is located on the inner aspect of the cell membrane. Adenylate cyclase is functionally coupled to various cell surface receptors by the regulatory actions of G proteins. As a result of binding to specific cell receptors, many peptide hormones incite a series of enzymatic reactions that produce an almost immediate increase in cAMP. Some hormones act to decrease cAMP levels and have an opposite effect.

Control of Hormone Levels

Hormone secretion varies widely during a 24-hour period. Some hormones, such as growth hormone (GH) and adrenocorticotropic hormone (ACTH), have diurnal fluctuations that vary with the sleep-wake cycle. Others, such as the female sex hormones, are secreted in a complicated cyclic manner. The levels of hormones such as insulin and antidiuretic hormone (ADH) are regulated by feedback mechanisms that monitor substances such as glucose (insulin) and water (ADH) in the body. The levels of many of the hormones are regulated by feedback mechanisms that involve the hypothalamic-pituitary-target cell system.

Hypothalamic-Pituitary Regulation

The hypothalamus and pituitary (*i.e.*, hypophysis) form a unit that exerts control over many functions of several endocrine glands as well as a wide range of other physiologic functions. These two structures are connected by blood flow in the hypophyseal portal system, which begins in the hypothalamus and drains into the anterior pituitary gland, and by the nerve axons that connect the supraoptic and paraventricular nuclei of the hypothalamus with the posterior pituitary gland.

Feedback Regulation

The level of many of the hormones in the body is regulated by negative feedback mechanisms. The function of this type of system is similar to that of the thermostat in a heating system. In the endocrine system, sensors detect a change in the hormone level and adjust hormone secretions so that body levels are maintained within an appropriate range. When the sensors detect a decrease in hormone levels, they initiate changes that cause an increase in hormone production; when hormone levels rise above the set point of the system, the sensors cause hormone production and release to decrease. For example, an increase in thyroid hormone is detected by sensors in the hypothalamus or anterior pituitary gland, and this causes a reduction in the secretion of TSH, with a subsequent decrease in the output of thyroid hormone from the thyroid gland.

Table 8.2: Some important hormones and role in body

Sr. No.	Source	Hormone Name	Action
1.	Hypothalamus	Corticotropin-releasing hormone (CRH) Thyrotropin-releasing hormone (TRH) Growth hormone-releasing hormone (GHRH) Gonadotropin-releasing hormone (GnRH)	Controls the release of pituitary hormones
2.	Anterior pituitary	Growth hormone (GH) Adrenocorticotropic hormone (ACTH) Thyroid-stimulating hormone (TSH) Follicle-stimulating hormone (FSH)	Stimulates growth of bone and muscle, promotes protein synthesis and fat metabolism, decreases carbohydrate metabolism Stimulates synthesis and secretion of adrenal cortical hormones Stimulates synthesis and secretion of thyroid hormone Female: stimulates growth of ovarian follicle, ovulation
3.	Posterior pituitary	Antidiuretic hormone (ADH) Oxytocin	Increases water reabsorption by kidney Stimulates contraction of pregnant uterus, milk ejection from breasts after childbirth
4.	Adrenal cortex	Mineralocorticosteroids	Increases sodium absorption, potassium loss by kidney
5.	Thyroid	Thyroid hormones: triiodothyronine (T3), thyroxine (T4)	Increase the metabolic rate; increase protein and bone turnover; increase responsiveness to catecholamines; necessary for fetal and infant growth and development
6.	Pancreatic islet cells	Insulin Glucagon Somatostatin	Lowers blood glucose by facilitating glucose transport across cell membranes of muscle, liver, and adipose tissue Increases blood glucose concentration by stimulation of glycogenolysis and glyconeogenesis Delays intestinal absorption of glucose

7.	Ovaries	Estrogen Progesterone	Affects development of female sex organs and secondary sex characteristics
			Influences menstrual cycle; stimulates growth of uterine wall; maintains pregnancy

THYROID HORMONE

The thyroid gland is a shield-shaped structure located immediately below the larynx in the anterior middle portion of the neck. Once inside the follicle, most of the iodide is oxidised by the enzyme peroxidase in a reaction that facilitates combination with a tyrosine molecule to form monoiodotyrosine and then diiodotyrosine.

Two diiodotyrosine residues are coupled to form thyroxine (T4), or a monoiodotyrosine and a diiodotyrosine are coupled to form triiodothyronine (T3). Only T4 and T3 are released into the circulation. There is evidence that T3 is the active form of the hormone and that T4 is converted to T3 before it can act physiologically.

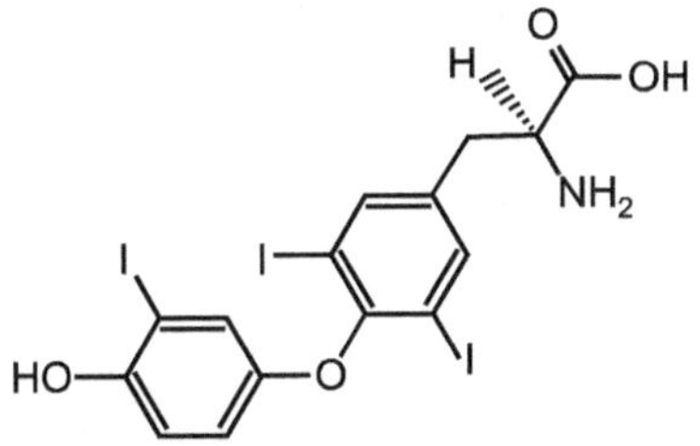

Triiodothyronine 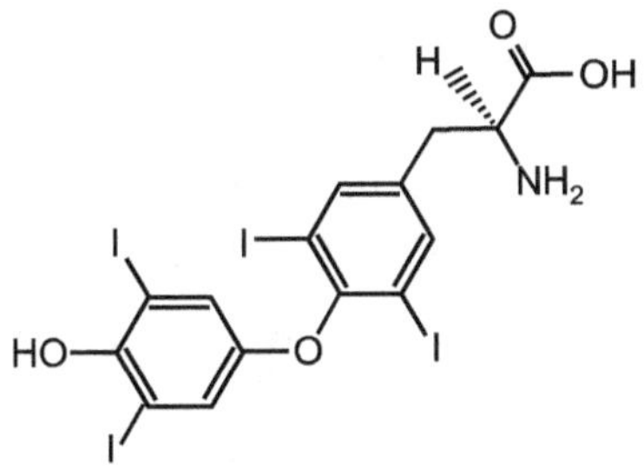 (T_3)

Triiodothyronine (T_4)

Other hormones of the thyroid glands are

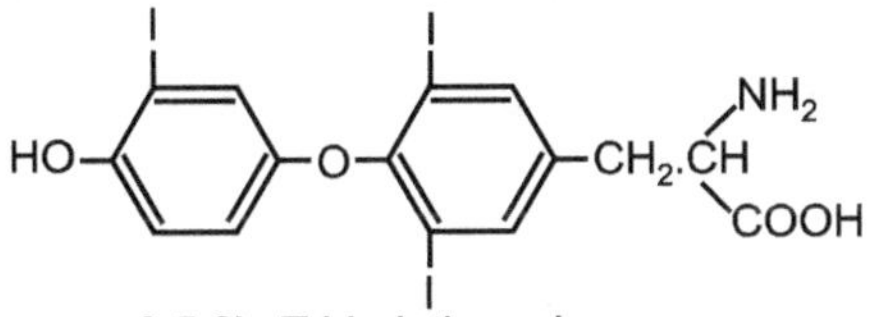

3,5,3' - Tri-iodothyronine

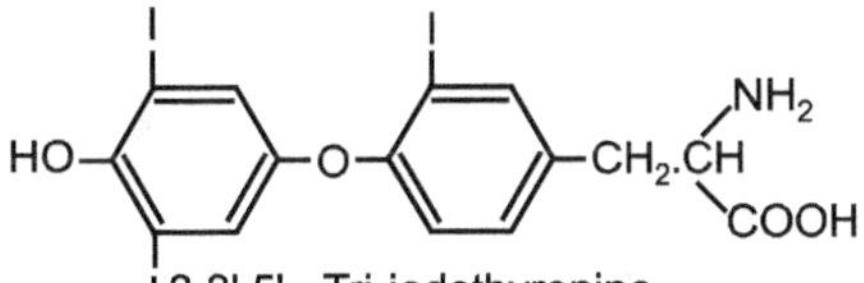

3,3',5' - Tri-iodothyronine

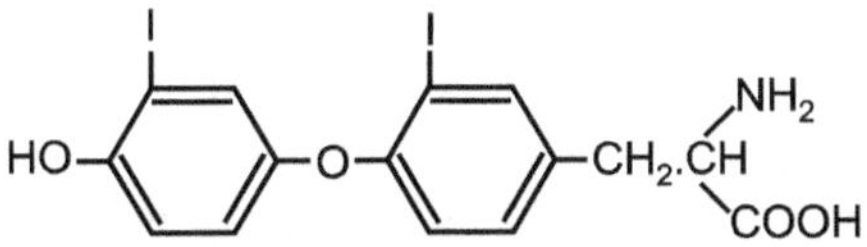

3,3' - Di-iodothyronine

Isolation

The thyroid gland is dried and treated twice with Ba(OH)$_2$ solution, first with 1.0 % solution and then with 40%. The so formed barium salt of thyroxine is suspended in 1% hot NaOH solution and treated with sodium sulphate solution to remove barium as BaSO$_4$. The thyroxine is obtained by the acidic hydrolysis of the sodium salt. Further purification may be carried out with alcohol and CH$_3$COOH. The hormone so obtained is a racemic mixture which can be resolved into *l*-isomer by trypsin.

Preparation

The thyroid preparations may be synthetic or of animal origin. The synthetic levothyroxine (T4) is used most frequently for thyroid replacement and suppression because it is cheap, less allergic, and stable and has a long duration of action whereas tri-iodothyronine (T3) is used in case of myxoedema coma because of its prompt action. A mixture of thyroxine and tri-iodothyronine in a ratio of 4:1 is available but is very expensive.

Constitution

1. Molecular formula - C$_{15}$H$_{11}$N$_{I4}$
2. It was found to contain one acidic group by the normal reactions such as it forms monoester.
3. On acetylation it forms mono-ester indicating the presence of either an –OH or –NH$_2$ group.

    But thyroxine on treatment with HONO gives a hydroxy acid with the .evolution of nitrogen showing the presence of -NH$_2$ group.

4. On catalytic reduction (H$_2$-Pd), it gives thyronine (C$_{15}$H$_{15}$NO$_4$) by replacing iodine atoms by hydrogen.

Constitution of thyronine (thyronin)

(i) The molecular formula is C$_{15}$H$_{15}$NO$_4$.

(ii) As thyronine gives a brick red colouration with Millon's reagent (Hg in HNO$_2$) indicating thereby the presence of hydroxyphenyl group.

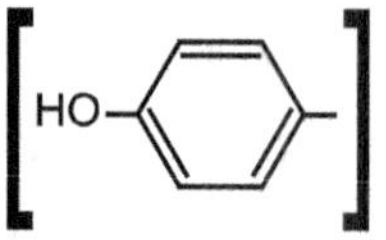

$$\left[HO-\underset{}{\bigcirc}- \right]$$

(iii) On treatment with ninhydrin, it gives blue colour showing the presence of α - amino acid.

(iv) On fusion with KOH at 300°, it yields quinol, p-hydroxybenzoic acid, a diphenyl derivative (HO- C$_6$H$_4$-O-C$_6$H$_4$-CH$_3$), oxalic acid and ammonia. These results clearly indicate that the thyronine molecule contains two benzene nuclei linked by an ether linkage (-C$_6$H$_4$-O-C$_6$H$_4$ -) and one of the nuclei carries a hydroxyl group in the para position to the ether linkage. So, the rest of the carbon atoms

(C_{15}–C_{12}=C_3) must be present in the side chain. Moreover, thyronine is also found to be an α-amino acid, so the part structure of thyronine may be either I or II.

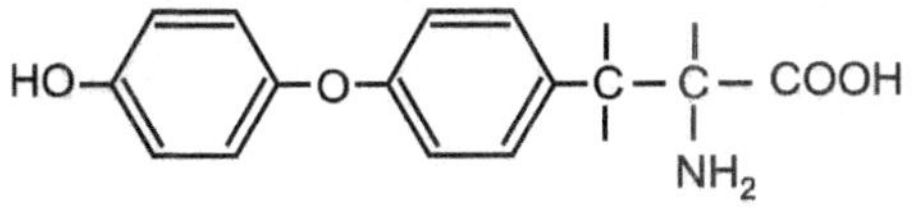

HO–⟨⟩–O–⟨⟩–C–C–COOH
         | |
         | NH$_2$

I. Straight side-chain

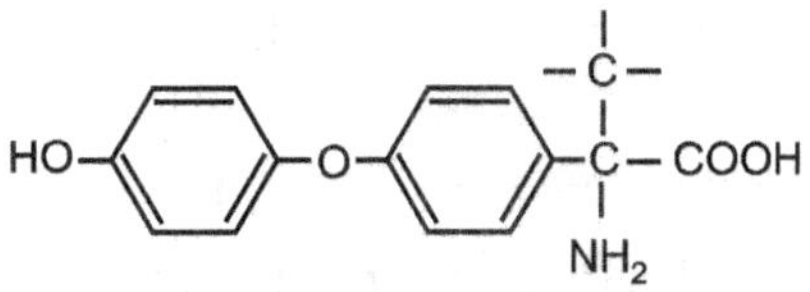

HO–⟨⟩–O–⟨⟩–C–COOH
              |
              NH$_2$
         (with –C– branch)

II. Branched side-chain

(v) Thyronine on boiling with HI gives tyrosine which clearly indicates that the side chain in thyronine is straight chain

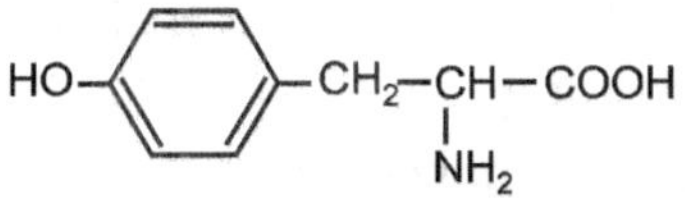

HO–⟨⟩–CH$_2$–CH–COOH
              |
              NH$_2$

Tyrosine

Thus the structure of thyronine is Ia.

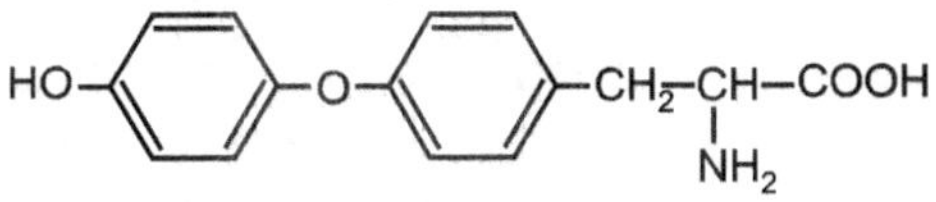

HO–⟨⟩–O–⟨⟩–CH$_2$–CH–COOH
                      |
                      NH$_2$

Ia   Thyronine

(vi) Thyroxine on fusion with alkali gives two pyrogallol compounds (replacement of iodine by –OH groups). The formation of pyrogallol derivatives clearly indicates that the two iodine atoms are in *o*-positions to the original hydroxyl group in each benzene nuclei. Thus the structure of thyroxine will be II.

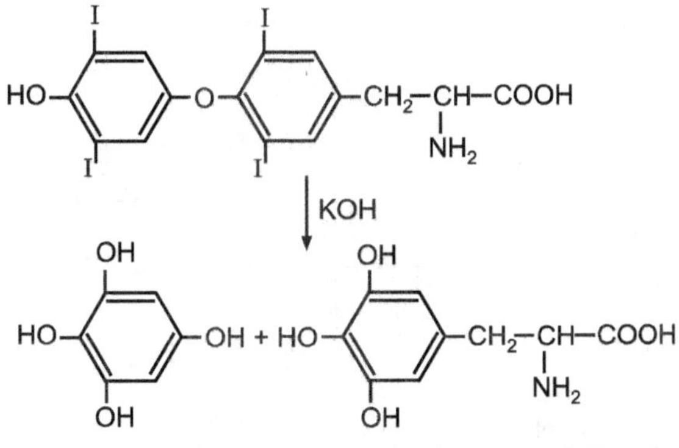

HO–⟨⟩(I,I)–O–⟨⟩(I,I)–CH$_2$–CH–COOH
                              |
                              NH$_2$

↓ KOH

HO–⟨⟩(OH,OH)–OH + HO–⟨⟩(OH,OH)–CH$_2$–CH–COOH
                                        |
                                        NH$_2$

(vii) The above structure can further be proved by the following specific reaction of iodinated phenols in both the ortho positions. Thyroxine on treatment with nitrous acid gives a yellow colour which deepens on boiling and changes to red on cooling followed by addition of ammonia

Thyroxine $\xrightarrow{\text{HONO}}$ Yellow colour $\xrightarrow{\text{Boil}}$ Colour deepens $\xrightarrow[\text{NH}_3]{\text{Boil}}$ Red

Biosynthesis of Thyroid Hormones

(1) **Uptake:** Once taken up by the thyroid gland, iodide undergoes a series of enzymatic reactions that converts it into active thyroid hormone. The first step is the transport of iodide into the thyroid gland by an intrinsic follicle cell basement membrane protein called the sodium/iodide symporter (NIS). This can be inhibited by such anions as SCN^-, TcO_4^-, and ClO_4^-.

(2) **Oxidation and iodination:** Iodide is then oxidised by thyroidal peroxidase to iodine, in which form it rapidly iodinates tyrosine residues within the thyroglobulin molecule to form monoiodotyrosine (MIT) and diiodotyrosine (DIT). This process is called iodide organification. Thyroidal peroxidase is transiently blocked by high levels of intrathyroidal iodide and blocked more persistently by thioamide drugs.

(3) **Coupling and Release and Conversion of T_4 to T_3 in periphery:** Two molecules of DIT combine within the thyroglobulin molecule to form L-thyroxine (T_4). One molecule of MIT and one molecule of DIT combine to form T3. In addition to thyroglobulin, other proteins within the gland may be iodinated, but these iodoproteins do not have hormonal activity. Thyroxine, T_3, MIT, and DIT are released from thyroglobulin by exocytosis and proteolysis of thyroglobulin at the apical colloid border. The MIT and DIT are deiodinated within the gland, and the iodine is reutilised. This process of proteolysis is also blocked by high levels of intra thyroidal iodide. The ratio of T_4 to T_3 within thyroglobulin is approximately 5:1, so that most of the hormone released is thyroxine. Most of the T_3 circulating in the blood is derived from peripheral metabolism of thyroxine.

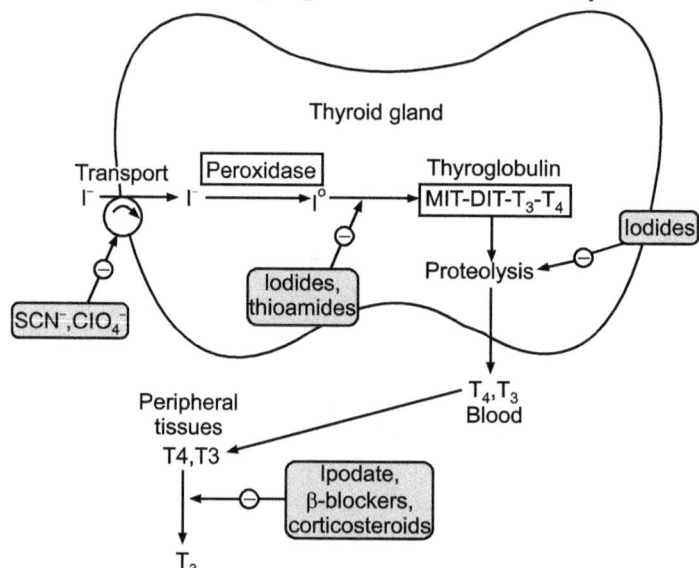

Fig 8.2 : Synthesis of thyroid hormones

[Structures of Thyroxine with Deiodination to Activation (3,5,3'-Triiodothyronine, T₃) and Inactivation (3,3'5'-Triiodothyronine, reverse T₃)]

Transport and Metabolism

T_4 and T_3 in plasma are reversibly bound to the plasma proteins primarily the thyroxine binding globulin (TBG). The protein binding protects the hormones from metabolism and excretion resulting in their long half lives in the circulation. Only about 0.03% of total T_4 and 0.3% of T_3 exist in the "free" form which is the form in which the hormones have metabolic activity. Beside TBG, transthyretin and albumin can also bind the thyroxine.

Thyroxine has a half life of 6-8 days and the same for T_3 is 1- 2 days. The half lives are increased in hypothyroidism and decreased in hyperthyroidism because of altered rates of metabolism. In condition where TBG is increased such as pregnancy or by contraceptives or estrogens, the concentration of total and bound hormone will increase but the concentration of free hormone and steady state elimination will be normal.

Regulation of Thyroid Function

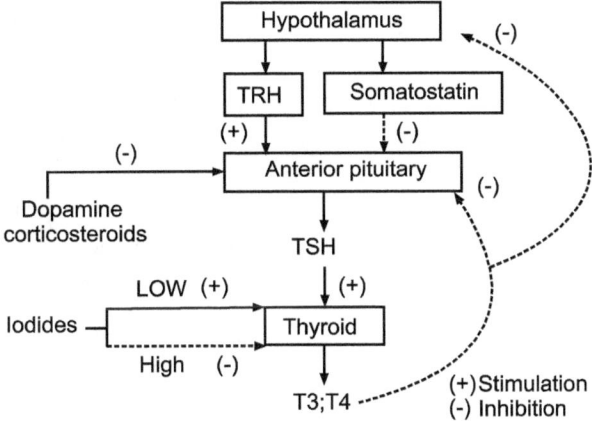

Fig. 8.3 : Regulation of thyroid

As is seen in **Fig. 8.3**, hypothalamus secretes thyrotropin releasing hormone (TRH) into the pituitary portal venous system. TRH stimulates the synthesis and release of thyroid stimulating hormone (TSH). TSH increases the synthesis and release of T_4 and T_3 via an adenylyl cyclase (cAMP) pathway. T_4 and T_3 act in a negative feedback fashion in the pituitary and hypothalamus to block the secretion of TSH and TRH respectively. Besides this, other drugs such as dopamine, steroids etc. also affect the thyroid function.

Synthesis of Thyroid Hormone

(i) By Harington and Barger in 1927.

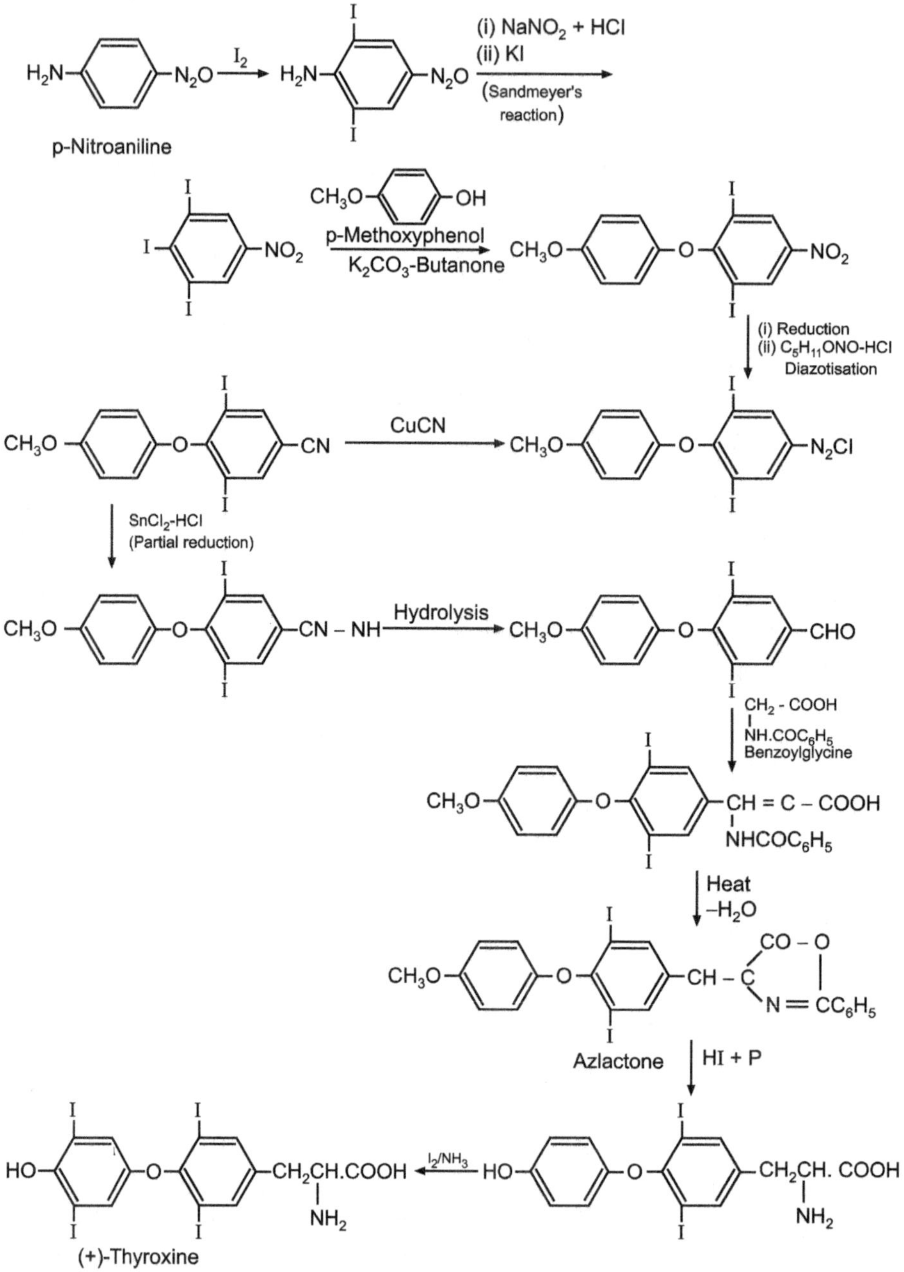

p-Nitroaniline $\xrightarrow{I_2}$ (diiodo intermediate) $\xrightarrow[\text{(ii) KI (Sandmeyer's reaction)}]{\text{(i) NaNO}_2 + \text{HCl}}$ 3,5-diiodo-4-iodo-nitrobenzene

$\xrightarrow[\text{K}_2\text{CO}_3\text{-Butanone}]{\text{CH}_3\text{O–C}_6\text{H}_4\text{–OH (p-Methoxyphenol)}}$ CH$_3$O–C$_6$H$_4$–O–C$_6$H$_2$I$_2$–NO$_2$

$\xrightarrow[\text{(ii) C}_5\text{H}_{11}\text{ONO-HCl Diazotisation}]{\text{(i) Reduction}}$ CH$_3$O–C$_6$H$_4$–O–C$_6$H$_2$I$_2$–N$_2$Cl

$\xrightarrow{\text{CuCN}}$ CH$_3$O–C$_6$H$_4$–O–C$_6$H$_2$I$_2$–CN

$\xrightarrow[\text{(Partial reduction)}]{\text{SnCl}_2\text{-HCl}}$ CH$_3$O–C$_6$H$_4$–O–C$_6$H$_2$I$_2$–CN–NH

$\xrightarrow{\text{Hydrolysis}}$ CH$_3$O–C$_6$H$_4$–O–C$_6$H$_2$I$_2$–CHO

$\xrightarrow[\text{Benzoylglycine}]{\text{CH}_2\text{-COOH, NH.COC}_6\text{H}_5}$ CH$_3$O–C$_6$H$_4$–O–C$_6$H$_2$I$_2$–CH=C(NHCOC$_6$H$_5$)–COOH

$\xrightarrow[-\text{H}_2\text{O}]{\text{Heat}}$ CH$_3$O–C$_6$H$_4$–O–C$_6$H$_2$I$_2$–CH–C(CO–O / N=CC$_6$H$_5$) (Azlactone)

$\xrightarrow{\text{HI + P}}$ HO–C$_6$H$_3$I–O–C$_6$H$_2$I$_2$–CH$_2$CH(NH$_2$)COOH

$\xleftarrow{\text{I}_2/\text{NH}_3}$ HO–C$_6$H$_4$–O–C$_6$H$_2$I$_2$–CH$_2$CH(NH$_2$)COOH

(+)-Thyroxine

The racemic mixture may be resolved by active formic acid.

(ii) Thyroxine was synthesised by Hems in 1949 in Glaxo Laboratories by a second method.

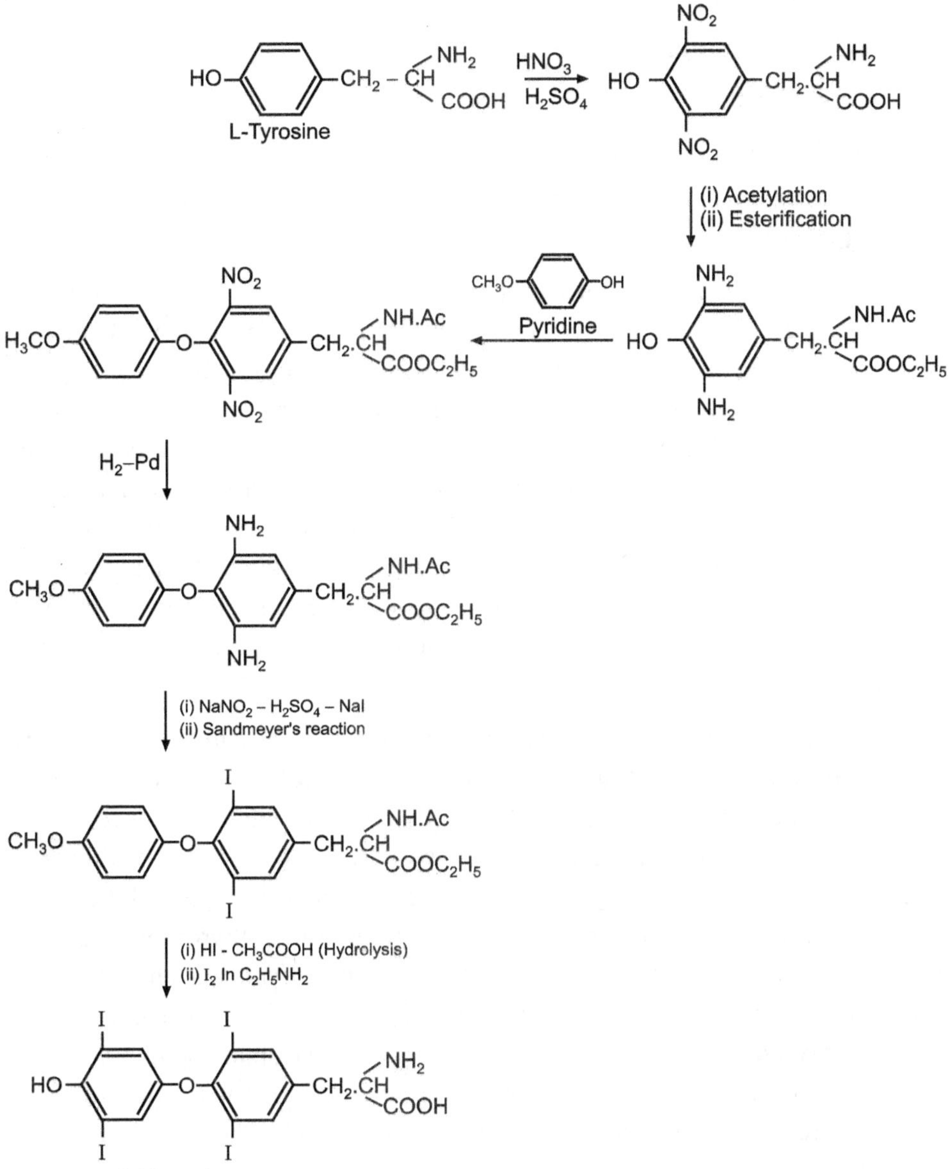

[Reaction scheme: L-Tyrosine → (HNO$_3$/H$_2$SO$_4$) → 3,5-dinitro-tyrosine → (i) Acetylation (ii) Esterification → diamino intermediate (after reduction shown) ...]

The synthesis proceeds through:

1. L-Tyrosine + HNO$_3$/H$_2$SO$_4$ → 3,5-dinitrotyrosine
2. (i) Acetylation (ii) Esterification → N-acetyl-3,5-dinitrotyrosine ethyl ester
3. + CH$_3$O–C$_6$H$_4$–OH / Pyridine → diaryl ether (with NO$_2$ groups)
4. H$_2$–Pd → diamino diaryl ether
5. (i) NaNO$_2$–H$_2$SO$_4$–NaI (ii) Sandmeyer's reaction → 3,5-diiodo diaryl ether
6. (i) HI–CH$_3$COOH (Hydrolysis) (ii) I$_2$ in C$_2$H$_5$NH$_2$ → **L-Thyroxine**

Structure Activity Relationship

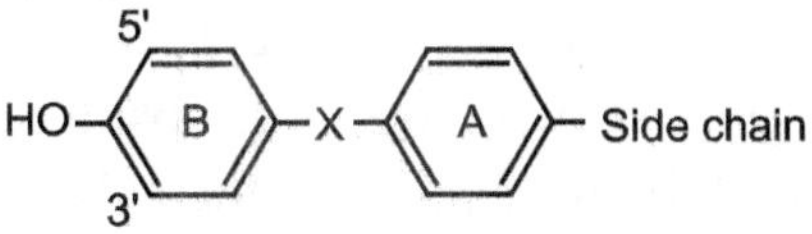

[Diagram: HO–(Ring B, positions 3',5')–X–(Ring A)–Side chain — Thyronine nucleus]

The SARs are discussed in terms of single structural variations of T4 in the

1. Alanine side chain,
2. 3- and 5-positions of the inner ring,
3. The bridging atom,
4. 3'- and 5'-positions of the outer ring, and
5. The 4'-phenolic hydroxyl group.

Aliphatic Side Chain

The naturally occurring hormones are biosynthesised from L-tyrosine and possess the L-alanine side chain. The L-isomers of T3 and T4 are more active than the D-isomers, the carboxylate ion and the number of atoms connecting it to the ring are more important for activity than is the intact zwetterionic alanine side chain. In the carboxylate series, the activity is maximum with the two-carbon acetic acid side chain but decreases with either the shorter formic acid or the longer propionic and butyric acid analogues. The ethylamine side chain analogues of T4 and T3 are less active than the corresponding carboxylic acid analogues. In addition, isomers of T3 in which the alanine side chain is transposed with the 3-iodine or occupies the 2-position were inactive in the rat antigoiter test, indicating a critical location for the side chain in the 1-position of the inner ring.

Alanine-side chain

The phenyl ring bearing the alanine side chain, called the inner ring or α-ring, is substituted with iodine in the 3 and 5 positions in T3 and T4. Removal of both iodine atoms from the inner ring to form 3',5'-T2 or 3'-T1 produces analogues devoid of T4 like activity, primarily because of the loss of the perpendicular orientation of diphenyl ether conformation. Retention of activity observed on replacement of the 3-and 5-iodine atoms with bromine implies that iodine does not play a unique role in thyroid hormone activity. Moreover, a broad range of hormone activity found with halogen free analogues indicates that a halogen atom is not essential for activity. In contrast to T3, 3'-isopropyl-3, 6-dimethyl, L-thyronine has the capacity to cross the placental membrane and exerts thyromimetic effect in the foetus after administration to the mother. This could prove to be useful in treating foetal thyroid hormone deficiencies or in stimulating lung development.

Substitution in the 3 and 5 positions by alkyl groups significantly larger and less symmetric than methyl groups, such as isopropyl and secondary butyl moieties, produces inactive analogues. These results show that 3, 5-disubstitution by symmetric, lipophilic groups not exceeding the size of iodine is required for activity.

Bridging Atom

Several analogues have been synthesised in which the ether oxygen bridge has been removed or replaced by other atoms. The biphenyl analogue of T4 formed by removal of the oxygen bridge, is inactive in the rat antigoiter test The linear biphenyl structure is a drastic change from the normal diphenyl ether conformation found in the naturally occurring hormones. Replacement of the bridging oxygen atom by sulphur or by a methylene group produces highly active analogues. This provides evidence against the Niemann quinoid theory, which postulates that the ability of a compound to form a quinoid structure in the phenolic ring is essential for thyromimetic activity, and emphasizes the importance of the three-dimensional structure and receptor fit of the hormones. Attempts to prepare amino- and carbonyl bridged analogues of T3, and T4 have been unsuccessful.

Phenolic Ring

The phenolic ring, also called the outer or β-ring, of the thyronine nucleus is required for hormonal activity. Variations in 3'- or 3',5'-substituents on the phenolic ring have dramatic effects on biological activity and affinity for the nuclear receptor. The unsubstituted parent structure of this series L-T2 possesses low activity. Substitution at the 3' ·position by polar hydroxyl or nitro groups causes a decrease in activity as a consequence of both lowered lipophilicity and intramolecular hydrogen bonding with the 4' –hydroxyl group. Conversely, substitution by nonpolar halogen or alkyl groups results in an increase in activity in direct relation to the bulk and lipophilicity of the substituent- for example, $F < Cl < Br < I$ and $CH, < CH_2CH_3, < CH(CH_3)_2$. Although 3'·isopropylthyronine is the most potent analogue, it results in a substantial decrease in activity, presumably as a result of the weak hydrogen bonding ability of the latter group. The retention of activity observed with the 4'-unsubstinued compound provides direct evidence for metabolic 4-hydroxylation as an activating step.

Introduction of a 4'-substituent that cannot mimic the functional role of a phenolic group such as a methyl group and that is not metabolically converted into a functional residue results in complete loss of hormonal actvity. The thyromimetic activity of the 4'-methyl ether was ready for metabolic cleavage to form an active 4'-hydroxyl analogue.

The pKa of 4'-phenolic hydroxyl group is 6.7 for T_4 (90% ionised at pH 7.4) and 8.5 for T_3, (-approximately 10% ionised). Greater acidity for T4 is due to its stronger affinity for plasma proteins which also results in it`s longer plasma half-life.

The 3' -substituent should be distal and the 5' - substituent should be proximal to the side - chain bearing ring in order to maintain the hormone molecule in the active conformation, as shown in the following figure.

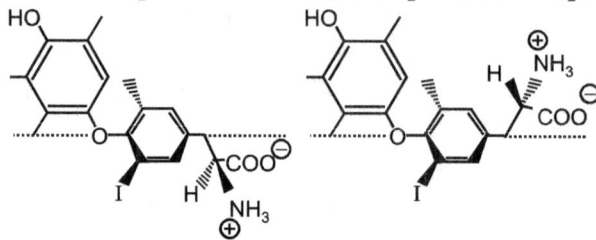

Structures of representative distal and proximal compounds

Side chain conformation of thyroid hormone: transoid (left) and Cisoid (right)

Mechanism of Action

Thyroid hormones, T4 and T3, dissociate from thyroid-binding proteins, enter the cell by diffusion or possibly by active transport. Within the cell, T4 is converted to T3 by 5'-deiodinase, and the T3 enters the nucleus, where T3 binds to a specific T3 receptor protein, Most of the effects of thyroid on metabolic processes appear to be mediated by activation of nuclear receptors that lead to increased formation of RNA and subsequent protein synthesis, eg, increased formation of Na_+/K_+ ATPase. This is consistent with the observation that the action of thyroid is manifested in vivo with a time lag of hours or days after its administration.

Actions of Thyroid Hormone : Thyroid hormone increases metabolism and protein synthesis, and it is necessary for growth and development in children, including mental development and attainment of sexual maturity.

1. **Metabolic Rate:** Thyroid hormone increases the metabolism of all body tissues except the retina, spleen, testes, and lungs. Lipids are mobilised from adipose tissue, and the breakdown of cholesterol by the liver is increased. Blood levels of cholesterol are decreased in hyperthyroidism and increased in hypothyroidism. Muscle proteins are broken down and used as fuel causing muscle fatigue that occurs with hyperthyroidism.

2. **Cardiovascular Function:** Cardiovascular and respiratory functions are strongly affected by thyroid function. Metabolism increases, there is an increase in oxygen consumption and production of metabolic end-products, accompanied by an increase in vasodilatation. Blood flow to the skin, is increased as a means of dissipating the body heat that results from the higher metabolism.

3. **Gastrointestinal Function:** Thyroid hormone enhances gastrointestinal function, causing an increase in motility and production of gastrointestinal secretions that often results in diarrhoea.

4. **Neuromuscular Effects:** Thyroid hormone has profound effects on neural control of muscle function and tone. In the hyperthyroid state, a fine muscle tremor is present. The cause of this tremor is unknown, but it may represent an increased sensitivity of the neural synapses in the spinal cord that control muscle tone.

5. **Other effects:** Thyroid hormones also affect skeletal muscle contraction, propulsive activity of gastrointestinal system and are required for maintenance of pregnancy and lactation.

PANCREATIC HORMONE

The endocrine pancreas in the adult human consists of approximately 1 million islets of Langerhans interspersed throughout the pancreatic gland. Within the islets, at least four hormone-producing cells are present. (Table 8.3) Their hormones include **insulin**, - an important storage and anabolic hormone of the body; **islet amyloid polypeptide (IAPP,** or **amylin**), - modulates appetite, gastric emptying, and glucagon and insulin secretion; **glucagon**- the hyperglycemic factor that mobilises glycogen stores; **somatostatin**- a universal inhibitor of secretory cells; and **pancreatic peptide**- a small protein that facilitates digestive processes by a mechanism not yet clarified.

Table 8.3 : Pancreatic islet cells and their secretory products

Cell Types	Approximate Percent of Islet Mass	Secretory Products
A cell (alpha)	20	Glucagon, proglucagon
B cell (beta)	75	Insulin, C-peptide, proinsulin, amylin
D cell (delta)	3-5	Somatostatin
F cell (PP cell)	< 2	Pancreatic polypeptide (PP)

Within pancreatic polypeptide-rich lobules of adult islets, located only in the posterior portion of the head of the human pancreas, glucagon cells are scarce (< 0.5%) and F cells make up as much as 80% of the cells.

Type 1: Diabetes Mellitus

The hallmark of type 1 diabetes is selective B-cell destruction and *severe* or *absolute* insulin deficiency. Administration of insulin is essential in patients with type 1 diabetes. Type 1 diabetes is further subdivided into immune and idiopathic causes. The immune form is the most common form of type 1 diabetes. Although most patients are younger than 30 years of age at the time of diagnosis, the onset can occur at any age. Type 1 diabetes is found in all ethnic groups, but the highest incidence is in people from northern Europe and from Sardinia. Susceptibility appears to involve a multifactorial genetic linkage but only 10-15% of patients have a positive family history.

Type 2: Diabetes Mellitus

Type 2 diabetes is characterized by tissue resistance to the action of insulin combined with a *relative* deficiency in insulin secretion. A given individual may have more resistance or more B-cell deficiency, and the abnormalities may be mild or severe. Although insulin is produced by the B cells in these patients, it is inadequate to overcome the resistance, and the blood glucose rises. The impaired insulin action also affects fat metabolism, resulting in increased free fatty acid flux and triglyceride levels and reciprocally low levels of high-density lipoprotein (HDL).

Individuals with type 2 diabetes may not require insulin to survive, but 30% or more will benefit from insulin therapy to control the blood glucose. It is likely that 10-20% of individuals in whom type 2 diabetes was initially diagnosed actually have both type 1 and type 2 or a slowly progressing type 1, and ultimately will require full insulin replacement. Although persons with type 2 diabetes ordinarily do not develop ketosis, ketoacidosis may occur as the result of stress such as infection or use of medication that enhances resistance, eg, corticosteroids. Dehydration in untreated and poorly controlled individuals with type 2 diabetes can lead to a life-threatening condition called *nonketotic hyperosmolar coma*. In this condition, the blood glucose may rise to 6-20 times the normal range and an altered mental state develops or the person loses consciousness. Urgent medical care and rehydration is required.

Type 3: Diabetes Mellitus

The type 3 designation refers to multiple *other* specific causes of an elevated blood glucose: non-pancreatic diseases, drug therapy, etc. For a detailed list the reader is referred to Expert Committee, 2003.

Type 4: Diabetes Mellitus

Gestational diabetes (GDM) is defined as any abnormality in glucose levels noted for the first time during pregnancy. Gestational diabetes is diagnosed in approximately 4% of all pregnancies in the USA. During pregnancy, the placenta and placental hormones create an insulin resistance that is most pronounced in the last trimester. Risk assessment for diabetes is suggested starting at the first prenatal visit. High-risk women should be screened immediately. Screening may be deferred in lower-risk women until the 24th to 28th week of gestation.

INSULIN HORMONE

Banting and Best discovered in 1923 that a factor, (which they called 'insulin') in the extract of the islets of Langerhans of the pancreas possessed hypoglycemic property and soon this came into use as a drug against diabetes to counteract hyperglycemia. Insulin is secreted from the beta-cells of islets of Langerhans.

Insulin is the only hormone known to have a direct effect in lowering blood glucose levels. The actions of insulin are promotes glucose uptake by target cells and provides for glucose storage as glycogen, prevents fat and glycogen breakdown and inhibits gluconeogenesis, and increases protein synthesis. Insulin acts to promote fat storage by increasing the transport of glucose into fat cells. It also facilitates triglyceride synthesis from glucose in fat cells and inhibits the intracellular breakdown of stored triglycerides.

Isolation

The pancreas of the slaughtered animal is immediately frozen and then it is minced and extracted with 80% ethanol containing some amount of phosphoric acid to adjust its pH at 3. The fats and Proteins are separated from the extract after centrifugation, the pH of the extract is then raised to about 8 by means of ammonia. The solution is filtered, the filtrate is acidified and then evaporated in vacuum to remove fatty materials. The solution in ethanol free from fatty material is treated with picric acid when insulin picrate is obtained. The insulin picrate is dissolved in acetone and insulin is reprecipitated as its hydrochloride. Further purification may be done by means of chromatography.

Insulin Secretion

There are various regulators of insulin secretion, glucose being the key regulator. Others include amino acids, ketones, various nutrients, gastrointestinal hormones and neurotransmitters. Glucose levels > 70mg/dl lead to secretion of insulin. Glucose and other nutrients when taken orally are more effective in causing insulin secretion than when given intravenously indicating the involvement of gastrointestinal hormones or chemical signals 'incretins' from the gut in secretion of insulin.

Step 1: First step involves entry of glucose into the pancreatic beta cell by the GLUT2 glucose transporter.

Step 2: After entry glucose is phosphorylated by glucokinase to glucose 6 phosphate (G6P) in cytoplasm of beta cell.

Step 3: G6P undergoes glycolysis to generate ATP.

Step 4: ATP generated here leads to inhibition of ATP sensitive K^+ ion channels. ATP sensitive K^+ channel has two proteins.

Step 5: Inhibition of K^+ channels induces beta cell membrane depolarization, which in turn leads to opening of voltage dependent Ca^{2+} channels. Ca^{2+} enters the cells and leads to release of insulin.

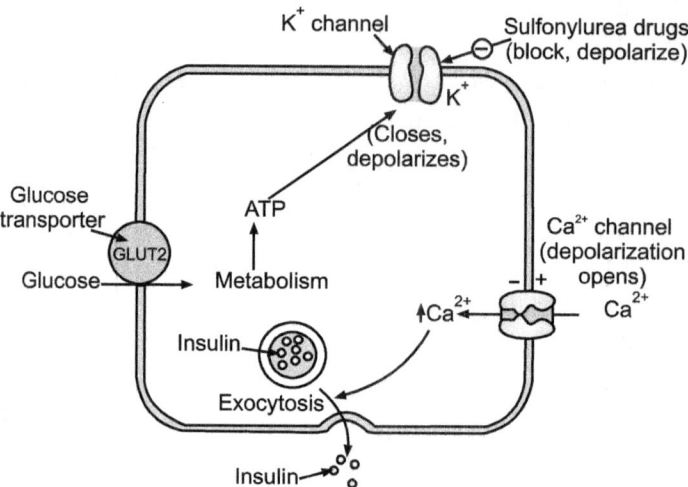

Fig. 8.4 : Insulin Secretion

Constitution

Insulin was the first protein whose amino acid sequence was worked out by **Sanger** et al in 1951-55. Moreover, insulin is one of the most complex proteins whose structures are established. Its structure was established in 1955 by Sanger for which he was awarded Nobel Prize in 1958; and associates (Brown et al. 1955). The important points which give insight into the structure of insulin are as follows.

1. Insulin, on complete hydrolysis gives 51 amino acids indicating the fact that it has 51 amino acid molecules. Qualitative studies of these amino acids revealed that they are of as much as 17 different types. Further quantitative studies of these 17 amino acids indicate the following numbers of the individual amino acid.

1.	Glycine (Gly)	4	10.	Threonine	1
2.	Alanine	3	11.	Lysine	1
3.	Valine	5	12.	Glutamic acid	4
4.	Leucine	6	13.	Glutamine	3
5.	Iso-leucine	1	14.	Asparagine	3
6.	Proline	1	15.	Arginine	1
7.	Phenylalanine	3	16.	Histidine	1
8.	Tyrosine	4	17.	Cysteine	2
9.	Serine	3		or cystine	3

2. By the use of FDNB (1-fluoro 2,4-dinitrobenzene) technique, Sanger established that glycine and phenylalanine are present as N-terminal residues. It means that insulin has two chains of polypeptides; one having glycine as the terminal amino acid and the other having phenylalanine as the terminal amino acid. Since insulin is found to have cystine the two chains might be linked with each other by disulphide bond.

3. On oxidation with peformic acid, insulin was oxidised to two peptides namely chain A and chain B. The two fractions were separated by electrophoresis or chromatography and degraded individually .

Fraction B : The chain B of insulin is found to be basic in nature and contains 30 amino acid residues. It was partially hydrolysed by means of different reagents (acids and enzymes) into various fragments of polypeptides. The fragments were separated by ion-exchange resins, by adsorption on charcoal and by ionophoresis. Further fractionation was achieved by paper chromatography.

The different polypeptide fragments are degraded by DNP method and thus the sequence of amino acids in various fragments are established.

Agent	Polypeptides
Acid	NH_2 NH_2 (on Asp and Glu) (i) Phe–Val–Asp–Glu–His–Leu–Cys–Gly (ii) Ser-His-Leu-V_t (iii) Ala-Glu (iv) Ala-Leu-Try (v) Tyr-Leu-Val-Cys-Gly (vi) Gly-Glu-Arg-G (vii) Gly-Phe (viii) Thr-Pro-Lys-Al
Pepsin	NH_2 NH_2 (on Asp and Glu) (i) Phe–Val–Asp–Glu–His–Leu–Cys–Gly–Ser–His–Leu (ii) Val-Glu-Ala-Leu (iii) Leu-Val-Cys-Gly-Glu-Arg-Gly-Phe (iv) Try-Thr-Pro-Lys-Ala
Chymotrypsin	(i) His-Leu-Cys-Gly-Ser-His-Leu (ii) Val-Glu-Ala-Leu-Tyr (iii) Leu-Val-Vys-Gly-Glu-Arg-Gly-Phe-Phe
Trypsin	(i) Gly-Phe-Phe-Tyr-Thr-Pro-Lys (ii) Ala

With the structure of the different polypeptides, the chain B is constructed by tracing the overlapping patterns of the different peptides isolated.

$$\begin{array}{c} \overset{NH_2}{|} \quad \overset{NH_2}{|} \\ \text{Phe-Val-Asp-Glu-His-Leu-Cy-Gly-Ser-His-Leu-Val-Glu-Ala-Leu-} \\ \text{Tyr-Leu-Val-Cy-Gly-Glu-Arg-Gly-Phe-Phe-Tyr-Thr-Pro-Lys-Ala} \\ | \\ SO_3H \end{array}$$

Fraction A: The chain A of insulin is found to be acidic and contains 21 amino acids. The sequence, of amino acids in chain A was elucidated in a similar manner and' was shown to be as below.

$$\begin{array}{c} \overset{NH_2}{|} \quad \overset{SO_3H}{|} \quad \quad \overset{SO_3H}{|} \\ \text{Gly-Ile-Val-Glu-Glu-Cy-Cy-Ala-Ser-Val-Cy-Ser-Leu-Tyr-Glu-Leu-Glu-Asp-Tyr-Tyr-Cy-Asp(NH}_2) \\ \quad\quad\quad\quad\quad\quad\quad\quad\quad\quad\quad\quad\quad\quad\quad\quad | \quad\quad\quad | \quad\quad | \; | \\ \quad\quad\quad\quad\quad\quad\quad\quad\quad\quad\quad\quad\quad\quad\quad\quad NH_2 \quad\quad NH_2 \quad\quad NH_2\; SO_3H \end{array}$$

4. The oxidation of insulin by means of performic acid to cysteic acid residues suggests the two chains must be linked through disulphide bridges. The positions of the disulphide bridges is established by getting peptides containing the cysteine residues intact from unoxidised insulin. Such fragments i.e. the fragments having disuilfide bonds are obtained in the following manner.

Insulin is hydrolysed by an enzyme in presence of thiol inhibitor such as N-ethyl maleimide (the inhibitor is used to check the cleavage of disulphide bonds) and the peptides containing the cystine residues having intact disulphide linkages are separated. The latter is oxidised to cysteic acid peptides which are separated and then identified by the usual DNP method. On the basis of the above type of reactions insulin is found to have the following three types of disulphide linkages.

$$\begin{array}{ccc}
\text{Leu-Val-Cy-Gly} & \text{His-Leu-Cy-Gly} & \text{Ser-Val-Cy} \\
| & | & | \\
S & S & S \\
| & | & | \\
S & S & S \\
| & | & | \\
\text{Tyr-Cy-Asp-NH}_2 & \text{Cy-Ala} & \text{Gly-Ileu-Val-Glu-Glu-Cy} \\
| & \text{II} & \text{III} \\
\end{array}$$

5. The A chain was found to contain four cysteic acid residues and the chain-B only two. Hence, the chain-A contains a disulphide ring and is linked to the chain-B by two disulphide bonds. Thus the complete structure of insulin may be represented as below.

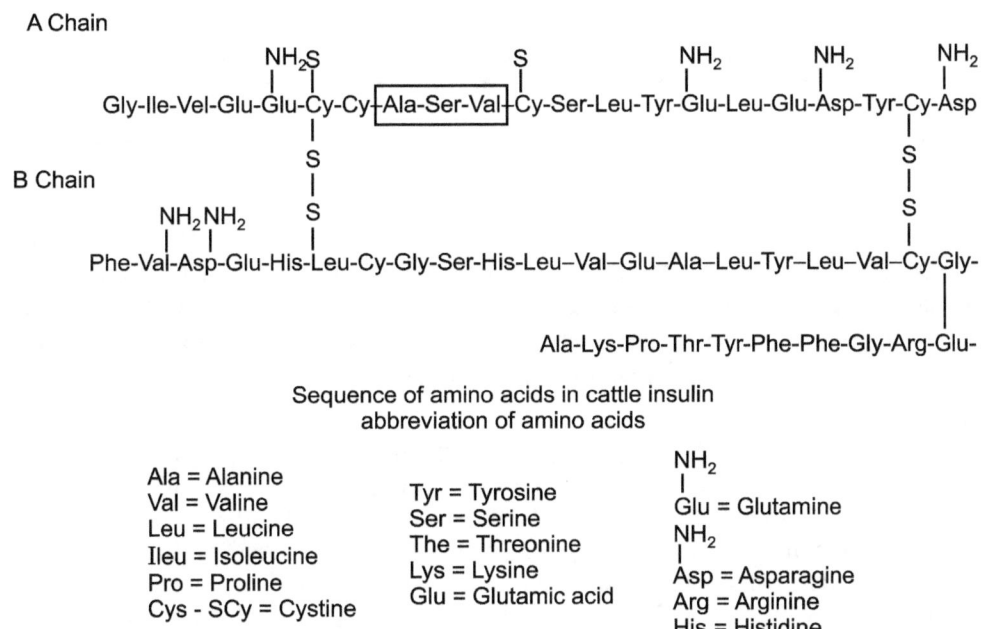

Sequence of amino acids in cattle insulin
abbreviation of amino acids

Ala = Alanine
Val = Valine
Leu = Leucine
Ileu = Isoleucine
Pro = Proline
Cys - SCy = Cystine

Tyr = Tyrosine
Ser = Serine
The = Threonine
Lys = Lysine
Glu = Glutamic acid

Glu = Glutamine
Asp = Asparagine
Arg = Arginine
His = Histidine

Biosynthesis of Insulin

The biosynthesis of insulin involves the conversion of its precursor preproinsulin (MW 11,500 nearly) to proinsulin (MW about 9.000) in the ribosome on the rough endoplasmic reticulum. Proinsulin has two polypeptide segments A and B, with disulphide bonds between A7 and B7, A20 and B19 and also between A6 and A11. These segments are connected by another inactive polypeptide (C-peptide). The molecule is also folded there. It is then transferred to the Golgi apparatus where the C-peptide is removed forming insulin (MW 5734) retaining the S·S bridges. Granulation of the insulin molecule takes place in the Golgi apparatus with the formation of hexamer crystals complexing with Zn (About 5% of proinsulin with low activity remains as such, and combines with Zn in the granule). This matures as it passes through the cytoplasm ultimately reaching the plasma membrane. It is then released into the extracellular fluid by a Ca^{2+} -dependent energy requiring process under appropriate stimulation.

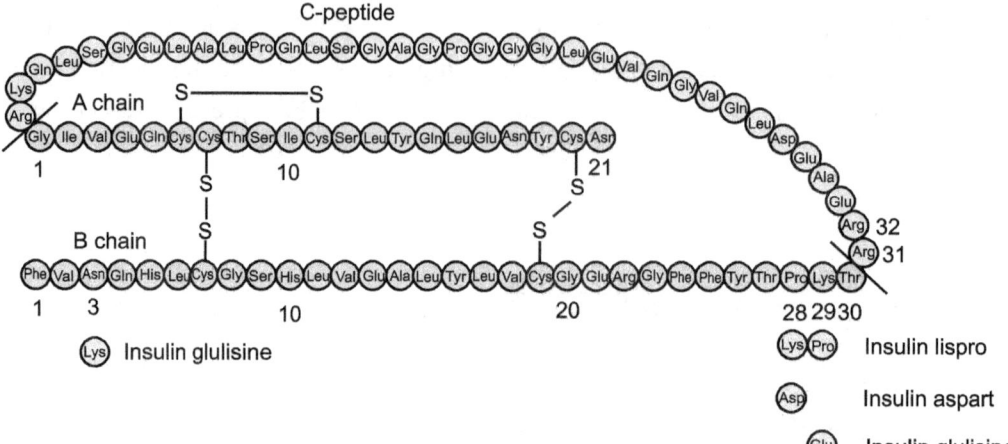

Fig. 8.5 : Structure of human proinsulin and some commercially available insulin analogs. Insulin is shown as the shaded (darker colour) peptide chains, A and B. Differences in the A and B chains and amino acids modifications for insulin asart, lispro, and glulisine are noted

Insulin Release

Insulin is produced by the pancreatic beta cells in the islets of Langerhans. The active form of the hormone is composed of two polypeptide chains—an A chain and a B chain. Active insulin is formed in the beta cells from a larger molecule called *proinsulin*. In converting proinsulin to insulin, enzymes in the beta cell cleave proinsulin at specific sites to form two separate substances: active insulin and a biologically inactive connecting peptide (C-peptide) chain that joined the A and B chains before they were separated. Active insulin and the inactive C-peptide chain are packaged into secretory granules and released simultaneously from the beta cell. The release of insulin from the pancreatic beta cells is regulated by blood glucose levels, increasing as blood glucose levels rise and decreasing when blood glucose levels decline. Secretion of insulin occurs in an oscillatory or pulsatile fashion.

Synthesis of Insulin

The synthesis of the two insulin chains were achieved after the long efforts of Katsoyannis and his co-workers in 1960. The main problems encountered during the synthesis of the two chains of insulin are

(i) The selection of the protecting groups,
(ii) The selection of the appropriate fragment to be eventually joined to the chains,
(iii) Some of the intermediates are extremely insoluble in the common solvents.
(iv) The formation of the correct disulphide bridges.

The approach of Katsoyannis (et al. 1964) for the synthesis of the two insulin chains may be summarised in *charts* 1-3. Simultaneously, Meienhofer (et al 1964) also reported, the synthesis of the two chains in a different manner, but here only the former approach is summarised. However, both of the approaches possess the following common characteristics.

(i) Most of the fragments, ranging from tri-to-deca-peptides are built up in a stepwise manner from the individual C-terminal amino acids and almost exclusively by the nitrophenyl ester method.

(ii) All the sulphydryl functions are protected by benzyl group.

The combination of the two chains A and B is developed by Du-Yu-Cang et. al (1961-65).

Synthesis of the A-Chain Insulin

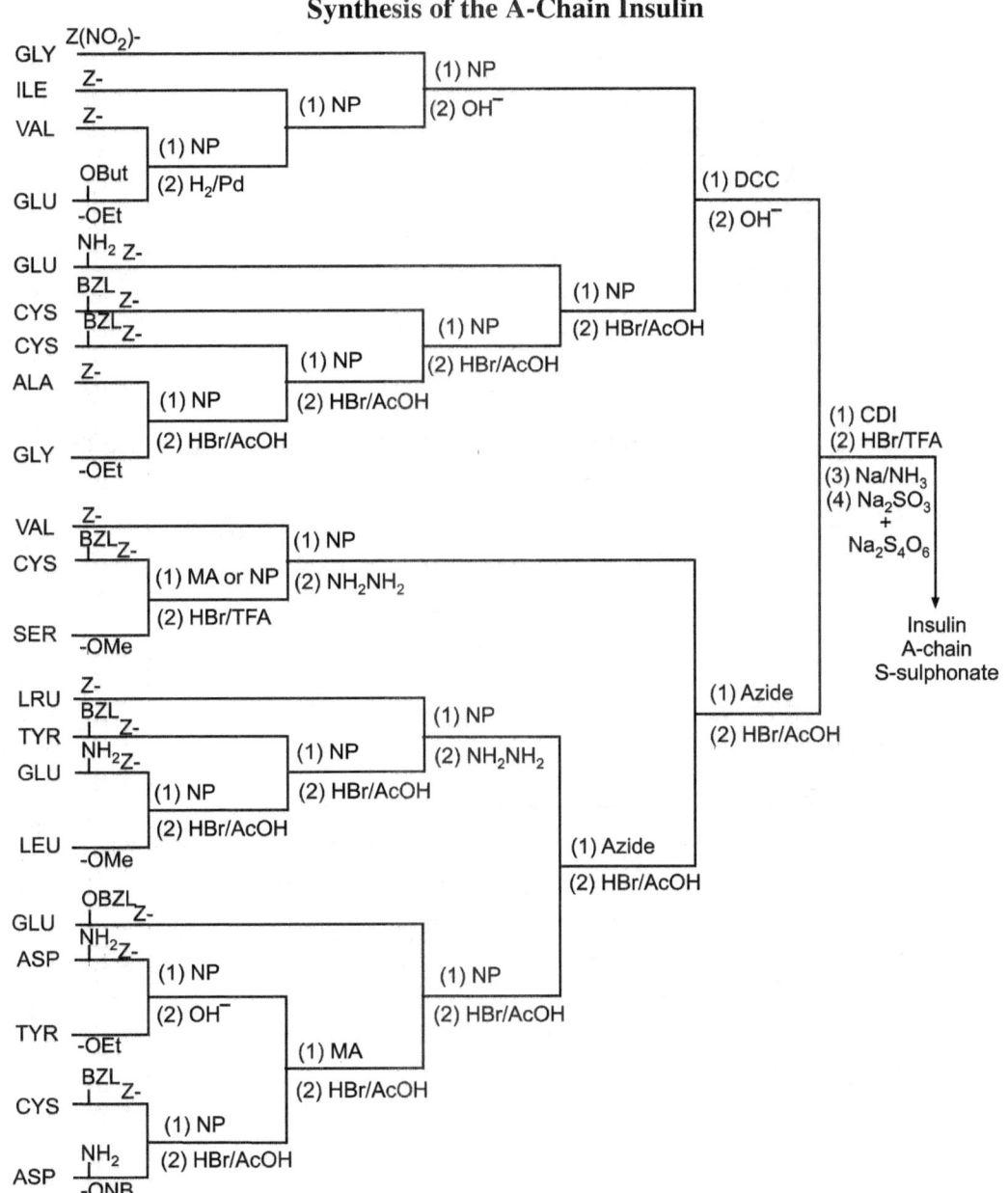

Synthesis of B_{1-9} and B_{10-3} Ammonia Acids of the B-chain of Insulin

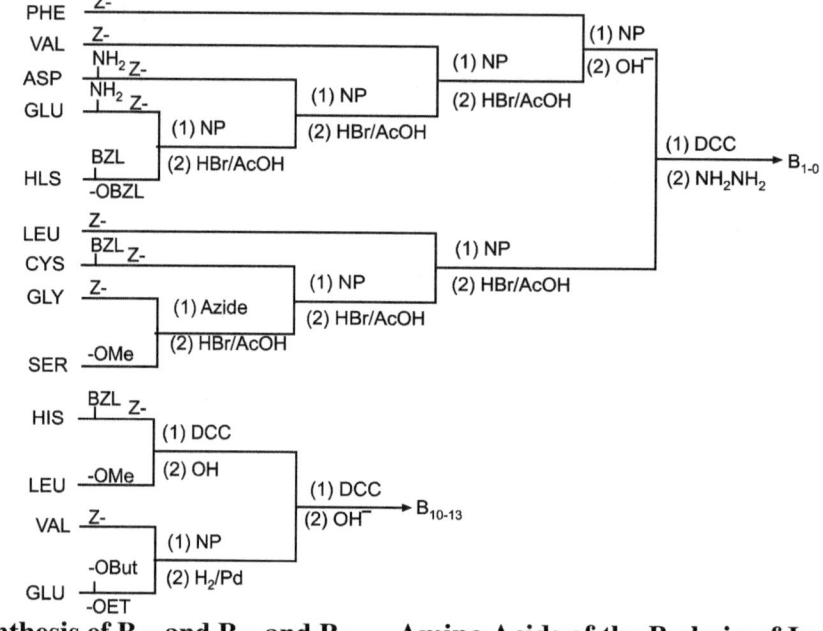

Synthesis of B_{14} and B_{20} and B_{21-30} Amino Acids of the B-chain of Insulin

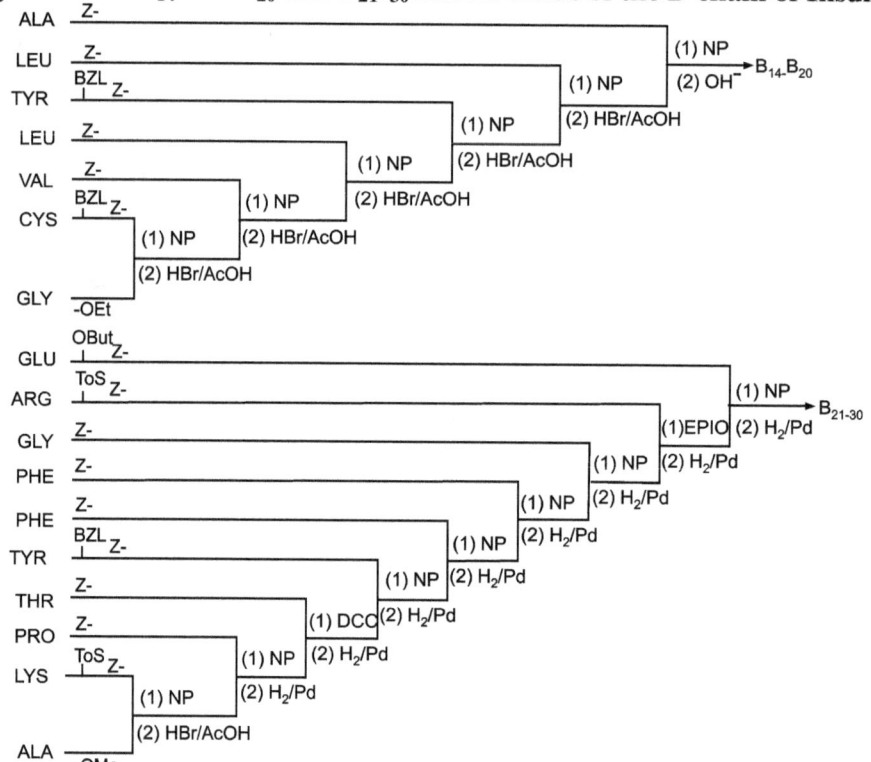

Synthesis of the B-chain Insulin

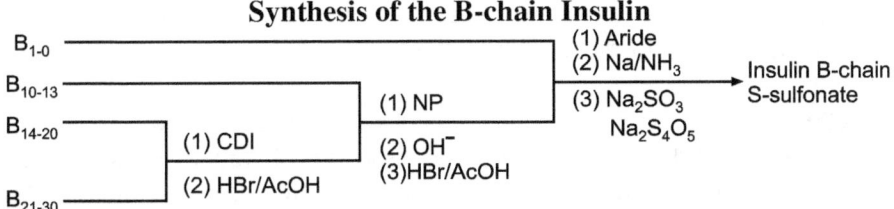

Structure Activity Relationship

In the rhombohedral crystal, the unit cell consists of six insulin molecules arranged as three equivalent dimers in three fold symmetry. The compact packing of the hexamer produces an oblate spheroid (Ca. 50°A wide. 35°A high), with polar amino acid side chains covering its surface. The two zinc ions are situated, 17°A apart, on the three fold crystal axis and coordinated to three equivalent β - 10 histidines. Perpendicular to threefold crystal axis are non-crystallographic twofold symmetry axes relating two dimers of the hexamer (O → Q) and the two monomers, molecules 1 and 2 of the dimer(O→P). The dimers constitute the asymmetric units. A detailed three dimensional structure of the monomeric insulin molecule appears in following Figure

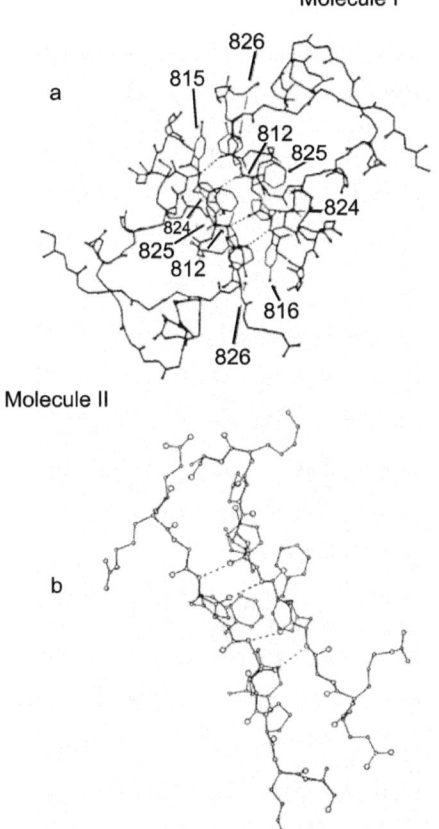

Fig. 8.6 : A 3-D structure of Insulin molecule

(i) **B-Chain:** Several residues of the beta chain are not required for full bioactivity. The first four to six and the last three residues (B28-30) are dispensable. As further residues from the COOH terminus (B27-B26 etc) are omitted one by one, the biological activity decreases gradually to desheptapeptide (B26-30)-insulin, which is totally inactive. Residues 24 - 26 occupy important parts of the receptor binding area of insulin.

(ii) **A-Chain:** The A chain cannot be shortened. Omission of A_1 glycine reduces the hormonal potency to less than 1% and omission of A21 asparagine abolishes all activity. However, replacement of A21 Asn by alanine preserves full bioactivity.

The A1 guanidinated insulin is the most active derivative. A positive charge increases (for A1 Lys and A1 Arg- insulin) and a negative charge decreases activities (for the A1 glu derivative)

(iii) **Fast acting Analogs:** Human insulin analog Lys [B28], Pro [B 29] (Lys - pro) has desirable pharmacokinetic and pharmacodynamic properties. Asp (B10) insulin (wherein the naturally occurring histidine at the 10 position of the B-chain is replaced by aspartic acid) is 3 - 4 times more active than that of human insulin.

(iv) **Slow acting Analogs:** Human diarginyl insulin Arg [B31], Arg [B32] is more slowly absorbed from subcutaneous tissues. Two extra arginines shift the isoelectric point from 5.4 to 7.0 thereby, giving an insoluble insulin. Glycine was substitued for Asparagine at A21. This modification extends the duration of action of the diarginyl insulin.

Distribution and Metabolism

Approximately 50% of the insulin released into the portal venous circulation is degraded by the liver. Rest enters the systemic circulation where it binds to the insulin receptor and stimulates the tyrosine kinase activity. Half life of natural insulin is 5-6 min in normal subject and in uncomplicated diabetics. Normal pattern of insulin secretion after a meal shows a rapid rise in the level of insulin in portal circulation, followed by parallel but smaller rise in peripheral circulation. Metabolism of insulin occurs primarily in liver, kidney and muscle.

Insulin Receptors and Target Cell Effects

To initiate its effects on target tissues, insulin binds to and activates a membrane receptor. It is the activated receptor that is responsible for the cellular effects of insulin. The insulin receptor is a combination of four subunits—a large alpha subunit that extends outside the cell membrane and is involved in insulin binding and a smaller beta subunit that is predominantly inside the cell membrane and contains a kinase enzyme that becomes activated during insulin binding. Activation of the kinase enzyme results in phosphorylation of the subunit, which in turn activates some enzymes and inactivates others, thereby directing the desired intracellular effect of insulin on glucose, fat, and protein metabolism.

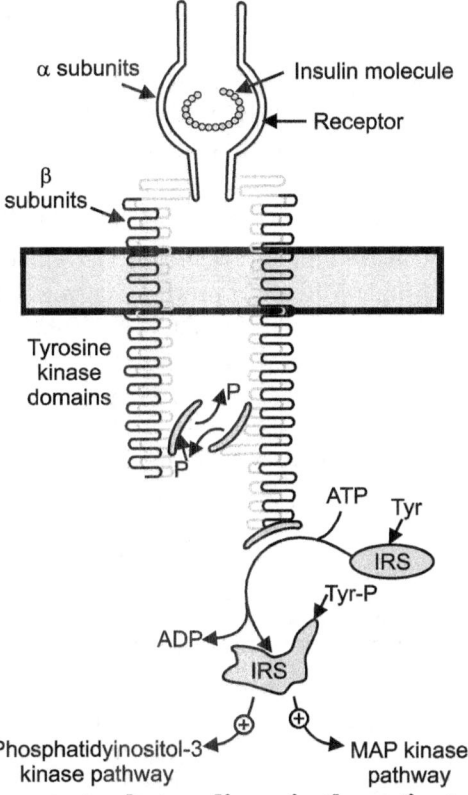

Fig. 8.7 : The insulin receptor heterodimer in the activated state. IRS, insulin receptor substrate; P-phosphate; tyr-tyrosine

Mechanism of Action

Insulin binds to a specific receptor on the surface of its target cells. The receptor is a large transmembrane glycoprotein complex belonging to the kinase-linked type 3 receptor super family and consisting of two α and two β subunits. Occupied receptors aggregate into clusters, which are subsequently internalised in vesicles, resulting in down-regulation. Internalised insulin is degraded in lysosomes, but the receptors are recycled to the plasma membrane.

- The signal transduction mechanisms that link receptor binding to the biological effects of insulin are complex. Receptor auto-phosphorylation, the first step in signal transduction, is a consequence of dimerisation, allowing each receptor to phosphorylate.
- Insulin receptor substrate (IRS) proteins undergo rapid tyrosine phosphorylation specifically in response to insulin and insulin-like growth factor-1 but not to other growth factors. The best characterised substrate is IRS-1, which contains 22 tyrosine residues that are potential phosphorylation sites. It interacts with proteins that contain a so-called SH2 domain, thereby passing on the insulin signal. Knockout mice lacking IRS-1 are hypo-responsive to insulin (insulin-resistant)

but do not become diabetic because of robust B-cell compensation with increased insulin secretion. By contrast, mice lacking IRS-2 fail to compensate and develop overt diabetes, implicating the IRS-2 gene as a candidate for human type 2 diabetes. Activation of phosphatidylinositol 3-kinase by interaction of its SH2 domain with phosphorylated IRS has several important effects, including recruitment of insulin-sensitive glucose transporters (Glut-4) from the Golgi apparatus to the plasma membrane in muscle and fat cells.

The long term actions of insulin entail effects on DNA and RNA, mediated partly at least by the Ras signalling complex. Ras is a protein that regulates cell growth and cycles between an active GTP-bound form and an inactive GDP-bound form. Insulin shifts the equilibrium in favour of the active form, and initiates a phosphorylation cascade that results in activation of mitogen-activated protein kinase, which in turn activates several nuclear transcription factors, leading to the expression of genes that are involved both with cell growth and with intermediary metabolism. Regulation of the rate of mRNA transcription by insulin provides an important means of modulating enzyme activity.

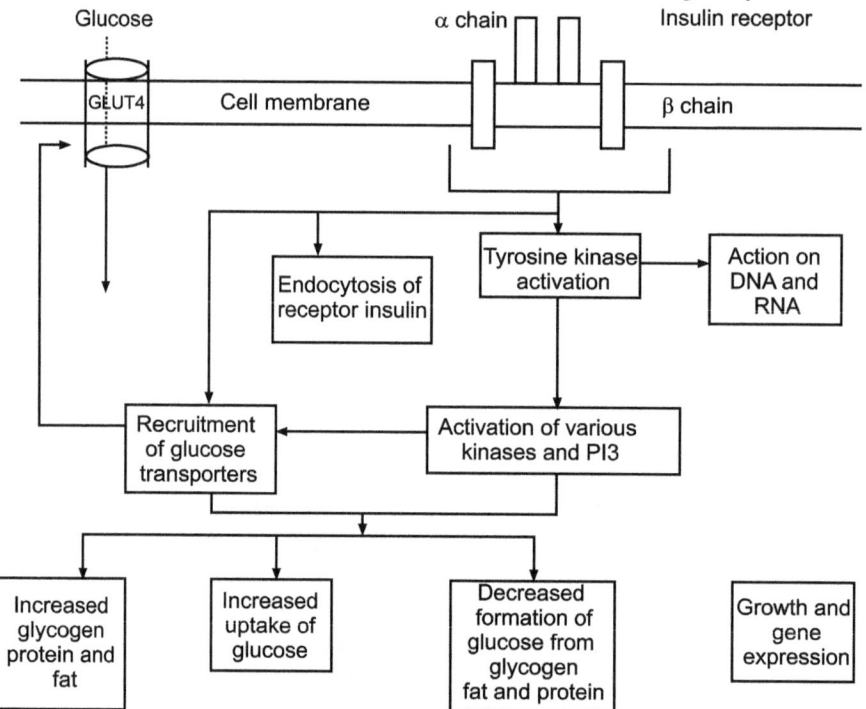

Fig 8.8: Mechanism of Action of Insulin

Pharmacological Actions

Insulin is the main hormone controlling intermediary metabolism, having actions on liver, muscle and fat. It is an anabolic hormone, its overall effect being to conserve fuel by facilitating the uptake and storage of glucose, amino acids and fats after a meal.

Effect of insulin on carbohydrate metabolism

Insulin influences glucose metabolism in most tissues, especially the liver, where it inhibits glycogenolysis and gluconeogenesis while stimulating glycogen synthesis. It also increases glucose utilisation, but the overall effect is to increase hepatic glycogen stores.

In muscle, unlike liver, uptake of glucose is slow and is the rate-limiting step in carbohydrate metabolism. The main effects of insulin are to increase facilitated transport of glucose via a transporter called Glut-4, and to stimulate glycogen synthesis and glycolysis.

Effect of insulin on fat metabolism

Insulin increases synthesis of fatty acids and triglycerides in adipose tissue and in liver. It inhibits lipolysis, partly via dephosphorylation of lipases. It also inhibits the lipolytic actions of adrenaline, growth hormone and glucagon by opposing their actions on adenylate cyclase.

Effect of insulin on protein metabolism

Insulin stimulates uptake of amino acids into muscle cells and increases protein synthesis. It also decreases protein catabolism and inhibits oxidation of amino acids in the liver.

Other metabolic effects of insulin

Other metabolic effects of insulin include transport of K^+, Ca^{2+}, nucleosides and inorganic phosphate into the cells.

Table 8.4 : Summary of action of insulin on various cells

Metabolism	Liver cells	Muscle cells	Adipose cells
Carbohydrate	↑↓ Gluconeogenesis ↓ Glycogenolysis ↑ Glycolysis ↑ Glycogenesis	↑ Glucose uptake ↑ Glycolysis ↑ Glycogenesis	↑ Glucose uptake ↑ Glycerol synthesis
Fat	↑ Lipogenesis ↓ Lipolysis	–	↑ Synthesis of triglycerides ↑ Fatty acid synthesis ↑ Lipolysis
Protein	↓ Protein breakdown	↑ Amino acid uptake ↑ Protein synthesis	–

GLUCAGON

Glucagon, pancreatic hormone that regulates glucose homeostatis was discovered by **Kimball** and **Murlin Glucagon** is synthesised in the A cells of the pancreatic islets of Langerhans. Glucagon is a peptide identical in all mammals. It consists of a single chain of *29 amino acids*, with a molecular weight of 3485. Selective proteolytic cleavage converts a large precursor molecule of approximately 18,000 MW to glucagon. One of the precursor intermediates consists of a 69-amino-acid peptide called glicentin, which contains the glucagon sequence interposed between peptide extensions.

Glucagon is extensively degraded in the liver and kidney as well as in plasma and at its tissue receptor sites. Because of its rapid inactivation by plasma, chilling of the collecting tubes and addition of inhibitors of proteolytic enzymes are necessary when samples of blood are collected for immunoassay of circulating glucagon. Its half-life in plasma is between 3 and 6 minutes, which is similar to that of insulin.

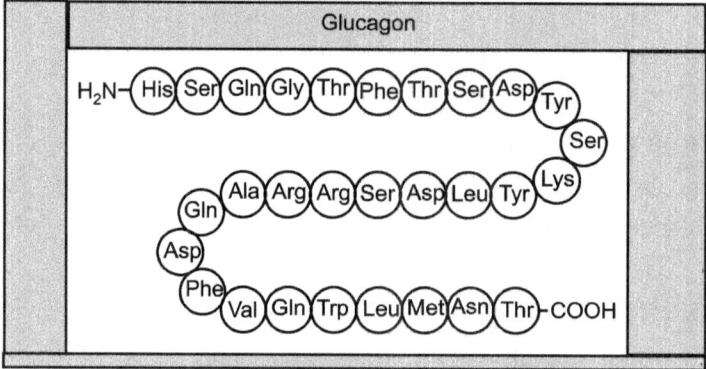

(a) Amino acid sequence of glucagon

His-Ser-Gln-Gly-Thr-Phe-Thr-Ser-Asp-Tyr-Ser-Lys-Tyr-Leu-Asp-Ser-Arg-Arg-Ala-Gln-Asp-Phe-Val-Gln-Trp-Leu-Met-Asn-Thr

Fig. 8.9 : (b) Structure of glucagon

Synthesis and Secretion

Glucagon is synthesised mainly in the A cell of the islets, but also in the upper gastrointestinal tract. It has considerable structural homology with other gastrointestinal tract hormones, namely secretin, vasoactive intestinal peptide and GIP. One of the main physiological stimuli to glucagon secretion is the concentration of amino acids, in particular L-arginine, in plasma. Therefore, it's secretion increases after ingestion of a high-protein meal, but when compared with insulin there is relatively little change in plasma glucagon concentrations throughout the day. Glucagon secretion is stimulated by low and inhibited by high concentrations of glucose and fatty acids in the plasma. Sympathetic nerve activity and circulating adrenaline stimulate glucagon release via β adrenoceptors. Parasympathetic nerve activity also increases secretion, whereas somatostatin, released from D cells adjacent to the glucagon-secreting A cells in the periphery of the islets, inhibits glucagon release.

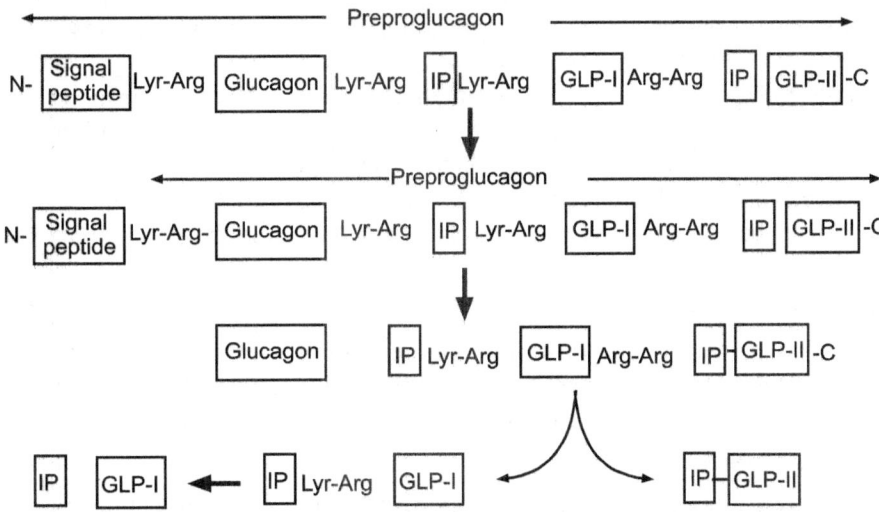

Fig 8.10 : Synthesis and secretion of Glucagon

Regulation of Secretion

Glucagon secretion is regulated by dietary glucose, insulin, amino acids, and fatty acids. The effect of glucose is lost in untreated or undertreated type 1 DM patients and in isolated pancreatic α cells, indicating that at least part of the effect is secondary to stimulation of insulin secretion. Somatostatin also inhibits glucagon secretion, as do free fatty acids and ketones. Most amino acids stimulate the release of both glucagon and insulin. This coordinated response to amino acids may prevent insulin-induced hypoglycemia in individuals who ingest a meal of pure protein. Secretion of glucagon also is regulated by the autonomic innervation of the islets. Stimulation of sympathetic nerves or administration of sympathomimetic amines increases glucagon secretion.

Mechanism of Action

Glucagon increases blood glucose and causes breakdown of fat and protein. It acts on specific G-protein-coupled receptors to stimulate adenylate cyclase, and consequently its actions are somewhat similar to β adrenoceptor-mediated actions of adrenaline. Unlike adrenaline, however, its metabolic effects are more pronounced than its cardiovascular actions. Glucagon is proportionately more active on liver, while the metabolic actions of adrenaline are more pronounced on muscle and fat. Glucagon stimulates glycogen breakdown and gluconeogenesis, and inhibits glycogen synthesis and glucose oxidation. Its metabolic actions on target tissues are thus the opposite of those of insulin. Glucagon increases the rate and force of contraction of the heart, although less markedly than adrenaline.

Pharmacologic Effects of Glucagon

(a) Metabolic Effects

The first six amino acids at the amino terminal of glucagon bind to specific receptors on liver cells. This leads to a G_s protein-coupled increase in adenylyl cyclase activity and the production of cAMP, which results in catabolism of stored glycogen and increases gluconeogenesis and ketogenesis. The immediate result of glucagon infusion is to raise blood glucose at the expense of stored hepatic glycogen. There is no effect on skeletal muscle glycogen, presumably due to the lack of glucagon receptors on skeletal muscle. Pharmacologic amounts of glucagon cause release of insulin from normal pancreatic B cells, catecholamines from pheochromocytoma, and calcitonin from medullary carcinoma cells.

(b) Cardiac Effects

Glucagon has a very potent inotropic and chronotropic effect on the heart, mediated by the cAMP mechanism described above. Thus, it produces an effect very similar to that of β-adrenoceptor agonists without requiring functioning β receptors.

(c) Effects on Smooth Muscle

Large doses of glucagon produce profound relaxation of the intestine. In contrast to the above effects of the peptide, this action on the intestine may be due to mechanisms other than adenylyl cyclase activation.

SOMATOSTATIN

Somatostatin was first discovered by Professor **R. Guillemin** in hypothalamic extracts. It was identified as a hormone that inhibited secretion of growth hormone. Somatostatin is a 14-amino-acid peptide secreted by a broad range of tissues, including pancreas, intestinal tract, hypothalamus and regions of the central nervous system outside the hypothalamus.

It inhibits growth hormone release in normal individuals. It has been shown to inhibit the release of glucagon, insulin, and gastrin. Exogenously administered somatostatin is rapidly cleared from the circulation, with an initial halflife of 1–3 minutes.

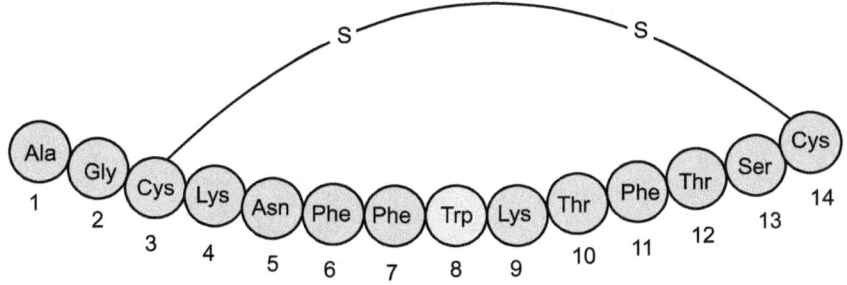

(a) Amino acid sequence of somatostatin

(b) Somatostatin structure

Fig. 8.11

Peptides have been synthesised that partially separate the various properties of somatostatin. A 7-aminoheptanoic acid derivative containing only four of the 14 amino acids of somatostatin has been found to block the effect of somatostatin.

Structure and Synthesis

Two forms of somatostatin are synthesized namely SS-14 and SS-28, reflecting their amino acid chain length. Both forms of somatostatin are generated by proteolytic cleavage of prosomatostatin, which itself is derived from preprosomatostatin. Two cysteine residules in SS-14 allow the peptide to form an internal disulfide bond.

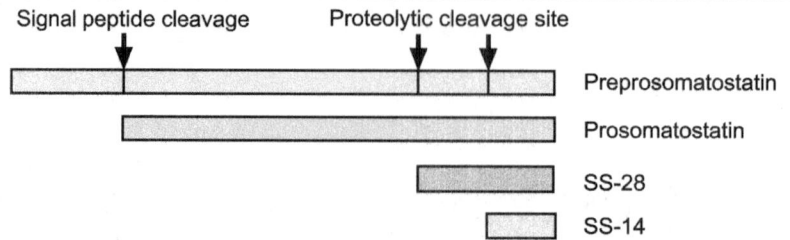

Fig. 8.12: Synthesis of the two forms of Somatostatin

The relative amounts of SS-14 versus SS-28 secreted depends upon the synthesising tissue. For example, SS-14 is the predominant form produced in the nervous system and apparently the sole form secreted from pancreas, whereas the intestine secretes mostly SS-28.

In addition to tissue-specific differences, the two forms of this hormone can have different biological potencies. SS-28 is roughly ten-fold more effective in inhibition of growth hormone secretion, but less potent that SS-14 in inhibiting glucagon release.

Receptors and Mechanism of Action

Five stomatostatin receptors have been identified and characterised. They are all members of the G protein-coupled receptor superfamily. Although all inhibit adenylyl cyclase, each of the receptors activates distinct signalling mechanisms within cells,. Four of the five receptors do not differentiate SS-14 from SS-28.

Physiologic Effects

Somatostatin acts by both endocrine and paracrine pathways to affect its target cells. A majority of the circulating somatostatin appears to come from the pancreas and gastrointestinal tract.

Effects on the Pituitary Gland

Somatostatin was named for its effect of inhibiting secretion of growth hormone from the pituitary gland. In experiments carried out on animals it was observed that all known stimuli for growth hormone secretion are suppressed by somatostatin administration. Additionally, animals treated with antisera to somatostatin and those that are genetically engineered to disrupt their somatostatin gene show elevated blood concentrations of growth hormone.

Ultimately, growth hormone secretion is controlled by the interaction of somatostatin and growth hormone releasing hormone, both of which are secreted by hypothalamic neurons.

Effects on the Pancreas

Cells within pancreatic islets secrete insulin, glucagon and somatostatin. Somatostatin appears to act in a paracrine manner to inhibit the secretion of both insulin and glucagon. It also suppresses pancreatic exocrine secretions, by inhibiting cholecystokinin-stimulated enzyme secretion and secretin-stimulated bicarbonate secretion.

Effects on the Gastrointestinal Tract

Somatostatin is secreted by scattered cells in the GI epithelium, and by neurons in the enteric nervous system. It inhibits secretion of many of the other GI hormones, including gastrin, cholecystokinin, secretin and vasoactive intestinal peptide.

In addition, somatostatin suppresses secretion of gastric acid and pepsin, lowers the rate of gastric emptying, and reduces smooth muscle contractions and blood flow within the intestine. Collectively, these activities seem to have the overall effect of decreasing the rate of nutrient absorption.

Effects on the Nervous System

Somatostatin has a neuromodulatory activity within the central nervous system, and appears to have a variety of complex effects on neural transmission. Injection of somatostatin into the brain of rodents leads to such things as increased arousal and decreased sleep, and impairment of some motor responses.

PANCREATIC POLYPEPTIDE

Pancreatic polypeptide (PP) is a polypeptide consisting of 36 amino acids and having a molecular weight about 4200 Da. It is secreted by PP cells of Langerhans islets in the endocrine pancreas predominantly in the head of the pancreas. The function of PP is to self-regulate pancreatic secretion activities (endocrine and exocrine). It also influences hepatic glycogen levels and gastrointestinal secretions.

Its secretion in humans increases after a protein meal, fasting, exercise, and acute hypoglycaemia and decreases by somatostatin and intravenous glucose.

Plasma PP is reduced in conditions associated with increased food intake and elevated in anorexia nervosa. Peripheral administration of PP has been shown to decrease food intake in rodents. It stimulates the gastric juice secretion, but inhibits the gastric secretion induced by pentagastrine. It is the antagonist of cholecystokinin and inhibits the pancreatic secretion which was stimulated by cholecystokinin. On fasting, PP serum concentration is 80 pg/ml; after the meal, it increases by 8 to 10; glucose and fats also induce PP's level increase, but on parenteral introduction of those substances, the level of hormones doesn't change. The administration of atropine, blocks the PP's after-meal secretion. The excitation of the vagus nerve, the administration of gastrin, secretin or cholecystokinin induce PP secretion.

The augmentation of PP secretion was observed in hormonal-active pancreatic tumors (insulin, glucagon), in Werner-Morryson syndrome, and in gastrinomas.

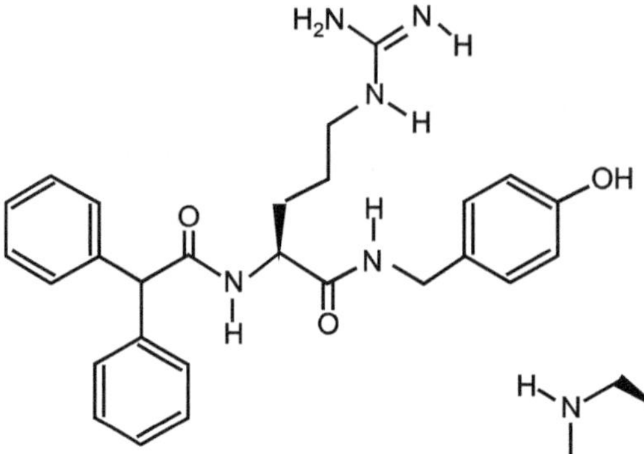

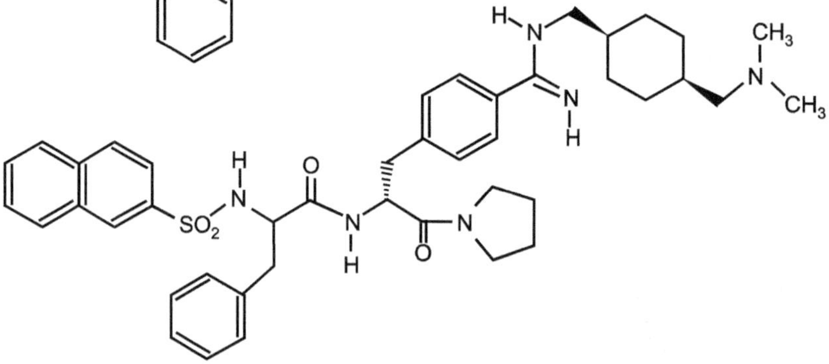

OXYTOCIN

Oxytocin is a peptide hormone secreted by the posterior pituitary that is responsible for milk ejection in lactating women. It may contribute to the initiation of labor. Oxytocin is released during sexual orgasm.

Chemical nature: Oxytocin is also an octapeptide (nonapeptide if cystine is considered as two cysteines). Oxytocin differs from vasopressin (ADH) in two amino acids, whereas six amino acids are the same. Oxytocin contains isoleucine and leucine in place of phenylalaninc and arginine present in ADH.

Structure

Oxytocin is a nine-amino-acid peptide composed of a six-amino-acid disulfide ring and a three membered tail. Oxytocin and vasopressin differ from vasotocin—the only posterior pituitary hormone found in nonmammalian vertebrates—by only one amino acid residue each.

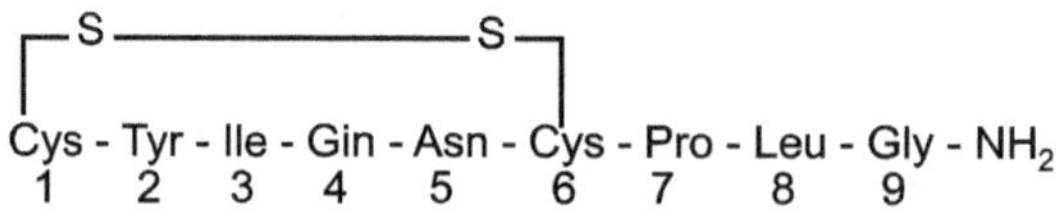

```
   ┌─S───────────S─┐
Cys - Tyr - Ile - Gln - Asn - Cys - Pro - Leu - Gly - NH₂
 1     2     3     4     5     6     7     8     9
```
Oxytocin

Isolation

The finely powdered posterior pituitary gland is extracted with ethanol or acetic acid and the resulting solution is treated with sodium chloride to coagulate all the proteins. The coagulated proteins are then treated with trichloroacetic acid to dissociate the various proteins, *viz* noradrenaline, oxytocin, vasopressin and other impurities. The proteins are separated from each other by means of paper chromatography and finally they are purified by means of electrophoresis.

Its structure was established independently by **du Vigneaud** (Nobel prize, 1955) and **H. Tuppy in 1953**. The important points for elucidating the structure of oxytocin may be formulated as below (H. Tuppy).

Constitution

1. The isoelectric point 7.7 of the oxytocin suggests that it has a free amino group and no free carboxyl group.

2. On complete hydrolysis with acid, it yields eight different amino acids in equimolecular amounts; namely glycine, leucine, iso-leucine, proline, cystine, tyrosine, aspartic acid, and glutamic acid, along with three moles of ammonia. The hydrolysis products indicate that oxytocin is built up of eight amino acids which have three amide $-CONH_2$ (which give ammonia molecule) groups. Since the molecular weight (1000) of oxytocin as determined by physical method corresponds to that of an octapeptide, oxytocin must be an octapeptide.

3. On oxidation with per-formic acid, oxytocin gives a disulphonic acid having molecular weight in the range of that of oxytocin disulphonic acid.

$$\text{Oxytocin} \xrightarrow{\text{HCOOOH}} \text{Oxytocin disulphonic acid}$$

4. This suggests that oxytocin is a cyclic compound and has a disulphide unit which is oxidised by performic acid to sulphonic acid in the following manner.

$$R-S-S-R \xrightarrow{\text{HCOOOH}} 2.RSO_3H$$

The - S - S - bond might be that of cystine molecule.

On controlled hydrolysis with hydrochloric acid, oxidised oxytocin gives two moles of cysteic acid, four dipeptides (I to IV) and two tripeptides (V and VI). The structure of the dipeptides and the amino end of the tripeptides were established by the usual methods. viz. treatment with FDNB followed by hydrolysis and identification of the DPN derivative by chromatography.

I	Asp – $CySO_3H$	IV	Ileu – Glu
II	$CySO_3H$ – Tyr	V	Tyr–(Glu, Ileu)
III	Leu – Gly	VI	$CySO_3H$ – (Leu, Pro)

With the knowledge of the structures of the dipeptides and the amino ends of the tripeptides, we can elucidate the partial structure of oxytocin according to the following points.

(a) From the sequence of the dipeptide IV, the structure of tripeptide V may be written as Va :Tyr-Ileu-Glu.

(b) From the knowledge of the structure of the dipeptide II, the structure Va may be extended as Vb : $CySO_3H$-Tyr-Ileu-Glu which also accounts for Va.

(c) From the knowledge of the structure of the dipeptide III, the structure of VI may be written as $CySO_3H$-pro-leu-Gly.

5. Partial hydrolysis of oxidised oxytocin with the enzyme proteinase (isolated from *Bacillus subtilis*) yields glycine amide and two acidic tetrapeptides VII and VIII; amino acid components and amino end groups of which are established by the usual methods.

$CySO_3H$ – (Glu, Tyr, Ileu);   Asp – ($CySO_3H$, Leu, Pro)
VII   VIII

The structure of the tetrapeptide VII has already been established in point 4 (b) as $CySO_3H$-Tyr-Ileu-Glu. Furthermore, from the structure of VI point 4 (c) the structure of VII may be extended as Asp - $CySO_3H$ - Pro -Leu -Gly. The formation of glycine amide indicates that glycine is present as an end group and hence the structure of VIII may be written as below.

Asp – $CySO_3H$ – Pro – Leu – Gly $(NH)_2$

6. On the basis of the structure of the two tetrapeptides and the fact that glycine is present as an end group the structure of oxidised oxytocin may be written as below.

$$CySO_3H - Tyr - Ileu - Glu \overset{NH_2}{\underset{|}{|}} Asp - CySO_3H - Pro - Leu \overset{NH_2}{\underset{|}{|}} Gly (NH_2)$$

The dotted lines indicate the points of cleavage of the oxidised oxytocin by means of the bacterial proteinase to the tetrapeptides VII and VIII and the glycine amide.

7. **Position of the amide groups:** The position of three amide groups is established by the following facts.

(a) As glycine is isolated as glycine amide in point 5, one of the amide groups must be present in glycine molecule.

(b) Out of the eight amino acids isolated from oxytocin only the glutamic and aspartic acids are monoaminodicarboxylic acids, so one of the carboxylic groups of each of these acids which is not involved in peptide linkage may only be present as amide groups.

8. The structure of oxidised oxytocin and its formation from oxytocin by means of performic acid without chain fission suggests the presence of S - S ring in the compound and hence oxytocin must have the structure as shown on the earlier page (assuming that a-carboxyl group of glutamic and aspartic acids are involved in the peptide linkages).

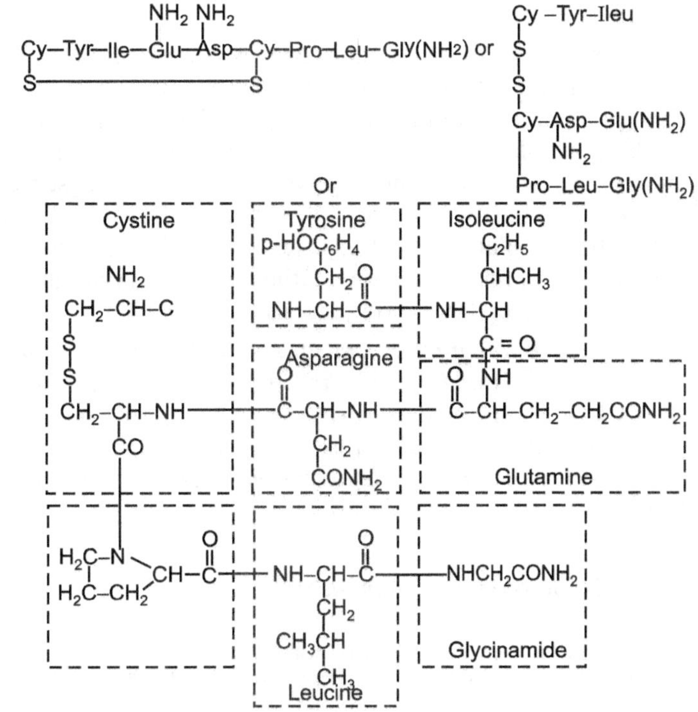

Cy—Tyr—Ile—Glu(NH₂)—Asp(NH₂)—Cy—Pro—Leu—Gly(NH₂) or

```
Cy—Tyr—Ileu
 S
 |
 S
 |
Cy—Asp—Glu(NH₂)
    |
    NH₂
Pro—Leu—Gly(NH₂)
```

Or

Cystine: NH₂–CH₂–CH–CO– ... –S–S–CH₂–CH–NH–

Tyrosine: p-HOC₆H₄–CH₂–NH–CH–C(=O)–

Isoleucine: C₂H₅–CH(CH₃)–NH–CH–C=O

Asparagine: –C(=O)–CH–NH–, CH₂–CONH₂

Glutamine: –C(=O)–CH–CH₂–CH₂CONH₂, NH

Proline: H₂C–N, H₂C–CH₂, CH–C(=O)–

Leucine: –NH–CH–C(=O)–, CH₂, CH₃CH, CH₃

Glycinamide: –NHCH₂CONH₂

9. Lastly the above structure of oxytocin is proved by a number of syntheses : only one of which is described below (V. du Vigneaud *et al.* 1959). The important points in the synthesis are as follows.

   (a) The amino group is protected by carbobenzoxy (Cbo) group which is introduced by treating the amino acid with carbobenzoxy chloride, $C_6H_5CH_2OCOCl$. The carbobenzoxy chloride is prepared from benzyl alcohol and phosgene.

   $$C_6H_5CH_2OH + ClCOCl \longrightarrow C_6H_5CH_2OCOl + HCl$$
   Phosgene

   (b) The amino acid whose amino group is protected by Cbo is condensed with the ester of other amino-acid molecule. The various esters used are ethyl (Et), benzyl (Bzl) and p-nitrophenyl (NP).

   (c) The protective group (Cbo) is removed by hydrogen bromide-acetic acid and the resulting product is treated with the ester of other amino acid whose amino group is protected by Cbo. These two steps are repeated till all the amino acid units present in oxytocin molecule are introduced.

   (d) The protective group is finally removed as toluene and carbon dioxide molecules either by catalytic reduction or by means of sodium in liquid ammonia.

   $$C_6H_5CH_2OCONH- \xrightarrow{H_2} C_6H_5CH_3 + CO_2 + H_2N-$$

Biosynthesis

Oxytocin is a cyclic nonapeptide that differs from vasopressin by only 2 amino acids. It is synthesized as a larger precursor molecule in cell bodies of the paraventricular nucleus, and to a lesser extent, the supraoptic nucleus in the hypothalamus. The precursor is rapidly converted by proteolysis to the active hormone and its neurophysin, packaged into secretory granules as an oxytocin-neurophysin complex, and secreted from nerve endings that terminate primarily in the posterior pituitary gland. In addition, oxytocinergic neurons that regulate the autonomic nervous system project to regions of the hypothalamus, brainstem, and spinal cord. Other sites of oxytocin synthesis include the luteal cells of the ovary, the endometrium, and the placenta.

Stimuli for oxytocin secretion include sensory stimuli arising from dilation of the cervix and vagina and from suckling at the breast. Estradiol stimulates oxytocin secretion, whereas the ovarian polypeptide relaxin inhibits release. Other factors that primarily affect vasopressin secretion also have some impact on oxytocin release (e.g., ethanol inhibits release, while pain, dehydration, hemorrhage, and hypovolemia stimulate release).

SYNTHESIS

The overall synthesis of oxytocin may be formulated in the abbreviated form as follows.

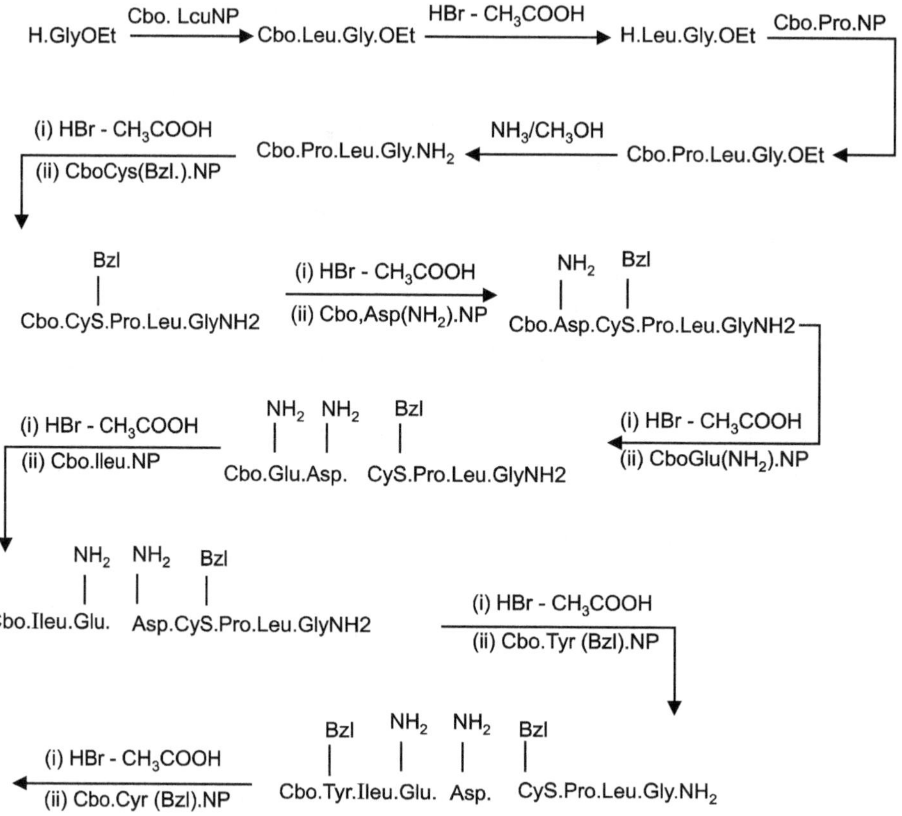

H.GlyOEt —Cbo.LcuNP→ Cbo.Leu.Gly.OEt —HBr - CH$_3$COOH→ H.Leu.Gly.OEt —Cbo.Pro.NP→

(i) HBr - CH$_3$COOH / (ii) CboCys(Bzl.).NP ← Cbo.Pro.Leu.Gly.NH$_2$ ←NH$_3$/CH$_3$OH— Cbo.Pro.Leu.Gly.OEt ←

Cbo.CyS(Bzl).Pro.Leu.GlyNH2 —(i) HBr - CH$_3$COOH / (ii) Cbo,Asp(NH$_2$).NP→ Cbo.Asp(NH$_2$).CyS(Bzl).Pro.Leu.GlyNH2

(i) HBr - CH$_3$COOH / (ii) Cbo.Ileu.NP ← Cbo.Glu(NH$_2$).Asp(NH$_2$).CyS(Bzl).Pro.Leu.GlyNH2 ←(i) HBr - CH$_3$COOH / (ii) CboGlu(NH$_2$).NP—

Cbo.Ileu.Glu(NH$_2$).Asp(NH$_2$).CyS(Bzl).Pro.Leu.GlyNH2 —(i) HBr - CH$_3$COOH / (ii) Cbo.Tyr(Bzl).NP→

←(i) HBr - CH$_3$COOH / (ii) Cbo.Cyr(Bzl).NP— Cbo.Tyr(Bzl).Ileu.Glu(NH$_2$).Asp(NH$_2$).CyS(Bzl).Pro.Leu.Gly.NH$_2$

Structure Activity Relationship

1. A 20 membered ring of neurohypophyseal hormone is essential for bioactivity. Non cyclic structures are inactive.

2. Analogs in which sulphur atoms for the disulfide bridges are replaced by CH_2 (carbon analogs), exhibit high activity.

3. The hydroxy group of tyrosine side chain; folded over the 20-membered ring of oxytocin acting cooperatively with the asparagine carboxamide group is considered to be the active element.

4. Introduction of 4 L-threonine, 7 -glycine increases the oxytocin activity several thousand fold.

Mechanism of Action

In the human myometrium, oxytocin acts *via* specific GPCRs, coupled to G_q and G_{11}, to activate the PLCβ-IP$_3$-Ca^{2+} pathway and enhance activation of voltage-sensitive Ca^{2+} channels. Oxytocin also increases local prostaglandin production, which further stimulates uterine contractions.

Oxytocin alters transmembrane ionic currents in myometrial smooth muscle cells to produce sustained uterine contraction. The sensitivity of the uterus to oxytocin increases during pregnancy. Oxytocin-induced myometrial contractions can be inhibited by -adrenoceptor agonists, magnesium sulfate, or inhalation anesthetics. Oxytocin also causes contraction of myoepithelial cells surrounding mammary alveoli, which leads to milk ejection. Without oxytocin-induced contraction, normal lactation cannot occur. Oxytocin has weak antidiuretic and pressor activity.

Physiological Roles of Oxytocin

Uterus: Because loss of pituitary oxytocin apparently does not compromise labor and delivery, the physiological role of oxytocin in pregnancy has been highly debated; however, the finding that the oxytocin antagonist atosiban (TRACTOCILE) is effective in suppressing preterm labor supports the physiological importance of oxytocin in this setting. Exogenous oxytocin stimulates the frequency and force of uterine contractions. The responsiveness to oxytocin roughly is directly proportional to the increase in spontaneous activity that constitutes the initiation of labor and is highly dependent on estrogen, which increases the expression of the oxytocin receptors. Thus, the uterus is more responsive to oxytocin in late pregnancy than in early pregnancy. Progesterone antagonizes the stimulant effect of oxytocin in vitro, and a decline in progesterone receptor signaling in late pregnancy may contribute to the normal initiation of human parturition.

Breast: Oxytocin plays an important physiological role in milk ejection. Stimulation of the breast through suckling or mechanical manipulation induces oxytocin secretion, causing contraction of the myoepithelium that surrounds alveolar channels in the mammary gland. This action forces milk from the alveolar channels into large collecting sinuses, where it is available to the suckling infant.

Cardio Vascular System: Oxytocin causes a marked but transient relaxation of vascular smooth muscle. When large amounts are adminstired, it can cause an antidiuretic effect. It can also supress the action of ACTH.

Adrenal Cortex Hormone (or Adrenocorticosteroids)

The adrenal glands are flattened, cap like structures located on the top of the kidneys. the inner core of which is known as *'Medulla'*.The medulla secretes catecholamines e.g. adrenaline, while the shell of the gland known as *'cortex'*, synthesizes steroids hormone known as **adrenal cortex hormone (or adrenocorticosteroids)**

The adrenal cortex synthesizes two classes of steroids

(a) **Glucocoticoids:** Glucocoticoids secreted from inner zone of cortex, namely *zona fasciculata and zona retiicularis,* have the important effect of elevating blood glucose level, besides their role in the metabolism of proteins and fats. The principal member is cortisol. Other less active compounds are corticosterone and deoxycorticosterone (DOC).

(b) **Mineralocoticoids:** These are secreted from the outer zone of the cortex, namely *zona glomerulosa.* These mainly effect electrolyte (Na-+. K+) levels in the extracellular fluid. The principal member is aldosterone. Other compounds with similar activity are deoxycorticosterone and corticosterone. Cortisol and cortisone also have this activity to a small extent.

(c) Androgens: Secreted from the same zone as glucocorticoids, these compounds have activity similar to sex hormones, but quite weak normally. The principal compound is dehydroepiandrosterone (DHEA).

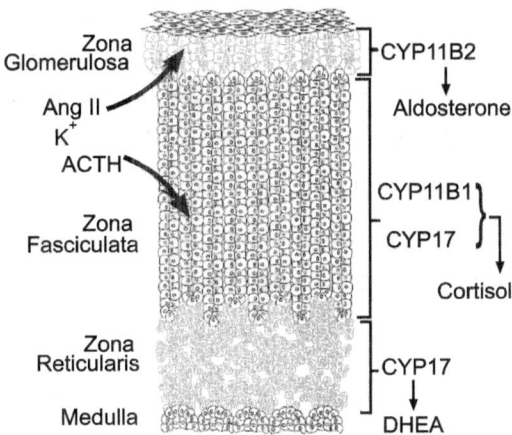

Fig. 8.13 : The adrenal cortex contains three anatomically and functionally distinct compartments

The major functional compartments of the adrenal cortex are shown, along with the steroidogenic enzymes that determine the unique profiles of corticosteroid products. Also shown are the predominant physiologic regulators of steroid production: AngII and K+ for the zona glomerulosa and ACTH for the zona fasciculata. The physiological regulator(s) of dehydroepiandrosterone (DHEA) production by the zona reticularis are not known, although ACTH acutely increases DHEA biosynthesis.

The natural adrenocortical hormones are steroid molecules produced and released by the adrenal cortex. They are also used for treatment of a variety of inflammatory and immunologic disorders. Secretion of adrenocortical steroids is controlled by the pituitary release of corticotropin (ACTH). Secretion of the salt-retaining hormone aldosterone is under the influence of angiotensin. Corticotropin has some actions that do not depend upon its effect on adrenocortical secretion. The hormonal steroids may be classified as those having important effects on intermediary metabolism (glucocorticoids), those having principally salt-retaining activity (mineralocorticoids), and those having androgenic or estrogenic activity. In the normal adult, in the absence of stress, 10–20 mg of cortisol is secreted daily. The rate of secretion follows a circadian rhythm governed by pulses of ACTH that peak in the early morning hours and after meals.

Isolation

The adrenal gland is extracted with alcohol or acetone. From the solution so obtained, adrenaline is removed by taking the advantage of its basic properties. Now the mixture of ACTH (after removing sex hormone) are separated from each other by means of combination of methods *viz* fractional crystallisation, partition coefficient and application of Girard's T or reagent. Further purification is done by chromatographic methods (adsorption or partition chromatography).

As these hormones are very sensitive to acids as well as alkalis, strong acid or alkline conditions should be avoided during their isolation.

Properties

All are colourless compounds, dextrorotatory and are very sensitive to alkali, They reduce in alkaline $AgNO_3$ solution due to presence of α ketol (α - hydroxyketone) group ($-CO.CH_2OH$). The ketonic group at C_{11} does not give normal ketonic reactions because of steric effects, e.g., it does not form oxime phenylhydrazone, semicarbazone, etc. The 11-keto group is resistant to catalytic reduction in neutral solution, but can be reduced in acid solution; it is readily reduced by $LiAlH_4$ to a hydroxyl group; and to methylene group by Clemmensen reduction.

Synthesis of Adrenocorticosteroids

Cholesterol undergoes clevage with an elimination of a 6-carbon fragment to form pregnenolone. Pregnenolone is the common precursor for the synthesis of all steroid hormones.

Conversion of cholesterol to pregnenolone is catalysed by cytochrome P_{450} side chain clevage enzyme. This reaction is promoted by ACTH. The enzymes-hydroxylases, dehydrogenases, isomerases and lyases associated with mitochondria or endoplasmic reticulum are responsible for the synthesis of steroid hormones. The metabolic pathway for the formation of major adrenocorticosteroids is given in the following Figure

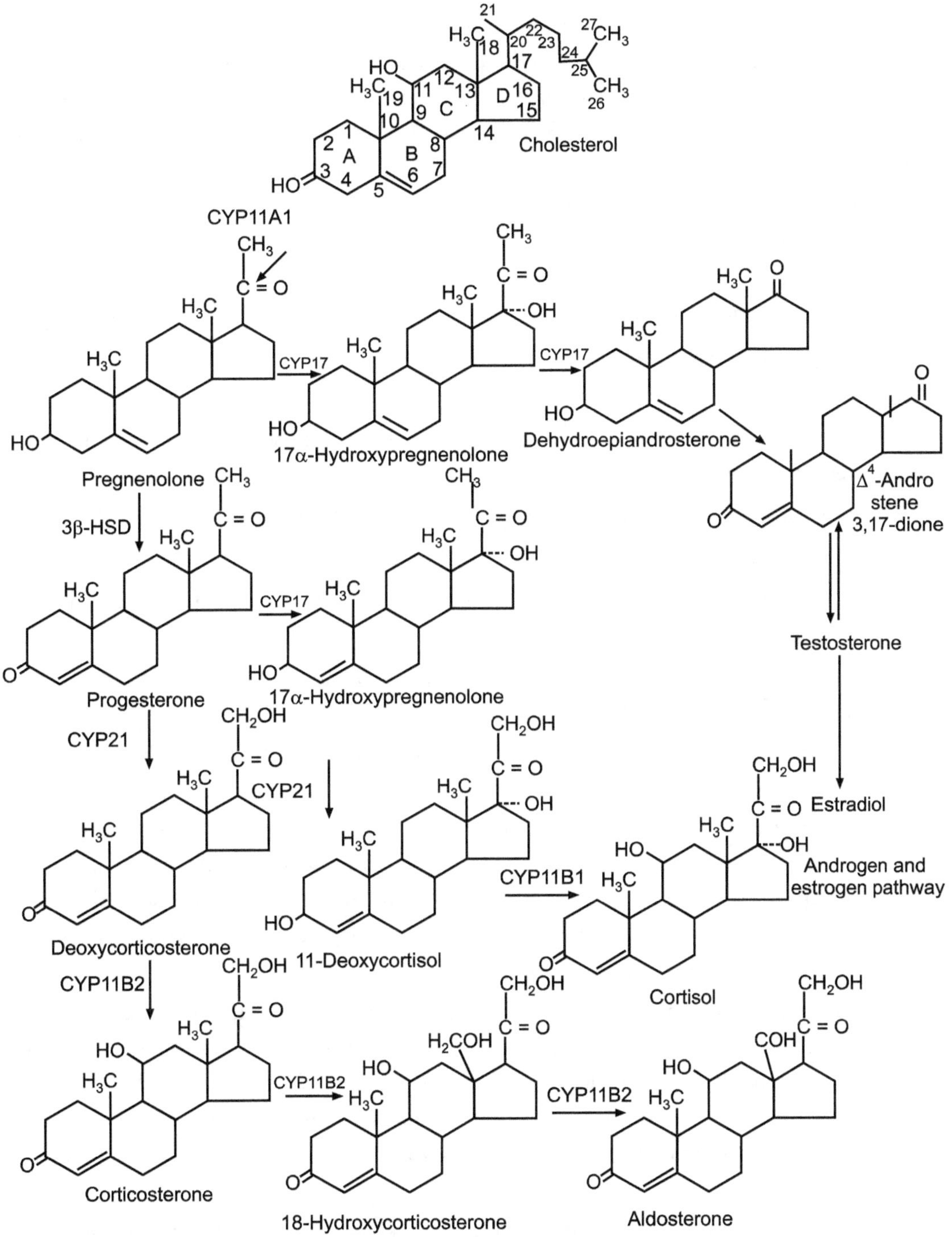

Pathways of corticosteroid biosynthesis

The steroidogenic pathways used in the biosynthesis of the corticosteroids are shown, along with the structures of the intermediates and products. The zona reticularis does not express 3β-HSD, and thus preferentially synthesizes DHEA, CYP11A1, cholesterol side-chain cleavage enzyme; 3 β--HSD, 3 β--hydroxysteroid dehydrogenase; CYP17, steroid 17α-hydroxylase; CYP21, steroid 21-hydroxylase; CYP11B2, aldosterone synthase; CYP11B1, steroid 11 β--hydroxylase.

Glucocorticoids

Glucocorticoids are secreted from inner zone of cortex, namely *zona fasciculata* and *zona reticularis*. The principal member is cortisol. Other less active compounds are ***corticosterone and deoxycorticosterone***

Structure of Cortisone

The chemistry and isolation of all the corticoids is mainly due to the researches of **Wintersteiner**, **Kendall** and **Reichstein**.

The structure of cortisone is derived by the following points

1. The molecular formula of cortisone is $C_{21}H_{29}O_5$.
2. It is very sensitive to alkali showing the presence of α, β-unsaturated ketonic group.
3. It contains one double bond, two ketonic, one primary alcoholic and one tertiary alcoholic group by normal tests.
4. It reduces alkaline silver nitrate and Fehling solution indicating the presence of α- ketol (-CO.CH$_2$OH) group.
5. On oxidation with chromic acid it gives adrenosterone. With the help of the absorption spectrum, adrenosterone and cortisone were found to contain ketonic group at position 3. They are α, β-unsaturated ketones. By comparing other steroid hormones (testosterone and progesterone) the double bond was found to be present between 4 and 5 carbon atom.
6. Adrenosterone on hydrogenation gives a triketone of known structure having M.P. 170°C. This triketone was found to be strongly androgenic in nature suggesting that it is a derivative of androstane - 3, 17-dione. This is further confirmed by the formation of androstane by reducing the triketone first by Clemmensen reduction and then by hydrogen. Hence cortisone is related to androstane.
7. Cortisone on oxidation with periodic acid yields a 17 - hydroxy acid indicating the position of the second hydroxyl group.

The structure of cortisone may be written as I which explain, all the above reactions.

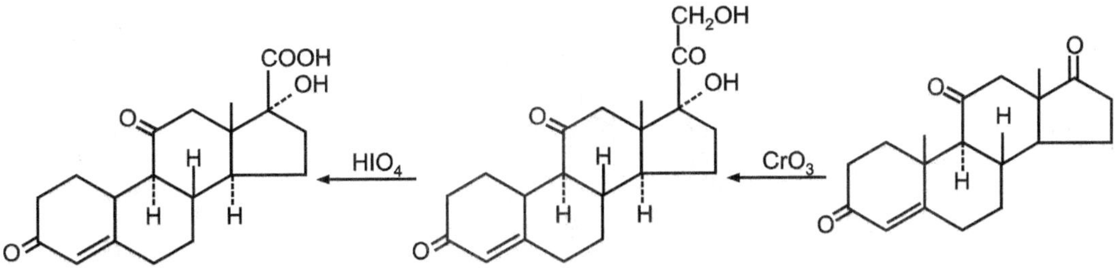

17-Hydroxy acid ← HIO$_4$ — Cortisone ← CrO$_3$ — Adrenosterone

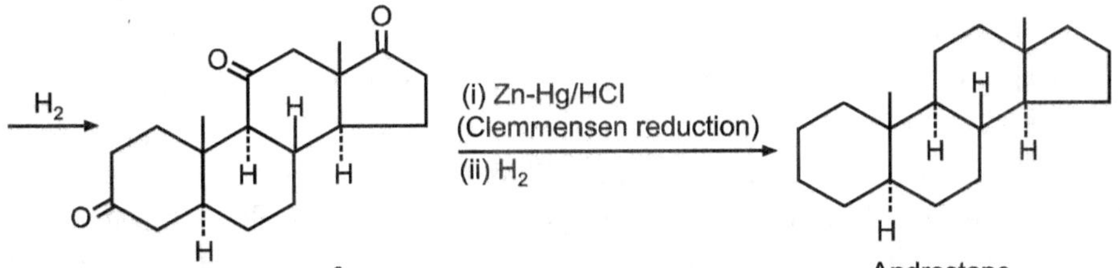

H$_2$ → Trike tone (M.P. 178°C) — (i) Zn-Hg/HCl (Clemmensen reduction) (ii) H$_2$ → Androstane

Cortisol

Cortisol, the most important glucocorticoid, has the same constitution as cortisone with the only difference that there is -OH group at C_{11} instead of ketonic group, so the structure of this can be derived on the same pattern as cortisone.

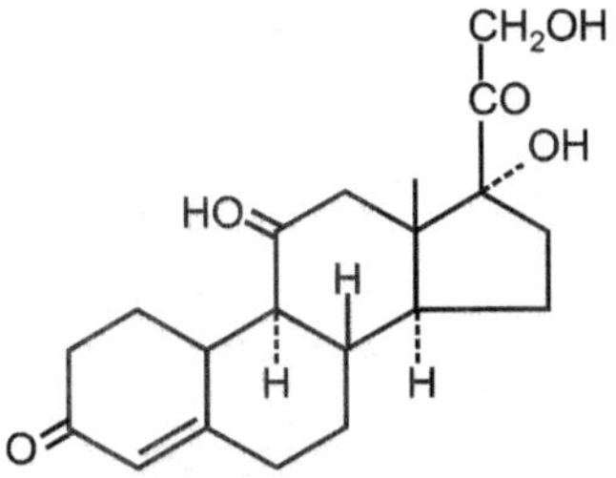

Cortisol

STRUCTURE ACTIVITY RELATIONSHIP

From the modification of cortisol molecule, following structure activity relationship has emerged.

(i) Modification in ring A.
(ii) Modification in ring B
(iii) Modification in ring C
(iv) Modification in ring D
(v) Modification in the side - chain at C-17.

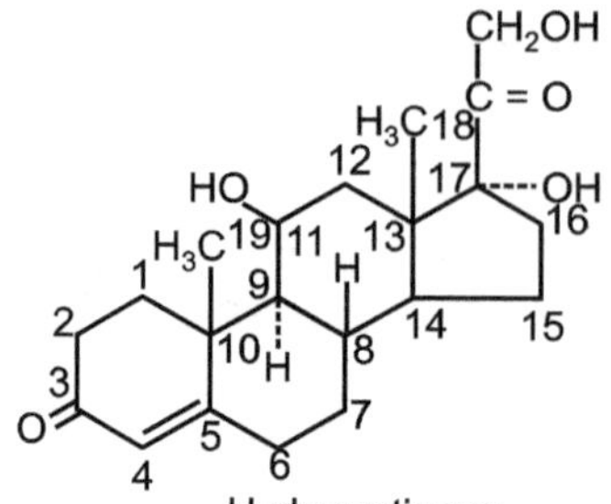

[Hydrocortisone structure]

Modification in ring A

1. The introduction of a double bond at C-1 leads to increased antiinflammatory activity e.g. betamethasone.
2. The introduction of 2 α-methyl group into cortisol enhances activity; a 2-bromosubstituent has no systemic effect.
3. Almost all active inflammatory steroids have a carbonyl group at C-3. The carbonyl group could be fused with heterocyclic moiety to yield "soft drug". A 3-spirofusedthiazolidine derivative (Compound a) was found active and this derivative reduced the thinning of the skin, generally found in corticosteroid. This is due to the fact, that such analogs bind to skin tissue through formation of disulfide bonds between prodrug and -SH containing amino acid residue in skin proteins.

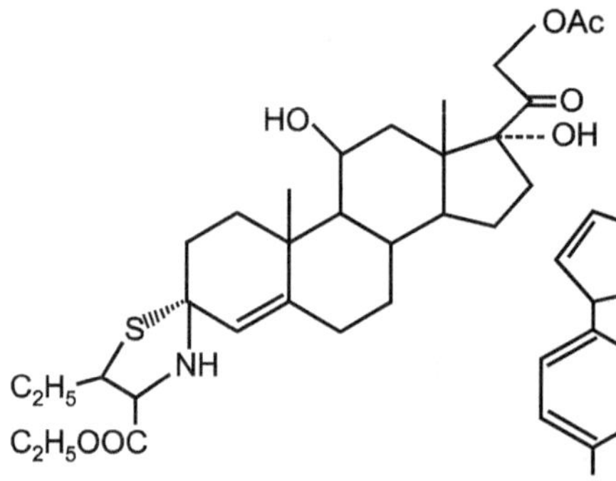

[Structures (a) and (b)]

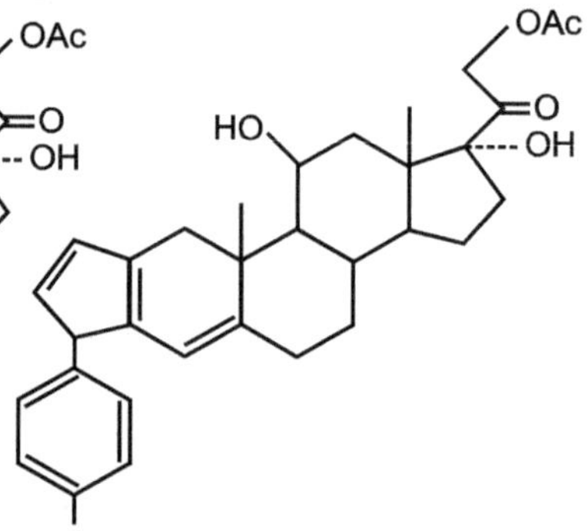

4. The Δ^4 double bond is important but not essential for antiinflammatory activity.
5. Ring A can be fused with pyrazole ring. Compound (2) has 2000 times the potency of cortisol, but lacks mineralocorticoid activity.

Modification in ring B

1. Substitution at 6 α position by hydrophobic groups, such as alkyl or halogens increases activity. 6 α - methyl, chloro and fluoro groups increases activity.
2. Substitution at 9 position have greatly influenced the anti-inflammatory potency of corticosteroids. The groups introduced were F, Cl, Br, I, -OH and CH_3. The activity of the compounds increases with increasing hydrophobic bonding of

the 9 α substituents. The function of the electron withdrawing group at C - 9 was to increase the acidity of the neighbouring 11β - hydroxysteroid which increases with increasing acidity of the 11β-hydroxy group.

3. Removal of the 19 angular methyl group decreases anti-inflammatory activity.

Modification in ring C
1. The C -11 oxygen group is not essential for anti-inflammatory activity. But it can be replaced by such groups (e.g Cl) which can be converted to the hydroxy group *in vivo*.
2. Ester substituents at C-12 have shown to impart anti-inflammatory property. Potency follows the order: propionyl > butyl > isovaleryl.

Modification in ring D
1. Presence of 16 α - hydroxy and 17 α - hydroxy groups resulted in potent compounds. These two groups could also form acetonide derivatives which are more potent than the corresponding 16, 17-dihydroxy derivatives.
2. At C-16, a carbonyl group increases topical activity and various esters have been prepared with increased local anti-inflammatory activity.
3. At C-16, introduction of chloro, methyl groups increases acidity.
4. The 17α- hydroxy group is not essential for activity. However, it can form ketals and esters to give compounds with increased activity.

Modification in the side chain at C- 17
1. The classical hydroxy-ethanone corticosteroidside chain attached at C-17 is not a requirement for activity. Tipredane, a 17-thioketal is a potent topical anti-inflammatory agent.

Tipredane

Fluticasone

2. Ketalization of the C -20 carbonyl group of corticosteroids with ethylene glycol gives ketals that retain anti-inflammatory activity.
3. Replacement of the hydroxyl group at C-21 by a chloro, fluoro increases activity.
4. Replacement of 21-carbons by sulphur fluticasone provided 21 thioesters, that have clinical activity.
5. Replacement of hydroxymethyl group with an aldehyde (compound 3) was active with some systemic absorption.
6. Acetonide formation across the 17, 20-diol arrangement led to more potent analogs compared to free diols.
7. The C-21 hydroxyl group is converted to various esters to give lipophillic compounds for repository use.

[Chemical structures: a fluorinated steroid with OHC, HO, OCOC₂H₅, F substituents; and Medrysone]

Mechanism of Action

The effects of the glucocorticoids are effected due to widely distributed glucocorticoid receptors. These proteins are members of the superfamily of nuclear receptors that includes steroid, sterol, thyroid, retinoic acid, and many other receptors with unknown or nonexistent ligands (orphan receptors). All these receptors in all possibility interact with the promoters of the target gene thereby regulating their transcription. In the absence of the hormonal ligand, glucocorticoid receptors are primarily cytoplasmic, in the form of oligomeric complexes with heat shock proteins (Hsp). The most important of these are two molecules of Hsp90, though other proteins are also involved. Free hormone from the plasma and interstitial fluid enters the cell and binds to the receptor, inducing conformational changes that allow it to dissociate from the heat shock proteins. The ligand-bound receptor complex is then actively transported into the nucleus, where it interacts with DNA and nuclear proteins. As a homodimer, it binds to glucocorticoid receptor elements (GRE) in the promoters of target genes.

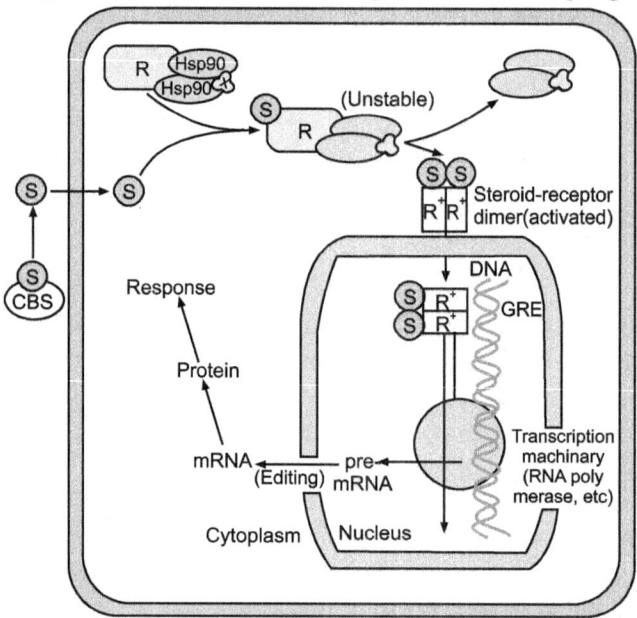

Fig. 8.14 : The interaction of a steroid, S and its receptor, R, and the subsequent events in a target cell

Physiologic Effects

The effects of glucocorticoids are dose-related and become magnified when large amounts are administered for therapeutic purposes. Other effects called "permissive" effects (a biochemical phenomenon in which the presence of one hormone is required in order for another hormone to exert its full effects on a target cell.) are also exhibited by glucocorticoids. For example, the response of vascular and bronchial smooth muscle to catecholamines is diminished in the absence of cortisol and restored by physiologic amounts of this glucocorticoid.

Metabolic Effects : The glucocorticoids influence carbohydrate, protein, and fat metabolism according to the dose administered. The same effects are responsible for some of the serious adverse effects associated with their use in therapeutic doses. Glucocorticoids are required for gluconeogenesis and glycogen synthesis in the fasting state.

Catabolic and Antianabolic Effects : Glucocorticoids stimulate protein and RNA synthesis in the liver; they have catabolic and antianabolic effects in lymphoid and connective tissue, muscle, fat, and skin. Catabolic and antianabolic effects on bone are the cause of osteoporosis in Cushing's syndrome and impose a major limitation in the long-term therapeutic use of glucocorticoids. In children, glucocorticoids reduce growth.

Anti-Inflammatory and Immunosuppressive Effects : Inflammation is characterised by the extravasation and infiltration of leukocytes into the affected tissue. These events are mediated by a complex series of interactions of white cell adhesion molecules with those on endothelial cells and are inhibited by glucocorticoids. A a single dose of a short-acting glucocorticoid results in the increase in the concentration of circulating neutrophils while the lymphocytes (T and B cells), monocytes, eosinophils, and basophils in the circulation decrease in number.

Other Effects : Glucocorticoids have important effects on the nervous system. Adrenal insufficiency causes marked slowing of the alpha rhythm of the EEG and is associated with depression. Increased amounts of glucocorticoids often produce behavioral disturbances in humans: initially insomnia and euphoria and subsequently depression.

MINERALOCORTICOIDS (ALDOSTERONE)

The most important mineralocorticoid in humans is aldosterone and is synthesised mainly in the zona glomerulosa of the adrenal cortex. ACTH produces a moderate stimulation of its release, but this effect is not sustained for more than a few days in the normal individual. Although aldosterone is no less than one third as effective as cortisol in suppressing ACTH, the quantities of aldosterone produced by the adrenal cortex and its plasma concentrations are insufficient to participate in any significant feedback control of ACTH secretion.

The most active and potent mineralocorticoid is aldosterone. It promotes Na^+ reabsorption at the distal convoluted tubules of kidney. Na^+ retention is accompanied by corresponding excretion of K^+, H^+ and NH_4^+ ions.

Structure Activity Relationship

1. Naturally occuring highly active mineralocorticoids have no OH function at postions 11 and 17. In fact, OH groups in any position reduce the sodium retaining activity of adrenocorticoid.

Aldosterone   11-Desoxycorticosterone

2. According to the hormone receptor binding studies, the C and D rings, involving positions 11, 12, 13, 16, 17, 20 and 21 are more important for binding than the rings A and B. More specifically, the α-surface of the rings A, C and D, as well as the 17 β-ketol side chain, is essential for sodium retaining activity.

3. Generally 9 α-F, 9 α-Cl and 9 α-Br substituents cause increased mineralocorticoid acticity where order of activity is F > Cl > Br.

4. Insertion of a 16 α-OH group results in reverse effect i.e., sodium excretion rather than Na^+ retention.

5. A double bond between position 1 and 2 (Δ^1- corticoids), also deccreases the activity.

6. 21-F, 16α-CH_3, 16β-CH_3, 16α-CH_3O, 16α-Cl, and 17α-OH groups are reported to inhibit the sodium retention property.

7. 12α-F, 2α-CH_3 and 21-OH groups moderately elevate the mineralocorticoid activity.

Regulation of Aldosterone Synthesis : The production of aldosterone is regulated by different mechanisms. These include rennin, angiotensin, potassium, sodium and ACTH.

Mechanism of Aldosterone Action : Aldosterone acts like other steroid hormones. It binds with specific receptors on the target tissue and promotes transcription and translation.

Pharmacological Effects

Aldosterone and other steroids with mineralocorticoid properties promote the reabsorption of sodium from the distal convoluted and cortical collecting renal tubules, loosely coupled to the excretion of potassium and hydrogen ion. Sodium reabsorption in the sweat and salivary glands, gastrointestinal mucosa, and across cell membranes in general is also increased. Excessive levels of aldosterone produced by tumors or overdosage with synthetic mineralocorticoids lead to hypernatremia, hypokalemia, metabolic alkalosis, increased plasma volume, and hypertension. Mineralocorticoids act by binding to the mineralocorticoid receptor in the cytoplasm of target cells, especially principal cells of the distal convoluted and collecting tubules of the kidney. The drug receptor complex activates a series of events. It is of interest that this receptor has the same affinity for cortisol, which is present in much higher concentrations in the extracellular fluid.

GONADAL HORMONE

The gonads (testes in males, ovaries in females) perform closely related dual functions

1. Synthesize sex hormones
2. Produce germ cells.

The steroid sex hormones are responsible for growth, development, maintenance and regulation of reproductive system. Sex hormones are essentially required for the development of germ cells.

Sex-hormones are usually classified as under

(i) **Oestrogens** (female or follicular hormones), e.g., **oestrone, oestriol, oestradiol, stilbesterol, hexesterol.** These are C-18 steroids. Ring A of steroid nucleus is phenolic in nature and is devoid of C-19 methyl group.

(ii) **Gestogens** (the corpus luteum hormones) e.g., **progesterone** is C-21 steroid.

(iii) **Androgens** (male hormones) *e.g.,* **androsterone, testosterone** or which are C-19 steroids.

The ovary has important gametogenic functions that are integrated with its hormonal activity. At puberty, the ovary begins a 30- to 40-year period of cyclic function called the menstrual cycle which involves regular episodes of bleeding that are its most obvious manifestation. It then fails to respond to gonadotropins secreted by the anterior pituitary gland. The cessation of cyclic bleeding is called the menopause.

The mechanism responsible for the onset of ovarian function at the time of puberty is thought to be neural in origin, because the immature gonad can be stimulated by gonadotropins already present in the pituitary and because the pituitary is responsive to exogenous hypothalamic gonadotropin releasing hormone.

Regulation of GnRH : The hypothalamus releases GnRH, a peptide that stimulate the anterior pitutary to secrete LH and FSH in males and females. This peptide controls and regulates both male and female reproduction as shown in following figure

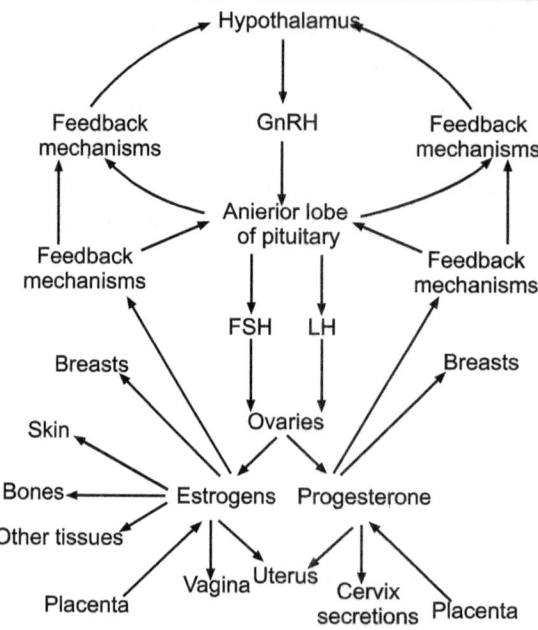

Fig. 8.15 : Regulation of GnRH

OESTROGENS OR FOLLICULAR HORMONES

The major estrogens produced by women are *estradiol (estradiol-17 beta, E2), estrone (E1), and estriol (E3)*. Estradiol is the major secretory product of the ovary. Although some estrone is produced in the ovary, most estrone and estriol are formed in the liver from estradiol or in peripheral tissues from androstenedione and other androgens. Estrogen-mimetic compounds are found in many plants, including saw palmetto, and soybeans and other foods. Studies have shown that eating these plant products may produce slight estrogenic effects. Additionally, some compounds used in the manufacture of plastics (bisphenols, alkylphenols, phthalate phenols) have been found to be estrogenic. During pregnancy, a large amount of estrogen is synthesised by the fetoplacental unit—consisting of the fetal adrenal zone, secreting androgen precursor, and the placenta, which aromatizes it into estrogen. The estriol synthesised by the fetoplacental unit is released into the maternal circulation and excreted into the urine.

Estrone

17 beta - estradiol : R =H
Ethinyl Estradiol : R = -C =CH

Estriol

Isolation of Oestrogens

These are usually present in combination with glucuronic acid, so the material is hydrolysed with concentrated HCl to get hormones in free state which are then extracted by means of organic solvents. These are then treated with Girard's reagent either T or P which forms water soluble compounds with the ketonic hormones leaving behind the non-ketonic one. Now the Girard derivatives are hydrolysed with HCl to give back the ketonic hormones.

Chemistry and Biosynthesis

Many steroidal and nonsteroidal compounds possess estrogenic activity (Table 4). The most potent endogenous estrogen is 17-estradiol, followed by estrone and estriol. The phenolic A ring is the principal structural feature responsible for selective, high-affinity binding to the estrogen receptors (ERs). Ethinyl substitutions at C17 increase oral potency by inhibiting first-pass hepatic metabolism.

Nonsteroidal compounds with estrogenic or antiestrogenic activity—including flavones, isoflavones (e.g., genistein), and coumestan derivatives—occur in plants and fungi. Synthetic agents—including pesticides (e.g.DDT), plasticizers (e.g., bisphenol A), and other industrial chemicals (e.g., polychlorinated biphenyls)—also have hormonal or antihormonal activity. While their affinity is relatively weak, their large number, bioaccumulation, and persistence in the environment raise concerns about their potential toxicity in humans and wildlife.

Steroidal estrogens arise from androstenedione or testosterone by aromatization of the A ring, a reaction catalyzed by aromatase (CYP19), an enzyme found in ovarian granulosa cells, testicular Sertoli and Leydig cells, adipose stroma, placental syncytiotrophoblast, preimplantation blastocysts, bone, various brain regions, and other tissues. Ovaries are the principal source of circulating estrogen in premenopausal women. Gonadotropins, acting *via* receptors that couple to the Gs-adenylyl cyclase–cyclic AMP pathway, increase the activities of aromatase and the cholesterol side-chain cleavage enzyme. The ovary contains the type I isoform of 17 β-hydroxysteroid dehydrogenase, which favours the production of testosterone and estradiol from androstenedione and estrone, respectively. In the liver, the type II isoform oxidises circulating estradiol to estrone, which then is converted to estriol. These estrogens are excreted in the urine along with their glucuronide and sulphate conjugates. In postmenopausal women, the principal source of circulating estrogen is adipose tissue stroma, where estrone is synthesised from dehydroepiandrosterone (DHEA) secreted by the adrenals. In men, the testes produce estrogens but extragonadal aromatization of circulating androstenedione and DHEA accounts for most circulating estrogens.

Local production of estrogens by the aromatization of androgens may play a causal role in the development or progression of diseases such as breast cancer. Estrogens also may be produced from androgens by CYP19 in the central nervous system (CNS) and other tissues and exert local effects near their production site (e.g., in bone they increase bone mineral density).

Steroidal Estrogens

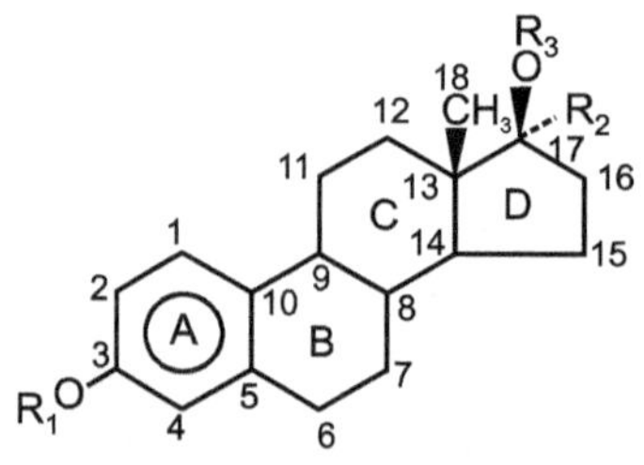

Derivative	R_1	R_2	R_3
Estradiol	–H	–H	–H
Estradiol valerate	–H	–H	$-C(=O)(CH_2)_3CH_3$
Ethinyl estradiol	–H	–C≡CH	–H
Mestranol	–CH$_3$	–C≡CH	–H
Estrone sulfate	–SO$_3$H	–*	= O*
Equilin	–H	–*	= O*

Non-steroidal Compounds with Estrogenic Activity

Diethylstilbestrol

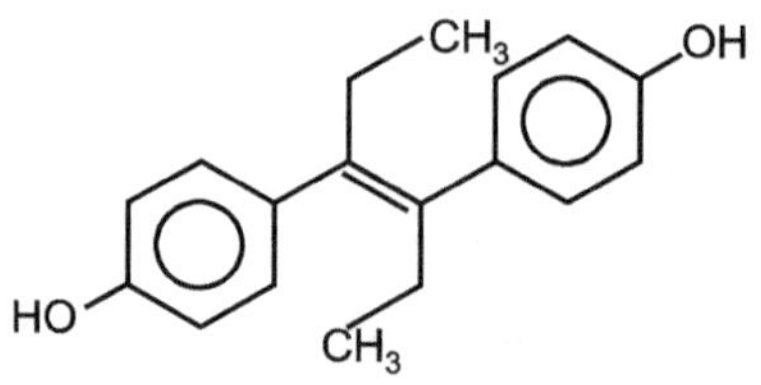

Bisphenol A

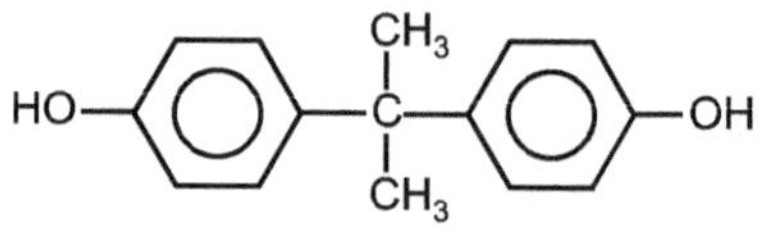

Genistein

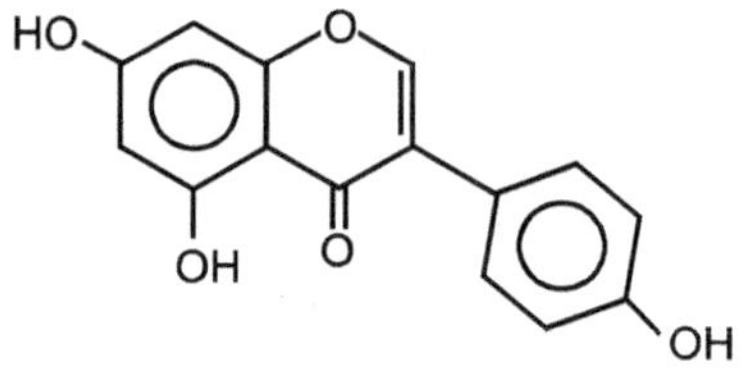

* Designates C17 ketone.
? Also contains 7, 8 double bond.

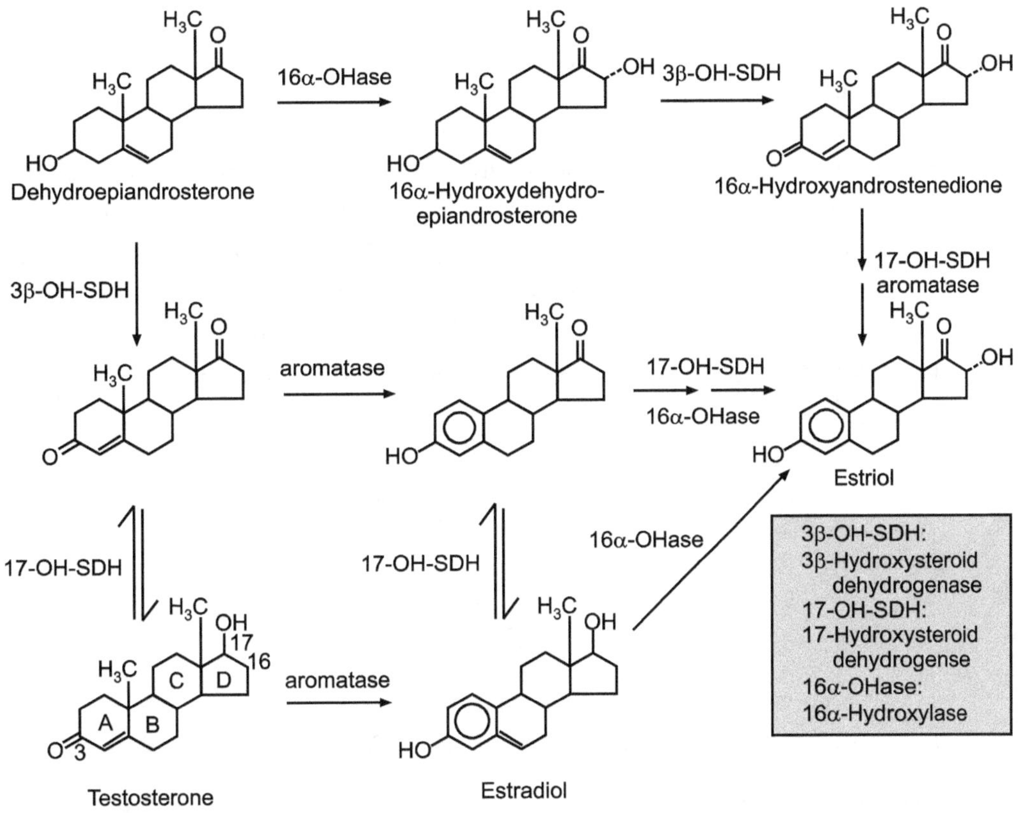

Biosynthetic Pathway for the estrogens

STRUCRURE ACIVITY RELATIONSHIP

1. 17 β-oestradiol is a potent oestrogenic agent. Many structural modifications of 17 β-estradiol were carried out since it rapidly gets oxidised to estrone, in liver and hence ineffective on oral administration. Adding a 17 α-alkyl group (particularly 17 α-ethinyl derivative) to oestradiol blocks this oxidation and makes the compound orally active. Another oestrogen, mestranol, which is used in oral contraceptives is synthesized by this similar route.

2. The esterifcation of 17 β-hydroxy and 3-hydroxy functions also prolongs the duration where slow rate of absorption is due to low water solubility. 3-benzoate 3, 17-dipropionate; 17-valerate and 17-cyclopentylpropionate are the ester forms most commonly used. Slow hydrolysis of these esters releases the free oestrogen over a prolonged period of time, hence ester forms are termed as prodrugs.

3. Steroidal nucleus is not an essential feature of oestrogenic activity.

4. The intensity of activity changes if route of adminstration is changed e.g. for oral route.

$$\text{Estriol} > \text{Estradiol} > \text{Estrone}$$

For subcutaneous route

$$\text{Estradiol} > \text{Estrone} > \text{Estriol}$$

5. Substitution on oestrone nucleus significantly modifies the oestrogenic activity.
   (a) Insertion of hydroxyl groups at 6, 7 and 11 positions diminishes the activity.
   (b) Removal of oxygen function at 3 and 17 position or epimerization to α configuration results in less active compounds.
   (c) Introduction of unsaturation in ring B, reduces activity.
   (d) Expansion of ring D in both, oestradiol and oestrone greatly reduces the activity.

D-homoestradiol

D-homoestradiol is less active than oestradiol

   (e) If ring D is removed in oestrone or oestradiol, activity remains the same.

6. The molecule should have a distance of about 8.55 Å between the groups that can form H-bonds (e.g. ketones, phenolic, and alcoholic hydroxyl groups).

7. A number of heterocyclic analogues of the oestrogens (steroidal) are being prepared and evaluated biologically. Among the most common are aza analogs. The -NH- group is isosteric to a methylene group.

Mechanism of Action

Plasma estrogens in the blood and interstitial fluid are bound to sex hormone-binding globulin, from which they dissociate to enter the cell and bind to their receptor. Two genes code for two estrogen receptor isoforms, alpha and beta, which are members of the superfamily of steroid, sterol, retinoic acid, and thyroid receptors. The estrogen receptors are found predominantly in the nucleus bound to heat shock proteins that stabilize them. Binding of the hormone to its receptor alters its conformation and releases it from the stabilizing proteins. The receptor-hormone complex forms homodimers that bind to a specific sequence of nucleotides called estrogen response elements (EREs) in the promoters of various genes and regulate their transcription. The ERE is composed of two half-sites arranged as a palindrome separated by a small group of nucleotides called the spacer. The interaction of a receptor dimer with the ERE also involves a number of nuclear proteins, the coregulators, as well as components of the transcription machinery. The receptor may also bind to other transcription factors to influence the effects of these factors on their responsive genes.

Pharmacological Action

Female Maturation

Estrogens are required for the normal sexual maturation and growth of the female. They stimulate the development of the vagina, uterus, and uterine tubes as well as the secondary sex characteristics. They stimulate stromal development and ductal growth in the breast and are responsible for the accelerated growth phase and the closing of the epiphyses of the long bones that occur at puberty.

Endometrial Effects

Estrogen also plays an important role in the development of the endometrial lining. When estrogen production is properly coordinated with the production of progesterone during the normal human menstrual cycle, regular periodic bleeding and shedding of the endometrial lining occur.

Cardiovascular Effects

Estrogens seem to be partially responsible for maintenance of the normal structure and function of the skin and blood vessels in women. Estrogens also decrease the rate of resorption of bone by promoting the apoptosis of osteoclasts and by antagonizing the osteoclastogenic and pro-osteoclastic effects of parathyroid hormone.

Effects on Blood Coagulation

Estrogens enhance the coagulability of blood. Many changes in factors influencing coagulation have been reported, including increased circulating levels of factors II, VII, IX, and X and decreased antithrombin III, partially as a result of the hepatic effects mentioned above. Increased plasminogen levels and decreased platelet adhesiveness have also been found.

Other Effects

Estrogens induce the synthesis of progesterone receptors. They are responsible for estrous behavior in animals and may influence behaviour and libido in humans. Administration of estrogens stimulates central components of the stress system, including the production of corticotrophin releasing hormone and the activity of the sympathetic system, and promotes a sense of well-being in women who are estrogen-deficient.

PROGESTERONE OR OESTROGENS OR CORPUS LUTEUM HORMONES

Progesterone is the most important progestin in humans (where progestin means favouring pregnancy). In addition to having important hormonal effects, it serves as a precursor to the estrogens, androgens, and adrenocortical steroids. It is synthesized in the ovary, testis, and adrenal from circulating cholesterol. Large amounts are also synthesized and released by the placenta during pregnancy.

Progesterone is a C_{21} steroid hormone. It belongs to a class of hormones called gestogens and is the major naturally occurring human progestgen. It was first isolated from sow ovaries by **W.M. Sllen** and his team. Professor George Washington, Comer and Allen also gave it the name **Progesterone** derived from *Progestational Steroidal Hormone*. Like other steroids, progesterone consist of four inter connected cyclic hydrocarbons. It consists ketone and oxygenated functional groups, as well as two methyl branches.

Properties

It is a white crystalline solid and is found in two forms α and β having M.P 120° and 121° respectively. These two forms have the same physiological activity, yield the same derivatives and are interconvertable.

Sources

Progesterone is produced in the adrenal glands, the gonads (specially after ovulation in the corpus luteum), the brain· and, during pregnancy. During the period of full corpus luteum activity, the human ovary produces about 1000 mg of progesterone daily.

Isolation

This hormone was first isolated in a pure form by **Butenandt and his co-workers (1934)**. The following procedure is adopted), for isolation.

The ovaries of pregnant pigs are finely ground and extracted with methanol. The extract thus obtained after dilution with water is filtered, to remove the undesirable matter (fatty matter). The hormone is extracted with the help of petroleum ether. The solvent petroleum ether is evaporated and residue is treated with ethanol, diluted with water and again extracted with petroleum ether. The progesterone is isolated in the ethernal phase leaving oesterone in the alcoholic portion. The petroleum ether fraction (which contain progesterone) is cooled at - 20°C and at this temperature progesterone gets crystallized.

Constitution

(a) Molecular Formula: $C_{21}H_{30}O_2$ has been ascertained by elementary analysis and molecular weight determination.

(b) Presence of Two Ketonic Groups: It form a dioxime with hydroxylamine, due to the presence of two ketonic groups.

$$C_{19}H_{30}(>\!\!C=O)_2 \xrightarrow{NH_2OH} C_{19}H_{30}(>\!\!C=N\!\!-\!\!OH)$$
Progesterone → Progesterone dioxime

(c) Presence of a Double Bond
  (i) On catalytic reduction, it form a dialcohol $C_{21}H_{36}O_2$ absorbing three molecules of hydrogen.
  (ii) Since four atoms of hydrogen are being used for the conversion of the two ketonic groups into two secondary alcoholic groups, the third molecule of hydrogen should have been added on the double bond to saturate it.

$$C_{19}H_{30}(\!\!>\!\!C=O)_2 \xrightarrow[\text{Cat. Redu.}]{NH_2OH} C_{19}H_{32}(\!\!>\!\!CHOH)_2$$

Progesterone   Dialcohol

(d) Presence of a Steroid Nucleus : The molecular formula of the parent hydrocarbon of progesterone is $C_{21}H_{36}$, it corresponds to the general formula C_nH_{2n-6}, thus showing progesterone to be a tetracyclic compound. i.e. contains a steroid nucleus. Moreover, the X-ray studies and its formation from cholesterol and stigmasterol confirm that it contains a steroid nucleus.

(e) Presence of α : β-unsaturated Ketonic System : Since progesterone is very sensitive to alkalies, it should be an α : β-unsaturated ketone which was further confirmed by its studies.

(f) Presence of $CH_3-\overset{\overset{O}{\|}}{C}-$Group: It undergo haloform reaction which indicates the presence of methyl ketonic group in this hormone.

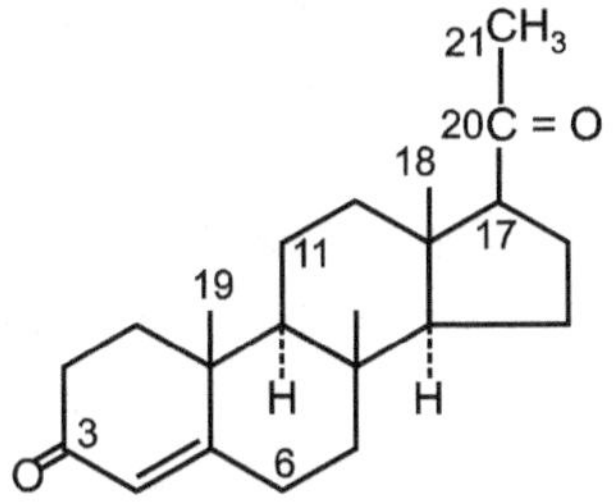

Progesterone

Biosynthesis and Secretion

Progesterone is secreted by the corpus luteum during the second half of the menstrual cycle under the stimulus of LH. After fertilisation, the trophoblast secretes hCG into maternal circulation, which also acts through the LH receptor to sustain the corpus luteum. During the second or third month of pregnancy, the developing placenta begins to secrete estrogen and progesterone in collaboration with the fetal adrenal glands, and thereafter the corpus luteum is not essential. Estrogen and progesterone then continue to be secreted in large amounts by the placenta throughout gestation.

STRUCTURE ACTIVITY RELATIONSHIP

Progestational activity appears to be restricted to molecules with a steroid nucleus. Progesterone is not effective orally due to its complete degradation during its one passage through liver. Further relatively, it has a short biological half-life (5 minutes). Therefore, attempts were made to prepare synthtic progestins which can be generally be divided into two main classes:

(a) 17 α-hydroxyprogesterone.
(b) 19-nortestosterone.

(a) 17 α-hydroxyprogesterone

Progesterone

1. Activity of 17 α-hydroxyprogesterone is increased by
   (a) Unsaturation at position 6 and 7,
   (b) Substitution of a methyl group or a halogen atom at sixth carbon, and
   (c) Introducing a methyl group at position 11.

   The above modification probably prevents the metabolic reduction of the two carbonyl groups and metabolic oxidation at position 6.

2. Substitution of a fluoro group at position 21 prevents hydroxylation at this point and enhances the oral effectiveness.

3. Inversion of the configuration at position 10 and 19 in proesterone leads to retroprogesterone which is more active parenterally and orally than progestrone. Further unsaturation at position 6 and 7 gives dyhydrogestrone which is orally active.

4. A progestin with prolonged duration of action is 16 α, 17-dihydroxyprogesterone acetophenide, in which androgenic and oestrogenic activities are absent when given parenterally.

(b) Modification of 19-nortestosterone derivatives.

1. Introduction of an alkyl group at C-17 of 19-nortestosterone prevents its oxidation to inactive compounds and increases its progestational activity.

   As in 17 α - ethinyl analog, by increasing its electron density ($C\equiv CH$) at C-17, one can simultaneously decrease its anabolic activity and promte good progestational activity e.g. ethisterone.

2. Removal of 19-CH_3 group (19-nor analog) further decreases its androgenic activity, e.g. norethisterone.

3. Following modiications of 19-nortestosterone leads to more effective progestins.
   (a) Substituting a chlorine atm at C-21 or by adding a methyl group at C-18 e.g.

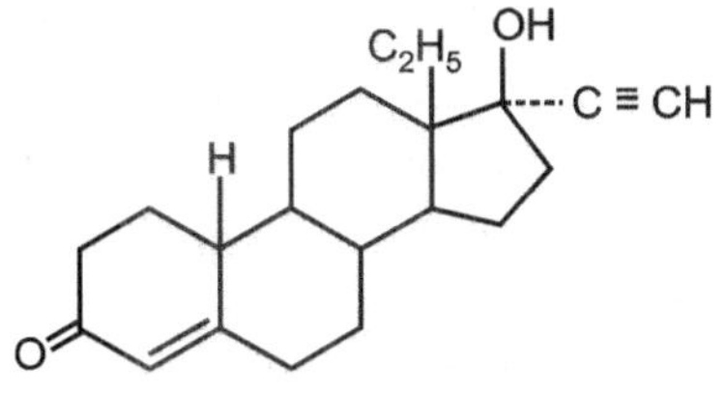

   Norgestrel

   (b) Unsaturation of the rings B or C.
   (c) Introduction of halogen or methyl at 6 α or 7 α positions e.g. Dimethisterone.
   (d) Acetylation of the 17 β -OH results in longer duration of action e.g Ethindiol diacetate.
   (e) Removal of the keto function at C-3, e.g. Lynestrenol.

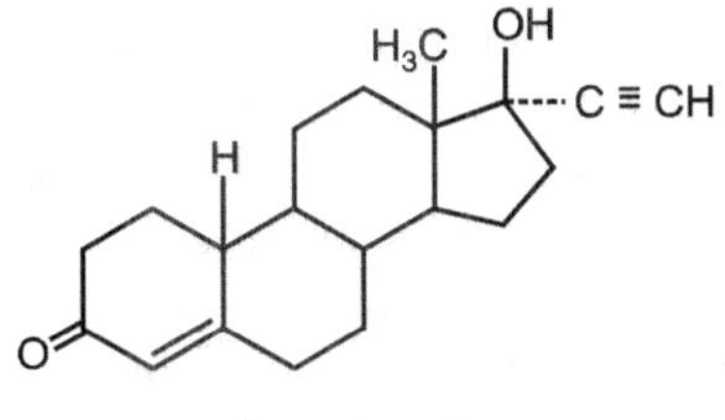

   Lynestrenol

Mechanism of Action

The mechanism of action of progesteroneis similar to that of other steroid hormones. Progestins enter the cell and bind to progesterone receptors that are distributed between the nucleus and the cytoplasm. The ligand-receptor complex binds to a progesterone response element (PRE) to activate gene transcription. The response element for progesterone appears to be similar to the corticosteroid response element, and the specificity of the response depends upon which receptor is present in the cell as well as upon other cell-specific receptor coregulators and interacting transcription factors. The progesterone-receptor complex forms a dimer before binding to DNA. Like the estrogen receptor, it can form heterodimers as well as homodimers between two isoforms: A and B. These isoforms are produced by alternative splicing of the same gene.

Effects of Progesterone on different body organs

Progesterone has little effect on protein metabolism. It stimulates lipoprotein lipase activity and favour fat deposition. The effects on carbohydrate metabolism are more marked.

Progesterone increases basal insulin levels and the insulin response to glucose. Progesterone can compete with aldosterone for the mineralocorticoid receptor of the renal tubule, causing a decrease in Na^+ reabsorption. This leads to an increased secretion of aldosterone by the adrenal cortex (eg, in pregnancy). Progesterone increases body temperature in humans.

Progesterone is responsible for the alveolobular development of the secretory apparatus in the breast. It also participates in the preovulatory LH surge and causes the maturation and secretory changes in the endometrium that are seen following ovulation.

Progesterone decreases the plasma levels of many amino acids and leads to increased urinary nitrogen excretion. It induces changes in the structure and function of smooth endoplasmic reticulum in experimental animals.

ANDROGEN (TESTOSTERONE)

In humans, the most important androgen secreted by the testis is testosterone. The main sources of this hormone are male urine and the testicular extract. In men, approximately 8 mg of testosterone is produced daily. About 95% is produced by the Leydig cells and only 5% by the adrenal. The testis also secretes small amounts of another potent androgen, dihydrotestosterone, as well as androstenedione and dehydroepiandrosterone, which are weak androgens. The Sertoli cells in the testis synthesize and secrete a variety of active proteins, including mullerian duct inhibitory factor, inhibin, and activin. Inhibin and activin appear to be the products of three genes that produce a common alpha subunit and two beta subunits, A and B. There are two inhibins (A and B), which contain the alpha subunit and one of the beta subunits. Activin stimulates pituitary FSH release and is structurally similar to transforming growth factor, which also increases FSH. The inhibins in conjunction with testosterone and dihydrotestosterone are responsible for the feedback inhibition of pituitary FSH secretion. (**Fig. 8.16**)

About 65% of circulating testosterone is bound to thier respective receptor i.e. sex hormone-binding globulin (SHBG). Circulating testosterone level is increased in plasma by estrogen, thyroid hormone, and in patients with cirrhosis of the liver. It is decreased by androgen and growth hormone and is lower in obese individuals. Most of the remaining testosterone is bound to albumin. Approximately 2% remains free and available to enter cells and bind to intracellular receptors. In men they may improve the sense of well-being and inhibit atherosclerosis. Testosterone or its active metabolite 5 alpha-dihydrotestosterone is responsible for the many changes that occur in puberty. In addition to the general growth-promoting properties of androgens on the body tissues, these hormones are responsible for penile and scrotal growth. Changes in the skin include the appearance of pubic, axillary, and beard hair. The sebaceous glands become more active, and the skin tends to become thicker and oilier. The larynx grows and the vocal cords become thicker, leading to a lower-pitched voice. Skeletal growth is stimulated and epiphysial closure accelerated, growth of the prostate and seminal vesicles is enhanced.Other effects include darkening of the skin, and increased skin circulation. Androgens play an important role in stimulating and maintaining sexual function in men. Androgens increase lean body mass and stimulate body hair growth and sebum secretion.

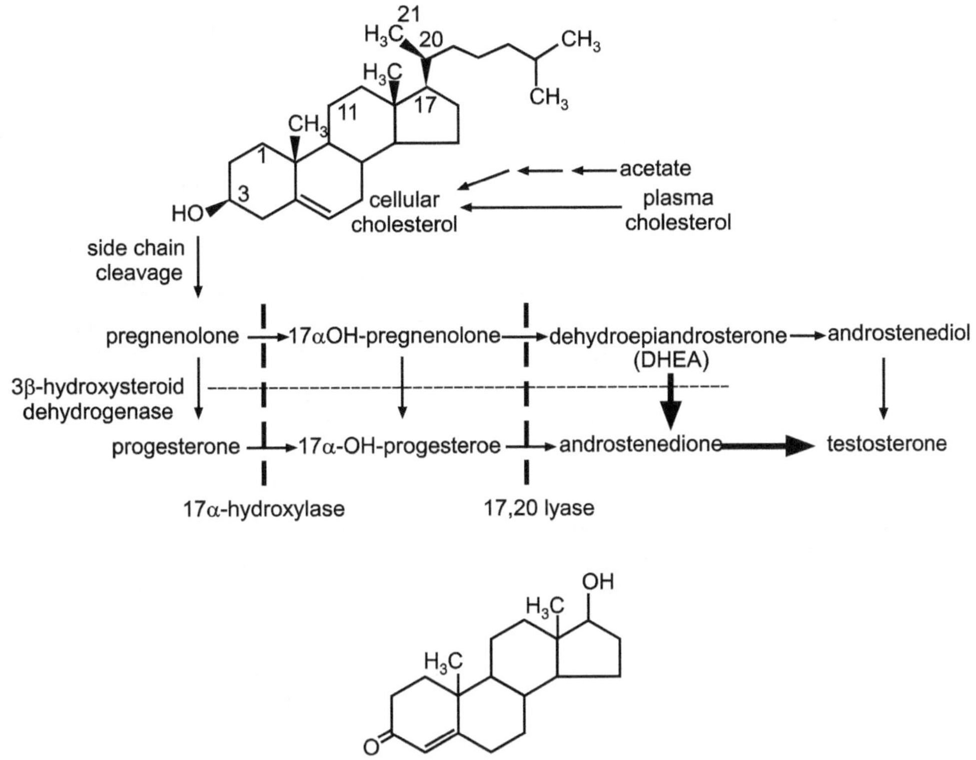

Fig. 8.16 : Pathway of synthesis of testosterone in the Leydig cells of the testes. Leydig cells express steroid 17α-hydroxylase (CYP17), which carries out sequential 17-hydroxylation and C17-20 lyase reactions in the biosynthetic pathway to produce androgens. Bold arrows indicate favoured pathways.

Isolation

Testosterone may be isolated from testes but to a very small amount because from 100 kg of testes nearly 10 mg testosterone may be obtained. The main problem in the isolation of this steroid is its instability in alkaline medium.

In the first step male urine is concentrated followed by its acidic hydrolysis. It is then treated with chloroform. The chloroform layer is separated and treated with KOH several times to remove impurities. And then treated with Girard reagent. The substance so obtained is extracted and hydrolysed to obtain pure testosterone.

Constitution

(a) **Molecular Formula :** $C_{19}H_{28}O_2$.

(b) **Presence of One Ketonic Group:** It reacts with hydroxyl amine to form mono-oxime which indicates the presence of one ketonic group.

$$C_{18}H_{28}(>C=O) \xrightarrow{NH_2OH} C_{18}H_{28}(>C=N-OH)$$
Testrosterone → Testosterone mono-oxide

(c) **Presence of One Secondary Alcoholic Group :** It gives the usual tests of one secondary alcohol which shows that testosterone contain one secondary alcoholic group.

(d) **Presence of One Double Bond**
  (i) The catalytic reduction of testosterone shows that it contains one double bond.
  (ii) In the above reaction testosterone absorbs two molecules of hydrogen, because two atoms of hydrogen are being used for the conversion of one ketonic group into secondary alcoholic group, thus the second molecule of hydrogen should have been added on the double bond to saturate it.

$$C_{18}H_{28}(\!\!>\!\!C=O)_2 \xrightarrow[\text{Cat. Redu.}]{2H_2} C_{18}H_{30}(\!\!>\!\!CHOH)_2$$

Testosterone   Secondary alcohol

(e) **Presence of a Steroid Nucleus :** The molecular formula of the parent hydrocarbon of testosterone is $C_{19}H_{32}$ which correspond to the general formula C_nH_{2n-6} thus confirming testosterone to be a tetracyclic compound i.e. it contains a steroid nucleus.

(f) **Evidence in Support of the Final Structure (oxidation view) :** It undergoes oxidation to form androst-4-en-3, 17-di-one which can be obtained by the oxidation of dehydroepiendrosterone.

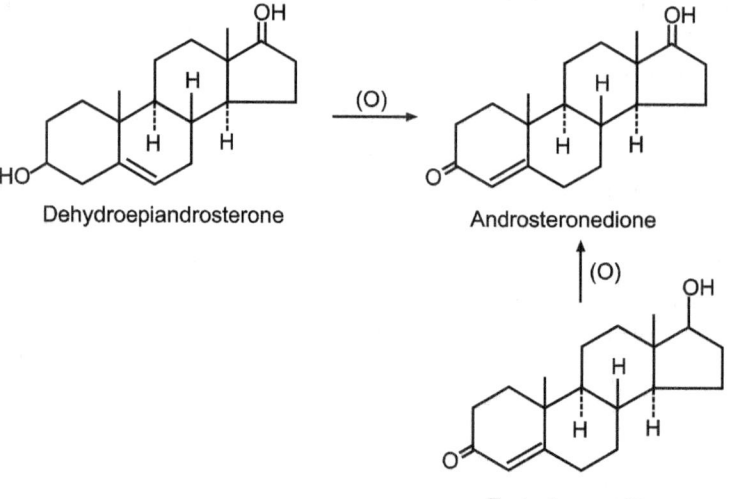

Structure Activity Relationship
1. The 17β-hydroxyl function is essential for androgenic and anabolic activity.
2. 1-Dehydroisomer of testosterone is a compound with potent biological action.

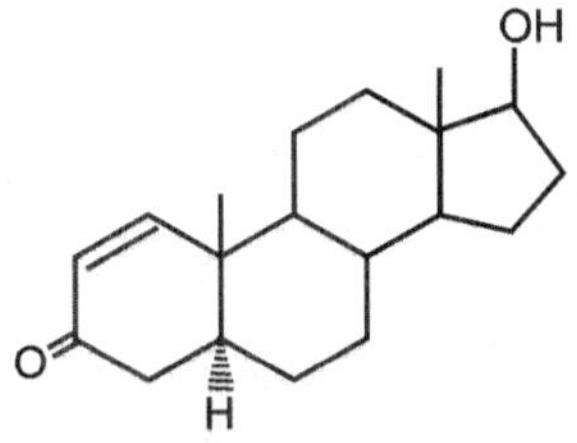

Dehydroisomer

3. Reduction of the A ring e.g. DHT (3-deoxy-2'-thymidinene) may increase the potency.
4. Changing the A/B trans stereochemistry (androsterone) to the A/B cis-etiochoanone drastically reduces both the anabolic and androgenic properties.
5. Introduction of C-17 α methyl group confers oral activity on testosterone.
6. 19-Nor testosterone (norandrolone) showed anabolic properties and only about 0.1 as androgenic testosterone.

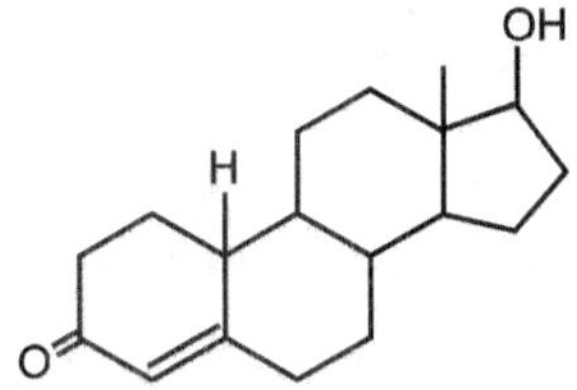

Norandrolone

7. Introduction of double bond at C1 produced agents with marked anabolic property. The acetate of 17 β hydroxy androsta-1,4-dien-3-one was as myotrophic as testosterone propionate but was much less androgenic. Introduction of unsaturation into the B, C and D rings has given rise to compounds with significant androgenic or anabolic activity.

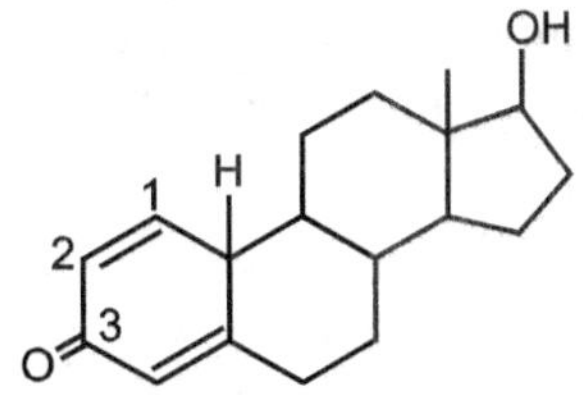

17 beta-hydroxy androsta-1,4-dien-3-one

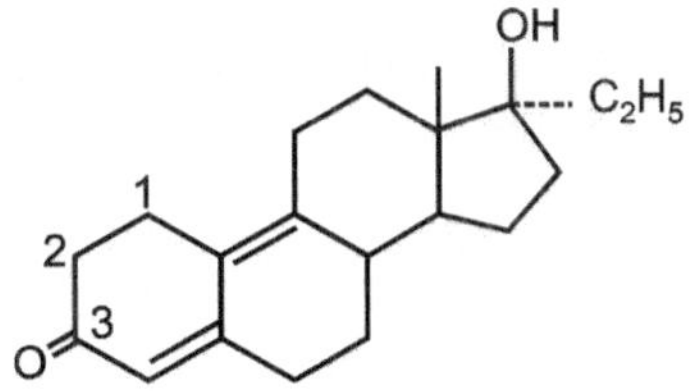

8. Alkylation of C1, C2, C7 and C18 has afforded compounds with chemical efficacy. Methanolone acetate, drostanolone, bolasterone exhibit pronounced anabolic activity.

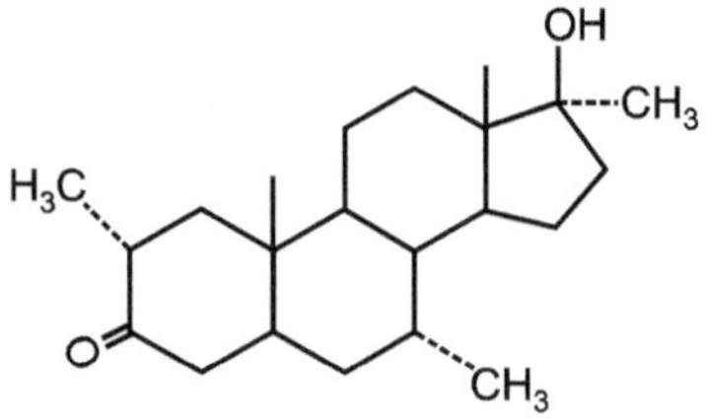

Drostanolone

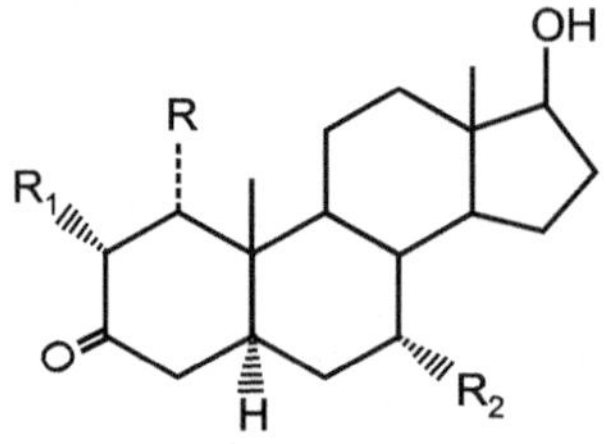

Methenolone
R = CH₃; R₁ = R₂ = H

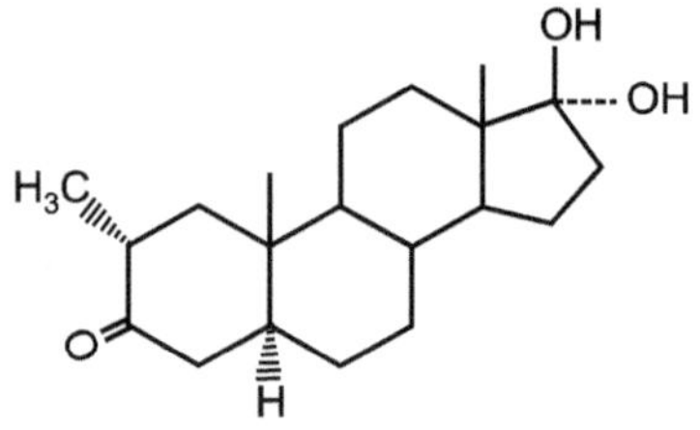

Bolasterone

9. Preparation of halogen, hydroxylated derivatives has resulted in weaker activity as compared to testosterone. However, α-fluoro derivative halotestin produced an oral anabolic effect 20 times that of 17 α-methyl testosterone.

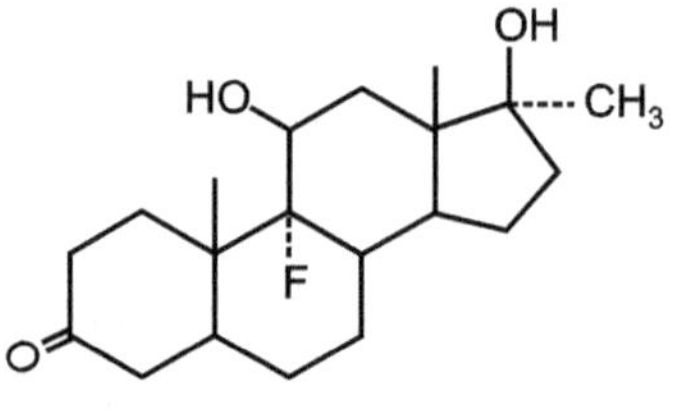

Halotestin

10. A number of androgen analogs in which an oxygen atom replaces one of the methylene groups in the steroid nucleus has oral anabolic activity.

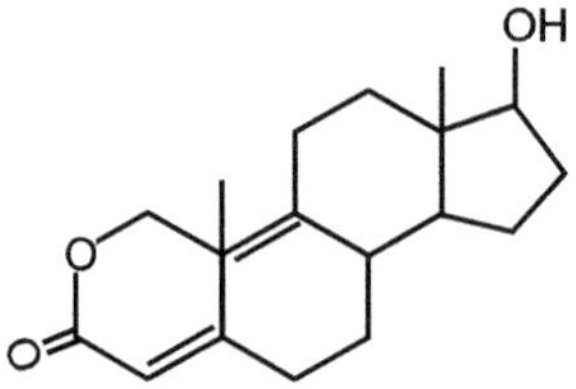

11. The 3-deoxy analogs have been found to be potent androgen. Several heterocyclic rings were then fused to ring A. The pyrazole (Stanazolol) and isoxazole (Androisoxazole) were much more active than 17 α-methyl testosterone. Androisoxazole exhibited an oral anabolic to androgenic ratio of 40.

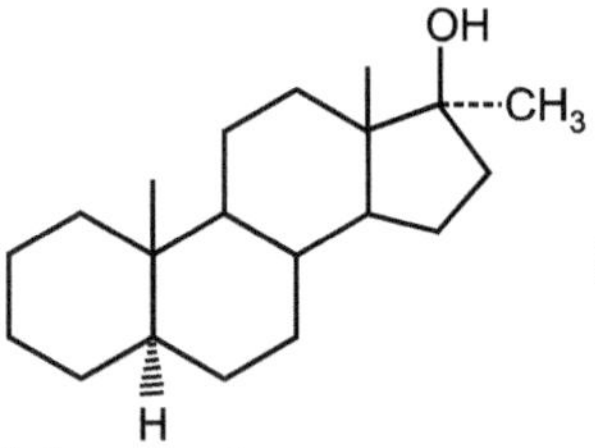

3-deoxy analogs

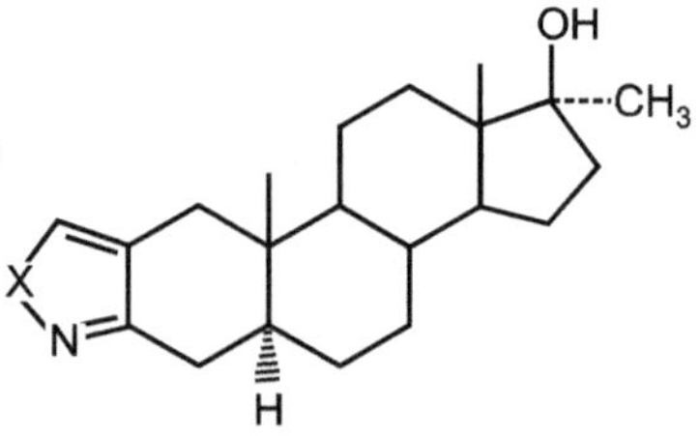

Stanazolol X=NH
Androisoxazole X=O

12. Esterification of testosterone markedly prolonged the activity. The acyl moiety is usually derived from a long chain aliphatic or arylaliphatic acids. The duration of action and the anabolic to androgenic ratio increased with the chain length of the ester group. In order of decreasing duration, the 17-β-esters are testosterone ethanate > cypionate > propionate > acetate

R = COCH$_2$CH$_3$ Testosterone Propionate;
R = -CO (CH$_2$)$_5$CH$_3$ Testosterone Enthanate;
R = -COCH$_2$CH$_2$—⟨ ⟩ Testosterone cypionate

Mechanisms of Action

Like other steroids, testosterone acts intracellularly in target cells. In skin, prostate, seminal vesicles, and epididymis, it is converted to 5 -dihydrotestosterone. In these tissues, dihydrotestosterone is the dominant androgen. The distribution of this enzyme in the foetus is different and has important developmental implications.

Testosterone and dihydrotestosterone bind to the intracellular androgen receptor, initiating a series of events similar to those described above for estradiol and progesterone, leading to growth, differentiation, and synthesis of a variety of enzymes and other functional proteins. In the male at puberty, androgens cause development of the secondary sex characteristics. In the adult male, large doses of testosterone—when given alone—or its derivatives suppress the secretion of gonadotropins and result in some atrophy of the interstitial tissue and the tubules of the testes.

Effects

In the male at puberty, androgens cause development of the secondary sex characteristics. In the adult male, large doses of testosterone when given alone or its derivatives suppress the secretion of gonadotropins and result in some atrophy of the interstitial tissue and the tubules of the testes. Since fairly large doses of androgens are required to suppress gonadotropin secretion, it has been postulated that inhibin, in combination with androgens, is responsible for the feedback control of secretion. In women, androgens are capable of producing changes similar to those observed in the prepubertal male. These include growth of facial and body hair, deepening of the voice, enlargement of the clitoris, frontal baldness, and prominent musculature. The natural androgens stimulate erythrocyte production.

The administration of androgens reduces the excretion of nitrogen into the urine, indicating an increase in protein synthesis or a decrease in protein breakdown within the body. This effect is much more pronounced in women and children than in normal men.

Direct effects of testosterone and indirect effects mediated by dihydrotestosterone or estradiol

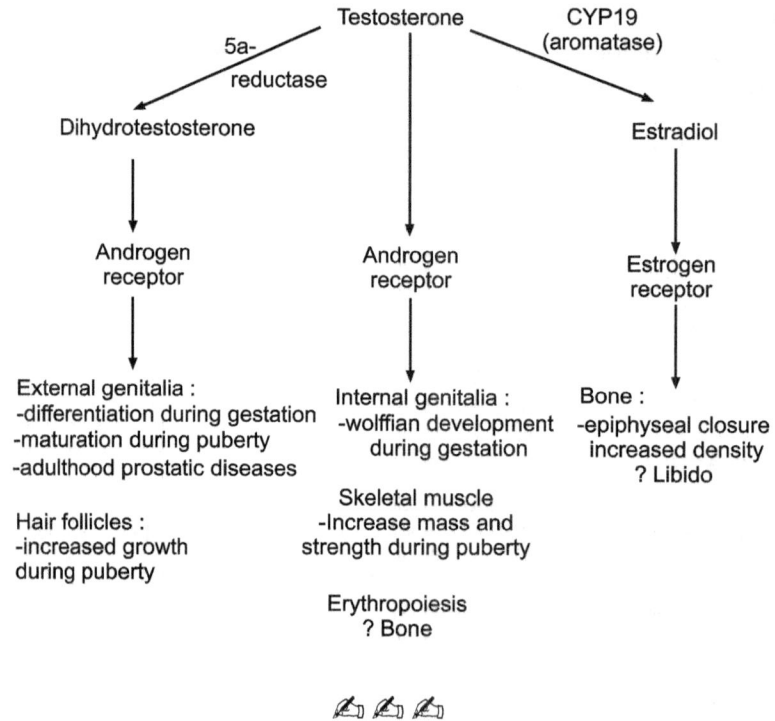

Chapter ... 9

PHARMACOLOGICAL SCREENING METHODS IN-VIVO AND IN-VITRO MODELS

Traditional medicines exist in every continent of the globe and is an integral part of every culture of the world. The most famous system of traditional medicines are the Chinese system of medicine in East Asia, Ayurveda in India, and formerly Galenic medicine in Europe.

For many decades, the discovery of drugs depended on screening. From the previous century until the 1960s, chemical compounds and natural products were tested in whole animal assays, and in the case of antibacterial and antitumor testing, the samples were tested in whole cell assays. Although screening was labour intensive and expensive, it was fruitful. A large number of successful drugs such as the cephalosporins, aminoglycosides, tetracyclines, macrolide antibiotics, doxyrubicin, etoposide, and other anticancer agents, steroids and drugs for use in the central nervous system and cardiovascular areas were discovered by screening. A single lead molecule identified in one company has, in many cases, kept several hundred industrial chemists and biologists busy for several years.

Screening natural products and a limited number of compound libraries fell out of favour in the early 1980s because very few useful new chemical entities were being identified. The concept of screening chemicals made in academic and industrial laboratories began to complement the screening of natural products. A large pool of compounds became available through the opening of Russia's borders. Academic chemists, who worked to establish new synthetic methods, became sources of chemical diversity for screening, as the compounds on their shelves, in many cases, had never been tested for biological activity. At the same time, progress in biotechnology allowed isolation of large amounts of pure proteins that were drug targets. Thus, testing chemical and natural product libraries against isolated enzymes and proteins became the preferred method for screening. Combinatorial synthesis of thousands of molecules became possible in the 1990s, and many companies tied combinatorial chemistry with high throughput screening. The use of microtiter plates made it possible to screen large numbers of samples while keeping reagent costs down.

In India, *Ayurveda*, *Siddha* and *Unani* systems of medicine provide health care for a large section of the population. The word **Ayurveda** is composed of two parts: Ayu (= life) and Veda (= knowledge). The origins of this science of life can be traced back to at somewhere around 6000 BC. The knowledge was passed on to successive generations by oral communication. Compared with modern anatomy and physiology, Ayurveda is based on certain fundamental doctrines, known as the *Darshanas*, such as the seven *Dhatus*. They can be described not exactly as organs but as body constituents. The three *Doshas: vata, pitta* and *kapha* are regulators of cell function in various ways. A balance of the three doshas is essential for maintaining health. Imbalance of the doshas results in disease. Drug therapy in Ayurveda is highly individualised. Both traditional Chinese and Ayurvedic medicine developed further in terms of formulations. There is also the tendency to adopt the modern forms of clinical trials.

Basic Consideration in Designing of High Throughput Screening (HTS)

With the need of careful coordination of activities between biologists, chemists, and computer and database specialists

and automation for high throughput screening, high throughput screening departments currently consist of a mixture of biologists, chemists, engineers, and computer and networking specialists. High throughput screening departments have become high technology departments. The promise of high throughput screening is that more leads will be identified and that these screening leads will be developed to make new chemical entities and eventually new drugs. During the last few years, the number of new chemical entities entering the marketplace has not increased greatly in spite of the increased throughput. The art of screening needs to be coupled to high throughput and ultra high throughput screening become effective throughput screening. The design of assays for high throughput screening (HTS) is anything but basic. To be effective in HTS, an assay must be robust, reproducible, and automatable. To make matters worse, these techniques must also support complex biological systems often involving engineered cell lines and always requiring comparison of results from hundreds of thousands of assay points.

Target Classes

Biological scientists will usually argue that the selection of the target for HTS is the most important decision. ''Screeners,'' on the other hand, may maintain that any target is a viable candidate for lead discovery if a proper screen is developed and it is run correctly. The selection of a therapeutically valid target and the assay used to elucidate it is not as clear-cut. Targets for HTS have historically come from basic scientific research in which years were spent discovering the details surrounding the manifestation of a disease or symptom. From these results, one could select key biological responses as steps for intervention. Most successful drugs on the market today are from validated and ''druggable'' targets of this type. Examples of these targets include enzymes (proteases, polymerases), interacting proteins, and receptors involved in signal transduction and transcriptional processes in the cell.

In such cases, the screen may be creating a tool to elucidate the function of the target and even its structure. Hence HTS is becoming an important tool in finding lead molecules for established targets and new chemical entities that serve to elucidate the pharmacology of novel disease targets.

Types of HTS Assays

Two basic assay formats are employed in HTS: in vitro biochemical assays and cell based assays. Targets that are routinely screened using in vitro formats include various enzymes, receptors, and protein - protein interaction assays. Cell based assays are utilised for targets that involve signal transduction pathways (including receptors) and in screens designed to identify antimicrobial agents. In both cases, the screens are generally carried out in 96- or 384-well microtiter plates using colorimetric, fluorescence, luminescence, and radiometric detection techniques to measure assay end points. Reporter assays (cell based) are widely employed to detect G-protein coupled receptor (GPCR) signaling and can be employed to detect interruptions in signaling as well as gene transcription and regulation. Functional cellular readouts, as the name implies, are more direct measures of cellular activity. The classic example is the direct measure of ion flux into cells using fluorescent dyes.

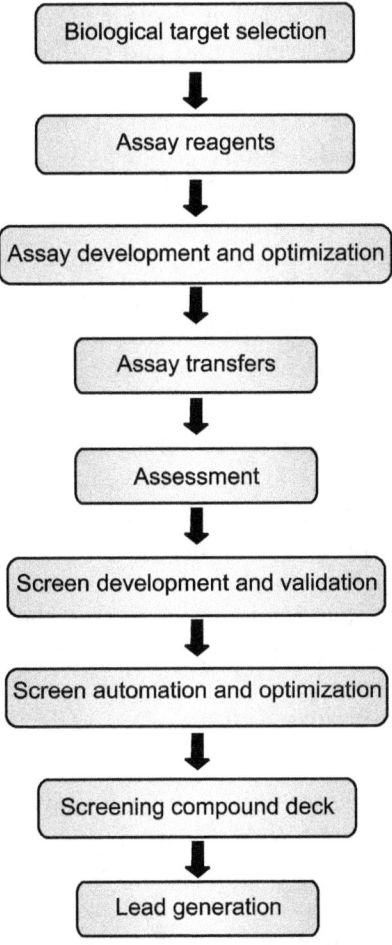

Figure 9.1 : Screen paradigm

Pharmacological Approaches in Modern Drug Discovery

The most important achievements of modern Western medicine were made in areas such as diagnosis, infectious diseases, endocrinology and medicinal chemistry. Medicinal chemistry as an important science started less than 100 years ago. The active principles of plants, mostly alkaloids, were isolated and were the starting point for syntheses, such as: morphine and papaverine from *Papaver somniferum* for synthetic analgesics and spasmolytics; atropine from *Atropa belladonna* for synthetic spasmolytics; cocaine from *Erythroxylon coca* for synthetic local anaesthetics; quinine and quinidine from *Cinchona succirubra* for synthetic anti malarial drugs and antiarrhythmics; ephedrine from *Ephedra sinica* for synthetic sysmpathicomimetics and sysmpathicolytics including β-blockers, xanthines like caffeine.

The classical way of pharmacological screening involves sequential testing of new chemical entities or extracts from biological material in isolated organs followed by tests in whole animals, mostly rats and mice but also higher animals if indicated. Most drugs in use nowadays in therapy have been found and evaluated with these methods. In the mid-1970s, receptor binding assays were introduced as an approach for compound evaluation by the development of radioligand binding assays, based on evaluation procedures and mathematical calculations provided by Schild. The reverse molecular pharmacological methodology includes cloning and expression of G-protein coupled receptors in mammalian cells and screening these cells for a functional response to cognate or surrogate agonists present in biological extract preparations, peptide libraries, and complex compound preparations.

The ligand binding assay is a powerful tool in the search for agonists and antagonists for novel receptors, and for identification of novel classes of agonists and antagonists for known receptors.

The classical approach has the advantage of relatively high relevance. If a compound has blood pressure lowering activity in hypertensive rats after oral dosage, the chances of activity in humans are high. Measurement of dose-response-curves, effects over a given period of time and comparison of the effects after intravenous and oral administration already give hints for pharmacokinetic data. This approach has the disadvantage that it is time consuming and requires relatively large amounts of the new compound.

SCREENING METHODS FOR VARIOUS PHARMACOLOGICAL ACTIVITY

Screening Methods for Respiratory Activity

In-Vitro Methods

Histamine (H1) receptor binding - Histamine is considered to play a major role in asthmatic attacks. H1-antagonists have been used since decades as therapeutic agents. This assay is used to determine the affinity of test compounds to the histamine H1 receptor by measuring their inhibitory activities on the binding of the H1 antagonist. Brains from guinea-pigs are homogenised in ice-cold Tris buffer (pH 7.5) in a Potter homogeniser (1 g brain in 30 ml buffer). The homogenate is centrifuged at 4°C for

10 min at 50 000 g. The supernatant is discarded, the pellet resupended in buffer, centrifuged as before, and the final pellets resupended in Tris buffer (1 g fresh weight/5 ml). Aliquots of 1 ml are frozen at −70 °C. In the competition experiment, 50 µl 3H-pyrilamine (one constant concentration of 2×10^{-9} M), 50 µl test compound (>10 concentrations, 10^{-5}–10^{-10} M) and 100 µl membrane suspension from guinea pig whole brain (approx. 10 mg wet weight/ml) per sample are incubated in a shaking bath at 25 °C for 30 min. Incubation buffer: 50 mM Tris-HCl buffer, pH 7.5. The reaction is stopped by rapid vacuum filtration through glass fibre filters. Thereby the membrane bound compound is separated from the free radioactivity. The retained membrane-bound radioactivity on the filter is measured after addition of 3 ml liquid scintillation cocktail per sample in a liquid scintillation counter.

In-Vivo Methods

Bronchospasmolytic activity in anesthetised guinea pigs

The method is based on registration of air volume changes of a living animal in a closed system consisting of the respiration pump, of the trachea and the bronchi as well as of a reservoir permitting measurement of volume or pressure of excess air. Administration of spasmogens like acetylcholine, histamine, bradykinin, serotonin, ovalbumin, PAF, substance P, methacholine or leukotrienes, results in contraction of bronchial smooth muscle. The method permits the evaluation of a drug's bronchospasmolytic effect by measuring the volume of air, which is not taken up by the lungs after bronchospasm.

Procedure

Guinea-pigs of either sex weighing 250–500 g are anaesthetised with 1.25 g/kg i.p. urethane. Pentobarbital (60 mg/kg s.c.) and alcuronium chloride (1 mg/kg s.c.) are to be preferred when the bronchospasm is elicited by PAF or substance P. Anesthesia has to be deep enough in order to prevent influence of spontaneous respiration. The trachea is cannulated by means of a two way cannula, one arm of which is connected to the respiratory pump and the other to a Statham P23 Db transducer. The animal is artificially respired using a Starling pump with an inspiratory pressure set at 90–120 mm of water, an adequate tidal volume of 3 ml/100 g body weight and a frequency of 60 strokes per minute. Excess air, not taken up by the lungs, is measured and recorded on a polygraph. Results are expressed as percent inhibition of induced bronchospasm over the control agonistic responses. The *ED*50 value is calculated.

Effect of arachidonic acid or PAF on respiratory function *in vivo*

Arachidonic acid is metabolised into thromboxane (TXA2) and prostacyclin (PGI2). TXA2 produced in the lung leads to bronchoconstriction, which is independent from circulating platelets and leukotrienes; TXA2 produced intracellularly in platelets induces a reversible thrombocytopenia. PGI2 produced in the vessel wall leads to the reduction of systolic and diastolic blood pressure.

Procedure

Male guinea pigs (Pirbright White) weighing 300–600 g are anesthetised with 60 mg/kg pentobarbital sodium (IP). One of the jugular veins is cannulated for the administration of spasmogen and test compound. Both external carotid arteries are cannulated; one is connected to a pressure transducer to register blood pressure, the other is used for blood withdrawal. The trachea is connected to a Starling pump with an inspiratory pressure set of 80 mm H_2O, an adequate tidal volume of approx. 10 ml/kg body weight and a frequency of 70–75 strokes/ min. Spontaneous respiration is inhibited by intravenous injection of pancuronium (4 mg/kg) or gallamine (2 mg/kg) on time. Percent inhibition or increase of bronchospasm, reduction of blood pressure, thrombocytopenia, leukocytopenia and hematocrit following test drug administration are calculated in comparison to control values before drug treatment. For the reduction of blood pressure, both the magnitude [mm Hg, systolic and diastolic] and the duration [min] are determined.

Bronchial Hyperreactivity

Symptoms like asphyctic convulsions resembling bronchial asthma in patients can be induced by inhalation of histamine or other bronchospasm inducing agents in guinea pigs. The challenging agents are applied as aerosols produced by an ultra-sound nebuliser.

Procedure

Ten male albino guinea pigs weighing 300–400 g per group are used. The inhalation cages consist of 3 boxes each ventilated with an air flow of 1.5 l/min. The animal is placed into box A to which the test drug or the standard is applied using an ultra-sound nebuliser LKB NB108 which provides an aerosol of 0.2 ml solution of the test drug injected by an infusion pump within 1 min. Alternatively, the animal is treated orally or subcutaneously with the test drug or the standard. Box B serves as a sluice through which the animal is passed into box C. There, the guinea pig is exposed to an aerosol of a 0.1% solution of histamine. Then, the animal is immediately withdrawn from the inhalation box. The aerosols are removed from the back wall of the boxes by applying low pressure. Percent increase of pre-convulsion time is calculated versus controls. *ED*50 values can be found, i.e. 50% of increase of pre-convulsion time.

Airway Microvascular Leakage

Plasma exudation in guinea-pig airways *in vivo* can be determined by Evans Blue dye and is fairly correlated with radiolabelled albumin.

Procedure

Female Dunkin-Hartley guinea pigs weighing 380–600 g are anesthetized with an initial dose of 1.5 g/kg urethane injected intraperitoneally Additional urethane is given intravenously 30 min later to achieve an appropriate level of anesthesia. A tracheal cannula is inserted into the lumen of the cervical trachea, a polyethylene catheter into the left carotid artery to monitor blood pressure and heart rate and another polyethylene catheter into the external jugular vein for administration of drugs. The animals are connected to a constant volume mechanical ventilator and then given an injection of 1.0–1.5 mg/kg suxamethonium (IV) to prevent interference with spontaneous respiration. The test compound (bradykinin receptor antagonist) is given intravenously. Ten min later, Evans Blue dye (20 mg/ml) is injected intravenously for 1 min. After 1 min, bronchoconstriction and microvascular leakage is induced by injection of bradykinin or by inhalation of bradykinin or PAF or vagal stimulation. Six min after induction of leakage, the thoracic cavity is opened, and a cannula is inserted into the aorta through a ventriculotomy. Perfusion is performed with 100–150 ml 0.9% saline at a pressure of 100–120 mm Hg in order to remove the intravascular dye from the systematic circulation. Blood and perfusion liquid are expelled through an incision in the right and left atrium. Subsequently, the right ventricle is opened, and the pulmonary circulation is perfused with 30 ml of 0.9% saline. Evans Blue dye concentration, expressed as ng/mg tissue, as well as lung resistance are compared by statistical means.

Antitussive Activity

Antitussive activity after irritant inhalation in guinea pigs results in cough which is thought to be caused by a reflex. The sensitive receptors are located in the bronchial tree, particularly in the bifurcation of the trachea. These receptors can be stimulated mechanically or chemically, e.g., by inhalation of various irritants.

Procedure of antitussive activity

Guinea pigs of either sex weighing 300–400 g are used. The animal is placed in a cylindrical glass vessel, with 2 tubes at either ends. One serves as the entrance of the aerosol, the other for its efflux. The latter tube has a side-arm connecting to a tambour, from which changes in pressure can be registered. A pinch-clamp with a variable screw is placed on the efflux tube beyond the side arm, permitting the regulation of the sensitivity of the system, so that the normal respiration is not registered, while the displacement of air in the enclosure caused by coughing of the animal is registered. The guinea pig is exposed to the aerosol of 7.5% citric acid in water for 10 min. Each animal is tested first to obtain the control response. The number of tussive responses is registered. One hour later, the test substance is applied either subcutaneously or orally, and 30 min later the guinea pig is subjected to the aerosol again. The number of coughs during 10 min is recorded. The number of coughs after treatment is expressed as percentage of the control period. Using various doses, *ED*50 values can be calculated.

Cough Induced by Mechanical Stimulation

After overnight fasting with water *ad libitum*, the guinea pigs are lightly anesthetised with 25% urethane (4 ml/kg IP) which induces surgical levels of analgesia without depressant effects on respiratory function. Analgesia is monitored throughout the experiment as the disappearance of head shaking in response to ear pinch. The animals are maintained at a constant body temperature of 37 °C by means of a heated plate. A thin steel wire is gently inserted into the trachea through a small incision near the cricoid cartilage. Coughs are evoked by pushing the steel wire to reach the bifurcation of the trachea 35 and 5 min before oral drug administration and 30, 60 and 120 min after treatment. One violent cough occurs upon each stimulation. Only those animals that respond to both mechanical stimulations before dosing are selected and then randomly assigned to receive the test drug at various doses or the standard (codeine 15, 30 and 60 mg/kg). Ten animals per dose are used.

SCREENING METHODS FOR EFFECTS ON BEHAVIOR AND MUSCLE COORDINATION

Open Field Test

The rats are observed in a square open field arena (68 × 68 × 45 cm) equipped with 2 rows of 8 photocells, sensitive to infrared light, placed 40 and 125 mm above the floor, respectively. The photocells are spaced 90 mm apart and the last photocell in a row is spaced 25 mm from the wall. Measurements are made in the dark in a ventilated, sound-attenuating box. Interruptions of photocell beams can be collected by a microcomputer and the following variables can be evaluated.

Motor activity: All interruptions of photo beams in the lower rows.

- **Peripheral motor activity:** Activation of photo beams in the lower rows, provided that the photo-beams spaced 25 mm from the wall were also activated.
- **Rearing:** All interruption of the photo beams in the upper rows.
- **Peripheral rearing:** Interruption of photo beams in the upper rows, provided that the photo beams spaced 25 mm from the wall were also activated.
- **Locomotion:** Successive interruptions of photocells in the lower rows when the animal is moving in the same direction.
- **Speed:** The time between successive photo beam interruptions during locomotion collected in 0.1 s categories.

Dose-response curves can be obtained for sedative and stimulant drugs, whereby the various parameters show different results. The effects of various doses are compared statistically with the values of controls and among themselves.

Hole-board Test

Mice of either sex (NMRI strain) with a weight between 18 and 22 g are used. The hole-board has a size of 40 × 40 cm. Sixteen holes with a diameter of 3 cm each are distributed evenly on the floor. The board is elevated so that the mouse poking its nose into the hole does not see the bottom. Nose-poking is thought to indicate curiosity and is measured by visual observation in the earliest description and counted by electronic devices in more recent modifications. Moreover, in the newer modifications motility is measured in addition by counting interruption of light beams. Usually, 6 animals are used for each dose and for controls. Thirty minutes after administration of the test compound the first animal is placed on the hole-board and tested for 5 min.

Inclined Plane

The plane consists of two rectangular plywood boards connected at one end by a hinge. One board is the base, the other is the movable inclined plane. Two plywood side panels with degrees marked on their surface are fixed on the base. A rubber mat with ridges 0.2 cm in height is fixed to the inclined plane which is set at 65 degrees. Male mice (Charles River strain) with a body weight between 20 and 30 g are used. The test compound or the standard are administered to groups of 10 mice either intraperitoneally or subcutaneously or orally. 30, 60 and 90 min thereafter, the mice are placed at the upper part of the inclined plane and are given 30 s to hang on or to fall off.

Evaluation

The peak time is determined as the time at which a compound produces the maximum performance deficit. At this time interval, a range of doses is tested using 10 animals per group. $ED50$ values are calculated.

Chimney test: Male mice (CD1, Charles River) weighing between 16 and 22 g are used in groups of 10 animals per dose. Pyrex-glass cylinders 30 cm long are required. The internal diameter varies with the animal's weight: for mice weighing 16 to 18 g, the diameter is 22 mm, for mice weighing 18 to 20 g, the diameter is 25 mm; for mice weighing 20 to 22 g, the diameter is 28 mm. Each tube has a mark 20 cm from its base. Initially, the tube is held in a horizontal position. At the end of the tube, near the mark, a mouse is introduced with the head forward. When the mouse reaches the other end of the tube, toward which it is pushed if necessary with a rod, the tube is moved to a vertical position. Immediately, the mouse tries to climb backwards and performs coordinated movements similar to an alpinist trying to pass through a chimney in the mountains. This gave the name for the test. The time required by the mouse to climb backwards out at the top of the cylinder is noted.

Evaluation

The $ED50$ (with 95% confidence limits), the dose for which 50% of the animals fail to climb backwards out of the tube within 30 s, is calculated by log-probit analysis.

Rotarod Method

The apparatus consists of a horizontal wooden rod or metal rod coated with rubber with 3 cm diameter attached to a motor with the speed adjusted to 2 rotations per minute. The rod is 75 cm in length and is divided into 6 sections by plastic discs, thereby allowing the simultaneous testing of 6 mice. The rod is in a height of about 50 cm above the table top in order to discourage the animals from jumping off the roller. Cages below the sections serve to restrict the movements of the animals when they fall from the roller. Male mice (CD-1 Charles River strain) with an weight between 20 and 30 g undergo a pretest on the apparatus. Only those animals which have demonstrated their ability to remain on the revolving rod for at least 1 minute are used for the test. The test compounds are administered intraperitoneally or orally. Thirty minutes after intraperitoneal or 60 min after oral administration the mice are placed for 1 min on the rotating rod. The number of animals falling from the roller during this time is counted.

SCREENING METHODS FOR ANTICONVULSANT ACTIVITY

Pentylenetetrazole (Metrazol) Induced Convulsions

Mice of either sex with a body weight between 18 and 22 g are used. The test compound or the reference drug is injected subcutaneously or intraperitoneally or given orally to groups of 10 mice. Another group of 10 mice serves as control. Fifteen min after sc.-injection, 30 min after i.p.-injection, or 60 min after oral administration – 60 mg/kg MTZ (Metrazol) are injected subcutaneously. Each animal is placed into an individual plastic cage for observation lasting 1 h. Seizures and tonic-clonic convulsions are recorded. At least 80% of the animals in the control group have to show convulsions. The number of protected animals in the treated groups is calculated as percentage of affected animals in the control group. ED_{50}-values can be calculated. Furthermore, the time interval between MTZ-injection and occurrence of seizures can be measured. The delay of onset is calculated in comparison with the control group.

Strychnine-induced Convulsions

The convulsing action of strychnine is due to interference with postsynaptic inhibition mediated by glycine. Glycine is an important inhibitory transmitter to motoneurons and interneurons in the spinal cord, and strychnine acts as a selective, competitive antagonist to block the inhibitory effects of glycine at all glycine receptors.

Groups of 10 mice of either sex having weight between 18 and 22 g are used. They are treated orally with the test compound or the standard (e.g. diazepam 5 mg/kg). One hour later the mice are injected with 2 mg/kg strychnine nitrate (IP). The time until occurrence of tonic extensor convulsions and death is noted during a 1 h period. With this dose of strychnine, convulsions are observed in 80% of the controls.

Evaluation

ED_{50}-values are calculated using various doses taking the percentage of the controls as 100%. For time-response curves the interval between treatment and strychnine injection varies from 30 to 120 min.

Isoniazid-induced Convulsions

Isoniazid can precipitate convulsions in patients with seizure disorders. The compound is regarded as a GABA-synthesis inhibitor.

Ten mice of either sex with a weight of 18 to 22 g are treated with the test compound or the standard (e.g. diazepam 10 mg/kg IP) by oral or intraperitoneal administration. Controls receive the vehicle only 30 min after IP or 60 min after oral treatment, the animals are injected with a subcutaneous dose of 300 mg/kg isoniazid (isonicotinic acid hydrazide). During the next 120 min, the occurrence of clonic seizures, tonic seizures and death is recorded.

SCREENING METHODS FOR ANTI-ANXIETY TEST

Light-dark Model

Mice and rats tend to explore a novel environment, but retreat from the aversive properties of a brightly-lit open field. In a two chambered system, where the animals can freely move between a brightly-lit open field and a dark corner, they show more crossings between the two chambers and more locomotor activity after treatment with anxiolytics. The numbers of crossings between the light and dark sites are recorded. The testing apparatus consists of a light and a dark chamber divided by a photocell-equipped zone. A partition containing a 13 cm long $\times$ 5 cm high opening separates the dark one third from the bright two thirds of the cage. The cage rests on an Animex® activity monitor which counts total locomotor activity. An electronic system using four sets of photocells across the partition automatically counts movements through the partition and clocks the time spent in the light and dark compartments. Naive male mice or rats are placed into the cage. The animals are treated 30 min before the experiment with the test drugs or the vehicle intraperitoneally and are then observed for 10 min. Groups of 6–8 animals are used for each dose.

Social Interaction in Rats

Male Sprague-Dawley rats (225–275 g body weight) are housed in groups of 5 animals The apparatus used for the detection of changes in social behaviour and exploratory behaviour consists of a Perspex open-topped box (51 $\times$ 51 cm and 20 cm high) with 17 $\times$ 17 cm marked areas on the floor. One hour prior to the test, two naive rats from separate housing cages are treated with the test compound orally. They are placed into the box (with 60 W bright illumination 17 cm above) and their behaviour is observed over a 10-min period by remote video recording. Two types of behaviour can be noted: social interaction between the animals is determined by timing the sniffing of partner, crawling under or climbing over the partner, genital investigation of partner, and following partner. Exploratory motion is measured as the number of crossings of the lines marked on the floor of the test box. Six pairs are used for each dose.

Elevated Plus Maze Test

The plus-maze consists of two open arms, 50 $\times$ 10 $\times$ 40 cm, and two enclosed arms, 50 $\times$ 10 $\times$ 40 cm, with an open roof, arranged so that the two open arms are opposite to each other. The maze is elevated to a height of 50 cm. The rats (200–250 g body weight) are housed in pairs for 10 days prior to testing in the apparatus. During this time the rats are handled by the investigator on alternate days to reduce stress. Groups consist of 6 rats for each dose. Thirty min after IP administration of the test drug or the standard, the rat is placed in the center of the maze, facing one of the enclosed arms. During a 5 min test period the following measures are taken: the number of entries into and time spent in the open and enclosed arms; the total number of arm entries. The procedure is conducted preferably in a sound attenuated room, with observations made from an adjacent room via a remote control TV camera.

Evaluation

Motor activity and open arm exploratory time are registered. The values of treated groups are expressed as percentage of controls. Benzodiazepines and valproate decrease motor activity and increase open arm exploratory time.

Staircase Test

In the staircase paradigm, step-climbing is purported to reflect exploratory or locomotor activity, while rearing behaviour is an index of anxiety. The number of rearings and steps climbed are recorded in a 5 min period. The dissociation of these parameters is considered to be characteristic for anxiolytic drugs. For experiments with mice the staircase is composed of five identical steps 2.5 cm high, 10 cm wide and 7.5 cm deep. The internal height of the walls is constant along the whole length of the staircase. Naïve male mice (Charles River strain) with a weight between 18 and 24 g are used. Each animal is used only once. The drug or the standard is administered orally 1 h or 30 min subcutaneously before the test. The animal is placed on the floor of the box with its back to the staircase.

The number of steps climbed and the number of rears are counted over a 3-min period. A step is considered to be climbed only if the mouse has placed all four paws on the step. In order to simplify the observation, the number of steps descended is not taken into account. After each test, the box has to be cleaned in order to eliminate any olfactory cues which might modify the behaviour of the next animal.

Evaluation

Twelve mice are used for the untreated control group, each drug group, and for the group receiving the standard. The average number of steps and rearings of the control group is taken as 100%. The values of treated animals are expressed as percentage of the controls.

SCREENING METHODS FOR HYPNOTIC ACTIVITY

Potentiation of Hexobarbital Sleeping Time

The test is used to elucidate CNS-active properties of drugs. Not only hypnotics, sedatives, and tranquilisers but also antidepressants at high doses are known to prolong hexobarbital induced sleep after a single dose of hexobarbital.

Procedure

Groups of 10 male NMRI-mice with an average weight of 18–22 g are used. They are dosed orally, IP or SC with the test compound or the reference standard (e.g. 3 mg/kg diazepam orally). Thirty min after IP or SC injection or 60 min after oral dosing 60 mg/kg hexobarbital is injected intravenously. The animals are placed on their backs on a warmed (37 °C) pad and the duration of loss of the righting reflex (starting at the time of hexobarbital injection) is measured until they regain their righting reflexes. Injection of 60 mg/kg hexobarbital usually causes anesthesia for about 15 min. If there is any doubt as to the reappearance of the righting reflex, the subject is placed gently on its back again and, if it rights itself within one minute, this time is considered as the endpoint.

Experimental Insomnia in Rats

Male Wistar rats (200–275 g) are prepared for chronic electroencephalographic and electromyographic recordings. Four silver/silver chloride epidural electrodes and two disc nuchal electrodes are implanted. A minimum of 10 days is allowed for recovery from surgery. The animals are placed into sound-attenuated recording chambers with grid floors. The frontal-occipital electroencephalogram and the electromyogram are recorded via nonrestraining recording leads on a polygraph and a tape recorder. On the control day, the animals are dosed with the vehicle and a control. Nonstress recording is obtained for 8 h. On the next day, the animals are again injected with the vehicle and then exposed to electric footshocks for 8 h. The footshock is delivered through the grid floor of the recording chamber using the EMG leads as in different electrodes, in the form of a 0.5 mA pulse of 15 ms width for 30 s at 1 Hz. During the footshock the EEG and EMG recording circuits are automatically interrupted. The delivery of electric footshock is triggered automatically by two adjustable timers. In this way, each shock period of 30 s is followed by an interval of 30 min. On the next day, the rats are dosed with the test compound or the standard and recordings are obtained during a shock session of 8 h.

SCREENING METHODS FOR BEHAVIOURAL TESTS

Catalepsy Antagonism in Chicken

Adult white Leghorn chicken are used. The animal is grasped with both hands whereby the left hand pushes the chicken slightly down and the right hand supports the animal from the ventral side. Immediately, the chicken is turned on its back and held with the right hand for 1 min. Usually, cataleptic numbness occurs immediately. The cataleptic state can be sustained by slight pushing the head of the animal on the table. After 1 min the right hand is carefully withdrawn. The chicken remains in the cataleptic state for several mins up to 1 h. The cataleptic rigour is interrupted by noise or fast movements of the observer. Clapping of the hands above the head arouses the chicken which jumps up and runs away. The chicken is always aroused by pulling on the wings. The animals are pretested in order to be sure about the cataleptic behaviour of an individual chicken.

As already found by previous investigators, the experiment can be repeated several times. Control studies showed that in untreated animals the phenomenon could be elicited 6 times every 30 min during a period 5 days. After the control experiments, the animals are injected IP with the test compound or the vehicle. The test is performed 4 times every 30 min during 2 h. The test is considered to be positive if the cataleptic rigour does not occur after treatment or is interrupted spontaneously within 1 min at least twice during the 2 h test period.

Tail Suspension Test in Mice

Male Balb/cJ mice weighing 20–25 g are used preferentially. They are housed in plastic cages for at least 10 days prior to testing in a 12 h light cycle with food and water freely available. Animals are transported from the housing room to the testing area in their own cages and allowed to adapt to the new environment for 1 h before testing. Groups of 10 animals are treated with the test compounds or the vehicle by intraperitoneal injection 30 min prior to testing. For the test, the mice are suspended on the edge of a shelf 58 cm above a table top by adhesive tape placed approximately 1 cm from the tip of the tail. The duration of immobility is recorded for a period of 5 min. Mice are considered immobile when they hang passively and completely motionless for at least 1 min.

SCREENING METHODS FOR LOCAL ANESTHETIC AGENTS

Conduction Anesthesia in the Sciatic Nerve of the Frog

Frogs (*Rana temporaria*) of either sex are used and are kept at 4 °C. The frog is decapitated with a pair of scissors. The skin is incised in the thigh region at both sides and the sciatic nerves are carefully exposed in the thigh, avoiding any stretching and injury of the nerve. The frog is suspended on a vertical board. Small pieces of white cotton are soaked with different concentrations of the test preparations (between 0.05% and 1%) or the standard and placed gently around the sciatic nerve for 1 min. Then the cotton swab is removed and the frog is placed with its extremities into a bath with 0.65% NaCl solution. This allows testing for duration and reversibility of the local anesthetic effect. One side is used for the test preparation and the other for the standard (e.g., 0.25% butanilicaine). Every 3 min the frog is removed from the bath and the toes of the legs or the ankle joint are pinched three times with a small forceps. The reflex contraction is abolished when conduction anesthesia is effective. The stimuli are repeated every 3 min until anesthesia vanishes. Two to five frogs are used for each concentration.

Evaluation

Time of onset and duration of anesthesia are recorded for each concentration. Time-response and dose-response curves can be established.

Conduction Anesthesia in the Sciatic Nerve of the Rat
Procedure
Male Wistar or Sprague Dawley rats weighing 125 to 175 g are used. The animal is suspended in a prone position by grasping the base of the tail and thoracic cage. A hind limb is extended to its full length and the depression for needle insertion is located by palpation with the left index finger. The site of injection is the area under the skin at the junction of the biceps femoris and the gluteus maximus muscles. The sciatic nerve is blocked in the mid thigh region with 0.2 ml of the drug solution administered by a 24- to 25-gauge needle attached to a 0.25 ml tuberculin syringe. Usually, a 1% solution of the test drug in 0.9% NaCl is used as a test solution. The other leg is used for a control drug (e.g., procaine or lidocaine). Immediately after the injection, repeated checks of the digit of the foot and the walking behaviour are performed. In the normal foot, the digits are wide apart, while in the blocked leg the digits of the foot are close together. Also the successful block is evidenced by dragging of the leg and an inability of the animal to use the leg in walking up the inclined wire mesh cover of the cage. After the time of block for each leg is noted, each animal is examined every 5 to 10 min in order to note the time of recovery.

Evaluation
From the data, averages for onset and duration of action are calculated, plus the frequency of blocks are noted.

Conduction Anesthesia on the Mouse Tail
Groups of 10 mice (NMRI-strain) of both sexes with a weight between 18 and 22 g are used for each dose. Before administration of the test compound or the standard the normal reaction time is determined. The animal is placed into a small cage with an opening for the tail at the rear wall. The tail is held gently by the investigator. By opening of a shutter, a light beam exerting radiant heat is directed to the proximal third of the tail. After about 6 s, the reaction of the animal is observed by the investigator. The mouse tries to pull the tail away and turns the head. The shutter is closed with a switch when the investigator notices this reaction. Mice with a reaction time of more than 6 s are not used in the test. The test compounds and the standard are injected in a volume of 0.1 ml on both sides in the area of the tail root. The animals are submitted to the radiant heat again after 10 min. The area of heating is about 1.5 cm distal to the injection site. For each individual animal the reaction time is noted.

SCREENING METHODS FOR ANTI-INFLAMMATORY, ANALGESIC AND ANTI-PYRETIC AGENTS

Methods for Analgesic Activity - (HAFFNER's Tail Clip Method)
Procedure
An artery clip is applied to the root of the tail of mice and the reaction time is noted. Male mice (Charles River strain or other strains) with a weight between 18 and 25 g are used. The control group consists of 10 mice. The test compounds are administered

subcutaneously to fed mice or orally to fasted animals. The test groups and the control group consist of 7–10 mice. The drug is administered 15, 30 or 60 min prior to testing. An artery clip is applied to the root of the tail (approximately 1 cm from the body) to induce pain. The animal quickly responds to this noxious stimuli by biting the clip or the tail near the location of the clip. The time between stimulation onset and response is measured by a stopwatch in 1/10 seconds increments.

Evaluation

A cut-off time is determined by taking the average reaction time plus 3 times the standard deviation of the combined latencies of the control mice at all time periods.

Radiant Heat Method

The animal is put into a small cage with an opening for the tail at the rear wall. The tail is held gently by the investigator. By opening of a shutter, a light beam exerting radiant heat is directed to the proximal third of the tail. For about 6 s the reaction of the animal is observed by the investigator. The mouse tries to pull the tail away and turns the head. With a switch the shutter is closed as soon as the investigator notices this reaction. Mice with a reaction time of more than 6 s are not used in the test. The escape reaction which is the endpoint of this test can be regarded as a complex phenomenon mediated by the brain. In contrast, the simple tail flick as an endpoint of this test may be mediated as a spinal reflex. Therefore the observation of the escape reaction can be regarded as a true assessment of the influence of the drug on the brain.

The test compounds and the standard are administered either orally or subcutaneously. The animals are submitted to the same testing procedure after 30, 60 and eventually 120 min.

Hot Plate Method

The paws of mice and rats are very sensitive to heat at temperatures which are not damaging the skin. The responses are jumping, withdrawal of the paws and licking of the paws. The time until these responses occur is prolonged after administration of centrally acting analgesics, whereas peripheral analgesics of the acetylsalicylic acid or phenyl-acetic acid type do not generally affect these responses.

Procedure

The method originally described by Woolfe and Mac Donald (1944) has been modified by several investigators. The following modification has been proven to be suitable:

Groups of 10 mice of either sex with an initial weight of 18 to 22 g are used for each dose. The hot plate, which is commercially available, consists of a electrically heated surface. The temperature is controlled for 55° to 56 °C. This can be a copper plate or a heated glass surface. The animals are placed on the hot plate and the time until either licking or jumping occurs is recorded by a stop-watch. The latency is recorded before and after 20, 60 and 90 min following oral or subcutaneous administration of the standard or the test compound.

Evaluation

The prolongation of the latency times comparing the values before and after administration of the test compounds or the values of the control with the experimental groups can be used for statistical comparison.

TAIL IMMERSION TEST

The method has been developed to be selective for morphine- like compounds. The procedure is based on the observation that morphine-like drugs are selectively capable of prolonging the reaction time of the typical tail-withdrawal reflex in rats induced by immersing the end of the tail in warm water at 55 °C.

Procedure

Young female Wistar rats (170–210 g body weight) are used. They are placed into individual restraining cages leaving the tail hanging out freely. The animals are allowed to adapt to the cages for 30 min before testing. The lower 5 cm portion of the tail is marked. This part of the tail is immersed in a cup of freshly filled water of exactly 55 °C. Within a few seconds the rat reacts by withdrawing the tail. The reaction time is recorded in 0.5 s units by a stopwatch. After each determination the tail is carefully dried. The reaction time is determined before and periodically after either oral or subcutaneous administration of the test substance, e.g., after 0.5, 1, 2, 3, 4 and 6 h. The cut off time of the immersion is 15 s. The withdrawal time of untreated animals is between 1 and 5.5 s. A withdrawal time of more than 6 s therefore is regarded as a positive response.

Evaluation

$ED50$ values can be calculated for each compound and time response curves (onset, peak and duration of the effect) are measured.

Formalin Test in Rats

Male Wistar rats weighing 180–300 g are administered 0.05 ml of 10% formalin into the dorsal portion of the front paw. The test drug is administered simultaneously either subcutaneously or orally. Each individual rat is placed into a clear plastic cage for observation. Readings are taken at 30 and 60 min and scored according to a pain scale. Pain responses are indicated by elevation or favouring of the paw or excessive licking and biting of the paw. Analgesic response or protection is indicated if both paws are resting on the floor with no obvious favouring of the injected paw.

Writhing Tests

Pain is induced by injection of irritants into the peritoneal cavity of mice. The animals react with a characteristic stretching behaviour which is called writhing. The test is suitable to detect analgesic activity although some psychoactive agents also show activity. Mice of either sex with a weight between 20 and 25 g are used. Phenylquinone in a concentration of 0.02% is suspended in a 1% suspension of carboxymethylcellulose.

An aliquot of 0.25 ml of this suspension is injected intraperitoneally. Groups of 6 animals are used for controls and treated mice. Preferably, two groups of 6 mice are used as controls. Test animals are administered the drug or the standard at various pretreatment times prior to phenylquinone administration. The mice are placed individually into glass beakers and five min are allowed to elapse. The mice are then observed for a period of ten min and the number of writhes is recorded for each animal. For scoring purposes, a writhe is indicated by stretching of the abdomen with simultaneous stretching of at least one hind limb. The formula for computing percent inhibition is: average writhes in the control group minus writhes in the drug group divided by writhes in the control group times 100%.

SCREENING METHODS FOR ANTI-INFLAMMATORY AGENTS

Inflammation has different phases: the first phase is caused by an increase of vascular permeability resulting in exudation of fluid from the blood into the interstitial space, the second one by infiltration of leukocytes from the blood into the tissues and the third one by granuloma formation. Accordingly, anti-inflammatory tests have to be divided into those measuring acute inflammation, subacute inflammation and chronic repair processes. In some cases, the screening is directed to test compounds for local application. The inflammatory process involves a series of events that can be elicited by numerous stimuli, e.g., infectious agents, ischemia, antigen-antibody interactions, chemical, thermal or mechanical injury. The response is accompanied by the clinical signs of erythema, edema, hyperalgesia and pain.

Ultraviolet Erythema in Guinea Pigs

Eighteen hours prior to testing, the animals are shaved on both flanks and on the back. Then they are chemically depilated by a commercial depilation product or by a suspension of barium sulfide. Twenty minutes later, the depilation paste and the fur are rinsed off in running warm water. On the next day, the test compound is dissolved (or suspended) in the vehicle and half the dose of the test compound is administered by gavage (at 10 ml/kg) 30 min before ultraviolet exposure. Control animals are treated with the vehicle alone. Four animals are used for each treatment group and control. The guinea pigs are placed in a leather cuff with a hole of 1.5 × 2.5 cm size punched in it, allowing the ultraviolet radiation to reach only this area. An original Hanau ultraviolet burner Q 600 is warmed up for about 30 min prior to use and placed at a constant distance (20 cm) above the animal. Following a 2 min ultraviolet exposure, the remaining half of the test compound is administered. The investigator has to protect himself/herself by gloves and ultraviolet glasses. The erythema is scored 2 and 4 h after exposure. The degree of erythema is evaluated visually by 2 different investigators in a double-blinded manner. The followings scores are given:

- 0 = no erythema
- 1 = weak erythema

- 2 = strong erythema
- 4 = very strong erythema

Vascular Permeability

Male Sprague-Dawley rats with a body weight between 160 and 200 g are used. The ventral sides of the animal are shaved. Five ml/kg of an 1% solution of Evan's blue are injected intravenously. One hour later the animals are dosed with the test compound orally or intraperitoneally or with the vehicle. Ten animals are used for each test group and the control. Thirty minutes later, the animals are briefly anaesthetised with ether and 0.05 ml of a 0.01% solution of test compounds under investigation is injected cutaneously at three sites both at the left and ventral side. Ninety minutes after the injection of test compounds, the animals are sacrificed by ether anesthesia. The abdominal skin is removed and the dye infiltrated areas of the skin are measured.

Evaluation

The diameter of the dye-infiltrated areas is measured in millimeters in two perpendicular directions and the mean values of all injection sites in one animal are calculated.

Croton-oil Ear Edema in Rats and Mice

For tests in mice, the irritant is composed as follows (v/v): 1 part Croton oil, 10 parts ethanol, 20 parts pyridine, 69 parts ethyl ether. For tests in rats, the following mixture is prepared (v/v): 4 parts Croton oil, 10 parts ethanol, 20 parts pyridine, 66 parts ethyl ether. The standards and the test compounds are dissolved in this solution. For tests in mice male, NMRI-mice with an weight of 22 g, for tests in rats male Sprague-Dawley rats with a weight of 70 g are used. Ten animals are used for controls and each test group. The test compounds are dissolved in a concentration of 0.03 mg/ml to 1 mg/ml for mice and in a 3 to 10 times higher concentration for rats in the irritant solution. On both sides of the right ear 0.01 ml in mice or 0.02 ml in rats are applied. Controls receive only the irritant solvent. The left ear remains untreated. The irritant is applied under ether anesthesia. Four hours after application the animals are sacrificed under anesthesia. Both ears are removed and discs of 8 mm diameter are punched. The discs are weighed immediately and the weight difference between the treated and untreated ear is recorded indicating the degree of inflammatory edema.

Paw Edema

Male or female Sprague-Dawley rats with a body weight between 100 and 150 g are used. The animals are starved overnight. To ensure uniform hydration, the rats receive 5 ml of water by stomach tube (controls) or the test drug dissolved or suspended in the same volume. Thirty minutes later, the rats are challenged by a subcutaneous injection of 0.05 ml of 1% solution of carrageenan into the plantar side of the left hind paw. The paw is marked with ink at the level of the lateral malleolus and immersed in mercury up to this mark. The paw volume is measured plethysmographically immediately after injection, again 3 and 6 h, and eventually 24 h after challenge.

Granuloma Pouch Technique

Male or female Sprague-Dawley rats with a body weight between 150 and 200 g are used. Ten animals are taken for controls and for test groups. The back of the animals is shaved and disinfected. With a very thin needle a pneumoderma is made in the middle of the dorsal skin by injection of 20 ml of air under ether anesthesia. Into the resulting oval airpouch 0.5 ml of a 1% solution of Croton oil in sesame oil is injected avoiding any leakage of air. Forty-eight hours later the air is withdrawn from the pouch and 72 h later any resulting adhesions are broken. Instead of croton oil 1 ml of a 20% suspension of carrageenan in sesame oil can be used as irritant. Starting with the formation of the pouch, the animals are treated every day either orally or subcutaneously with the test compound or the standard. For testing local activity, the test compound is injected directly into the air sac at the same time as the irritant. On the 4th or the 5th day the animals are sacrificed under anesthesia. The pouch is opened and the exudate is collected in glass cylinders. Controls have an exudates volume between 6 and 12 ml, which is reduced dose dependent in the treated animals.

Granuloma Formation

Male Wistar rats with an average weight of 200 g are anaesthetised with ether. The back skin is shaved and disinfected with 70% ethanol. An incision is made in the lumbar region. By a blunted forceps subcutaneous tunnels are formed and a sterilised cotton pellet is placed on both sides in the scapular region. The pellets are either standardised for use in dentistry weighing 20 mg or pellets formed from raw cotton which produce a more pronounced inflammation than bleached cotton. The animals are treated for 7 days subcutaneously or orally. Then, the animals are sacrificed, the pellets prepared and dried until the weight remains constant. The net dry weight, i.e. after subtracting the weight of the cotton pellet is determined.

SCREENING METHODS FOR ANTI-PYRETIC DRUGS

Antipyretic Testing in Rats

The subcutaneous injection of Brewer's yeast suspension is known to produce fever in rats. A decrease in temperature can be achieved by administration of compounds with antipyretic activity. A 15% suspension of Brewer's yeast in 0.9% saline is prepared. Groups of 6 male or female Wistar rats with a body weight of 150 g are used. By insertion of a thermocouple to a depth of 2 cm into the rectum the initial rectal temperatures are recorded. The animals are fevered by injection of 10 ml/kg of Brewer's yeast suspension subcutaneously in the back below the nape of the neck. The site of injection is massaged in order to spread the suspension beneath the skin. The room temperature is kept at 22–24 °C. Immediately after yeast administration, food is withdrawn. 18 h post challenge, the rise in rectal temperature is recorded.

The measurement is repeated after 30 min. Only animals with a body temperature of at least 38 °C are taken into the test. The animals receive the test compound or the standard drug by oral administration. Rectal temperatures are recorded again 30, 60, 120 and 180 min post dosing.

Antipyretic Testing in Rabbits

Lipopolysaccharides from Gram-negative bacteria, e.g. *E. coli*, induce fever in rabbits after intravenous injection. Rabbits of both sexes and of various strains with a body weight between 3 and 5 kg can be used. The animals are placed into suitable cages and thermocouples connected with an automatic recorder are introduced into the rectum. The animals are allowed to adapt to the cages for 60 min. Then 0.2 ml/kg containing 0.2 µg lipopolysaccharide are injected intravenously into the rabbit ear. Sixty min later the test compound is administered either subcutaneously or orally. Body temperature is monitored for at least 3 h.

SCREENING METHODS FOR ANTI-DIABETIC AGENTS

Pancreatectomy in Dogs

Male Beagle dogs weighing 12–16 kg are used. The animal is anesthetised with an intravenous injection of 50 mg/kg pentobarbital sodium and placed on its back. After removal of the fur and disinfection of the skin a midline incision is made from the xyphoid process reaching well below the umbilicus. Bleeding vessels are ligated and the abdomen is entered through the linea alba. The falciform ligament is carefully removed and the vessels ligated. A self-retaining retractor is applied. By passing the right hand along the stomach to the pylorus, the duodenum with the head of the pancreas is brought into the operating field. First, the mesentery at the unicate process is cut and the process itself is dissected free. The glandular tissue is peeled off from the inferior pancreatico-duodenal artery and vein. The vessels themselves are carefully preserved.

Alloxan Induced Diabetes

Rabbits weighing 2.0 to 3.5 kg are infused via the ear vein with 150 mg/kg alloxan monohydrate (5.0 g/100 ml, pH 4.5) for 10 min resulting in 70% of the animals to become hyperglycemic and uricosuric. The rest of the animals either die or are only temporarily hyperglycemic.

Streptozotocin Induced Diabetes

Male Wistar rats weighing 150–220 g fed with a standard diet are injected with 60 mg/kg streptozotocin (Calbiochem) intravenously. As with alloxan, three phases of blood glucose changes are observed. Initially, blood glucose is increased, reaching values of 150–200 mg% after 3 hours. Six–eight hours after streptozotocin, the serum insulin values are increased up to 4 times, resulting in a hypoglycemic phase which is followed by persistent hyperglycemia. Severity and onset of diabetic symptoms depend on the dose of streptozotocin. After the dose of 60 mg/kg IV, symptoms occur after 24–48 h with hyperglycemia up to 800 mg%, glucosuria and ketonemia. Histologically, the beta-cells are degranulated or even necrotic. A steady state is reached after 10–14 days allowing to use the animals for pharmacological tests.

Insulin Deficiency due to Insulin Antibodies

Bovine insulin, dissolved in acidified water (pH 3.0), is incorporated in a water-oil emulsion based on complete Freund's adjuvant or a mixture of paraffin oil and lanolin. A dose of 1 mg insulin is injected in divided doses subcutaneously to male guinea pigs weighing 300–400 g. Injections are given at monthly intervals and the guinea pigs are bled by cardiac puncture two weeks after the second and subsequent doses of antigen. It is possible to get 10 ml blood from every animal once a month. Intravenous injection of 0.25–1.0 ml guinea pig antiinsulin serum to rats induces a dose-dependent increase of blood glucose reaching values up to 300 mg%. This effect is unique to guinea pig anti-insulin serum and is due to neutralisation by insulin antibodies of endogenous insulin secreted by the injected animal. In this way a state of insulin deficiency is induced. It persists as long as antibodies capable of reacting with insulin remain in the circulation. Slow rate intravenous infusion or intraperitoneal injection prolongs the effect for more than a few hours. However, large doses and prolonged administration accompanied by ketonemia, ketonuria, glucosuria, and acidosis are fatal to the animals. After lower doses, the diabetic syndrome is reversible after a few hours.

GLOSSARY

Active transport: Active transport is the transport of a solute across a biological membrane from low to high concentration that requires the expenditure of (metabolic) energy.

Address-message concept: Address-message concept refers to compounds in which part of the molecule is required for binding (address) and part for the biological action (message).

ADME: Abbreviation for Absorption, Distribution, Metabolism, Excretion.

Addiction: Addiction can be defined as a habitual form of behaviour. It need not be harmful. For example, one can be addicted to eating chocolate or watching television without suffering more than a bad case of toothache or a surplus of soap operas.

Affinity: Affinity is the tendency of a molecule to associate with another. The affinity of a drug is its ability to bind to its biological target (receptor, enzyme, transport system, etc.) For pharmacological receptors it can be thought of as the frequency with which the drug, when brought into the proximity of a receptor by diffusion, will reside at a position of minimum free energy within the force field of that receptor.

For an agonist (or for an antagonist) the numerical representation of affinity is the reciprocal of the equilibrium dissociation constant of the ligand-receptor complex denoted K_A, calculated as the rate constant for offset (k_{-1}) divided by the rate constant for onset (k_1).

Agonist: An agonist is an endogenous substance or a drug that can interact with a receptor and initiate a physiological or a pharmacological response characteristic of that receptor (contraction, relaxation, secretion, enzyme activation, etc.).

Allosteric binding sites: Allosteric binding sites are contained in many enzymes and receptors. As a consequence of the binding to allosteric binding sites, the interaction with the normal ligand may be either enhanced or reduced.

Allosteric enzyme: An allosteric enzyme is an enzyme that contains a region to which small, regulatory molecules ("effectors") may bind in addition to and separate from the substrate binding site and thereby affect the catalytic activity.

On binding the effector, the catalytic activity of the enzyme towards the substrate may be enhanced, in which case the effector is an activator, or reduced, in which case it is a de-activator or inhibitor.

Allosteric regulation: Allosteric regulation is the regulation of the activity of allosteric enzymes.

Alkaloids: Nitrogen-containing organic compounds of plant origin; often basic, and having intense biological activity.

Alkalosis: A metabolic condition in which the capacity of the body to buffer OH⁻ is diminished; usually accompanied by an increase in blood pH.

Amino-acid residue (in a polypeptide): When two or more amino acids combine to form a peptide, the elements of water are removed, and what remains of each amino acid is called anamino-acid residue. Amino-acid residues are therefore structures that lack a hydrogen atom of the amino group (-NH-CHR-COOH), or the hydroxy moiety of the carboxy group (NH_2-CHR-CO-), or both (-NH-CHR-CO-); all units of a peptide chain are therefore amino-acid residues. (Residues of amino acids that contain two amino groups or two carboxy groups may be joined by isopeptide bonds, and so may not have the formulas shown). The residue in a peptide that has an amino group that is free, or at least not acylated by another amino-acid residue (it may, for example, be acylated or formylated), is called N-terminal; it is the N-terminus. The residue that has a free carboxy group, or at least does not acylate another amino-acid residue, (it may, for example, acylate ammonia to give -NH-CHR-CO-NH_2), is called C-terminal.

Symbols for amino acids (use of the one-letter symbols should be restricted to the comparison of long sequences) :

A	Ala	Alanine
B	Asx	Asparagine or aspartic acid
C	Cys	Cysteine
D	Asp	Aspartic acid
E	Glu	Glutamic acid
F	Phe	Phenylalanine
G	Gly	Glycine
H	His	Histidine
I	Ile	Isoleucine
K	Lys	Lysine
L	Leu	Leucine
M	Met	Methionine
N	Asn	Asparagine
P	Pro	Proline
Q	Gln	Glutamine
R	Arg	Arginine
S	Ser	Serine
T	Thr	Threonine
V	Val	Valine
W	Trp	Tryptophan
Y	Tyr	Tyrosine
Z	Glx	Glutamine or glutamic acid

Analog: An analog is a drug whose structure is related to that of another drug but whose chemical and biological properties may be quite different.

Antibacterial Agent: A synthetic or naturally occurring agent which can kill or inhibit the growth of bacterial cells.

Antibiotic: An antibacterial agent derived from a natural source (e.g. penicillin from *Penicillium* mold).

Antagonist: An antagonist is a drug or a compound that opposes the physiological effects of another. At the receptor level, it is a chemical entity that opposes the receptor-associated responses normally induced by another bioactive agent.

Antimetabolite: An antimetabolite is a structural analog of an intermediate (substrate or coenzyme) in a physiologically occurring metabolic pathway that acts by replacing the natural substrate thus blocking or diverting the biosynthesis of physiologically important substances.

Antisense molecule: An antisense molecule is an oligonucleotide or analog thereof that is complementary to a segment of RNA (ribonucleic acid) or DNA (deoxyribonucleic acid) and that binds to it and inhibits its normal function.

Angstrom (Å): A unit of length (10^{-8} cm) used to indicate molecular dimensions.

Anhydride: The product of the condensation of two carboxyl or phosphate groups in which the elements of water are eliminated to form a compound with the general structure R–X–O–X–R, where X is either carbon or phosphorus.
$$\begin{array}{cc} \| & \| \\ O & O \end{array}$$

ATP (adenosine triphosphate): A ribonucleoside 5'-triphosphate functioning as a phosphate group donor in the cell energy cycle; carries chemical energy between metabolic pathways by serving as a shared intermediate coupling endergonic and exergonic reactions.

ATP synthase: An enzyme complex that forms ATP from ADP and phosphate during oxidative phosphorylation in the inner mitochondrial membrane or the bacterial plasma membrane, and during photophosphorylation in chloroplasts.

ATPase: An enzyme that hydrolyzes ATP to yield ADP and phosphate; usually coupled to some process requiring energy.

Autacoid: An autacoid is a biological substance secreted by various cells whose physiological activity is restricted to the vicinity of its release; it is often referred to as local hormone.

Autoreceptor: An autoreceptor, present at a nerve ending, is a receptor that regulates, via positive or negative feedback processes, the synthesis and/or release of its own physiological ligand.

Bacteriostatic: Bacteriostatic drugs inhibit the growth and multiplication of bacteria, but do not directly kill them (e.g. sulfonamides, tetracyclines, chloramphenicol).

Bactericidal: Bactericidal drugs irreversibly damage and kill bacteria, usually by attacking the cell wall or plasma membrane (e.g. penicillins, cephalosporins, polymyxins).

Bioassay: A bioassay is a procedure for determining the concentration, purity, and/or biological activity of a substance (e.g., vitamin, hormone, plant growth factor, antibiotic, enzyme) by measuring its effect on an organism, tissue, cell, enzyme or receptor preparation compared to a standard preparation.

Bioisostere: A bioisostere is a compound resulting from the exchange of an atom or of a group of atoms with another, broadly similar, atom or group of atoms. The objective of a bioisosteric replacement is to create a new compound with similar biological properties to the parent compound. The bioisosteric replacement may be physicochemically or topologically based.

Bioprecursor prodrug: A bioprecursor prodrug is a prodrug that does not imply the linkage to a carrier group, but results from a molecular modification of the active principle itself. This modification generates a new compound, able to be transformed metabolically or chemically, the resulting compound being the active principle.

Biotransformation: Biotransformation is the chemical conversion of substances by living organisms or enzyme preparations.

CADD: Computer-assisted drug design.

Carrier-linked prodrug (Carrier prodrug): A carrier-linked prodrug is a prodrug that contains a temporary linkage of a given active substance with a transient carrier group that produces improved physicochemical or pharmacokinetic properties and that can be easily removed *in vivo*, usually by a hydrolytic cleavage.

Cascade prodrug: A cascade prodrug is a prodrug for which the cleavage of the carrier group becomes effective only after unmasking an activating group.

Catabolism: Catabolism consists of reactions involving endogenous organic substrates to provide chemically available energy (e.g., ATP) and/or to generate metabolic intermediates used in subsequent anabolic reactions.

Catabolite: A catabolite is a naturally occurring metabolite.

Citric Acid Cycle: A cyclic system of enzymatic reactions for the oxidation of acetyl residues to carbon dioxide, in which formation of citrate is the first step; also known as the Krebs cycle or tricarboxylic acid cycle (TCA cycle).

Chromatography: A process in which complex mixtures of molecules are separated by many repeated partitionings between a flowing (mobile) phase and a stationary phase.

Clone: A clone is a population of genetically identical cells produced from a common ancestor. Sometimes, "clone" is also used for a number of recombinant DNA (deoxyribonucleic acid) molecules all carrying the same inserted sequence.

Codon: A codon is the sequence of three consecutive nucleotides that occurs in mRNA which directs the incorporation of a specific amino acid into a protein or represents the starting or termination signals of protein synthesis.

Coenzyme: A coenzyme is a dissociable, low-molecular weight, non-proteinaceous organic compound (often nucleotide) participating in enzymatic reactions as acceptor or donor of chemical groups or electrons.

Combinatorial synthesis: Combinatorial synthesis is a process to prepare large sets of organic compounds by combining sets of building blocks.

Combinatorial library: A combinatorial library is a set of compounds prepared by combinatorial synthesis.

CoMFA: (*Comparative Molecular Field Analysis*). Comparative molecular field analysis (CoMFA) is a 3D-QSAR method that uses statistical correlation techniques for the analysis of the quantitative relationship between the biological activity of a set of compounds with a specified alignment, and their three-dimensional electronic and steric properties. Other properties such as hydrophobicity and hydrogen bonding can also be incorporated into the analysis.

Computational chemistry: Computational chemistry is a discipline using mathematical methods for the calculation of molecular properties or for the simulation of molecular behaviour.

Computer-assisted drug design (CADD): Computer-assisted drug design involves all computer-assisted techniques used to discover, design and optimize biologically active compounds with putative use as drugs.

Congener: A congener is a substance literally *con-* (with) *generated* or synthesized by essentially the same synthetic chemical reactions and the same procedures. Analogs are substances that are analogous in some respect to the prototype agent in chemical structure. Clearly congeners may be analogs or vice versa but not necessarily. The term congener, while most often a synonym for homologue, has become somewhat more diffuse in meaning so that the terms congener and analog are frequently used interchangeably in the literature.

Co-operativity: It is the interaction process by which binding of a ligand to one site on a macromolecule (enzyme, receptor, etc.) influences binding at a second site, e.g. between the substrate binding sites of an allosteric enzyme. Cooperative enzymes typically display a sigmoid (S-shaped) plot of the reaction rate against substrate concentration. (See also allosteric binding sites).

3D-QSAR: Three-dimensional Quantitative Structure-Activity Relationship: A three-dimensional quantitative structure-activity relationship is the analysis of the quantitative relationship between the biological activity of a set of compounds and their spatial properties using statistical methods.

De novo design: *De novo* design is the design of bioactive compounds by incremental construction of a ligand model within a model of the receptor or enzyme active site, the structure of which is known from X-ray or nuclear magnetic resonance (NMR) data.

Distomer: A distomer is the enantiomer of a chiral compound that is the less potent for a particular action. This definition does not excude the possibility of other effect or side effect of the distomer.

Dependence: A compulsive urge to take a drug for psychological or physical needs. The psychological need is usually why the drug was taken in the first place (to change one's mood) but physical needs are often associated with this. This shows up when the drug is no longer taken leading to psychological withdrawal symptoms (feeling miserable) and physical withdrawal symptoms (headaches, shivering, etc.) Dependence need not be a serious matter if it is mild and the drug is non-toxic e.g., dependence on coffee). However, it is a serious matter if the drug is toxic and/or shows tolerance. Examples: opiates, alcohol, barbiturates, diazepams.

Dextrorotatory isomer: A stereoisomer that rotates the plane of plane-polarized light clockwise.

Docking studies: Docking studies are molecular modeling studies aiming at finding a proper fit between a ligand and its binding site.

Double-blind study: A double-blind study is a clinical study of potential and marketed drugs, where neither the investigators nor the subjects know which subjects will be treated with the active principle and which ones will receive a placebo.

Double prodrug (or pro-prodrug): A double prodrug is a biologically inactive molecule which is transformed *in vivo* in two steps (enzymatically and/or chemically) to the active species.

Drug: A drug is any substance presented for treating, curing or preventing disease in human beings or in animals. A drug may also be used for making a medical diagnosis or for restoring, correcting, or modifying physiological functions (e.g., the contraceptive pill).

Drug disposition: Drug disposition refers to all processes involved in the absorption, distribution, metabolism and excretion of drugs in a living organism.

Drug latentiation: Drug latentiation is the chemical modification of a biologically active compound to form a new compound, which *in vivo* will liberate the parent compound. Drug latentiation is synonymous with prodrug design.

Drug targeting: Drug targeting is a strategy aiming at the delivery of a compound to a particular tissue of the body.

Dual action drug: A dual action drug is a compound which combines two desired different pharmacological actions at a similarly efficacious dose.

ED$_{50}$: The ED$_{50}$ is the mean effective dose of a drug necessary to produce a therapeutic effect in 50 per cent of the test sample.

Efficacy: Efficacy describes the relative intensity with which agonists vary in the response they produce even when they occupy the same number of receptors and with the same affinity. Efficacy is not synonymous to intrinsic activity. Efficacy is the property that enables drugs to produce responses. It is convenient to differentiate the properties of drugs into two groups, those which cause them to associate with the receptors (affinity) and those that produce stimulus (efficacy). This term is often used to characterise the level of maximal responses induced by agonists. In fact, not all agonists of a receptor are capable of inducing identical levels of maximal responses. Maximal response depends on the efficiency of receptor coupling, i.e., from the cascade of events, which, from the binding of the drug to the receptor, leads to the observed biological effect.

Elimination: Elimination is the process achieving the reduction of the concentration of a xenobiotic including its metabolism.

Electrophoresis: Movement of charged solutes in response to an electrical field; often used to separate mixtures of ions, proteins, or nucleic acids.

Enantiomers: Stereoisomers that are non-superimposable mirror images of each other.

Endocrine Glands: Groups of cells specialised to synthesise hormones and secrete them into the blood to regulate other types of cells.

Enzyme: An enzyme is a macromolecule, usually a protein, that functions as a (bio) catalyst by increasing the reaction rate. In general, an enzyme catalyses only one reaction type (reaction selectivity) and operates on only one type of substrate (substrate selectivity). Substrate molecules are transformed at the same site (regioselectivity) and only one or preferentially one of chiral a substrate or of a racemate is transformed (enantioselectivity[special form of stereoselectivity]).

Enzyme induction: Enzyme induction is the process whereby an (inducible) enzyme is synthesised in response to a specific inducer molecule. The inducer molecule (often a substrate that needs the catalytic activity of the inducible enzyme for its metabolism) combines with a repressor and thereby prevents the blocking of an operator by the repressor leading to the translation of the gene for the enzyme.

Enzyme repression: Enzyme repression is the mode by which the synthesis of an enzyme is prevented by repressor molecules. In many cases, the end product of a synthesis chain (e.g., an amino acid) acts as a feed-back corepressor by combining with an intracellular aporepressor protein, so that this complex is able to block the function of an operator. As a result, the whole operation is prevented from being transcribed into mRNA, and the expression of all enzymes necessary for the synthesis of the end product enzyme is abolished.

Eudismic ratio: Eudismic ratio is the potency of the eutomer relative to that of the distomer.

Eutomer: The eutomer is the enantiomer of a chiral compound that is the more potent for a particular action.

Extraction: Extraction is an important step in studies involving the discovery and isolation of active compounds of plant materials.

Genome: A genome is the complete set of chromosomal and extrachromosomal genes of an organism, a cell, an organelle or a virus; the complete DNA (deoxyribonucleic acid) component of an organism.

Gluconeogenesis: The biosynthesis of a carbohydrate from simpler, noncarbohydrate precursors such as oxaloacetate or pyruvate.

Glycoside: Glycosides are (usually) non-reducing compounds, on hydrolysis by reagents or enzymes yield one or more reducing sugars among the products of hydrolysis

Glycerophospholipid: An amphipathic lipid with a glycerol backbone; fatty acids are ester-linked to Gl and C-2 of glycerol, and a polar alcohol is attached through a phosphodiester linkage to C-3.

Glycolipid: A lipid containing a carbohydrate group.

Glycolysis: The catabolic pathway by which a molecule of glucose is broken down into two molecules of pyruvate.

Glycoprotein: A protein containing a carbohydrate group.

Glycosidic Bonds: Bonds between a sugar and another molecule (typically an alcohol, purine, pyrimidine, or sugar) through an intervening oxygen or nitrogen atom; the bonds are classified as O-glycosidic or N-glycosidic, respectively.

Glyoxylate Cycle: A variant of the citric acid cycle, for the net conversion of acetate into succinate.

Hansch analysis: Hansch analysis is the investigation of the quantitative relationship between the biological activity of a series of compounds and their physicochemical substituent or global parameters representing hydrophobic, electronic, steric and other effects using multiple regression correlation methodology.

Hapten: A hapten is a low molecular weight molecule that contains an antigenic determinant but which is not itself antigenic unless combined with an antigenic carrier.

Hard drug: A hard drug is a non-metabolisable compound, characterised either by high lipid solubility and accumulation in adipose tissues and organelles, or by high water solubility. In the lay press, the term "Hard Drug" refers to a powerful drug of abuse such as cocaine or heroin.

Heteroreceptor: A heteroreceptor is a receptor regulating the synthesis and/or the release of mediators other than its own ligand.

High-Performance Liquid Chromatography (HPLC): Chromatographic procedures, often conducted at relatively high pressures, using automated equipment that permits refined and highly reproducible profiles.

Homologue: The term homologue is used to describe a compound belonging to a series of compounds differing from each other by a repeating unit, such as a methylene group, a peptide residue, etc.

Hormone: A hormone is a substance produced by endocrine glands, released in very low concentration into the bloodstream, and which exerts regulatory effects on specific organs or tissues distant from the site of secretion.

Hormone Receptor: A protein in, or on the surface of, target cells that binds a specific hormone and initiates the cellular response.

Hydrogen Bond: A weak electrostatic attraction between one electronegative atom (such as oxygen or nitrogen) and a hydrogen atom covalently linked to a second electronegative atom.

Hydrophilicity: Hydrophilicity is the tendency of a molecule to be solvated by water.

Hydrophobicity: Hydrophobicity is the association of non-polar groups or molecules in an aqueous environment which arises from the tendency of water to exclude non polar molecules.

Hydrolysis: Cleavage of a bond, such as an anhydride or peptide bond, by the addition of the elements of water, yielding two or more products.

Intrinsic activity: Intrinsic activity is the maximal stimulatory response induced by a compound in relation to that of a given reference compound.

Inverse agonist: An inverse agonist is a drug which acts at the same receptor as that of an agonist, yet produces an opposite effect. Also called negative antagonists.

Isosteres: Isosteres are molecules or ions of similar size containing the same number of atoms and valence electrons, e.g., $O2-$, $F-$, Ne.

In vitro: "In glass"; that is, in the test tube.

In vivo: "In life"; that is, in the living cell or organism.

Ion channel: An integral membrane protein that provides for the regulated transport of a specific ion, or ions, across a membrane.

Isomers: Any two molecules with the same molecular formula but a different arrangement of molecular groups.

Isozymes: Multiple forms of an enzyme that catalyze the same reaction but differ from each other in their amino acid sequence, substrate affinity, V_{max}, and/or regulatory properties; also called isoenzymes.

LD_{50}: The LD50 is the mean lethal dose of a drug required to kill 50 per cent of the test sample.

Lead discovery: Lead discovery is the process of identifying active new chemical entities, which by subsequent modification may be transformed into a clinically useful drug.

Lead generation: Lead generation is the term applied to strategies developed to identify compounds which possess a desired but non-optimised biological activity.

Lead optimisation: Lead optimisation is the synthetic modification of a biologically active compound, to fulfill all stereoelectronic, physicochemical, pharmacokinetic and toxicological parameters required for clinical usefulness.

Levorotatory Isomer: A stereoisomer that rotates the plane of plane-polarized light counterclockwise.

Ligand: A small molecule that binds specifically to a larger one; for example, a hormone is the ligand for its specific protein receptor.

Lipophilicity: Lipophilicity represents the affinity of a molecule or a moiety for a lipophilic environment. It is commonly measured by its distribution behaviour in a biphasic system, either liquid-liquid (e.g., partition coefficient in octan-1-ol/water) or solid/liquid (retention on reversed-phase high performance liquid chromatography (RP-HPLC) or thin-layer chromatography (TLC) system).

Medicinal chemistry: Medicinal chemistry is a chemistry-based discipline, also involving aspects of biological, medical and pharmaceutical sciences. It is concerned with the invention, discovery, design, identification and preparation of biologically active compounds, the study of their metabolism, the interpretation of their mode of action at the molecular level and the construction of structure-activity relationships.

Metabolism: The term metabolism comprises the entire physical and chemical processes involved in the maintenance and reproduction of life in which nutrients are broken down to generate energy and to give simpler molecules (catabolism) which by themselves may be used to form more complex molecules (anabolism).

In case of heterotrophic organisms, the energy evolving from catabolic processes is made available for use by the organism. In medicinal chemistry the term metabolism refers to the biotransformation of xenobiotics and particularly drugs.

Metabolite: A metabolite is any intermediate or product resulting from metabolism.

Me-too drug: A me-too drug is a compound that is structurally very similar to already known drugs, with only minor pharmacological differences.

Molecular graphics: Molecular graphics is the visualisation and manipulation of three-dimensional representations of molecules on a graphical display device.

Molecular modeling: Molecular modeling is a technique for the investigation of molecular structures and properties using computational chemistry and graphical visualisation techniques in order to provide a plausible three-dimensional representation under a given set of circumstances.

Mutagen: A mutagen is an agent that causes a permanent heritable change (i.e., a mutation) into the DNA (deoxyribonucleic acid) of an organism.

Mutual prodrug: A mutual prodrug is the association in a unique molecule of two, usually synergistic, drugs attached to each other, one drug being the carrier for the other and vice versa.

New Chemical Entity: A new chemical entity (NCE) is a compound not previously described in the literature.

Non-classical isostere: Same meaning as Bioisostere.

Nucleic acid: A nucleic acid is a macromolecule composed of linear sequences of nucleotides that perform several functions in living cells, e.g., the storage of genetic information and its transfer from one generation to the next DNA (deoxyribonucleic acid), the expression of this information in protein synthesis (mRNA, tRNA) and may act as functional components of subcellular units such as ribosomes (rRNA).

RNA (ribonucleic acid) contains D-ribose, DNA contains 2-deoxy-D-ribose as the sugar component.

Nucleoside: A nucleoside is a compound in which a purine or pyrimidine base is bound via a N-atom to C-1, replacing the hydroxy group of either 2-deoxy-D-ribose or of D-ribose, but without any phosphate groups.

The common nucleosides in biological systems are adenosine, guanosine, cytidine, and uridine (which contain ribose) and deoxyadenosine, deoxyguanosine, deoxycytidine and thymidine (which contain deoxyribose).

Nucleotide: A nucleotide is a nucleoside in which the primary hydroxy group of either 2-deoxy-D-ribose or of D-ribose is esterified by orthophosphoric acid.

Oligonucleotide: An oligonucleotide is an oligomer resulting from a linear sequences of nucleotides.

Oncogene: An oncogene is a normal cellular gene which, when inappropriately expressed or mutated, can transform eukaryotic cells into tumour cells.

Orphan drug: An orphan drug is a drug for the treatment of a rare disease for which reasonable recovery of the sponsoring firm's research and development expenditure is not expected within a reasonable time. The term is also used to describe substances intended for such uses.

Partial agonist: A partial agonist is an agonist which is unable to induce maximal activation of a receptor population, regardless of the amount of drug applied.

Pattern recognition: Pattern recognition is the identification of patterns in large data sets using appropriate mathematical methodologies.

Peptidomimetic: A peptidomimetic is a compound containing non-peptidic structural elements that is capable of mimicking or antagonizing the biological action(s) of a natural parent peptide. A peptidomimetic does no longer have classical peptide characteristics such as enzymatically sessile peptidic bonds.

Peptoid: A peptoid is a peptidomimetic that results from the oligomeric assembly of N-substituted glycines.

Pentose Phosphate Pathway: A pathway that serves to interconvert hexoses and pentoses and is a source of reducing equivalents and pentoses for biosynthetic processes; present in most organisms. Also called the phosphogluconate pathway.

Pharmacokinetics: Pharmacokinetics refers to the study of absorption, distribution, metabolism and excretion (ADME) of bioactive compounds in a higher organism.

Pharmacophore (pharmacophoric pattern): A pharmacophore is the ensemble of steric and electronic features that is necessary to ensure the optimal supramolecular interactions with a specific biological target structure and to trigger (or to block) its biological response.

A pharmacophore does not represent a real molecule or a real association of functional groups, but a purely abstract concept that accounts for the common molecular interaction capacities of a group of compounds towards their target structure. The pharmacophore can be considered as the largest common denominator shared by a set of active molecules. This definition discards a misuse often found in the medicinal chemistry literature which consists of naming as pharmacophores simple chemical functionalities such as guanidines, sulfonamides or dihydroimidazoles (formerly imidazolines), or typical structural skeletons such as flavones, phenothiazines, prostaglandins or steroids.

Pharmacophoric descriptors: Pharmacophoric descriptors are used to define a pharmacophore, including H-bonding, hydrophobic and electrostatic interaction sites, defined by atoms, ring centers and virtual points.

Placebo: A placebo is an inert substance or dosage form which is identical in appearance, flavor and odour to the active substance or dosage form. It is used as a negative control in a bioassay or in a clinical study.

Potency: Potency is the dose of drug required to produce a specific effect of given intensity as compared to a standard reference.

Prodrug: A prodrug is any compound that undergoes biotransformation before exhibiting its pharmacological effects. Prodrug can thus be viewed as drugs containing specialised non-toxic protective groups used in a transient manner to alter or to eliminate undesirable properties in the parent molecule .

Quantitative Structure-Activity Relationships (QSAR): Quantitative structure-activity relationships are mathematical relationships linking chemical structure and pharmacological activity in a quantitative manner for a series of compounds. Methods which can be used in QSAR include various regression and pattern recognition techniques.

Receptor: A receptor is a molecule or a polymeric structure in or on a cell that specifically recognizes and binds a compound acting as a molecular messenger (neurotransmitter, hormone, lymphokine, lectin, drug, etc.).

Receptor mapping: Receptor mapping is the technique used to describe the geometric and/or electronic features of a binding site when insufficient structural data for this receptor or enzyme are available. Generally the active site cavity is defined by comparing the superposition of active to that of inactive molecules.

Second messenger: A second messenger is an intracellular metabolite or ion increasing or decreasing as a response to the stimulation of receptors by agonists, considered as the "first messenger". This generic term usually does not prejudge the rank order of intracellular biochemical events.

Site-specific delivery: Site-specific delivery is an approach to target a drug to a specific tissue, using prodrugs or antibody recognition systems.

Soft drug: A soft drug is a compound that is degraded *in vivo* to predictable non-toxic and inactive metabolites, after having achieved its therapeutic role.

Structure-activity relationship (SAR): Structure-activity relationship is the relationship between chemical structure and pharmacological activity for a series of compounds.

Structure-based design: Structure-based design is a drug design strategy based on the 3D structure of the target obtained by X-ray or NMR.

Structure-property correlations (SPC): Structure-property correlations refers to all statistical mathematical methods used to correlate any structural property to any other property (intrinsic, chemical or biological), using statistical regression and pattern recognition techniques.

Systemic: Systemic means relating to or affecting the whole body.

Therapeutic Index (Or Ratio): The therapeutic index is the ratio of a drug's undesirable effects with respect to its desirable effects and is therefore a measure of how safe that drug is. Usually this involves comparing the dose levels leading to a toxic effect with respect to the dose levels leading to a therapeutic effect. The larger the therapeutic index, the safer the drug.

To be more precise, the therapeutic index compares the drug dose levels which lead to toxic effects in 50 per cent of cases studied, with respect to the dose levels leading to maximum therapeutic effects in 50 per cent of cases studied. This is a more reliable method of measuring the index since it eliminates any peculiar individual results.

Tolerance: Repeat doses of a drug may result in smaller biological results. The drug may block or antagonize its own action and larger doses are needed for the same pharmacological effect. Alternatively, the body may 'learn' how to metabolise the drug more efficiently. Again larger doses are needed for the same pharmacological effect, increasing the chances of toxic side-effects. Examples: morphine, hexamethonium.

Teratogen: A teratogen is a substance that produces a malformation in a foetus.

Topliss tree: A Topliss tree is an operational scheme for analog design.

Transition-state analog: A transition-state analog is a compound that mimics the transition state of a substrate bound to an enzyme.

Xenobiotic: A xenobiotic is a compound foreign to an organism (xenos [greek] = foreign).

INDEX

Chemotherapeutic Index	1.3-1.4
Salvarsan	1.3
Therapeutic Index	1.4, 1.40
LD50	1.4, 1.34, 1.40, 4.40
ED50	1.4, 1.40, 9.5 – 9.7, 9.9-9.10, 9.17
Structure–Activity Relationship (SAR)	1.2, 1.4
Quantitative Structure–Activity Relationship (QSAR)	1.4
Drug Discovery Process	1.10
Bioisosterism	1.16
Toxicology	1.2, 1.34-1.35, 7.10
Dose response Curve	1.36, 1.40, 9.4, 9.8, 9.14
Passive Diffusion	1.37-1.38, 5.31
Toxicity Studies	1.34, 1.39
Acute Toxicity Studies	1.39 - 1.40
Sub-acute Toxicity Studies	1.41
Chronic Toxicity Studies	1.42
Kegg's Pathway	2.2
Glycolysis	2.2 – 2.3
Citric Acid Cycle	2.4-2.6
Krebs Cycle	2.4-2.6
Shikimic Acid Pathway	2.6-2.7
Acetate Mevalonate/ Isoprenoid Pathway	2.8-2.10
Microwave Extraction Technology	3.2
Instrumentation of Microwave Extraction Technology	3.4
Supercritical Fluids	3.7
Supercritical Fluid Extraction	3.7
Critical Temperature	3.8
Critical Pressure	3.8

Triple Point	3.8
Ultrasonic Extraction	3.11
Cavitation	3.11
Solid Phase Micro-Extraction	3.14 – 3.17
Chemotherapy	5.1, 5.2, 6.1
Antibiotic	1.14, 4.7, 4.35, 5.1, 9.1
Penicillin	1.3, 1.6, 1.8, 1.28, 5.2-5.5
Biosynthesis of Penicillin	5.5-5.7
Structure of Penicillin	5.7-5.11
Mechanism of Action of Penicillin	5.11-5.12
Cephalosporins	5.12-5.14
Structure of Cephalosporins	5.15-5.17
Mechanism of Action of Cephalosporins	5.18
Griseofulvin	5.19
Biosynthesis of Griseofulvin	5.19 -5.20
Mechanism of Action of Griseofulvin	5.20
Bacitracin	5.20-5.21
Aztreonam	5.21-5.22
Polymyxin	5.22-5.23
Chloramphenicol	5.23-5.27
Tetracyclines	5.28-5.31
Macrolides	5.31-5.33
Clindamycin	5.33-5.34
Linezolid	5.35
Aminoglycosides	5.35, 5.39-5.40
Streptomycin	5.36-5.38
Biosynthesis	6.1
Alkaloids	2.2, 4.4, 4.7, 4.35, 4.39, 4.43, 6.1, 7.4, 7.7, 9.4
Colchicine	6.1, 6.3, 6.5
Thiamine	6.2
Piperine	3.6, 4.13 - 4.14, 6.2, 6.4-6.5

Classification of Alkaloids	6.3-6.6
Dragendorff's Test	6.7
Mayer's Test	6.7
Hager's Test	6.7
Wagner's Test	6.8
Tannic Acid Test	6.8
Biosynthesis of Alkaloids	6.8
Tropane Alkaloids	6.9
Thin Layer Chromatography	6.11
Extraction of Tropane Alkaloids	6.13
Mechanism of Action of Tropane	6.14-6.15
Quinoline	6.19
Quinine	6.19
Quinidine	6.19
Cinchonine	6.19
Cinchonidine	6.19
Isolation of Quinoline Alkaloids	6.20-6.22
Biosynthesis of Quinine	6.23-6.24
Fluorescence Test	6.25
Thalleioquin Test	6.25
Erythroquinine Test	6.26
Herpathite Test	6.26
Mechanism of Action of *Cinchona* Alkaloids	6.28
Mechanism of Action of Quinidine	6.28
Opium Alkaloids	6.30
Classification of Opium Alkaloids	6.31-6.32
Properties of Opium Alkaloids	6.33
Heroin	6.34
Apomorphine	6.34
Morphine	6.34
Codiene	6.34

Isolation of Opium Alkaloids	6.35-6.37
Biosynthesis of Opium Alkaloids	6.38-6.39
Ergot Alkaloids	6.44
Classification of Ergot Alkaloids	6.44-6.46
Isolation of Ergot Alkaloids	6.48-6.49
Biosynthesis of Ergot Alkaloids	6.50-6.51
Vinca (Catharanthus) Alkaloids	6.53-6.54
Classification of *Vinca* Alkaloids	6.54-6.55
Isolation of *Vinca* Alkaloids	6.56
Biosynthesis of *Vinca* Alkaloids	6.56-6.58
Vinblastine	6.59
Vincristine	6.59
Vinorelbine	6.59
Pyrrolizidine Alkaloids	6.60
Isolation of Pyrrolizidine Alkaloids	6.61
Biosynthesis of Pyrrolizidine Alkaloids	6.62-6.63
Glycosides	6.64
Classification and Nomenclature of Glycosides	6.64 - 6.66
Isolation of Glycosides	6.68-6.69
Chemical Tests for Glycosides	6.69-6.72
Cardiac Glycoside	6.73
Chemical Test of Cardiac Glycoside	6.78
Isolation of Cardiac Glycoside	6.79
Biosynthesis of Cardiac Glycoside	6.80
Anthraquinone Glycosides	6.85
Types of Anthraquinone Glycoside	6.86
Cascara	6.87 - 6.88
Ayurveda	9.1-9.2
High Throughput Screening	9.2
Types of HTS Assays	9.3
Pentobarbital	9.5,9.6,9.21

Bronchial Hyperreactivity	9.6
Antitussive Activity	9.7
Open Field Test	9.8
Hole-board Test	9.8
Chimney test	9.9
Rotarod Method	9.9
Light-dark Model	9.11
Elevated Plus Maze Test	9.11
Staircase Test	9.12
Tail Suspension Test	9.14
HAFFNER's Tail Clip Method	9.15-9.16
Radiant Heat Method	9.16
Hot Plate Method	9.16
Tail Immersion Test	9.17
Formalin Test	9.17
Writhing Test	9.17
Granuloma Pouch Technique	9.20
HPLC (High Performance Liquid Chromatography)	4.4, 4.6, 4.13, 4.34
Instrumentation of HPLC	4.6
Application of HPLC	4.7
HPLC Specification	4.8
High Performance Thin Layer Chromatography (HPTLC)	4.17
HPTLC Applications	4.18
GC- MS	3.16, 3.18, 4.27 – 4.29\
Application of GC- MS	4.29
Instrumentation of GC- MS	4.34
LC-MS	4.33
LC-MS Applications	4.35
Gel Electrophoresis	4.38
Who Guidelines for Herbal Drugs Standardisation	4.40
Good Agricultural/Manufacturing Practices	4.44

Tracer Technique	7.1
Criteria for Tracer Technique	7.3
Methods in Tracer Technique	7.5
Applications of Tracer Technique	7.8
Radiography	7.11
Autographic Techniques	7.13
Hormones	8.1
Classification of Hormones	8.4
Mechanisms of Action of Hormones	8.6
Thyroid Hormone	8.9
Pancreatic Hormone	8.19
Insulin Hormone	8.21
Glucagon	8.34
Somatostatin	8.36
Pancreatic Polypeptide	8.39
Oxytocin	8.40
Adrenal Cortex Hormone (or Adrenocorticosteroids)	8.46
Glucocorticoids	8.50
Mineralocorticoids (Aldosterone)	8.55
Gonadal Hormone	8.57
Oestrogens or Follicular Hormones	8.58
Progesterone or Oestrogens or Corpus Luteum Hormones	8.63
Androgen (Testosterone)	8.68

www.ingramcontent.com/pod-product-compliance
Lightning Source LLC
Chambersburg PA
CBHW060309240426
43661CB00059B/2702